Lecture Notes in Computer Science

Lecture Notes in Artificial Intelligence   14157

Founding Editor

Jörg Siekmann

Series Editors

Randy Goebel, *University of Alberta, Edmonton, Canada*
Wolfgang Wahlster, *DFKI, Berlin, Germany*
Zhi-Hua Zhou, *Nanjing University, Nanjing, China*

The series Lecture Notes in Artificial Intelligence (LNAI) was established in 1988 as a topical subseries of LNCS devoted to artificial intelligence.

The series publishes state-of-the-art research results at a high level. As with the LNCS mother series, the mission of the series is to serve the international R & D community by providing an invaluable service, mainly focused on the publication of conference and workshop proceedings and postproceedings.

Fabian Meder · Alexander Hunt ·
Laura Margheri · Anna Mura · Barbara Mazzolai
Editors

Biomimetic and Biohybrid Systems

12th International Conference, Living Machines 2023
Genoa, Italy, July 10–13, 2023
Proceedings, Part I

 Springer

Editors
Fabian Meder (iD)
Italian Institute of Technology
Genoa, Italy

Laura Margheri (iD)
Italian Institute of Technology
Genoa, Italy

Barbara Mazzolai (iD)
Italian Institute of Technology
Genoa, Italy

Alexander Hunt (iD)
Portland State University
Portland, OR, USA

Anna Mura (iD)
Radboud University
Nijmegen, The Netherlands

ISSN 0302-9743   ISSN 1611-3349 (electronic)
Lecture Notes in Artificial Intelligence
ISBN 978-3-031-38856-9   ISBN 978-3-031-38857-6 (eBook)
https://doi.org/10.1007/978-3-031-38857-6

LNCS Sublibrary: SL7 – Artificial Intelligence

This Springer imprint is published by the registered company Springer Nature Switzerland AG
The registered company address is: Gewerbestrasse 11, 6330 Cham, Switzerland

Preface

These proceedings contain the papers presented at the 12th International Conference on Biomimetic and Biohybrid Systems (Living Machines 2023) in Genoa, Italy, July 10–13, 2023. The international conferences in the Living Machines series focus on the intersection of research on novel life-like technologies inspired by the scientific investigation of biological systems, biomimetics, and research that seeks to interface biological and artificial systems to create biohybrid systems. The conference aims to highlight the most exciting research in both fields united by the theme of "Living Machines."

Gaining a deep understanding of the essence of life is an essential prerequisite for advancing artificial technology. There are two fundamental principles to consider. Firstly, technology should serve life and living beings. Its development should aim to improve the well-being and quality of life of all living organisms. Secondly, as researchers, our primary objective should be the development of sustainable technologies that harmoniously integrate with Earth's ecosystems and the inherent life within them. The escalating environmental pollution and resulting climate changes pose significant challenges that must be addressed. This situation presents humanity with an unprecedented and monumental challenge, arguably the greatest we have ever encountered. As researchers, it is imperative for us to look deeper into how living systems solve issues and explore ways to translate these solutions into technology.

By studying and emulating the strategies and mechanisms found in living systems, we can strive to develop innovative technologies that are not only efficient and functional but also environmentally friendly and sustainable. This approach requires a multidisciplinary effort, combining knowledge from biology, ecology, engineering, and other relevant fields. The Living Machines conference embodies and promotes this vision by bringing together researchers from various disciplines such as engineering, biology, computational science, and materials science. These researchers propose technical solutions that draw inspiration from a wide range of biological mechanisms found in nature. These mechanisms span from the nervous system to motion, sensing, and materials in plants and animals. The conference also encompasses biohybrid systems, where artificial technology directly interacts with biological systems.

The Living Machines conference series was first organized by the Convergent Science Network (CSN) of biomimetic and biohybrid systems to provide a mechanism for ensuring this communication. It is a focal point for gathering world-leading researchers and the presentation and discussion of cutting-edge research at the boundary of biology and engineering. This year's Living Machines conference upheld this esteemed legacy by showcasing biologists and engineers who have dedicated their careers to advancing biomimetic and biohybrid systems. Furthermore, the event provides an opportunity to introduce and support numerous young researchers in this rapidly expanding field. This emphasis on nurturing emerging talent ensures continued growth and innovation within the realm of biomimetics and biohybrid systems.

The papers in these proceedings encompass the research submissions to the conference, and from these submissions, a careful selection was made for oral and poster presentations. The articles underwent rigorous evaluation, with an average of 2.7 reviewers per paper, conducted in a single-blind review process. A total of 66 papers were received, and the acceptance rate for publication in the proceedings was 87%. This indicates that a significant portion of the submitted research met the standards set by the conference organizers and reviewers. Moreover, the 180 reviewers who contributed to the evaluation provided authors with detailed comments, typically offering comprehensive suggestions rather than brief, superficial responses. To illustrate the depth of the review process, one article received over 100 comments from a reviewer. This level of engagement demonstrates the commitment of the reviewers to support the authors by offering valuable suggestions for improving their work. Following revisions, most papers underwent a second round of review. The meticulous evaluation and revision process ensures that the papers included in these proceedings represent a high standard of research in the field of biomimetic and biohybrid systems.

The main conference was a three-day in-person meeting with single-track oral presentations and six plenary talks taking place in Genoa, Italy, preceded by a one-day event with four workshops and four tutorials. The conference venue, the Aquarium of Genoa, was selected to further underline the importance of life for the conference where the participants were surrounded by over 800 animal and vegetal species and over 15000 living specimens in one of Europe's biggest aquariums. This setting added an immersive and enriching dimension to the conference, aligning with its focus on biomimetic and biohybrid systems. The plenary speakers were Peter Fratzl (Max Planck Institute of Colloids and Interfaces, Germany), Eleni Stavrinidou (Linköping University, Sweden), Marco Dorigo (Université Libre de Bruxelles, Belgium), Oussama Khatib (Stanford University, USA), Kyu-Jin Cho (Seoul National University, South Korea), and Olga Speck (University of Freiburg, Germany). Session themes included: Bioinspired materials, actuators, sensors I+II; Human-robot interaction, rehabilitation and learning; Joints and muscles; Biohybrid systems and interactions; Invertebrate locomotion and perception mechanisms; Computational tools and modelling; Bioinspiration under water; and Biomimetics analyzed. Additionally, a Science Café was organized on "Living Machines: the Origin and the Future" that was open to the public and moderated by Nicola Nosengo, Chief Editor, Nature Italy.

We wish to thank the many people that were involved in making Living Machines 2023 possible. The conference would not have been possible without the dedication, efforts, and support of numerous individuals. Additional guidance and support were provided by the Living Machines International Advisory Board. We would also like to thank the authors and speakers who contributed their valuable work to the conference. A significant acknowledgment goes to the reviewers who dedicated their time and expertise. Lastly, we would like to express our gratitude to the volunteers, sponsors, and all other individuals who contributed their time, resources, and support to ensure the smooth running of Living Machines 2023.

June 2023   Fabian Meder
                                                                        Alexander Hunt
                                                                        Laura Margheri
                                                                            Anna Mura
                                                                      Barbara Mazzolai

Organization

General Chair

Barbara Mazzolai   Istituto Italiano di Tecnologia, Italy

Program Chairs

Fabian Meder   Istituto Italiano di Tecnologia, Italy
Alexander Hunt   Portland State University, USA

Local Organization

Laura Margheri   Istituto Italiano di Tecnologia, Italy

Communication Chairs

Giuliano Greco   Istituto Italiano di Tecnologia, Italy
Anna Mura   Radboud University, The Netherlands
Valeria Delle Cave   Istituto Italiano di Tecnologia, Italy

Workshop and Tutorial Chairs

Wenqi Hu   Max-Planck-Institute for Intelligent Systems,
     Germany
Li Wen   Beihang University, China

International Steering Committee

Minoru Asada   Osaka University, Japan
Joseph Ayers   Northeastern University, USA
Hillel Chiel   Case Western Reserve University, USA
Mark Cutkosky   Stanford University, USA
Marc Desmulliez   Heriot-Watt University, UK

José Halloy	Université Paris Cité, France
Koh Hosoda	Osaka University, Japan
Alexander Hunt	Portland State University, USA
Holger G. Krapp	Imperial College London, UK
Cecilia Laschi	National University of Singapore, Singapore
Nathan Lepora	University of Bristol, UK
Uriel Martinez-Hernandez	University of Bath, UK
Barbara Mazzolai	Istituto Italiano di Tecnologia, Italy
Fabian Meder	Istituto Italiano di Tecnologia, Italy
Anna Mura	Radboud University, The Netherlands
Tony Prescott	University of Sheffield, UK
Roger Quinn	Case Western Reserve University, USA
Masahiro Shimizu	Osaka University, Japan
Thomas Speck	Albert-Ludwigs-Universität Freiburg, Germany
Nicholas Szczecinski	West Virginia University, USA
Falk Tauber	Albert-Ludwigs-Universität Freiburg, Germany
Paul F. M. J. Verschure	Radboud University, The Netherlands
Vasiliki Vouloutsi	Technology Innovation Institute, United Arab Emirates
Victoria Webster-Wood	Carnegie Mellon University, USA

Reviewers

Andrew Adamatzky	University of the West of England, UK
Ian Adams	Case Western Reserve University, USA
Adepapo Alabi	University of Cincinnati, USA
Emanuel Andrada	University of Jena, Germany
Yasmin Ansari	Scuola Superiore Sant'Anna, Italy
Paolo Arena	University of Catania, Italy
Serena Armiento	Istituto Italiano di Tecnologia, Italy
Daniel Aukes	Arizona State University, USA
Jessica Ausborn	Drexel University, USA
Robert Baines	Yale University, USA
Simeon Bamford	Istituto Italiano di Tecnologia, Italy
Giacinto Barresi	Istituto Italiano di Tecnologia, Italy
Anil Bastola	University of Nottingham, UK
Lucia Beccai	Istituto Italiano di Tecnologia, Italy
Sofia Belardinelli	University of Naples Federico II, Italy
Paolo Bollella	University of Bari, Italy
Brandon Caasenbrood	Eindhoven University of Technology, The Netherlands

Genci Capi	Hosei University, Japan
Ragesh Chellattoan	Istituto Italiano di Tecnologia, Italy
Ziyu Chen	Technical University of Munich, Germany
Tiffany Cheng	University of Stuttgart, Germany
Francesca Ciardo	Istituto Italiano di Tecnologia, Italy
Kliton Cikalleshi	Istituto Italiano di Tecnologia, Italy
David Correa	University of Waterloo, Canada
Marco Crepaldi	Istituto Italiano di Tecnologia, Italy
Mark Cutkosky	Stanford University, USA
Giulia D'Angelo	Istituto Italiano di Tecnologia, Italy
Simon Danner	Drexel University, USA
Doris Danninger	Johannes Kepler University Linz, Austria
Riddhi Das	Istituto Italiano di Tecnologia, Italy
Edoardo Datteri	University of Milan, Italy
Cem Balda Dayan	Max Planck Institute for Intelligent Systems, Germany
Emanuela Del Dottore	Istituto Italiano di Tecnologia, Italy
Osman Yirmibeşoğlu	Yale University, USA
Volker Dürr	Bielefeld University, Germany
Matt Ellis	University of Sheffield, UK
Muhammad Farhan	Helmholtz-Zentrum Hereon, Germany
Isabella Fiorello	Istituto Italiano di Tecnologia, Italy
Daniel Flippo	Kansas State University, USA
Fabrizio Gabbiani	Baylor College of Medicine, USA
Luigi Garaffa	University of Padua, Italy
Marcello Garcia	University of the Basque Country, Spain
Benoît Girard	Pierre and Marie Curie University, CNRS, France
Evripidis Gkanias	University of Edinburgh, UK
Axel Gorostiza	University of Cologne, Germany
Benjamin Gorrisen	KU Leuven, Belgium
Lorenzo Guiducci	Max Planck Institute for Colloids, Germany
Wesley Guo	Stanford University, USA
Tamar Gutnick	Okinawa Institute of Science and Technology, Japan
Joe Hays	United States Naval Research Laboratory, USA
Shinishi Hirai	Ritzumeikan University, Japan
Alexander Hunt	Portland State University, USA
Bohyun Hwang	Korea Aerospace University, South Korea
Jacqueline Hynes	Brown University, USA
Auke Ijspeert	EPFL, Switzerland
Hiroyuki Ishii	Waseda University, Japan
Ludger Jansen	University of Rostock, Germany

Alejandro Jimenez-Rodriguez	University of Sheffield, UK
Seonggung Joe	Istituto Italiano di Tecnologia, Italy
Julie Jung	University of Utah, USA
Behnam Kamare	Istituto Italiano di Tecnologia, Italy
Lorenzo Kinnicutt	Boston University College of Engineering, USA
Holger Krapp	Imperial College London, UK
Sebastian Kruppert	University of Freiburg, Germany
Maarja Kruusmaa	Tallinn University of Technology, Estonia
Cecilia Laschi	National University of Singapore, Singapore
Florent Le Moël	University of Edinburgh, UK
Binggwong Leung	Vidyasirimedhi Institute of Science and Technology, Thailand
Junnan Li	Technical University of Munich, Germany
Vittorio Lippi	University of Freiburg, Germany
Matteo Lo Preti	Istituto Italiano di Tecnologia, Italy
Kees Lokhorst	Wageningen University, The Netherlands
Huub Maas	University of Amsterdam, The Netherlands
Michael Mangan	University of Sheffield, Opteran, UK
Stefano Mariani	Istituto Italiano di Tecnologia, Italy
Andrea Marinelli	Istituto Italiano di Tecnologia, Italy
Marcos Maroto	Charles III University of Madrid, Spain
Edgar A. Martinez Garcia	Universidad Autónoma de Ciudad Juárez, Mexico
Uriel Martinez-Hernandez	University of Bath, UK
Arianna Mazzotta	Istituto Italiano di Tecnologia, Italy
Stu McNeal	Portland State University, USA
Edoardo Milana	University of Freiburg, Germany
Stefano Mintchev	ETH Zurich, Switzerland
Charanraj Mohan	Istituto Italiano di Tecnologia, Italy
Sumit Mohanty	AMOLF, The Netherlands
Alessio Mondini	Istituto Italiano di Tecnologia, Italy
Sara Mongile	Istituto Italiano di Tecnologia, Italy
Kenneth Moses	Case Western Reserve University, USA
Anna Mura	Radboud University, The Netherlands
Indrek Must	University of Tartu, Estonia
Giovanna Naselli	Istituto Italiano di Tecnologia, Italy
Noel Naughton	University of Illinois, USA
Nir Nesher	Hebrew University of Jerusalem, Israel
Huu Nhan Nguyen	JAIST, Japan
Jasmine Nirody	University of Chicago, USA
William Nourse	Case Western Reserve University, USA
Luca Padovani	University of Rome, Italy
Luca Patanè	University of Messina, Italy

Linda Paterno	Scuola Superiore Sant'Anna, Italy
Andrew Philippides	University of Sussex, UK
Telmo Pievani	University of Padua, Italy
Maria Pozzi	University of Siena, Italy
Saravana Prashanth Murali Babu	SDU Biorobotics, Denmark
Thorsten Pretsch	Fraunhofer IAP, Germany
Boris Prilutsky	Georgia Tech, USA
Qiukai Qi	University of Bristol, UK
Roger Quinn	Case Western Reserve University, USA
Nicholas Rabb	Tufts University, USA
Giulio Reina	Politecnico di Bari, Italy
Leonardo Ricotti	Scuola Superiore Sant'Anna, Italy
Shane Riddle	Case Western Reserve University, USA
Donato Romano	Scuola Superiore Sant'Anna, Italy
Taher Saif	University of Illinois Urbana-Champaign, USA
Vanessa Sanchez	Stanford University, USA
Francisco Santos	Radboud University, The Netherlands
Rob Scharff	Hong Kong University of Science and Technology, China
Milli Schlafly	Northwestern University, USA
Andrew Schulz	Georgia Tech, USA
Marianna Semprini	Istituto Italiano di Tecnologia, Italy
Kim Seungwon	KIST, South Korea
Ebrahim Shahabishalghouni	Istituto Italiano di Tecnologia, Italy
Edoardo Sinibaldi	Istituto Italiano di Tecnologia, Italy
Thomas Speck	University of Freiburg, Germany
Osca Sten	Istituto Italiano di Tecnologia, Italy
Germán Sumbre	ENS Paris, France
Xuelong Sun	University of Lincoln, UK
Gregory Sutton	University of Lincoln, USA
Nicholas Szczecinski	West Virginia University, USA
Falk Tauber	University of Freiburg, Germany
Yonas Teodros Tefera	Istituto Italiano di Tecnologia, Italy
Thomas George Thuruthel	University College London, UK
Kadri-Ann Valdur	University of Tartu, Estonia, Imperial College London, UK
Lorenzo Vannozzi	Scuola Superiore Sant'Anna, Italy
Julian Vincent	Heriot-Watt University, UK
Francesco Visentin	University of Verona, Italy
Francesco Wanderlingh	University of Genoa, Italy
Barbara Webb	University of Edinburgh, UK
Victoria Webster-Wood	Carnegie Mellon University, USA

Nick Willemstein   University of Twente, The Netherlands
Wenci Xin   National University of Singapore, Singapore
Zachary Yoder   Max Planck Institute for Intelligent Systems,
                          Germany
Yichen Zhai   University of California San Diego, USA
Xingwen Zheng   University of Tokyo, Japan
Bowen Zhu   Westlake University, China

Contents – Part I

Bioinspiration Under Water

Invertebrate Locomotion and Perception Mechanisms and Thereof Inspired Systems

Contents – Part II

Computational Tools and Modelling

Biomimetic Research Analyzed

Human-Robot Interaction, Rehabilitation, and Learning

Simple Synthetic Memories of Robotic Touch

Pablo J. Salazar[✉] and Tony J. Prescott

Department of Computer Science and Sheffield Robotics,
University of Sheffield, Sheffield S1 4DP, UK
{pjsalazarvillacis1,t.j.prescott}@sheffield.ac.uk

Abstract. It has been previously demonstrated in robots that the mimicking of functional characteristics of biologic memory can be beneficial for providing accurate learning and recognition in circumstances of social human-robot-interaction. The effective encoding of social and physical salient features has been demonstrated through the use of Bayesian Latent Variable Models as abstractions of memories (Simple Synthetic Memories). In this work, we explore the capabilities of formation and recall of tactile memories associated to the encoding of geometric and spatial qualities. Compression and pattern separation are evaluated against the use of raw data in a nearest neighbour regression model, obtaining a substantial improvement in accuracy for prediction of geometric properties of the stimulus. Additionally, pattern completion is assessed with the generation of 'imagined touch' streams of data showing similarities to real world tactile observations. The use of this model for tactile memories offers the potential for robustly perform sensorimotor tasks in which the sense of touch is involved.

Keywords: Tactile memories · Robot touch · Latent variable space · Tactile data generation

1 Introduction

The emulation of the known functionality of biological memory systems represents an area of great potential towards the development of flexible and adaptive autonomous systems. Developing robotic systems able to effectively store memories from experiences contributes to the achievement of complex tasks through the use of contextual information on sensorimotor control. High-level abstractions of memory involve the reproduction of essential features such as compression of sensory data, pattern separation, and pattern completion [5]. These characteristics have inspired the development of computational memory models for spatial navigation [2] using Time Restricted Boltzmann Machines mimicking the structure and functionality of the Hippocampus; and in the context of social interaction with robots [11] characterising the aforementioned features trough Gaussian Process Latent Variable Models (GP-LVMs) [8] as the core for the development of Synthetic Autobiographical Memory Systems.

F. Meder et al. (Eds.): Living Machines 2023, LNAI 14157, pp. 3–15, 2023.
https://doi.org/10.1007/978-3-031-38857-6_1

The formation and recall of memories in multiple sensory modalities have exploited the robustness of Bayesian Latent Variable Models [18], being able to produce meaningful representations of sensory data through non-linear dimensionality reduction and uncertainty quantification [4]. Prescott et al. [12] proposed the establishment of this family of models as Simple Synthetic Memories (SSMs). Active compression of high-dimensional data, creation of fantasy memories, and recovering of observations from latent spaces were explored for: face recognition, audition, action discrimination and tactile interactions. For the sense of touch, the data were obtained when the interacting human applied four different types of touch on the artificial skin of the robot. Results showed that the touch SSM was able to accurately recognise the type of tactile stimulus, therefore providing memory abstractions for passive tactile stimulation. Learned representations present the potential to be included in a closed loop for human-robot interaction, allowing speech and emotion-related facial expressions to be generated according to the context of the incoming tactile sensations.

The development of robotic systems able to interact with the environment requires the use of multiple sensing modalities. Incorporating the sense of touch to such systems has led to improvements in grasping, manipulation, and exploration of material and geometric properties. Tactile sensing involves the transduction of physical magnitudes akin to mechanoreception processes occurring in biological touch. The dimensionality of tactile data depends on the number of touch-sensitive elements contained in the sensing device. These tactile elements generally present a distribution within the artificial skin in a manner that the overlapping receptive fields deliver a highly correlated multidimensional signal in accordance to skin deformation. The formation of tactile memories can be related to the reduction of redundancies, and reveal invariances through compression of sensory signals.

It has been previously demonstrated that linear dimensionality reduction of systematically collected tactile data involving orientation and sensor position produces a structured manifold. The generated manifold reflects regularities from the observational space with the potential to support accurate perception of magnitudes for sensorimotor control [1]; specifically in the discrimination of angle and position of the sensor with respect to the edge of an object using non-parametric models in supervised learning [14]. Alternatively, non-linear dimensionality reduction has been studied in the context of learning a manifold to relate tactile data and actions for object recognition [17]. In addition, in [16] data efficiency in tactile exploration was addressed with online learning through the update of a GPLVM model with an intelligent policy for data collection by analysing similarities of incoming tactile data in the latent variable space.

Although non-linear dimensionality reduction for sensorimotor tasks has provided meaningful representations as an aid to perception, the use of GPLVMs as tactile memories with the capability to mimic the functionality of biological memories remains to be examined. In this work, we show that the formation of tactile memories previously demonstrated to provide accurate perception in a social interaction setting can be extended to the perception of magnitudes related to the execution of sensorimotor tasks. Specifically, we evaluate functional characteristics of memory such as compression, pattern separation, and pattern completion of tactile memories that encode geometric and spatial qualities. We show that improvements in accuracy of a nearest neighbour regressor can be achieved through the effective contextual separation capabilities of the SSM. Additionally, sensory observations related to 'imagined touch' are generated from the latent representations of test data. These generated tactile percepts appear to be noticeably similar to the real streams of data.

2   Methods

2.1   Robotic Setting

The systematic collection of tactile data containing implicit information regarding edge orientation and relative sensor position require a robotic platform able to perform movements with precision, and a tactile sensor mimicking the operation of mechanoreception. The robotic system (Fig. 1a), previously used for the execution of a tactile exploratory procedure [15], consists of a Cartesian robot with a soft biomimetic tactile sensor as the end effector.

Robotic Platform. The formation of tactile memories that encode spatial quantities requires a robotic platform able to perform precise and accurate movements within the horizontal plane. The "Yamaha XYX" Cartesian robot produces highly accurate movements of approximately $20\,\mu\mathrm{m}$, thus being able to produce a consistent positioning of the sensor for the systematic collection of tactile data. The contact between the sensor and the surface of the object requires discrete vertical movements (taps onto the surface). This interaction with the object is performed with the action of an "Actuonix P-16" linear actuator. This device acts as a prismatic joint in a range of 50 mm. The actuator does not produce precise and consistent vertical movements. However, the produced motion of the actuator allows the collection of tactile data in a less structured setting, being able to record signals more likely to occur in a real world setting.

Biomimetic Tactile Sensor. Tactile data is acquired through the use of a TacTip sensor [3] mounted on the robotic platform. The TacTip is a soft biomimetic optical tactile sensor. The device consists of a 40 mm-diameter compliant dome containing a distributed array of 127 markers inside the dome filled with a clear compliant acrylic polymer. A 3D printed structure is attached to the dome enclosing a webcam pointing towards the markers. The camera provides samples at 20 frames per second with a resolution of 640×480 pixels. The detection and tracking of the markers is achieved through computer vision techniques [9], delivering a continuous stream of data consisting of the horizontal and vertical positions of each of the markers. Therefore, delivering a 254-dimensional array per sample associated to the recorded position of each marker.

(A)   (B)

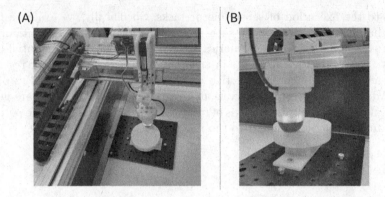

Fig. 1. Robotic setting. A) The Robotic platform consists of a Yamaha "XYX" robot and an Actuonix P-16 linear actuator vertical displacements. B) TacTip sensor [3] with the stimulus for data collection.

2.2   Tactile Data Acquisition

The collection of data for the formation and recovery of tactile memories is systematically performed with the execution of discrete taps onto the periphery of the surface of an object. The object for tactile interaction is a 3D printed 2.5D flat surface with a circular shape, as depicted in Fig. 1b. The object was selected given that circular flat surfaces contain the majority of the possible relative edge orientations to be encoded in the latent space. Edge orientations are represented by the relative angle between the sensor and the edge of the object. Thus, for each relative orientation a set of taps are executed from a position of -9 mm to 5 mm in steps of 1 mm where the 0 mm position is located at the edge of the object.

The data acquisition procedure consists of aligning the centre of the compliant dome of the sensor to a distance of 9 mm relative to the edge of the object. Consecutively, a vertical displacement of 4 mm towards the surface is performed with a duration of 0.6 s. This time duration is taken into account from the beginning of the displacement until the fulfilment of the time. Thereafter, a vertical movement directed to the initial position is executed (Fig. 2a); at this stage, the data is recorded for 0.4 s. Subsequently, a pause of 1 s is set to make sure the shape of the compliant component of the sensor is restored. After a discrete tap is executed, the Cartesian robot performs a displacement of 1 mm in a direction towards the centre of the object following the radial axis of the constant movement angle relative to the orientation to be perceived (Fig. 2b). This procedure is repeated until the sensor reaches the final radial position (5 mm from the edge to the centre) for angles from 0 to 342° in steps of 18°. Therefore, obtaining 20 constant angle sets composed of taps from 17 equidistant positions; providing 340 discrete taps for training. Samples of the collected data can be observed in Fig. 2c, along with the distribution of the internal markers of the TacTip sensor (Fig. 2d)

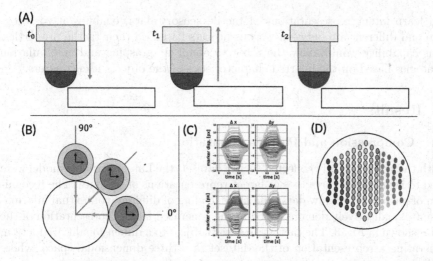

Fig. 2. Data collection procedure. A) Execution of a tap over the stimulus. B) Direction of sensor displacement for the collection of multiple taps for each edge orientation. C) Tactile data for taps located at 2 mm from the edge to the centre for 0 and 90° orientations. D) Internal marker distribution of the sensor.

2.3   Bayesian Latent Variable Model

The formation of tactile memories involves inferring latent representations from tactile sensory data and incorporating a generative component for recall and the generation of imagined touch. Gaussian Process Latent Variable models (GPLVMs) offer a powerful tool for nonlinear dimensionality reduction [7,8]. These unsupervised learning models derive latent representations of the data through a generative mapping function, where observations (y) are related to latent variables (x) through the equation $y = f(x) + \epsilon$, with ϵ representing Gaussian noise. The Bayesian variant of the model (BGPLVMs) allows for further data compression through the use of inducing points to handle larger datasets [18]. Importantly, these low-dimensional latent variable descriptions of high-dimensional data exhibit properties akin to biological memory, including compression, pattern separation, and pattern completion [4]. In our study, we employed the implementation of GPLVM from the GPy library [6] to train the Simple Synthetic Memory (SSM). The model utilized an RBF kernel with automatic relevance determination, as well as white noise and bias kernels. The latent representations were initialized through principal component analysis, and the positions of the latent points were optimized using the kernel hyperparameters.

The application of latent variable models, such as Gaussian Process Latent Variable models (GPLVMs), extends beyond theoretical considerations and finds practical utility in interactive scenarios. For instance, in the field of human-robot interaction, these models can enhance the robot's ability to perceive and interact with its environment. Consider a scenario where a robot is equipped with tactile sensors to explore and interact with objects. By employing GPLVMs, the robot can learn latent representations of tactile sensory data, enabling it to recognize and differentiate between various objects based on their tactile properties. This capability would allow the robot to adapt its grasping and manipulation strategies based on the inferred characteristics of the objects it encounters.

3   Results

3.1   Compression and Pattern Separation

With the systematically collected tactile dataset, the Latent Variable model were used to form tactile memories as latent representations of the data. The recognition of patterns from raw data, and the encoding of different contextual information are qualitatively demonstrated in the generated latent representation of the data, shown in Fig. 3. The tactile data was subject to a dimensionality reduction, generating a representation of the dataset in a three dimensional space, where each data-point is equivalent to the memory of a tap over the stimulus.

The encoded information within the manifold is related to the variables that were used to conduct the data acquisition. Figure 3a, c present the projection of the SSM on latent dimensions 0 and 1. The distribution of taps associated to different angles reveals a pattern separation over the latent dimension 1 (Fig. 3a). Similarly, as observed in Fig. 3c, the taps related to sensor position are distributed over the latent dimension 0. Pattern separation of tap representations is more evident on taps collected in positions from −9 mm (labelled as class 0) to taps on the edge of the object, i.e. 0 mm (labelled as class 10), denoting similarity between taps as the data is acquired towards the centre of the object. Additionally, Fig. 3b, d, can be seen as a illustration of the data collection process in which the different edge orientations are radially distributed (Fig. 3b), and where the positions of the sensor preserve the acquisition arrangement (Fig. 3d).

The quantification of pattern recognition and separation was performed through K-NN regressor models for raw data and compressed data. Taking into account the memory feature of encoding consistency, we used the same representations of memory to train and test a nearest neighbour regression model. The performance of the regression model, as a proxy for evaluating the compression and pattern separation of the SSM was quantified through the use of the R^2 score and the Mean Absolute Error (MAE) of test data predictions.

Table 1. Performance metrics for nearest neighbour regression model with data from the latent space.

Metric	Angle	Position
R^2 (Raw)	0.824	0.983
R^2 (SSM)	0,992	0.985
M.A.E (Raw)	24.49 [deg]	0.46 [mm]
M.A.E (SSM)	2,54 [deg]	0,34 [mm]

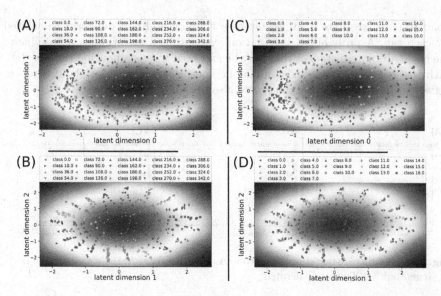

Fig. 3. Latent Representation of tactile memories. Compressed representation labelled as angle classes in the manifold, depicting latent dimensions: A) 0 and 1 B) 1 and 2. Representation labelled as position classes in the manifold, depicting latent dimensions: C) 0 and 1. D) 1 and 2. Each point is associated to a tap, the background intensities correspond to the uncertainty of predicting observations from latent variables.

The coefficient of determination (R^2 score) provides insight into the goodness of fit of the model, thereby enabling an assessment of the model's ability to accurately predict unseen samples based on the extent of explained variance. The highest attainable score is 1. The R^2 score for angle and position indicate that a robust compression and pattern separation has been achieved. A high coefficient of determination can lead to accurate predictions, reflected in the obtained mean absolute error. Table 1 shows an increase in performance for the regression of both variables by effect of due to the pattern recognition property of the BGPLVM. Additionally, a relevant increase in performance for angle regression can be noticed. This improvement in accuracy reflects the pattern separation capabilities of the SSM.

3.2   Pattern Completion

The reconstruction of tactile observations from partial information was achieved through the generative mapping function of the Bayesian Latent Variable Model. In this work, taps from the test dataset were subject to dimensionality reduction trough the SSM. This compressed data was used to generate observation data, i.e. tactile data from the execution of a discrete tap. The produced data may be regarded as imagined touch given that no actions are required for its generation. The existence of differences between train and test observations were taken into account to quantify the correctness of the generated data. The mean of the point-to-point absolute distance between training and test data was calculated for each tap. A probability distribution was obtained to establish a baseline of the mean absolute distances that may be expected when comparing the real data with the generated data. In a similar manner, distributions for the differences between real and generated data were also obtained.

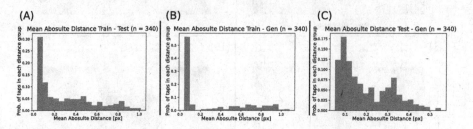

Fig. 4. Probability distributions for mean absolute distance: A)Train vs Test. B) Train vs Generated. C) Test vs Generated.

Figure 4 presents the probability distributions as representations of the mean distance between taps for: train and test data (Fig. 4a); train and generated data (Fig. 4b); test and generated data Fig. 4c. These metrics can be considered as a quantification of the error between observations. Differences between real and generated data should be expected due to the existence of differences from train and test real data. As expressed in Table 2, the minimum error for train vs test observational data denotes a difference of 0.007 pixels with respect to the train vs generated data. Samples of the minimum error obtained from the train vs gen. distribution (Fig. 4b) can be observed in Fig. 5; the similarity of the generated data with respect to the real data can be visually corroborated with a congruent displacement of the internal markers of the sensor. Similarly, the difference of 0.020 pixels corresponding to the minimum error from the test vs gen. distribution (Fig. 4c) substantiate the resemblance of the tactile observations presented in Fig. 6.

The observation data with the maximum error of train vs generated data (Fig. 7) provides a notion of the type of differences that might be expected. Although the majority of internal markers of generated data show a similar displacement compared to observations from the train dataset, some markers display differences in amplitude, specially following a displacement similar to the tap data of the test set. A similar effect can be noticed in the sample of maximum difference between test vs generated data (Fig. 8). However, in this case, the tap of the generated dataset appears to have more similarity to the observation from the train dataset than to the tap data from the test set.

A Mann-Whitney U test [10] was conducted to determine whether that samples from the obtained distributions come from the same population. The mean of absolute distances were assigned to three groups. Group 1: Train vs Test M.A.D; Group 2: Train vs Gen. M.A.D; Group 3: Test vs Gen. M.A.D. A critical value

Table 2. Maximum and minimum values for the mean of the absolute distances between real and generated observations.

Metric	Train vs Test	Train vs Gen.	Test vs Gen.
Min. M.A.D.	0.032 [px]	0.039 [px]	0.052 [px]
Max. M.A.D.	1.013 [px]	1.082 [px]	0.551 [px]

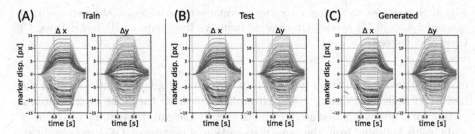

Fig. 5. Samples of tactile data for the minimum mean distance between train and generated data (0.039 pixels). Observation from: A) Train dataset, B) Test dataset, C) Generated dataset.

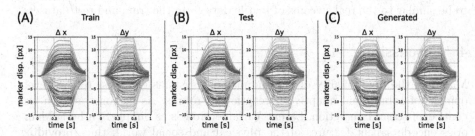

Fig. 6. Samples of tactile data for the minimum mean distance between test and generated data (0.052 pixels). Observation from: A) Train dataset, B) Test dataset, C) Generated dataset.

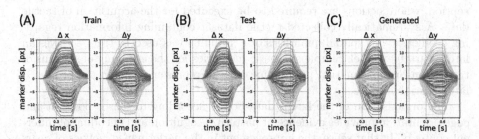

Fig. 7. Samples of tactile data for the maximum mean distance between train and generated data (1.082 pixels). Observation from: A) Train dataset, B) Test dataset, C) Generated dataset.

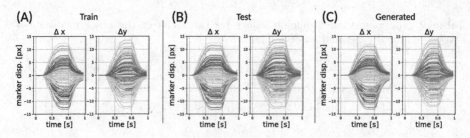

Fig. 8. Samples of tactile data for the maximum mean distance between test and generated data (0.551 pixels). Observation from: A) Train dataset, B) Test dataset, C) Generated dataset.

of $\alpha = 0.01$ was set to avoid type I errors, i.e. obtaining false positives. With the null hypothesis that Group 1 and Group 2 come from the same distribution, a p-value of 0.093 was calculated. Similarly, with the null hypothesis of Group 1 and Group 3 coming from the same distribution, a p-value of 0.052 was obtained. For both cases there is weak evidence that the mean of the absolute distances do not come from the same population. Thus, failing to reject the null hypothesis. Qualitatively, these results are consistent with the similarity quantification as presented in Figs. 5, 6, 7 and 8, where the generated tactile observations appear to be similar to the real streams of tactile data from the train and test datasets.

4   Discussion

Matching the functionality of biologic memory systems gives rise to the development of robust and adaptive perception in robots. As demonstrated in the context of social interaction, Latent Variable Models as Simple Synthetic Memories encode salient features of the physical and social world; thus, providing an efficient encoding of high-dimensional streams of data, and generative capabilities for the reconstruction of observation sensory data given a cue. These insights of memory formation and recall from social interaction were tested in the context of physical interaction, specifically in a setting of robotic tactile perception, where actions are required to be executed for the acquisition of tactile data. A systematically collected tactile dataset containing information regarding geometric and spatial quantities of a stimulus was used to train a Bayesian latent variable model. Simple synthetic memories for the encoding of streams of tactile sensory information provide meaningful representations in the produced latent variable space.

The organisation of the latent data-points according to sensor position and edge orientation provides evidence of pattern recognition and encoding of different contexts. In that sense, the improvement in the performance metrics of nearest neighbour regression using compressed data compared to raw data reveals the effects of pattern separation in the latent space. Recall and generation of tactile memories was attained through the generative capabilities of the SSM.

The similarity of the observations between the generated dataset with respect to the train and test dataset was evaluated by calculating a metric related to the error between real and generated data. As errors between train and test data appear to be present due to the response of the linear actuator that executes vertical movements in data acquisition, we could determine that the errors of train and test touch vs imagined touch followed similar probability distributions. This outcome was confirmed with the application of a Mann-Whitney U test, determining that distributions of train-gen. error and test-gen. error might come from the same population. Additionally, the similarity between real and generated data was depicted by showing the samples in which the minimum and maximum error was obtained (Figs. 5, 6, 7 and 8), demonstrating a similar and congruent pattern of displacement of the internal markers of the sensor.

The use of Simple Synthetic Memories of touch may be considered as an abstraction of the posterior parietal cortex of non human primates where convergence of cutaneous and proprioceptive inputs appear to take place [13]. In robotic systems, the encoding of spatial and geometric qualities from tactile data can support the completion of complex sensorimotor tasks by providing robust representations of memories and generating 'imagined touch' streams of data for planning optimal movements in the execution of tasks such as grasping, manipulation and tactile property exploration.

To provide a practical example, let's consider the potential application of SSMs in tactile perception for robots. By encoding memories within the tactile sensory modality, SSMs can enable robots to efficiently capture and process tactile information. Imagine a robot equipped with tactile sensors on its fingertips, which can detect and gather rich tactile data from interactions with objects or surfaces. To make sense of this data and generate meaningful representations, the robot can employ SSMs, utilizing Gaussian Process Latent Variable models (GPLVMs) to derive low-dimensional latent representations of the tactile data.

These SSMs trained on tactile data could enable the robot to perform various tasks related to tactile perception. For example, the robot could learn to recognize different textures by encoding tactile memories of various surfaces. When presented with a new tactile stimulus, the robot could use pattern completion techniques to reconstruct the complete texture based on a partial cue. This ability would be particularly useful when exploring unfamiliar objects or environments. Furthermore, SSMs can facilitate pattern separation, enabling the robot to distinguish between different tactile patterns. This would allow the robot to recall distinct patterns of interaction, even if they share some similarities in terms of tactile properties. By leveraging the memory capabilities of SSMs, the robot could navigate its environment, manipulate objects, and interact with humans using tactile information in a more human-like and context-aware manner.

While the practical example described above demonstrates the potential of SSMs in tactile perception for robots, further research and development are needed to realize this application fully. Future works could focus on training SSMs specifically for tactile data, exploring different strategies for encoding and processing tactile information, and evaluating the performance of SSM-based tactile perception systems in real-world robotic scenarios. By incorporating SSMs into tactile perception, robots could enhance their ability to interact with the physical world and engage in tasks that require tactile sensitivity opening new possibilities for robotic applications.

Acknowledgments. This work was supported by European Union's Horizon 2020 MSCA Programme under Grant Agreement No. 813713 NeuTouch and by the EU Horizon 2020 FET Flagship programme through the Human Brain Project (HBP-SGA3, 945539).

Competing Interests. TJP is a director and shareholder in two robotics companies-Consequential Robotics Ltd. and Bettering Our Worlds (BOW) Ltd. These companies are not expected to benefit from this publication. PJS has no competing interests.

References

1. Aquilina, K., Barton, D.A., Lepora, N.F.: Principal components of touch. In: Proceedings - IEEE International Conference on Robotics and Automation, pp. 4071–4078. Institute of Electrical and Electronics Engineers Inc., September 2018. https://doi.org/10.1109/ICRA.2018.8461045
2. Boorman, L.W., Damianou, A.C., Martinez-Hernandez, U., Prescott, T.J.: Extending a hippocampal model for navigation around a maze generated from real-world data. In: Wilson, S.P., Verschure, P.F.M.J., Mura, A., Prescott, T.J. (eds.) LIVINGMACHINES 2015. LNCS (LNAI), vol. 9222, pp. 441–452. Springer, Cham (2015). https://doi.org/10.1007/978-3-319-22979-9_44
3. Chorley, C., Melhuish, C., Pipe, T., Rossiter, J.: Development of a tactile sensor based on biologically inspired edge encoding. In: 2009 International Conference on Advanced Robotics, ICAR 2009 (2009)
4. Damianou, A., Ek, C.H., Boorman, L., Lawrence, N.D., Prescott, T.J.: A top-down approach for a synthetic autobiographical memory system. In: Wilson, S.P., Verschure, P.F.M.J., Mura, A., Prescott, T.J. (eds.) LIVINGMACHINES 2015. LNCS (LNAI), vol. 9222, pp. 280–292. Springer, Cham (2015). https://doi.org/10.1007/978-3-319-22979-9_28
5. Evans, M.H., Fox, C.W., Prescott, T.J.: Machines learning - towards a new synthetic autobiographical memory. In: Duff, A., Lepora, N.F., Mura, A., Prescott, T.J., Verschure, P.F.M.J. (eds.) Living Machines 2014. LNCS (LNAI), vol. 8608, pp. 84–96. Springer, Cham (2014). https://doi.org/10.1007/978-3-319-09435-9_8
6. GPy: GPy: A Gaussian process framework in PyThon (2014). http://github.com/SheffieldML/GPy
7. Lawrence, N.: Probabilistic non-linear principal component analysis with gaussian process latent variable models. J. Mach. Learn. Res. **6**, 1783–1816 (2005)
8. Lawrence, N.D.: Gaussian process latent variable models for visualisation of high dimensional data. In: Advances in Neural Information Processing Systems (2004)
9. Lepora, N.F., Aquilina, K., Cramphorn, L.: Exploratory tactile servoing with active touch. IEEE Robot. Autom. Lett. **2**(2), 1156–1163 (2017). https://doi.org/10.1109/LRA.2017.2662071

10. Mann, H.B., Whitney, D.R.: On a test of whether one of two random variables is stochastically larger than the other. Ann. Math. Stat. **18**(1), 50–60 (1947). http://www.jstor.org/stable/2236101

11. Martinez-Hernandez, U., Damianou, A., Camilleri, D., Boorman, L.W., Lawrence, N., Prescott, T.J.: An integrated probabilistic framework for robot perception, learning and memory. In: 2016 IEEE International Conference on Robotics and Biomimetics, ROBIO 2016, pp. 1796–1801 (2016). https://doi.org/10.1109/ROBIO.2016.7866589

12. Prescott, T.J., Camilleri, D., Martinez-Hernandez, U., Damianou, A., Lawrence, N.D.: Memory and mental time travel in humans and social robots. Philos. Trans. Roy. Soc. B Biol. Sci. **374**(1771), 20180025 (2019). https://doi.org/10.1098/rstb.2018.0025

13. Sakata, H., Shibutani, H., Kawano, K.: Neural correlates of space perception in the parietal association cortex of the monkey. In: Brain and Behaviour, Pergamon, pp. 291–298, January 1981. https://doi.org/10.1016/b978-0-08-027338-9.50047-5

14. Salazar, P.J., Prescott, T.J.: Deep Gaussian processes for angle and position discrimination in active touch sensing. In: Cañamero, L., Gaussier, P., Wilson, M., Boucenna, S., Cuperlier, N. (eds.) SAB 2022. LNAI, vol. 13499, pp. 41–51. Springer, Cham (2022). https://doi.org/10.1007/978-3-031-16770-6_4

15. Salazar, P.J., Prescott, T.J.: Tactile and proprioceptive online learning in robotic contour following. In: Pacheco-Gutierrez, S., Cryer, A., Caliskanelli, I., Tugal, H., Skilton, R. (eds.) TAROS 2022. LNAI, vol. 13546, pp. 166–178. Springer, Cham (2022). https://doi.org/10.1007/978-3-031-15908-4_14

16. Stone, E.A., Lepora, N.F., Barton, D.A.: Learning to live life on the edge: online learning for data-efficient tactile contour following. In: IEEE International Conference on Intelligent Robots and Systems, pp. 9854–9860. Institute of Electrical and Electronics Engineers Inc., September 2020. https://doi.org/10.1109/IROS45743.2020.9341565. arXiv:1909.05808

17. Tanaka, D., Matsubara, T., Ichien, K., Sugimoto, K.: Object manifold learning with action features for active tactile object recognition. In: IEEE International Conference on Intelligent Robots and Systems, pp. 608–614. IEEE, September 2014. https://doi.org/10.1109/IROS.2014.6942622

18. Titsias, M.K., Lawrence, N.D.: Bayesian Gaussian process latent variable model. J. Mach. Learn. Res. **9**, 844–851 (2010). JMLR Workshop and Conference Proceedings

Distributed Adaptive Control for Virtual Cyborgs: A Case Study for Personalized Rehabilitation

S. Kahali[✉], T. Ngo, T. S. Mandahar, E. Martínez-Bueno, O. Guerrero-Rosado,
H. López-Carral, I. T. Freire, A. Mura, and P. F. M. J. Verschure

Donders Institute for Brain, Cognition and Behaviour, 6525 GD Nijmegen, The Netherlands
sajad.kahali@donders.ru.nl

Abstract. As robotics and artificial intelligence have become greatly advanced, cyborgs are often envisioned as the next step in human evolution. Once only a fictional concept, nowadays, cyborg systems can be used to support people with neurological impairments and enhance their quality of life. Recent technological advances have given rise to numerous novel solutions for neurorehabilitation, in which combining wearable exoskeletons and virtual reality-based exercises has emerged as a promising technique. Nonetheless, there is often a lack of a control architecture that effectively integrates and coordinates the adaptation of different modules within such VR-robotic synergistic rehabilitative systems. In this pilot study, we propose a multi-level adaptive coaching paradigm based on the notion of 'virtual cyborgs' and evaluate its core components. By modeling the digitized representations of exoskeleton-assisted human subjects and providing adaptation through a distributed control architecture, we aim to establish a groundwork for personalized interventions that are more accessible than available treatments.

Keywords: Cyborg · Adaptive Control · Cognitive Architecture · Virtual Reality · Rehabilitation Robotics

1 Introduction

The current digital era calls for human augmentation resulting from advancements in fields such as artificial intelligence and biotechnology. According to modern theorists, the merging process of humans and technologies into cyborgs is already taking place and is no longer a futuristic concept [1, 2]. The term 'cyborg' was first coined in 1960 by Clynes and Kline [3], referring to a living organism whose capabilities are restored or augmented beyond its typical restrictions with built-in artificial components [2–4]. Biology and technology should be integrated tightly for such a human-machine hybrid to be called a 'cyborg' [2, 5]. Cyborgs are usually depicted in science fiction as going beyond human abilities and having visible mechanical extensions. However, theorists suggested that any mechanical, chemical or digital tool used to partially regenerate or unburden any human sensorimotor or cognitive process can also be regarded as part of a cyborg system [2].

F. Meder et al. (Eds.): Living Machines 2023, LNAI 14157, pp. 16–32, 2023.
https://doi.org/10.1007/978-3-031-38857-6_2

Medical advancements like bionic limbs, wearable exoskeletons, brain stimulation, retina and cochlear implants, vaccines, and pharmaceuticals to alter the psychological states of people with neurological disorders are all influenced by the idea of cyborgs [5, 6]. Among neurological diseases causing acquired disability globally, stroke is the most common [7]. Severely impaired motor and cognitive functions that follow stroke often inhibit full and autonomous participation in activities of daily living [8]. Due to the frequent lack of sufficient recovery and patients' quality of life [9], it has become crucial to develop rehabilitative treatments that are tailor-made to stroke patients and more effective in targeting particular impairments [10–12].

Robot-assisted neurorehabilitation has a relatively long history in promoting neuro-motor recovery via intensive, repetitive, and task-oriented training of the paretic limbs while reducing the workload of healthcare practitioners [13, 14]. The use of robotic devices in aiding individuals with motor deficits has been proven a fruitful approach to hasten functional recovery [14, 15]. Exoskeletons are commonly used devices for movement rehabilitation with mechanical structures mirroring the skeletal structures of human extremities [16]. An exoskeleton can form a cyborg when being worn by a human body for either power augmentation or motion assistance [13].

Besides robotics, virtual reality (VR) has gained increased traction from healthcare practitioners in recent years [16] thanks to its inherent utility of engaging patients in embodied and task-specific training [17]. VR isolates users from physical reality into a controllable and customizable virtual world where therapists can manipulate various sensory stimuli to achieve rehabilitative goals [16–18]. In addition, VR-based training effectively fosters neuroplasticity and post-stroke recovery through skills acquisition, retention, and generalization [18]. Thus, rehabilitation enhanced by VR technologies often outperform standard care [18–20], and this holds not only for the motor domain but can be generalized as a holistic strategy that enhances cognitive functions [21].

While robotics and VR have led to groundbreaking healthcare approaches, further progress is required for these technologies to have a significant impact, especially in terms of adaptive and personalized interventions. In conventional practice, clinicians typically prescribe exercises to their patients based on preliminary assessment, which have been shown as an unreliable predictor of recovery outcomes [22]. Additionally, individualized rehabilitation has been demonstrated to shorten treatment time, lower re-hospitalization risk, and improve exercise adherence [9–11]. Hence, there is a need to move away from a one-size-fits-all strategy and adapt task difficulty and assistance modalities to each affected individual [11]. On the one hand, contemporary cyborgs are often equipped with extended sensors, allowing them to incorporate functionalities for both quantitative monitoring of movements and optimally administrating tailor-made interventions [23]. This entails both opportunities and challenges regarding the seamless integration of organic and machine components as an effective cyborg may require extensive knowledge about the specific individual involved in the system [24]. On the other hand, serious games – a prevalent type of VR healthcare content [25, 26] – can facilitate contextual experiences due to the variability of behavioral responses [26]. This could mean adjusting training scenarios to the user's intents or needs [27].

Considering that individualized neurorehabilitation is desirable and promising, plus the combination of different assisting modalities might have a greater impact than a single approach, we propose to incorporate the VR-based training exercises from the clinically-validated Rehabilitation Gaming System (RGS) [27] into a cyborg system with digitized neuroprosthesis. To overcome the challenge of delivering a customized experience to every participant, we utilize a trending user-modeling paradigm for fast and reliable decision-making in digital healthcare – the digital twin (DT) [28]. DT is a virtual representation that – through bi-directional data flows – reproduces, monitors, predicts, and enhances in real-time the processes and features of a connected real-world living entity [29, 30]. Modeling a DT of a bionically-augmented human (i.e., a cyborg) is possible in VR. In this paper, we suggested the notion of a 'virtual cyborg' – the digital counterpart of an exoskeleton coupled with a human user. The human-exoskeleton combination can be represented in VR as a human avatar 'wearing' an exoskeleton made of pure bits of information [32]. The human avatar and the virtual exoskeleton are characterized using digital readings pertaining to movements, forces, and other measurements that make such entities equivalent to the unique ones in the real world. Besides increasing the accessibility of rehabilitative solutions, this hybrid approach enables more intuitive human-machine interactions and improves the assist-as-needed aspect of virtual neuroprosthetic devices [14, 30].

Modeling an effective virtual cyborg involves more than just imitating the external structure of its real-world counterpart. A body's internal states (e.g., muscular fatigue, cognitive load) should be considered as it interacts with its surroundings [31]. Hence, kinematics data from users' actual movements as well as their internal states should be updated in synchrony. At the same time, the dynamic assistance of neuroprosthetic devices and real-time displays of the VR-based training context can directly influence users' physiological states and performance, resulting in closed-loop feedback. This synergistic system then can help in adaptive interventions best suited to each patient's functional status and recovery progress [30].

This pilot study serves as the first step towards a more comprehensive solution currently being developed under the REhabilitation based on HYBrid neuroprosthesis project (REHYB, https://rehyb.eu). The main objectives of REHYB are to maximize the rehabilitation efficiency and improve the quality of life of stroke survivors. These objectives are accomplished through a VR-based rehabilitation program approved by clinicians that estimates patients' user models from various motion and physiological sensors and offer multi-modal assisting devices, including an upper-body exoskeleton and an EMG-based functional electrical stimulation (FES). The exoskeleton, the FES, and the VR-based environment (RGS) are coordinated within a control system serving the role of a rehabilitation coach that delivers adequate motor and cognitive aids. In this exploration, we focus solely on the bio-inspired design of such a coaching system before integrating it into the REHYB ecosystem with actual sensors and actuators. In other words, rather than equipping subjects with a real exoskeleton and FES device, we bypass the FES and embed a functioning virtual exoskeleton into the RGS system. Physiological data used to drive control signals is also simulated instead of retrieved from stroke patients through sensors. Although the effectiveness of the entire REHYB paradigm is not fully demonstrated in this preliminary study, we expect to develop and optimize the system's core modules that operate towards fulfilling the proposed principles of personalized, internally-driven adaptive control.

Figure 1 depicts a general overview of the user-centered coaching system employed in this paper. The main modules explored in this work include: 1) the first-order need-based, closed-loop feedback control based on the patient's simulated physiological states; and 2) the second-order adaptive control delivered by the system's outputs – i.e., the virtual exoskeleton embedded in the virtual environment and the parameters of RGS's task difficulty.

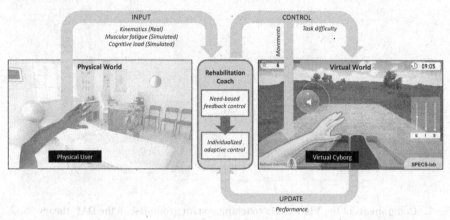

Fig. 1. General overview of the VR-robotic synergistic coaching system for individualized rehabilitation. The real-world user's movements (left) are monitored and translated into the virtual world (right). The rehabilitation coach (middle) serves as a control interface between the physical and virtual worlds. Control signals from the rehabilitation coach are used to drive the virtual exoskeleton (gray-bordered zone) and are coupled with the actual tracked movements to form the final virtual movement.

Conceptual Framework for Distributed Adaptive Control. The rehabilitation coach is built following the Distributed Adaptive Control (DAC) cognitive architecture [32, 33]. DAC provides a control framework comprising biologically-constrained models of sensorimotor and cognitive functions. It has become a standard in the domains of behavior-based robotics [34] and VR neurorehabilitation [35]. The DAC framework views the human brain as a distributed control system constituting parallel, tightly-coupled layers: Somatic, Reactive, Adaptive, and Contextual. These layers cooperate and compete to guide the virtual cyborg's individualized adaptation to its contextual VR environment (RGS) (see Fig. 2).

The Somatic layer resembles the virtual cyborg's body. It defines inputs acquired from the virtual environment, internally-generated needs, and the movement control of both the human avatar and the virtual exoskeleton. The Reactive layer comprises sensorimotor control loops representing the cyborg's internal needs (i.e., stabilizing cognitive load and muscular fatigue or maximizing perceived success in performing motor and cognitive functions). Those predefined closed-loop systems are triggered by changes in cognitive load or muscular fatigue, modulate RGS training parameters, and dynamically regulate exoskeleton supports. The Adaptive layer acquires a state space describing interaction context between the virtual cyborg and its environment and estimates the intent-driven trajectory to reach a target. It also adequately shapes actions based on outputs of other modules (i.e., user's intents, simulated physiological states, and rehabilitative goals). The Contextual layer relies on given clinical data and historical game events to predict the users' performance. Performance estimation is an essential first step to adapt the task difficulty of RGS training scenarios.

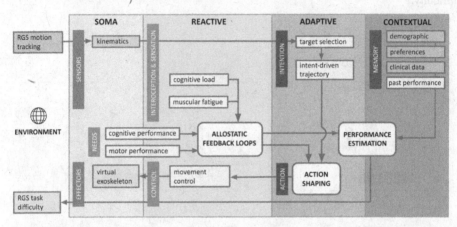

Fig. 2. Components of the VR-robotic coaching system grounded on the DAC theory. Modules are either inherent sensorimotor and cognitive attributes of the virtual cyborg (i.e., perception, internal needs, intention, memory, and action control) or environmental properties responsive to its goals and needs (motion tracking and adaptive task difficulty). RGS stands for Rehabilitation Gaming System. In the full REHYB system, cognitive load and muscular fatigue can be measured using physiological sensors and machine learning algorithms.

Control Theories Based on Task Performance, Task Difficulty, and Internal States. This study's ultimate objectives are to design and optimize a rehabilitation experience that is best suited to an individual's functional status and recovery goals. The desired situation might be a state in which participants actively engage in an exercise where their capacities – or, in other words, attainable performance – are balanced with how challenging the exercise is. The psychologist Mihaly Csikszentmihalyi has coined the term "flow" to describe such an optimal experience [36, 37] (see Fig. 3a). Likewise, the Yerkes-Dodson law [38] presents the relationship between mental arousal and task performance by postulating that optimal performance is reached when a participant experiences an intermediate arousal level. Performance deteriorates when the arousal levels are insufficient or excessive [38] (see Fig. 3b).

Both the flow theory and Yerkes-Dodson law demonstrate how humans, as living organisms, operate based on maintaining balanced physiological states, also known as principles of homeostasis and allostasis [39, 40]. While homeostasis can refer to any organismic activity used to preserve a desired level of internal conditions, allostasis is defined as maintaining overall stability through varying internal control parameters to ensure the adequate matching between one's needs and environmental resources [38]. Several previous works have applied these mechanisms to computationally resemble core behavioral systems driven by physiological needs [41–43] (see Fig. 3c–d).

With this pilot study, we aim to develop solutions based on these control theories that can contribute to comprehensive adaptive rehabilitation. We suggest that different individuals performing training exercises with different difficulty levels might require different physiological conditions to optimize performance. For instance, demanding tasks may benefit from a low level of fatigue to facilitate concentration, whereas tasks requiring perseverance might call for higher cognitive load to boost motivation. Thus, in order to provide efficacy, training sessions must maintain the balance between task difficulty, cognitive load and muscular fatigue levels, and task performance.

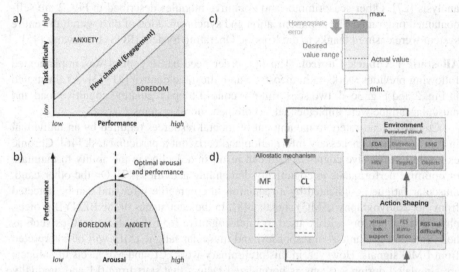

Fig. 3. Control theories based on performance, task difficulty, and internal states. a) Flow theory. The flow channel (gray zone) represents where the arousal level is balanced. b) Yerkes-Dodson law. Task performance is maximized when the arousal level is not too low or too high. c) The state of balance is reached when the actual cognitive load or fatigue value (red dashed line) falls within the desired range (blue zone); otherwise, a corrective tendency to bring back balance will be triggered (red arrow). d) The allostatic mechanism adjusts the cognitive aspects of RGS difficulty to address cognitive load (CL). Muscular fatigue (MF) is stabilized through both motor difficulty modulators and exoskeleton assistance. In the complete REHYB system, CL is interpreted from electrodermal activity (EDA) and heart rate variability (HRV), while MF could be deduced from electromyography (EMG) signals. Reproduced from [36, 38, 42, 43].

We hypothesize that 1) measures of cognitive load and muscular fatigue can inform us about the equilibrium between users' performance and the challenge their exercises represent. Furthermore, 2) given simulated physiological data, through the dynamic adaptation of the virtual exoskeleton's assistance and task difficulty, the desired levels of cognitive load or fatigue of subjects will be more likely to stay within their target range in comparison to those of ones trained with a fixed level of exoskeleton aids and game challenges. Likewise, the highest attainable performance is expected when the adaptive coaching system is in use.

2 Methods

We developed a "Hit, Grasp, Place" (HGP) RGS game tailored for neurorehabilitation as the training context of this study. In this desktop game, a series of colored spheres approach from the horizon toward the user, who must grasp and release them in the basket of the corresponding color to get points (Fig. 1, left). The game was primarily built using the Unity game engine (Unity Technologies, USA) [44] and benefits from a variety of technologies such as low-immersive VR, depth-sensing motion tracking via Azure Kinect device (Microsoft, USA), and machine learning algorithms for scene analysis [27]. Other sensorimotor and cognitive modules described in Fig. 2 are self-contained programs. The communication and synchronization of data within the entire system were ensured thanks to the Robotic Operating System (ROS) framework [45].

Allostatic Feedback Control. The first-order need-based control was implemented following previous works in homeostatic and allostatic control [41–43]. As illustrated in Fig. 2 and Fig. 3c–d, two sensorimotor control loops regulating cognitive load and muscular fatigue were implemented as core behavioral systems.

Cognitive load refers to the amount of mental resources required by an individual in order to process necessary information and carry out a particular task [46]. Chronic exposure to excessive cognitive load can result in a decline in the ability to maintain or optimize performance in cognitively demanding activities [47]. On the other hand, muscular fatigue is indicated by a reduction in contractile force and can be detected from electromyography (EMG) signals [48]. In the later stages of the REHYB project, physiological sensors will be used to infer cognitive load (CL) from metrics such as heart rate and galvanic skin responses, and muscular fatigue (MF) will be interpreted from EMG signals. However, in this preliminary work, CL and MF levels of subjects are simulated during sessions as normalized factors that start from 0.1 and gradually increase over time until they reach the maximum value of 1. The variability in task performance of the subject will affect this value. Although fatigue and cognitive load can both contribute to motor coordination and motor planning, distinct feedback loops can be established as the difficulty parameters linked to trained motor and cognitive functions are manipulated independently within the RGS environment. Likewise, the indicators of successful achievements in performing motor and cognitive subtasks are measured independently. For instance, an unsuccessful reach to a target will lead to a drop in motor performance and increased MF, whereas correctly putting a sphere onto a basket of the corresponding color shows an improvement in cognitive performance and subsequently decreases CL. Further exploration of machine and deep learning techniques might allow for the estimation of CL and MF from physiological data and will further distinguished these two core behavioral systems [49, 50].

Computationally, CL (which regulates the cognitive aspects of game difficulty) and MF (which adjusts aids from the virtual exoskeleton and motor difficulty level) were represented by error-based, closed-loop feedback controllers which determine an ideal value range of CL or MF as two minimum and maximum setpoints (SPs) and evaluate whether the actual condition (i.e., process variable - PV) is within that range. The coaching system only exhibits regulation when PV goes below the minimum SP or above the maximum SP, and the homeostatic errors (e) – i.e., the intensity of the tendency to bring back a balanced state – are calculated by the discrepancy between PV and the closest homeostatic threshold (Fig. 3c). For instance, once high muscular fatigue is detected, the adaptive rehabilitation coach will send control signals to lower the motor difficulty of the HGP training scenario and increase the virtual exoskeleton support. Similarly, a low level of cognitive load will trigger an increment in the HGP game's cognitive difficulty (Fig. 3d). Thus, given a timestep t, a constant increment unit b, and the change Δp in normalized performance (with respect to the maximum achievable performance), the PVs of CL or MF will be updated as follows:

$$PV_{t+1} = PV_t + b + \Delta p_t \tag{1}$$

On top of such evaluation of the homeostatic balance of CL and MF conditions, the rehabilitation coach constantly monitors generated homeostatic errors and distributes adaptation efforts based on the corresponding attained performance. Given a timestep t and the change Δp in normalized performance, the supports based on CL and MF are weighed by the gain factor K. K is updated following the below equation:

$$K_{t+1} = K_t \cdot (1 + \Delta p_t) \tag{2}$$

The end goal is to inform the whole VR-robotic synergistic system about how each of its components should provide support M to individual patients at each timestep t. M can be computed in a similar manner with a proportional-integral controller where the current perceived homeostatic error is integrated with the cumulative average of past errors over time to generate the final control signal. If the PV is below the minimum SP or above the maximum SP, the minimum SP or the maximum SP will be used to calculate errors, respectively.

$$M_t = K_t \cdot (|PV_t - SP_t| + \frac{1}{t} \cdot \sum_{j=0}^{t} |PV_j - SP_j|) \tag{3}$$

Future implementations can leverage this allostatic feedback controller and progress towards constructing a complete proportional-integral-derivative (PID) controller, in which the gains for each of the PID terms can be tuned using advanced methods such as evolutionary algorithms or neural networks.

Virtual Exoskeleton Embedded in RGS. In response to stroke patients' decreased range of motion, an essential function of a rehabilitative coaching system is to support subjects in performing movements they cannot execute independently. In the absence of a real exoskeleton, this function can be done by manipulating the virtual experience through modeling a virtual exoskeleton and mapping the tracked movements from subjects with its simulated assistance. The first step towards developing a functioning virtual exoskeleton with adaptive movement control is to determine the participant's arm's three-dimensional (3D) coordinates inside the RGS virtual environment after incorporating all motion data from various sources. In Fig. 4a, the "tracked" red dots resemble the virtual hand, elbow, and shoulder positions, resulting from real motion captured by the Azure Kinect depth-sensing camera. In the rehabilitation context, this information indicates the actual movements made by individuals with partial motor disabilities. The "target" position (green dot) represents the coordinates of where the users should reach in order to intercept a target successfully. To identify whether an existing virtual sphere is the subject's goal target, we generated the relative distance from all spheres available in the virtual environment to the virtual arm and assumed the closest one as the possible target.

The final 3D position P_{mapped} of the virtual arm (black dot) after applying the assistance given by the rehabilitation coach was determined as a linear interpolation between the $P_{tracked}$ position detected from the movement conducted by the subject and the targeted position P_{target}:

$$P_{mapped} = (1 - \theta).P_{tracked} + \theta.P_{target} \tag{4}$$

In which, θ can be defined as a mapping factor of the tracked and target movements and is expressed as the virtual exoskeleton's effects on the subject's movements. θ is determined based on the control signal M from allostatic closed-loop feedback control as follows:

$$\theta = M.Min((1 - (P_{tracked} - P_{target})/r), 0) \tag{5}$$

r is a tuning constant used in the activation of the virtual exoskeleton's assistance. It was determined as the size of an interaction zone that subjects' hands need to enter to authenticate their intention to reach the target sphere (see Fig. 4, light blue circle). If $P_{tracked}$ - P_{target} is larger than r, the $(P_{tracked} - P_{target})/r$ term would be greater than 1 and no control would be applied. With this, the exoskeleton support will not be executed when the virtual hand is too far from the target.

We employed the actualization of mapped movements using inverse kinematics. Inverse kinematics is the process of calculating joint parameters needed to place the endpoint (i.e., the virtual hand) of an animated kinematic chain in a given position and orientation relative to the starting point (i.e., the virtual shoulder), utilizing multiple trigonometric formulas [53]. The advantage of using inverse kinematics is that only the origin and destination of the motion are required, with the detailed motion of each connected component being implicitly computed (Fig. 4b).

Adaptive Modulation of RGS Game Difficulty. RGS integrates a machine learning algorithm for adaptive difficulty, which dynamically alters the complexity of the VR training context [28]. As shown in previous studies, this strategy has demonstrated beneficial impacts on stroke patients' recovery speed and motivation [26, 52]. The main advantage of this approach is that it takes performance as the sole input and moves away from ad-hoc, one-on-one mappings of indicators of success, addressed motor and cognitive functions, and game parameters for difficulty modulation.

Below is the code snippet of the adaptive difficulty algorithm for three arbitrary difficulty modulators (DMs). A Multi-layer Perceptron (MLP) regressor was used to predict performance at the next timestep based on a given configuration of those DMs. The algorithm will continuously search for the most optimal DM combinations until the predicted outcome reaches a desired target performance value. This target performance derives from the difficulty level commanded by the allostatic control module. For instance, if the adaptive rehabilitation coach sends an inquiry to decrease the task difficulty by a certain percentage, the algorithm will lower its expectation of achievable performance at the next timestep by decreasing the desired performance accordingly. A

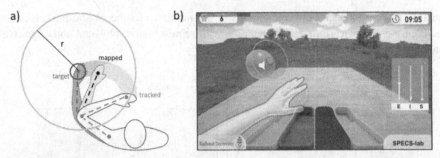

Fig. 4. Implementation of the virtual exoskeleton. Dark blue circle represents the virtual hand's 3D coordinates that could lead to a successful sphere grasp. Light blue circle indicates the "intention zone" that triggers exoskeleton assistance when reached by the virtual hand. a) Mapping actual tracked movements, fatigue-based support, and intent-driven target trajectory. b) The virtual exoskeleton (gray-bordered zone) overrides movements of the arm avatar to actualize the mapped movement. The sliders shows the assisting command given by allostatic control (E), the size of "intention zone" (I), and the adjusted difficulty of HGP game ("S"). All gizmos and sliders are hidden from subjects during sessions.

random set of corresponding DMs is initialized and used to predict an upcoming value of either cognitive or motor performance. When the prediction output is lower than what is desired, the system keeps generating another set of DMs. If the DMs are predicted to be able to deliver the expected outcome, the system will break the loop and changes in those game parameters will be applied.

```
while True:
    bestDM1 = random.randint(0, 10)/10
    bestDM2 = random.randint(0, 10)/10
    bestDM3 = random.randint(0, 10)/10
    predictedPerformance = MLPRegressor.predict([[bestDM1, bestDM2,
    bestDM3]])

    if accuracy > 0.7:
        if predictedPerformance < desiredPerformance:
            bestDM1 = random.randint(0, 10)/10
            bestDM2 = random.randint(0, 10)/10
            bestDM3 = random.randint(0, 10)/10
        else:
            break
```

Ten different configurations for task challenges have been implemented within the HGP training exercise, consisting of multiple parameters for modulating motor and cognitive difficulty levels. For instance, if a participant struggles to execute the full motion range of the paretic arm, the horizontal and vertical distribution ranges of virtual spheres (i.e., their dispersion from the center of the scene), the sizes of spheres and baskets, or the approaching speed of spheres will be more prioritized than other cognitive difficulty modulators. Examples of modulators that affect the complexity level of cognitive demands are the interval between spheres or the number of spheres and baskets' colors. Figure 5 shows various HGP scenarios with representative physical and cognitive challenges combinations.

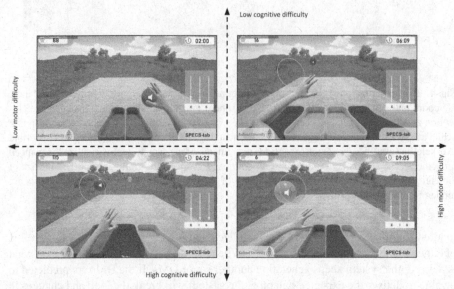

Fig. 5. HGP scenarios with different configurations of motor and cognitive challenges. Top left: low motor difficulty (small baskets and narrow horizontal range of sphere distribution) and low cognitive difficulty (only one color of spheres and baskets). Top right: higher motor difficulty (increased number of baskets and a wider range of required movements) and low cognitive difficulty. Bottom left: low motor difficulty and higher cognitive difficulty (more colors of spheres and baskets). Bottom right: high motor and cognitive challenges.

3   Results

To test our hypotheses on the effectiveness of the employed adaptation modules, we implemented two versions of the coaching system: one offers adaptive regulation of game difficulty and supports from the virtual exoskeleton (i.e., the adaptive coaching system), and the other constantly delivers the same HGP game challenges and fixed assistance to subjects regardless of either their CL and MF levels or performances (i.e., the static coach). We collected $n = 10$ healthy, informed subjects for both versions of the rehabilitation coach. Each subject played the HGP game twice on two different days and the order in which they tried the two systems was randomized. All training sessions had a fixed duration of 10 min. Each timestep started when a new sphere was launched into the virtual environment, and data collected from all sessions were limited to the first 330 timesteps for consistency.

Validation of Correlated Control Parameters. First, in order to validate whether the adaptive coaching system properly regulated RGS task difficulty according to the simulated CL and MF data, we picked out three representative trials with different conditions of CL and MF and evaluated the visualized assisting patterns (Fig. 6). We observed that an unstable cognitive performance and satisfactory motor achievements could lead to a condition with high CL and low MF (Fig. 6, left), resulting in a drastic decrease in cognitive challenges of the HGP game and a maximum level of motor difficulty, as well as little support provided by the virtual exoskeleton. Conversely, a condition with low CL and high MF (Fig. 6, middle) is the outcome of low motor performance and high cognitive performance. Such physiological conditions triggered a reduction in motor difficulty and increased exoskeleton assistance sufficiently. At the same time, the cognitive difficulty remained high. It is worth mentioning here that subjects can increase their cognitive performance while making no improvements in motor tasks by using the healthy limb to catch the target, which is informed to them in the beginning of the session.

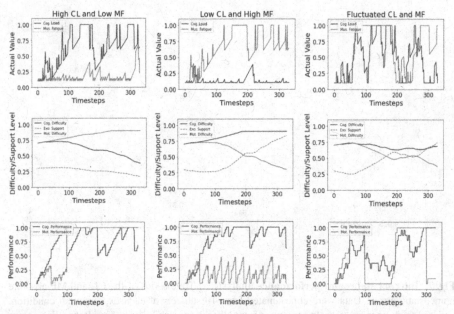

Fig. 6. Representative scenarios of closed-loop feedback control based on cognitive load (CL) and muscular fatigue (MF). The simulated actual values (process variables) of CL or MF of a feedback loop results from changes in obtained performance. Those given data are used to regulate supports from the training context and assisting devices. This, in turn, affects the achievability of an improved success rate.

Analyses on Stabilizing Simulated Internal States and Performance Maximization. We proceeded to analyze the efficacy of dynamically adjusting the extent of support from the HGP scenario and the virtual exoskeleton. Time series of homeostatic errors and achieved performance of subjects undergoing adaptive rehabilitation are extracted and compared to the same information from subjects receiving a fixed game difficulty of 0.7 and a constant assistance of 0.3 from the virtual exoskeleton.

As expected, the adaptive coaching system could maintain internal stability with fewer deviations caused by the lack of insufficient responses (see Fig. 7a). We also observed a significant superiority in cognitive performance exhibited by the adaptive coaching paradigm. However, there is no difference in motor performance between the two experimental conditions (Fig. 3b). Mann-Whitney tests were carried out to assess the significance of the preliminary results. When comparing two groups, both CL and MF homeostatic errors as well as obtained cognitive performance show p-values worthy of consideration (< 0.01). On the contrary, motor performance shows no superiority of the adaptive coach over the static supports.

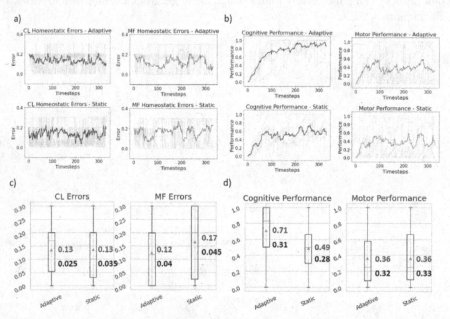

Fig. 7. Internal states and performance analysis. a) Time series of the CL and MF absolute homeostatic errors. Data were concatenated from 10 subjects of each experimental condition. Colored thick lines represent mean errors from all sessions, while each thin, dashed line comes from an individual trial. b) Similar to a) but in the case of cognitive and motor performance. c) Box plots of homeostatic errors and attained performance grouped by experimental condition. Green numbers indicate mean values of errors, and black numbers indicate standard deviations. d) Similar to c) but in the case of cognitive and motor performance.

Performance of the MLP Regressor. In order to evaluate the performance prediction module, we analyzed the histogram of prediction errors. We calculated the prediction errors by subtracting the predicted performance from the obtained performance. Both resulting histograms of prediction errors display a bias towards underestimation (see Fig. 8) with immoderate deviations, especially in the case of cognitive performance. For motor performance, the central tendency of prediction errors was near zero, while for cognitive performance, it was close to 0.25. This suggests that the MLP regressor demonstrates relatively accurate performance across sessions, but lacks consistency.

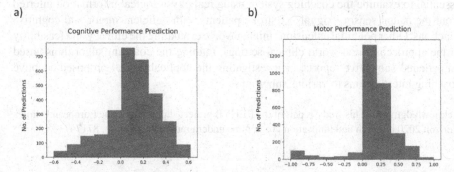

a)

Cognitive Performance Prediction

b)

Motor Performance Prediction

Fig. 8. Histograms of prediction errors. a) Errors of predicted versus obtained performance in the case of cognitive sub-task. Data were concatenated from 10 subjects undergoing adaptive training. b) Similar to a) but in the case of motor performance.

The stability of the MLP regressor should be enhanced in future works, especially by feeding more data from real stroke patients and examining prediction errors that are above 0.5 or below -0.5. Once the nature and potential causes of those extreme values are well understood, we may come up with either new ways to tune model parameters or changes to the experimental protocols.

4   Discussion and Conclusion

In this study, individualistic motor and cognitive disabilities, as well as intrinsic well-beings of participating subjects, are addressed through monitoring their internal states and rehabilitative performances during training sessions. The information is leveraged to adaptively control virtual cyborgs representing the exoskeleton-assisted subjects in VR. In contrast to predetermining a fixed level of task difficulty and motor assistance, we show results from the first exploration of a distribute adaptive control system that might serve as a foundation of tailor-made rehabilitative solutions that are anticipated to be more affordable, optimal, and personalized.

We aimed to investigate how our approach could enhance the efficiency of such adaptive training interventions by accommodating the internal states of participating subjects. In order to validate the main modules of our adaptive coaching system, we compared the cognitive load and fatigue levels as well as task performance of healthy subjects undergoing dynamically regulated support to ones with unchanged exercises. The results of our study indicate that the adaptive coaching system has successfully maintained an optimal level of simulated cognitive load and fatigue while achieving more excellent average performance. This pilot study serves as the initial exploration of how to design effective individualized adaptation under the scheme of VR-robotic synergistic neurorehabilitation, offering potential to further research in this field.

Future research may focus on more precise methods for dynamically calculating the motor and cognitive success rates based on relevant game events or on training sessions that might be brief or lengthy, depending on the demands of patients. It is also essential to examine the coaching system using real physiological information inferred from the actual sensory signals of stroke patients with deficient motor and cognitive functions. Other potential extensions might involve evaluating the efficacy and feasibility of the approach in real-world clinical settings, refining the coaching algorithms based on patients' subjective reports, or investigating the applicability of proposed adaptive coaching interventions to various subgroups.

Acknowledgment. This study is part of the REHYB project supported by the European Union's Horizon 2020 research and innovation programme under grant agreement no. 871767.

References

1. Haraway, D.J.: A Cyborg Manifesto: Science, Technology, and Socialist-Feminism in the Late Twentieth Century. Cyborgs and Women: The Reinvention of Nature (1991)
2. Clark, A.: Natural-Born Cyborgs: Minds, Technologies, and the Future of Human Intelligence. Oxford University Press, Oxford (2004)
3. Clynes, M.E., Kline, N.S.: Cyborgs and space. Astronautics **14**(9), 26–27 (1960)
4. Ramoğlu, M.: Cyborg-computer interaction: designing new senses. Design J. **22**, 1215–1225 (2019)
5. Warwick, K.: Cyborgs. In: Encyclopedia of Applied Ethics, pp. 699–704 (2012)
6. Papakonstantinou, E., et al.: The medical cyborg concept. EMBnet J. **27**, 1005 (2022)
7. Adamson, J., Beswick, A., Ebrahim, S.: Is stroke the most common cause of disability? J. Stroke Cerebrovasc. Dis. **13**(4), 171–177 (2004)
8. Heshmatollah, A., Mutlu, U., Koudstaal, P.J., Ikram, M.A., Ikram, M.K.: Cognitive and physical impairment and the risk of stroke – a prospective cohort study. Sci Rep **10**(1), 6274 (2020)
9. Di Carlo, A.: Human and economic burden of stroke. Age Ageing **38**(1), 4–5 (2009)
10. Caramenti, M., Bartenbach, V., Gasperotti, L., da Fonseca, L.O., Berger, T.W., Pons, J.L.: Challenges in neurorehabilitation and neural engineering. Biosyst. Biorobot. (2016)
11. Norouzi-Gheidari, N., et al.: Feasibility and preliminary efficacy of a combined virtual reality, robotics and electrical stimulation intervention in upper extremity stroke rehabilitation. J. Neuroeng. Rehabil. **18**(1), 1–10 (2021)
12. Semprini, M., et al.: Technological approaches for neurorehabilitation: from robotic devices to brain stimulation and beyond. Front. Neurol. **9**, 212 (2018)
13. Marchal-Crespo, L., Reinkensmeyer, D.J.: Review of control strategies for robotic movement training after neurologic injury. J. Neuroeng. Rehabil. **6**(1), 1–15 (2009)
14. Watanabe, H., et al.: Efficacy and safety study of wearable cyborg HAL (hybrid assistive limb) in hemiplegic patients with acute stroke (EARLY GAIT study): protocols for a randomized controlled trial. Front Neurosci **15**, 666562 (2021)
15. Bertani, R., Melegari, C., De Cola, M.C., Bramanti, A., Bramanti, P., Calabrò, R.S.: Effects of robot-assisted upper limb rehabilitation in stroke patients: a systematic review with meta-analysis. Neurol. Sci. **38**(9), 1561–1569 (2017). https://doi.org/10.1007/s10072-017-2995-5
16. Bai, S., Christensen, S.: Biomechanical HRI modeling and mechatronic design of exoskeletons for assistive applications. In: Human Modeling for Bio-Inspired Robotics: Mechanical Engineering in Assistive Technologies (2017)

17. Zeiler, S.R., Krakauer, J.W.: The interaction between training and plasticity in the poststroke brain. Curr. Opin. Neurol. **26**(6), 609 (2013)
18. Massetti, T., et al.: The clinical utility of virtual reality in neurorehabilitation: a systematic review. J. Cent. Nerv. Syst. Dis. **10** (2018)
19. Maier, M., Rubio Ballester, B., Duff, A., Duarte Oller, E., Verschure, P.F.M.J.: Effect of specific over nonspecific VR-based rehabilitation on poststroke motor recovery: a systematic meta-analysis. Neurorehabil. Neural Repair **33**(2), 112–129 (2019)
20. Ballester, B.R., et al.: A critical time window for recovery extends beyond one-year poststroke. J. Neurophysiol. **122**(1) (2019)
21. Ballester, B.R., et al.: Adaptive VR-based rehabilitation to prevent deterioration in adults with cerebral palsy. In: International Conference on Virtual Rehabilitation (2019)
22. Maier, M., Bañuelos, N.L., Ballester, B.R., Duarte, E., Verschure, P.F.M.J.: Conjunctive rehabilitation of multiple cognitive domains for chronic stroke patients in virtual reality. In: IEEE International Conference on Rehabilitation Robotics (2017)
23. Nijland, R.H.M., van Wegen, E.E.H., Harmeling-van der Wel, B.C., Kwakkel, G.: Accuracy of physical therapists' early predictions of upper-limb function in hospital stroke units: the EPOS study. Phys. Ther. **93**(4), 460–469 (2013)
24. Zanatta, F., Giardini, A., Pierobon, A., D'Addario, M., Steca, P.: A systematic review on the usability of robotic and virtual reality devices in neuromotor rehabilitation: patients' and healthcare professionals' perspective. BMC Health Serv Res **22**(1), 523 (2022)
25. Webster-Wood, V.A., et al.: Biohybrid robots: recent progress, challenges, and perspectives. Bioinspir. Biomimet. **18**(1) (2022)
26. Djaouti, D., Alvarez, J., Jessel, J.-P.: Classifying serious games: the G/P/S model. In: Handbook of Research on Improving Learning and Motivation Through Educational Games: Multidisciplinary Approaches, pp. 118–136 (2011)
27. McClarty, K.L., Orr, A., Frey, P.M., Dolan, R.P., Vassileva, V., McVay, A.: A literature review of gaming in education. Gaming Educ. **1**, 1–35 (2012)
28. Nirme, J., Duff, A., Verschure, P.F.M.J.: Adaptive rehabilitation gaming system: on-line individualization of stroke rehabilitation. In: Annual International Conference of the IEEE Engineering in Medicine and Biology Society, pp. 6749–6752. IEEE (2011)
29. Cameirão, M.S., i Badia, S.B., Zimmerli, L., Oller, E.D., Verschure, P.F.M.J.: The rehabilitation gaming system: a virtual reality based system for the evaluation and rehabilitation of motor deficits. Virtual Rehabilitation, pp. 29–33. IEEE (2007)
30. Barricelli, B.R., Casiraghi, E., Fogli, D.: A survey on digital twin: definitions, characteristics, applications, and design implications. IEEE access **7**, 167653–167671 (2019)
31. Croatti, A., Gabellini, M., Montagna, S., Ricci, A.: On the integration of agents and digital twins in healthcare. J. Med. Syst. **44**, 1–8 (2020)
32. Stinear, C.M., et al.: Predicting recovery potential for individual stroke patients increases rehabilitation efficiency. Stroke **48**(4), 1011–1019 (2017)
33. Gaggioli, A., Vettorello, M., Riva, G.: From cyborgs to cyberbodies: the evolution of the concept of techno-body in modern medicine. PsychNology J. **1**(2), 75–86 (2003)
34. Verschure, P.F.M.J.: Distributed adaptive control: a theory of the mind, brain, body nexus. Biolog. Inspir. Cogn. Archit. **1**, 55–72 (2012)
35. Verschure, P.F.M.J., Voegtlin, T., Douglas, R.J.: Environmentally mediated synergy between perception and behaviour in mobile robots. Nature **425**(6958), 620–624 (2003)
36. Maffei, G., Santos-Pata, D., Marcos, E., Sánchez-Fibla, M., Verschure, P.F.M.J.: An embodied biologically constrained model of foraging: from classical and operant conditioning to adaptive real-world behavior in DAC-X. Neural Netw. **72**, 88–108 (2015)
37. Verschure, P.F.M.J.: Neuroscience, virtual reality and neurorehabilitation: brain repair as a validation of brain theory. In: Annual International Conference of the IEEE Engineering in Medicine and Biology Society, pp. 2254–2257. IEEE (2011)

38. Csikszentmihalyi, M.: Flow: The Psychology of Optimal Experience (1990)
39. Kawabata, M., Mallett, C.J.: Flow experience in physical activity: examination of the internal structure of flow from a process-related perspective. Motiv Emot **35**, 393–402 (2011)
40. Yerkes, R.M., Dodson, J.D.: The relation of strength of stimulus to rapidity of habit-formation (1908)
41. Sterling, P., Eyer, J.: Allostasis: a new paradigm to explain arousal pathology. In: Handbook on Life Stress, Cognition, and Health, pp. 629–649 (1988)
42. McEwen, B.S., Wingfield, J.C.: The concept of allostasis in biology and biomedicine. Horm Behav. **43**(1), 2–15 (2003)
43. Vouloutsi, V., Lallée, S., Verschure, P.F.M.J.: Modulating behaviors using allostatic control. Biomimet. Biohybrid Syst.: Living Mach. **2013**, 287–298 (2013)
44. Guerrero-Rosado, O., Verschure, P.F.M.J.: Robot regulatory behaviour based on fundamental homeostatic and allostatic principles. Procedia Comput. Sci. **190**, 292–300 (2021)
45. Ngo, T., Guerrero, O., Freire, I.T., Verschure, P.F.M.J.: Homeostatic and allostatic principles for behavioral regulation in desert reptiles: a robotic evaluation. Biomimet. Biohybrid Syst.: Living Mach. **2022**, 332–344 (2022)
46. Haas, J.K.: A history of the unity game engine. Diss. Worcester Polytechnic Institute, p.483 (2014)
47. S. A. I. Laboratory: Robotic operating system. CA, USA (2018)
48. Paas, F., Van Gog, T., Sweller, J.: Cognitive load theory: New conceptualizations, specifications, and integrated research perspectives. Educ. Psychol. Rev. **22**, 115–121 (2010)
49. Holtzer, R., Shuman, M., Mahoney, J.R., Lipton, R., Verghese, J.: Cognitive fatigue defined in the context of attention networks. Aging Neuropsychol. Cogn. **18**(1), 108–128 (2010)
50. Cifrek, M., Medved, V., Tonković, S., Ostojić, S.: Surface EMG based muscle fatigue evaluation in biomechanics. Clin. Biomech. **24**(4), 327–340 (2009)
51. Wang, J., Sun, S., Sun, Y.: A muscle fatigue classification model based on LSTM and improved wavelet packet threshold. Sensors **21**(19), 6369 (2021)
52. Jaiswal, A., Zadeh, M.Z., Hebri, A., Makedon, F.: Assessing fatigue with multimodal wearable sensors and machine learning. arXiv:2205.00287 (2022)
53. Aristidou, A., Lasenby, J., Chrysanthou, Y., Shamir, A.: Inverse kinematics techniques in computer graphics: A survey'. In: Computer graphics forum, pp. 35–58 (2018)
54. da Silva Cameirão, M., Bermúdez i Badia, S., Duarte, E., Verschure, P.F.M.J.: Virtual reality based rehabilitation speeds up functional recovery of the upper extremities after stroke: a randomized controlled pilot study in the acute phase of stroke using the rehabilitation gaming system. Restor. Neurol. Neurosci. **29**(5), 287–298 (2011)

Robotic Active Tactile Sensing Inspired by Serotonergic Modulation Using Active Inference

Filip Novicky[1(✉)], Joshua Offergeld[2], Simon Janssen[2], and Pablo Lanillos[2,3]

[1] Donders Institute for Brain, Cognition and Behavior,
Department of Neurophysics, Radboud University, Nijmegen, The Netherlands
`filip.novicky@donders.ru.nl`
[2] Donders Institute for Brain, Cognition and Behavior,
Department of Artificial Intelligence, Radboud University,
Nijmegen, The Netherlands
[3] Cajal International Center for Neuroscience,
Spanish National Research Council (CSIC), Madrid, Spain

Abstract. When faced with uncertainty in the world, biological agents actively sense the environment to acquire the most informative input to fulfil their tasks. Actions are performed to adjust bodily sensors to maximize the collected information, which is usually known as active sensing. For instance, rodents continuously adjust the speed and amplitude of whisking to better identify objects and body location in space, which ultimately regulates navigation. Whilst, the internal mechanism that drives active sensing in humans is still under research, recent evidence points towards neuromodulators, such as serotonin, that influence whether the habitual behaviour is preferred over sensor adjustments to trigger exploration. Here, we present an active tactile-sensing model for a robot inspired by the serotonergic function viewed from the uncertainty minimization perspective. To mechanistically explain this neuromodulatory function, we associated it with precision parameters regulating habitual behaviour and tactile encoding based on previous findings. We qualitatively evaluated the model using an experiment inspired by the gap-crossing paradigm but tailored to a humanoid with tactile sensing. Behavioural switch timing results show the strong dependencies between active sensing and precision regulation. Ultimately, this work discusses how the neural microcircuitry regulates active sensing, hence opening future research of such neuromodulatory processes translated to robotics active sensing and perception.

Keywords: Active Sensing · Active Perception · Active Inference · Serotonin · Precision · Neurorobotics

---

F. Novicky, J. Offergeld and S. Janssen—Contributed equally to this work and share the first authorship.

F. Meder et al. (Eds.): Living Machines 2023, LNAI 14157, pp. 33–55, 2023.
https://doi.org/10.1007/978-3-031-38857-6_3

1   Introduction

Perception is not passive. Biological agents actively explore the world by select-
ing such actions that inform them about the world, given their embodied constraints. Whilst this active sensing process is not yet fully understood (Bajcsy et
al. 2018; Meera et al. 2022), recent findings in neuroscience point to neuromodulators, such as serotonin, to be strongly involved. In humans, serotonin has been
suggested to be involved in the sensitivity of sensory processing (Homberg et al.
2016) and perceptual decision making—by tracking sensory uncertainty (Bang et
al. 2020). But regarding active sensing a revealing study comes from exploratory
functions of rodents (Azarfar et al. 2019), where it has been shown that while
wild type rodents, with normal levels of serotonin, show a switch from a large to
a small amplitude of their whiskers when they touch an object—to acquire more
information—, rodents with altered levels of serotonin (i.e., knock-out serotonin
mice, SERT-/-) do not present this behaviour. This may mean that SERT-/-
rodents have their active sensing mechanism turned off. We suggest that the
changes in the exploratory behaviour can be understood as an uncertainty minimization strategy that is triggered by switching to a more efficient mode of
collecting data under higher uncertainty.

We hypothesize that abnormal active sensing behaviour can be accounted
for through aberrant precision modulation (i.e., broadly inverse covariance) in
two ways: modulating incoming sensory input (via reducing sensory precision)
or modulating habitual behaviours (increasing habitual precision). The sensory
precision dictates how accurately a stimulus will be encoded in the brain and
how much information it provides for an apt inference. Habitual precision, on
the other hand, modulates habits that are selected a priori without considering
current input (Miller et al. 2019). Habits have the advantages that they do not
require the complex computations of policy selection. Hence, we suggest that
proper precision modulation is at the core of producing active sensing behaviour.

Here, we present a robotic active perception computational model inspired
by the serotonin-based active sensing observed in rodents. Our work follows from
previous research on active sensing where – from the computational point of view
– this behaviour relates to uncertainty minimization or information gain maximization (Yang et al. 2016; Martinez-Hernandez et al. 2017; Parr et al. 2021).
Our model thus extends on these theories via providing precision parameters as a
neuromodulatory function that regulates this behaviour—see (Parr and Friston
2017; Parr et al. 2022).

While rodents active sensing differs from human tactile sensing, there are
some relevant connections, such as how tactile information is obtained through
habitual versus exploratory behaviours. Disentangling this mechanism may provide a new direction in tactile active perception, particularly in robotics applications, such as navigation (Rasouli et al. 2020) and object recognition (Kaboli et
al. 2017). Besides, our model can be specifically used to translate its theoretical
findings into animal or human behaviour via the deployment of the model in a
humanoid robot.

Hence, to validate the model, we deployed the model on a humanoid robot and designed an exploration experiment inspired by rodent navigation via the so-called gap-crossing paradigm (Voigts et al. 2008). The humanoid robot relies only on somatosensory (tactile) data with a broad movement amplitude (i.e., randomly moving robot's hands in the air) to maximize the range of where the stimulation can come from. Active sensing is then considered when a small range of movement around a more informative stimulus is selected. This is consistent with previous computational models that understand active sensing as information gain behaviour (Yang et al. 2016; Parr et al. 2021). We found that optimal levels of precision lead to more informative behaviour, while dysregulations of these move the agent to suboptimal behaviour where information gained from an object are missed, causing an agent to be ignorant about the environment. Thus, indicating the strong connection between precision modulation and optimal active sensing behaviours. The specific contribution of our model lies in applying the uncertainty minimization perspective in active tactile-sensing, and its demonstration in a humanoid.

2   Methods

Our model is grounded on the Active Inference (Friston et al. 2017) (AIF) mathematical framework—see (Lanillos et al. 2021) for a survey on robotic applications. Particularly, we used the discrete state space AIF to model the robot's behaviour. Thus, we first briefly describe active inference and then the model used for active sensing.

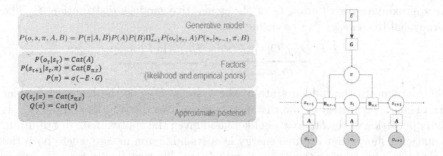

Fig. 1. *General factor graph of the POMDP behind the discrete active inference model of the agent.* On the left panel, the equations specify the generative model. The generative model is thus a joint probability of outcomes, states, and model parameters. The right panel shows the graphical representation of the same generative model. This figure has been adapted from (Friston et al. 2017). The terms o, s, π and τ refer to outcomes, hidden states, policies, and time-steps respectively. Model parameters are labeled as A, B and E which relates to likelihood and transition matrices, and a habitual vector, respectively. Lastly, $Cat(.)$ specifies a categorical distribution, and σ is a softmax function.

2.1   Agent Model

We modelled the agent dynamics and action selection using the discrete Partially-Observable Markov Decision Process (POMDP) formalism. The POMDP structure provides a mapping from outcomes to hidden states, and across time-steps, referring to likelihood and transition functions. The structure is specified in Fig. 1. The agent has a hidden state s that evolves through time depending on the transition function B and is updated given the observation o at each time step. The agent has a mapping (likelihood) of observations given the state.

2.2   Active Inference

Action selection is modelled under the AIF mathematical framework, a corollary theory of the free energy principle. The free energy principle assumes that all living systems follow a simple process of self-organization which is to minimize the surprisal value (Friston 2010). Variational free energy ($\mathcal{F}$) then works as an upper-bound on this value (Friston et al. 2017):

$$\mathcal{F} \geq -\ln P(o) \tag{1}$$

where $\mathcal{F}$ is the free energy, o denotes outcomes or input data and $P(o)$ represents the surprisal in probabilistic terms. This equation states that minimizing the free energy minimizes the surprisal as well (Oliver et al. 2021). The reason we do not minimize the surprisal directly is due to its intractability when scaling beyond very low-dimensional distributions (Da Costa et al. 2020). The variational free energy bound combats this mathematical pit via the use of variational inference (Blei et al. 2017), an approximate Bayesian inference that uses an approximate distribution Q of the generative model's distribution P. The variational free energy can be defined as:

$$\mathcal{F} = \underbrace{D_{KL}[Q(s)||P(s)]}_{Complexity} - \underbrace{E_{Q_{(s)}}(\ln P(o|s))}_{Accuracy} \tag{2}$$

where s denotes the hidden state of the system, D_{KL} is the Kullback-Leibler divergence that measures the distance between two distributions and $E_{Q_{(s)}}$ is the expectation of the observation likelihood given the approximate distribution. Equation 2 shows that the free energy is at its minimum in case where both the complexity and accuracy term are equal to zero. The complexity term compares the approximate posterior distribution $Q(s)$ with the model's prior distribution $P(s)$. This value is minimized when the model's prior knowledge only explains the new stimulation forming the posterior. The accuracy term assures the agent of inferring those (hidden) states that can explain the stimuli o the most. It is computed by averaging over the posterior approximate distribution $Q(s)$ the likelihood function of the model. Without the complexity term, the accuracy would lead to observations overfitting, and without the accuracy term the agent would ignore the outside world and focus on the model's beliefs without updating them. Hence, free energy is a balance of exploitation (i.e., fulfilling our priors) and exploration (i.e., inferring the most informative hidden states).

Action Selection. We define the agent's action selection as computing the optimal policy π, given the combination of the habitual behaviours E^1 (i.e. a behaviour occurring automatically, without a complex inference) and the optimization of the Expected Free Energy (G) of executing a plan of actions in the future[2]:

$$\pi = \arg\max \; Q(\pi) = \arg\max \; \sigma\big[\rho \ln E(\pi) - G(\pi)\big] \qquad (3)$$

where ρ is the precision parameter that modulates the interplay between habitual policies and new computed optimal policies, given the model and new observations. The σ represents a softmax function that in a discrete state representation transforms the objective values into probabilities. Thus, the policy with the higher probability is selected.

To enable the agent to plan actions ahead (Lanillos et al. 2021), we used the Expected Free Energy (EFE) objective function G, which predicts the free energy value in the next time-point (Kaplan and Friston 2018):

$$G(\pi) = \underbrace{D_{KL}[Q(s_\tau|\pi)||P(s_\tau)]}_{Risk} - \underbrace{E_{Q(s_\tau|\pi)P(o_\tau|s_\tau)}[\ln \; P(o_\tau|s_\tau, A)]}_{Ambiguity} \qquad (4)$$

where π is a policy/plan (i.e. a sequence of actions), τ is a time point, and A represents the likelihood function of the model. The terms risk and ambiguity closely follow the terms complexity and accuracy from Eq. 2, respectively. A relevant difference between the free energy F and G is that the latter is sampled from the predictive posterior distribution. This means that the agent predicts the consequences of its actions and calculates the deviance from surprise based on these. The risk calculates the posterior value of a hidden state in the next time-step, given a policy selected at a given moment that is compared to the prior beliefs of the agent. This assures a selection of such a policy that leads to fulfilling the priors. On the other hand, the ambiguity term functions similarly to the accuracy term mentioned above, but the likelihood is predictive (over the next time step) based on the averaged approximate distribution of an expected hidden state given a policy $Q(s_\tau|\pi)$. This means that the ambiguity term selects those policies that are most informative.

---

[1] E can be provided by the designer or learned and encodes the agent's preferences given by evolution.

[2] Note that the EFE is a generalization of the variational free energy conditioned on an action plan or policy.

2.3 Precision Modulation

As described in the introduction, we suggest that active sensing is modulated by neurotransmitters, such as serotonin, which we assimilate to sensory precision or habitual precision. Sensory precision modulates the likelihood function of the model, while the habitual precision modulates policy selection (through EFE computation).

Likelihood Modulation. Sensory precision ζ modulates the impact of the sensory input.

$$A = \sigma(\zeta \ln(\mathbf{A} + \epsilon)) \tag{5}$$

where σ represents a softmax function, and ϵ is some arbitrary small number that prevents a mathematical error due to taking a logarithm of 0. The bold matrix $\mathbf{A}$ denotes a distribution shown in Fig. 2 (shown in the middle panel) and represents the likelihood mapping between states and observations. Since only those columns linked to tactile sensing have a non-uniform distribution, the equation above then implicitly modulates only these columns, as the inverse temperature parameter ζ cannot modulate the uniform distribution.

Policy Selection Modulation. The habitual precision parameter ρ is described in Eq. 3 of action selection. The E vector prespecifies a preference over the habitual policy, and thus the precision parameter can only minimize or maximize the difference, but not shift it around and make a habitual preference for a small movement policy. High ρ thus indicates a strong preference for the broad range of movement, while low ρ makes the habitual preferences disappear.

2.4 Model Tailored to Robotic Tactile Active Sensing

Our active sensing model is described in Fig. 2. Inspired by the gap-crossing paradigm in rodents (Voigts et al. 2008), we designed the robotic model with two hidden factors, which describe the state: object appearance (or context) and arm position. The former hidden factor is split into four states. Three states (indicated with black, grey, and white boxes) reflect three different positions of where the object can be detected. The fourth hidden state assumes that no object can be detected. For the hidden factor arm position, we specify five different arm positions. Note the three middle positions are duplicated so we can provide a back and forth movement in a discrete space, as much as in whisking movement. Therefore, the arm positions are represented by eight different states. There is one outcome modality in the model, which is associated with touch. The outcome is then either being touched or not. Following the outcome modalities and hidden states, we can provide likelihood functions, specifying the probability of being touched, given a specific context and arm position. If the agent infers that there is no stimulus around, the likelihood function is completely uniform and thus

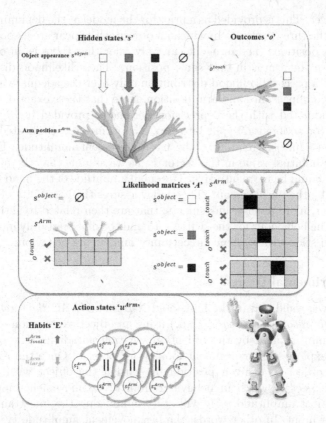

Fig. 2. *The generative model of active sensing in the Nao humanoid.* The model contains two hidden factors: object appearance and arm position. The former indicates where the object will appear in the environment, defined by the arm position. There are three objects that can be linked to three distinct arm positions, and also a case when there is no object which is what the agent believes at the beginning of every trial. Next, there are 5 arm positions, where the middle three positions are duplicated due to the sinewave-like behaviour (i.e., going back and forth). There is only one outcome modality, touch, which takes a boolean value of either touched or untouched. The likelihood matrices depend on what context (i.e., object appearance) is inferred. We defined the likelihood function A in an uncertainty-minimization environment, where the motivation for the agent to explore an object (where the stimulation is sensed) is defined by a uniform likelihood distribution except for the part where the hand can sense an object. In the matrix, the black colour relates to high probability, while white boxes are of low probability. The grey boxes represent uncertain distribution. Lastly, we specified two policies. The first one, which has a higher habitual value, is related to a complete hand circle which is a logical way of exploring the (uncertain) world as fully as possible. The second policy provides some nuances on how to escape the former policy and stick with the most certain outcome related to a given arm position. This policy has a lower habitual value and therefore its selection depends on the uncertainty minimization behaviour. These actions are then derived from transition matrices B specified in Fig. 1.

uninformative[3]. This is provided as a prior for the model at the beginning of every trial. Next, the three positions in which an object can appear are associated with distinct arm positions (i.e. an agent can only infer that there is an object in a position when the arm is in that same position). These likelihood distributions then provide a precise likelihood distribution only over the adequate association of the object's appearance and arm position. Note that these exact distributions are then modulated with the ζ precision parameter provided in Eq. 5. Lastly, the policies (or actions) are split into two. The former one (indicated in yellow colour in the figure) is related to the large movement amplitude. This policy has a higher habitual value in the vector E, as we assume that the bigger hand movements should be more intuitive. The small amplitude of the hand movement is indicated by the purple colour. This policy assures the possibility of switching to the smaller, more precise, movements, that are then related to active sensing strategies. The behaviour for the switch is to find the most certainly interpretable outcome and stick with it, hence uncertainty minimizing behaviour.

2.5 Experimental Design

The model was validated in the humanoid Nao robot (*NAO the humanoid and programmable robot — Aldebaran*, n.d.) using an object exploration experiment using one limb, inspired by the rodents navigation paradigm. The goal of the robot is to explore the environment looking for objects. Once the robot infers there is an object in a given position by sensing the object with the touch sensor, we expect a switch in behaviour from broad movement amplitude to small movement amplitude as it will start minimizing the uncertainty over a more certain input. In other words, the big movement amplitude is used when the environment is more uncertain and all inputs are equally uncertain. The object provides more certainty to the agent, hence it makes sense that the agent will stay around more certain inputs with a small movement amplitude.

To test distinct tactile exploratory processes under precision modulation, we conducted experiments in which a Nao robot moves its arm back and forth as hard-coded based on our model (see Fig. 2). The experiments contain 40 time-steps (with one exception of 80 time-steps), where a time step is simply defined by an arm position. Hence, during a single experiment, the robot moves its arm 40 times. Each time-step takes approximately 2.5 s (communication speed between the robot and the host computer and the robot physically

---

[3] It might seem counter-intuitive that without any stimulation, the agent does not recognize that nothing has been touched, but rather increases the uncertainty of the world. This is motivated by the so-called dark room problem (Friston et al. 2012; Baltieri and Buckley 2019) that resolves a problem in the free energy that states that, if agents minimize the uncertainty of the world, why not stay in completely dark environments which should provide completely predictable stimuli (i.e., always dark)? The answer is that perceiving darkness is highly ambiguous, therefore we treat no stimulation in the same way and build likelihood matrices in such a way that increases uncertainty over sensing no-stimulation signals while the stimulation outcomes provide higher certainty of causes.

moving between two states), which means that running an experiment takes approximately one minute and forty-five seconds. The Nao robot will always start with the first arm position. After the 8th time-step, we introduce an object (the researcher's hand) at a specific arm position.

2.6 Implementation

To implement the model that we described in Sect. 2.1, we used the open-source 'pymdp' package (Heins et al. 2022). This software implements active inference agents in discrete time, state, and action spaces. To translate the model into the physical Nao robot we used the NAOqi driver. Thus, we developed the interface between the NAOqi SDK and the pymdp algorithm to control the robot. Since the NAOqi software only runs on Python 2.7 and the python model needs to be implemented in Python 3 because of the pymdp library, we implemented a socket module to communicate observations from the physical robot to the model and the actions from the model to the robot.

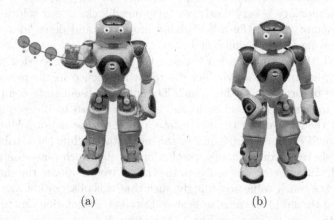

(a)   (b)

Fig. 3. *Illustrations of the Nao robot used for the experiments.* a) A particular arm position of the Nao robot in the experiment. The red dots indicate all states of the robot, where the most right arm position is referred to as arm position 1 and the most left arm position is referred to as arm position 5. The darker red line indicates the trajectory between arm positions and the dots indicate a movement down and up again to sense the environment. b) The location of the touch sensor on the back of the robot's right hand indicated by a red circle. The touch sensor is a capacitive sensor that can distinguish between two different states: touched and not touched. (Color figure online)

Furthermore, the acting and sensing computations of the robot were subdivided into parallel threads to allow the robot to sample faster in the environment when moving the arm down and up in a particular state, thereby increasing the probability that a touch is observed. The acting thread was responsible for moving the robot's arm and for interacting with the model script. To move the robot's arm, we used the motion module of the Nao robot (ALMotion) to access the joints of the robot's right shoulder. In accordance with the model, five arm positions have to be specified and the three middle positions have to be duplicated, so the robot can move back and forth between states in discrete space (see Fig. 3a)[4]. When the right hand arrives in a new state, it will slightly move down (0.1 rad vertically) in order to sense whether there is an object in the state. Afterward, it will move up again and continue to the next state.

The sensing thread was responsible for registering whether the touch sensor of the robot is touched and updating the variables in the script accordingly. To register a touch, we used a touch sensor on the back of the robot's right hand. In particular, we only used the middle touch sensor on the back of the robot's hand, which is a capacitive sensor with a binary output (touched or not touched) (see Fig. 3b for the location of this touch sensor in red). The touch sensor is always facing down (angle is 1.74 rad) (see Fig. 3a for the positioning of the hand in a particular state). By accessing the memory of the Nao robot (ALMemory) and reading out the value for the back touch sensor on the right hand, we could infer whether the sensor was touched (value is 1) or not (value is 0)[5]. Because reading from memory is very costly, we introduced locks in our solution to only read from memory when the robot's hand moves up and down in a state and not when moving between different states.

In general, the communication between the two scripts proceeded as follows: first, the acting thread read whether the robot is touched in the previous state and sent this observation to the model. The model subsequently computed the next action for the robot to execute and sent this action to the acting thread. This thread then moved to the next state, based on the action. Afterward, it moved the hand down and up again in this next state, while the sensing thread simultaneously read from memory whether or not the touch sensor on the robot was touched. If the sensor was touched, the thread would update the shared variable storing the touch value accordingly, such that this observation was available for the acting thread in the next time step. Detailed information on the software implementation can be found in Fig. 7, Appendix A.1.

3   Results

First, based on observations from the simulations, we evaluated behavioural and perceptual differences depending on the precision modulation parameter (ζ and ρ) values that are the hypothesized homologues of serotonergic neuromodulation and that affects active sensing behaviour. Second, based on the simulations we introduced a qualitative analysis studying the robot NAO behaviour with low and high ζ values, combined with low and high ρ values.

---

[4] Note that the movement of the robot's arm is only horizontal. Therefore, we could fix the joint position of the shoulder pitch to 0.1 rad. For the shoulder roll, we chose to evenly space the joint positions between 0.2 and −1.0 rad, such that the shoulder roll has to move 0.3 rad between states.

[5] We also used the speech module of the Nao robot (ALTextToSpeech) to have an auditory cue which could indicate whether the sensor was touched.

3.1   Simulations

We analyzed the experiment in simulation for 13 different ζ values and 13 different ρ values, selected to capture the whole range of potential behaviours. All of the experiments followed the structure as described above, meaning 40 time-steps per experiment, where after the 8th time step we simulated object appearance at arm position 4. We thus ran 169 (13 × 13) experiments, 8 times each. Note that for the simulated experiments, the starting arm position is randomized. These experiments show numerical differences in tactile exploratory behaviour under distinct precision modulation. Specifically, we focused on i) the time when the (behavioural) switch from a large to small hand movement amplitude; and ii) the switch of the object appearance posterior occurs after introducing the object.

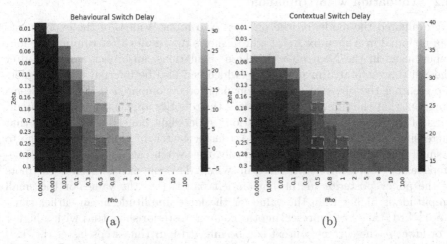

(a)   (b)

Fig. 4. *Numerical analyses of the active sensing behaviour.* Figure (a) represents a time delay of behaviour switch. Figure (b) shows a time delay of inferred contextual switch. Based on these analyses, we decided to simulate four precision combination in the humanoid that are represented in the dashed green squares in both heatmaps. (Color figure online)

Figure 4a represents the time it takes to switch from a large to a small hand movement amplitude from the moment an object has been touched. Here, we can see that the increase of ζ and decrease of ρ gradually speeds up the switch. Figure 4b represents the same problem, but for inferring the correct context (i.e. that an object is located at arm position 4). This has been calculated as a time difference from an object has been touched to the point where context 4 (a context where an object is believed to appear to arm position 4) has a higher posterior probability than context 1 (the initial context where no object is believed to be in front of the humanoid). As shown in the figure above, all cases show a gradual change in the same manner for both precision parameters. Based on these analyses, we selected four different cases where behaviour is distinct from each other. This is highlighted in dashed green boxes of Fig. 4, which were then applied in the humanoid. Based on this finding, we also conclude that there is a strong binding of lower sensory precision with stronger habitual behaviour, at least in tactile detection and exploratory domain, as these two appear to modulate the behaviour in the same manner. This is because the effects of these two precision terms provide the same function when it comes to a temporal delay of active sensing. Given the methodological structure of (Azarfar et al. 2019) that compared animals with high and normal levels of serotonin, the upper-left and bottom-right green dashed boxes can be regarded as a behaviour from the wild-type animals, providing the baseline model. The other two boxes then demonstrate a behaviour of agents with higher levels of serotonin.

3.2 Validation with Humanoid

We evaluated the model on the physical Nao robot. Videos of the experiments can be found in Appendix A.3. Figure 5 shows the results after running the four experiments in the Nao robot. In these simulations, an object appeared after the 8th time-step at arm position 4 (which can also be inferred from the plots representing the observation and arm position). Compared to Fig. 4, it seems apparent that the simulated results with the robotics application are consistent. First of all, the plots of the arm position (upper-right panels) show a trend that increasing ζ or decreasing ρ leads to a faster switch in policy from a large to a small movement amplitude. Specifically, the switch can happen up to 8 time-steps faster (representing one full arm swing). This can also be seen in the plots of the policy posterior in the bottom-left panels (i.e. the value for the small amplitude is higher than the value for the large amplitude at an earlier time-step). Next, the plots representing the context posterior show that with a higher ζ or lower ρ, the correct context can be inferred four time-steps faster (i.e. half an arm swing).

In addition to testing whether the simulation results when varying ζ and ρ can be validated in experiments with the Nao robot, we also conducted an experiment to see whether behaviour is similar when the robot is touched in different arm positions. Results between touching the robot in arm position 3 (see Fig. 6a) and in arm position 4 (see Fig. 5c) under the same precision parameters show that this is indeed the case. Namely, the switch between policies occurs at the same time (considering it takes one time-step longer to see the change in policy for Fig. 6a) and also the context posteriors for the respective arm position (i.e. 'Touched right' (red line) in Fig. 5c and 'Touched middle' (yellow line) in Fig. 6a) seem to increase with a similar trend. The difference after time-step 32 is due to a missed sensory stimulation. The missed sensory stimulation also provides an interesting case where the consequences of unreliable sensors affect active sensing. This then leads to a longer exploration and a sudden drop in the context posterior. This indicates a loss of confidence in the agent's beliefs about understanding the newly acquired structure of the environment, causing it to explore for longer.

Lastly, we conducted a longer experiment with 80 time-steps (see Fig. 6b), where we switched from touching the robot in arm position 2 to arm position 3 after 30 time-steps (indicated by the red line). As can be seen in the plot for the context posterior (bottom-right panel), the robot was able to correctly infer the change in the context (i.e. the context of being touched in arm position 2 goes down after 30 time-steps and the context of being touched in arm position 3 goes up) and adapted its behaviour accordingly (i.e. after time-step 30, the robot switches back to large movement amplitude and after time-step 45, the robot switches to a small movement amplitude around arm position 3). These results suggest that the model can quickly adapt to new information, as a switch in arm position leads to a switch in behaviour and posterior probabilities. Doing so, we just touched the surface of the robotics application for the neuro-scientific research, but such extensions can inform neuroscience and psychology research more about the assumptions originating from these fields, such as adaptive behavioural switching in an environment where objects are not stationary, something that the gap-crossing paradigm does not consider.

4   Discussion

We studied the behaviour of a humanoid robot with serotonergic depletion using the active inference framework (Adams et al. 2013; Friston et al. 2017; Da Costa et al. 2020) – where we associated serotonin with a modulation of sensory or habitual precision.

Although this work was inspired by rodent behaviour with serotonin alteration (Azarfar et al. 2019), humans also show a similar aspect of switching from a coarse-grained action execution to a more fine-grained one – once an object or environment is being explored. The more detailed behaviour provides more information about the texture or shape, or even motion of the object (Ryan et al. 2021). In our case, we focused on exploratory strategies in the tactile domain which extends current neuroscientific and psychological research focusing on exploration mostly in vision (Najemnik and Geisler 2005, 2008; Renninger et al. 2007). We also extend this by focusing on subtle changes in neuromodulation – specifically serotonin – and show that to fully comprehend how we are able to resolve uncertainty in the world via adjusting our sensors, neuromodulatory systems also have to be investigated.

There are, however, other computational models focusing on the function of serotonin. Most of them are developed under the reinforcement learning framework focusing on assertive behaviour (Daw et al. 2002; Doya 2002; Dayan and Huys 2008; Cools et al. 2011). These models thus analyze the exploitative behaviour, i.e., how to behave to collect the least punishment. Our model – where we modelled (consequences of) altered levels of serotonin via habitual and sensory precision in order to bias exploratory behaviour – seems to be compatible with previous models as well. In particular, (Dayan and Huys 2008) suggested that modulating the reward value – in order to promote assertive behaviour linked to serotonin (Dayan and Huys 2009) – limits the exploration of cases

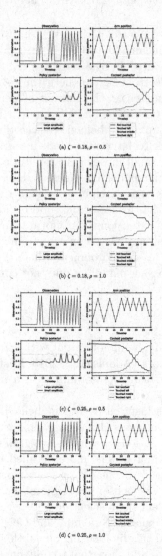

(a) $\zeta = 0.18, \rho = 0.5$

(b) $\zeta = 0.18, \rho = 1.0$

(c) $\zeta = 0.25, \rho = 0.5$

(d) $\zeta = 0.25, \rho = 1.0$

Fig. 5. *Application of the generative model in a humanoid.* This figure represents the experiments conducted in the Nao robot for different values of ζ and ρ, where an object appears in arm position 4 after the 8th time-step. For each experiment, the top-left panels labeled as 'Observation' represent whether or not the robot is touched for every time-step. Here, a value of 1 means that a sensor was triggered, while a value of 0 says that no touch was sensed. The top-right panels 'Arm Position' represent the (discrete) position of the hand per time-step. There are five hand positions that can be reached. These graphs nicely show the switch from the large amplitude to the small one. The bottom-left panels represent the 'Policy Posterior' for the large amplitude (yellow) and small amplitude (purple). Lastly, the bottom-right panels 'Contextual posterior' represent the posterior probabilities for four different contexts in which the agent can find itself. It starts with the preference over 'Not touched' and eventually switches to 'Touched right', which is the context where a hand was touched at position 4 as specified above. (Color figure online)

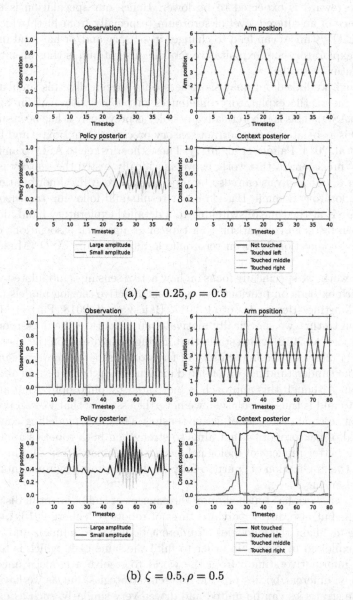

(a) $\zeta = 0.25, \rho = 0.5$

(b) $\zeta = 0.5, \rho = 0.5$

Fig. 6. *Additional simulations in the robot.* The template of results is the same as in Fig. 5. Figure (a) represents an interesting case when an object appeared at the arm position 3; and one stimulation at the 32nd time-step was missed, leading to more exploration compared to Fig. 5c. In addition, this led to a sudden drop in context posterior. Figure (b) is slightly different, as there are 80 time-steps instead of 40 as in previous experiments. The red lines here specify when a context was changed (i.e., when a researcher's hand position appeared at a different position). (Color figure online)

where the reward is expected to be lower. Hence our speculation is that the consequence of an altered level of serotonin (especially from birth which is the case of SERT-/- mice) can lead to changes in sensory and/or habitual precision. Aligning exploratory and exploitative models of serotonin is thus an interesting field for future research.

Although we linked our analysis to serotonin specifically, this simulation can also test the tactile exploratory differences in people with Autism Spectrum Disorder (ASD). This is theoretically possible, as previously it has been suggested that ASD is associated with aberrant sensory precision (Van Boxtel and Lu 2013; Lawson et al. 2014; Palmer et al. 2017). These theories relate ASD to an increase in sensory precision. In this work, as we specifically tested the sensory precision parameter ζ, our analysis can also be used to explore ASD abnormalities in the tactile exploratory domain. Based on our results and following the theories, we hypothesize that the time of switching to a detailed exploratory hand movement will happen faster in comparison to a typical group. Such associations can also deepen the connection between serotonergic alterations in ASD (Muller et al. 2016).

In our work, we specifically focus on how active sensing is modulated via serotonin which extends on previous assumptions of active sensing models (Yang et al. 2016; Martinez-Hernandez et al. 2017; Bajcsy et al. 2018; Parr et al. 2021). In addition to this, we specifically motivate our model via the dark-room problem (Friston et al. 2012) which states that having no information (i.e., not sensing any object) increases the uncertainty of the world rather than decreasing it via holding some understanding (or a related hidden state) that is certain about such a situation. Although this approach is motivated by philosophy (Sun and Firestone 2020) and is thus speculative, we nevertheless show that we can use it as a motivation to create a model of active sensing. Thus, our modelling contributes to the field of neurorobotics that aims to strengthen both robotics applications and create better replicas of biological agents (Krichmar 2018; Tani and White 2022) via the application of (purposefully built) uncertain environments to trigger active sensing.

Lastly, our work has touched upon the concept of embodiment in distinct living systems but also distinct architectures of robots (Glenberg 2010; Lux et al. 2021). We highlight the analogies of different bodies (c.f., humans and rodents) that are exploited by agents in order to fulfil the same task, which is to collect the most informative stimuli from the world to resolve a model's uncertainty of it. Surely, different bodies provide different strategies, but as we have shown here, some strategies can be united and driven very similarly, such as exploring an environment using whiskers or hand movement. In robotics, there are several distinct architectures of robots to fulfil distinct tasks (Rubio et al. 2019). Although this is outside the scope of this paper, we hope to motivate future researchers to play with the concept of embodiment and see what strategies are universal across several bodies, and what changes lead to different neural encodings, for instance.

4.1 Limitation

Here we consider several limitations of our work that are worth mentioning. First, the difference between hand movement and animal whisking is obviously distinct, and the fact that both are used for tactile exploration can be misleading from the neuroscientific point of view, as these processes are encoded with different importance (i.e. it is less important to lose one whisker but more tragic to lose a human arm). For instance, the speed of whisking during object exploration is up 25 Hz (Berg and Kleinfeld 2003), which is a speed that cannot be reached by a hand. However, the model is simplified enough to justify the use of both models for both species independently, and the link should be further tested to suggest whether this generalization is possible. Furthermore, while the model works with discrete actions—which can be action primitives—its extension to continuous control could be interesting for robot exploration tasks. The models combining discrete and continuous domains have been shown in (Parr et al. 2021, 2022). As a final practical consideration, we acknowledge that the touch sensors on the Nao robot are not suited for object exploration, as reliable stimulation of the touch sensor only occurred when using a researcher's hand (see also Appendix A.2).

5   Conclusion

We described an active sensing model inspired by serotonergic modulation under the active inference framework. Particularly, we designed a generative model to perform tactile exploration in a humanoid robot. While the presented robotic model is still far away from human tactile exploration we suggested some possible relations. Specifically, we have shown that to resolve uncertainty in the environment, the influence of high sensory and/or low habitual precision on the inference process leads to a faster appearance of an active sensing behaviour. Moreover, our findings also contribute to scrutinizing the vast functions of serotonin (Berger et al. 2009) that in our case are associated with the aforementioned parameters. Next, we highlight that it might be a complex task to dissociate the effect of habitual behaviour with imprecise sensory estimation at least in active sensing. Whether this is a universal criterion of behaviour and thus extends to other behavioural processes such as social cognition (Lockwood and Klein-Flügge 2021) or reward learning (Lindström et al. 2021), and whether these are regulated via serotonin in the same manner, should be further tested.

Acknowledgement. FN was supported by the EU H2020 MSCA ITN project 'Serotonin and Beyond' (N 953327). We thank Tansu Celikel and Thomas Parr for their helpful discussions.

A   Appendix

A.1   Python Scripts

The scripts that we used in order to simulate the experiment and run the experiment in the Nao robot can be found on the following GitHub page: https://github.com/SimonJanssen1/Serotonin-based-active-sensing.git

In order to generate the heatmaps in Sect. 3.1, we used a Jupyter Notebooks file in which we iterated through different combinations of ζ and ρ parameters, while simulating a touch in arm position 4. We also used the scripts as explained in Sect. 2.6 (see also Fig. 7 for a visual description of the software architecture) in order to conduct the experiment with the Nao robot. Next, we simulated the script communicating with the Nao robot to test whether the architecture is working correctly. In this script, the general architecture is the same with an acting and sensing thread and some shared variables. However, instead of communicating with the robot to sense the environment and execute actions, the script simulates these behaviours. For simulating touch, we defined three options: 1) simulating touch at specific time-steps, which could be indicated by means of a list, 2) simulating touch in a specific arm position, or 3) simulating touch randomly, where a probability of touch could be specified.

A.2   Experiment with Different Sensory Stimulation

In addition to the experiments with the Nao robot presented in Sect. 3.2, we conducted another experiment where we touched the robot in arm position 4 with a metal object instead of using a researcher's hand. Because the robot has capacitive sensors on the back of the right hand, it should still be able to sense a touch when using a metal object. However, Fig. 8 shows that this is not the case. Namely, the robot only registers a touch four times, whereas we expected it to register a touch every time the arm was at position 4. These results thus show that the back touch sensor on the hand of the Nao robot was not very sensitive to touch with materials other than a hand.

A.3   Experiment Videos

During the experiments, we also recorded the humanoid's behaviour. These results can be found under the following link: https://drive.google.com/drive/folders/1QFmy1nHtQlmWxmKPZa-kbgj84FBJ9Q6n?usp=sharing.

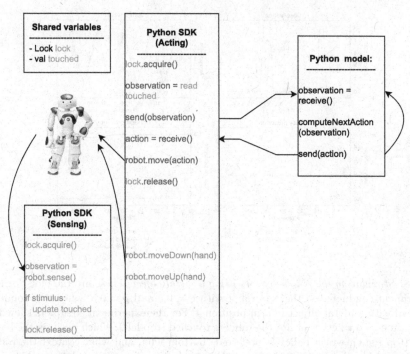

Fig. 7. *The software architecture of the Nao robot to conduct the experiment.* The script that interacts with the robot consists of two different threads that are responsible for acting and sensing, respectively. The acting thread reads an observation from the shared variable storing the touch value, which it sends to the python model. The python model subsequently computes the next action for the robot, given the observation, and sends this action back to the acting thread, which uses it to move to the next state. When in the new state, the robot moves its arm down and up again, during which the sensing thread is also active and records whether or not the touch sensor of the robot is touched. If the robot's sensor is touched, the sensing thread will make sure to update the shared variable storing the touch value accordingly, such that the acting thread can send the observation to the python model in the next time step.

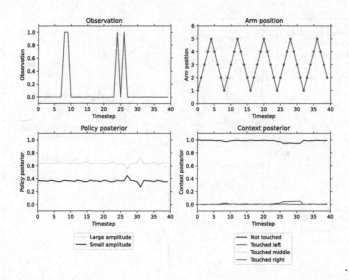

Fig. 8. *Stimulating the Nao's sensors using a metal object.* These are the plots for the experiment conducted in the Nao robot with $\zeta = 0.5$ and $\rho = 0.5$, where the robot is touched with a metal object in arm position 4. For the experiment, the plots show for every time-step whether or not the robot is touched (top left), which position the hand is in (top right), which policy is preferred (bottom left), and what context the robot believes it is in (bottom right). As can be seen in the observation plot, touching the robot is often not registered and results in unreliable behaviour.

References

Adams, R.A., Shipp, S., Friston, K.J.: Predictions not commands: active inference in the motor system. Brain Struct. Funct. **218**, 611–643 (2013)

Azarfar, A., Zhang, Y., Alishbayli, A., Schubert, D., Homberg, J.R., Celikel, T.: Serotonergic development of active sensing. BioRxiv, 762534 (2019)

Bajcsy, R., Aloimonos, Y., Tsotsos, J.K.: Revisiting active perception. Auton. Robot. **42**, 177–196 (2018)

Baltieri, M., Buckley, C.L.: The dark room problem in predictive processing and active inference, a legacy of cognitivism? In: Artificial Life Conference Proceedings, pp. 40–47 (2019)

Bang, D., et al.: Sub-second dopamine and serotonin signaling in human striatum during perceptual decision-making. Neuron **108**(5), 999–1010 (2020)

Berg, R.W., Kleinfeld, D.: Rhythmic whisking by rat: retraction as well as protraction of the vibrissae is under active muscular control. J. Neurophysiol. **89**(1), 104–117 (2003)

Berger, M., Gray, J.A., Roth, B.L.: The expanded biology of serotonin. Annu. Rev. Med. **60**, 355–366 (2009)

Blei, D.M., Kucukelbir, A., McAuliffe, J.D.: Variational inference: a review for statisticians. J. Am. Stat. Assoc. **112**(518), 859–877 (2017)

Cools, R., Nakamura, K., Daw, N.D.: Serotonin and dopamine: unifying affective, activational, and decision functions. Neuropsychopharmacology **36**(1), 98–113 (2011)

Da Costa, L., Parr, T., Sajid, N., Veselic, S., Neacsu, V., Friston, K.: Active inference on discrete state-spaces: a synthesis. J. Math. Psychol. **99**, 102447 (2020)

Daw, N.D., Kakade, S., Dayan, P.: Opponent interactions between serotonin and dopamine. Neural Netw. **15**(4–6), 603–616 (2002)

Dayan, P., Huys, Q.J.: Serotonin in affective control. Annu. Rev. Neurosci. **32**, 95–126 (2009)

Dayan, P., Huys, Q.J.M.: Serotonin, inhibition, and negative mood. PLoS Comput. Biol. **4**(2), e4 (2008)

Doya, K.: Metalearning and neuromodulation. Neural Netw. **15**(4–6), 495–506 (2002)

Friston, K.: The free-energy principle: a unified brain theory? Nat. Rev. Neurosci. **11**(2), 127–138 (2010)

Friston, K., FitzGerald, T., Rigoli, F., Schwartenbeck, P., Pezzulo, G.: Active inference: a process theory. Neural Comput. **29**(1), 1–49 (2017)

Friston, K., Thornton, C., Clark, A.: Free-energy minimization and the dark-room problem. Front. Psychol. **130** (2012)

Friston, K.J., Parr, T., de Vries, B.: The graphical brain: belief propagation and active inference. Netw. Neurosci. **1**(4), 381–414 (2017)

Glenberg, A.M.: Embodiment as a unifying perspective for psychology. Wiley Interdisc. Rev.: Cogn. Sci. **1**(4), 586–596 (2010)

Heins, C., et al.: pymdp: a python library for active inference in discrete state spaces. arXiv preprint arXiv:2201.03904 (2022)

Homberg, J.R., Schubert, D., Asan, E., Aron, E.N.: Sensory processing sensitivity and serotonin gene variance: insights into mechanisms shaping environmental sensitivity. Neurosci. Biobehav. Rev. **71**, 472–483 (2016)

Kaboli, M., Feng, D., Yao, K., Lanillos, P., Cheng, G.: A tactile-based framework for active object learning and discrimination using multimodal robotic skin. IEEE Robot. Autom. Lett. **2**(4), 2143–2150 (2017)

Kaplan, R., Friston, K.J.: Planning and navigation as active inference. Biol. Cybern. **112**(4), 323–343 (2018)

Krichmar, J.L.: Neurorobotics-a thriving community and a promising pathway toward intelligent cognitive robots. Front. Neurorobot. **12**, 42 (2018)

Lanillos, P., et al.: Active inference in robotics and artificial agents: survey and challenges. arXiv preprint arXiv:2112.01871 (2021)

Lawson, R.P., Rees, G., Friston, K.J.: An aberrant precision account of autism. Front. Hum. Neurosci. **8**, 302 (2014)

Lindström, B., Bellander, M., Schultner, D.T., Chang, A., Tobler, P.N., Amodio, D.M.: A computational reward learning account of social media engagement. Nat. Commun. **12**(1), 1311 (2021)

Lockwood, P.L., Klein-Flügge, M.C.: Computational modelling of social cognition and behaviour—a reinforcement learning primer. Soc. Cogn. Affect. Neurosci. **16**(8), 761–771 (2021)

Lux, V., Non, A.L., Pexman, P.M., Stadler, W., Weber, L.A., Krüger, M.: A developmental framework for embodiment research: the next step toward integrating concepts and methods. Front. Syst. Neurosci. **15**, 672740 (2021)

Martinez-Hernandez, U., Dodd, T.J., Evans, M.H., Prescott, T.J., Lepora, N.F.: Active sensorimotor control for tactile exploration. Robot. Auton. Syst. **87**, 15–27 (2017)

Meera, A.A., Novicky, F., Parr, T., Friston, K., Lanillos, P., Sajid, N.: Reclaiming saliency: rhythmic precision-modulated action and perception. arXiv preprint arXiv:2203.12652 (2022)

Miller, K.J., Shenhav, A., Ludvig, E.A.: Habits without values. Psychol. Rev. **126**(2), 292 (2019)

Muller, C.L., Anacker, A.M., Veenstra-VanderWeele, J.: The serotonin system in autism spectrum disorder: from biomarker to animal models. Neuroscience **321**, 24–41 (2016)

Najemnik, J., Geisler, W.S.: Optimal eye movement strategies in visual search. Nature **434**(7031), 387–391 (2005)

Najemnik, J., Geisler, W.S.: Eye movement statistics in humans are consistent with an optimal search strategy. J. Vis. **8**(3), 4 (2008)

Nao the humanoid and programmable robot | aldebaran (n.d.). https://www.aldebaran.com/en/nao

Oliver, G., Lanillos, P., Cheng, G.: An empirical study of active inference on a humanoid robot. IEEE Trans. Cogn. Dev. Syst. **14**(2), 462–471 (2021)

Palmer, C.J., Lawson, R.P., Hohwy, J.: Bayesian approaches to autism: towards volatility, action, and behavior. Psychol. Bull. **143**(5), 521 (2017)

Parr, T., Friston, K.J.: Uncertainty, epistemics and active inference. J. R. Soc. Interface **14**(136), 20170376 (2017)

Parr, T., Limanowski, J., Rawji, V., Friston, K.: The computational neurology of movement under active inference. Brain **144**(6), 1799–1818 (2021)

Parr, T., Pezzulo, G., Friston, K.J.: Active Inference: The Free Energy Principle in Mind, Brain, and Behavior. MIT Press, Cambridge (2022)

Parr, T., Sajid, N., Da Costa, L., Mirza, M.B., Friston, K.J.: Generative models for active vision. Front. Neurorobot. **15**, 651432 (2021)

Rasouli, A., Lanillos, P., Cheng, G., Tsotsos, J.K.: Attention-based active visual search for mobile robots. Auton. Robot. **44**(2), 131–146 (2020)

Renninger, L.W., Verghese, P., Coughlan, J.: Where to look next? Eye movements reduce local uncertainty. J. Vis. **7**(3), 6 (2007)

Rubio, F., Valero, F., Llopis-Albert, C.: A review of mobile robots: concepts, methods, theoretical framework, and applications. Int. J. Adv. Rob. Syst. **16**(2), 1729881419839596 (2019)

Ryan, C.P., Bettelani, G.C., Ciotti, S., Parise, C., Moscatelli, A., Bianchi, M.: The interaction between motion and texture in the sense of touch. J. Neurophysiol. **126**(4), 1375–1390 (2021)

Sun, Z., Firestone, C.: The dark room problem. Trends Cogn. Sci. **24**(5), 346–348 (2020)

Tani, J., White, J.: Cognitive neurorobotics and self in the shared world, a focused review of ongoing research. Adapt. Behav. **30**(1), 81–100 (2022)

Van Boxtel, J.J., Lu, H.: A Predictive Coding Perspective on Autism Spectrum Disorders, vol. 4. Frontiers Media SA (2013)

Voigts, J., Sakmann, B., Celikel, T.: Unsupervised whisker tracking in unrestrained behaving animals. J. Neurophysiol. **100**(1), 504–515 (2008)

Yang, S.C.-H., Wolpert, D.M., Lengyel, M.: Theoretical perspectives on active sensing. Curr. Opin. Behav. Sci. **11**, 100–108 (2016)

Detecting Human Distraction from Gaze: An Augmented Reality Approach in the Robotic Environment

Panagiotis Zaparas, Panagiotis Katranitsiotis[✉], Konstantinos Stavridis, and Petros Daras

The Visual Computing Lab - Centre for Research and Technology Hellas/Information Technologies Institute, Thessaloniki, Greece
{pan.zap,pkatranitsiotis,staurid,daras}@iti.gr

Abstract. The investigation of human signals has been a topic of research since the advent of technology enabled their acquisition. Signals like gaze can reveal part of the human brain mechanisms. To facilitate the research of the analysis of these signals, researchers are developing and publishing datasets. This paper introduces the Augmented Reality DISTraction dataset (ARDIST), a novel dataset for processing human gaze. The primary objective of this dataset is to provide the scientific community with a resource that researchers can use to assess the distraction/attention levels of individuals performing specific tasks in the Robotic environment. The experiment was designed based on the latest findings in the field of neuroscience to include a diverse range of variables that affect human attention levels. Furthermore, the dataset can be utilized to model the human gaze signal under the influence of significant factors.

Keywords: Gaze dataset · Human Attention detection · Augmented Reality

1 Introduction

Throughout the human era, machines have become a vital part of almost every human activity. Scientists have explored how people interact with machines in order to provide safe machines and robotic frameworks that are accident-free and are able to increase productivity. The human ability to maintain concentration throughout the entire collaboration is a crucial factor in achieving an effective human-robot interaction scheme.

Human concentration can be affected in multiple ways and by numerous factors: internal such as motives, mood, interest and emotion or external such as visual, auditory or even olfactory stimulus. Likewise, the mental workload of the

The work presented in this paper was supported by the European Commission under contract H2020 - 101016953 CoRoSect.

subject affects its ability to remain concentrated and could result in negative implications [13,15,16]. Currently, two types of attention are commonly distinguished in the literature: bottom-up and top-down attention, or stimulus-driven and goal-oriented attention [5,6,11]. Top-down attention refers to the voluntary allocation of attention to certain features, objects, or regions in space and on the other hand bottom-up attention is not voluntarily directed. Salient stimuli can attract attention, even though the subject had no intentions to attend to these stimuli [14].

Subsequently, during human-robot collaboration tasks, human attention can easily be disturbed, therefore the need to monitor the attention level of humans has risen. In the current literature, the gaze is used as a tool to measure concentration level for a wide variety of tasks and also as a mechanism for controlling the task completion [2,8,9]. The use of gaze is not limited only to measuring and predicting the attention level. It can also be utilized in user interfaces for virtual and augmented reality technologies, by loading only the essential visual stimulus that is dictated by the gaze and still retain a pleasant experience for the user.

Numerous research studies have shown that the scientific community has long-standing interest in the study of gaze [1,4,12,17]. Researchers have created a variety of datasets that captured gaze behaviour under various circumstances in order to extract fruitful gaze patterns. These datasets involve gathering participant's gaze data over a predetermined time period, usually during an experiment in which the participant is either engaged in free viewing mode or completing a specific task.

Various studies in the literature introduced gaze annotated datasets for several scientific purposes. The MIT300 dataset was proposed in [10] and is the first dataset that recorded human-eye movements to predict the salient areas of a visual stimulus. It contains three hundred (300) depicting natural indoor and outdoor views. The eye movements were recorded using the ETL 400 ISCAN which records at a frequency of 240HZ. The proposed dataset was designed with the objective of being used as a benchmark for saliency prediction models. In a similar line of work, the well-known dataset is the CAT2000 in [3] which contains 4000 images from a variety of 20 categories. The number of participants stands at 120 from which the eye movements were recorded. This dataset has the purpose of boosting the research on saliency and conducting behavioural studies regarding bottom-up visual attention.

An impressive dataset is the EGO4D in [7], which is a massive worldwide egocentric video dataset with over 3000 h hours of daily-life activity video and over 9000 people partaking in its data accumulation. A portion of the data is accompanied by audio, 3D meshes of the environment stereo, eye gaze and even synchronized videos from multiple egocentric cameras at the same event. Wearable glasses equipped with eye-tracking technology, named Pupil Labs, were used for the collection of the gaze data. The dataset was designed with the objective of being used in a variety of fields, such as in an episodic memory system, hand and object interactions in the view of how the object change when being interacted, audio-visual diarization, social interactions and forecasting.

To the best of the authors' knowledge, the introduced dataset, ARDIST, is the first dataset that can be utilized for modelling the gaze signal to reveal patterns capable of predicting the levels of human attention, which is the major contribution of the current study. Moreover, an Augmented Reality (AR) industrial environment simulation dataset is being proposed to enable the ARDIST creation. In particular, a participant is assigned the specific task of supervising a virtual robot performing the pick and place task and marking any missteps the robot makes. The introduced dataset can further boost research in human attention prediction using the Machine Learning (ML) and Deep Learning (DL) paradigms. The ARDIST dataset is publicly available as well as a demonstration video of the experiment to facilitate its replication on the following link https://vcl.iti.gr/dataset/ardist/.

2   The ARDIST Dataset

The goal of the ARDIST dataset is to provide gaze annotations that can be ultimately be employed for training deep learning models in order to reveal complicated gaze patterns. These models are intended to evaluate the attention level of humans during human-robot collaboration schemes, thus achieving safer and more efficient cooperation between machines and people.

2.1   Experimental Setup

To create the augmented reality (AR) experience and to collect gaze data with respect to the augmented objects, the HoloLens 2 glasses and the Unity3D, an open-source game development tool, were utilized.

The participant's role during the experiment was to observe the AR robot that was carrying out the pick-and-place assignment, as depicted in Fig. 1. In particular, the augmented robot is engaged in the task of placing cubes, which can be either green or red, into designated boxes that correspond to their colors. Whenever the placement of the cube is in the wrong box the participant needs to press a designated button and therefore to annotate the incorrect movement. Several distractions were added through the aforementioned procedure in order to measure the distraction level of the participant while supervising the robot's task. Despite numerous distractions, the participant had to pay attention and stay focused on the job at hand. These distractions were purposefully added to the setting to resemble a real-world situation where humans and robots collaborate. The participant who wore the head-mounted augmented reality device, Microsoft's HoloLens 2, was instructed to press a keyboard button whenever the robot committed an error. Thereby, the action label was formulated and provided the ground truth for the dataset (distracted/not distracted subject), as depicted in Fig. 2.

The experiment was divided into five segments, each lasting for one minute and featuring a different type and level of distraction. In order to acquire a diverse set of gaze data that could be used to train deep learning models in

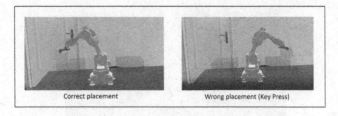

Fig. 1. Visual representation of actions.

Fig. 2. Experimental Setup.

assessing the attention levels of humans during human-robot collaboration, these segments were designed to simulate a variety of scenarios over the course of the corresponding cooperation. The first segment was designed to familiarize the participant with the AR setup and the movements of the robot and therefore contained no errors made by the robot nor distractions for the participant.

The second segment included both errors made by the robot and exclusively visual distractions for the participant. These visual distractions were in the form of a kinetic object that caused a visual stimulus, with the aim of decreasing the participant's attention on the robot. A representation of this scenario is depicted in Fig. 3.

The third segment consisted of both robot errors and solely auditory distractions for the participant, in the form of busy street noises (e.g. ambulance sirens, vehicle horns, etc.).

The fourth segment incorporated robot errors and both of the aforementioned distractions (visual and auditory) in order to further decrease the participant's attention level.

Fig. 3. Visual Distraction.

The fifth and final segment comprised robot errors and an increased cognitive load on the participant. This was achieved by continuously subtracting 7, starting from 1000 [13], until the end of the fifth segment (which also lasted 1 min), while simultaneously supervising and labeling the robot errors. A summarization of the above is presented in Table 1.

Table 1. Experimental Design.

Segments	1	2	3	4	5	Total
Iterations	40	40	40	40	40	200
Proper	40	27	27	27	27	148
Errors	0	13	13	13	13	52
Distractions	0	10	7	15	0	32
Visual	0	10	0	10	0	20
Audio	0	0	7	5	0	13

2.2 The ARDIST Description

In total, 50 participants were able to conduct the experiment. Further demographic analysis of the dataset is presented in Table 2. During the 5-minute experiment, each discrete recording was designed to have 200 executions of the pick and place task, out of which 52 executions resulted in errors by the robot. Except for the first segment, each subsequent segment of the recording included 40 repetitions of the task, out of which 13 executions resulted in errors. A total of 10,000 repetitions of the pick and place task were performed, during the entire experiment, out of which 2600 executions corresponded to errors, as presented in Table 3. The experiment also revealed that on average, there were 1.83 fixations when the minimum distance was set to 0.1 and the minimum duration to 0.1 s. The maximum number of fixations observed per task repetition was 5, and the minimum was 1. This represents the summary from the first version of the experiment.

Table 2. Demographics.

Gender	Male	39
	Female	11
Age	Mean	31.4
	Min	24
	Max	48

Table 3. Task Repetitions.

Executions			
Per subject		In Total	
Proper	Error	Proper	Error
148	52	7400	2600

3   Conclusion and Future Work

In this work, we presented our ongoing work on a novel, augmented reality based, gaze dataset which has the potential to be utilized for further studying the human gaze patterns and human attention levels in relation to the intensity and type of distractions. We outlined the current status of our collected dataset and the equipment used for data recording, as well as their types, methods employed, all of which were conceptualized through the use of Unity3D game development engine and HoloLens 2. This work aims to contribute towards the evolution and efficiency of human-robot collaboration.

For future work, the potential of discovering gaze patterns that reveal the levels of human attention will be explored. In particular, several gaze modeling methods will be applied oriented to the temporal and the spatial dimensions of the human signal. Moreover, a variety of machine and deep learning algorithms will be utilized in comparison for the prediction task. In addition, a systematic study will be conducted to gain insights into how distraction factors influence the levels of human attention. Since providing the hololens device can be costly prohibited, a research line of work will be established to replace the gaze signal with face photo captured by cameras in the robotic environment. Further research directions in analyzing human signals and automatically detect human intentions can boost human-robot collaboration schemes.

References

1. Argyle, M., Cook, M.: Gaze and mutual gaze (1976)
2. Ballard, D.H., Hayhoe, M.M.: Modelling the role of task in the control of gaze. Vis. Cogn. **17**(6–7), 1185–1204 (2009)
3. Borji, A., Itti, L.: Cat 2000: a large scale fixation dataset for boosting saliency research. arXiv preprint arXiv:1505.03581 (2015)

4. Calder, A.J., et al.: Reading the mind from eye gaze. Neuropsychologia 40(8), 1129–1138 (2002)
5. Carrasco, M.: Visual attention: the past 25 years. Vision. Res. 51(13), 1484–1525 (2011)
6. Connor, C.E., Egeth, H.E., Yantis, S.: Visual attention: bottom-up versus top-down. Curr. Biol. 14(19), R850–R852 (2004)
7. Grauman, K., et al.: Ego4D: around the world in 3,000 hours of egocentric video. In: Proceedings of the IEEE/CVF Conference on Computer Vision and Pattern Recognition, pp. 18995–19012 (2022)
8. Hessels, R.S., van Doorn, A.J., Benjamins, J.S., Holleman, G.A., Hooge, I.T.: Task-related gaze control in human crowd navigation. Attention Percept. Psychophys. 82(5), 2482–2501 (2020)
9. Jovancevic, J., Sullivan, B., Hayhoe, M.: Control of attention and gaze in complex environments. J. Vis. 6(12), 9 (2006)
10. Judd, T., Durand, F., Torralba, A.: A benchmark of computational models of saliency to predict human fixations (2012)
11. Katsuki, F., Constantinidis, C.: Bottom-up and top-down attention: different processes and overlapping neural systems. Neuroscientist 20(5), 509–521 (2014)
12. Li, Y., Liu, M., Rehg, J.: In the eye of the beholder: gaze and actions in first person video. IEEE Trans. Pattern Anal. Mach. Intell. 45, 6731–6747 (2021)
13. Mingardi, M., Pluchino, P., Bacchin, D., Rossato, C., Gamberini, L.: Assessment of implicit and explicit measures of mental workload in working situations: implications for industry 4.0. Appl. Sci. 10(18), 6416 (2020)
14. Pinto, Y., van der Leij, A.R., Sligte, I.G., Lamme, V.A., Scholte, H.S.: Bottom-up and top-down attention are independent. J. Vis. 13(3), 16 (2013)
15. Posner, M.I., Petersen, S.E.: The attention system of the human brain. Annu. Rev. Neurosci. 13(1), 25–42 (1990)
16. Robertson, I.H., Ward, T., Ridgeway, V., Nimmo-Smith, I.: The structure of normal human attention: the test of everyday attention. J. Int. Neuropsychol. Soc. 2(6), 525–534 (1996)
17. Sibert, L.E., Jacob, R.J.: Evaluation of eye gaze interaction. In: Proceedings of the SIGCHI Conference on Human Factors in Computing Systems, pp. 281–288 (2000)

Learning Time and Recognition Rate Improvement of CNNs Through Transfer Learning for BMI Systems

Goragod Pogthanisorn[1]([✉]), Ryota Takahashi[1], and Genci Capi[2]

[1] Graduate School of Science and Engineering, Hosei University, Tokyo, Japan
goragod.pongthanisorn.3w@stu.hosei.ac.jp
[2] Department of Mechanical Engineering, Hosei University, Tokyo, Japan

Abstract. Brain-Machine Interface (BMI) is a control paradigm involving using brain signal to generate control commands for other devices. A non-invasive method of brain signal recording such as Electroencephalogram (EEG) is widely used. Modern approaches for BMI tend to utilize Deep Learning (DL) such as Convolutional Neural Network (CNN) to extract essential features as well as improve the classification accuracy. Nonetheless, EEG is a subject dependent signal wherein individuals exhibit a distinct signal pattern even when performing identical tasks. In addition, DL requires a huge amount of data which leads to longer training time. In this paper we propose transfer learning (TL) to improve the recognition rate and reduce the training time of BMI systems. We implement multiple conditions to evaluate the TL performance. The experiments using competition IV b2 dataset mental imaginary tasks and the dataset collected in our lab for several grasping hand motions are utilized to evaluate the TL performance.

Keywords: Brain-Machine Interface · Transfer learning · Convolutional Neural Network · Electroencephalogram

1 Introduction

Brain Machine Interface (BMI) utilizes the brain signals to control machines. BMI is expected to improve the quality of life of disabled and elderly people by providing an alternative way of interacting with the real-world environment. Nonetheless, BMI application does not limit communication. [1] utilized BMI for rehabilitation purposes which include motion and speech. [2] proposed an algorithm to detect a seizure from the brain signals. [3] proposed mental state detection, while in [4] an algorithm to realize the current emotion of the subject using brain signals is presented.

There are many types of brain signals but the Electroencephalogram (EEG) is the most widely used. EEG signal is measured by placing the electrodes in the specific location of the subject's scalp and measuring an electrical signal produced by the brain.

A robust BMI system required an accurate classifier since EEG is low signal-to-noise ratio (SNR) by nature. Many researchers have addressed this issue and proposed

F. Meder et al. (Eds.): Living Machines 2023, LNAI 14157, pp. 63–76, 2023.
https://doi.org/10.1007/978-3-031-38857-6_5

algorithms to enchant system performance. Traditional BMI system tends to utilize Linear Discriminant Analysis (LDA), K-nearest Neighborhood (K-NN) [5], or Support Vector Machine (SVM) [6] as a context classifier. However, the traditional approach require an intensive preprocessing to remove noise from original signals. Moreover, feature engineering of EEG is not trivial task for BMI systems as well.

Recent BMI systems utilize DL approach for context classification of brain signals, such as CNN, since it produces higher accuracy compared to traditional methods [7]. A robust DL model requires a large amount of dataset in order to generate the informative feature. This leads to significant increasing of a training time. To ease the issue, several techniques are used including TL. Instead of having the model trained from scratch, a pre-trained model which has already trained with base dataset, is further trained with additional information. Typical TL approach involves a fine-tuning of the feature extraction layers' parameters such as, weights and bias to the target dataset. All or only specific layers parameters can be *frozen*, mean the model's parameter will not be updated during learning.

The work from [8] applied TL to Motor Imaginary (MI) tasks, which refer to mentally perform a movement without physically execution. Their results show that TL helped obtained higher accuracy while training time is reduced. [9] improve the BMI performance using fine-tuning method for each convolutional layer. [10] introduced a cross sleep stage dataset TL for BMI using transformer-based approach. Their experiments involved fine-tuning the inner and outer block of their model.

Nonetheless, previous research evaluated only a single modality dataset. It is not shown whether the improvement obtained from TL is universal across all modalities. TL method needs further investigation not only in modality, but also the effect of freezing convolutional layers. In this work, we verify the performance of the TL and the frozen feature extraction layers condition in two datasets: 1) BCI competition IV b2 dataset for MI tasks and 2) CapiLab Dataset. BCI competition IV b2 dataset contains 3 EEG channels targeting two mental tasks from 9 subjects [11]. CapiLab Dataset [12] targeting a different right hand grasping motions. The data was obtained from 19 EEG channels of four male subjects. The evaluation results using multiple conditions of TL show a significant improvement in terms of: 1) accuracy improvement and 2) learning time reduction.

2 Datasets and Deep Learning Model

The datasets which were used to verify conditional TLs are BCI Competition IV2b [11] and CapiLab Dataset [12]. These 2 datasets target different tasks. While [11] focuses on EEG signals during imagination of left or right-hand motions, [12] focuses on real motion of right-hand grasping different objects which is called Motor Execution (MO) task. The 2 datasets utilize 10–20 system for electrode placement. The details of these datasets including recording technique are discussed.

The CNN model for classification and preprocessing technique of target signal is also explained in this section.

2.1 Datasets

BCI Competition Dataset 2b. The dataset was recorded by [11] at Graz university of technology, Austria which is online and available under CC BY-ND license. The sampling rate is 250 Hz. 0.5–100 Hz Bandpass filter was applied to remove any artifact that may be contained in the signal. Another 50 Hz notch filter was applied to remove AC line noise from the signal. The recording consists of 2 sessions, a screening for practicing imagination and smiley feedback for testing. Each subject needs to perform 2 sessions without feedback and 3 sessions with feedback. One session contains 6 runs, and each run contains 10 trials. Before each run, ECoG was recorded for further use. The time scheming of recording was described in Fig. 1.

During the screening, subjects were instructed to imagine a movement of either hand in the same direction of the arrow shown on the screen. Before the trial starts, a fixate arrow appears on the screen for 3 s. During this time, an alert sound is played before the cue period (1 s) as the subjects are ready to imagine. Then the arrow and direction will appear on the screen for 4 s. Finally, 1-s pause is performed, and another 1 s rest. That concludes a single trial.

During smiley feedback, the imagination practice result is put to test. The subjects rather than displaying a fixated cross then the arrow with direction, the smiley face will appear on the screen. At the start, the smiley face appears on the screen for 3.5 s. The alerting sound is played to make subjects ready. Within 4.5 s, the subjects need to use their imagination to move the smiley face in the correct direction on the screen indicated by color (green is correct and red otherwise).

The complete timeline of both screening and feedback is shown in Fig. 2.

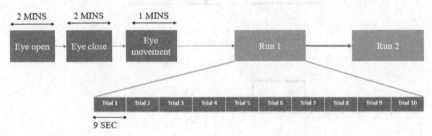

Fig. 1. Time scheming in one session for both with and without feedback. (Adapted from [11])

CapiLab Dataset. The dataset was obtained from the Assistive Robotic Laboratory, Hosei university of Japan [12]. 4 male subjects participated in the recording session. The record paradigm was inspired by the previous dataset but targeted the movement of the right hand. The recording device is Mitsar EEG 201 with 19 input channels. 19 electrodes are placed according to the standard 10–20 system. The signals are sampled at 500 Hz and 50 Hz notch filter was applied to remove AC line noise. Channel A1 and A2 serve as references.

The subjects need to perform 3 sessions to complete the recording. In single sessions, the subjects performed 12 trials. The subjects need to perform 12 sessions on different days to prevent fatigue for 3 days. This dataset maps the EEG signal to grasping 2

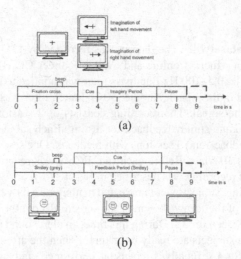

Fig. 2. Timing scheme of the paradigms: (a) screening trial (b) smiley feedback trial [11]

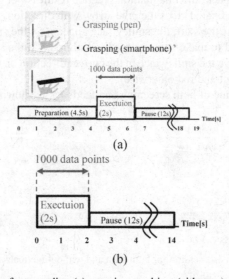

Fig. 3. Timing scheme for recording (a) grasping an object (either pen or smartphone) (b) idle.

objects, a pen, and a smartphone, with different gestures and idle. While grasping pen and smartphone has similar timing scheme, the idle task does not have a preparation period, as shown in Fig. 3.

Before recording, the subjects were instructed to look at the screen all the time and refrain as much as possible from blinking during the execution of grasping (2 s). At the start, the target object appears on the screen indicating the task that subjects are required to perform the progress bar on the left side of the screen is appear at the same time. The virtual object will gradually move toward the virtual hand on the screen and finally touch the virtual hand. That indicates that signal sampling has started. When the virtual object touches the virtual hand on the screen, the virtual hand starts grasping the virtual object. At the same time, an actual object is placed and the subject replicates the movement. The sampling period is 2 s long and followed by a 12-s rest period before the next trial starts.

Preprocessing. EEG data are prone to various noises. Therefore, noise is removed by applying 8.0–30.0 Hz [10] for BCI Competition IV2b dataset and 0.5–40.0 Hz for CapiLab dataset. However, for BCI Competition IV2 dataset sampled all periods of data from start of the experiment. Hence, only a portion of data relevant to the MI task are only processed.

General approaches for enchanting MI task classification are using either Continuous Wavelet Transform (CWT) or or-time Fourier Transform (STFT). Accordingly, to [15–17], CWT outperforms SFTF in terms of classification accuracy. Therefore, CWT is selected as a preprocessing for BCI competition IV2b dataset. The main purpose of applying CWT is to extract target spatial features from EEG signals [16]. EEG spatial features can be divided into different bands called α (alpha), β (beta), θ (theta), δ (delta), and γ (gamma). δ waves consider the slowest ranging from 0.5–4Hz. This band is associated with the deep sleep stage. θ waves, ranging from (4–8Hz) are produced during some state of sleep and when focusing. α waves, ranging from 8–14 Hz are produced when the subject mental state is relaxed, eyes close yet does not fall asleep. β waves, ranging from 14–30 Hz associated with normal and active concentrations. Finally, γ wave, above 30 Hz strongly correlated to the visual stimuli [20]. For BCI competition IV2b dataset, CWT was applied to all channels (C3, C4, and Cz) and extracted feature α (8–13) and β (13–30) bands. The extracted features are then combined creating a feature map from both bands and then used as input of the CNN.

Classifier. CNN is a highly accurate machine learning algorithm that was originally used in image processing applications. But recently, CNN became one of the best options to decode a brain signal. However, the general model for EEG is still not satisfying in terms of performance. Since EEG in different tasks is heavily contaminated by noise. Generally, the CNN model will be designed/fine-tuned for specific tasks.

To classify completely different tasks in our work (MI and MO), we utilized 2 CNN models for each dataset model A and B for CapiLab dataset and BCI competition IV2b, respectively.

Model A. The model is inspired by EEGNet [18] which consists of 6 convolutional blocks and 1 fully-connected block. The single convolutional block is one convolutional layer (with ReLU activation) and a max pooling layer. Except for the first block, which contains another spatial convolutional layer to reduce the length of spatial features. Finally, the features are fed to 3 fully connected layers with SoftMax activation at the final layer. Figure 6 shows the overall architecture of model A and a sample input.

Model B. The architecture of this model is based on AlexNet [19], which is a well-known CNN architecture for computer vision applications. We modify the classification layer of the network to align with the target class of the dataset. Additionally, the input of the network was slightly adjusted from the to a size of $227 \times 227 \times 3$, which corresponds to the BCI competition IV2b dataset with CWT's dimension. The overall model architecture and a sample input are shown in Fig. 7. The model was trained using a dataset of EEG signals recorded during MI tasks and achieved a high classification accuracy on test data (Figs. 4 and 5).

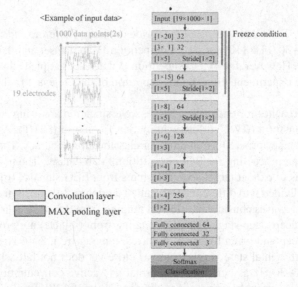

Fig. 4. Model A structure for decoding CapiLab dataset

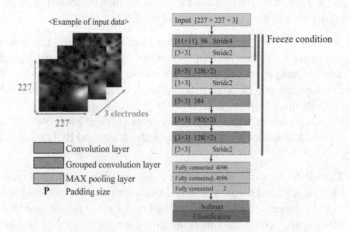

Fig. 5. Model B structure for decoding BCI competition IV2b dataset

3   Experiment Setting

3.1   Condition Setting for Transfer Learning

CNN improves accuracy by repeatedly updating parameters such as weights and bias during training. Nonetheless, weights and other parts are initialized randomly. Therefore, randomness is considered one of the factors which affect the training time. The practical approach is that the model should not be trained from the initial state but reuse some pre-trained model weights (with or without bias) [8]. In TL, each convolutional layer can be fine-tuned or set to a frozen layer. Fine-tuning of learning refers to re-adjusting parameters such as transferred weights with new data while frozen layer parameters are not updated during the training process.

In this work, we performed fine tuning with freezing conditions (line on the right side of Fig. 6 and 7), as follow:

- *C1*: The first convolution layer is frozen (red line).
- *C2*: The first and second convolution layers are frozen (green line).
- *C3*: All layers except for classification head are frozen (blue line).

These conditions were applied to CapiLab and BCI competition IV2b dataset. The results of these conditions are compared and verified. To obtain an actual performance of the final output, K-fold cross-validation technique is used. K-fold cross-validation technique is widely used to evaluate the performance of the trained model. The key idea is to segment the training data accordingly to k segment. Then used 1 of that segment as validation data while k–1 segment is used as training data. Finally, an average of accuracy is computed and utilized.

Condition for BCI Competition IV2b Dataset
For the BCI competition IV2b dataset, the conditions are simply source and target subjects where the source refers to the data used to train the model while the target is the subject that uses the pre-trained model to train their data. The configurations of the source-target are shown in Table 1. For training, Adam [21] with a learning rate of 1e-3 is used as an optimizer. The loss function is Binary Cross Entropy since we only have 2 classes. The batch size is 76, the epochs are 500 and the number of folds is 6. However, the model tends to be overfitted if it is overly trained using the dataset. Therefore, if the validation loss is not improved more than 6 epochs, the training process is terminated.

Condition for CapiLab Dataset.   There are 2 experiments on transfer learning in this dataset. The first experiment is the source-target evaluation (similar to the previous dataset). 3 Subjects data are used to create the pre-train model and the fourth Subject's data used to train the new model using TL. CapiLab dataset contains 12 sessions for each subject. One subject performs 4 sessions in 1 day to prevent fatigue.

The second experiment is an extension of experiment 1 which is only conducted using Subject 1 data. The purpose of this experiment is to evaluate a feasibility of controlling the robot hand using the classifier obtained from previous experiments. Figure 6 show overall step of the second experiment.

First step, the TL model of subject 1 obtained after experiment 1. Next, Subject 1 performed another 1 sessions of data recording. This data is then divided into training and

Table 1. Conditional transfer learning based on source and target subject

Source Subjects	Target Subject
Subject 4–9	Subject 1 Subject 2 Subject 3
Subject 1–3 and 7–9	Subject 4 Subject 5 Subject 6
Subject 1–6	Subject 7 Subject 8 Subject 9

testing data then performed conditional TL similar to the previous experiment. Finally, the result is evaluated. The data records in this step call *Testing data* In the next step, Subject 1 perform another 3 sessions of data recording (on the same day as first step). But this time, the data will not be used to train the model. The model needs to classify the target action from the data. This simulated the scenario where the model is fine-tune and testing on the real operation. The data records in this step call *Same-day* In the final step, we would like to evaluated the effect of different day EEG data on the TL model. Therefore, we record another 3 sessions and evaluate the accuracy of the TL model on this data. The data correct in this session is called *Another-day*.

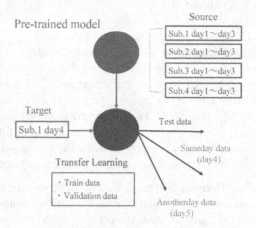

Fig. 6. Overall steps of experiment

4   Results and Discussion

The experiments are executed on a desktop PC with AMD Ryzen7 5800X CPU, NVIDIA GeForce RTX 3060 GPU, and 16.0 GB of RAM.

4.1   BCI Competition IV2b Results

In the experiment, each model is trained with the defined conditional TL for all cases (36 models, 4 model for each subject). The results indicate an improvement in accuracy when applying transfer learning to the model training. The defined conditional TL improve the classification accuracy for almost all subjects except for Subject 9. In the case of Subject 9, the accuracy is not improved by TL, but the difference is very small as shown on Fig. 7.

Nonetheless, there still no concrete confirmation from the evaluation result which TL condition yield the highest result. In case of Subject 1 and 5, C1 condition outperform other conditions. While C2 produce higher accuracy on Subject 3 and 7. Finally, C3 is most effective for Subject 2, 4, 6 and 8.

The results of training time indicates that transfer learning is highly effective in reducing the training time. The shortest training time is achieve on C2 conditions for Subject 1, 2, 3, 4 and 6. In C3, Subject 5, 6, 7 and 9 produce shortest training time. Interestingly, the time difference between C1, C2 and C3 is not significant despite the number of layers need to be trained (Tables 2 and 3).

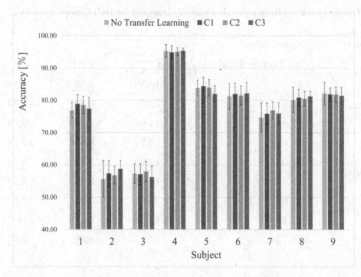

Fig. 7.   Source-target experiment with different conditions for BCI Competition IV2b dataset

4.2   CapiLab Dataset Result

There are two experiments performed in this dataset, source-target transfer learning and additional data transfer learning of Subject 1. This experiment follows the previous experiment protocol. The main different is that previous dataset is MI task while CapiLab dataset is ME task, an actual movement.

Experiment 1 Source-target with Condition Transfer Learning
Figure 7 shows a summary of accuracy results of the source-target experiment. In this

Table 2. Accuracy (%) from condition transfer learning for BCI Competition IV2b dataset

Target Subject	Condition			
	No Transfer Learning	C1	C2	C3
1	76.90	**78.89**	78.52	77.41
2	55.64	57.30	56.72	**58.73**
3	57.31	57.08	**57.92**	56.25
4	95.32	94.86	95.05	**95.36**
5	83.83	**84.32**	83.92	81.98
6	81.25	81.94	81.48	**82.13**
7	74.72	75.88	**76.90**	75.93
8	80.13	80.83	80.53	**81.23**
9	**82.13**	81.85	81.81	81.39

Table 3. Training time (s) from condition transfer learning for BCI Competition IV2b dataset

Target Subject	Condition			
	No Transfer Learning	C1	C2	C3
1	18.73	10.38	**8.22**	8.65
2	16.61	9.59	**6.52**	6.70
3	15.36	11.67	**8.86**	9.05
4	17.61	10.74	**8.64**	9.27
5	21.03	10.90	8.96	**8.74**
6	19.48	11.11	8.59	**8.53**
7	17.60	9.74	7.21	**7.10**
8	17.16	12.54	**10.79**	11.35
9	19.76	11.13	8.89	**8.57**

case, transfer learning improves the accuracy of all subjects, especially C1 condition outperforms other transfer learning in all subjects. However, Subjects 1 and 3 results are slightly different compared to C3 condition. Table 4 shows a detailed accuracy result for all conditions. Not surprisingly, C3 gave the best result the training time since the training layer is only classification head which is simple 3-fully connected layers. The detailed training time is described on Table 5 (Fig. 8).

Experiment 2 Additional Data on Subject 1

This is an extension of experiment 1. The TL model is evaluated on two different types of unknown data, as discussed in Sect. 3.1. The conditional TL model from previous experiments was obtained and further performed TL on additional Subject 1 data. The

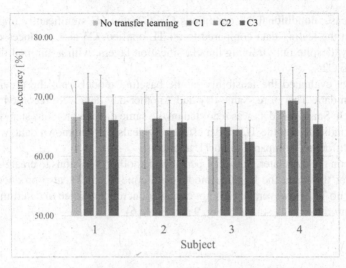

Fig. 8. Source-target experiment with different conditions for CapiLab dataset

Table 4. Accuracy (%) from condition transfer learning for CapiLab dataset

Target Subject	Condition			
	No Transfer Learning	C1	C2	C3
1	66.59	**69.06**	68.52	66.05
2	64.35	**66.28**	64.35	65.66
3	59.95	**64.89**	64.43	62.42
4	67.67	**69.29**	68.06	65.35

Table 5. Training time (s) from condition transfer learning for CapiLab dataset

Target Subject	Condition			
	No Transfer Learning	C1	C2	C3
1	13.76	10.19	7.21	**4.73**
2	12.54	7.82	5.89	**4.56**
3	11.74	8.63	5.85	**4.30**
4	14.66	10.69	7.74	**5.54**

three sessions' data, totaling 36 instances (12 instances per class), was divided into 30 training data and 6 testing data, and the baseline model was obtained.

In this case, conditional TL conditions C1, C2, and C3 significantly improve the accuracy on the testing data compared to no TL applied. C3 also produces the highest accuracy, despite only training the classification layers, with a minimal difference compared to C2.

Next, we evaluated the feasibility of the baseline model from the previous step on unknown data. Therefore, Same-day and Another-day data were recorded for three sessions each. Same-day data was recorded on the same day the previous step was done. The results indicate that the TL model effectively deals with unknown data, with more than a 3% difference compared to no TL applied.

Finally, on the days later, Subject 1 performed another 3 sessions to create Another-day data. For this data, the baseline model with conditional TL also produced better results than no TL. However, there is not enough concrete evidence to determine which conditions produce the best result (Fig. 9 and Table 6).

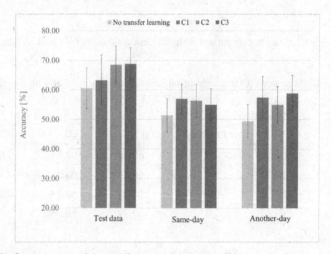

Fig. 9. Accuracy of date-different additional condition on CapiLab dataset

Table 6. Accuracy (%) from date-different additional condition for CapiLab dataset

Conditions	Conditions			
	No transfer learning	C1	C2	C3
Test data	60.49	63.27	68.52	**68.83**
Same-day	51.39	**56.94**	56.33	54.94
Another-day	49.38	57.41	54.94	**58.80**

5   Conclusion

In this work, we proposed a TL method to improve the accuracy and reduce the training time of BMI systems. We verified the performance of TL in two datasets. We defined 3 conditions regarding which layers weight and bias are not updated. The results showed that the TL improves an accuracy in most cases and significantly improves training time under different conditions. TL is also effective for dealing with unknown data as seen in experiment 2 of CapiLab Based on the application, we can select the solution from the trade-off between training time and the final model's accuracy. However, there is no concrete evidence of the best condition for a specific task. Therefore, we plan to utilize an optimization algorithm such as genetic algorithms or reinforcement learning to adjust the condition layers or fine-tune the parameters of the network.

References

1. Bamdad, M., Zarshenas, H., Auais, M.A.: Application of BCI systems in neurorehabilitation: a scoping review. Disabil. Rehabil. Assist. Technol. **10**, 355–364 (2015)
2. Aghazadeh, R., Montagna, F., Benatti, S., Rossi, D., Frounchi, J.: Compressed sensing based seizure detection for an ultra low power multi-core architecture. In: 2018 International Conference on High Performance Computing & Simulation (HPCS) (2018)
3. Vézard, L., Legrand, P., Chavent, M., Faïta-Aïnseba, F., Trujillo, L.: EEG classification for the detection of mental states. Appl. Soft Comput. **32**, 113–131 (2015)
4. Gannouni, S., Aledaily, A., Belwafi, K., Aboalsamh, H.: Emotion detection using electroencephalography signals and a zero-time windowing-based epoch estimation and relevant electrode identification. Sci. Rep. **11** (2021)
5. Bhattacharyya, S., Khasnobish, A., Chatterjee, S., Konar, A., Tibarewala, D.N.: Performance Analysis of LDA, QDA and KNN algorithms in left-right limb movement classification from EEG Data. In: 2010 International Conference on Systems in Medicine and Biology (2010)
6. Ines, H., Slim, Y., Noureddine, E.: EEG classification using support vector machine. In: 10th International Multi-Conferences on Systems, Signals & Devices 2013 (SSD13) (2013)
7. Wang, J., Yu, G., Zhong, L., Chen, W., Sun, Y.: Classification of EEG signal using convolutional neural networks. In: 2019 14th IEEE Conference on Industrial Electronics and Applications (ICIEA) (2019)
8. Xu, G., et al.: A deep transfer convolutional neural network framework for EEG signal classification. IEEE Access **7**, 112767–112776 (2019)
9. Li, M.-A., Xu, D.-Q.: A transfer learning method based on VGG-16 convolutional neural network for MI classification. In: 2021 33rd Chinese Control and Decision Conference (CCDC) (2021)
10. Kim, D., Woo, Y., Jeong, J., Kim, D.-K., Lee, J.-G.: Sleep stage classification for inter-institutional transfer learning. In: 2021 International Conference on Information and Communication Technology Convergence (ICTC) (2021)
11. BCI Competition IV Homepage. https://www.bbci.de/competition/iv. Accessed 12 Dec 2021
12. Pongthanisorn, G., Shirai, A., Sugiyama, S., Capi, G.: Combination of reinforcement and deep learning for EEG channel optimization on brain-machine interface systems. In: 2023 International Conference on Artificial Intelligence in Information and Communication (ICAIIC) (2023)
13. Leeb, R., Lee, F., Keinrath, C., Scherer, R., Bischof, H., Pfurtscheller, G.: Brain-computer communication: MOTIVATION, AIM, and impact of exploring a virtual apartment. IEEE Trans. Neural Syst. Rehabil. Eng. **15**, 473–482 (2007)

14. BNCI Horizon 2020. http://bnci-horizon-2020.eu/database/data-sets. Accessed 30 Jan 2023
15. Chen, Z., Wang, Y., Song, Z.: Classification of motor imagery electroencephalography signals based on image processing method. Sensors **21**, 4646 (2021)
16. Chaudhary, S., Taran, S., Bajaj, V., Sengur, A.: Convolutional neural network based approach towards motor imagery tasks EEG signals classification. IEEE Sens. J. **19**, 4494–4500 (2019)
17. Lee, H.K., Choi, Y.-S.: Application of continuous wavelet transform and convolutional neural network in decoding motor imagery brain-computer interface. Entropy **21**, 1199 (2019)
18. Lawhern, V.J., Solon, A.J., Waytowich, N.R., Gordon, S.M., Hung, C.P., Lance, B.J.: EEGNet: a compact convolutional neural network for EEG-based brain–computer interfaces. J. Neural Eng. **15**, 056013 (2018)
19. Krizhevsky, A., Sutskever, I., Hinton, G.E.: ImageNet classification with deep convolutional neural networks. Commun. ACM **60**, 84–90 (2017)
20. Abo-Zahhad, M., Ahmed, S.M., Abbas, S.N.: A new EEG acquisition protocol for biometric identification using eye blinking signals. Int. J. Intell. Syst. Appl. **7**, 48–54 (2015)
21. Kingma, D.P., Ba, J.: Adam: a method for stochastic optimization. arXiv preprint arXiv:1412.6980 (2014)

Optimization of EMG-Derived Features for Upper Limb Prosthetic Control

Dario Di Domenico[1,2](✉) , Francesca Paganini[1,3] , Andrea Marinelli[1,4] ,
Lorenzo De Michieli[1] , Nicoló Boccardo[1,5] , and Marianna Semprini[1]

[1] Rehab Technologies Lab, Italian Institute of Technology,
Via Morego, 30, 16163 Genova, Italy
dario.didomenico@iit.it
[2] Department of Electronics and Telecommunications, Politecnico di Torino,
10124 Turin, Italy
[3] Department of Mechanical and Process Engineering, University of Applied Science
Offenburg, 77652 Offenburg, Germany
[4] Bioengineering Lab, University of Genova, DIBRIS, Genova, Italy
[5] Open University Affiliated Research Centre at Istituto Italiano di Tecnologia
(ARC@IIT), Genova, Italy

Abstract. Polyarticulated active prostheses constitute a promising
solution for upper limb amputees. The bottleneck for their adoption
though, is the lack of intuitive control. In this context, machine learning
algorithms based on pattern recognition from electromyographic (EMG)
signals represent a great opportunity for naturally operating prosthetic
devices, but their performance is strongly affected by the selection of
input features. In this study, we investigated different combinations of
13 EMG-derived features obtained from EMG signals of healthy individuals performing upper limb movements and tested their performance for
movement classification using an Artificial Neural Network. We found
that input data (i.e., the set of input features) can be reduced by more
than 50% without any loss in accuracy, while diminishing the computing
time required to train the classifier. Our results indicate that input features must be properly selected in order to optimize prosthetic control.

Keywords: EMG features · Machine Learning · Myocontrol ·
Prosthetic control

1 Introduction

With the loss of a hand, the level of autonomy and ability to perform work, social,
and activities of daily living (ADLs) can be significantly reduced. Prosthetic
devices have evolved over time from simple mechanical and passive devices to
more sophisticated mechatronic systems designed to be controlled by human
intentions, often by means of electronic sensors able to detect electromyographic

D. Di Domenico and F. Paganini—These authors contributed equally to this work.

F. Meder et al. (Eds.): Living Machines 2023, LNAI 14157, pp. 77–87, 2023.
https://doi.org/10.1007/978-3-031-38857-6_6

(EMG) activity of the residual limb [9]. Myoelectric prostheses thus translate muscle activity into information used to control the movements of the prosthetic limb. The control is proportional, meaning that the higher the EMG signal, the faster the prosthesis moves [1]. This allows the amputee to control the force and speed of movement by varying the intensity of muscle contraction.

Today, the most common upper extremity prosthetic control strategy available on the market, still relies on two muscle contractions. Since controlling multiple joints simultaneously is still a challenge, the control is generally limited to a single DoF at a time. Switching from one joint movement to another is typically accomplished through simultaneous contraction of the flexor and extensor muscles of the wrist (co-contraction) [14].

Researchers are thus investigating new techniques based on pattern recognition and machine learning algorithms to improve control strategies and make prosthetic devices more reliable and naturally activated [3]. In this scenario, EMG signal is typically processed and turned into input for the control algorithm. Current research aims at increasing the accuracy of predicting human intentions from EMG-derived features, as the number of degrees of freedom (DoFs) for prosthetic movements increases [9]. Many control algorithms have been proposed but the main problems remain accurate signal detection and fast processing (for a review, see [5]). In particular, the literature is lacking of studies addressing the choice of training method and the composition of the training dataset [5].

To address these issues, we here aim to tackle the composition of the input dataset and we study the relationship between muscle activation and generated movements during reaching and grasping tasks, by examining the key components of EMG signals and with the goal of better understanding the key biomechanical elements of upper limb movements in healthy subjects. The final goal is to determine which control algorithm inputs (i.e., *EMG-derived features*) are more appropriate to both increase the accuracy of the control algorithm and reduce the computational effort. This study could have a crucial impact for the control of upper limb prostheses.

2   Materials and Methods

2.1   Subjects and Experimental Setup

Thirteen healthy participants (8 males, aged 29.7 ± 3.8 years) voluntarily took part to the experiments after having signed an informed consent. The Italian Institute of Research Ethics Committee approved the study protocol and procedures, assessing that all the requirements of the Declaration of Helsinki were followed.

Myoelectric activity was measured by recording EMG signals via high-density surface EMG with a portable 64-channels amplifier (Sessantaquattro, OT Bioelettronica, Torino, Italy) to which two 32-channels electrode grids were connected. The two grids were attached to the forearm of the subject proximally 5cm below the olecranon. The first patch (electrodes 1–32) was placed on flexor muscles of the fingers, while the second patch (electrodes 33–64) was placed on the extensor muscles of the fingers. The position of the patches was decided in order to cover the entire circumference of the forearm. Grids were configured with 8 × 4 electrodes, with an inter-electrode distance of 10mm. The first grid was placed over flexor extrinsic hand muscles, in the mid of the ventral side of the forearm, while the second grid was placed over extensor extrinsic hand muscles on the dorsal side of the forearm, in the first proximal third of the forearm. Ulna palpation was used as a reference, as well as muscle palpation during prescribed contraction actuating the muscles of interest. The signal was sampled at 2000 Hz and A/D converted on 24 bits.

2.2 Experimental Protocol

This study is based on two datasets: one used to evaluate whether and how different EMG-derived features convey the same information about the underlying movement generated (dataset-1); and one used to test the efficacy of such combinations for prosthetic control (dataset-2).

To create dataset-1, 10 of the recruited subjects were asked to perform 16 tasks, which ranged from simple hand gestures like Hand Opening (HO) or Hand Closing (HC), Wrist Extension and Flexion (WE and WF) or Wrist Supination and Pronation (WS and WP), to more complex tasks which involved reaching and grasping of objects of different shapes (i.e., Cylindrical grasp, Spherical grasp, Tri-digital grasp, Thumb opposition, Frontal reaching, Cylindrical reaching, Spherical reaching, Pour a water glass, Screw a bottle cap, Bring an object to mouth). Each gesture was repeated 10 times and muscular activities were captured by the Sessantaquattro device (OTBioelettronica, Torino, Italy) equipped with two matrices of EMG sensors (4X8), as represented in Fig. 1.

To create dataset-2, high-density EMG signals were acquired from 3 subjects while performing 10 repetition of simple hand gestures (HO, HC, WP, WS, WF, WE) and rest. The data was acquired such that for each repetition of each movement, only the transitory phase and the steady state phase of maximal contraction were included, with each repetition consisting of approximately 2s. The acquisition thus started as the subject was performing the movement and continued during the steady state. At this point, the subject was required to keep contracting the muscle until the end of the 2s of acquisition; after the acquisition was stopped the subject could relax the muscle to avoid fatigue. For each movement this process was repeated 10 times.

2.3 Signal Processing and EMG-Derived Features Extraction

For both datasets, the raw EMG signals acquired were preprocessed with a 4th order Butterworth bandpass filter with a low cutoff frequency 20 Hz and a high cutoff frequency 500 Hz.

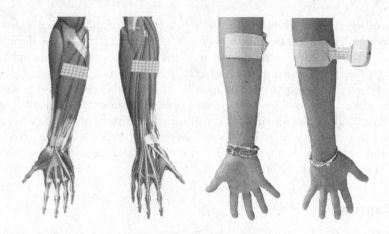

Fig. 1. Experimental setup.

EMG-derived features were extracted from the preprocessed EMG signals using a sliding-window of 200ms (400 samples) with an increment of 50ms (100 samples). To allow a comparison between different conditions, the features were then normalized by subtracting the minimum value of each EMG channel and by dividing for the difference between the maximum range.

The selected EMG-derived features are the most used in prosthetic applications [8,11] and are presented in Table 2. All data processing was performed using Matlab (Mathworks).

2.4   Combinations of EMG-Derived Features

To evaluate whether pairs of features share a similar content of information about the underlying movement, we calculated their Cross Correlation (CC). CC was calculated for each couple of features that were extracted from dataset-1, then the mean CC across all tasks and all subjects was calculated. Combinations of EMG-derived features were then calculated according to CC results as follows. First, groups of features with high correlation were identified, then different combinations were created using one or more features per group, taking into account all the possible combinations.

2.5   Evaluation of EMG-Derived Features Combinations

Dataset-2 was used to test the performance of different combinations of EMG-derived features for movement classification, i.e., for operating a prosthetic device. To this end, features were extracted from dataset-2 and then supplied to a machine learning classifier (Artificial Neural Network: ANN [4]). For each group of hyperparameters the dataset was randomly split in training set (Tr=80%) and test set (Ts=20%). The hyperparameters of the ANN classifier were optimized using a grid search strategy [7]. In particular, the number of layers was

Table 1. Name and formula of the EMG-derived features.

	Feature name	Formula
1	Mean Square (MS)	$\frac{1}{N}\sum_{i=1}^{N} x_i^2$
2	Root Mean Square (RMS)	$\sqrt{\frac{1}{N}\sum_{i=1}^{N} x_i^2}$
3	Mean Absolute Value (MAV)	$\frac{1}{N}\sum_{i=1}^{N} \mid x_i \mid$
4	Difference Absolute Standard Deviation (DABS)	$\sqrt{\frac{1}{N-1}\sum_{i=2}^{N} (x_i - x_{i-1})^2}$
5	Waveform Length (WL)	$\sum_{i=1}^{N-1} \mid x_{i+1} - x_i \mid$
6	Maximum Fractal Length (MFL)	$\log(\sqrt{\sum_{i=2}^{N}(x_i - x_{i-1})^2})$
7	Zero Crossing (ZC)	$\sum_{i=2}^{N} \mathrm{sgn}(-x_{i-1}x_i)$
8	Slope Sign Change (SSC)	$\sum_{i=2}^{N} \mathrm{sgn}[-(x_i - x_{i-1})(x_{i-1} - x_{i-2})]$
9	Willison Amplitude (WA)	$\sum_{i=2}^{N} \mathrm{sgn}(\mid x_i - x_{i-1} \mid -x_{std})$
10	Myopulse Percentage Rate (MPR)	$\sum_{i=1}^{N} \mathrm{sgn}(\mid x_i \mid -x_{std})$
11	Logarithm Detector (LD)	$\exp(\frac{1}{N}\sum_{i=1}^{N} \log \mid x_i \mid)$
12	V-Order (V3)	$\sqrt[3]{\frac{1}{N}\sum_{i=1}^{N} x_i^3}$
13	Mean Absolute Value Slope (MAVS)	$\frac{\sum_{i=2}^{N/2} \mid x_i \mid - \sum_{i=N/2+1}^{N} \mid x_i \mid}{N/2}$

changed between 1 and 2. The number of neurons varied between 8 and 64 with logarithmic scale of base 2. The learning rate varied logarithmically with scale 10 between 1e-6 and 1e-3. The batch-size varied between 4 and 16 with a logarithmic scale of base 2. The aforementioned parameters were optimized for each subject on Tr. Moreover, Adam optimizer [6] was used to iteratively update network weights based on training data (Table 1).

To evaluate the performance of the classifier on the Ts and measure the accuracy of predictions and computing time, the ANN was trained on Tr using various combinations of features as input. This process was repeated 100 times as the training process of the network is not stochastic, thus the robustness of the classifier was also tested. Such method, combined with the generalization of the neural network helped to avoid overfitting [13].

The computational effort was analyzed by measuring the required computing time at the end of each iteration. It must be underlined that it is evaluated on the basis of the time required by the code to compute the features on the whole dataset-2. Therefore, this assessment reflects the time needed to compute the same set of EMG-derived features in the application of real-time prosthetic control.

To assess statistical difference among performance obtained with different combination of features, the following steps were taken. First, data normality was tested with Kolmogorov-Smirnov test. Then, we run a one-way analysis of variance (either ANOVA or Kruskal-Wallis) using COMBINATION (i.e., combinations of features) as between factor, for accuracy and computing time separately. Post-hoc analysis was performed using Tukey-Kramer procedure. The significant level was set at p = 0.05.

3 Results

3.1 Identification of Optimal Sets of Features

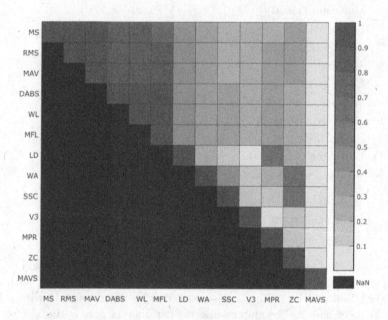

Fig. 2. Cross-correlation among pairs of EMG-derived features.

Figure 2 shows CC among pairs of features. It emerges that EMG-derived features can be grouped into 4 sets, each identified by a value of CC >60% among each couple of features. The identified groups of features are thus the following:

- Group 1: MS, RMS, MAV, DABS, WL, MFL
- Group 2: LD, MPR
- Group 3: ZC, SSC
- Group 4: ZC, WA

Following identification of redundant features, we defined different sets of them, using only one feature from each group in different possible combinations.

From the first group, the RMS was identified as the best feature, since it is the most widespread in prosthetic applications [2] and it was the only feature used for its group. For groups 2-3-4 all the possible permutations were tested.

The obtained combinations are listed in Table 2, Combination-0 being the combination with all the 13 features. These combinations were then used with dataset-2 to feed the ANN classifier and evaluate both its accuracy and computing time.

Table 2. Combinations of EMG-derived features.

Combination	Features
Combination 0	All features
Combination 1	RMS, SSC, WA, LD, V3, MAVS
Combination 2	RMS, SSC, WA, MPR, V3, MAVS
Combination 3	RMS, ZC, WA, MPR, V3, MAVS
Combination 4	RMS, ZC, WA, LD, V3, MAVS
Combination 5	RMS, ZC, SSC, WA, MPR, LD, V3, MAVS
Combination 6	RMS, ZC, MPR, V3, MAVS
Combination 7	RMS, ZC, LD, V3, MAVS
Combination 8	RMS, SSC, ZC, MPR, V3, MAVS
Combination 9	RMS, SSC, ZC, LD, V3, MAVS

3.2 Evaluation of Performance of Different Sets of Features

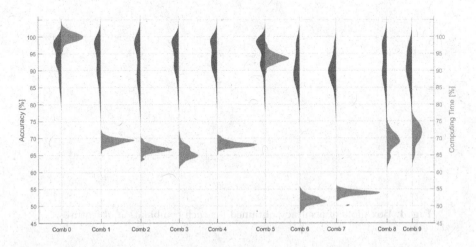

Fig. 3. Accuracy and computing time for each combination of features. The computing time is normalized relative to the mean computing time of combination-0.

Figure 3 displays accuracy and computing time for each combination of features, with the computing time being normalized relative to the mean computing time of Combination 0. Table 3 compares the accuracy and computing times of each combination of features, reporting their median, mean and standard deviation (std).

Table 3. Median, mean and standard deviation of accuracy and computing time of each combination of features.

Combination:	0	1	2	3	4	5	6	7	8	9
Median Accuracy	94.38	93.75	93.75	94.38	94.38	95.31	90.00	89.38	90.63	90.63
Mean Accuracy	93.31	92.66	92.48	93.63	93.93	93.55	90.06	88.77	90.01	90.11
Std Accuracy	5.58	6.20	6.24	5.22	4.96	5.94	6.10	6.17	8.38	6.61
Median Computing Time	99.79	69.08	66.72	65.51	68.08	93.66	51.59	53.81	69.10	71.38
Mean Computing Time	100.00	69.93	66.67	66.06	68.76	96.34	51.83	53.66	68.79	71.08
Std Computing Time	7.08	9.19	2.34	2.82	4.84	11.36	1.81	1.47	3.25	3.07

Accuracy. Figure 4 shows, for each combination of features, accuracy results across the 100 runs with each combination. Kruskal-Wallis test results indicated a significant effect of COMBINATION ($p \ll 0.05$, Bonferroni corrected) and post-hoc analysis indicated that for several pairs of combinations accuracy was not significantly different. Interestingly, we found that accuracy of combination-0 did not differ from that of combinations 3 ($p = 0.99$), 4 ($p = 0.65$) and 5 ($p = 0.94$), indicating that the same level of accuracy can be reached with a smaller number of features.

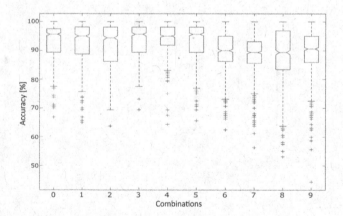

Fig. 4. Box-plots of accuracy obtained for each combination of features.

Computing Time. Figure 5 shows the computing time required for each combination of features, each run 100 times. ANOVA results indicated a significant effect of COMBINATION ($p \ll 0.05$, Bonferroni corrected) and post-hoc analysis indicated that computing time was significantly different for each pair of combinations with the exception of combination 2 and 3 and of 4 and 8. Importantly, all combinations showed a significantly smaller computation time with respect to that of combination-0 3, indicating that reducing the number of input features directly affects the computation effort.

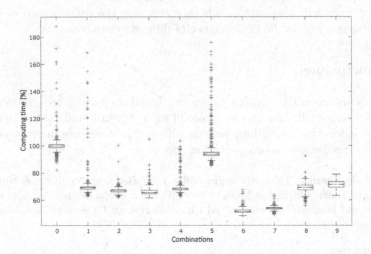

Fig. 5. Box-plots of computing time obtained for each combination of features.

By considering these results and that of accuracy, it emerges that combinations 3 and 4 are the more desirable as they both minimize the computing time, while showing no significant difference in performance with combination-0. In particular, combination-4 appears as the optimal choice due to its consistency in leading to highest accuracy values, as indicated by its low standard deviation (Table 3).

4   Discussion

In this study, we investigated how to improve prosthetic control by optimizing the sets of input features to be fed to the classifier. Specifically, we aimed to maximize the prediction accuracy of a pattern recognition algorithm, i.e. ANN, based on the input EMG features, while at the same time minimizing the computational effort, here measured through the computing time required by the machine learning algorithm. We found that optimal performance can be obtained with a subset of 6 features, e.g. combination-3 and combination-4.

This study has some limitations. First, CC does not directly quantify the amount of information carried by each feature. However, it still indicates which sets of features can be considered as redundant and thus which ones can be discarded in favor of quicker computing times. Future development of this study will explore feature selection by quantifying the information content of each combination of features (e.g., using Shannon Mutual Information [12]). Another limitation lies in the absence of a true prosthetic device and of amputated subjects among the study participants. However, we here aimed at evaluating the classifier performance, which, according to our previous studies, does not change in case of control of a virtual or real prosthetic hand, and also behaves similarly for able bodied and amputated individuals [3,10].

Future work will also explore whether and how the combination of EMG-derived features affects the performance of different classifiers.

5 Conclusions

This study indicates that prosthetic control based on pattern recognition algorithms is strongly affected by the choice of input features and that such choice should be guided by taking into account different performance metrics, such as accuracy of prediction and computation effort.

Acknowledgements. The authors gracefully acknowledge their colleagues Inna Forsiuk, Simone Tanzarella, Simon Müller-Cleve, Michele Canepa for their support in data collection, and Massimiliano Iacono and Chiara Bartolozzi for useful discussions.

References

1. Cordella, F., et al.: Literature review on needs of upper limb prosthesis users. Front. Neurosci. **10**, 209 (2016). publisher: Frontiers Media, SA
2. De Luca, C.J.: The use of surface electromyography in biomechanics. J. Appl. Biomech. **13**(2), 135–163 (1997). publisher: Human Kinetics Inc
3. Di Domenico, D., et al.: Hannes prosthesis control based on regression machine learning algorithms, pp. 5997–6002. IEEE (2021)
4. Dreiseitl, S., Ohno-Machado, L.: Logistic regression and artificial neural network classification models: a methodology review. J. Biomed. Inform. **35**(5–6), 352–359 (2002). publisher: Elsevier
5. Fougner, A., Stavdahl, Ø., Kyberd, P.J., Losier, Y.G., Parker, P.A.: Control of upper limb prostheses: terminology and proportional myoelectric control: a review. IEEE Trans. Neural Syst. Rehabil. Eng. **20**(5), 663–677 (2012). publisher: IEEE
6. Kingma, D.P., Ba, J.: Adam: a method for stochastic optimization. arXiv preprint arXiv:1412.6980 (2014)
7. Lerman, P.: Fitting segmented regression models by grid search. J. R. Stat. Soc. Ser. C: Appl. Stat. **29**(1), 77–84 (1980). publisher: Oxford University Press
8. Luu, D.K., et al.: Deep learning-based approaches for decoding motor intent from peripheral nerve signals. Front. Neurosci. **15**, 667907 (2021). publisher: Frontiers Media SA
9. Marinelli, A., et al.: Active upper limb prostheses: a review on current state and upcoming breakthroughs. Prog. Biomed. Eng. **5**(1), 012001 (2023). https://doi.org/10.1088/2516-1091/acac57. publisher: IOP Publishing
10. Marinelli, A., et al.: Performance evaluation of pattern recognition algorithms for upper limb prosthetic applications, pp. 471–476. IEEE (2020)

11. Nguyen, A.T., et al.: A portable, self-contained neuroprosthetic hand with deep learning-based finger control. J. Neural Eng. **18**(5), 056051 (2021). https://doi.org/10.1088/1741-2552/ac2a8d. arXiv:2103.1345
12. Shannon, C.E.: Communication theory of secrecy systems. Bell Syst. Tech. J. **28**(4), 656–715 (1949), publisher: Nokia Bell Labs
13. Srivastava, N., Hinton, G., Krizhevsky, A., Sutskever, I., Salakhutdinov, R.: Dropout: a simple way to prevent neural networks from overfitting. J. Mach. Learn. Res. **15**(1), 1929–1958 (2014). publisher: JMLR. org
14. Vujaklija, I., Farina, D., Aszmann, O.C.: New developments in prosthetic arm systems. Orthop. Res. Rev. **8**, 31–39 (2016). publisher: Taylor & Francis

Bioinspired Materials, Actuators, Sensors

A 3D-Printed Thermoresponsive Artificial Venus Flytrap Lobe Based on a Multilayer of Shape Memory Polymers

Falk J. Tauber[1,2]([envelope]) [iD], Fabian Scheckenbach[1], Mario Walter[3], Thorsten Pretsch[3] [iD], and Thomas Speck[1,2,4] [iD]

[1] Plant Biomechanics Group (PBG) Freiburg, Botanic Garden of the University of Freiburg, Freiburg im Breisgau, Germany
falk.tauber@biologie.uni-freiburg.de
[2] Cluster of Excellence livMatS @ FIT – Freiburg Center for Interactive Materials and Bioinspired Technologies, University of Freiburg, Freiburg im Breisgau, Germany
[3] Synthesis and Polymer Technology Division, Fraunhofer Institute for Applied Polymer Research IAP, Potsdam, Germany
[4] Freiburg Center for Interactive Materials and Bioinspired Technologies (FIT), University of Freiburg, Freiburg im Breisgau, Germany

Abstract. Plant motion patterns and structures have inspired designers, researchers and engineers for centuries. Recent advancements in analyzing and manufacturing technologies have allowed for a deeper understanding of biological principles and their application to bioinspired engineered systems. This has advanced 3D printing of thermoresponsive materials, like shape memory polymers. These materials enable the translation and creation of complex bioinspired mobile structures. In this study, we use novel 3D printable shape memory polymers in a multi-material, multilayer system to create double curved surfaces that can change their curvature from concave to convex, like the lobes of a Venus flytrap. The artificial trap lobes can be manufactured by identifying suitable material combinations, bonding methods and programming parameters. In this study, the system parameters to achieve a motion and the closing behavior in response to a temperature change are characterized. The resulting trap lobe represents a successful translation of the prestress ratios and layered morphology found in the biological model into an autonomous artificial Venus flytrap.

Keywords: artificial Venus flytrap · shape memory · snapping mechanics · biomimetics

1 Introduction

Plants, as sedentary organisms at the mercy of their environment, have developed a variety of mechanisms and materials to respond to and cope with a changing environment. As a result, they provide a wealth of ideas for mechanisms and materials that can be used as inspiration for new systems [1–3]. The rather young research field of plant-inspired

F. Meder et al. (Eds.): Living Machines 2023, LNAI 14157, pp. 91–108, 2023.
https://doi.org/10.1007/978-3-031-38857-6_7

robotics focuses on the translation of principles behind growth, actuation, autonomy, energy efficiency, and sustainability of plants into technology. One of the most prominent role models for plant motions is *Dionaea muscipula*, commonly known as Venus flytrap (Fig. 1A).

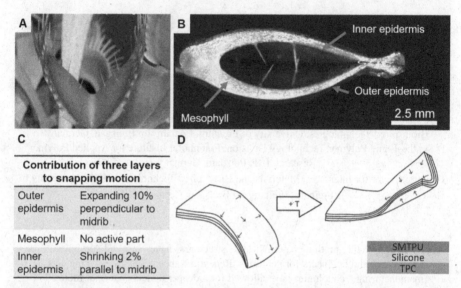

Fig. 1. *Dionaea muscipula* traps (A) technically represent a multilayer material system with three main layers: outer epidermis (outside), mesophyll (middle) and inner epidermis (inside) forming the trap (B, cross section). The prestresses in a ready to snap trap (A) are necessary for a fast snapping motion. The layers (B) contribute differently to the trap closure (C). The three-layer setup and the different expansion ratios will be translated into a multilayer, multi-material trap lobe demonstrator, in which a shape memory thermoplastic polyurethane (SMTPU) and thermoplastic copolyesters elastomer (TPC) connected via non-active silicone layers represent the three different layers of the biological model and mimic their contribution to the motion. (Figures in A and B are reprinted from publication [4], with permission from PNAS).

Dionaea muscipula is a carnivorous plant that possesses specialized snapping traps. These traps consist of two bilaterally symmetric, doubly curved trapezoidal lobes connected by a midrib, which typically close within 100–500 ms (Fig. 1A) [5–8]. The closure of the trap is initiated by a first turgor change-based slower motion, followed by a second passive, fast motion, which is triggered by the release of stored elastic energy causing an abrupt geometric change of the trap lobes. This change causes the lobes to snap-buckle from a concave to a convex state (viewed from the outer lobe side) [5–8]. The trap consists of three main tissue layers: outer epidermis, mesophyll and inner epidermis (Fig. 1B). Sachse et al. (2020) determined the mechanical behavior of the three tissue layers during closure and their contribution to trap closure via 3D digital image correlation measurements in combination with a finite element simulation meta study [4]. They identified, that the closure is driven by a simultaneous expansion of the outer epidermis by 10% and a shrinkage of the inner epidermis by 2%. The mesophyll has no active part in the closure (Fig. 1C). Sachse et al. (2020) pointed out that the traps must be in a ready-to-snap state for rapid closure. This is achieved by differences in internal hydraulic prestress between the layers, which are released during the fast closing motion. This is reflected in the expansion and contraction ratios of the different layers during the motion. This confirmed the assumptions of Forterre et al. (2005) that a prestress ratio of 3:1 of the outer to the inner epidermis plays a role in the rapid closure of the traps [9].

This unique mechanism of trap closure in *Dionaea muscipula* is a fascinating combination of both active and passive motions, and has been the subject of much research in the fields of biomechanics and materials science. In recent years, advances in 3D printing technology allowed researchers to create intricate and complex artificial structures, including those that mimic the mechanics of the Venus flytrap. These artificial Venus flytraps (AVF) translate the snap buckling motion during trap closure into technical demonstrators. So far, there are more than a dozen different systems using different materials and operating principles, ranging from carbon fiber prepregs actuated by springs or magnets made of shape memory alloys [10–12], to pneumatic versions based on flexible silicone [13], trap lobes based on hygroscopic materials utilizing changes in humidity [14] as well as silver nanowire/polydimethylsiloxane composites traps utilizing offset displacement introducing snap-through instabilities to part of the actuator structure resulting in fast snapping motions actuated via joule heating [15]. Other AVFs are described as thermoresponsive 3D printed monolayer systems [16], and multilayer systems that respond to different environmental stimuli [17]. There are even bio-hybrid systems, in which soft electrodes are attached to a trap of the plant and used to trigger the closing of the tarp lobes to utilize the trap as a small gripper [18]. The newest AVF systems utilize meta-materials as skeletons and actuators of the trap lobes [19]. However, none of these systems incorporates the multilayer morphology and prestresses necessary for fast snapping of the biological model as highlighted by Forterre et al. (2005) and Sachse et al. (2020). Their translation will enable the creation of an even more lifelike AVF. Thermally active materials are best suited to realize the individual components and behaviors because they can actively expand and contract. A multilayer system from such materials can be used to construct a thermally activated AVF trap lobe.

In this paper, we investigate the design and fabrication of a thermally actuated AVF trap consisting of a multilayer of different materials (Fig. 1D). Through a combination of innovative design, thermoactive materials, and 3D printing techniques, we have developed a structure that is capable of mimicking the natural movement of the Venus flytrap. The system provides a thermoresponsive platform for future research in the fields of biomimetics and soft robotics. This paper will provide a detailed overview of the design and fabrication process, as well as an analysis of the structure's mechanical properties and potential applications.

2 Concept of a Thermoresponsive Multilayer AVF (TMA)

The three-layer setup of biological role model and their different contributions to the snapping motion are translated into a multilayer, multi-material trap lobe demonstrator. The thermoresponsive multilayer AVF (TMA) trap lobe should have a concave shape like the biological model at room temperature and should snap into a convex shape when the temperature is increased. Following the biological model, the multilayer should have a prestress ratio along the axes of 3:1 in the resting state [4, 9]. The three layers represent the outer epidermis (layer 1), mesophyll (layer 2) and the inner epidermis (layer 3) (Fig. 1B). Three different materials are bonded together in such a way that two functional layers (layer 1 and 3) are connected via a flexible layer (layer 2) (Fig. 1D). Layer 1 requires a material with a low coefficient of thermal expansion (CTE) and a high modulus of elasticity (Young's modulus), the elastic modulus must be as independent of temperature as possible. However, layer 1 must also contract above a certain temperature. The actuating layer 3, on the other hand, requires a material with a high CTE whose Young's modulus at room temperature is higher but at high temperatures lower than that of the material of layer 1. Thus, the combination of two different CTEs and Young's moduli is decisive for the curvature inversion during a snapping motion. Both materials are bonded with a flexible intermediate layer, layer 2. This acts as a fixed-length spacer, converting a change in length of the materials into a curvature of the system. The bonding of layer 1 to layer 2, as well as of layer 2 to layer 3, is not implemented as further adhesive layers, if possible, but as a form-fit of the materials to each other (see Sect. 3.3 for details). A curvature inversion should be achieved in a temperature range of 60 °C to 70 °C and should be reversible.

According to these requirements, three different materials were chosen for the creation of the TMA trap lobe. The system consisted of a 3D printed shape memory thermoplastic polyurethane (SMTPU) (inner epidermis) and a 3D printed thermoplastic copolyesters elastomer (TPC) (outer epidermis) connected via a non-active silicone layer (mesophyll). The silicone layer acts only as a support spacer structure, since it has no active part in the movement.

3 Characterization of Multilayer Material and Bonding

3.1 Material Characterization

The Fraunhofer Institute for Applied Polymer Research (IAP) developed the SMTPU 3D printing material for layer 1. The filament had a diameter of 1.75 mm and was characterized by a Young's modulus of 233 MPa at 23 °C. After appropriate thermomechanical treatment, the material exhibits a 2-way shape memory effect with a lower switching temperature of about 38 °C and an upper switching temperature of approximately 65 °C. A commercially available 0.5 mm thick silicone membrane was selected for layer 2, with a usable temperature range from −60 °C to 230 °C. For layer 3, the 3D printing filament FlexiFil TPC from Formfutura with a 1.75 mm diameter was selected. It has a Young's modulus of 95 MPa, a melting temperature of 180 °C, high flexibility (with a maximum elongation of 530%) and high long-term heat resistance.

In order to estimate the behavior of the materials under thermal load, the material properties were first determined on a Hegewald & Peschke universal testing machine with an integrated temperature chamber (Table 1). For material testing, ten 10 mm wide and 290 mm long strips were prepared from each material. Silicone strips were cut from a membrane with 0.5 mm thickness. For SMTPU and TPC the strips were 3D printed with an E3D tool changer Fused Filament Fabrication (FFF) printer with a thickness of 0.6 mm (SMTPU) and 0.4 mm (TPC). The Young's modulus was measured at room temperature and at 70 °C with a strain rate of 25 mm/min up to 60% strain. The CTE was measured with an initial strain of 1% at room temperature and under constant load of 0.1 N when heated to 70 °C. The resulting change in expansion can be taken as an approximation of CTE. This is given in relative length fractions in millions per degree Celsius [10^{-6}/K].

Table 1. Material properties at room temperature (23 °C) and upper testing temperature (70 °C) n = 10

Material	Young's modulus [MPa]	Coefficient of thermal expansion (CTE) [10^{-6}/K]	Creep [%]
SMTPU	253.0 ± 12.9^{a}	187.1 ± 26.7^{c}	–
	1.4 ± 0.2^{b}		
Silicone	5.0 ± 0.4	336.0 ± 101.2	–
TPC	90.0 ± 2.6^{a}	235.8 ± 6.0	16.0 ± 1.4^{a}
	82.5 ± 8.4^{b}		46.2 ± 4.0^{b}

a: Measurement at 23 °C. b: Measurement at 70 °C. c: unprogrammed material

The results of the material characterization are in accordance with our requirements for a multilayer trap lobe. The SMTPU has a lower Young's modulus at higher temperatures. The silicone generally has a lower Young's modulus than the other two materials at all temperatures tested. The TPC has a lower Young's modulus than the SMTPU at room temperature and a higher Young's modulus at 70 °C. The CTE of the materials is also similar and the silicone does not interfere with the TPC. Therefore, the materials are ideal for the fabrication of a multilayer trap lobe.

3.2 Characterization of Two-Way Shape Memory Effect

The SMTPU exhibits in addition to the 1-way effect, like a number of shape memory polymers also a 2-way effect. In the case of the 2-way effect, reversible deformation occurs during both heating and subsequent cooling [20–22]. The two-way effect can be further divided into two categories: the intrinsic two-way effect and the extrinsic two-way effect. While in the intrinsic two-way effect both the low and high temperature shapes are stored in the material, an external actuator generates the extrinsic two-way effect. In the case of the extrinsic two-way effect, the material is therefore pre-stretched again after each one-way effect [21]. However, care must be taken to ensure that the restoring force of the spring is not too great. Otherwise, the shape memory effect will be inhibited.

The two-way shape memory effect was investigated under stress-free conditions, as layer 1 should contract in response to a rise in temperature. The characterization was conducted in a Memmert CTC256 climate chamber (Fig. 2A). To characterize the samples, a temperature program, which increased the heat from 65 °C to 69 °C in 0.5 °C increments, was chosen. In between each heating step was a cooling step, which reverted back to 20 °C. Each heating and cooling step was set for 20 min, followed by a 20-min holding step to ensure an even temperature distribution throughout the chamber. Fifteen identically prepared SMTPU strips were tested, which all had a 200 mm length, 10 mm width and 0.6 mm thickness. During each cooling step, a return to the original length

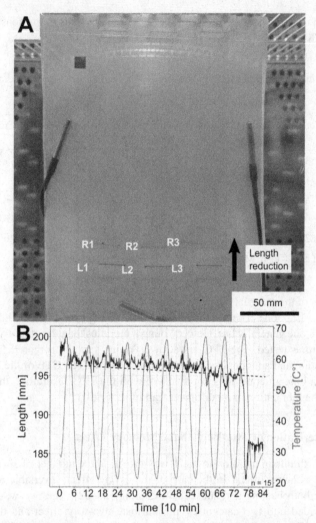

Fig. 2. Characterization of the two-way shape memory effect under stress-free conditions. A) Thermally triggered length change of the shape memory specimens. L1, L2 and L3 denote the initial length of the three studied SMTPU specimens. R1, R2 and R3 denote the corresponding obtained length after heating to 69.5 °C. A significant length reduction can be seen in all three specimens. In this figure, the image at 69.5 °C with an opacity of 25% was superimposed on the image with the initial length. B) Average length change of the 15 specimens over 10 heating steps. A linear increase in length reduction up to heating step 8 can be seen (dotted line). At each heating step, a decrease of 2–3 mm in the measured length can be seen which is reversed by the seventh heating step when the temperature drops. From the eighth heating on, the length change is about twice as large at 4.5 mm, and the measured length remains at a lower level of about 195 mm even after the temperature drop. At heating step 10, an average length change of about 14.5 mm is measured.

took place (Fig. 2B). A maximum length reduction of up to 14.5 mm was observed after the tenth heating step, which equals a 7.25% length reduction. The characterization confirms the applicability of the SMTPU as a contracting layer 1 for the TMA trap lobe. As layer 3, functions as external actuator for the SMTPU the extrinsic two-way effect was chosen as modus operandi, as the one-way shape memory effect seen during the last actuation generates the highest contraction. During each cooling step, a return to the original length took place.

3.3   Characterization of Bonding Strength

For the identification of a suitable bonding agent and method, small multilayer samples (50×50 mm^2) were produced and the delamination strength was determined in a peel-off measurement (at 30 mm/s for 60 mm distance) (Fig. 3A). An improved form-fit of thermoplastic materials and silicones at room temperature could be achieved with the use of aminopropyltriepoxysilane (APTES) [23, 24]. Both materials were treated with plasma, the activated thermoplastic was placed in a 1% or 10% APTES solution. The APTES binds to the reactive groups and increases the number of possible binding partners. The two activated surfaces were then placed on top of each other and incubated for a few minutes, allowing covalent bonds to form, thus achieving a good form closure. This method can be used to achieve a bond without the need for an additional adhesive layer, which would introduce its own material properties into the system. In addition to testing the bonding with APTES, a flexible cyanoacrylate adhesive (Loctite 4850) and a combination of roughened and smooth surfaces were tested. Loctite 4850 has a modulus of elasticity of 515 MPa to 675 MPa when polymerized and shows a temporary reduction in strength of about 75% when heated to 70 °C. To enhance the bonding strength of the SMTPU and silicone, the surface of the SMTPU was roughened with sand paper. In the bonding area of 50×50 mm^2 the silicone was scribed with a grid pattern. Table 2 gives an overview of the different method combinations.

Table 2. Investigated bonding methods

Material combination	Bonding	Surfaces treatment	Abbreviation
TPC - silicone	–	Plasma	ToA
TPC - silicone	1% APTES solution	Plasma	TA
TPC - silicone	10% APTES solution	Plasma	TA10
SMTPU - silicone	–	Plasma	SoA
SMTPU - silicone	1% APTES solution	Plasma	SA
SMTPU - silicone	10% APTES solution	Plasma	SA10
SMTPU - silicone	Loctite 4850	Plasma	SLP
SMTPU - silicone	Loctite 4850	Plasma, sanded SMTPU surface	SLP2
SMTPU - silicone	Loctite 4850	Plasma, sanded SMTPU, silicone carved with laser cutter	SLP3

After plasma treatment, all samples showed a slightly increased adhesion force. The use of APTES significantly increased the bonding strength in all cases, as shown by the increased force necessary for delamination (Fig. 3B). However, the combination of SMTPU and silicone with APTES showed significantly lower bonding strengths and low long-term stability compared to TPC silicone with 10% APTES solution (median value of 21.4 N). The best bonding results for SMTPU and silicone were achieved by roughening the surfaces of both materials and using Loctite. The SLP3 variant achieved the significantly highest delamination force of 13.0 N (median) for silicone and SMTPU. Based on these preliminary tests, a combination SLP3 with TA10 was selected for the production of the TMA trap lobes.

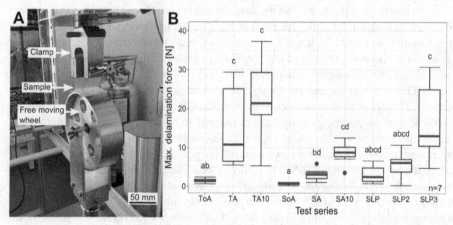

Fig. 3. Characterization of delamination strength. A) Peel-off setup. A 50×50 mm^2 bilayer specimen was attached to a free moving wheel via double-sided adhesive tape. The silicone layer was pulled upwards with 30 mm/s for a distance of 60 mm delaminating the two layers. B) Average delamination forces of different bonding methods. The test series ToA, TA and TA10 denote bonding methods of TPC with silicone without APTES (ToA), with 1% APTES (TA) and 10% APTES (TA10). Equivalently, SoA, SA and SA10 denote bonding of SMTPU with silicone without APTES (SoA), with 1% APTES (SA) and 10% APTES (SA10). SLP, SLP2 and SLP3 denote the bonding when SMTPU was bonded with silicone using a plasma treatment, Loctite 4850 and a mechanical press. SLP represents a bonding without roughened contact surfaces, SLP2 is a bonding with contact surfaces roughened by sandpaper, and SLP3 is a bonding in which the silicone was roughened with a laser cutter and the SMTPU was roughened with sandpaper. The lowest delamination forces were measured for the test series ToA with a median value of 1.6 N and SoA with 0.8 N. The highest delamination forces were measured for the test series TA with a median value of 10.8 N, TA10 with 21.4 N, SA10 with 8.6 N and SLP3 with 13.0 N. Significance levels were determined using a Kruskal Wallis test, different letters correspond to a significant difference in the achieved delamination force with p-values below 0.05.

4 Construction and Characterization of Thermoresponsive Multilayer AVF (TMA) Trap Lobe

4.1 Multilayer Construction

The chosen materials and identified bonding methods allow the construction of TMA trap lobes. In order to transfer the prestress differences seen in the biological model and to achieve its concave curvature, the active layers must be prestretched prior to bonding to introduce the stresses into the multilayer. Therefore, a biaxial stretching device was developed for the production of the multilayers (Fig. 4A).

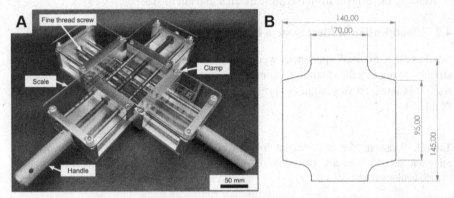

Fig. 4. Biaxial stretched multilayer production. A) The biaxial stretching device consists of two crossed detachable uniaxial stretchers. The materials were fixed with the clamps and could be stretched in two directions using the four fine-thread screws. B) The sketch of material layer indicates the overall dimensions. The areas to be stretched were 70 mm and 95 mm wide, respectively. The rounded corners were optimized for an optimal distribution of the tension according to the method of Mattheck's triangle of tension.

The production process for one exemplary sample is briefly described in the following. For the active layers, 140×145 mm^2 sheets of TPC and SMTPU were printed with different thicknesses. The silicone sheets were laser cut into 100×100 mm^2 samples and a grid pattern was scribed on one side. The SMTPU sheets were programmed, i.e. stretched by 100%|50% along the axes (horizontal stretch | perpendicular stretch). For which they were fixated in the biaxial stretcher stretched and heated to 80 °C for 20 min in the climatic chamber. After cooling, the programmed specimen was cut to 100×100 mm^2. The smooth side of the SMTPU created during printing was cleaned with isopropanol, roughened with sandpaper, activated in the plasma device, and ATPES and Loctite4850 bonded to the structured side of the silicone. The TPC sheet was cleaned with isopropanol and its surface was activated in the plasma device. The TPC was fixated in the biaxial stretcher, treated side up, and stretched 20%|10% along the axes. The silicone side of the bilayer was cleaned with isopropanol and activated in the plasma device. The silicone side of the SMTPU silicone bilayer was then bonded to the TPC and the air was removed. After an incubation period of 16 h, the resulting multilayer module was removed from the biaxial stretcher and cut to a sample size of 50×50 mm^2 or 100×100 mm^2. This procedure was used to prepare all samples. The preparation process of one TMA trap lobe can briefly summarized in six steps:

1. 3D printing of SMTPU and TPC layers.
2. Laser cut and carve grid onto one side of 100×100 mm^2 silicone squares.
3. Program SMTPU at 80 °C, bond SMTPU and silicone with Loctite4850 to form a bilayer.
4. Treat TPC with 10% APTES solution and prestretch.
5. Activate silicone side of bilayer via plasma and attach to TPC, rake out air and incubate for 16h at room temperature.
6. Remove the trilayer from the film stretcher and cut to size.

4.2 Identification of Ideal System Parameters to Achieve Curvature Inversion

Smaller 50×50 mm^2 specimens were first prepared in order to identify the ideal prestretch parameters for obtaining a concave orientation that snap buckles on temperature rise. This involved varying not only the preload but also the thickness of the materials (Table 3).

Table 3. Parameter for small biaxial stretched models to determine ideal material programming and prestretch values. The prestretch values are given in percentage (horizontal stretch | perpendicular stretch).

Demonstrator model	Thicknesses [mm]		Biaxial SMTPU programming [%]	Biaxial prestretch TPC [%]	n
	SMTPU	TPC			
P1	0.6	0.2	100|50	20|10	3
P2	0.6	0.6	50|33	20|14	4
P3	0.6	0.6	50|17	21|7	4

In the climate chamber, the three lines of demonstrator models were heated from room temperature (23 °C) to 70 °C for 20 min to analyze their response to a rise in temperature and to record the curvature inversion and angular change. For bending angle K measurements, two setups were used to photograph the demonstrator at 23 °C and 70 °C (Fig. 5A). The angular change in reaction to a rise in temperature was analyzed using video recordings (Fig. 5C).

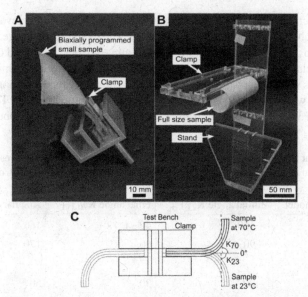

Fig. 5. Setup for the bending angle measurements. A) Clamping device of the 50×50 mm^2 pre-test series. B) Stand with clamp in which two full size multilayers can be fixed at the same time for motion and bending angle analysis. C) Sketch of curvature measurement in the multilayer models. The curvature angles are measured at room temperature and when heated to 70 °C.

The two specimens of P1 showed a curvature inversion (Table 4). To note, here one specimen coiled up when heated to 63 °C and collapsed along the diagonal at 70 °C. Already 1 min after complete folding of the specimen, it starts to open again. After 13 min the specimen was unfolded again, a curvature inversion did not take place in this case (Fig. 6A–C). The other two specimens in the series were examined clamped on one side and showed a curvature inversion with a bending angle of 160° and 170°, respectively (Table 4). In all three specimens of the test series, the SMTPU separated from the silicone at 70 °C, and shape recovery was limited to the TPC silicone bilayer. Three P2 specimens showed curvature inversion within 4 min, but no snapping behavior could be identified (Fig. 6D–F). Furthermore, instead of a reset, a detachment of the SMTPU from the silicone was observed. In the fourth P2 specimen the SMTPU layer detached from the silicone during heating after 15 min and thus curvature inversion could not be measured.

All P3 specimens showed a snapping behavior and a curvature inversion with a mean angular change 73.75° ± 12.93° (Table 4). They showed a change in curvature from a lateral to a longitudinal curvature within 3 min (Fig. 6G–I). Instead of reforming, the SMTPU detached from the silicone at 70 °C in the center after 15 min. Although detachment was visible, the parameter combination chosen for the P3 demonstrators was the only one in which all specimens showed complete curvature reversal. Therefore, the parameters of P3 were chosen to construct the final version of the trap lobes.

Table 4. Angular change of different biaxially stretched demonstrator models in response to a rise in temperature. In tests marked with (–) the measurement was not possible due to delamination.

Demonstrator model	Initial angle K_{23} [°]	Final angle K_{70} [°]	Angular change [°]
P1	−120	40	160
	−90	60	170
	–	–	–
P2	−20	30	50
	−20	35	55
	0	40	40
	–	–	–
P3	−90	0	90
	−80	0	80
	0	70	70
	−5	50	55

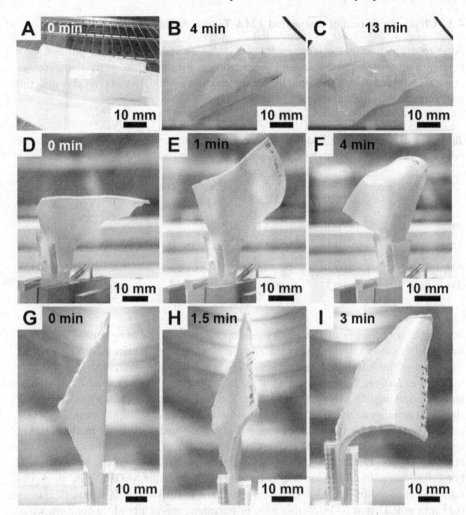

Fig. 6. Temperature response of demonstrator models with different parameter combination. A–C) Exemplary temperature response of P1 specimen (A). The motion started immediately at reaching 70 °C and after 4 min at 70 °C the specimen was folded up completely (B). The multilayer increases its curvature by roll up when heated to 63 °C (A) and at 70 °C it inverts its curvature (B). After 13 min, the SMTPU layer detaches from the silicone layer, the expansion of the TPC unfolds, and the TMA lobe recovers its original shape (C). D–F) Exemplary curvature change of a P2 specimen. Motion started immediately and was finished after 4 min. D: Initial curvature alignment. E: Intermediate state during heating. F: Heated specimen with inverted curvature orientation. The P2 test series shows curvature inversion behavior during heating. However, it was not observed to return to its original shape. The layers started to detach at the corners after 15 min (E). G–I) Exemplary curvature change of P3 specimen. Motion started immediately and was finished after 3 min. G: Initial curvature alignment. H: Intermediate state during heating. I: Heated specimen with inverted curvature orientation. The P3 test series shows a snapping behavior during the curvature inversion motion while heating up to 70 °C. Each specimen was heated for 20 min.

4.3   Characterization of Optimized TMA Trap Lobe Models

After identification of the ideal parameters, full-size specimens were built and their bending angle inversion was measured. Furthermore, we studied the material thicknesses at which a curvature can still be achieved, optimizing not only weight but also material consumption during production. (Table 5).

Table 5. Parameter for optimized TMA trap lobe models with varying thicknesses. The prestretch values are given in percentage (horizontal stretch I perpendicular stretch).

Demonstrator model	Thicknesses [mm]		Biaxial SMTPU programming [%]	Biaxial prestretch TPC [%]
	SMTPU	TPC		
O1	0.13	0.53	50I17	20I7
O2	0.13	0.33	50I17	20I7
O3	0.13	0.37	50I17	20I7
O4	0.33	0.56	50I17	20I7

Similar to the previous test series the temperature response of optimized TMA trap lobe models was characterized in the climate chamber for 20 min and in case of O3 for 45 min. The different demonstrators were heated from room temperature (23 °C) to 70 °C to analyze their response to a rise in temperature and to record the curvature inversion and angular change (cf. Fig. 5B). The four optimized TMA trap lobe models showed a bending angle of 125° (O1) (after 4 min), 170° (O2) (after 4 min), 140° (O3) (after 5 min) and 314° (O4) (after 14 min) (Table 6). The demonstrator models O1, O2 and O4 showed a recovery of 40°, 30° and 10° after 2 min of continuous heating at 70 °C. For demonstrator O3, heating continued for 25 min and a recovery of 10° was measured. For O1 no curvature inversion was observed. Even when the SMTPU-TPC thickness ratio was changed from 0.13 mm to 0.53 mm (O1), to 0.13 mm to 0.33 mm (O2) or to 0.13 mm to 0.37 mm (O3), no inversion of curvature was achieved. In contrast, when the thickness ratio of SMTPU to TPC was 0.33 mm to 0.56 mm (O4), both curvature inversion and buckling behavior were observed. During the test runs, no detachment behavior was observed for specimens D1, D2 and D4. In specimen D3, two (small) areas were identified where the SMTPU detached from the silicone at the center of the clamp and on the opposite side. The highest achieved angular change was observed in demonstrator O4, which also shows as only snap buckling (Fig. 7). As such, the parameter combination and chosen thickness ratios were identified as the ideal system configuration to achieve an autonomous artificial Venus flytrap lobe.

Table 6. Exemplary angular changes of optimized TMA trap lobe models in response to rise in temperature.

Demonstrator model	Initial angle K_{23} [°]	Final angle K_{70} [°]	Angular change [°]	Recovery angle K_{rec} [°]
O1	−255	−130	125	40
O2	−280	−110	170	30
O3	−270	−130	140	10
O4	−220	94	314	10

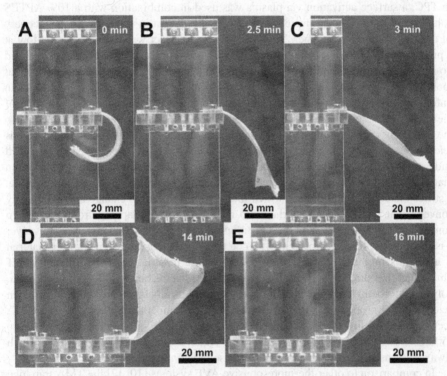

Fig. 7. Characterization of optimized TMA trap lobe motion in response to a rise in temperature to 70 °C. Exemplary motion sequence of O4 specimen. At room temperature, the specimen is in the initial concave state (A). An increase in temperature to 70 °C initiates the curvature inversion motion (B) with a visible snap (C) and further closure, achieving a final angular change of 314° (D) at 14 min. After 2 min at constant temperature of 70 °C a relaxation of 10° was observed (E).

5 Discussion

In the TMA trap lobe we successfully transferred the multilayer morphology, the pre-stress ratios and the snap buckling behavior of *Dionaea muscipula* trap into a thermoresponsive multi material, multilayer technical demonstrator. Curvature inversion of the trap lobes was achieved via a specifically designed and prestretched doubly curved multilayer. The designed models are based on the three layered morphology of *Dionaea muscipula* and its contribution to closure motion as highlighted by Forterre et al. (2005) and Sachse et al. (2020). Within our study, several parameters were investigated to achieve a technical multilayer capable of a curvature inversion and snapping motion, i.e. the variations in bonding techniques, prestretch and programming as well as thickness ratios of the different layers.

The desired goal, a snap buckling capable multilayer module (demonstrator O4), was implemented with SMTPU programming of 50%|17%, TPC preload of 20%|7% and a thickness ratio of 3:2. A successful bonding of the different layers was achieved by utilizing Loctite 4850 for bonding SMTPU and silicone. For the bonding of silicone to TPC, a surface activation via plasma was used in combination with a 10% APTES solution treatment. The extrinsic 2-way effect via TPC was used for the shape recovery of the shape memory polymer. The intrinsic 2-way effect was found to be too low at a programing of 100%, so only a small angular change would have been expected and no snap buckling. In contrast to the O1-O3, O4 showed a snap buckling behavior, but took almost triple the time. While the others changed their angular curvature in an unfolding motion within 4 min but stopped and did not inverse curvature. In spite of the successful snap buckling behavior of sample O4, it was not possible to recover to the initial shape. This could be due to an impurity in the bonding or an inhomogeneous release of prestresses. In order to investigate this, further specimens must be produced and examined. Although a snapping back process could be demonstrated with the chosen material selection, this is only one possible material combination. Instead of silicone, a stiffer material could be used, which inhibits its own length change and completely converts that of the other materials into curvature. After snapping from concave to convex, the force generated by the TPC might not support the shape recovery - as layer 2 is flexible, the force vector is likely to be towards the curvature - if a stiffer material is used, this might be circumvented. One possible material could be a flexible PET film, which has already been used to create AVF systems before [17, 25]. In addition, polytetrafluoroethylene (PTFE) can be investigated as an abutment. Teflon offers even better thermal properties than TPC, with a melting temperature of 325 °C to 335 °C, accompanied by low creep behavior and a suitable Young's modulus of 400 MPa to 750 MPa. The use of PTFE might enable the creation of a self-resetting system, which always returns to its original shape in response to varying temperatures.

In comparison to other thermoresponsive AVF systems [10, 17] the TMA trap lobe system presented here is the first to translate the layered morphology and prestress ratios of a biological model to achieve curvature inversion and snap buckling in response to a rise in temperature. The combination of different thermoresponsive materials into one TMA trap lobes multilayer system represents the first step toward building a fully autonomous temperature responsive AVF.

6   Conclusion

Complex multi material structures can be used to build artificial bioinspired systems, which perform complex motion sequences. In this study, we developed and character-ized a thermoresponsive multilayer artificial Venus flytrap (TMA) trap lobe. The basic multilayer structure and prestress ratios were abstracted form a biological model. We used different prestretch ratios and thicknesses of our three materials to enable the formation of a double curved surface. This novel multilayer made out of shape memory TPU (SMTPU), silicone and TPC was used to create an artificial Venus flytrap trap lobe, like the trap of the biological model *Dionaea muscipula*. When heating the lobes above 70 °C, they snap from a concave to convex configuration. Here we investigated the suitable materials, prestretch ratios and bonding methods to achieve the double curved surfaces. We characterized the temperature response and angular changes. This revealed that a prestretch ratio as in the biological role model and a thickness ratio from 3:2 SMTPU to TPC was necessary to achieve a curvature inversion and snap buckling. This novel thermoresponsive AVF trap lobe will enable us to build autonomous AVF systems and support structures for soft machines performing complex motion sequences in the future. The soft autonomous system could be used for example as a support structure for soft solar harvesters protecting them against unfavorable environmental conditions, or as soft autonomous gripper that reacts to changing environmental condition by closing the system and securing the payload.

Acknowledgement. Funded by the Deutsche Forschungsgemeinschaft (DFG, German Research Foundation) under Germany's Excellence Strategy – EXC-2193/1 – 390951807. We thank the AG Technik of the Institute for Biology 2 of University of Freiburg for the construction of the biaxial stretching device. This work was supported by Fraunhofer Cluster of Excellence "Programmable Materials" under PSP elements 40-01922-2500-00002 and 40-03420-2500-00003. T.P. wishes to thank the European Regional Development Fund for financing a large part of the laboratory equipment (project 85007031).We thank Laura Mahoney from the *liv*MatS Writer studio for spellchecking and improving the manuscript.

References

1. Meder, F., Armiento, S., Naselli, G.A., et al.: Biohybrid generators based on living plants and artificial leaves: influence of leaf motion and real wind outdoor energy harvesting. Bioinspir. Biomim. **16**, 055009 (2021). https://doi.org/10.1088/1748-3190/ac1711
2. Mazzolai, B., Laschi, C.: A vision for future bioinspired and biohybrid robots. Sci. Robot. **5** (2020). https://doi.org/10.1126/scirobotics.aba6893
3. Mazzolai, B., Laschi, C., Dario, P., et al.: The plant as a biomechatronic system. Plant Sig. Behav. **5**, 90–93 (2010). https://doi.org/10.4161/psb.5.2.10457
4. Sachse, R., Westermeier, A., Mylo, M., et al.: Snapping mechanics of the Venus flytrap (*Dionaea muscipula*). Proc. Natl. Acad. Sci. U.S.A. **117**, 16035–16042 (2020). https://doi.org/10.1073/pnas.2002707117
5. Westermeier, A.S., Sachse, R., Poppinga, S., et al.: How the carnivorous waterwheel plant (*Aldrovanda vesiculosa*) snaps. Proc. Biol. Sci. **285** (2018). https://doi.org/10.1098/rspb.2018.0012
6. Poppinga, S., Bauer, U., Speck, T., et al.: Motile traps. In: Ellison, A., Adamec, L. (eds.) Carnivorous Plants: Physiology, Ecology, and Evolution, pp. 180–193. Oxford University Press (2018). https://doi.org/10.1093/oso/9780198779841.003.0014
7. Poppinga, S., Kampowski, T., Metzger, A., et al.: Comparative kinematical analyses of Venus flytrap (Dionaea muscipula) snap traps. Beilstein J. Nanotechnol. **7**, 664–674 (2016). https://doi.org/10.3762/bjnano.7.59

8. Poppinga, S., Joyeux, M.: Different mechanics of snap-trapping in the two closely related carnivorous plants *Dionaea muscipula* and *Aldrovanda vesiculosa*. Phys. Rev. E **84**, 041928–041935 (2011). https://doi.org/10.1103/PhysRevE.84.041928

9. Forterre, Y., Skotheim, J.M., Dumais, J., et al.: How the Venus flytrap snaps. Nature **433**, 421–425 (2005). https://doi.org/10.1038/nature03185

10. Kim, S.-W., Koh, J.-S., Lee, J.-G., et al.: Flytrap-inspired robot using structurally integrated actuation based on bistability and a developable surface. Bioinspir. Biomim. **9**, 36004 (2014). https://doi.org/10.1088/1748-3182/9/3/036004

11. Zhang, Z., Chen, D., Wu, H., et al.: Non-contact magnetic driving bioinspired Venus flytrap robot based on bistable anti-symmetric CFRP structure. Compos. Struct. **135**, 17–22 (2016). https://doi.org/10.1016/j.compstruct.2015.09.015

12. Zhang, Z., Li, X., Yu, X., et al.: Magnetic actuation bionic robotic gripper with bistable morphing structure. Compos. Struct. **229**, 111422 (2019). https://doi.org/10.1016/j.compstruct.2019.111422

13. Pal, A., Goswami, D., Martinez, R.V.: Elastic energy storage enables rapid and programmable actuation in soft machines. Adv. Funct. Mater. **30** (2019). https://doi.org/10.1002/adfm.201906603

14. Lunni, D., Cianchetti, M., Filippeschi, C., et al.: Plant-inspired soft bistable structures based on hygroscopic electrospun nanofibers. Adv. Mater. Interfaces (2020). https://doi.org/10.1002/admi.201901310

15. Wu, S., Baker, G.L., Yin, J., et al.: Fast thermal actuators for soft robotics. Soft Robot. **9**, 1031–1039 (2022). https://doi.org/10.1089/soro.2021.0080

16. Riley, K.S., Ang, K.J., Martin, K.A., et al.: Encoding multiple permanent shapes in 3D printed structures. Mater. Des. **194**, 108888 (2020). https://doi.org/10.1016/j.matdes.2020.108888r

17. Tauber, F.J., Auth, P., Teichmann, J., et al.: Novel motion sequencés in plant-inspired robotics: combining inspirations from snap-trapping in two plant species into an artificial venus flytrap demonstrator. Biomimetics **7**, 99 (2022). https://doi.org/10.3390/biomimetics7030099

18. Li, W., Matsuhisa, N., Liu, Z., et al.: An on-demand plant-based actuator created using conformable electrodes. Nat. Electron. **4**, 134–142 (2021). https://doi.org/10.1038/s41928-020-00530-4

19. Tauber, F.J., et al.: Unit cell based artificial Venus flytrap. In: Hunt, A., et al. (eds.) Biomimetic and Biohybrid Systems. Living Machines 2022. LNCS, vol. 13548, pp. 1–12. Springer, Cham (2022). https://doi.org/10.1007/978-3-031-20470-8_1

20. Bothe, M., Pretsch, T.: Two-way shape changes of a shape-memory poly (ester urethane). Macromol. Chem. Phys. **213**, 2378–2385 (2012). https://doi.org/10.1002/macp.201200096

21. Langbein, S., Czechowicz, A.: Formgedächtnistechnik: Entwickeln, Testen und Anwenden, 2nd überarbeitete und erweiterte Auflage. Springer, Wiesbaden (2021). https://doi.org/10.1007/978-3-658-17904-5

22. Chalissery, D., Schönfeld, D., Walter, M., et al.: Fused filament fabrication of actuating objects. Macromol. Mater. Eng. **307**, 2200214 (2022). https://doi.org/10.1002/mame.202200214

23. Sunkara, V., Park, D.-K., Hwang, H., et al.: Simple room temperature bonding of thermoplastics and poly (dimethylsiloxane). Lab Chip **11**, 962–965 (2011). https://doi.org/10.1039/c0lc00272k

24. Carrell, C.S., McCord, C.P., Wydàllis, R.M., et al.: Sealing 3D-printed parts to poly (dimethylsiloxane) for simple fabrication of Microfluidic devices. Anal. Chim. Acta **1124**, 78–84 (2020). https://doi.org/10.1016/j.aca.2020.05.014

25. Esser, F., et al.: Adaptive biomimetic actuator systems reacting to various stimuli by and combining two biological snap-trap mechanics. In: Martinez-Hernandez, U., et al. (eds.) Living Machines 2019. LNCS (LNAI), vol. 11556, pp. 114–121. Springer, Cham (2019). https://doi.org/10.1007/978-3-030-24741-6_10

Charge-Dependent Flexural Rigidity of a Conductive Polymer Laminate for Bioinspired Non-thermal Compliance Modulation

Yauheni Sarokin[1]([✉]) [iD], Vadim Becquer[2], Eric Cattan[2] [iD], Alvo Aabloo[1] [iD], and Indrek Must[1] [iD]

[1] University of Tartu, 50411 Tartu, Estonia
{yauheni,alvo.aabloo,indrek.must}@ut.ee
[2] Polytechnic University Hauts de France, 59313 Valenciennes, France
{vadim.becquer,eric.cattan}@uphf.fr

Abstract. Material-level stiffness modulation allows for the creation of controllable energy-dissipating structures for auxiliary and training exoskeletons and the manipulation of delicate objects and tissues. These use cases require simple control systems and disfavour thermally driven solutions. Many natural mechanisms that involve stiffness modulation rely on reversible charge-driven modifications of internal constituents, inspiring the development of analogous technologies. This paper investigates flexural rigidity variation in an electronically conducting polymer (PEDOT:PSS) laminate concurrently with bending actuation. The flexural rigidity of the laminate increased by 45% as a result of a low input voltage (1.7 V) application. The addition of an ion-diffusion promoter (polyethylene oxide) amplified the stiffness response with minimal effect on actuation. The rapid response (up to 15 s), non-thermal working mechanism, safe materials, and simple control make this solution an attractive interface to various forms of life.

Keywords: Stiffness modulation · Electronically conducting polymers · Capacitive laminate

1 Introduction

Reversible cross-linking of proteins is a chemically mediated variable stiffness approach evolved in natural tissues to respond to varying physiological conditions. For example, the stiffness of the wing hinges of insects is increased through the formation of tyrosine crosslinks in the resilin protein (and decreased by selective degradation via the tyrosinase enzyme) [1]. Reversible cross-linking of proteins can be seen as nature's solution to change material elastic properties on demand. Reversible chemical modulation of material parameters is not widespread in engineering. The technologies for varying stiffness can generally be classified into two categories. The first group, structural stiffness, involves interaction between structural elements while preserving material properties,

F. Meder et al. (Eds.): Living Machines 2023, LNAI 14157, pp. 109–116, 2023.
https://doi.org/10.1007/978-3-031-38857-6_8

e.g., folding, electrostatic, hydraulic, pneumatic, and jamming mechanisms [2–9]. The second group of mechanisms involves changes in material properties, e.g., phase/glass transition of alloys/polymers [10–13], and electro/magnetorheological fluids [14, 15], i.e., not chemically modulated. The application of these exampled technologies in contact with the living domain can be restricted by bulkiness, complicated control systems, and the involvement of temperatures beyond physiological limits. Electrochemically mediated reversible elasticity modulation can provide a large range of stiffness modulation at a constant temperature, satisfying the requirements for human-interfaced application and inspiring the development of robotic materials for adaptive scenarios analogous to muscles and tendons in nature.

Taking inspiration from natural charge-driven chemically modulated elasticity modulation, we investigate a comparable approach in electronically conductive polymers (ECPs). The alteration in mechanical properties of ECPs involves the following two phenomena. The first effect concerns the changes in the length and conformation of the polymeric backbone at different charge densities (by injection of electronic charge externally), resulting in changes in various material properties [16]. The change in volume has motivated the use of ECPs as actuators [17]. The second effect is an osmotic expansion of ECP caused by the influx of solvent molecules due to concentration modulation [16]. Upon injection of electronic charge to ECP, the charge is balanced by electrolyte ions, resulting in a decrease of ion concentration in bulk and thus promoting the influx of solvent to equalise the concentration. We investigated the stiffness variation of an actuating three-layer laminate consisting of two layers of ECP separated by a layer of solid polymer electrolyte (SPE) [17]. As ECP, we use poly (3, 4-ethylenedioxythiophene)polystyrene sulfonate (PEDOT:PSS), commercially available for various flexible electronics solutions. PEDOT:PSS-based wearable sensors have demonstrated excellent safety in direct contact with the living domain, including humans [18]. The charge-dependent stiffness of the PEDOT:PSS actuator was measured in previous studies through a tensile test and expressed as longitudinal elastic modulus [19]. Subsequent research has demonstrated the variation in stiffness of ECPs upon actuation, which is attributed to changes in the geometric configuration (topology of the contact surface) [20]. However, our experimental approach is characterized by the calculation of the actuator's variable flexural rigidity using a bending test, which accounts for the combined effects of changes in the second moment of inertia and elastic modulus of the laminate layers. Possible use cases in wearable robotics need linear as well as bending modes of stiffness modulation and actuation to accommodate complex geometries at a large degree of freedom. Linear mode is challenging to be integrated into textile due to practical challenges in arranging a two-electrode system. In laminates, two electrodes are effectively arranged, yet developing mirror-symmetrical processes in opposite electrodes upon charge injection. In bending actuation, mirror-symmetric strain at opposite surfaces is beneficial, yet, vice versa, the opposite-direction stiffness modulation at opposite layers tends to cancel each other out. However, the charge-dependent stiffness is not completely symmetric to charge, and stiffness modulation is commonly needed complementary to actuation, thus motivating us to investigate the charge-dependent stiffness of an actuating laminate symmetrical to the center plane.

Upon electronic charge introduction, ECPs exchange ions with the ion reservoir (electrolyte solution bulk). As suggested recently [17], the addition of ion mobility promoters to the ECP blend enhances electrochemical properties by providing more effective ion pathways and a more accessible ion reservoir. This work introduced polyethylene oxide (PEO) to PEDOT:PSS electrodes to investigate if ion mobility promoters also result in enhanced stiffness-modulation performance.

The bioinspired mechanism of ECP stiffness variation is attractive for its non-thermal mechanism and good reversibility. The metal-free construction of the system (except for contacts) and chemically safe constituents further justify use in wearable applications. The infinite deformation degree of freedom (not the case of conventional robotic solutions) provided by non-thermal bending actuators allows more complex and intricate movements (assist or dissipate energy opposing motion) in human-interfaced applications, leading to improved performance of wearable devices.

2 Experimental

2.1 Laminate Fabrication

The fabrication of the laminate based on PEDOT:PSS/PEO followed the layer-by-layer procedure previously published. Here the fabrication is described in brief, please refer to [21, 22] for in-detail description.

Materials: poly(ethylene glycol) methyl ether methacrylate (PEGM, M_n = 500 g mol^{-1}), poly(ethylene glycol) dimethacrylate (PEGDM, Mn = 750 g mol^{-1}), ammonium persulfate (APS, 98%), and cyclohexanone (>99.8%) were purchased from Sigma-Aldrich and used as received. PEDOT:PSS aqueous solution (Clevios PH1000, solids content 1.0–1.3 wt %) was purchased from Heraeus Precious Metals GmbH & Co. Nitrile butadiene rubber (NBR), the initiator dicyclohexyl peroxydicarbonate (DCPD) and 1-ethyl-3-methylimidazolium bis (trifluoromethanesulfonyl) imide (EMImTFSI 99.9%) were supplied by LANXESS, Groupe Arnaud and Solvionic, respectively.

The procedure consists of successive stacking of electrodes and an ionically conducting membrane, followed by final polymerization. Both PEDOT:PSS and PEDOT:PSS/PEO electrodes were prepared by casting [23, 24]. The PEDOT:PSS solution for electrode casting was prepared by adding mPEG composed of 50 wt % PEGM monomer and 50 wt % PEGDM crosslinker, ranging from 0–60% in terms of solids content in commercial Clevios PH1000 PEDOT:PSS in aqueous solution. Ammonium persulfate as a radical initiator for PEO precursors was added to the solution with respect to 3 wt% mPEG. After mixing the PEDOT:PSS solution with the PEO precursors and ammonium persulfate in the above proportions, the solution is casted into the mold at an ambient temperature of 50 °C, and the water is evaporated from the solution, allowing the first electrode layer to form.

2.2 Flexural Rigidity Measurement

The measurement set up is shown in Fig. 1. The laminate was mounted between electrically conductive terminals forming a cantilever beam with a free length $L = 10$ mm and width $w = 2$ mm. The thickness of the laminate was 40 μm. A small contact force offset (approximately 180 μN) is applied to the laminate to prevent discontinuity in sinusoidal force measurements so that the force sensor will always contact the laminate. The clamped laminate was subjected to bending at the distal end, perpendicular to the surface, to displacement δ using a voice coil actuator driven with $f = 1$ Hz sine wave. The resulting force F was registered using a custom force sensor attached at the tip of the voice coil actuator. The force sensor is constructed out of two 350-Ω strain gauges in half-Wheatstone configuration, according to the previously developed system [25].

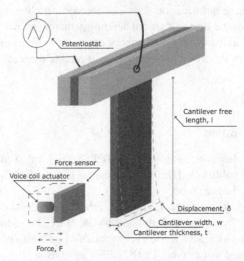

Fig. 1. Measurement set up, showing arrangement of the variable-stiffness laminate (in black) cantilevered between conducting clamps (terminals) and bent using a voice-coil-actuator carrying with force sensor attached.

Flexural rigidity is calculated as a product of second moment of inertia, I, and elastic modulus, E, according to Euler-Bernoulli theorem [26] as follows:

$$EI = FL^3/3\delta_{max}, \qquad (1)$$

where δ_{max} is the deflection of the beam at the point of application of the force. The sinusoidal displacement was $\delta_{max} = 0.36$ mm. Due to the very high compliance of the 40 μm thick laminate, the effect of the blocking force on the voice coil actuator movement was negligible.

The clamps were connected to a BioLogic BP-300 potentiostat. The laminate was charged by applying a voltage stepwise, with each voltage step 100 mV ranging from 0 V to 1.7 V. After each voltage step, a sinusoidal strain was applied for one minute (60 sinusoidal cycles), and the corresponding sinusoidal force was recorded. The force signal was sampled using a National Instruments USB-6218 data acquisition device and LabView 20.0.1 software. The signal was processed by Fourier transform to extract the force amplitude (twice the value of force F amplitude).

3 Results and Discussion

The scanning electron micrograph of the ECP-based laminate cross-section is depicted in Fig. 2A, showing a uniform thickness of 47 μm. The structure of the electrodes was homogenous, whereas the ionically permeable membrane shows a characteristic structure, potentially influenced by the cryo-fracture preparation.

A comparison between raw signals at different voltages in three consecutive experiments on a same sample is presented in Fig. 2B, showing good repeatability. The most prominent effect was the large potential-dependent offset, corresponding to blocking force. Blocking force is equal to the force acting on the force sensor subtracting the initial force offset. The sine wave amplitude differences in subsequent experiments are negligible, indicating that the redox reaction occurring within the bulk is reversible.

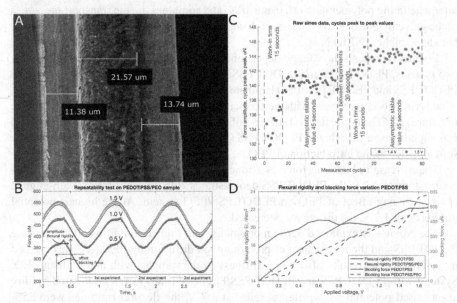

Fig. 2. Results of variable flexural rigidity measurements. (A) Scanning electron micrograph of the cross-section of PEDOT:PSS/PEO laminate. (B) Results of repeatability test on PEDOT:PSS/PEO sample. Raw force signal data repeated in three consecutive experiments with 3 different applied voltages within each experiment: 0.5, 1.0 and 1.5 V. (C) Peak to peak values of raw force sine cycles annotating rate of flexural rigidity variation. (D) Result of flexural rigidity and blocking force measurements as a function of applied.

The cantilevered laminate was bent from its free end using a voice coil actuator driven by a 1-Hz sinusoidal voltage. Minor distortions from sine are visible, particularly at lower applied voltage levels, possibly corresponding to sliding contact between the force sensor and the contacting point at the laminate or to a slight buckling motion of the close-to-straight laminate. At higher potentials, this artefact disappeared, indicating a better-defined geometry.

Figure 2C depicts a typical transient course of the sinusoidal force peak-to-peak amplitude in response to a small (100-mV) abrupt (at $t = 0$) change in applied voltage. The laminate assumed a new stable level of force amplitude (and thus the level of flexural rigidity) in about 15 s, preserving the newly achieved value during the subsequent 45-s of the experiment.

The actuation of the structure is facilitated by the phenomena that occur simultaneously in the polymer matrix but reciprocally: reduction and oxidation reactions occur at the opposite electrodes, causing contraction in the oxidized ECP electrode and expansion in the reduced electrode. The above-mentioned redox reactions are bringing to the electrodes structural (second moment of inertia due to volume expansion/contraction in ECP-based electrodes) and intrinsic (elastic properties due to polymer backbone conformation changes) variations.

The SPE membrane, which serves as an ion reservoir, is based on a semi-interpenetrating polymer network (semi-IPN) and combines the ion transport properties of the polyethylene oxide (PEO) network with the mechanical properties of linear nitrile butadiene rubber (NBR) [17].

Figure 2D presents the voltage-dependence of flexural rigidity and blocking force for two systems, PEDOT:PSS and PEDOT:PSS/PEO. The elastic moduli of the uncharged PEDOT:PSS and PEDOT:PSS/PEO laminates were 1.66 GPa and 1.53 GPa, respectively, which is in a good agreement with the elasticity of free-standing PEDOT:PSS films in the literature [27]. The initial flexural stiffness of the PEDOT:PSS/PEO sample (16.3 nN m^2) was slightly lower than that of PEDOT:PSS (17.7 nN m^2), which might indicate shallow softening due to the introduction of PEO.

The increase in blocking force as a function of applied voltage is also clearly pronounced: up to 1.2 V, the PEDOT:PSS demonstrates 26% higher stiffness, well-aligned to the softening effect of PEO on PEDOT:PSS/PEO system. At the highest potential difference of 1.7 V, the difference decreased.

The previously explained dense morphology and limited ion diffusivity in pristine PEDOT:PSS and the mechanism of promoting ion diffusion by PEO [28] was verified by comparing the results of bending stiffness of the samples with and without PEO. Systems with PEDOT:PSS and PEDOT:PSS/PEO electrodes increased flexural rigidity at increased potential by a different ratio: at 1.7 V, the flexural rigidities were 25% and 46%, respectively, higher from the uncharged state, as shown in Fig. 2D. Stiffness variation was thus more affected by the introduction of PEO, compared to blocking force. Consequently, more accessible ion reservoirs and more effective ion mobility pathways positively affect stiffness modulation magnitude.

4 Conclusions

The modulation of stiffness was investigated in a symmetric laminate with two ECP electrodes, and it was found that blending PEO with PEDOT:PSS substantially increased the amplitude of flexural rigidity variation. However, while the introduction of PEO resulted in softening of the material and decreased blocking force, the effect was more pronounced for flexural rigidity modulation.

The results of these studies open a new perspective for a non-thermal stress-controlled approach at the material level for variable stiffness applications. In particular, the engagement of ECPs and the mechanism of reversible redox reaction-based stiffness variation simultaneously to electroactive actuation is a new material-level approach for exosuits. The thin-film configuration of the laminate and low applied driving signal potential (less than 1.7 V) further confirms the suitability. The rate at which the flexural rigidity varies depends on the laminate's thickness; therefore, even faster responses could be achieved by thinner laminates.

Simple, reversible, and non-thermal control, substantial flexural stiffness variation (up to 46%) and fabrication in thin film configuration suggest that ECPs in combination with ion diffusion promoters are very suitable for wearable applications and can be used as compliant joints allowing stiffening or softening of the joint. This material-level technology promises limitless degrees of freedom which is very important for anatomically determined structures without strictly fixed axes of locomotion. This thin laminate scalable variable-stiffness technology is promising for exosuits, mainly because this laminate has the potential for being embedded into and combined with textiles.

Acknowledgements. This research was supported by the Estonian Research Council grants PRG1498 and PRG1084, and H2020 project TWINNIMS (Grant agreement 857263) and Kristjan Jaak Scholarship for short study visits (provided by Estonian Ministry of Education and Research and the Education and Youth Board).

References

1. Partlow, B.P., Applegate, M.B., Omenetto, F.G., Kaplan, D.L.: Dityrosine cross-linking in designing biomaterials. ACS Biomater. Sci. Eng. **2**(12), 2108–2121 (2016)
2. Hayes, G.J., Liu, Y., Genzer, J., Lazzi, G., Dickey, M.D.: Self-folding origami microstrip antennas. IEEE Trans. Antennas Propag. **62**, 5416–5419 (2014)
3. Henry, C., McKnight, G.: Cellular variable stiffness materials for ultra-large reversible deformations in reconfigurable structures. In: Smart Structures and Materials 2006: Active Materials: Behavior and Mechanics, vol. 6170, pp. 536–547 (2006)
4. Krishnan, G.: Kinematics of a generalized class of pneumatic artificial muscles. J. Mech. Robot. **7**(4), 041014 (2015)
5. Tabata, O.: Micro fabricated tunable bending stiffness devices. Sens. Actuators, A: Phys. **89**, 119–123 (2001)
6. Brown, E.: Universal robotic gripper based on the jamming of granular material. Proc. Natl. Acad. Sci. **107**, 18809–18814 (2010)
7. Faisal, T.R.: The impact of tissue morphology, cross-section and turgor pressure on the mechanical properties of the leaf petiole in plants. J. Bionic Eng. **7**, S11–S23 (2010)
8. Chen, Y.: Multi-turn, tension-stiffening catheter navigation system. In: 2010 IEEE International Conference on Robotics and Automation, pp. 5570–5575. IEEE Xplore, Anchorage (2010)
9. Ota, T.: A highly articulated robotic surgical system for minimally invasive surgery. Ann. Thorac. Surg. **87**(4), 1253–1256 (2009)
10. Shan, W.: Soft-matter composites with electrically tunable elastic rigidity. Smart Mater. Struct. **22**(8), 085005 (2013)

11. McEvoy, M.: Thermoplastic variable stiffness composites with embedded, networked sensing, actuation, and control. J. Compos. Mater. **49**(15), 1799–1808 (2015)
12. Loeve, A.: Polymer rigidity control for endoscopic shaft-guide 'Plastolock'-a feasibility study. J. Med. Devices **4**(4), 045001 (2010)
13. Hodgson, D.: Shape memory alloys. In: ASM International, Metals Handbook, 10th edn., vol. 2, pp. 897–902 (1990)
14. Manti, M.: Stiffening in soft robotics: A review of the state of the art. IEEE Robot. Autom. Mag. **23**(3), 93–106 (2016)
15. Jolly, M.: Properties and applications of commercial magnetorheological fluids. J. Intell. Mater. Syst. Struct. **10**(1), 5–13 (1999)
16. Bay, L.: Mechanism of actuation in conducting polymers: osmotic expansion. J. Phys. Chem. B **105**(36), 8492–8497 (2001)
17. Maziz, A.: Top-down approach for the direct synthesis, patterning, and operation of artificial micromuscles on flexible substrates. ACS Appl. Mater. Interfaces. **8**(3), 1559–1564 (2016)
18. Savagatrup, S., et al.: Plasticization of PEDOT:PSS by common additives for me-chanically robust organic solar cells and wearable sensors. Adv. Funct. Mater. **25**(3), 427–436 (2015)
19. Rohtlaid, K., et al.: Asymmetric PEDOT:PSS trilayers as actuating and sensing linear artificial muscles. Adv. Mater. Technol. **6**(3), 2001063 (2021)
20. Mutlu, R., Alici, G.: Artificial muscles with adjustable stiffness. Smart Mater. Struct. **19**(4), 045004 (2010)
21. Rohtlaid, K.: PEDOT:PSS-based micromuscles and microsensors fully integrated in flexible chips. Smart Mater. Struct. **29**(9), 09LT01 (2020)
22. Rohtlaid, K.: Poly(3,4-ethylenedioxythiophene):Poly(styrene sulfonate)/polyethylene oxide electrodes with improved electrical and electrochemical properties for soft microactuators and microsensors. Adv. Electron. Mater. **5**(4), 1800948 (2019)
23. Yan, H.: Highly conductive and transparent poly(3,4-ethylenedioxythiophene)/poly(4-styrenesulfonate) (PEDOT/PSS) thin films. Polym. J. **41**(12), 1028–1029 (2009)
24. Okuzaki, H.: Electrically driven PEDOT/PSS actuators. Synth. Met. **159**(21–22), 2233–2236 (2009)
25. Must, I.: A variable-stiffness tendril-like soft robot based on reversible osmotic actuation. Nat. Commun. **10**(1), 1–8 (2019)
26. Gere, J.M., Goodno, B.J.: Mechanics of Materials. Cengage learning, Boston (2009)
27. Greco, F.: Ultra-thin conductive free-standing PEDOT/PSS nanofilms. Soft Matter **7**(22), 10642–10650 (2011)
28. Fu, K.: Mixed ion-electron conducting PEO/PEDOT:PSS miscible blends with intense electrochromic response. Polymer **184**, 121900 (2019)

A 3D-Printed Biomimetic Porous Cellulose-Based Artificial Seed with Photonic Cellulose Nanocrystals for Colorimetric Humidity Sensing

Kliton Cikalleshi[1,2] (iD), Stefano Mariani[1](✉) (iD), and Barbara Mazzolai[1](✉) (iD)

[1] Bioinspired Soft Robotics Laboratory, Istituto Italiano di Tecnologia, 16163 Genova, Italy
{stefano.mariani,barbara.mazzolai}@iit.it
[2] The Biorobotics Institute, Scuola Superiore Sant'Anna, 56025 Pontedera, Italy

Abstract. Distributed sensing of environmental parameters is going towards solutions that are more efficient by taking inspiration from flying plant seeds. Yet, present technologies mostly rely on electronics, and they are often heavy and not biodegradable. Here, we develop a biodegradable and porous material, based on cellulose acetate and lignin, and characterize its degree of porosity. We use this material to 3D print lightweight and porous artificial fliers inspired by *Ailanthus altissima* seeds. By 3D printing, we can tailor in a precise way the morphology of the artificial flier that strongly influences its aerodynamic behavior. We add a cellulose-based photonic crystal for humidity sensing of topsoil by optical readout. These artificial flyers are biomimetic, lightweight and biodegradable and have the same mass (~22.4 mg) and descent speed (~0.64 m/s) of the natural seeds, thus constituting a novel approach for perspective distributed monitoring of relevant environmental parameters (i.e., humidity).

Keywords: Porous cellulose artificial seed · Photonic cellulose nanocrystals · Colorimetric humidity sensing

1 Introduction

Bioinspired deployable sensor networks for spatio-temporal monitoring of environmental parameters are gaining much attention and study lately [1–3]. Among several biological models, flying plant seeds are becoming more and more attractive for this application scenario. These plant seeds constitute a model of morphological computation found in nature [4]. It is, in fact, their morphology and structural features that give them the ability to passively fly and be dispersed by the wind, without the need of any energy input from inside [5].

Acer samara seeds were taken as inspiration to develop deployable auto-rotating sensors for wildfire detection [6], or airborne sensors for gathering atmospheric parameters, as temperature, air pressure, relative humidity and wind speed along their descent [7].

The original version of this chapter was previously published without open access. A correction to this chapter is available at
https://doi.org/10.1007/978-3-031-38857-6_33

F. Meder et al. (Eds.): Living Machines 2023, LNAI 14157, pp. 117–129, 2023.
https://doi.org/10.1007/978-3-031-38857-6_9

These solutions strongly rely on electronics, which generate e-waste; moreover, they are heavy and energy consumptive. *Taraxacum* seeds were chosen as a model by Iyer et al. to build battery-free sensing devices [1]. Although they are lightweight and solar powered, they are based on electronics and not biodegradable materials. *Tristellateia* seeds acted as a source of bioinspiration for Kim et al. to develop battery-free electronic and colorimetric microfliers for ultraviolet exposure and pH sensing [2], that were not biodegradable. Yoon et al. developed colorimetric fliers inspired by *Tristellateia* and *Taraxacum* seeds for sensing pH, heavy metal concentrations, ultraviolet exposure, humidity and temperature [3]. These fliers are biodegradable, yet some reagents used for sensing are not biodegradable and may be even toxic (e.g., S-8028, containing Cobalt dichloride). *Alsomitra macrocarpa* seed was taken as a model for developing fully biodegradable artificial seeds for visual pH sensing of rainwater [8].

The aim of the present work is to develop biomimetic, deployable, lightweight, fully biodegradable and 3D printed artificial seeds for the sensing of an environmental parameter, such as humidity, via optical readout. The artificial seeds are bioinspired by *Ailanthus altissima* seeds and they are made of porous cellulose acetate (CA). A sensor layer, made of photonic cellulose nanocrystals (CNC), is applied on one side of the artificial seed for humidity sensing of topsoil.

Porous tissues, i.e., aerenchyma, are common in plants, and they are also present in flying seeds [9], likely with the aim of enhancing lightness. We think it is important to reproduce this feature artificially and to tailor the positioning of porous structures' by means of 3D printing. Cellulose acetate was dissolved in acetone [10] and mixed with lignin particles, which were later removed by water (pores formation by leaching technique). The degree of porosity was then characterized. Both cellulose acetate and lignin are biodegradable, as reported in literature [11–13].

Next, we employed the porous material for the 3D printing of an artificial seed bioinspired by *Ailanthus altissima* seed, also referred as samara. Differently from an *Acer* samara seed, which falls by autorotating around its vertical axis, *Ailanthus altissima* samara rotates both around its longitudinal axis and its vertical axis [14]. Moreover, *Ailanthus altissima* seed has another important flight mode, that is tumbling, that allows it to travel on the xy plane without the need for the wind [15, 16]. *Ailanthus altissima* seed is constituted of an actual seed part, placed at the center of an eye shaped wing. The wing has a twisted structure, with one side being twisted, to help lateral transport even if on the ground [14]. We performed a morphometric and aerodynamic analysis on natural *Ailanthus altissima* seeds. Based on the extracted data, we designed and 3D printed biomimetic *Ailanthus altissima* seeds using the previously developed material. We, then, analyzed the morphometry and aerodynamics of the artificial seeds to check their compliance with the natural seeds. The process of designing, 3D printing and testing took place iteratively until a behavior similar to the natural seeds was reached.

We developed a photonic crystal based on Cellulose Nanocrystals (CNCs) [17] for colorimetric sensing of humidity [18]. The sensor was added on the artificial *Ailanthus altissima* seed for the monitoring of humidity oscillation by analyzing the changes of the reflected color through a spectrometer-based and/or colorimetric analysis.

2   Experimental

2.1   Preparation and Characterization of the Porous Cellulose-Based Material for 3D Printing

A number of four solutions made of distinct ratios of cellulose acetate (30000 MW) (Sigma-Aldrich, Germany), and lignin (Alkaline) (TCI Europe N.V., Japan), were prepared.

First, a cellulose acetate batch solution was prepared by mixing in a beaker cellulose acetate in acetone at 30% w/w. The beaker was closed with Parafilm and aluminum foil and was put on a magnetic stirrer (Thermo Fisher Scientific Inc., USA) at 50 °C at 30 rpm for 1 h. The batch solution was split into 4 parts in which different amounts of lignin were added: 0, 33.3, 50, 66.6% of the cellulose acetate weight. Each new solution, unless the first, was closed and stirred at 50 °C at 30 rpm for 1 h.

The four solutions were used as 3D printing material for the Direct Ink Writing (DIW) process on a 3D-Bioplotter (EnvisionTEC, USA and Germany). Printing temperature and build plate temperature were set at 20 °C, printing speed was set at 25 mm/s and the diameter of the used nozzle was 0.4 mm. The four compositions were printed at different pressures: 1.2, 1.4, 1.8, 2.2 bar for the 0, 33.3, 50, 66.6% solutions, respectively, because of the increasing viscosity of the cellulose acetate-lignin solutions. For brevity, we will refer to these solutions as 0-lig, 33-lig, 50-lig and 66-lig.

Square specimens (10 × 10 mm base) with three different thicknesses, 0.1, 0.5, 1 mm, (5 specimens per thickness), were printed for each of the 4 compositions, using the preset printing parameters; for a total of 60 specimens. They were then dried in oven (Vacutherm, Thermo Electron LED GmbH, Germany) at 70 °C for 30 min, to let all the acetone evaporate. Then, they were weighted with an analytical balance (Practum, Sartorius AG, Germany). The thickness of the square specimens was measured with a digital caliper (RS PRO 150 mm Digital Caliper, RS Components Ltd., UK) to derive the volume. Consequently, each specimen was put in a plastic petri dish filled with deionized water and left at rest for intervals of 1 h, 4 times, and for one last interval of the duration of 16 h, to allow the release of lignin in water, (5 intervals for a total of 20 h). After each interval, the specimens were dried, first with adsorbent paper, then in oven (Vacutherm, Thermo Electron LED GmbH, Germany) at 70 °C for 30 min, and their weight was measured with an analytical balance (Practum, Sartorius AG, Germany).

The evolution of weight in time was recorded and computed. Moreover, with the measured weights and volumes, porosity of the specimens was derived by the following relationship:

$$P = 1 - \rho/\rho_{AC} \tag{1}$$

where P is the porosity of the specimen, ρ is its density and ρ_{AC} is the density of cellulose acetate as reported by the manufacturer (1.3 g/cm^3).

2.2   From Natural Flying Seeds to 3D Printed Artificial Flying Seeds

Ailanthus altissima seeds were collected from a tree in Morego (Genoa, Italy). The morphometric analysis was performed on n. 8 seeds. Dimensions of the seeds, i.e., longitudinal length (L_L), transversal length (L_T), wing thickness (Th_w), seed capsule thickness (Th_s) and diameter (D), were measured using a digital caliper (RS PRO 150 mm Digital Caliper, RS Components Ltd., UK). Mass of the seeds (M) was assessed with an analytical balance (Practum, Sartorius AG, Germany). Wing surface (S) was estimated with ImageJ from pictures of the *Ailanthus altissima* seeds taken with a camera (1280 × 800 pixels) of a Samsung A40 (South Korea) smartphone (Fig. 2c). The wing loading (W/S) was calculated from the weight value (W) of the seed and the wing surface (S). Microscope images of the wing were taken with a digital microscope (KH-8700, Hirox, Japan).

An aerodynamic analysis in laboratory conditions was performed to determine the descent speed (v_d) in the spirally twisted flight mode of n. 8 *Ailanthus altissima* seeds. The seed was released from rest, in a laboratory without active ventilation, from a height of 2.95 m and allowed to fall freely. The flight of the seed was recorded by a camera of a Samsung A40 (South Korea) with a resolution 1280 × 800 pixels. The mean v_d was calculated considering the time elapsed between the frame of the release and the frame in which the seed touches the ground. Each individual seed was tested 3 times, giving a total of 24 drops.

For the biomimetic design of the *Ailanthus altissima* artificial seed, a top view picture of a natural seed was taken with the camera (1280 × 800 pixels) of a Samsung A40 (South Korea) smartphone. The picture was used for the extraction of a vector file of the contours, with the free and open-source vector graphics editor Inkscape. The vector file of the contours was consequently imported in the 3D CAD modeling software Siemens NX, and the design of the artificial samara seed was developed taking into consideration the morphometric analysis performed on the natural seed. For the 3D printing of the artificial seed, a Direct Ink Writing (DIW) process was employed with the 3D printer Bioplotter (EnvisionTEC, USA). The CAD model was converted in STL format, sliced with Perfactory RP software and imported in the 3D printer software VisualMachine, where the build instructions were set. The material used for the printing of the artificial *Ailanthus altissima* seeds was the 50-lig solution and the set printing parameters were those above-mentioned for that composition.

The same morphometric and aerodynamic analysis conducted on the natural *Ailanthus altissima* seeds were conducted also on the 3D printed 50-lig artificial seed. Subsequently, the same seed was put in deionized water for 20 h for lignin removal, dried with adsorbent paper and in oven (Vacutherm, Thermo Electron LED GmbH, Germany) at 70 °C for 30 min. Again, morphometrics and aerodynamics were conducted on the artificial seeds. In addition, an estimation of porosity was performed by considering the nominal value of the volume derived from the CAD model and the mass derived from measurements.

2.3 Cellulose Nanocrystals (CNCs) Photonic Crystal Humidity Sensor Fabrication and Characterization

Cellulose nanocrystals (CNCs) were purchased from Cellulose Lab (Canada). CNC were prepared by hydrolysis with sulfuric acid and they had the following features: width 5–20 nm and length 100–250 nm. CNCs were dissolved in deionized water (7.5% w/w) and magnetically stirred (1000 rpm for 72 h). Then Glycerol (5% w/w) was added to the CNCs solution and magnetically stirred (1000 rpm for 72 h). The solution (3 ml) was then casted in circular plastic Petri (3 cm in diameter). After evaporation at room temperature (20 °C) for 2–3 days, free-standing films with iridescent and photonic colors were obtained.

A square section of the CNC photonic crystal film (4 × 4 mm) was cut using a razor blade and attached onto the artificial seed using a 1 μL of Cellulose Acetate in acetone (30% w/w) as glue.

The reflectance and the shift of the photonic bandgap over different humidity variations (30%, 60% and 90%) were analyzed through spectrometry using an optical setup previously described [19] and consisting of: spectrometer FLAME-S-XR1-ES (200–1025 nm) (Ocean Insight, USA), light source SciSun 300 Solar Simulator (Sciencetech, Canada) working at 0.5 Sun (0.5 mW/cm^2); and a bifurcated fiber-optic probe (diameter = 600 μm) (Ocean Optics, USA). Light exiting from the light source is fed through one arm of the bifurcated fiber-optic probe orthogonally to CNC surface and the reflected light was collected through the other arm of the bifurcated fiber-optic probe into the spectrometer that yields the reflectance spectra. A protected silver mirror (Thorlabs, USA) was used for normalization. Relative humidity was changed (30%, 60% and 90%) using a climatic chamber (CTC256, Memmert GmbH, Germany) with the temperature fixed at 30 °C.

The colorimetric changes of the photonic bandgap over different humidity value (30%, 60% and 90%) were also captured by a Logitech Brio Stream, Logitech (Swiss), orthogonally placed onto the artificial *Ailanthus altissima* seed, and elaborated with Editor Video (Windows). CIE 1931 chromaticity diagram was plotted from spectral data using an online tool [20]. Colorimetric analysis of the CNC photonic crystal over the explored humidity variations was carried using ImageJ software analysis [21].

3 Results

3.1 Characterization of the Porous Cellulose Material

Weight loss due to lignin release was recorded over a period of 20 h for the four cellulose acetate-lignin compositions (0, 33.3, 50, 66.6% lignin) and for three different thicknesses (0.1, 0.5, 1 mm), as shown in Fig. 1.

For the 0-lig specimens (Fig. 1a) a very slight decrease in mass, constant in time, is observed, due to degradation of the cellulose acetate network. A mean mass loss of 3.8, 5.3 and 4.7% is recorded for thicknesses of 0.1, 0.5 and 1 mm, respectively. Porosity of the 0-lig specimens went from a mean initial value of 29.1, 47.7, 48.4% to a mean final value of 31.8, 50.5, 50.9%, for thicknesses of 0.1, 0.5 and 1 mm, respectively, as shown in Table 1.

In the 33-lig specimens (Fig. 1b) a greater loss was measured, due to the removal of most of the lignin, in addition to the degradation of CA. The mean recorded loss was 36.1, 32.9 and 30.5% for 0.1, 0.5 and 1 mm thicknesses respectively. If we correct these values with the percentages found for the pure CA (0-lig), we obtain a mean loss of 32.3, 27.5 and 25.7% respectively, caused by lignin release only. This indicates a residual fraction of lignin, 1, 5.8 and 7.6% respectively, still trapped in the CA network, as can be seen visually in Fig. 1e. The final mass of the 0.1 mm specimens is reached within the first hour of lignin release in water, due to the high surface to volume ratio. While for the 0.5 and 1 mm specimens, 90 and 81% of the total loss, respectively, happened in the first hour, indicating a slower release for lower surface to volume ratios. Final mean porosities for the 33-lig specimens were 68.5, 66.2, 58.9% for 0.1, 0.5 and 1 mm thicknesses respectively, as shown in Table 1.

As regards the 50-lig specimens (Fig. 1c), the recorded mean loss in mass was 53.5, 54.2 and 53.7% of the initial masses for 0.1, 0.5 and 1 mm thicknesses, respectively. Correcting with the degradation percentage of pure CA, the mean mass loss provided only by lignin releases were 49.7, 48.8 and 49.0% respectively. Only 0.3, 1.2 and 1% of lignin, respectively, stayed inside the cellulose acetate network, indicating a greater release of lignin due to a less packed CA network. Within the first hour, the mean mass loss of the 0.1 mm specimens was complete, while for the 0.5 mm specimens was 91% of the total mass loss. For the 1 mm specimens it was just 69% in the first hour and went over 90% after only 3 h. Porosity reached the values of 79.8, 73.3, 76.3 for 0.1, 0.5, 1 mm thickness, respectively, as shown in Table 1.

The 66-lignin specimens exhibited the major loss in weight: 69.6, 68.7 and 69.1% for 0.1, 0.5 and 1 mm thicknesses, respectively. The corrected mean values were 65.8, 63.3 and 64.4% respectively, with a fraction of residual entrapped lignin of 0.8, 3.3 and 2.2%. For the first hour, 99% of the total mass loss was reached for the 0.1 mm specimen, 93% for the 0.5 mm specimen and only 59% for the 1 mm specimen. Porosity increased to a maximum value of 89.1, 85.5 and 84.5 for 0.1, 0.5 and 1 mm thickness specimens, respectively, as shown in Table 1.

3.2   From Natural Flying Seeds to Artificial Flying Seeds

The morphometric analysis performed on n. 8 natural *Ailanthus altissima* seeds led to dimensions (Fig. 2a), that were used for the design and fabrication of the artificial seed. The longitudinal length (L_L) was 51.3 ± 1.6 mm, the transversal length (L_T) was 9.0 ± 0.7 mm, the wing thickness (Th_w) was 0.18 ± 0.02 mm, the seed capsule thickness (Th_s) was 1.7 ± 0.1 and its diameter (D) was 5.8 ± 0.2 The mean mass (M) measured for the natural seeds was 22.6 ± 2.2 mg. The mean of the measured wing surfaces (S) resulted in 319 ± 17 mm^2 and led to a wing loading (W/S) of 0.69 ± 0.08 N/m^2.

The aerodynamic analysis was intended to establish the descent speed of *Ailanthus altissima* seeds derived from the spirally twisted flight mode because this was the most frequent descent mode. The mean descent speed was 0.64 ± 0.12 m/s. Other flight modes were observed in addition to twisted spiral: tumbling, simple rotation and dead weight.

The morphometric and aerodynamic data acquired from *Ailanthus altissima* seed were used to design an artificial seed that could have the same characteristics. The design and fabrication workflow is shown in Fig. 2e. The vector file of the contour of a photographed model seed was slightly modified in the 3D CAD software to fit the mean dimensions extracted by the morphometric analysis of the natural seeds. The curls of the wing were not realized. A number of 8 artificial *Ailanthus altissima* seeds were printed using the 4 cellulose acetate-lignin solutions previously tested and their weights were measured. The 50-lig composite was the chosen material for the development of the final artificial seed. That is because the mass of the seed printed with it was nearly double the mass of the natural seed, and upon lignin removal in water half of the mass

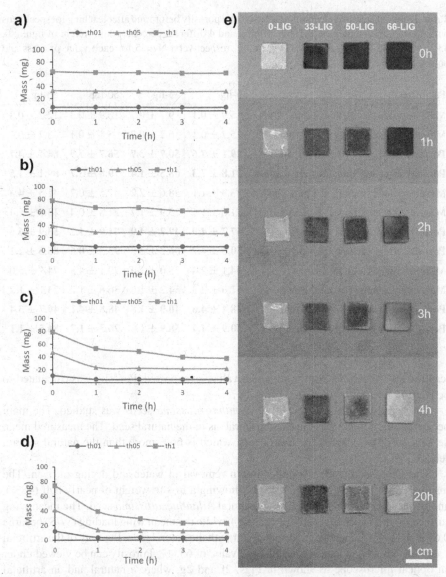

Fig. 1. Evolution of weight over time for square specimens of different cellulose acetate-lignin composition. (A) Mass loss over 4 h of 0% lignin-cellulose acetate specimens. (B) Mass loss over 4 h of 33.3% lignin-cellulose acetate specimens. (C) Mass loss over 4 h of 50% lignin-cellulose acetate specimens. (D) Mass loss over 4 h of 66.7% lignin-cellulose acetate specimens. (E) Evolution over a period of 20 h of 4 specimens (1 mm thick) with the following initial lignin percentage, from left to right: 0, 33.3, 50, 66.7%.

was lost, giving a final mass similar to that of the natural seed. The printed *Ailanthus altissima* seeds resulted in a mean mass of 43.0 ± 1.8 mg. The wing surface (S) was 320 ± 11 mm², right as the wing surface of the natural seed, while the wing loading (W/S)

Table 1. Initial and final mean values of mass and porosity before and after leaching for specimens with 3 different thicknesses (0.1, 0.5, 1 mm), and 4 different percentages in weight of lignin: 0, 33.3, 50, 66.6%, (0-lig, 33-lig, 50-lig, 66-lig, respectively. $N = 5$ for each value of mass and porosity)

Parameters	0-lig	33-lig	50-lig	66-lig
Mass as printed (mg), th. 0.1 mm	5.9 ± 0.1	9.7 ± 0.7	10.9 ± 0.3	12.2 ± 0.3
Mass after leaching (mg), th. 0.1 mm	5.7 ± 0.1	6.2 ± 0.2	5.1 ± 0.1	3.7 ± 0.1
Porosity as printed (%), th 0.1 mm	**29.1 ± 7.6**	**50.7 ± 3.7**	**56.7 ± 7.9**	**64.1 ± 4.7**
Porosity after leaching (%), th. 0.1 mm	**31.8 ± 7.3**	**68.5 ± 1.4**	**79.8 ± 3.7**	**89.1 ± 1.5**
Mass as printed (mg), th. 0.5 mm	33.3 ± 1.1	38.6 ± 2.2	47.5 ± 0.7	41.5 ± 4.3
Mass after leaching (mg), th. 0.5 mm	31.6 ± 1.1	25.9 ± 1.7	21.8 ± 0.4	13.0 ± 1.4
Porosity as printed (%), th. 0.5 mm	**47.7 ± 4.9**	**49.7 ± 4.9**	**41.9 ± 1.2**	**53.9 ± 6.5**
Porosity after leaching (%), th. 0.5 mm	**50.5 ± 4.7**	**66.2 ± 3.5**	**73.3 ± 0.6**	**85.5 ± 2.1**
Mass as printed (mg), th. 1 mm	64.1 ± 2.4	78.0 ± 1.4	79.1 ± 4.5	74.7 ± 5.0
Mass after leaching (mg), th. 1 mm	61.0 ± 2.3	54.2 ± 1.6	36.6 ± 1.7	23.1 ± 1.7
Porosity as printed (%), th. 1 mm	**48.4 ± 4.6**	**40.9 ± 1.8**	**48.8 ± 4.1**	**49.7 ± 3.4**
Porosity after leaching (%), th. 1 mm	**50.9 ± 4.4**	**58.9 ± 1.6**	**76.3 ± 1.7**	**84.5 ± 1.1**

resulted in 1.32 ± 0.08 N/m^2, a doubled value, as expected. Porosity was calculated to be 33.5%.

The aerodynamics of n. 8 50-lig *Ailanthus altissima* seeds was studied. The main occurring flight mode was the twisted spiral, as in the natural seed. The measured mean descent speed (v_d) was 1.07 ± 0.11 m/s, which is 66% more than the natural samara seeds.

The same seed was tested after lignin removal in water and drying in oven. The resulting mass (M) was 22.4 ± 1.1 mg, showing a loss in weight of nearly half (48%), and it was identical to the mass of the natural *Ailanthus altissima* seed. The mean wing surface (S) did not change (320 ± 11 mm^2), while the mean wing loading (W/S) became 0.69 ± 0.04 N/m^2, in quite good agreement with the natural seed. Porosity of the artificial seeds was greatly enhanced, reaching the value of 65.4%. Porosity can be viewed under an optical microscope as shown in Figs. 2f and 2g, where a natural and an artificial porous wing are compared.

The mean descent speed (v_d) of the twisted spiral flight mode of the porous artificial samara seeds was measured to be 0.64 ± 0.03 m/s, the same as the natural. A comparison of the mean morphometric and aerodynamic data between the 3 seeds (natural, 50-lig artificial, porous artificial), can be found in Table 2.

3.3 Humidity Sensing with CNC Optical Crystals

Figure 3a shows the coupling of the CNC photonic crystal (square 4×4 mm, weight 7 mg) with the porous cellulose acetate based artificial *Ailanthus altissima* seed.

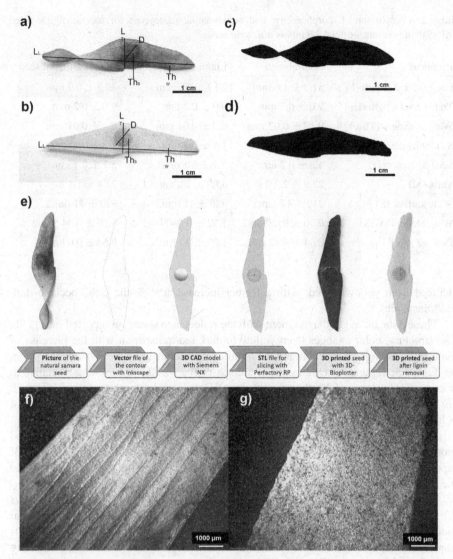

Fig. 2. Development of the artificial seed from the natural *Ailanthus altissima* seed. a) Dimensions of the natural seed. b) Dimensions of the artificial porous seed. c) Image binarization of the surface of the natural seed for the calculation of wing surface and wing loading. d) Image binarization of the surface of the artificial seed for the calculation of wing surface and wing loading. e) Workflow of the development of the artificial *Ailanthus altissima* seed. f) Micrograph of the wing of the natural seed and g) artificial seed (scalebar 1000 μm).

Figure 3a shows a sequence of pictures of the CNC film exposed to different humidity conditions (30, 60 and 90%) proving structural color changes in the visible spectrum. At %RH of 30% the CNC showed a yellow color. As %RH increased to 60% the CNC

Table 2. Comparison of morphometric and aerodynamic parameters for natural, lignin filled artificial and porous artificial *Ailanthus altissima* seeds.

Parameters	Natural seed	Lignin artificial seed	Porous artificial seed
Longitudinal length (L_L)	51.3 ± 1.6 mm	49.3 ± 0.7 mm	49.3 ± 0.7 mm
Transversal length (L_T)	9.0 ± 0.7 mm	9.0 ± 0.2 mm	9.0 ± 0.2 mm
Wing thickness (Th_W)	0.18 ± 0.02 mm	0.2 ± 0.01 mm	0.2 ± 0.01 mm
Seed thickness (Th_S)	1.7 ± 0.1 mm	1.5 ± 0.2 mm	1.5 ± 0.2 mm
Seed diameter (D)	5.8 ± 0.2 mm	5.7 ± 0.1 mm	5.7 ± 0.1 mm
Mass (M)	22.6 ± 2.2 mg	43.0 ± 1.8 mg	22.4 ± 1.1 mg
Wing surface (S)	319 ± 17 mm2	320 ± 11 mm2	320 ± 11 mm2
Wing loading (W/S)	0.70 ± 0.08N/m2	1.32 ± 0.08 N/m2	0.69 ± 0.04 N/m2
Descent speed (v_d)	0.64 ± 0.12 m/s	1.07 ± 0.11 m/s	0.64 ± 0.03 m/s

changed from yellow to red; with a further increase at 90% the CNC became dark red/transparent.

These data are in good agreement with the reflectance spectrum reported in Fig. 3b. The structural color changes from yellow to dark red/transparent with the increase of humidity is owing to the swelling of the multilayer structure caused by water adsorption.

Figure 3c reports the calibration of the sensor (i.e., %RH *vs* wavelength relative to maximum reflectance of the photonic bandgap). Data from the spectra reported in Fig. 3b are shown superimposed on a CIE 1931 diagram in Fig. 3d, proving the possibility of being colorimetrically discriminated.

The CNC colors at %RH 30, 60 and 90% extracted from Fig. 3a were also analyzed plotting the histogram in the blue channel using ImageJ software [21] (Fig. 3e). Figure 3f reports the colorimetric calibration of the sensor (i.e., %RH vs pixels value relative to the maximum intensity).

In summary, the CNC photonic crystal sensor coupled with the artificial *Ailanthus altissima* seed showed promising applicability for colorimetric humidity environmental monitoring using both spectrometer analysis and colorimetric image processing techniques. In perspective, statistical validation and an on-field measurement of the humidity using the colorimetric calibration will be carried out.

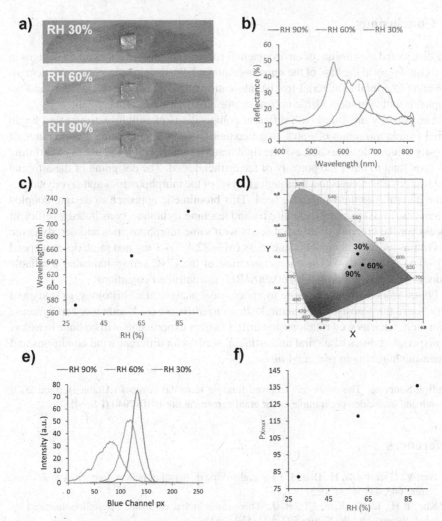

Fig. 3. Colorimetric humidity sensing characterization. a) Picture of the porous artificial *Ailanthus altissima* seed with the square (4 × 4 mm) CNC photonic crystal humidity sensor over relative humidity variations (30, 60 and 90%). b) Reflectance spectrum of the CNC photonic crystal humidity sensor at 30, 60 and 90% relative humidity. c) Calibration %RH vs wavelength (nm) relative to the maximum reflectance values recorded in (b). d) Spectral data from b) represented in a CIE 1931 diagram of the color perceived by the human eye. e) Colorimetric analysis of the CNC photonic crystal humidity sensor pictures (using ImageJ software) in the blue channel over relative humidity variations (30, 60 and 90%). f) Calibration %RH vs px value relative to maximum intensity values recorded in (e).

4 Conclusions

The distributed monitoring of environmental parameters poses even more challenges in the technologies at the base of the sensors employed. We developed a porous, biodegradable and 3D printable material for the fabrication of biomimetic artificial fliers and we coupled it with a biodegradable optical sensor based on CNC nanocrystals.

The porosity measured with different compositions of cellulose acetate and lignin varied from a minimum of ~30% to a maximum of ~90%, indicating a wide range of porosity achievable. The choice of the right material composition and use of 3D printing was important to tailor the porosity of the artificial seed. The designing of the artificial seed was possible thanks to a thorough analysis of the morphometrics and aerodynamics of the natural *Ailanthus altissima* seed. This biomimetic approach to design, coupled with the use of 3D printing technologies and leaching technique, constituted an efficient process for the creation of artificial seeds with same morphometries and aerodynamic behavior as the natural model (same mass (M) ~22.4 ± 1.1 mg and same descent speed (v_d) ~0.64 ± 0.03 m/s). The characterization of the CNC sensor indicated a reliable readout of relative humidity (30, 60, 90%RH) in controlled conditions.

Future work will include more morphological analysis, i.e., histology, to study and characterize the porosity of the natural *Ailanthus altissima* seed, and more aerodynamic parameters, such as seed rotations and drift. Outdoor experiments will be done to assess the dispersal abilities of natural and artificial seeds with different wind conditions and to measure humidity in real conditions.

Funding Sources. This work has received funding from the European Union Horizon 2020 research and innovation programme under grant agreement no. 101017940 (I-Seed).

References

1. Iyer, V., Gaensbauer, H., Daniel, T.L., et al.: Wind dispersal of battery-free wireless devices. Nature **603**, 427–433 (2022)
2. Kim, B.H., Li, K., Kim, J.T., et al.: Three-dimensional electronic microfliers inspired by wind-dispersed seeds. Nature **597**, 503–510 (2021)
3. Yoon, H-J., et al.: Biodegradable, three-dimensional colorimetric fliers for environmental monitoring. Sci. Adv. **8**(51), eade3201 (2022)
4. Mazzolai, B., Mariani, S., Ronzan, M., et al.: Morphological computation in plant seeds for a new generation of self-burial and flying soft robots. Front. Robot. AI **8**, 797556 (2021)
5. Seale, M., Nakayama, N.: From passive to informed: mechanical mechanisms of seed dispersal. New Phytol. **225**, 653–658 (2020)
6. Pounds, P., Singh, S.: Samara: Biologically inspired self-deploying sensor networks. IEEE Potentials **34**(2), 10–14 (2015)
7. Bolt, M., Prather, J.C., Horton, T., et al.: Massively deployable, low-cost airborne sensor motes for atmospheric characterization. Wirel. Sens. Netw. **12**, 1–11 (2020)
8. Wiesemüller, F., Meng, Z., Hu, Y. et al.: Transient bio-inspired gliders with embodied humidity responsive actuators for environmental sensing. Front. Robot. AI **9**, 1011793 (2022)
9. Takahashi, H., Yamauchi, T., Colmer, T.D., Nakazono, M.: Aerenchyma formation in plants. In: van Dongen, J.T., Licausi, F. (eds.) Low-Oxygen Stress in Plants. PCM, vol. 21, pp. 247–265. Springer, Vienna (2014). https://doi.org/10.1007/978-3-7091-1254-0_13

10. Pattinson, S.W., Hart, A.J.: Additive manufacturing of cellulosic materials with robust mechanics and antimicrobial functionality. Adv. Mater. Technol. **2**(4), 1600084 (2017)
11. Sakai, K., et al.: Biodegradation of Cellulose Acetate by *Neisseria sicca*. Biosci. Biotechnol. Biochem. **60**(10), 1617–1622 (1987)
12. Buchanan, C.M., Gardner, R.M., Komarek, R.J.: Aerobic biodegradation of cellulose acetate. J. Appl. Polym. Sci. **47**, 1709–1719 (1993)
13. Buswell, J.A., Odier, E., Kirk, K.: Lignin biodegradation. Crit. Rev. Biotechnol. **6**(1), 1–60 (1987)
14. Kowarik, I., Säumel, I.: Biological flora of Central Europe: Ailanthus altissima (Mill.) Swingle. Perspect. Plant Ecol. Evol. Syst. **8**, 207–237 (2007)
15. Matlack, G.R.: Diaspore size, shape, and fall behavior in wind-dispersed plant species. Am. J. Bot. **74**(8), 1150–1160 (1987)
16. Vincent, L., Liu, Y., Kanso, E.: Shape optimization of tumbling wings. J. Fluid Mech. **889**, A9 (2020)
17. Parker, R.M., Zhao, T.H., Frka-Petesic, B., Vignolini, S.: Cellulose photonic pigments. Nat. Commun. **13**, 3378 (2022)
18. Yao, K., Meng, Q., Bulone, V., Zhou, Q.S.: Flexible and responsive chiral nematic cellulose nanocrystal/poly(ethylene glycol) composite films with uniform and tunable structural color. Adv. Mater. **29**(28), 1701323 (2017)
19. Mariani, S., et al.: moldless printing of silicone lenses with embedded nanostructured optical filters. Adv. Funct. Mater. **30**, 1906836 (2019)
20. Sci-Sim CIE 1931. https://sciapps.sci-sim.com/CIE1931.html. Accessed 24 Mar 2023
21. Schneider, C.A., Rasband, W.S., Eliceiri, K.W.: NIH Image to ImageJ: 25 years of image analysis. Nat. Methods **9**(7), 671–675 (2012)

FRESH-Printing of a Multi-actuator Biodegradable Robot Arm for Articulation and Grasping

Avery S. Williamson[1] , Wenhuan Sun[1] , Ravesh Sukhnandan[1] , Brian Coffin[2] , Carmel Majidi[1] , Adam Feinberg[2,3] , Lining Yao[4] , and Victoria A. Webster-Wood[1,2,5(✉)]

[1] Department of Mechanical Engineering, Carnegie Mellon University, Pittsburgh, PA 15218, USA
vwebster@andrew.cmu.edu
[2] Department of Biomedical Engineering, Carnegie Mellon University, Pittsburgh, PA 15218, USA
[3] Department of Materials Science and Engineering, Carnegie Mellon University, Pittsburgh, PA 15218, USA
[4] Human-Computer Interaction Institute, School of Computer Science, Carnegie Mellon University, Pittsburgh, PA 15218, USA
[5] McGowan Institute for Regenerative Medicine, Carnegie Mellon University, Pittsburgh, PA 15218, USA
http://engineering.cmu.edu/borg

Abstract. The recent popularity of soft robots for marine applications has established a need for the reliable fabrication of actuators that enable locomotion, articulation, and grasping in aquatic environments. These actuators should also reduce the negative impact on sensitive ecosystems by using biodegradable materials such as organic hydrogels. Freeform Reversible Embedding of Suspended Hydrogels (FRESH) printing can be used for additive-manufacturing of small-scale biologically derived, marine-sourced hydraulic actuators by printing thin-wall structures out of sustainably sourced calcium-alginate hydrogels. However, controlling larger alginate robots with complex geometries and multiple actuation mechanisms remains challenging due to the reduced strength of such soft structures. For tethered hydrogel hydraulic robots, a direct interface with fluid lines is necessary for actuation, but the drag forces associated with tethered lines can quickly overcome the actuation force of distal and extremity structures. To overcome this challenge, in this study, we identify printing parameters and interface geometries to allow the working fluid to be channeled to distal components of FRESH-printed alginate robots and demonstrate a proof-of-concept biodegradable robotic arm for small object manipulation and grasping in marine environments.

Keywords: 3D printing · Hydrogel actuators · Biodegradability · Sustainability · Shape morphing · Soft robotics

Supplementary Information The online version contains supplementary material available at https://doi.org/10.1007/978-3-031-38857-6_10.

F. Meder et al. (Eds.): Living Machines 2023, LNAI 14157, pp. 130–141, 2023.
https://doi.org/10.1007/978-3-031-38857-6_10

1 Introduction

Soft robots have broad applications in human and environmental monitoring due to their ability to interact more safely with organisms than their traditional rigid counterparts [1]. Compliant actuators have seen broad adoption in wearable devices [2–4], swimming [5–11, 33] and crawling robots [10–13], grippers [14, 15], and tentacles [15, 33]. Recently, many researchers have endeavored to move their robotic systems beyond the lab, deploying robotic devices capable of adapting to locomotion in both amphibious and terrestrial environments [9–11, 16, 34].

However, many of the materials used in soft robotics may pose risks to fragile marine ecosystems. Most conventional soft robot materials rely on plastics and elastomers [17]. These may bioaccumulate in coastal ecosystems if robotic systems fail during deployment. Furthermore, small-scale marine robots may be accidentally ingested by native life [18, 19]. In particular, turtles, petrels, and other marine life can experience strongly adverse outcomes from ingesting non-digestible materials [18–21].

Biologically sourced and biodegradable materials are of growing interest in soft robotics to help minimize the risk of deploying soft robots in sensitive environments [1, 8, 11, 15, 17]. Biologically sourced actuators can span a spectrum from bio-derived plastic devices [23–25] to biotic muscle-based actuators [5, 12, 13]. Using plant-derived materials, researchers have developed pneumatic [26] and electrohydraulic [27] actuators that can biodegrade in natural environments. However, these actuators have been primarily tested in air. Biohybrid actuators that incorporate natural muscle tissue can operate in aquatic and marine ecosystems depending on the cell or tissue type [9–11, 16]. However, the metabolic and environmental conditions must be precisely regulated to maintain functionality, which currently prevents deployment outside of a research laboratory.

For marine applications, we have recently demonstrated that biodegradable, biologically sourced hydraulic actuators can be fabricated using Freeform Reversible Embedding of Suspended Hydrogels (FRESH) [15, 28]. These structures maintain functionality with minimal loss in range of motion over 100s of cycles, then degrade completely within a week of incubation on an ambient marine environment. FRESH enables the direct 3D printing of biologically relevant hydrogel inks featuring hydrophilic, porous, polymer networks. This printing method expands the geometric design freedom of printed structures and allows for more complex geometries to be fabricated than with methods such as casting that require removal from a mold or post-casting assembly [15]. In this way, FRESH-printing is advantageous over alternative manufacturing methods. Common printing materials include alginate, fibrin, collagen type I, and Matrigel [28]. For marine applications, alginate, a polysaccharide derived from seaweed that is naturally biodegradable, is compatible with FRESH printing [29]. Alginate can be ionically cross-linked using multivalent cations (e.g., Ca^{2+}), resulting in a physical gel with tunable mechanical properties [22]. Using biologically derived alginate hydrogel inks, we have previously created proof-of-concept demonstrations for bending and linear actuators, small-scale robotic grippers, and multi-actuator structures for end-effector positioning. These actuators are fully biodegradable, can undergo reversible shape and stiffness morphing, and are safely edible by marine organisms [15]. Whereas this prior work demonstrated that FRESH-printed alginate actuators were reliable, biodegradable, and even edible, all actuators were interfaced with driving syringe pumps at a single fixed base. Our prior preliminary attempts to interface more distal actuators on complex structures with independent tubing found that the actuators could not overcome the tube stiffness, which greatly restricted motion.

To overcome this limitation, in this work, we present the application of FRESH printing to larger, multi-actuator biodegradable robots with internal fluidic routing for independent control of distal actuators. We tested the ability of FRESH printing to create straight and angled fluidic channels using an alginate bioink and identified channel geometries needed for perfusion (Fig. 2H, 3A). Additionally, we designed, printed, and tested a proof-of-concept robotic arm with four degrees of freedom for end effector positioning and independent control of a distal soft grasper via internal routing. To our knowledge, this proof-of-concept work presents the first 3D-printed biodegradable robotic arm created using biologically sourced marine-derived materials.

2 Experimental Materials and Methods

Materials. Sodium alginate (mannuronic to guluronic acid (M/G) ratio = 1:3, Allevi), Alcian Blue (Alfa Aesar), gelatin Type B (Fisher Chemical), Pluronic F-127 (Sigma-Aldrich), gum arabic (Sigma-Aldrich), hydrochloric acid (HCl) (1N, Fisher Chemical), calcium chloride ($CaCl_2$) (Fisher Chemical), water-resistant glue (Ultra-Gel Control Super Glue, Loctite) were used as received.

2.1 Alginate Bioink Preparation

Preparation of the alginate bioink was performed as previously described [15]. Briefly, the alginate bioink was prepared by solubilizing sodium alginate powder in heated (65 °C) deionized water to a concentration of 4% w/v and mixing using a magnetic stirrer. Alcian Blue powder was added to the bioink at a concentration of 0.02% (w/v) to allow the hydrogel to be visible during testing.

2.2 Preparation of Gelatin Support Bath

The gelatin support bath was prepared following previous work [15, 29–31]. Briefly, 2.0% (w/v) gelatin Type B, 0.25% (w/v) Pluronic F-127, and 1.0% (w/v) gum arabic were thoroughly mixed in 50% (v/v) ethanol solution at 70–80 °C using magnetic stirring. The solution was adjusted to 5.55–5.57 pH by adding 1N HCl dropwise while monitoring pH with a benchtop pH meter (Apera Instruments). This precursor solution was stirred overnight in a temperature-controlled room (21–24 °C) using an overhead stirrer at 550–575 rpm. After stirring, the gelatin slurry was washed three times with 0.1% (w/v) $CaCl_2$. Finally, the slurry solution was diluted to a concentration of 0.05% (w/v) $CaCl_2$, vortexed, centrifuged at 2000 g for 5 min immediately before printing.

2.3 FRESH Printing of Alginate Robot Components

Methods for modeling, slicing, and printing alginate robots were adapted from Sun et al. [15] and prior literature [29–31] (Fig. 1). Briefly, all digital models in this study were created using Solidworks (Dassault Systèmes) and converted to Geometric codes (G-code) using Slic3r (http://slic3r.org) (16 mm/s print speed, 50 μm layer height). Perimeter-only features were used through the walls of the structure. A full slicer configuration profile is accessible in the supplemental materials.

All 3D printing was performed using a Replistruder V4 on a desktop CoreXY 3D printer (Elf, Creativity Technology). A 5 mL gastight syringe (Model 1005TLL, Hamilton) with a G30 blunt-tip needle (DN-05-LP-30, Bestean) was loaded with the bioink before printing, and excess air bubbles were expelled. Printing wells were vacuum formed from thermoplastic polycarbonate material to house the gelatin slurry suspension and fixed to the printer bed with double-sided tape (Fig. 1A). For structures less than 30 mm in the z direction, the 1-inch G30 needle was attached directly to the Hamilton syringe via a Luer-lock connection. A compound needle was fabricated to achieve printed structures exceeding 30 mm by inserting a 1-inch G30 needle into the open end of a 1-inch G23 needle via a press fit and connecting to the Hamilton syringe via a Luer-lock connection on the G23 needle.

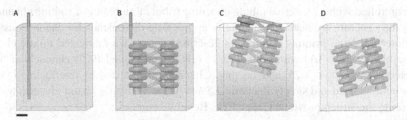

Fig. 1. FRESH-printing process of a typical alginate structure. (A) Gelatin slurry filled printing well with a G30 needle represented in purple. (B) Newly printed structure incubating in slurry at room temperature. (C) Slurry liquefication in 37 °C water bath and released printed structure. (D) Retrieved part in fresh 2.5% (w/v) $CaCl_2$ solution.

During printing, alginate structures were crosslinked by the 0.05% (w/v) $CaCl_2$ remaining in the slurry to ensure filament fusion and increase hydrogel strength. The printing times for the gripper, linear actuator structure, and compound structure were 27 min, 2 h 25 min, and 5 h 49 min respectively. Immediately following printing, the components were incubated in the printing wells at room temperature for 60 min (Fig. 1B). The wells were then transferred to a watertight container with 2.5% (w/v) $CaCl_2$ solution and incubated in a 37 °C water bath for 60 min for slurry liquefaction and part retrieval (Fig. 1C) as described previously [15]. Subsequently, the printed alginate components were transferred to a fresh 2.5% (w/v) $CaCl_2$ solution and incubated overnight at room temperature (Fig. 1D).

2.4 Interfacing FRESH-Printed Alginate Components with External Pressure Control and Measurement Systems

After cross-linking, the structure's base was adhered to a 5 mm thick silicone block for handling and subsequent interfacing with an external pressure control system using Loctite. To create the interface, a pin was first used to penetrate the silicone and actuator membrane. The pin was removed, and a blunt-tipped G25 needle was inserted through the opening and held in place by the silicone block. A 3 mm diameter PTFE tube was connected to the interface needle on one end and a 5 ml syringe on the other. Pressurization of the control line was performed by manually withdrawing and infusing fluid into the printed structure. While this proof-of-concept study did not fully characterize the maximum pressure withstood by the system, previous experiments [15] have demonstrated that the working pressure of the gripper bellows falls between 0.1 and 0.14 kPa. The pressurization of the system was measured with the use of an in-line Microfluidic Sensor Reader (Elveflow) with an acquisition sampling rate of up to 100 Hz and a 11 bit resolution. Data was tracked and analyzed using Elveflow Sensor Interface software.

2.5 Design and Testing of FRESH-Printed Channels for Fluid Routing

To fabricate larger, composite alginate robot structures in which actuators can be individually controlled without external tubing impeding robot motion, fluidic routing channels within the structure are needed. To identify appropriate dimensions for channels using the printer, ink, and printing parameters described above, we fabricated fluidic channel test blocks (Fig. 3A) with both straight (180°) and angled (90°) channels at five diameters: 0.7, 0.85, 1, 1.25, and 1.5 mm. Channels were tested by interfacing a G25 needle with one end and slowly injecting 2.5% w/v $CaCl_2$ dyed with red glycerin while monitoring the structure with a Canon EOS Rebel T7 camera.

2.6 Design and Testing of a FRESH-Printed Alginate Robot Arm

A soft, multi-actuator robot arm and end effector were created by incorporating the components developed by Sun et al. [15] and the FRESH-printed channels described above (Fig. 2A, B, C, D). The arm is composed of a base, with three parallel linear actuators to provide four degree-of-freedom positioning (Fig. 2E, F, G), a FRESH-printed channel to bring fluid to the end effector for separate control (Fig. 2H), and a soft grasper (Fig. 2I). To achieve watertightness for all actuators and channels, slicing parameters and printing orientation was critical. The hydrogel filament deposition was designed to progress along the axial direction of the arm during printing. The wall thickness for all bellows structures was set to 600 μm, and the inner face of the gripper was printed with a wall thickness of 700 μm in the slicing program. The fluid channel for gripper control was printed along the central axis of symmetry of the three linear actuators with a channel diameter of 2 mm and wall thickness of 1.5 mm.

A pilot trial was performed to assess the range of motion, positioning, and grasping capabilities of the proof-of-concept FRESH-printed alginate robot arm. The FRESH-printed structure was mounted to the silicone block as described and secured using Loctite (Fig. 4E). The silicone block was suspended in a 500 mL bath of 2.5% w/v

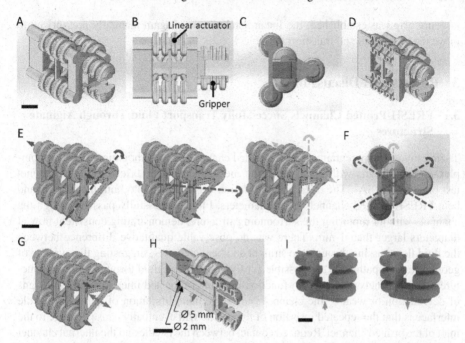

Fig. 2. Soft, multi-actuator robot arm for articulation and grasping. (A) Isometric view of compound structure featuring 3 linear truss actuators, internal routing channels, and distal single-channel gripper. (B) Side view of the compound structure. (C) Top view of the compound structure. (D) Cross-sectional of compound structure highlighting hollow bellows of linear actuators. Scale bar: 5 mm. (E) Isometric model of multi-actuator truss component demonstrating 3 rotational degrees of freedom. The axis of rotation achieved by pressurizing an individual linear actuator is denoted in like colors. Scale bar: 5 mm. (F) Rotational degrees of freedom overlaid on the top-down view of the structure. (G) Isometric model of multi-actuator truss component demonstrating 1 translational degree of freedom by actuating all linear bellows together. (H) Cross-sectional view of compound structure highlighting FRESH-printed channel enabling hydraulic actuation of distal structures. Internal channel diameter of 2 mm. Outer column diameter of 5 mm. Scale bar: 5 mm. (I) Isometric model of single channel gripper component. During infusion, the gripper jaws will bend in (left), and during withdrawal, they will bend out (right). Scale bar: 2 mm. (Color figure online)

$CaCl_2$ from a wire frame so that the structure could move freely in the solution (see supplemental materials). A G25 blunt-tipped needle was inserted directly into each linear actuator using the interface methods described above. For the gripper actuation line, a G25 needle was inserted into the base of the structure only until it penetrated the funnel-shaped chamber leading to the embedded channel (Fig. 2G). We first tested and measured the range of motion of the entire structure by manually pressurizing the linear actuator control lines independently and monitoring with a Canon EOS Rebel T7 camera. We then tested the grasping ability of the gripper by manually oscillating pressure from the open to the closed position. To demonstrate the strength and stability of the robot arm, we manually positioned various objects within the grasping range of the open gripper and pressurized the system to grasp and hold the object securely. When a secure grip was established, the linear actuators were again manually pressurized to move the entire arm and transport the object.

3 Results and Discussion

3.1 FRESH-Printed Channels Successfully Transport Fluid Through Alginate Structures

To investigate the potential use of embedded channels in the fabrication of larger, complex alginate robots with distal actuation mechanisms, we fabricated fluidic channel test blocks (Fig. 3A). The dyed $CaCl_2$ solution was injected into both the straight and bent FRESH-printed channels at all diameters. Fluid successfully passed through the channels without rupturing the surrounding structure, demonstrating consistent flow at diameters larger than 1 mm. There was no observable qualitative difference between the fluid flow passing through the straight and bent channels, suggesting that a range of geometries and pathways are possible for the transport of fluid through alginate structures. The channels continued to function even after repeated injections with no signs of degradation or wear to the channel walls. The main limitation of the direct needle interface is that the repeated insertion of the needle will eventually cause damage to the inlet of the printed channel. Reduced contact between the needle and the internal channel walls improves the life of the printed part. This was implemented in the design of the compound structure by incorporating a hollow chamber within the base block into which the needle may be inserted. Fluid in this chamber is funneled into the smaller channel, rather than having the needle directly contact the internal walls of the channel. Further studies should investigate the impact of channel diameter, length, and path geometry on the laminar flow of hydraulic fluid. Consideration should also be given to the effect that high pressure flow has on the walls of the surrounding structures to determine if shear stress and pressure are a limiting factor to what can be achieved with FRESH-printed channels in alginate robots. As a proof-of-concept, this method of FRESH-printing fluid channels eliminates the need for externally tethered interfaces and enables the actuation of distal components on complex alginate robots.

3.2 Compound FRESH-Printed Structure for Articulation and Grasping

After demonstrating the capability of FRESH-printed channels to transport fluid through alginate structures, we designed and tested a proof-of-concept robot arm comprised of a linear truss structure and a distal gripper. The resulting structure was 20.33 mm × 22.34 mm × 31.05 mm and weighed 2.05 g. The actuation of the linear truss elements was achieved through a direct needle interface, while the distal gripper was actuated through a channel running from the base of the structure through a central support column (Fig. 2G). The FRESH-printed robot arm successfully deflected the structure in 4 degrees of freedom with a maximum deflection angle of approximately 25° (± 1°) from the central axis (Fig. 4A). Future experiments should more specifically quantify independent gripper deflection, maximum linear actuator extension, and the motion of the arm in 3D space.

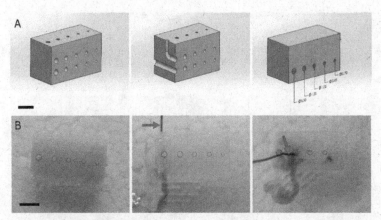

Fig. 3. Schematic of functional microfluidics channels embedded in a 3D FRESH-printed block. (A) Isometric CAD model view of test block with a series of embedded microfluidics channels (left), cross sectional view of 180° and 90° bend internal channels (middle), and dimensioned view of a range of channel diameters (right). Scale bar: 5 mm. (B) Top view of FRESH-printed test block (left), demonstration of dyed fluid flow through 180° channel (middle), and demonstration of dyed fluid flow through 90° bend channel (right). Red arrows indicate the G25 needle which has been interfaced with the channel. Scale bar: 5 mm. (Color figure online)

The robot arm was also capable of controlled grasping through the opening and closure of the distal gripper (Fig. 4B). Articulation and grasping were performed repeatedly in aquatic conditions; the arm manipulated multiple small objects within the environment. Previous experiments have tested the strength of the gripper by securely holding an M3 nut weighing 0.11 g [15]. We repeated this action with the compound arm to demonstrate that there has been no qualitative functionality lost in terms of grip strength (Fig. 4C) and that the arm can sustain a grip on objects at least 5% of its own weight. Future experiments will further validate this by performing force or pressure measurements and comparing to literature values [15].

The combined capabilities of the multi-actuator truss and gripper elements of this structure allow for the robot arm to interact with its environment and perform tasks, including picking up, transporting, and releasing small objects (Fig. 4D). Additional video of articulation and grasping performed by the robot arm are available in the supplemental materials. While the arm performed well in the aqueous environment when removed from the solution and held in air, it was unable to support its own weight and buckled (Fig. 4E). This observation supports what previous reports have established; the unfavorable mechanical properties of alginate-based hydrogels prevent long-term functionality external to an aqueous environment [15]. Articulation and grasping in air and interaction with larger and heavier objects in solution may be more achievable by introducing fiber reinforcements and composite materials to improve the structure's mechanical properties [15, 17, 29, 33].

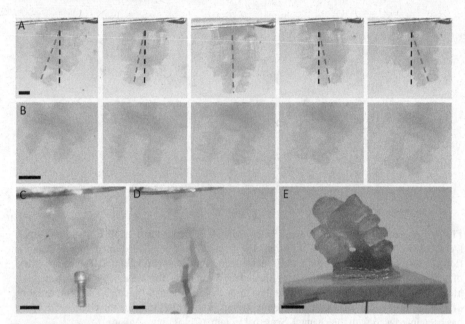

Fig. 4. FRESH-printed robot arm demonstrating complex articulation and grasping. (A) Actuation of the FRESH-printed robot arm produces deflection to the left and right. Scale bar: 5 mm. (B) Actuation of the distal gripper between open and close from left to right. Scale bar: 5 mm. (C) FRESH-printed robot arm securely grasping M3 screw. Scale bar: 5 mm. (D) Actuation of FRESH-printed robot arm allows for the interaction and manipulation of objects within the aquatic environment. Scale bar: 5 mm. (E) FRESH-printed robot arm adhered to silicone block while external to the aqueous environment. Scale bar: 5 mm.

4   Conclusion

Here we presented a proof-of-concept for embedding fluidic channels within alginate structures using FRESH-printing methods to enable the fabrication of multi-actuator robots. The complex actions and tasks performed by the robot arm in this work would not be possible without the combined capabilities of both the linear actuator truss structure and the inclusion of an independently controlled distal gripping mechanism. The functionality of the gripper specifically is enabled by the introduction of embedded FRESH-printed channels to transport hydraulic fluid from the needle interface point to the point of actuation. This reduces the need for externally tethered lines which cause detrimental drag forces and can hinder movement or damage the structure. The functionality of this printed structure suggests that increasingly complex and larger robot limbs can be fabricated using this method without as many challenges typically associated with the scaling of soft hydrogel parts. These findings help to further advance the potential future use of soft biodegradable actuators in marine ecosystems as non-disruptive exploratory robots.

Acknowledgements. This research was supported in part by grants from the NSF DBI 2015317 as part of the NSF/CIHR/ DFG/FRQ/UKRI-MRC Next Generation Networks for Neuroscience

Program, the Presidential Fellowship in the College of Engineering at Carnegie Mellon University, the Collaborative Fellowship from the Department of Mechanical Engineering at Carnegie Mellon University, and funding award no. HQ00342110020 from the National Defense Education Program. Manuscript copy-editing for clarity and grammar after initial drafting was assisted by Grammarly. All edited content was reviewed by the authors.

Supporting Information. Supporting information including supplemental videos and slicer configuration profiles is available online.

References

1. Laschi, C., Mazzolai, B., Cianchetti, M.: Soft robotics: technologies and systems pushing the boundaries of robot abilities. Sci. Robot. **1**(1) (2016)
2. Webster-Wood, V.A., et al.: Organismal engineering: toward a robotic taxonomic key for devices using organic materials. Sci. Robot. **2**(12) (2017). https://doi.org/10.1126/scirobotics.aap9281
3. Kim, J., Park, J., Lee, J.: Biohybrid microsystems actuated by cardiomyocytes: microcantilever, microrobot, and micropump. In: IEEE International Conference on Robotics and Automation, Pasadena, CA (2008)
4. Legant, W.R., Pathak, A., Yang, M.T., Deshpande, V.S., McMeeking, R.M., Chen, C.S.: Microfabricated tissue gauges to measure and manipulate forces from 3D microtissues. Proc. Natl. Acad. Sci. U.S.A. **106**, 10097–10102 (2009)
5. Holley, M.T., Nagarajan, N., Danielson, C., Zorlutuna, P., Park, K.: Development and characterization of muscle-based actuators for self-stabilizing swimming biorobots. Lab Chip **16**, 3473–3484 (2016)
6. Williams, B.J., Anand, S.V., Rajagopalan, J., Saif, M.T.A.: A self-propelled biohybrid swimmer at low Reynolds number. Nat. Commun. **5**, 3081 (2014)
7. Nawroth, J.C., et al.: A tissue-engineered jellyfish with biomimetic propulsion. Nat. Biotechnol. **30**, 792–797 (2012)
8. Paschal, T., Bell, M.A., Sperry, J., Sieniewicz, S., Wood, R.J., Weaver, J.C.: Design, fabrication, and characterization of an untethered amphibious sea urchin-inspired robot. IEEE Robot. Autom. Lett. **4**(4), 3348–3354 (2019)
9. Hwang, J., Wang, W.D.: Shape memory alloy-based soft amphibious robot capable of seal-inspired locomotion. Adv. Mater. Technol. **7**(6) (2022). ISSN: 2365709X. https://doi.org/10.1002/admt.202101153
10. Ren, K., Yu, J.: Research status of bionic amphibious robots: a review. Ocean Eng. **227** (2021). https://doi.org/10.1016/j.oceaneng.2021.108862
11. Milana, E., Raemdonck, B.V., Cornelis, K., et al.: EELWORM: a bioinspired multimodal amphibious soft robot. IEEE Xplore (2020). https://doi.org/10.1109/RoboSoft48309.2020.9115989
12. Inoue, N., Shimizu, M., Hosoda, K.: Self-organization of a joint of cardiomyocyte-driven robot. In: Duff, A., Lepora, N.F., Mura, A., Prescott, T.J., Verschure, P.F.M.J. (eds.) Biomimetic and Biohybrid Systems. Living Machines 2014. LNCS, vol. 8608, pp. 402–404. Springer, Cham (2014). https://doi.org/10.1007/978-3-319-09435-9_43
13. Webster, V.A., Hawley, E.L., Akkus, O., Chiel, H.J., Quinn, R.D.: Effect of actuating cell source on locomotion of organic living machines with electrocompacted collagen skeleton. Bioinspir. Biomim. **11**, 036012 (2016)

14. Hao, Y., Wang, T., Ren, Z., et al.: Modeling and experiments of a soft robotic gripper in amphibious environments. Int. J. Adv. Robot. Syst. **14**(3) (2017). ISSN: 17298814. https://doi.org/10.1177/1729881417707148

15. Sun, W., et al.: Biodegradable, sustainable hydrogel actuators with shape and stiffness morphing capabilities via embedded 3D printing. Under Rev. (2023). Pre-print embargoed until 6/1/2023

16. Baines, R.L., Booth, J.W., Fish, F.E., Kramer-Bottiglio, R.: Toward a bio-inspired variable-stiffness morphing limb for amphibious robot locomotion. In: IEEE International Conference on Soft Robotics, RoboSoft 2019, pp. 704–710 (2019)

17. Sun, W., Schaffer, S., Dai, K., Yao, L., Feinberg, A., Webster-Wood, V.: 3D printing hydrogel-based soft and biohybrid actuators: a mini-review on fabrication techniques, applications, and challenges. Front. Robot. AI (2021). https://doi.org/10.3389/frobt.2021.673533

18. Clause, A.G., Celestian, A.J., Pauly, G.B.: Plastic ingestion by freshwater turtles: a review and call to action. Sci. Rep. **11**(1), 5672 (2021). https://doi.org/10.1038/s41598-021-84846-x

19. Nelms, S.E., et al.: Plastic and marine turtles: a review and call for research. ICES J. Mar. Sci. **73**(2), 165–181 (2016). https://doi.org/10.1093/icesjms/fsv165

20. Meaza, I., Toyoda, J.H., Wise J.P.: Microplastics in sea turtles, marine mammals and humans: a one environmental health perspective. Front. Environ. Sci. **8** (2021). https://doi.org/10.3389/fenvs.2020.575614

21. Ryan, P.G.: Ingestion of plastics by marine organisms. In: Takada, H., Karapanagioti, H.K. (eds.) Hazardous Chemicals Associated with Plastics in the Marine Environment. THEC, vol. 78, pp. 235–266. Springer, Cham (2016). https://doi.org/10.1007/698_2016_21

22. Hecht, H., Srebnik, S.: Structural characterization of sodium alginate and calcium alginate. Biomacromol **17**(6), 2160–2167 (2016). https://doi.org/10.1021/acs.biomac.6b00378

23. Kheirikhah, M.M., Rabiee, S., Edalat, M.E.: A review of shape memory alloy actuators in robotics. In: Ruiz-del-Solar, J., Chown, E., Plöger, P.G. (eds.) RoboCup 2010: Robot Soccer World Cup XIV. LNCS, vol. 6556, pp. 206–217. Springer, Heidelberg (2011). https://doi.org/10.1007/978-3-642-20217-9_18

24. Lendlein, A., Gould, O.E.: Reprogrammable recovery and actuation behaviour of shape-memory polymers. Nat. Rev. Mater. **4**, 116–133 (2019)

25. Youn, J.-H., et al.: Dielectric elastomer actuator for soft robotics applications and challenges. Appl. Sci. **10**, 640 (2020)

26. Polygerinos, P., et al.: Soft robotics: review of fluid-driven intrinsically soft devices; manufacturing, sensing, control, and applications in human-robot interaction. Adv. Eng. Mater. **19**, 1700016 (2017)

27. Shin, S.R., et al.: Electrically driven microengineered bioinspired soft robots. Adv. Mater. **30**, 1704189 (2018)

28. Hinton, T.J., et al.: Three-dimensional printing of complex biological structures by freeform reversible embedding of suspended hydrogels. Sci Adv. **1**, 1–10 (2015). https://doi.org/10.1126/sciadv.1500758

29. Sun, W., Tashman, J.W., Shiwarski, D.J., Feinberg, A., Webster-Wood, V.: Long-fiber embedded hydrogel 3D printing for structural reinforcement. ACS Bio-Mater. Sci. Eng. **8**(1), 303–313 (2022)

30. Lee, A., et al.: 3D bioprinting of collagen to rebuild components of the human heart. Science **365**(6452), 482 (2019)

31. Mirdamadi, E., Tashman, J.W., Shiwarski, D.J., Palchesko, R.N., Feinberg, A.W.: Emergence of FRESH 3D printing as a platform for advanced tissue biofabrication. ACS Biomater. Sci. Eng. **5**, 010904 (2020)

32. Won, P., Ko, S.H., Majidi, C., W. Feinberg, A., Webster-Wood, V.: Biohybrid actuators for soft robotics: challenges in scaling up. Actuators **9**, 96 (2020). https://doi.org/10.3390/act9040096

33. Patterson, Z.J., Sabelhaus, A.P., Chin, K., Hellebrekers, T., Majidi, C.: An untethered brittle star-inspired soft robot for closed-loop underwater locomotion. In: 2020 IEEE/RSJ International Conference on Intelligent Robots and Systems, pp. 8758–8764 (2020)
34. Patel, D.K., et al.: Highly dynamic bistable soft actuator for reconfigurable multimodal soft robots. Adv. Mater. Technol. **8**(2), 2201259 (2023)

Wrinkle-Free Sewing with Robotics: The Future of Soft Material Manufacturing

E. Fontana[1], M. Farajtabar[1,2], G. Marchello[1(✉)], M. Lahoud[1], H. Abidi[1],
A. Meddahi[1], K. Baizid[1], M. D'Imperio[1], and F. Cannella[1]

[1] Istituto Italiano di Tecnologia, 16163 Genoa, Italy
{eleonora.fontana,gabriele.marchello,marcel.lahoud,
syed.abidi,amal.meddahi,khelifa.baizid,ferdinando.cannella}@iit.it
[2] Department of Mechanical and Manufacturing Engineering at University of
Calgary, Calgary, Alberta AB T2N 1N4, Canada
mohammad.farajtabar@ucalgary.ca

Abstract. Sewing flexible materials such as textiles and clothing can be challenging due to their tendency to wrinkle easily and their non-linear mechanical behaviour. Conventional methods in industrial plants are performed by workers and can be labour-intensive and time-consuming. Therefore, the interest in robotic solutions has grown in the last decade. In this paper, we propose a flexible and reliable robotic solution that can autonomously remove wrinkles from fabric. This method was designed as a part of a robotic cell capable of sewing together two different textiles, used in the manufacturing of cyclist garments. The robotic system employs two compliant soft fingers to stretch the fabric and a vision system to identify the wrinkles to flatten. The design of the fingers is bio-inspired, mimicking the adaptability and dexterity of biological systems, hence improving the gripping performance while reducing the risk of damage to the fabric. The developed vision system performs instance segmentation to identify the wrinkles on the fabric, and then identifies the best places to apply the gripper to flatten the tissue. This two-step process is iterated until wrinkles on the surface do not affect the final sewn product. Such a methodology is highly flexible and has no hard requirements, as the vision system requires only an RGB camera, and the fingers are 3D-printed, an affordable and common manufacturing process. Consequently, the system proposed in this paper can be easily employed in a wide variety of industrial scenarios, improving the productivity and the welfare of the workers.

Keywords: Soft materials manipulation · Autonomous sewing ·
Wrinkles flattening

1 Introduction

Wrinkles in nature can be observed in various forms, offering intriguing insights into the complexity and beauty of the natural world. They can manifest in dif-

---

E. Fontana and M. Farajtabar—These authors contributed equally.

© The Author(s) 2023
F. Meder et al. (Eds.): Living Machines 2023, LNAI 14157, pp. 142–155, 2023.
https://doi.org/10.1007/978-3-031-38857-6_11

ferent scales, from the microscopic to the macroscopic, and are often the result of intricate processes and interactions. In biological systems, wrinkles can be observed in various organisms and they play their own pivotal role. For example, in the human brain, wrinkles allow for a greater density of neurons and enhanced cognitive abilities; or wrinkles on leaves of plants help reduce water loss and increase light absorption. Unfortunately, wrinkles appearing on fabrics and textiles do not have the same beneficial effects and are actually unwanted consequence of manipulation. In fact, the sewing of these materials can be challenging, as they tend to wrinkle easily, affecting the overall appearance and durability of the final product. In order to overcome this issue, flattening wrinkles during the sewing process is crucial. Therefore, in recent years, the use of robotics technology in the sewing process has received increased attention as a potential solution to this problem. Conventionally, different methods are adopted to flatten wrinkles in flexible materials during the sewing process, including the use of steam or heat, mechanical pressure, and manual smoothing. However, these methods are often labour-intensive and time-consuming. Conversely, robotics technology offers a promising solution to this problem, as it can automate the process of flattening wrinkles in flexible materials [1,2]. The efforts to employ robots in the production line of soft materials like clothes started decades ago [3]. As one of the earliest attempts, Gershon investigated a parallel decomposition of robotic sewing tasks involving interaction with a dynamic environment [4]. They decomposed the sewing task into four concurrent processes including a vision-based contour tracker, tension sensing to measure the fabric tension, a feeding mechanism to pass the fabric under the needle, and the sewing machine. Vision-based techniques are amongst the most popular approaches adopted to identify wrinkles appearing on the surface of fabrics. Initially, such features have been identified by applying Gabor filters that label the abrupt changes in intensity at different orientations as wrinkles [5]. Similarly, Sun et al. initially developed an identification method employing the wavelet filters [6]. A few years later, Sun et al. modified their method by processing 2.5D depth maps [7]. Consequently, the height and width of the wrinkles were identified by geometrical means. It has been further refined to compute the surface curvatures in order to finally detect and quantify the wrinkles [8,9].

In fabric handling tasks performed by robots, the end-effector plays a crucial role as it directly interacts with the fabric. The design, structure, and material of the end-effector significantly impact the grasping performance. Hence, it was essential to develop suitable end-effectors for robots specifically tailored to fabric handling applications [10]. Various designs have been extensively studied, which can be grouped mainly into three classes according to the adopted grasping technology: physical adsorption, adhesion and mechanical clamping. The design of grippers belonging to the first category includes vacuum suction, or electrostatic adhesion, and they are widely employed to pick a single sheet of fabric from a stack [11,12]. Conversely, the adhesion-based grippers are characterised by the addition of an adhesive media, such as polyurethane [13,14]. Finally, mechanical clamping grippers heavily rely on the friction between the fingertip of the gripper and the fabric [15,16]. This solution allows for a high variety of designs, mainly made of rigid or soft materials [17–19].

In this paper, a fully automated approach to flatten wrinkles on fabrics manipulated in industrial plants is proposed. It requires an RGB camera, a hoop to hold the fabric in position, and a robotic arm equipped with a parallel jaw gripper with soft fingers. Grippers with compliant fingers are designed to mimic the adaptability and dexterity of biological systems, making them an ideal candidate for biomimetic and biohybrid applications [20]. The use of soft materials in gripper design has the potential to enhance gripping performance while reducing the risk of damage to delicate objects. The soft fingers of the gripper can conform to the shape of the object being grasped, thereby improving grip stability. In addition, the compliance of the fingers can be controlled to optimize the performance of the gripper for a given task. These features make soft grippers an attractive option for applications such as robotic surgery, prosthetics, and industrial automation [21]. It is possible to create more natural and intuitive interactions between machines and humans, by integrating soft grippers into biohybrid systems. Therefore, the development of grippers with soft fingers has significant potential to advance the field of biomimetics and biohybrid systems [22]. The design of the soft fingers adopted in this work has been thoroughly studied to achieve high-quality results. The shape of fingers, the material they are made of and the way they are employed take inspiration from human fingers. The design of this device is tailored to the task to fulfil and the elasticity of the tissue, as the fingers have to be soft enough to be compliant with the fabric, yet not too stiff to break or damage it. Having a bio-inspired design enables the development of the wrinkles removal technique, which requires first the identification of the wrinkles on the fabric. The step is implemented by performing instance segmentation on the images of the fabric constrained by the hoop. This step is necessary to prevent the gripper from dragging the fabric out of the working area and hence having no effects on the wrinkles. Subsequently, similarly to the manual process, the fingers are driven over the fabric, spread open and outward, consequently stretching the fabric. This routine has to be iteratively applied in order to flatten the whole surface, therefore the best strategy has to be derived. Consequently, it was implemented as a hierarchy scheduling algorithm that defines the ordered sequence of points on the fabric at which to iteratively apply the gripper and stretch the fabric. After every iteration, the wrinkles have to be identified, quantifying the number of pixels on the image corresponding to the wrinkles. The process is iterated until the amount of these labelled pixels drops below a threshold set after evaluating the corresponding manual operation. Such a methodology results to be highly flexible, as it is not dependent on any specific hardware characteristics and it just requires a set of images of the manipulated fabric. The presented work was developed as part of *SOFTMANBOT*, a cross-sectorial project funded by the European Union Horizon 2020 research and innovation program. The project aims to design a robotic cell to automate the manipulation and assembly of two textile components (*i.e.* a foam pad and an elastic fabric) used in the production of cycling garments at Decathlon industrial plant. One of the main problems to tackle by the project relies on the difficulties of handling flexible objects, which results in changes of shape, requiring continuous adjustments of the applied forces. Moreover, the manufacturing process of cyclist garments is further hindered by the layered structure of the soft materials under manipulation, having their elastic behaviours mutually affected [23].

The paper is divided into four sections: in Sect. 2 the proposed methodology and the developed software architecture are presented, Sect. 3 illustrates the results of the implementation and test of the experimental setup; and finally, a brief discussion of the results and suggestions for future works are presented in Sect. 4.

2   Methodology

The present section describes the developed methodology to tackle the flattening of the wrinkles on soft materials, with a focus on the design of the fingers and the software implementation. In particular, the methodology was tailored on a fabric composed of polyamid (PA) and elastane (EA).

2.1   Soft Compliant Fingers

An essential part of this work concerns the design of a gripper with soft fingers capable of manipulating the fabric, by stretching it and consequently flattening the wrinkles. Conventionally, the operator has to hold a portion of fabric and stretch it before feeding it to the sewing needle. A schematic representation of the conventional methodology is reported in Fig. 1.

However, such a methodology is highly complex to be replicated reliably by a robotic solution, as the operating space around the sewing needle is very limited. Hence, in order to develop a robotic solution, the wrinkles removal and the sewing processes had to be separated. The clamping mechanism holds firmly the fabric and the fingers are applied outside the hoop, preventing the creation of further wrinkles due to the spring-back effect of the fabric elasticity (Fig. 2).

Consequently, this design is highly suitable to be automated, having the robots flattening the wrinkles without any obstacle. The design of the fingers was inspired by the gestures usually performed by humans to stretch small surfaces. Two fingers of the same hands are applied across the wrinkle to flatten, and are then spread open (Fig. 3/0). Such a process was set at the base of the design of the soft fingers. Initially, multi-pegs fingers were evaluated, but unfortunately they required wide operational areas, and hence poorly replicated the human operation (Fig. 3/1–2). Consequently, the single-peg design was selected, and the performance of different models were evaluated, by varying the material in elasticity and softness (Fig. 3/3–6). The properties of the different designs are reported in Table 1.

The initial designs of the finger (Fig. 3.1 and Fig. 3.2) were comprised of four and two rigid fingers, which had to be installed in pairs on the parallel jaw of

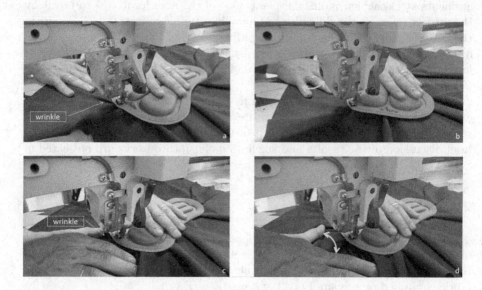

Fig. 1. Representation of the conventional wrinkle removal methodology. The operator grabs a small portion of the fabric, stretches it and feeds it under the sewing needle.

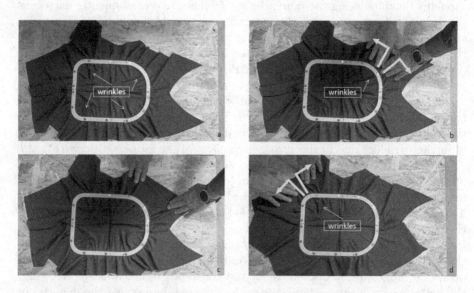

Fig. 2. Representation of the wrinkle removal solution set at the base of the automated process. A hoop is employed to hold tightly the fabric and the fingers are applied outside the hoop to stretch the fabric and thus removing the wrinkles.

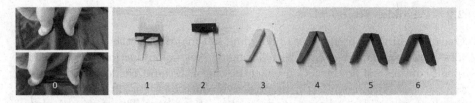

Fig. 3. Gallery of the different designs of the soft fingers. On the left and labelled with 0, the motion performed by the hand inspiring the design of the fingers. The fingers are ordered from left to right according to increasing softness.

Table 1. Technical properties of different designs of the soft fingers.

Fingers model	Material	Additional Info
1	Polylactic Acid (PLA)	–
2	Polylactic Acid (PLA)	–
3	Nylon 12	Selective Laser Sintering (SLS)
4	Tango Black Plus	Shore A 80
5	Tango Black Plus	Shore A 60
6	Tango Black Plus	Shore A 25

the gripper. The other models feature the same simplified design, consisting of a single prong, but with variable stiffness (Fig. 3.3, Fig. 3.4, Fig. 3.5, and Fig. 3.6). The first three prototypes were designed with a rigid structure to firmly pull the fabric, varying only the number of prongs and length, by controlling the force applied by the manipulator equipped with the gripper. Conversely, the last three finger designs were manufactured with the same material (*i.e.* Tango Black Plus), but with varying degrees of softness. This feature ensures deformation as soon as the fingers come into contact with rigid surfaces with the same applied force.

In order to test all the prototypes, the different designs were mounted on the wrist of the UR5 robot by using the compliance controller. This tool runs a ROS-controller that implements Forward Dynamics Compliance Control (FDCC) on a set of joints, *i.e.* a hybrid between force control and impedance control. This type of control is applied in the case the manipulator is in contact with rigid external surfaces, thus enabling the robot to follow surfaces, dampening the impacts and gaining collaborative behaviour. Such control technique was carefully selected as in the case of high normal force applied to the fabric, it may happen that a finger has to slide over the fabric. Conversely, an encompass coupling would grasp firmly the fabric and possibly damage the fabric in a similar scenario. Such a controller was kept constant and used to test the behaviour of the different designs of fingers, by evaluating their deformation, the grip on the fabric and the capability of removing wrinkles.

2.2   Wrinkles Removal

One of the direct consequences of handling soft materials is the creation of wrinkles. However, the presence of wrinkles hinders tissue production and lowers the quality of the final product. Consequently, one of the most challenging aspects of the automation of manufacturing processes concerns the ability to stretch fabrics, flatten wrinkles and prevent the creation of new ones. Therefore, a clamping mechanism consisting of two plastic circles housing magnets was designed and realised. The magnets ensure that the attractive force between the two hoops is strong enough to hold the fabric in place, without hindering its stretching. Moreover, the position of the hoops on the workbench is constrained on the workbench by a system of pull-up solenoids, which prevent any unwanted movements of the clamping mechanism and misalignments.

In this paper, we proposed an autonomous two-step iterative method to flatten the wrinkles, based on identification and stretching. The first stage is implemented through instance segmentation, a deep learning-based approach that can detect objects in images and demarcate their boundaries. The system employs Mask R-CNN [24] and has been trained to identify wrinkles and the centre of seams, $i.e.$, the cross-section of pieces of fabric (Fig. 4).

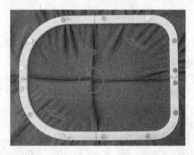

Fig. 4. The instance segmentation technique was trained to detect two classes of features: the wrinkles on the fabric highlighted by the arrows, and the center of the seams, circled in red. (Color figure online)

The developed approach was implemented via transfer learning, $i.e.$, by using the pre-trained set of weights derived from the COCO dataset. The deep network was then trained for 200 epochs on a set of 350 different images, which were recorded by using a greyscale camera sensor installed on the robotic gripper. This method not only maps the pixels corresponding to the wrinkles, but also produces in output the coordinates, the area, the dimension and the orientation of the different wrinkles. The results of the identification system are then set in input to the wrinkle removal algorithm. Unfortunately, it may happen to detect wrinkles outside the region of interest (ROI) limited by the hoops of the clamping mechanism, and that hence do not affect the quality of the outcome. Therefore, a filtering process is first applied: the hoop clamping the fabric is identified in the raw image, its contour is extracted and used to filter out the wrinkles identified within the ROI (Fig. 5).

Fig. 5. Schematic representation of the filtering process applied to detect any possible wrinkle outside the ROI, delimited by the hoops of the clamping mechanism. The wrinkles identified out of the hoop are subsequently filtered out.

After filtering the wrinkles, the ROI is split into eight radial sub-areas (Fig. 6), and the density of the wrinkles in each of them is computed. These values are fed in input to a dynamic hierarchy scheduling algorithm that assigns the highest priority to the areas containing the highest density value. Then, a specific point out of the clamping mechanism is assigned to each sub-area, thus defining the gripper application points.

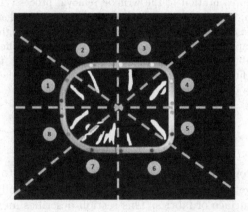

Fig. 6. Schematic representation of the algorithm designed to derive the strategy to best flatten the wrinkles. The ROI limited by the hoop is split into eight radial sub-areas in order to compute the density of the wrinkles in each of them.

The gripper equipped with the two soft fingers is then applied to the predefined grasping point, corresponding to the sub-area with the highest priority assigned by the dynamic hierarchy scheduling algorithm. Consequently, the gripper gently pulls and stretches the fabric outward, avoiding any damage to the fabric (Fig. 7).

The presence of the clamping mechanism guarantees that the fabric does not return to its original state after the manipulation is performed and the wrinkles are therefore removed correctly. The two-step methodology is iterated until the number of pixels labelling the wrinkles drops below a threshold, finely identified by analysing the conventional manually manufactured fabric. This value was selected not null, since small wrinkles are crucial for the high quality of the final product, as they prevent the garments from stretching too much and then breaking open when worn and deformed.

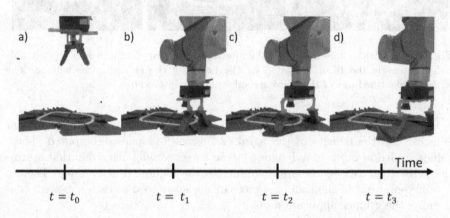

Fig. 7. Graphical representation of the wrinkle removal process. The gripper is first moved over the cloth, in order to take an image for the wrinkle identification ($t = t_0$). Once the wrinkles are identified, the density is estimated for the eight different regions, and the sub-area to apply the gripper is selected. The gripper is then lowered exerting pressure over the fabric in the pre-defined grasping point ($t = t_1$). Therefore, the gripper spreads the fingers open creating tension ($t = t_2$) and the end-effector pulls the fabric outward in order to flatten the wrinkles ($t = t_3$).

3   Results

In this paper, we proposed an innovative design of soft fingers to be equipped on a robotic gripper, together with the methodology to automatically flatten wrinkles appearing on the surface of fabrics. This section describes an evaluation of the design process and the results obtained from the wrinkle removal technique.

3.1   Soft Compliant Fingers

Six different 3D-printed soft finger prototypes were designed and manufactured, differing in material, length, thickness and elasticity (Fig. 3). Various tissue manipulation routines were then performed to verify which of the prototypes was the most suitable for the application presented in this paper. The same robotic routine described in Fig. 7 was then performed with all the different finger types, to assess their behaviour. It became clear that prototypes with a high degree of deformation were more likely to hold the tissue, preventing it from slipping and escaping the grip. The deformation of the various prototypes responding to the same manipulator process is shown in Fig. 8.

Fig. 8. Gallery of the deformation experienced by the different designs of the soft fingers. Each prototype was mounted on the gripper and used to perform the same robotic routine. The softer the fingers, the higher the observed deformation.

Regarding elasticity, the level of fabric damage was considered to be of primary importance. By increasing the force applied by the manipulator it was deduced that the softer the gripper fingers, the less damage the fabric suffered. In fact, testing the first three prototypes with greater stiffness showed that, especially after prolonged use, marks of manipulation and stretching remained evident on the fabric. Conversely, fingers that were too soft were not able to pull the fabric tight enough to remove creases cleanly. Consequently, the finger prototype realised with Tango Black Plus material with Shore A 60 was found to be the best candidate. Its unique features make it highly appropriate for fabric manipulation, as it offers a suitable level of flexibility without being overly rigid and hence damaging the fabric to stretch.

3.2 Wrinkles Removal

The identification of the best model of soft fingers enabled the tests of the wrinkle removal methodology. At the beginning of every iteration, the camera mounted on the wrist of the manipulator was positioned over the fabric to take an image and process it to detect the wrinkles and center of the stitches. The results of the identification process are depicted in Fig. 9.

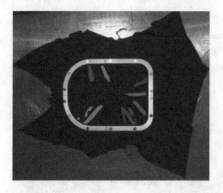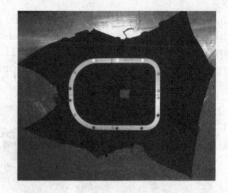

Fig. 9. Schematic representation of the results of the detection. On the left, the wrinkles detected within the hoop delimiting the ROI are highlighted. On the right, the centre of the stitches is detected.

The density of wrinkles identified in the ROI was thus computed for each sub-area. These values were then fed in input to the dynamic hierarchy scheduling algorithm, which prioritizes the selection of the sub-area to stretch based on the associated density values. Thus, the region with the highest density was selected for the first iteration, during which the soft fingers gripper stretches the fabric outward in order to mitigate the wrinkles in that area. After each iteration, the camera captured a new image to assess the density of wrinkles within the ROI once again, enabling the following step of the wrinkle removal process. This task is performed until the number of pixels labelling the wrinkles drops below a pre-determined threshold. In Fig. 10, it is possible to appreciate the results of five consecutive manipulation routines. Each pair of identification-manipulation tasks takes about 13 s, with the software run on a workstation with Intel Core i7 11700K at 3.60 GHz, 23 GB of RAM, and an NVidia QUADRO RTX A4000 of 16 GB as GPU.

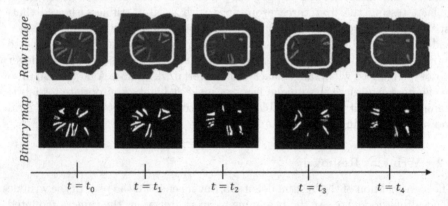

Fig. 10. Schematic representation of the results of the wrinkles removal module. The top row depicts the original images, with a coloured mask highlighting the wrinkles. The bottom row highlights only the pixels assigned to the wrinkles. The different time points are obtained after applying the manipulation routine.

It clearly emerges how the number of total wrinkles, and thus the quantity in each of the eight sub-regions, progressively decreases over the course of the iterations, without thereby affecting the quality of the final stitched product.

A video showing the results of here discussed automated tasks is available at https://youtu.be/c72TGHsyfOo.

4   Conclusions

Automating the industrial production of clothes is still a task far from being achieved, due to the complexity of robotic manipulation of soft objects, as fabric fold-over, wrinkles and uncertainty in localization are crucial issues, intrinsic to the material nonlinear mechanical behaviour. However, in this paper, we proposed a robotic system capable of removing wrinkles on the surface of fabrics. This system is based on the thorough design of soft compliant fingers equipped on a robotic gripper, and the wrinkle removal algorithm. The latter was conceived as an iterative methodology, alternating between the identification of wrinkles using a simple RGB camera and the robotic routine of stretching the fabric and then flattening the wrinkles.

A wide variety of soft fingers was evaluated, varying the design, the number of prongs, their size and stiffness. Rigid fingers were proven to have a high slip and to damage and scratch the fabric in the case of prolonged use. Conversely, highly flexible materials ensure a high adhesion between the fingers and the surface, allowing the fabric to be stretched tightly. Consequently, the designed soft fingers played a key role in the wrinkle removal methodology. The system thus developed is characterised by great flexibility, as it does not depend on any specific hardware requirements. Furthermore, the developed vision system can be applied to a wide variety of scenarios, as it has to be trained on a gallery of images of the tissue to be manipulated. The soft finger material was carefully adjusted to the elasticity of the fabric. However, different materials can be investigated to produce fingers that can best stretch other types of fabric. In addition, the fingers were 3D printed, a common and cost-effective manufacturing process that facilitates the design of the best finger implementation. Lastly, the developed pieces of software are computationally efficient, hence do not require powerful workstations to run.

The robotic solution presented in this paper was proven to be highly effective, flexible and easy to deploy. Therefore, it may be implemented in different scenarios, contributing to the automation of manufacturing processes that are labour-intensive and require a high level of accuracy. Consequently, the adoption of such autonomous systems can contribute to increased productivity, while improving the welfare of the workers.

Acknowledgements. This work is funded via European Union's Horizon 2020 Research and Innovation project 'SOFTMANBOT' (under grant agreement no 869855). Special thanks to Decathlon Italia for their help and support, in particular to Pierpaolo Rotondi and Alberto Mereu.

References

1. Jimenez, P., Torras, C.: Perception of cloth in assistive robotic manipulation tasks. Nat. Comput. **19**, 409–431 (2020)
2. Lin, X., Wang, Y., Huang, Z., Held, D.: Learning visible connectivity dynamics for cloth smoothing. In: Conference on Robot Learning, 256–266 (2022)
3. Nocentini, O., Kim, J., Bashir, Z.M., Cavallo, F.: Learning-based control approaches for service robots on cloth manipulation and dressing assistance: a comprehensive review. J. NeuroEng. Rehabil. **19**(1), 1–25 (2022)
4. Gershon, D.: Parallel process decomposition of a dynamic manipulation task: robotic sewing. IEEE Trans. Robot. Autom. **6**(3), 357–367 (1990)
5. Yamazaki, K., Inaba, M.: A cloth detection method based on image wrinkle feature for daily assistive robots. In: Proceedings of the IAPR Conference on Machine Vision Applications (IAPR MVA 2009), Keio University, Yokohama, Japan, pp. 366–369 (2009)
6. Sun, J., Yao, M., Xu, B., Bel, P.: Fabric wrinkle characterization and classification using modified wavelet coefficients and support-vector-machine classifiers. Text. Res. J. **81**(9), 902–913 (2011)
7. Sun, L., Aragon-Camarasa, G., Rogers, S., Siebert, J.: Accurate garment surface analysis using an active stereo robot head with application to dual-arm flattening. In: 2015 IEEE International Conference on Robotics and Automation (ICRA), pp. 185–192 (2015)
8. Sun, L., Camarasa, G.A., Khan, A., Siebert, P.: A precise method for cloth configuration parsing applied to single-arm flattening. Int. J. Adv. Robot. Syst. **13**(2), 70 (2016)
9. Sun, L., Aragon-Camarasa, G., Rogers, S., Siebert, J.: Autonomous clothes manipulation using a hierarchical vision architecture. IEEE Access **6**, 76646–76662 (2018)
10. Su, J., Wang, N., Zhang, F.: A design of bionic soft gripper for automatic fabric grasping in apparel manufacturing. Text. Res. J. **93**(7–8), 1587–1601 (2023)
11. Feng, W.Q., Hu, Y.L., Li, X.R., et al.: Robot end effector based on electrostatic adsorption for manipulating garment fabrics. Text. Res. J. **92**, 691–705 (2022)
12. Digumarti, K.M., Cacucciolo, V., Shea, H., et al.: Dexterous textile manipulation using electroadhesive fingers. In: The IEEE/RSJ International Conference on Intelligent Robots and Systems (IROS) Electronic Network, vol. 27, pp. 6104–6109 (2021)
13. Zhang, T., Liang, T., Yue, X., Sameoto, D.: Integration of thermoresponsive velcro-like adhesive for soft robotic grasping of fabrics or smooth surfaces. In: 2nd IEEE International Conference on Soft Robotics (RoboSoft), pp. 120–125 (2019)
14. Ku, S., Myeong, J., Kim, H.Y., Park, Y.L.: Delicate fabric handling using a soft robotic gripper with embedded microneedles. IEEE Robot. Autom. Lett. **5**(3), 4852–4858 (2020)
15. Su, J., Shen, J., Lyu, J.: Arrangement of soft fingers for automatic grasping of fabric pieces of garment. Text. Res. J. **92**(1–2), 143–159 (2022)
16. Su, J., Shen, J., Zhang, F.: Grasping model of fabric cut pieces for robotic soft fingers. Text. Res. J. **92**(13–14), 2223–2238 (2022)
17. Ku, S., Myeong, J., et al.: Delicate fabric handling using a soft robotic gripper with embedded microneedles". IEEE Robot. Autom. Lett. **5**, 4852–4858 (2020)
18. Su, J., Wang, N., Zhang, F.: A design of bionic soft gripper for automatic fabric grasping in apparel manufacturing. Text. Res. J. **93**, 1587–1601 (2023)

19. Teeple, C.B., Werfel, J., Wood, R.J.: Multi-dimensional compliance of soft grippers enables gentle interaction with thin, flexible objects. In: ICRA (2022)
20. Majidi, C.: Soft robotics: a perspective-current trends and prospects for the future. Soft Robot. **1**(1), 5–11 (2014)
21. Ciuti, G., Rateni, G.: Design and development of a soft robotic gripper for manipulation in minimally invasive surgery: a proof of concept. Meccanica **50**, 2855–2863 (2015)
22. Laschi, C., Mazzolai, B., Cianchetti, M.: Soft robotics: technologies and systems pushing the boundaries of robot abilities. Sci. Robot. **1**(1) (2016)
23. Lahoud, M., et al.: Robotic manipulation system for multi-layer fabric stitching. In: International Design Engineering Technical Conferences and Computers and Information in Engineering Conference, vol. 85437 (2021)
24. He, K., Gkioxari, G., Dollár, P., Girshick, R.: Mask R-CNN. In: Proceedings of the IEEE International Conference on Computer Vision, pp. 2961–2969 (2017)

Bioinspired Soft Actuator Based on Photothermal Expansion of Biodegradable Polymers

Luca Cecchini[1,2(✉)] , Stefano Mariani[1(✉)] , Nicola M. Pugno[2,3(✉)] ,
and Barbara Mazzolai[1(✉)]

[1] Bioinspired Soft Robotics Laboratory, Istituto Italiano di Tecnologia,
Via Morego 30, 16163 Genova, Italy
{luca.cecchini,stefano.mariani,barbara.mazzolai}@iit.it
[2] Laboratory for Bioinspired, Bionic, Nano, Meta Materials and Mechanics,
Department of Civil, Environmental and Mechanical Engineering,
University di Trento, Via Mesiano 77, 38123 Trento, Italy
nicola.pugno@unitn.it
[3] School of Engineering and Materials Science, Queen Mary University of London, Mile End
Road, London 1 4NS, UK

Abstract. The combined effects of thermo-sensitive and photothermal materials present novel actuation strategies for wireless application and the use of sustainable energy sources, such as the sunlight. To understand the operating features of multifunctional materials, bioinspired multi-layer actuators represent a simple solution as a testing platform. Here, we report the fabrication of a bilayer photothermal and biodegradable bending actuator, based on thermal expansion of polycaprolactone-lignin blend, 3D printed on cellulose acetate substrate. When the actuator is irradiated with 300 mW/cm^2 of simulated solar irradiance, it shows a change in curvature of 25.34%, with a bending moment of $\sim$80.2 μN $\cdot$ m and with a characteristic actuation time of 30 s. Moreover, the photothermal blend shows a conversion efficiency of 13.5%. Due to the photothermal and biodegradability properties, the actuator could be used as a battery-free tool for different tasks, in a scenario where no contamination of the environment is required.

Keywords: Actuator · Photothermal · Biodegradable · Bioinspiration · Soft robotics

1 Introduction

Soft actuators in the robotics field have recently attracted attention for their low-cost in fabrication, adaptability, and deformability [1, 2]. Compared with their rigid counterparts, soft robotic devices show a range of notable improvements in safe interaction,

The original version of this chapter was previously published without open access. A correction to this chapter is available at
https://doi.org/10.1007/978-3-031-38857-6_33

Supplementary Information The online version contains supplementary material available at https://doi.org/10.1007/978-3-031-38857-6_12.

F. Meder et al. (Eds.): Living Machines 2023, LNAI 14157, pp. 156–164, 2023.
https://doi.org/10.1007/978-3-031-38857-6_12

complex motions through dynamic shape change and resilience to unstructured environments [3, 4]. Inspired by nature, it is also possible to define a new paradigm in which a robot should be able to evolve selectively in a specific scenario, adapting its morphology according to environmental stimuli and biodegrade at the end of its life cycle [5]. Moreover, an autonomous system should be able to embody chemical or electrical energy sources directly within its materials and structures, rather than requiring separate battery packs [6].

In this framework, bioinspiration represents a role model in the design of multifunctional tools to emulate the highly sophisticated and interconnected systems of natural organisms, such as animals and plants. For instance, the Geraniaceae seeds (e.g., Pelargonium and Erodium genus') promote their germination exploiting the deformable properties of the bilayer structures, in which bending and twisting occur through exploiting the expansion of an active tissue coupled with an inert material [7, 8].

Multi-layer actuators represent a simple solution as a testing platform for multifunctional materials. Several actuators for soft robotics are demonstrated in literature, such as grasping, lifting, locomotion and soil-exploration [8–10]. The inclusion of photothermal properties in thermo-sensitive structures permits to power the actuator from the environmental illumination as a wireless system, without requiring any battery onboard.

Inspired by the bilayer and tissue structure of Geraniaceae seeds, we present a bending photothermal actuator, composed by biodegradable polymers: Polycaprolactone-PluronicF127-Lignin (PPL) blend [11–13] printed using Fused Deposition Modeling (FDM) on a cellulose acetate (CA) substrate [14]. We combined the thermal expansion of polycaprolactone (PCL), with the photothermal properties of lignin [15], to induce a local expansion of tissues and, consequently, a local photothermal strain. Pluronic F127 is mainly used as surfactant to better homogenize the blend and to increase the printability properties. The actuator shows a reversible bending behavior when it is subjected to 300 mW/cm^2 of simulated solar irradiance, in which the change in curvature is $\Delta\kappa = 24.3 \pm 1.3$ m^{-1} (25.34% of relative variation). The bending actuator provides a static moment of M = 80.2 ± 5.3 μN $\cdot$ m.

2 Materials and Methods

2.1 Materials and Chemicals

PCL (Number average molar mass 80 kg/mol) was purchased from ThermoFisher Scientific (Massachusetts, USA). Alkaline lignin was purchased from Tokyo Chemical Industry (Japan). Pluronic F127 and acetic acid (CH$_3$COOH, 99.8%) were purchased from Merck Millipore (Massachusetts, USA). CA 25 μm thick film was purchased from Goodfellow GmbH (Germany).

2.2 Methods

We proceed to describe chronologically the procedures used for the realization and characterization of the photothermal actuator. The methods are presented in the order they were performed.

Preparation of PPL Blend. The PPL blend was prepared using solvent casting method, mixing 6.5 g of PCL, 0.5 g of Pluronic F127, 0.5 g or 2 g of alkaline lignin (7% w/w and 17% w/w with respect the total weight of the blend) with 10 ml of acetic acid. The solution was continuously stirred at 200rpm with a temperature of T = 80 °C for 48 h. Next, the solvent was removed via evaporation, keeping the temperature constant at T = 150 °C for 60 min.

4D Printing of the Bending Actuator. We extruded the solid and homogeneous blend with FDM printer (3DBioplotter, EnvisionTEC) using the following printing conditions: nozzle internal diameter 0.3 mm, temperature 150 °C, needle offset 0.24 mm, pressure 6 bar, speed 22 mm/s, pre-flow 0.05 s, post-flow −0.05 s. Hence, we fabricated the actuator depositing aligned fibers of PPL with distance between strands 1.5 mm on a CA film. Finally, the CA-PPL sheet is cut using CO_2 laser cutter (Beamo, FLUX) with relative power 20 (defined by Beam Studio GUI) and cutting speed 8 mm/s.

Plasma Activation. To promote adhesion between the two polymers, we activated the CA surface using air plasma (Tergeo, Pie Scientific). The plasma time was set to 60 s, power setpoint to 75 W, gas setpoint 30 sccm (cm^3/min) and base vacuum to 0.50 mbar.

Photothermal Characterization. FDM printed PPL samples (1 cm × 1 cm × 300 μm) were irradiated under solar spectrum SciSun 300 Sun Simulator (Sciencetech, Canada) at different powers (100–300 mW/cm^2). Samples were suspended in air using Teflon tweezers to avoid any thermal diffusion in the sample holder. Power densities of the simulated sunlight were verified using an RS PRO solar energy meter (RS, UK). The variation of temperature due to photothermal effect was carried out with an IR thermal camera (A700, FLIR Systems, USA). The experiments were performed in ambient air (T = 25 °C, 30% RH).

Curvature Evaluation. The actuator was exposed to 300 mW/cm^2 of simulated solar irradiance (SciSun 300 Sun Simulator Sciencetech, Canada), while simultaneously video recording the variation of radius (Logitech Brio Stream, Logitech). To ensure complete thermalstability, the samples were exposed for 5 min. To evaluate the variation of curvature, all the video-data are post-processed using ImageJ software [16]. The experiments were performed in ambient air (T = 25 °C, 30% RH measured using RS PRO RS-325A Digital Hygrometer). The evaluation of curvature variation due to hygroscopic effect was performed in climatic test chamber (CTC256, Memmert GmbH), fixing the temperature T = 30 °C and changing RH from 30% to 90%.

Static Moment Test. For the moment evaluation, force is measured with 10 g sensitive load cell (Futek LSB200, USA), calibrated using samples with a weight force equal to 0.59 mN. Solar irradiance was selected using the Sun Simulator SciSun 300 (Sciencetech, Canada). The measurement consists in putting in contact with a suspended load cell the CA-PPL bilayer sample (1 cm × 2 cm, width and length, respectively) and subsequently the actuator is irradiated cyclically (period 15 min with 50% duty cycle) from 0 to 300 mW/cm^2. The experiments were performed in ambient air (T = 25 °C, 30% RH measured using RS PRO RS-325A Digital Hygrometer. According to the experimental setup, the moment was evaluated assuming that $M = 1/2\ F \cdot L$.

Photography. Photographs were taken using a digital camera (D7100, Nikon, Japan).

Data Analysis. The normality of data distribution was tested with the Shapiro–Wilk test; normally-distributed data were analyzed with ANOVA followed by LSD post hoc with Bonferroni correction and expressed as average ± standard error. Non-normally distributed data were analyzed with the Kruskal–Wallis test followed by pairwise Wilcox post hoc test with Holm correction and expressed as median ±95% confidence interval. Each experiment has been performed in triplicate (n = 3), if not differently indicated. The data were analyzed and plotted in Origin (Version 2019b, 32bit).

3 Results

3.1 Evaluation of the Photothermal Conversion Efficiency of PPL Blend

We first verified the photothermal properties of PPL blend, comparing the photothermal conversion efficiency of two different samples dispersing in the PCL polymer matrix respectively 7% and 17% w/w of alkaline lignin.

We tested the robustness of the effect changing irradiance with 12.5 min illumination cycle with 50% of duty cycle. Figure 1 shows an increase of temperature due to photothermal effect, when the specimens were subjected to 100 mW/cm^2 of simulated solar irradiance. Figure 1A shows that PCL did not present any photothermal properties, while PPL samples with 7% and 17% w/w of lignin reach in both cases a temperature peak of $T_M = 42.5 \pm 0.7\,°C$ in $\tau = 87.6 \pm 2.5$ s.

Since the samples with different amount of lignin did not show a statistically significant variation (paired t-test p* > 0.05), we selected the PPL solution with lower dispersion grade, because an increase of lignin dispersant in PCL polymeric matrix will make the blend more brittle and it will reduce the processability and the printability [17].

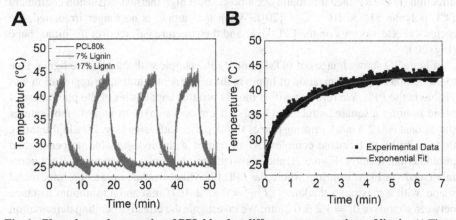

Fig. 1. Photothermal properties of PPL blend at different concentrations of lignin. A) Time behavior of photothermal effect (12.5 min illumination cycle with 50% of duty cycle) under 100 mW/cm^2 of simulated solar irradiance input. B) Exponential fit of the temperature variation ($R^2 = 0.98$) used for the evaluation of the photothermal conversion efficiency in 7% w/w lignin sample.

Consider the thermal kinetic of a solid body that exchanges heat with the environmental air in natural convection regime, it was possible to evaluate the photothermal conversion efficiency (η) [18, 19] from the exponential fit of the temperature dynamics (Fig. 1B):

$$T(t) = T_0 + \Delta T\left(1 - e^{-t/\tau}\right)$$

$$\eta = \frac{\Delta T}{\tau} \frac{\rho c_p h}{J_0\left(1 - 10^{-\alpha}\right)}.$$

where T_0 is the initial environmental temperature, ΔT is the temperature variation from the initial to the saturation value, τ is the characteristic rising time, ρ the density, c_p the specific heat capacity, h the thickness of the sample, J_0 the simulated solar irradiance, α the absorption coefficient.

To evaluate η, we assumed that the impinging light is completely absorbed by the PPL ($\alpha = +\infty$) and we consider in first approximation that the density and the specific heat capacity are mainly governed by PCL properties ($\rho = 1120$ kg m^{-3}, $c_p = 2.2$ J g^{-1} K^{-1} [20]). Hence, knowing that the sample thickness is h $= 0.30 \pm 0.01$ mm, T, $T_0 = 25$ °C, $\Delta T = 17.5$ °C, $\tau = 87.6$ s, the experimental PCE is equal to $\eta = 13.5\%$.

3.2 Fabrication of the Photothermal Actuator

We proceed with the manufacturing of the bending actuator, FDM printing on a plasma activated cellulose acetate substrate the PPL blend (Fig. 2A). When the actuator is irradiated, the photothermal element will determine a local increase of temperature in the actuator. Subsequently, the PPL layer will anisotropic expand along the printing direction (Fig. 2B) since it is mainly composed by a high thermal expansion coefficient PCL polymer (16×10^{-5} °C^{-1} [20]). When the sample is no longer irradiated, the reciprocal effect occurs on the PPL layer and the structure will recover its initial shape (Fig. 2C).

Figure 2D shows images of FDM printed PPL sample with 7% alkaline lignin. Due to the complete homogenization of lignin in the acetic acid solution, no aggregation was visible in the PPL. We further verified the 3D printing capabilities of the photothermal blend printing a squared structure (1 cm × 1 cm × 3 mm) with honeycomb features (hexagonal side 2.5 mm). Printing planes shows perfect adhesion (Fig. 2D), highlighting the possibility to fabricate complex 3D structures with biodegradable properties and photothermal features. Figure 2E shows two different samples of bending soft actuators fabricated via FDM printing, where the PPL fiber-like structures present a trapezoidal shape, with a maximum thickness of $h_F = 0.37 \pm 0.07$ mm and a minimum distance between strands of $d_F = 1.2 \pm 0.2$mm. We investigate the effective bending deformation of the structure due to photothermal expansion of the PPL.

3.3 Kinematics and Static of the Photothermal Actuator

In Fig. 3 is reported the curvature of the actuator exposed to 300 mW/cm^2 of simulated solar irradiance. The initial curvature in the idle condition was equal to $\kappa_0 = 83.3 \pm 2.3$ m^{-1} (Fig. 3A). After the illumination, the actuator reaches the thermal equilibrium in 30 ± 2.5 s with a curvature $\kappa_1 = 59.0 \pm 3.4$ m^{-1} (Fig. 3B). Coming back to the

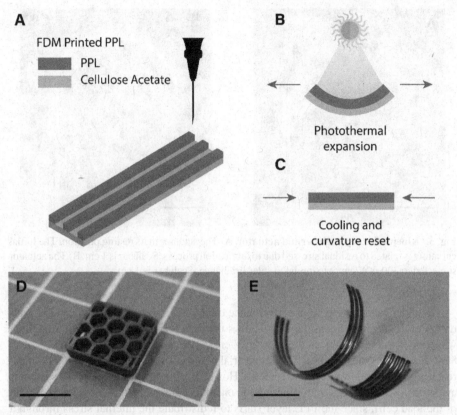

Fig. 2. Sketch and working principle of the photothermal bending actuator. A) Representation of the fabrication process to realize the PPL-CA actuator. In particular, the PPL blend is extruded on a CA substrate with aligned tracks. B) Working principle of the actuator during solar illumination. When the sample is irradiated, there will be an increase of temperature in the whole actuator. Then, the PPL region will anisotropic expand due to the thermal expansion properties of PCL. C) Working principle of the actuator without illumination. Due to the decrease of temperature, the PPL layer shows anisotropic contraction, recovering its initial curvature. D) 3D printed honeycomb sample. Scalebar is 1 cm. E) Two different samples of soft actuators. Scalebar is 2 cm.

idle state, the curvature reaches the initial value $\kappa_2 = 83.3 \pm 1.6$ m^{-1} in 30.0 ± 2.5 s (tested on n = 5 different samples). Therefore, the actuator shows a reversible bending behavior mediated by the photothermal effect, showing 25.34% in change of curvature. Considering that cellulose acetate is a hygroscopic material [21], we verified the effective hygroscopic behavior of the actuator measuring the variation of curvature when it is subjected to variation of relative humidity from 30% to 90%. The actuator showed 1% of curvature variation, value that is one order of magnitude lower with respect to the curvature variation induced by the photothermal effect. Hence, we have observed that, in a first approximation, the actuator is predominantly powered by the thermal expansion mechanism.

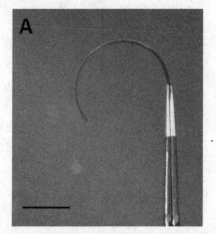
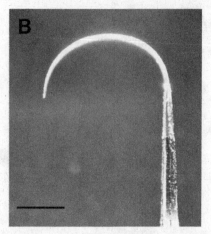

Fig. 3. Kinematics of photothermal actuator. A) The actuator in its resting position. The initial curvature is related to residual stressed due to fabrication process. Scalebar is 1 cm. B) The actuator subjected to 300 mW/cm^2 of simulated solar irradiance. Scalebar is 1 cm.

To understand the effective performance of CA-PPL, we performed the static evaluation of the beam moment. Figure 4 shows the time behavior of the bending moment when the actuator is subjected to 300 mW/cm^2. The moment reaches a peak of $M = 80.2 \pm 5.3$ μN · m (tested on 5 different trials). As in the curvature case, the moment reaches its saturation value in 30.0 ± 2.5 s. However, the main limitation of the system is evident after 5 cycles of 1 min illumination under an external load (constrained reaction of the load cell), since the PPL layer starts to redistribute the internal stress through a

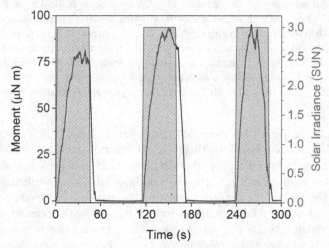

Fig. 4. Moment of the photothermal actuator as function of time exposed to 300 mW/cm^2 of simulated solar irradiance.

deformation of the entire body, due to the low melting point of the PCL component (T_M = 60 °C [20]) in the PPL blend.

4 Conclusions

We presented a photothermal bilayer composed by biodegradable polymers, for the creation of a sunlight-driven bending actuator. Thanks to the synergic combination of photothermal properties of lignin and the thermal expansion of polycaprolactone, a bending actuator can be manufactured through versatile 3D printing, involving commonly available materials in the market (e.g., PCL and Pluronic F127) and in nature (e.g., cellulose-based and lignin). Moreover, we verified that the photothermal PPL blend can be 3D printed via FDM method. The actuator shows reversible deformation, featuring a 30 ± 2.5 s response time, associated with a ~25% change in curvature and a moment of 80.2 ± 5.3 $\mu N \cdot m$, when samples are exposed to 300 mW/cm² irradiation. However, the requirement of high solar irradiance implies that when the actuator is subjected to an external load the PPL blend begins to deform plastically after 5 illumination cycles, due to the melting of the polymer. To overcome this problem, a numerical analysis on the thermo-mechanical effects will be necessary to design properly a reliable actuator for environmental applications (i.e., grasping, lifting, locomotion and soil-exploration). A biodegradable and photothermal actuator offers an original and concrete possibility to operate in different scenarios where no contamination of the environment is required, with systems driven by wireless and renewable energy sources.

Acknowledgement. This work has received funding from the European Union Horizon 2020 research and innovation program under grant agreement No 101017940 (I-Seed).

References

1. Rus, D., Tolley, M.: Design, fabrication and control of soft robots. Nature **521**, 467–475 (2015)
2. Wang, J., Chortos, A.: Control strategies for soft robot systems. Adv. Intell. Syst. **4**, 2100165 (2022)
3. Lee, C., et al.: Soft robot review. Int. J. Control Autom. Syst. **15**(1), 3–15 (2016). https://doi.org/10.1007/s12555-016-0462-3
4. Laschi, C., Mazzolai, B., Cianchetti, M.: Soft robotics: technologies and systems pushing the boundaries of robot abilities. Sci. Robot. **1**, eaah3690 (2016)
5. Mazzolai, B., Laschi, C.: A vision for future bioinspired and biohybrid robots. Sci. Robot. **5**, 38 (2020)
6. Aubin, C.A., Gorissen, B., Milana, E., et al.: Towards enduring autonomous robots via embodied energy. Nature **602**, 393–402 (2022)
7. Mazzolai, B., et al.: Morphological computation in plant seeds for a new generation of self-burial and flying soft robots. Front. Robot. AI **26**(8), 797556 (2021)
8. Cecchini, L., Mariani, S., Ronzan, M., Mondini, A., Pugno, N.M., Mazzolai, B.: 4D printing of humidity-driven seed inspired soft robots. Adv. Sci. **10**, e2205146 (2023)

9. Shin, B., et al.: Hygrobot: a self-locomotive ratcheted actuator powered by environmental humidity, Sci. Robot. **3**, eaar2629 (2018)

10. Yoon, C.: Advances in biomimetic stimuli responsive soft grippers. Nano Converg. **6**(1), 20 (2019)

11. Hartmann, F., Baumgartner, M., Kaltenbrunner, M.: Becoming sustainable, the new frontier in soft robotics. Adv. Mater. **33**, 2004413 (2021)

12. Diniz, I.M.A., et al.: Pluronic F-127 hydrogel as a promising scaffold for encapsulation of dental-derived mesenchymal stem cells. J. Mater. Sci. Mater. Med. **26**, 153 (2015). https://doi.org/10.1007/s10856-015-5493-4

13. Wang, H.-M., Yuan, T.-Q., Song, G.-Y., Sun, R.-C.: Green Chem. **23**, 3790–3817 (2021)

14. Erdal, N.B., Hakkarainen, M.: Degradation of cellulose derivatives in laboratory, man-made, and natural environments. Biomacromol **23**(7), 2713–2729 (2022)

15. Li, J., et al.: Lignin: a sustainable photothermal block for smart elastomers. Green Chem. **24**, 823–836 (2022)

16. https://imagej.nih.gov/ij/

17. Tian, J., Yang, Y., Song, J.: Grafting polycaprolactone onto alkaline lignin for improved compatibility and processability. Int. J. Biol. Macromol. **141**, 919–926 (2019). ISSN 0141–8130. https://doi.org/10.1016/j.ijbiomac.2019.09.055

18. Breitenborn, H., et al.: Quantifying the photothermal conversion efficiency of plasmonic nanoparticles by means of terahertz radiation. APL Photon. **4**, 126106 (2019)

19. Mariani, S., Cecchini, L., et al.: A bioinspired plasmonic nanocomposite actuator sunlight-driven by a photothermal-hygroscopic effect for sustainable soft robotics. Adv. Mater. Technol., 2202166 (2023)

20. Wurm, A., Merzlyakov, M., Schick, C.: reversible melting during crystallization of polymers studied by temperature modulated techniques (TMDSC, TMDMA). J. Therm. Anal. Calorim. **60**, 807–820 (2000)

21. Khoshtinat, S., Carvelli, V., Marano, C.: Characterization and modeling the hygroscopic behavior of cellulose acetate membranes. Cellulose **29**, 2175–2186 (2022)

Anisotropic Actuation in Salty Agarose Gel Actuators

Pedram Tootoonchian[ID], Levent Bahçeci[ID], and Bilge Baytekin[(✉)][ID]

Chemistry Department and UNAM, Bilkent University, 06800 Ankara, Turkey
b-baytekin@fen.bilkent.edu.tr

Abstract. When hydrogels that can reversibly dehydrate/rehydrate are physically combined with a constant water supply, the cycles can be controlled by on/off states and the positions of an external light source. The shrinking upon dehydration upon illumination causes bending towards the light source, and rehydration in the light-off state restores the initial shape. This simple material feedback mechanism mimics the self-regulating heliotropism (sun tracking) and nyctinasty (leaf opening) movements of plants. In this work, we show the effect of some common salts on the bending behavior of actuators entirely made of hydrogel. The 'salty' actuators exhibit different motion kinetics regarding the unique chemical characteristics of each ion. We display that this chemistry of ions also enables us to program the kinetics in a single actuator using the differences in evaporation/diffusion rate of water in the salty gels. This programmability of the motion in a hydrogel actuator with the inclusion of salts can be used to achieve complex behavior observed in living organisms straightforwardly.

Keywords: Plant Robots · Hydrogels · Material Feedback · Soft Robots

1 Introduction

Autonomy and self-regulation are the two essential features of the living [1–5]. Being inspired by living plants' motions directed by various external stimuli – such as temperature, light, pH, and touch – soft roboticists have developed many soft material analogs capable of mimicking these motions [6–9]. Among these, stimuli-responsive hydrogels are particularly interesting since they provide an aqueous environment similar to the living systems by which external stimuli can be effectively transmitted and used [10–16]. The previous works of our group displayed two forms of self-regulating artificial plant robots that could mimic living plants' nyctinasty and heliotropism movements under the illumination of light. In the first work [17], shape-memory nitinol springs were used as the thermo-responsive feedback material. The plant robots were formed using a 3D printed stem, and these springs arranged in unique geometries followed the light source without an external power source or programming. The light-harvesting efficiencies of the solar panels placed as the 'leaves' was enhanced by 30–110% through this self-regulated phototropic motion, Fig. 1a. However, the design was made of hard materials, limiting further soft robotics applications. In the second work [18], we designed a soft,

© The Author(s), under exclusive license to Springer Nature Switzerland AG 2023
F. Meder et al. (Eds.): Living Machines 2023, LNAI 14157, pp. 165–172, 2023.
https://doi.org/10.1007/978-3-031-38857-6_13

self-regulating plant-like robot. The body was made of cellulose paper, and agarose hydrogels were used as the actuators. Based on the volume change of the gel network of the gel upon dehydration/hydration of the gel, a phototropic and nyctinastic behavior could be obtained, similar to that of the previous robot, as shown in Fig. 1b. Although the robots were composed of only paper and agarose gel, the kinetics of the motion could be controlled by the amount of the gel, its position on the paper, and gel concentration.

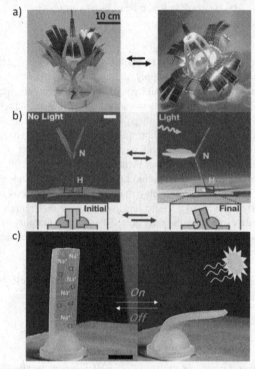

Fig. 1. Three different designs for the artificial heliotropic plant robot. a) An optomechanical feedback-based robot actuated by nitinol springs [17]. b) Paper-bodied plant robot tracking light based on dehydration and shrinking of the gel facing toward the IR light source (gels are applied on both sides of the two junctions) [18]. c) A gel actuator in which the effect of different ions can be studied. The scale bar for b and c represents 1 cm. (This work)

In the work we present here, we show an additional level of complexity by adding the gels some common salts by mixing the salts in the pre-gel solution. Upon gelation, the salts remain trapped in the gel network. The 'salty' gels have significantly different dehydration/hydration rates than the 'unsalted' ones. The type of added ions controls the magnitude of this difference and its direction (faster/slower cycles). In addition to their type, the concentration of the ions can lead to significant changes in the bending rate (Fig. 1c). These parameters can be used to achieve sequential and anisotropic bending actuators and complex-design plant robots.

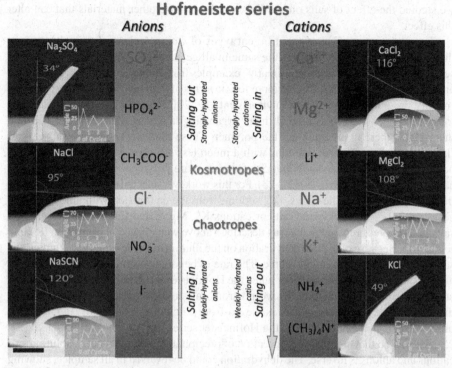

Fig. 2. The effect of salts on the gel bending pattern. In anions, weakly-hydrated ions bend faster compared to strongly-hydrated ones. On the other hand, cations show an opposite behavior where gels doped with strongly-hydrated ions bend faster. The yellow inset graphs illustrate the dehydration/rehydration cycles for which the bending angle remained constant upon dehydration in each consecutive cycle. The photos were taken after 30 min of light illumination. Scale bar = 1 cm.

2 Results and Discussion

The preparation of the salty gel actuators is a straightforward process. A weighed amount of salt is dissolved in water to obtain a 0.10–0.30 M solution. Then, a proper amount of agarose is added to the solution (to make a 5.0 w/w% gel) and is heated to 90 °C until complete dissolution. After that, the pre-gel solution is transferred to a 3D-printed mold and is left to gel for 30 min.

In a typical setup for displaying actuation, we fixed the gels in a metastable vertical position in a container. The gel was kept hydrated by keeping the bottom of the gel immersed in water. Exposure to a lamp (IR, 250 W; General Electric) affected the gel actuation. When the light was on, the water evaporation rate was faster than the gel rehydration; therefore, the gel bent towards the light. When the light was off, the gel was rehydrated and swelled back to its initial position. The bending was captured by a camera throughout the whole process. The distance of the light from the gel was optimized (30 cm away from the gel) so that the gel did not deform plastically. Incorporating additives such as silver nanoparticles could enhance the thermal sensitivity of the gels. However, since we studied the effect of salts on bending, we did not use other materials that can alter this effect.

To compare the effect of the different types of cations/anions of the salt, we kept the total ionic strength of the ions the same in all gel samples. We used the Hofmeister series of ions to select a few representative examples from numerous possible cations and anions. This series shows the behavior of ions in terms of their help to solubilize polymers (mainly proteins) in an aqueous environment [19, 20]. According to this series, some ions keep water molecules around them, organizing layers of water as a shell around themselves, thereby precipitating the polymer. These ions are known as 'salting out' (kosmotropes). In contrast, the ions with a much less affinity for water molecules and help solubilize the solute (polymer) by forming more polymer-solvent interaction are called 'salting in' (chaotropes) [21–23]. For this work, we selected the anions and cations that are 'extremes' in the series, i.e., sodium from the cation side with anions SCN^-, Cl^-, and SO_4^{2-}, and chloride salts of cations K^+, Mg^{2+}, and Ca^{2+} were chosen. The salty gel samples prepared in the way described above were placed in front of an IR lamp for 30 min. Because of the fast dehydration on the illuminated side of the gel samples, the samples bent towards the light source. The rate of bending was recorded as the bending angle vs. time. The gel bends faster when the Hofmeister series of the cations and anions are considered for the anions (as we go from sulfate to thiocyanate). In contrast, in the cations, the gel bends slower as we go from calcium to potassium (Fig. 2). This observation is in accordance with the Hofmeister series reported by Mazzini et al. [24, 25], who stated that the 'forward' direction of precipitating polymers out of solution – of cations and anions is inverse. The dehydration could be reversed in all samples, showing that the salty gels can be used as actuators, controlled by light and ion type.

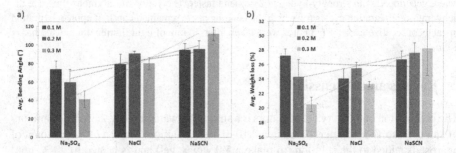

Fig. 3. The effect of the concentration of ions on the bending of the gel. a) The higher the concentration, the higher the effect on bending. b) Average weight loss of gel having different concentrations of ions due to evaporation of water.

In addition, the concentration of ions added to the gel affects the solute-solvent interaction. As the concentration of ions increases, the observed effect on the bending increases. We studied the ion concentrations between 0.1 M, below which the ion effect was less significant, and 0.3 M, above which the presence of the salts starts to prevent agarose gelation. The average bending angle upon 30 min of illumination (Fig. 3a) and the weight loss of the gel upon illumination (how much water is evaporated) were recorded (Fig. 3b). This data helped us to design anisotropic-bending actuators in the next step.

3   Application

Patterning stimuli-responsive gels is an approach to getting complex architectures, actuators, and robots made up of these gels [26–30]. Many successful approaches exist to fast-responding complex architectures of such gels. An exciting example is a plant-inspired hydrogel-elastomer actuator that mimics the anisotropic actuation of the growth stages of cacti [31]. However, most include bilayer structures that are harder to manufacture and can delaminate, micron-sized thickness requiring microfabrication that is harder to scale up, or doping with transition metals [32–34]. Therefore, we predicted that our easy-to-prepare, cheap, scalable salty gels could be exploited to make more complex architectures that work on the principle of different bending rates. We prepared gels with different salts 'added to different parts,' as shown in Fig. 4, and illuminated them from the top for 30 min.

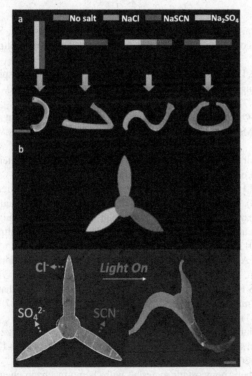

Fig. 4. a) Anisotropic bending of agarose hydrogel leading to different 3D shapes – the gels contain sodium salts of different anions at various locations. b) Anisotropic bending of a three-legged actuator. The thickness of the actuator is 2.5 mm. The three-legged actuator was manufactured through stepwise pouring/gelation of the salty gels in the compartments of the respective 3D mold. Scale bar = 1 cm.

4   Conclusion and Perspective

The phototropic motion of the plants is controlled by the difference in the reversible swelling and shrinkage of cells on the opposite side of the shoot of a plant. This swelling/shrinking results from the turgor pressure signaled by the hormone Auxin. Plants use transpiration to regulate the osmotic flow necessary to maintain and control the turgor pressure. In our artificial plants, we see how different salts (solutes) can regulate 'transpiration' (evaporation) by interacting with the gel polymer.

The use of stimuli-responsive hydrogels for soft robotics applications is rapidly expanding [35–38]. The swelling/deswelling of hydrogel actuators can be combined with other materials, such as elastomers, to obtain anisotropic bending and shape change or tropic motion similar to those observed in nature [31]. Our study shows the ions which are essential in plant metabolism and motion [39, 40] can be used to regulate the actuation of hydrogels. We, therefore, envisage the pioneering work using salts for sensing and actuation in soft robots [41, 42] can be expanded using the chemistry of ions.

References

1. Keplinger, C., Sun, J., Foo, C.C., Rothemund, P., Whitesides, G.M., Suo, Z.: Stretchable, transparent ionic conductors. Science **341**(6149), 984–988 (2013). https://doi.org/10.1126/science.1240228
2. Zheng, J., Xiao, P., Le, X., Lu, W., Théato, P., Ma, C., et al.: Mimosa inspired bilayer hydrogel actuator functioning in multi-environments. J. Mater. Chem. C. **6**, 1320–1327 (2018). https://doi.org/10.1039/C7TC04879C
3. Tang, J., Yin, Q., Qiao, Y., Wang, T.: Shape morphing of hydrogels in alternating magnetic field. ACS Appl. Mater. Interfaces **11**(23), 21194–21200 (2019). https://doi.org/10.1021/acsami.9b05742
4. Sun, J.Y., Keplinger, C., Whitesides, G.M., Suo, Z.: Ionic skin. Adv. Mater. **26**(45), 7608–7614 (2014). https://doi.org/10.1002/adma.201403441
5. Kim, C.C., Lee, H.H., Oh, K.H., Sun, J.Y.: Highly stretchable, transparent ionic touch panel. Science **353**(6300), 682–687 (2016). https://doi.org/10.1126/science.aaf8810
6. Sadeghi, A., Tonazzini, A., Popova, L., Mazzolai, B.: A novel growing device inspired by plant root soil penetration behaviors. PLoS ONE **9**(2), e90139 (2014). https://doi.org/10.1371/journal.pone.0090139
7. Meder, F., et al.: A perspective on plant robotics: from bioinspiration to hybrid systems. Bioinspir. Biomim. **18** (015006) (2023). https://doi.org/10.1088/1748-3190/aca198
8. Meder, F., Babu, S.P.M., Mazzolai, B.: A plant tendril-like soft robot that grasps and anchors by exploiting its material arrangement. IEEE Robot. Autom. Lett. **7**, 5191–5197 (2022). https://doi.org/10.1109/LRA.2022.3153713
9. Cecchini, L., Mariani, S., Ronzan, M., Mondini, A., Pugno, N.M., Mazzolai, B.: 4D printing of humidity-driven seed inspired soft robots. Adv. Sci. **10**(2205146), 1–12 (2023). https://doi.org/10.1002/advs.202205146
10. He, X., et al.: Synthetic homeostatic materials with chemo-mechano-chemical self-regulation. Nature **487**(7406), 214–218 (2012). https://doi.org/10.1038/nature11223
11. Wang, E., Desai, M.S., Lee, S.W.: Light-controlled graphene-elastin composite hydrogel actuators. Nano Lett. **13**(6), 2826–2830 (2013). https://doi.org/10.1021/nl401088b
12. Shastri, A., McGregor, L.M., Liu, Y., Harris, V., Nan, H., Mujica, M., et al.: An aptamer-functionalized chemomechanically modulated biomolecule catch-and-release system. Nat. Chem. **7**(5), 447–454 (2015). https://doi.org/10.1038/nchem.2203

13. Qin, M., et al.: Bioinspired hydrogel interferometer for adaptive coloration and chemical sensing. Adv. Mater. **30** (1800468) (2018). https://doi.org/10.1002/adma.201800468

14. Zhao, Y., Xuan, C., Qian, X., Alsaid, Y., Hua, M., et al.: Soft phototactic swimmer based on self-sustained hydrogel oscillator. Sci. Robot. **4**(33), 1–11 (2019). https://doi.org/10.1126/scirobotics.aax7112

15. Lee, Y., Song, W.J., Sun, J.Y.: Hydrogel soft robotics. Mater. Today Phys. **15**, 100258 (2020). https://doi.org/10.1016/j.mtphys.2020.100258

16. Wang, T., Huang, J., Yang, Y., Zhang, E., Sun, W., Tong, Z.: Bioinspired smart actuator based on graphene oxide-polymer hybrid hydrogels. ACS Appl. Mater. Interfaces **7**(42), 23423–23430 (2015). https://doi.org/10.1021/acsami.5b08248

17. Baytekin, B., Cezan, S.D., Baytekin, H.T., Grzybowski, B.A.: Artificial heliotropism and nyctinasty based on optomechanical feedback and no electronics. Soft Robot. **5**(1), 93–98 (2018). https://doi.org/10.1089/soro.2017.0020

18. Cezan, S.D., Baytekin, H.T., Baytekin, B.: Self-regulating plant robots: bioinspired heliotropism and nyctinasty. Soft Robot. **7**(4), 444–450 (2020). https://doi.org/10.1089/soro.2019.0036

19. Hofmeister, F.: Zur Lehre von der Wirkung der Salze. Archiv f. experiment. Pathol. u. Pharmakol **25**, 1–30 (1888). https://doi.org/10.1007/BF01838161

20. Kunz, W., Henle, J., Ninham, B.W.: "Zur Lehre von Der Wirkung Der Salze" (about the Science of the Effect of Salts): Franz Hofmeister's Historical Papers. Curr. Opin. Colloid Interface Sci. **9**(1–2), 19–37 (2004). https://doi.org/10.1016/j.cocis.2004.05.005

21. Kang, B., Tang, H., Zhao, Z., Song, S.: Hofmeister series: insights of ion specificity from amphiphilic assembly and interface property. ACS Omega **5**(12), 6229–6239 (2020). https://doi.org/10.1021/acsomega.0c00237

22. Okur, H.I., et al.: Beyond the Hofmeister series: ion-specific effects on proteins and their biological functions. J. Phys. Chem. B **121**(9), 1997–2014 (2017). https://doi.org/10.1021/acs.jpcb.6b10797

23. Rogers, B.A., Okur, H.I., Yan, C., Yang, T., Heyda, J., Cremer, P.S.: Weakly hydrated anions bind to polymers but not monomers in aqueous solutions. Nat. Chem. **14**(1), 40–45 (2022). https://doi.org/10.1038/s41557-021-00805-z

24. Mazzini, V., Craig, V.S.J.: What is the fundamental ion-specific series for anions and cations? Ion specificity in standard partial molar volumes of electrolytes and electrostriction in water and non-aqueous solvents. Chem. Sci. **8**(10), 7052–7065 (2017). https://doi.org/10.1039/c7sc02691a

25. Mazzini, V., Craig, V.S.J.: Correction: what is the fundamental ion-specific series for anions and cations? Ion specificity in standard partial molar volumes of electrolytes and electrostriction in water and non-aqueous solvents (Chemical Science (2017) **8** (7052–7065). 10.1039/C7. Chem. Sci. **10**(11), 3430–3433 (2019). https://doi.org/10.1039/C9SC90050K

26. Jeon, S.J., Hauser, A.W., Hayward, R.C.: Shape-morphing materials from stimuli-responsive hydrogel hybrids. Acc. Chem. Res. **50**(2), 161–169 (2017). https://doi.org/10.1021/acs.accounts.6b00570

27. Chen, Y., et al.: Light-driven bimorph soft actuators: design, fabrication, and properties. Mater. Horizons **8**(3), 728–757 (2021). https://doi.org/10.1039/d0mh01406k

28. van Manen, T., Janbaz, S., Zadpoor, A.A.: Programming the shape-shifting of flat soft matter. Mater. Today **21**(2), 144–163 (2018). https://doi.org/10.1016/j.mattod.2017.08.026

29. Xue, P., Bisoyi, H.K., Chen, Y., Zeng, H., Yang, J., Yang, X., et al.: Near-infrared light-driven shape-morphing of programmable anisotropic hydrogels enabled by mxene nanosheets. Angew. Chemie - Int. Ed. **60**(7), 3390–3396 (2021). https://doi.org/10.1002/anie.202014533

30. Zhang, X., Xue, P., Yang, X., Valenzuela, C., Chen, Y., Lv, P., et al.: Near-infrared light-driven shape-programmable hydrogel actuators loaded with metal-organic frameworks. ACS Appl. Mater. Interfaces **14**(9), 11834–11841 (2022). https://doi.org/10.1021/acsami.1c24702

31. Bastola, A.K., Rodriguez, N., Behl, M., Soffiatti, P., Rowe, N.P., Lendlein, A.: Cactus-inspired design principles for soft robotics based on 3D printed hydrogel-elastomer systems. Mater. Des. **202**, 109515 (2021). https://doi.org/10.1016/j.matdes.2021.109515

32. Qin, H., Zhang, T., Li, N., Cong, H.P., Yu, S.H.: Anisotropic and self-healing hydrogels with multi-responsive actuating capability. Nat. Commun. **10**(1), 1–11 (2019). https://doi.org/10.1038/s41467-019-10243-8

33. Zhu, Q.L., Du, C., Dai, Y., Daab, M., Matejdes, M., Breu, J., et al.: Light-steered locomotion of muscle-like hydrogel by self-coordinated shape change and friction modulation. Nat. Commun. **11**(1), 1–11 (2020). https://doi.org/10.1038/s41467-020-18801-1

34. Erol, O., Pantula, A., Liu, W., Gracias, D.H.: Transformer hydrogels: a review. Adv. Mater. Technol. **4**(4), 1–27 (2019). https://doi.org/10.1002/admt.201900043

35. Chen, M., Wang, Y., Zhang, J., Peng, Y., Li, S., Han, D., et al.: Stimuli-responsive DNA-based hydrogels for biosensing applications. J. Nanobiotechnology **20**(40), 1–22 (2022). https://doi.org/10.1186/s12951-022-01242-x

36. Wang, H., Wang, X., Lai, K., Yan, J.: Stimulus-responsive DNA hydrogel biosensors for food safety detection. Biosensors **13**(3), 320 (2023). https://doi.org/10.3390/bios13030320

37. Shi, Q., Liu, H., Tang, D., Li, Y., Li, X.: Bioactuators based on stimulus-responsive hydrogels and their emerging biomedical applications. NPG Asia Mater. **11**(64) (2019). https://doi.org/10.1038/s41427-019-0165-3

38. Liu, S., Li, X., Han, L.: Recent developments in stimuli-responsive hydrogels for biomedical applications. Biosurface Biotribology **8**(4), 290–306 (2022). https://doi.org/10.1049/bsb2.12050

39. DeFalco, T.A., Bender, K.W., Snedden, W.A.: Breaking the code: Ca^{2+} sensors in plant signaling. Biochem. J. **425**(1), 27–40 (2010). https://doi.org/10.1042/BJ20091147

40. Ho, C.H., Lin, S.H., Hu, H.C., Tsay, Y.F.: CHL1 functions as a nitrate sensor in plants. Cell **138**(6), 1184–1194 (2009). https://doi.org/10.1016/j.cell.2009.07.004

41. Li, H., Li, L., Zhang, H., Wei, J., Xu, Z., Chen, T.: Cell differentiation-inspired, salt-induced multifunctional gels for an intelligent soft robot with an artificial reflex arc. ACS Appl. Mater. Interfaces **15**(4), 5910–5920 (2023). https://doi.org/10.1021/acsami.2c20172

42. Wang, X., Li, X., Wang, B., Chen, J., Zhang, L., Zhang, K., et al.: Preparation of salt-induced ultra-stretchable nanocellulose composite hydrogel for self-powered sensors. Nanomaterials **13**(1), 157 (2023). https://doi.org/10.3390/nano13010157

Soft Electroactive Suction Cup with Dielectric Elastomer Actuators for Soft Robotics

Armin Jamali[1,2](✉) [ID], Dushyant Bhagwan Mishra[1,2] [ID],
Prathyusha Sriperumbuduri[1,2] [ID], Robert Knoerlein[1], Frank Goldschmidtboeing[1,2] [ID],
and Peter Woias[1,2] [ID]

[1] Laboratory for the Design of Microsystems, Department of Microsystems Engineering
(IMTEK), University of Freiburg, Freiburg im Breisgau, Germany
`armin.jamali@imtek.uni-freiburg.de`
[2] Cluster of Excellence livMatS, University of Freiburg, Freiburg im Breisgau, Germany

Abstract. Soft grippers, made of flexible and deformable materials, are used to
grasp and manipulate objects and represent a rapidly growing area in the field of
soft robotics. Inspired by nature, biomimetic soft grippers are designed to mimic
the gripping and manipulation capabilities of biological organisms, such as octopus
tentacles or human fingers. These grippers use soft and flexible materials that can
conform to the shape of objects and provide gentle, yet strong gripping forces. For
the design and actuation of such a gripper, dielectric elastomer actuators (DEAs)
are suitable candidates, as they are made of thin elastomer layers sandwiched
between compliant electrode layers. They are, hence, at the same time elastic,
deformable and capable of performing actuation. In this paper, we present the
development of an electroactive suction cup made with DEAs. We explain the
novel concept and design of the soft backbone and its necessity for the suction
mechanism. We present a demonstrator and characterize the deflection of the
membrane under different voltages.

Keywords: Dielectric Elastomer Actuators · Soft Robotics · Soft Grippers ·
Artificial Muscles · Electroactive Polymers · Biomimetic · Suction Cup

1 Introduction

Soft robotics is an emerging field of robotics focusing mainly on designing and building
robots from soft and flexible materials, in contrast to the traditional rigid materials used
in conventional robots. These soft robots are highly adaptable and can change shape
to perform various tasks, making them ideal for applications in different fields such as
healthcare, manufacturing, and exploration [1]. Biomimetic soft robotics draws inspiration from nature. For example, plant-inspired robotics mainly focus on the functional
principles of plants such as *Dionaea muscipula* (Venus flytrap) [2]. This field, however, is
not limited to the realm of plants. Soft-bodied animals such as octopuses and worms are
highly adaptable and can move through complex environments with ease. By mimicking
these physical properties and behaviors of these organisms, soft robotics researchers are

F. Meder et al. (Eds.): Living Machines 2023, LNAI 14157, pp. 173–183, 2023.
https://doi.org/10.1007/978-3-031-38857-6_14

creating robots that can move and manipulate objects in ways that traditional robots cannot [3]. In recent years, advances in materials science and manufacturing techniques have enabled researchers to create sophisticated soft robots driven by different actuation mechanisms that can perform tasks such as grasping delicate objects in a safe manner, similar to humans or animals [4, 5].

Among the actuation mechanisms, we can mention electrically responsive, magnetically responsive, thermally responsive, pressure-driven, and explosive actuators [5–7]. Electroactive polymers (EAPs) are a diverse group of such polymeric material systems that change in dimensions (size or shape) when stimulated by an electric field. They have been investigated widely as potential candidates for soft robotic grippers and artificial muscles [8]. A sub-group of EAPs are Dielectric Elastomer Actuators (DEAs), as used in this research work. DEAs are made up of a thin layer of elastomer sandwiched between two compliant electrodes. When a voltage is applied to the electrodes, the elastomer layer becomes polarized and high electrical field leads to an electrostatic force that compresses the elastomer layer in the direction of the electric field and, hence, expands it in a planar direction (Fig. 1). The direction of the actuation is shown in Fig. 1b. DEAs have several advantages over traditional actuators, while they are very flexible, lightweight, show high energy density, have self-sensing characteristics, and are capable of generating large forces. In addition, they are compatible with traditional electronic devices and can be integrated with electric drivers [6, 9]. Therefore, they are studied and used for a wide range of applications, including soft robotics, haptic feedback devices [10], and artificial muscles [11].

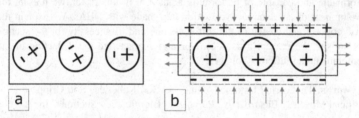

Fig. 1. Schematic of the actuation mechanism of DEAs; a) the actuator not connected to the voltage source, and b) the elastomer in an electric field

In this work, we focused on DEA grippers for soft robots, inspired by the suction mechanism of the suction cups. Octopus suckers are a remarkable biological adaptation found in the tentacles of octopuses and other cephalopods. These structures are used for grasping and manipulating objects. Each octopus arm is covered with hundreds of suckers, which are circular, muscular structures surrounded by a flexible rim called the infundibulum. When the infundibulum is pressed against an object, the circular muscle contracts, creating a low-pressure region within the sucker. This low pressure causes the suction cup to adhere to the object, creating a strong grip that allows the octopus to manipulate the object with precision [12]. In this suction mechanism, maintaining the seal between the sucker rim and the substrate (the object to be grasped onto) is crucial, since the suction cup should form an enclosed cavity with the substrate. The actuation of the suction cup is basically happening through a volume increase of the sucker, thus reducing the pressure inside the cavity. The negative pressure generated inside the suction cup results in an attachment of the sucker to the object, as long as the seal does not break [13].

There are several studies on the development of suction cups with different mechanisms. Among them, it is noteworthy to mention adhesive patches developed by Baik et al. in 2017 and 2018 [14, 15] and also the skin-adhesive wearable electronics with octopus-inspired micro suckers by Chun et al., 2019 [16]. Another great research is presented by Follador et al., 2014, in which they produced DEA hydraulic assisted suction cups with a dielectric elastomer actuation mechanism mimicking the *vulgaris* octopi's suckers. [17]. For actuation, they used common DEAs, which are made of acrylic elastomers (including VHB 4910) [6]. Although the VHB tapes show relatively large deformations, they generally need a rigid frame to hold their form and to keep the pre-stretch of the elastomer which is necessary for the actuation. Nevertheless, the need for an external rigid frame may in a way or another question the softness of the actuator.

The main focus of our research is to find a way to design and fabricate DEA suction cups with no need of external hard frames. As a solution for omitting the rigid frame, in our previous work, we presented a bending finger actuator made of DEAs with 5 active layers and backbones made of polymethyl methacrylate (PMMA) sheets embedded in the topmost passive layer. For that, we demonstrated how the implementation of the backbone caused the actuator to bend. We developed two bending fingers facing each other, lifting and holding objects [18].

Here, we present the proof of concept for a fully soft suction cup, by implementing a compliant ring made of soft silicone as the flexible backbone without using an external rigid frame for actuation. The idea of implementing a flexible ring made of PDMS to create an off-plane deflection was also presented by Jiaqi et al., 2020 [19], however, in their work, the off-plane deformation of the membrane does not make a pressure change under the actuator. They used the soft DEA ring to generate pressure in the liquid dielectric which causes the membrane, filled with the liquid dielectric, to buckle up and give a haptic feedback to the user. In our design, the suction ring is attached to a planar DEA and forms a DEA membrane. The deflection of the membrane results in a change in the volume inside the suction ring, which changes the pressure inside the suction cup.

2 Design and Fabrication

2.1 Design

The design of the suction cup is the combination of the ideas of a planar actuator and a ring-shaped backbone (Fig. 2). A simple planar actuator expands in the surface plane direction when voltage is applied. However, when a ring is attached to one surface of the actuator, the surface inside the ring cannot expand in-plane. Therefore, the trapped area deflects out-of-plane to fulfill both the increase of area and also the mechanical restriction inside the ring. As a result, the combination of the planar DEA and the ring forms a suction cup, in which the internal pressure is changed via the out-of-plane movement of the DEA. As depicted in Fig. 2, this deflection is either convex or concave, or irregular. The convex and concave deflection is favorable for the suction mechanism, as it results in a straightforward increase or decrease of the volume. In the convex mode, the volume of the cavity -the volume enclosed between the rings, substrate, and the membrane- increases, resulting in a pressure drop. In the concave actuation mode, the suction cup is first activated, and then it touches the substrate. After forming a seal with the substrate, the voltage is set back to zero. The elastic energy of the membrane pushes the membrane back to the relaxed state, causing the enclosed volume to increase and the pressure to decrease accordingly.

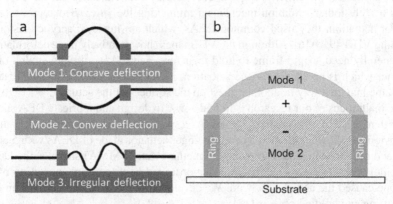

Fig. 2. The out-of-plane deflection of the membrane; a) possible deflection modes, and b) illustration of the volume change of the suction cup

The aforementioned design was simulated with COMSOL Multiphysics® to verify the expected deflection as a function of the design parameters, as shown in Fig. 3. In this 2D axis-symmetric model, the suction cup with four active layers is connected to 6 kV. The dimensions of the actuator, including the thickness of each layer is as shown in Fig. 4. Furthermore, the mechanical parameters of the used materials are mentioned in the Fabrication section (Table 1), where we discuss the material selection. In Fig. 3a, the cross-section of the actuator is depicted under no voltage. The volume under the actuator is shown with the label "cavity", and the vertical rectangle is the cross-section of the ring. The slight deformation of the membrane is due to the weight of the membrane. In this design, gravity gives a convex preform which directs the actuation in mode 2 (Fig. 2). Figure 3b presents the out-of-plane deformation of the membrane under voltage.

2.2 Fabrication

For the fabrication of the suction cup, we followed the procedure explained in our last work to make an active planar actuator [20]. The deposition of the dielectric layer was done with a spin-coating machine, while the electrode layers, with an approximate thickness of 5 μm were made of carbon powder, dry-brushed directly onto the elastomer. As depicted in Fig. 4, the yellow layers are the active silicone elastomers sandwiched between the carbon black electrodes. The passive silicone layers, depicted in green, cover and protect the first and the last electrode layers. The ring, made of ECOFLEX™₀₀₋₅₀ (for ease of referencing, we call the material Ecoflex50) and depicted in blue, is attached

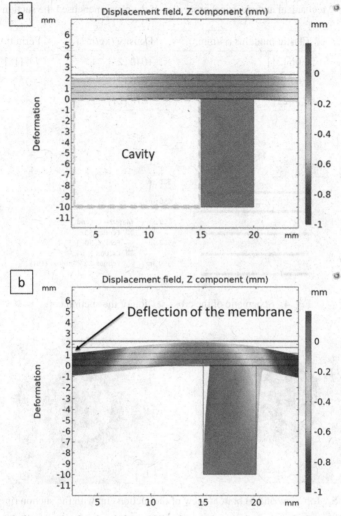

Fig. 3. Simulation results for the deformation of a suction cup; a) no voltage condition, and b) actuation with 6 kV.

to the actuator by another passive layer made of Ecoflex30, shown in green. The application of silicones from the same family allows the bonding of the suction ring to the DEA. Ecoflex50 is 1.67 times stiffer than Ecoflex10T (mixture of Ecoflex10 and SILI-CONE THINNER™) [21]. Although Ecoflex50 is a soft and compliant material, it plays the role of the stiff backbone for the Ecoflex10. In other words, the Ecoflex 50, restricts the planar deformation of the Ecoflex10, however, it does not make the actuator rigid.

The fabricated suction cup is shown in Fig. 5. The black area is where the electrode layers are embedded, and the two extended black parts are designed for the contact to the voltage source.

Table 1. Mechanical and electrical properties of the elastomers used the suction cup.

Material	Elastic modulus (N/mm^2)	Density (kg/m^3)	Permittivity
Ecoflex10T	0.06 [21]	1040 [21]	4.4 [18]
Ecoflex30	0.07 [21]	1070 [21]	-
Ecoflex50	0.1 [21]	1070 [21]	-

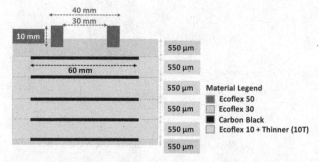

Fig. 4. Schematic of the cross-section of the suction cup

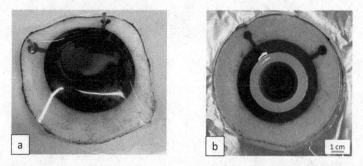

Fig. 5. Top-view and b) bottom-view of the suction cup with the suction ring

3   Measurements

For the test and characterization of the suction cup, a dedicated measurement setup was developed. The high voltage is provided by a voltage amplifier (*10HVA24-P1, ULTRAVOLT*), which is powered by a power supply. A data acquisition module (National Instrument, NI-DAQ) serves as an interface between the computer and the measurement setup. The commands for the voltage signal are sent from the computer to the NI-DAQ, which sends the input control-voltage to the high-voltage amplifier. Then, the feedback-voltage from the amplifier is sent back to the NI-DAQ module and from there to the computer. In a graphical user interface, the command signals are programmed for controlling the voltage over time, and the feedback signals from the amplifier are plotted in real-time. Based on the real-time plots, the breakdown-voltage of the actuator is detected.

For characterizing the bending curvature of the activated suction cup, a laser sensor (*scanCONTROL 3002–25/BL, Micro-Epsilon*) was implemented. For future work, the bending curvature can be used for measuring the change in volume. In Fig. 6 the signal flow of the measurement setup is explained.

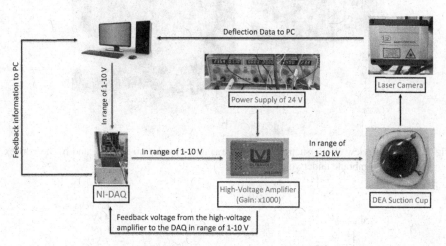

Fig. 6. Measurement setup for characterizing the suction cup

In this part, we present the behavior of the suction cup under voltages from zero to the DEA breakdown-voltage, while monitoring the deflection of the actuator with a focus on the area restricted by the silicone ring. Figure 7 shows the close-up view of and activated versus inactivated suction cup. It should be noted that blue line is the measurement line from the laser sensor. As mentioned before, due to gravity, the membrane initially (under no voltage) takes a convex form. Therefore, the applied voltage only increases the curvature of the concave bending without changing the deflection mode. For every voltage point, the deflection profile of the actuator is recorded. The results are shown in Fig. 8. Moreover, the maximum vertical deflection of the membrane for the applied voltages are depicted in Fig. 9. As shown in the figure, the suction cup broke down electrically at about 7.5 kV.

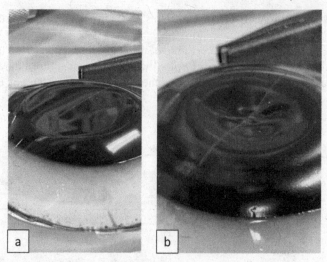

Fig. 7. Close-up view of the suction cup; a) the actuator under no voltage, and b) the convex bending of the membrane under voltage

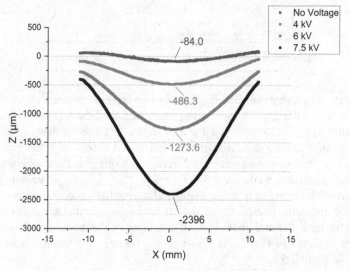

Fig. 8. Deflection profile of the membrane of the actuator

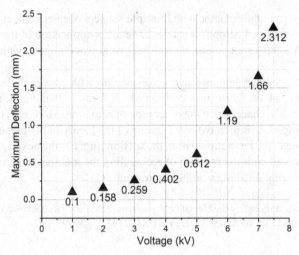

Fig. 9. Maximum deflection of the membrane, measured at the center of the area restricted by the silicone ring

4 Summary and Outlook

In this paper, we presented the development of an electroactive suction cup with DEAs. We implemented the backbone idea in form of a suction ring to restrict the planar expansion of the membrane. This restriction resulted in an off-plane deflection of the membrane which changes the volume enclosed within the suction cup, thereby changing the pressure of the enclosed fluid which is necessary for the attachment of the suction cup to an object. The advantage of implementing the suction ring made of silicone, is that it plays the role of the hard backbone for the actuator, while having the soft attributes of silicones. Afterwards, the fabrication of the suction cup with the ring was explained, and the possible actuation modes of this design were discussed. Finally, we presented a demonstrator for the proof of concept and showed the membrane deflection for different voltages from zero to the breakdown-voltage.

The measurements shown in this study are the preliminary results for the proof of concept for a fully soft electroactive suction cup. Therefore, mainly the deflection of the membrane was studied. For the future work, the first and foremost step is the development of an asset for monitoring the pressure inside the cavity of the sucker. The pressure drop can give a good estimation of the attachment force and is an important factor to optimize the dimensions of the suction cup, since the initial volume plays a significant role in the amount of pressure drop during actuation. The next step will be development of a measurement setup for measuring the attachment force using a force gauge and a frame to hold the specimen.

After measuring the pressure drop and the attachment force, we would like to modify the shape of the suction ring to improve its sealing quality. Here, we need more inspiration from the anatomy of the octopus. When the sucker is characterized and optimized, we will miniaturize the suction cup to have multiple cups on one actuator. This enables the actuator to adapt to the geometry of the object. And finally, by combining the idea of the bending finger and the actuator with multiple suckers, we get another step closer to the fabrication of artificial octopus tentacles. The other application of the actuator with multiple suckers is the development of electroactive gloves equipped with electroactive suction cups.

In this paper, we have demonstrated a suction cup with convex deflection. For the future work, we work on fabrication designs which form an initial concave curvature. With that, we can also characterize the other type of actuation. Moreover, the simulation result shown in Fig. 3, was merely for validation of the theory of off-plane deflection of the membrane due to the restriction within the suction ring. For the next step, we develop the simulation model with the purpose of reconciling the measurement and simulation results and optimizing the design of the suction cup.

Acknowledgement. Funded by the Deutsche Forschungsgemeinschaft (German Research Foundation) under Germany's Excellence Strategy – EXC-2193/1 – 390951807.

References

1. Li, J., Liu, L., Liu, Y., Leng, J.: Dielectric Elastomer Spring-Roll Bending Actuators: Applications in Soft Robotics and Design. Soft Rob. (2019). https://doi.org/10.1089/soro.2018.0037

2. Esser, F.J., Auth, P., Speck, T.: Artificial Venus Flytraps: A Research Review and Outlook on Their Importance for Novel Bioinspired Materials Systems. Front. Robot. AI (2020). https://doi.org/10.3389/frobt.2020.00075

3. Xie, R., Su, M., Zhang, Y., Li, M., Zhu, H., Guan, Y.: PISRob: A Pneumatic Soft Robot for Locomoting Like an Inchworm. In: 2018 IEEE International Conference on Robotics and Automation (ICRA). 2018 IEEE International Conference on Robotics and Automation (ICRA), Brisbane, QLD, 21.05.2018 - 25.05.2018, pp. 3448–3453. IEEE (2018 - 2018). https://doi.org/10.1109/ICRA.2018.8461189

4. Hwang, G.W., Lee, H.J., Da Kim, W., Yang, T.-H., Pang, C.: Soft Microdenticles on Artificial Octopus Sucker Enable Extraordinary Adaptability and Wet Adhesion on Diverse Nonflat Surfaces. Advanced science (Weinheim, Baden-Wurttemberg, Germany) (2022). https://doi.org/10.1002/advs.202202978

5. Kappel, P., Kramp, C., Speck, T., Tauber, F.J.: Application-Oriented Comparison of Two 3D Printing Processes for the Manufacture of Pneumatic Bending Actuators for Bioinspired Macroscopic Soft Gripper Systems. In: Hunt, A., Vouloutsi, V., Moses, K., Quinn, R., Mura, A., Prescott, T., Verschure, P.F.M.J. (eds.) Biomimetic and Biohybrid Systems, vol. 13548. Lecture Notes in Computer Science, pp. 54–67. Springer International Publishing, Cham (2022)

6. El-Atab, N., et al.: Soft Actuators for Soft Robotic Applications: A Review. Advanced Intelligent Systems (2020). https://doi.org/10.1002/aisy.202000128

7. Shintake, J., Cacucciolo, V., Floreano, D., Shea, H.: Soft Robotic Grippers. Adv. Mater. (2018). https://doi.org/10.1002/adma.201707035

8. Bogue, R.: Artificial muscles and soft gripping: a review of technologies and applications. Ind. Robot. (2012). https://doi.org/10.1108/01439911211268642

9. Carpi, F. (ed.): Dielectric elastomers as electromechanical transducers. Fundamentals, materials, devices, models and applications of an emerging electroactive polymer technology. Elsevier, Amsterdam (2008)

10. Ji, X., et al.: Untethered Feel-Through Haptics Using 18-μm Thick Dielectric Elastomer Actuators. Adv. Funct. Mater. (2021). https://doi.org/10.1002/adfm.202006639
11. Wang, Y., et al.: Dielectric elastomer actuators for artificial muscles: A comprehensive review of soft robot explorations. Resources Chemicals and Materials (2022). https://doi.org/10.1016/j.recm.2022.09.001
12. Tramacere, F., Beccai, L., Kuba, M., Gozzi, A., Bifone, A., Mazzolai, B.: The morphology and adhesion mechanism of Octopus vulgaris suckers. PLoS ONE (2013). https://doi.org/10.1371/journal.pone.0065074
13. Kier, W.M., Smith, A.M.: The structure and adhesive mechanism of octopus suckers. Integr. Comp. Biol. (2002). https://doi.org/10.1093/icb/42.6.1146
14. Baik, S., Da Kim, W., Park, Y., Lee, T.-J., Ho Bhang, S., Pang, C.: A wet-tolerant adhesive patch inspired by protuberances in suction cups of octopi. Nature (2017). https://doi.org/10.1038/nature22382
15. Baik, S., Kim, J., Lee, H.J., Lee, T.H., Pang, C.: Highly Adaptable and Biocompatible Octopus-Like Adhesive Patches with Meniscus-Controlled Unfoldable 3D Microtips for Underwater Surface and Hairy Skin. Advanced science (Weinheim, Baden-Wurttemberg, Germany) (2018). https://doi.org/10.1002/advs.201800100
16. Chun, S., et al.: Water-Resistant and Skin-Adhesive Wearable Electronics Using Graphene Fabric Sensor with Octopus-Inspired Microsuckers. ACS Appl. Mater. Interfaces. (2019). https://doi.org/10.1021/acsami.9b04206
17. Follador, M., Tramacere, F., Mazzolai, B.: Dielectric elastomer actuators for octopus inspired suction cups. Bioinspir. Biomim. (2014). https://doi.org/10.1088/1748-3182/9/4/046002
18. Jamali, A., Knoerlein, R., Goldschmidtboeing, F., Woias, P.: Development of a Scalable Soft Finger Gripper for Soft Robots. In: DEVELOPMENT OF A SCALABLE SOFT FINGER GRIPPER FOR SOFT ROBOTS. Hilton Head Workshop 2022: A Solid-State Sensors, Actuators and Microsystems Work-shop, Hilton Head, USA (2022)
19. Ma, J., et al.: A Haptic Feedback Actuator Suitable for the Soft Wearable Device. Appl. Sci. (2020). https://doi.org/10.3390/app10248827
20. Jamali, A., Knoerlein, R., Goldschmidtboeing, F., Woias, P.: Development and Characterization of a Soft Bending Actuator. In: Hunt, A., Vouloutsi, V., Moses, K., Quinn, R., Mura, A., Prescott, T., Verschure, P.F.M.J. (eds.) Biomimetic and Biohybrid Systems, vol. 13548. Lecture Notes in Computer Science, pp. 152–156. Springer International Publishing, Cham (2022)
21. KauPo Plankenhorn e.K.: ECOFLEX® SERIE (2020)

Miniature Soil Moisture Sensors
for a Root-Inspired Burrowing Growing Robot

Emanuela Del Dottore[1]([⊠]) [iD], Alessio Mondini[1] [iD], Davide Bray[2] [iD],
and Barbara Mazzolai[1]([⊠]) [iD]

[1] Bioinspired Soft Robotics Lab, Istituto Italiano di Tecnologia (IIT),
Via Morego 30, 16163 Genova, Italy
{emanuela.deldottore,barbara.mazzolai}@iit.it
[2] School of Engineering and Applied Sciences, Harvard University, Cambridge, MA 02138,
USA

Abstract. This paper shows the implementation of miniature sensors for soil moisture measurement and their integration in a root-inspired burrowing growing robot. Three kinds of sensors are combined to estimate the water content in soil: a resistivity sensor composed of two brass electrodes, a commercial air humidity sensor interfaced with the soil by a filter membrane of PTFE with polyester scrim, and an RGB sensor used for visible reflectance spectroscopy. We show their integration and embeddability in a burrowing growing robot based on additive manufacturing with a 4 cm probe diameter. The multimodal sensing strategy has been characterized and tested in clay and sand medium at different water content. Results show that the resistive sensor works in all the tested ranges but is prone to failure due to electrode-soil contact issues. The air humidity sensor works accurately in a range of water content less than 5% (dry conditions), and the RGB sensor works in the 5–20% range. We propose a statistical approach for soil moisture estimation that combines all three technologies and demonstrate that we can accurately predict the water content in our experimental soils, clay and sand, with better performance in clay (Root Mean Square Error, RMSE = 0.38). The proposed miniaturized multimodal sensing strategy can enable long-term, in-situ soil moisture monitoring functionalities in self-deployable robots for precision agriculture and forestry applications.

Keywords: Soil Moisture Sensor · RGB Sensor · Burrowing Robot · Growing Robot

1 Introduction

Precision agriculture and digital farming are management strategies increasingly used for the proven advantages in providing economic, environmental, and product quality enhancement due to a more correct and measured use of fertilizers, pesticides, and

Supplementary Information The online version contains supplementary material available at https://doi.org/10.1007/978-3-031-38857-6_15.

water [1–3]. Fundamental to a reliable process is the demand for accurate and timely information directly from the field [4]. In the air, inexpensive monitoring stations on the market guarantee accurate measurements of e.g., temperature, humidity, wind, and they include fixed and mobile Wireless Sensors Networks to increase spatial data resolution [5]. In contrast, sensor solutions for soil analysis are still quite limited today, especially for systems capable of monitoring parameters in real-time in a non-invasive way [6].

Among many soil parameters [7], monitoring volumetric humidity is essential in several applications. Maintaining a balanced soil water content is necessary for agriculture, meteorological, climatologic, and hydrologic applications [8]. The typical approach for soil moisture measurements accounts for sampling and laboratory analyses [9]. However, these are slow, expensive, discontinuous, and not punctual. Alternative methods use spaceborne/airborne remote sensing, static/mobile proximal sensing, and in-situ/ground sensors [10]. Several sensors have been developed for in-situ installation and continuous monitoring in recent decades. The most adopted measurement techniques include soil resistivity sensors, tensiometers, dielectric (capacity, Time Domain Reflectometry, and Frequency Domain Reflectometry), and optical techniques [9]. They all are relatively bulky, with complicated reading electronics requiring in-field calibration to achieve the desired accuracy [11].

Soil is a challenging environment for exploration and monitoring. The acceleration of climate change demands more attention for below-ground monitoring because of the impact of soil-living organisms in carbon recycling. Equipping a robotic probe with moisture sensors could help realize self-deployable monitoring stations for soil and subsoil ecosystem monitoring [12]. Recently, bioinspiration has attracted attention for application in geotechnical studies [13]. In particular, earthworm-inspired [14–16] and growing [17–20] robots have been demonstrated to be viable solutions for burrowing granular mediums [21]. In burrowing robotic systems, preserving reduced dimensions is important to guarantee efficient underground locomotion [22]. This requirement implies a compact sensing system, in terms of sensor dimension and conditioning electronics, combined with low energy consumption.

This paper investigates a multimodal sensing strategy for sensor selection and integration in a root-inspired growing robot that moves through a layer-by-layer additive manufacturing process [17]. That means the growing robot can be adopted as an autonomous soil penetrometer for, e.g., agriculture or forestry subsoil long-time monitoring. We propose a robotic tip design that integrates different soil moisture sensors: (i) a resistivity sensor to measure soil impedance by a couple of electrodes shaped like the root tip to remain in contact with the soil during growth; (ii) a digital air humidity sensor interfaced with the soil through a filter cap; and (iii) an optical reflectance sensor based on an RGB digital sensor combined with a white LED. We provide a preliminary sensor characterization for different soil types and prospect a potential strategy for their usage in the growing robot.

2   Materials and Methods

2.1   Root-Inspired Growing Robot

Taking inspiration from the ability of plants to explore by growing at their apical extremities, an integrated 3D printing mechanism for robotic roots has recently been proposed [17]. The system integrates a customized 3D printer based on Fused Deposition Modeling (FDM) inside the artificial root to extrude thermoplastic material and thus add material from the robotic tip, imitating the apical growth of plant roots (Fig. 1).

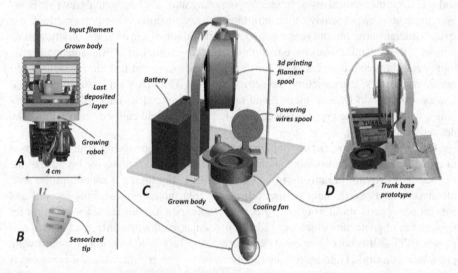

Fig. 1. Root-inspired growing robot prototype. (A) The assembled growing robot without the tip. Its main components are a heater that melts the filament and two motors, one for feeding the filament and one for rotation, to permit the filament plotting. (B) Growing robot tip with embedded soil moisture sensors. (C) CAD assembly of the growing robot base with the main components: the spool of the 3d printing filament that is passively unrolled during growth; a cooling fan to guarantee the fast set of the material after printing, the battery with the spool for powering wires release; and the grown body connected to the growing robot. (D) The developed prototype of the trunk-like base of the growing system.

The growth system comprises a tubular body, a deposition mechanism (Fig. 1A), and a sensorized tip (Fig. 1B) that monitors soil moisture and controls the material deposition process. The deposition mechanism consists of an extruder and a plotting unit. The extruder includes a feed mechanism that pulls a thermoplastic filament from a spooler and pushes it through a tube to the heater. The latter melts the filament and extrudes it through a nozzle. The plotting unit (Fig. 1A) enables the rotation of the robotic tip permitting the circular deposition of the extruded filament at the tip level. This pushes the tip into the medium (providing the necessary force to penetrate) while simultaneously building the body of the root (see Supporting Video). The system is controlled by three parameters: feed speed, plotting speed, and heating temperature.

To grow into soil, the system needs high reliability and efficiency, combined with a small dimension to reduce energy needs for penetration. The growing robot proposed here has a diameter of 40 mm. A limitation in using FDM as an enabling technology for growing robots is the heating temperature necessary to process thermoplastic filaments and build the robot's body. The system loses most of its energy in the heating/cooling process. Moreover, reaching high temperatures affects the motor's efficiency, leading to breakdowns. We employ a constant airflow generated by a fan in the trunk-like base (Fig. 1C and Fig. 1D). This airflow facilitates air circulation within the tip, directing it towards the soil and partially returning it to the filament inlet. This arrangement has two purposes: first, it helps prevent the rising of the system's temperature, and second, it helps the filament to return to a solid state which allows pushing forward the robotic tip. In this implementation, we tested Polylactic acid (PLA) and Polycaprolactone (PCL) filaments in an artificial granular medium (Polyoxymethylene – Copolymer, POM-C) and topsoil to verify their usability. The authors previously used PLA filament and demonstrated to provide good mechanical properties to the built body. However, it needs a high melting temperature (about 180 °C), possibly stressing the system and affecting soil moisture locally due to the high temperature. PCL filament is here evaluated as an alternative due to its lower melting point (about 60 °C).

2.2 Sensorized Robotic Tip

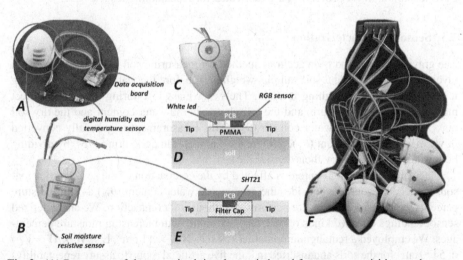

Fig. 2. (A) Prototypes of the sensorized tip, electronic board for sensor acquisition, and sensor board for the digital air humidity sensor. (B) A highlight of the brass electrodes for the resistive sensor and the filter cap for the digital humidity sensors. (C) A highlight of the RGB sensor. (D) Schematic section view of the RGB sensor. (E) Schematic section view of the digital sensor. (F) The five sensorized root tips realized for tests.

A sensory solution suitable for integration into the robotic root must be dimensionally scalable, have reduced signal conditioning electronics to facilitate scalability, require low computational cost, and reach high accuracy. With this in mind, we selected some promising technologies and integrated all of them into the artificial root tip for their investigations (Fig. 2A):

- A resistive sensor (Fig. 2B). It is formed by two brass electrodes (similar to [23]) of dimensions 3×14 mm and distant 3 mm each, connected in a voltage divider configuration with a fixed resistance of 10 MΩ and acquired through an analog-to-digital converter integrated into the embedded microcontroller. The electrical resistance of the soil measured varies with the percentage of humidity contained.
- A reflectance sensor (Fig. 2C and Fig. 2D) composed of a white LED light (LTW-C191TS5 by Lite-On) and an RGB color sensor with I2C digital interface (VEML6040 by Vishay) integrated on a PCB board and directed towards the ground through a circular aperture of 8 mm in diameter closed by a PMMA window in the tip. It measures the light reflected by the soil supposed to change with water content.
- A digital air humidity sensor (Sensirion SHT21 by Sensirion). It measures the humidity of the interstitial air of the soil. It is decoupled from the soil by a filter membrane of PTFE with polyester scrim (Fig. 2E) that helps to protect the sensor against water, dust, particles, and other contaminants.

The tip of the robot is designed with a shape mimicking real plant root tips to facilitate soil penetration [24] and is manufactured in nylon by 3D printing (ProX SLS 6100 by 3D Systems Inc., USA). The electrodes for measuring humidity are made of brass by CNC machining. Five prototypes are fabricated for repeatability tests (Fig. 2F).

2.3 Sensors Characterization

The gravimetric method is an accurate method for measuring soil water content [25]. It involves taking a physical soil sample, weighing it before the water is lost, and drying it in an oven before weighing it again. The water mass lost during drying is a direct measure of the soil moisture, and the ratio between the water content and the dry soil mass is the gravimetric water content (θ_m). This measurement is generally converted in volumetric water content (θ_v), a reference parameter in agriculture [25], by dividing both water and dry soil by their density [26].

The volumetric water content is affected by the compaction of the soil. For this reason, in the following, we consider the gravimetric water content (θ_m) as soil moisture percentage, and experiments are performed without soil compaction. We characterized sensor readings into two kinds of soil, clay and sand, with increasing moisture percentages. We employed a rectangular container ($29.6 \times 16.8 \times 11$ cm^3, L $\times$ W $\times$ H $= V_C$) of 5470 cm^3 for the soils and inserted in it the five artificial roots (to assure repeatability) connected to a PC for data acquisition. We dried about 10 kg of each soil in an oven at 100 °C for 36 h. Subsequently, the soil aggregates were broken and filtered with a sieve with a mesh of 2×2 mm holes. Five experimental groups were defined in clay ($i = 1$, 2, 5, 10, and 20) and six in sand ($i = 0.4$, 1, 2, 5, 10, and 20). The lowest percentage (0.4%) was unfeasible to reach in clay. Each group represents the mass percentage of water introduced starting from the dry soil (m_{ds}). The water mass (m_{w_i}) is obtained as the percentage of m_{ds}:

$$m_{w\_i} = \frac{i \cdot m_{ds}}{100}. \tag{1}$$

When this water mass is added to the dry soil, the total mass of the wet soil (m_{ws}) becomes:

$$m_{ws} = \frac{i + 100}{100} \dot{m}_{ds}, \tag{2}$$

and the corresponding volumetric moisture at each percentage can eventually be calculated as:

$$\theta_{v\_i} = \frac{m_{w\_i}/\rho_w}{V_s}, \tag{3}$$

with ρ_w water density (997 kg/m^3).

The experiments were done by increasing water content, taking the soil of the previous group, and adding the missing water mass. At each test: (1) the soil was mixed with water; (2) a first layer of 40 mm was deposited in the container; (3) the five artificial roots were cleaned from soil residuals and inserted in a vertical position by exerting a slight pressure in order to secure them in position and ensure contact of their surface with the soil; (4) the container was filled with the necessary soil to reach the predefined volumetric level (V_C); (5) the container was covered in order to contain the evaporation of the water.

Three repetitions were performed with five artificial roots resulting in 15 measurements for each humidity group in each soil with an acquisition time window of ~15 min each (sampling rate 10 Hz). Three roots were used for sensor characterization (Sect. 3.1) and two for validation (Sect. 3.3). To be sure all the sensors reached a steady state, we collected values from the last 5 min of acquisition and averaged them.

3 Results and Discussion

3.1 Soil Moisture Sensor Characterization

Sensor reading results are plotted in Fig. 3A-C for the tested soils. Values of red, green, and blue channels obtained from the RGB sensor are summed together to get the white value plotted in the figure. Since not all the groups are normally distributed, and variances are not equal, we performed a Kruskal-Wallis test to analyze the differences between the groups (Fig. 3D-F). We can observe that the air humidity sensor works only in dry soil, $0 < \theta_m < 5\%$. Above that range, the sensor saturates because the soil's water content reaches a level where the interstitial air is at 100% humidity. On the contrary, the RGB sensor displays a low signal-to-noise ratio for $\theta_m < 5\%$, thus, it is insensitive to low humidity levels. The resistive sensor, as expected, can cover the whole range, albeit with an irregular standard deviation over the groups. This is due to electrode-soil contact issues that alter the measurement. The small dimension of the electrodes chosen for embeddability in the robot tip further amplifies this effect. For this reason, the resistive sensor suffers from low accuracy and risks becoming an unreliable measurement in many cases. However, in both soils, humidities up to 1% significantly differ from the 5% with the resistive sensor, allowing to distinguish between dry soil, within the range $0 \leq \theta_m < 2\%$, and wet soil, within the range $2 \leq \theta_m \leq 20\%$.

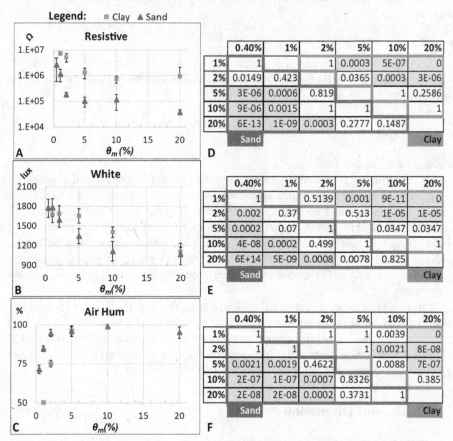

Fig. 3. Sensor characterization. (A-C) Mean values and standard deviation for the different sensors: (A) resistive, (B) white light obtained as the summation of the RGB channels, and (C) digital air humidity sensor. In (D-F), the pairwise comparative analysis was performed on the (D) resistive, (E) white, and (F) air humidity sensor acquisitions, both soil types. After Bonferroni correction, we applied $\alpha = 0.003$ to define the level of significance (colored cells in the table have p-value < α). (Color figure online)

3.2 Robot Growing Results

PCL and PLA filaments have been studied as growing materials. In particular, PCL has been selected for its low melting point (about 60 °C) that could, in theory, bring advantages in terms of energy (lower energy is spent in heating the material), stress for the system (motors are less subjected to high temperature, and so they degrades less), and moisture measurement (high-temperatures evaporate water around the tip). As a drawback, from the experiments, we observed it generates high internal friction (between the last deposited layers and the printing unit) that stresses the plotting motor much faster than PLA (Fig. 4A). The duty cycle with PCL has trend lines with a slope greater than the one reached with PLA and doubles the duty cycle with PLA in topsoil (Table 1). The resulting duty cycle becomes more irregular, leading to high spikes due to the stickiness of PCL, which causes slippage in the growing mechanism. This slippage results in uneven growth of the body structure and subsequently leads to variations in friction between the growing mechanism and the structure. This high friction of the PCL is even higher when not completely cold. Because of the low melting temperature with PCL (reducing the thermal exchange with the environment), cooling is difficult to achieve, even with high ventilation. Thus, in these conditions, PLA-based filaments guarantee a longer system lifespan and can facilitate penetration with respect to PCL. On the other hand, the employment of PLA can overheat the system during growth. This effect must be mitigated by improving dissipation (e.g., increasing ventilation). In our experiments, we tested up to 15 cm penetration in both granular medium and topsoil with PCL (Fig. 4C, D) and PLA material (Fig. 4E, F) (see Supplementary Video).

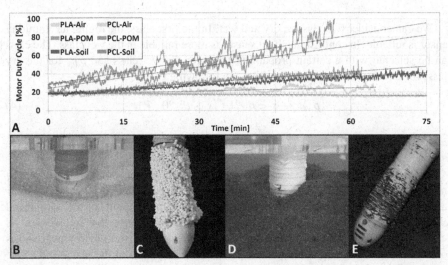

Fig. 4. (A) Duty cycles of the plotting motor during growth in the air (Air), topsoil (Soil), and artificial granular medium (POM), obtained with PLA and PCL. (B-E) Examples of penetration tests performed with the growing robot in (B-C) POM-C to emulate granular soil using PCL filament for body construction: (B) initial state, (C) final configuration (~15 cm length); and (D-E) in topsoil using PLA: (D) initial configuration, (E) final structure of ~15 cm length.

3.3 Validation

Based on the presented sensor characterization, we propose a preliminary approach for moisture estimation to verify the feasibility of adopting multimodal sensing in the robot.

Table 1. Duty cycle (%) of plotting motor obtained from the fitting functions gained from the experimental tests (Fig. 4A) performed into topsoil (Soil), artificial granular medium (POM), and air (Air). Ratios between the estimated duty cycle reached when growing with PCL and PLA are calculated and shown in the table for comparison. The Root Mean Square Error (RMSE) is evaluated for the linear fitting model. A less accurate prediction is obtained with PCL with respect to PLA because of greater irregularities of the duty cycle.

min	PLA_{Air}	PCL_{Air}	$\frac{PCL_{Air}}{PLA_{Air}}$	PLA_{POM}	PCL_{POM}	$\frac{PCL_{POM}}{PLA_{POM}}$	PLA_{Soil}	PCL_{Soil}	$\frac{PCL_{Soil}}{PLA_{Soil}}$
30	17.7	21.1	1.2	30.1	47.4	1.6	27.0	55.2	2.0
60	16.4	24.6	1.5	42.1	70.6	1.7	36.3	82.1	2.3

	Linear fitting of the duty cycle shown in Fig. 4A:					
	Air		POM		Soil	
	Fitting line	RMSE	Fitting line	RMSE	Fitting line	RMSE
PLA	y = -0.0419x + 18.942	1.15	y = 0.4008x + 18.054	1.91	y = 0.311x + 17.658	2.40
PCL	y = 0.1176x + 17.567	3.85	y = 0.7733x + 24.173	4.78	y = 0.8977x + 28.242	7.10

We can consider two classes, dry and wet. In the first class, the digital air humidity sensor is reliable. In contrast, the light sensor is more reliable in the wet class. The class can be selected with a certain probability (p_{wet} for the wet class and p_{dry} for the dry class) from the resistive measure as from the following pseudocode:

$$p_{wet} \leftarrow \underline{s} < th_l?1 : (\underline{s} > th_u?0 : P) \tag{4}$$

$$p_{dry} \leftarrow 1 - p_{wet} \tag{5}$$

In Eq. (4), $\underline{s}$ is the normalized resistive value (upper bound rounded to 10^7 Ω), th_l and th_u are the threshold values that must be defined from a calibration process. In our case, they are obtained as the lower and upper bound (mean ± std) of the normalized resistive values at $\theta_m = 2\%$, which marks the boundary between dry and wet soil as defined in Sect. 3.1. P is the probability that $\underline{s}$ comes from a wet environment and is considered equal to the p-value obtained from calibration. From the pair 2%-5%, we have p-value = 0.036 borderline in clay and p-value = 0.819 in the sand (Fig. 3D). In Eq. (4), p_{wet} is assigned as: if $\underline{s}$ is below the lower threshold, p_{wet} equals 1. If $\underline{s}$ is greater than the upper threshold p_{wet} equals 0, P otherwise.

The humidity can be estimated with a fitting model with class-specific weights (or probabilities, p_{wet} and p_{dry}):

$$p_{dry}\dot{y}_a + p_{wet}\dot{y}_w \tag{6}$$

The characterization from Sect. 3.1 is here used to define the calibration curves for y_a and y_w (see Fig. 5A, B). y_a, fitting function for the dry class that uses the normalized value (saturation to 100%) from the air sensors, and y_w, fitting function for the wet class,

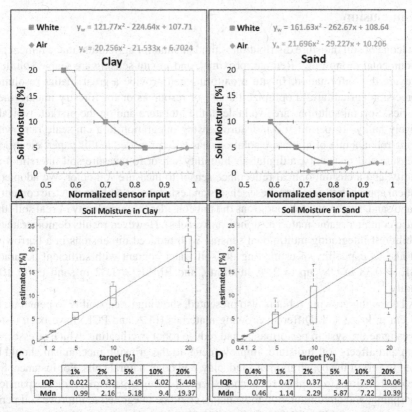

Fig. 5. (A-B) Calibration curves are obtained with a polynomial fitting for the soil moisture as a function of the normalized light and digital humidity sensors mean values acquired in (A) clay and (B) sand. (C-D) Humidity estimated with Eq. (4)–(6). In Eq. (4) we used $(th_l, th_u) = (0.2, 0.6)$ in clay, and $(th_l, th_u) = (0.01, 0.02)$ in sand. In the box and whisker plots, the red line suggests the target line of best fit. The tables below each graph show the IQR and median (Mdn) used to estimate the precision and accuracy of results, respectively. (Color figure online)

that uses the normalized value (upper limit rounded to 2000 lx) of white channel from the RGB sensors.

Results of humidity estimation are shown in Fig. 5C, D. If we consider the error as the difference between the target humidity (θ_m) and the median value (Mdn), in clay, we get Mdn $\approx$ target θ_m reaching high accuracy (RMSE = 0.38) and high precision (IQR < 1.5 for $\theta_m \leq 5\%$) that slightly degrade with increasing humidity (increasing IQR). In sand, we reach a resolution of $\theta_m \leq 5\%$ with high accuracy (RMSE = 0.49) and good precision (IQR < 3.5), whereas performance decreases in wet conditions ($\theta_m \geq 10\%$), where the target θ_m – Mdn > > 1 and IQR is large (RMSE = 1.32 up to $\theta_m = 10\%$, and RMSE = 4.1 up to $\theta_m = 20\%$). This is perhaps induced by the less compactibility of sand with respect to clay: in wet condition, sand does not compact but fill the voids with water, whereas grains in clay tend to aggregate.

4 Conclusion

Knowledge of soil moisture distribution is fundamental for agriculture management and environmental monitoring. Remote, proximal, and in-situ sensing are viable solutions to provide this information. In-situ monitoring can provide a great spatial resolution for precision agriculture to optimize the use of resources or for forestry management strategies. Several solutions are available in the literature and on the market, typically relatively bulky. To permit soil moisture sensing integration in a cm-scale burrowing growing robot, a mix of miniature solutions has been proposed in this paper: electrodes to measure soil resistivity, a digital air humidity sensor to measure soil interstitial air humidity, and a custom optical reflectance sensor to measure soil color. We adopted a statistical approach to combine these sensors and estimate the soil gravimetric content in clay and sand. Experimental conditions did not consider the complexity of real soil (that can also contain organic material, stones, and cracks). However, results demonstrate the feasibility of integrating multimodal sensing with reduced dimensions in a burrowing robot and its capability of estimating the soil water content with sufficient accuracy: RMSE = 0.38 in clay up to 20% humidity, and RMSE = 1.32 in sand up to 10% humidity.

A burrowing growing robot is also presented, showing its capability to penetrate up to 15 cm in loose soil. Different growing materials (PLA and PCL) have been tested to investigate the system performance and reduce robot overheating, which stresses the system and affects soil moisture. Improvements to the growing mechanism should be applied to permit the penetration of sand, clay, and other natural soils. For instance, following suggestions from plant roots and other soil-living organisms, radial expansion, tip morphing, and circumnutation movements could be integrated to improve soil penetration performances [22, 27, 28]. Such self-deployable robots with soil exploration and monitoring abilities could be employed as distributed systems in a soil sensor network for agriculture and forestry applications.

Acknowledgments. This work has received funding from the European Research Council (ERC) under the European Union's Horizon 2020 Research and Innovation Programme Grant Agreement No. 101003304 (I-Wood).

References

1. Mulla, D.J.: Twenty five years of remote sensing in precision agriculture: key advances and remaining knowledge gaps. Biosys. Eng. **114**, 358–371 (2013). https://doi.org/10.1016/j.biosystemseng.2012.08.009
2. Shafi, U., Mumtaz, R., García-Nieto, J., Hassan, S.A., Zaidi, S.A.R., Iqbal, N.: Precision agriculture techniques and practices: from considerations to applications. Sensors (Switzerland). **19**, 3796 (2019). https://doi.org/10.3390/s19173796
3. Shamshiri, R.R., et al.: Research and development in agricultural robotics: a perspective of digital farming. Int. J. Agric. Biol. Eng. **11**, 1–14 (2018). https://doi.org/10.25165/ijabe.v11i4.4278

4. Tsouros, D.C., Bibi, S., Sarigiannidis, P.G.: A review on UAV-based applications for precision agriculture. Information **10**, 349 (2019). https://doi.org/10.3390/info10110349
5. Thakur, D., Kumar, Y., Kumar, A., Singh, P.K.: Applicability of wireless sensor networks in precision agriculture: a review. Wirel. Pers. Commun. **107**(1), 471–512 (2019). https://doi.org/10.1007/s11277-019-06285-2
6. Fan, Y., et al.: A critical review for real-time continuous soil monitoring: advantages, challenges, and perspectives. Environ. Sci. Technol. **56**, 13546–13564 (2022). https://doi.org/10.1021/acs.est.2c03562
7. Adamchuk, V.I., Hummel, J.W., Morgan, M.T., Upadhyaya, S.K.: On-the-go soil sensors for precision agriculture. Comput. Electron. Agric. **44**, 71–91 (2004). https://doi.org/10.1016/j.compag.2004.03.002
8. Vereecken, H., et al.: Soil hydrology: recent methodological advances, challenges, and perspectives. Water Resour. Res. **51**, 2616–2633 (2015). https://doi.org/10.1002/2014WR016852
9. Su, S.L., Singh, D.N., Baghini, M.S.: A critical review of soil moisture measurement. Measurement **54**, 92–105 (2014)
10. Babaeian, E., Sadeghi, M., Jones, S.B., Montzka, C., Vereecken, H., Tuller, M.: Ground, proximal, and satellite remote sensing of soil moisture. Rev. Geophys. **57**, 530–616 (2019). https://doi.org/10.1029/2018RG000618
11. Hardie, M.: Review of novel and emerging proximal soil moisture sensors for use in agriculture. Sensors (Switzerland) **20**, 1–23 (2020). https://doi.org/10.3390/s20236934
12. Dottore, E.D., Mazzolai, B.: Perspectives on computation in plants. Artif. Life 1–15 (2023). https://doi.org/10.1162/artl_a_00396
13. Martinez, A., et al.: Bio-inspired geotechnical engineering: principles, current work, opportunities and challenges. Géotechnique. **72**, 1–19 (2021). https://doi.org/10.1680/jgeot.20.P.170
14. Ortiz, D., Gravish, N., Tolley, M.T.: Soft robot actuation strategies for locomotion in granular substrates. IEEE Robot. Autom. Lett. **4**, 2630–2636 (2019). https://doi.org/10.1109/LRA.2019.2911844
15. Niiyama, R., Matsushita, K., Ikeda, M., Or, K., Kuniyoshi, Y.: A 3D printed hydrostatic skeleton for an earthworm-inspired soft burrowing robot. Soft Matter **18**, 7990–7997 (2022). https://doi.org/10.1039/d2sm00882c
16. Das, R., Babu, S.P.M., Visentin, F., Palagi, S., Mazzolai, B.: An earthworm-like modular soft robot for locomotion in multi-terrain environments. Sci Rep. **13**, 1571 (2023). https://doi.org/10.1038/s41598-023-28873-w
17. Sadeghi, A., Mondini, A., Mazzolai, B.: Toward self-growing soft robots inspired by plant roots and based on additive manufacturing technologies. Soft Rob. **4**, 211–223 (2017). https://doi.org/10.1089/soro.2016.0080
18. Naclério, N.D., Hubicki, C.M., Aydin, Y.O., Goldman, D.I., Hawkes, E.W.: Soft robotic burrowing device with tip-extension and granular fluidization. In: 2018 IEEE/RSJ International Conference on Intelligent Robots and Systems (IROS), pp. 5918–5923. IEEE, Madrid (2018). https://doi.org/10.1109/IROS.2018.8593530
19. Sadeghi, A., Del Dottore, E., Mondini, A., Mazzolai, B.: Passive morphological adaptation for obstacle avoidance in a self-growing robot produced by additive manufacturing. Soft Rob. **7**, 85–94 (2020). https://doi.org/10.1089/soro.2019.0025
20. Naclerio, N.D., et al.: Controlling subterranean forces enables a fast, steerable, burrowing soft robot. Sci. Robot. **6**, eabe2922 (2021). https://doi.org/10.1126/scirobotics.abe2922
21. Wei, H., et al.: Review on bioinspired planetary regolith-burrowing robots. Space Sci. Rev. **217**(8), 1–39 (2021). https://doi.org/10.1007/s11214-021-00863-2

22. Ruiz, S., Or, D., Schymanski, S.J.: Soil penetration by earthworms and plant roots—mechanical energetics of bioturbation of compacted soils. PLoS ONE **10**, e0128914 (2015). https://doi.org/10.1371/journal.pone.0128914

23. Mazzolai, B., et al.: A miniaturized mechatronic system inspired by plant roots for soil exploration. IEEE/ASME Trans. Mechatron. **16**, 201–212 (2011). https://doi.org/10.1109/TMECH.2009.2038997

24. Mishra, A.K., Tramacere, F., Guarino, R., Pugno, N.M., Mazzolai, B.: A study on plant root apex morphology as a model for soft robots moving in soil. PLoS ONE. **13**, e0197411 (2018). https://doi.org/10.1371/journal.pone.0197411

25. Dobriyal, P., Qureshi, A., Badola, R., Hussain, S.A.: A review of the methods available for estimating soil moisture and its implications for water resource management. J. Hydrol. **458–459**, 110–117 (2012). https://doi.org/10.1016/j.jhydrol.2012.06.021

26. Schmugge, T.J., Jackson, T.J., McKim, H.L.: Survey of methods for soil moisture determination. Water Resour. Res. **16**, 961–979 (1980)

27. Kolb, E., Legué, V., Bogeat-Triboulot, M.-B.: Physical root–soil interactions. Phys. Biol. **14**, 065004 (2017). https://doi.org/10.1088/1478-3975/aa90dd

28. Del Dottore, E., Mondini, A., Sadeghi, A., Mattoli, V., Mazzolai, B.: An efficient soil penetration strategy for explorative robots inspired by plant root circumnutation movements. Bioinspir. Biomim. **13**, 015003 (2017)

Soft Tubular Strain Sensors for Contact Detection

Kevin Dai[1], Abirami Elangovan[1], Karen Whirley[1],
and Victoria A. Webster-Wood[1,2,3(✉)]

[1] Department of Mechanical Engineering, Carnegie Mellon University,
Pittsburgh, USA
vwebster@andrew.cmu.edu
[2] Department of Biomedical Engineering, Carnegie Mellon University,
Pittsburgh, PA, USA
[3] McGowan Institute for Regenerative Medicine, Carnegie Mellon University,
Pittsburgh, PA, USA

Abstract. Sensing and actuation are intricately connected in soft robotics, where contact may change actuator mechanics and robot behavior. To improve soft robotic control and performance, proprioception and contact sensors are needed to report robot state without altering actuation mechanics or introducing bulky, rigid components. For bioinspired McKibben-style fluidic actuators, prior work in sensing has focused on sensing the strain of the actuator by embedding sensors in the actuator bladder during fabrication, or by adhering sensors to the actuator surface after fabrication. However, material property mismatches between sensors and actuators can impede actuator performance, and many soft sensors available for use with fluidic actuators rely on costly or labor-intensive fabrication methods. Here, we demonstrate a low-cost and easy-to manufacture-tubular liquid metal strain sensor for use with soft actuators that can be used to detect actuator strain and contact between the actuator and external objects. The sensor is flexible, can be fabricated with commercial-off-the-shelf components, and can be easily integrated with existing soft actuators to supplement sensing, regardless of actuator shape or size. Furthermore, the soft tubular strain sensor exhibits low hysteresis and high sensitivity. The approach presented in this work provides a low-cost, soft sensing solution for broad application in soft robotics.

Keywords: Soft robotics · Strain sensor · Contact detection

This work was supported by NSF DBI2015317 as part of the NSF/CIHR/DFG/FRQ/UKRI-MRC Next Generation Networks for Neuroscience Program and by the NSF Research Fellowship Program under Grant No. DGE1745016. Any opinions, findings, and conclusions or recommendations expressed in this material are those of the authors and do not necessarily reflect the views of the National Science Foundation.

F. Meder et al. (Eds.): Living Machines 2023, LNAI 14157, pp. 197–215, 2023.
https://doi.org/10.1007/978-3-031-38857-6_16

1   Introduction

Sensing and actuation are critical to enabling robots to interact with their environments. Actuators are used for locomotion, manipulation of external objects, and modification of the robot's internal state or configuration. Sensors can close the loop for robotic control by providing feedback about the environment or the robot's internal state. While significant research has gone into developing sensors and actuators for traditionally rigid robots, the field of soft, bioinspired robots has received less attention in developing sensorized actuators. Soft, bioinspired robots must deal with additional design constraints over their rigid counterparts due to using flexible materials, which can preclude the usage of many existing actuators and sensors [4,11]. Examples of actuators that have been developed to meet the needs of soft robotics include fluidic artificial muscles [15], dielectric actuators [7], and shape-memory alloys and polymers [5].

Of the available soft actuators, fluidic artificial muscles, such as the McKibben actuator, provide an accessible and well-characterized solution for soft robotic actuation. Fluidic artificial muscles demonstrate high power densities and can be easily manufactured at a low cost using commercially available components, without the need for specialized tooling [15]. These fluidic actuators are typically composed of an elastomer, such as a latex balloon, and selectively stiffened reinforcement, such as a braided mesh, that constrains the inflation of the elastomer when pressurized [9,10]. Sensors have been designed for integration with McKibben actuators and other fluidic artificial muscles by embedding resistive or capacitive sensing elements within the actuator's elastomer [6,8,16] or by mounting to the actuator's external surface [17]. However, these sensors are primarily intended to measure the length of the actuator. They may not provide additional sensing functionality, such as detecting contact along the actuator's length, which could be helpful for robotic manipulation. Furthermore, these sensors may suffer from complex fabrication methods or large form factors that limit their usage as soft robots utilize higher numbers of sensorized actuators. For creating accessible soft robots for applications such as grasping, where multiple fluidic actuators may be assembled together in close proximity [3], sensors with small form factors and facile integration with actuators are needed.

An ideal sensor not only requires a small form factor and easy integration with different actuators without affecting actuation, but also needs to be easy to manufacture. Since a common mode of failure in fluidic artificial muscles is due to fatigue failure of the elastomer [9], sensors should also accommodate the replacement or repair of elastomeric components, which may preclude the integration of sensors within the elastomer. Compact and easy-to-manufacture strain sensors can be formed by filling commercially available elastomer tubing with conductive fluids for either resistive or capacitive sensing [2,14,18], without requiring dedicated tooling. Such a sensor could then be wrapped around a McKibben actuator for detecting actuator strain or external contact, while enabling the facile repair of the actuator's elastomer components. For tubular sensors to be most effective, they should have a high fill volume with minimal air gaps within the tube and high connectivity between the internal conductive fluid and external electrical connections. However, sealing the ends of these tubular sensors during the manufacturing process can be challenging, resulting in either large air gaps within the liquid or in fluid leakage when inserting solid conductive leads into the ends of the sensor. Additionally, existing tubular sensors reported in the literature require each sensor to be manufactured individually, which is time-consuming and increases production costs.

In this paper, we present a novel manufacturing technique that enables the rapid sequential manufacturing of multiple tubular strain gauges without significant fluid leakage by using hollow syringe needles to serve as conductive leads. We characterize the tubular strain gauge's resistive response and hysteresis. In addition, we demonstrate the capability of a helically-wound tubular strain gauge to detect contact during grasping with a toroidally-shaped McKibben actuator. As these sensors are low-cost, easy-to-manufacture, and easily mountable to a wide array of actuators, they have far-reaching potential in soft robotics by providing proprioception for internal state estimation and contact detection. These capabilities will enable sensorized actuators to enhance soft robotic performance in applications such as grasping, manipulating, and exploring external environments.

2   Methods

The presented tubular strain gauge uses a novel manufacturing method that enables the rapid sequential production of multiple sensors while maintaining a low part count. The strain gauge is fabricated by filling elastomer tubing with a conductive fluid, eutectic gallium-indium (EGaIn). Strain sensors of two different lengths were fabricated and characterized to acquire their resistance-strain response and mechanical stress-strain hysteresis response. In addition, one specimen of the longer strain sensor was attached to a McKibben actuator for evaluating both electromechanical hysteresis and contact detection.

2.1   Sensor Design and Fabrication

The strain gauge has a simple design with few components. In brief, hollow elastomer tubing is filled with an electrically-conductive fluid, EGaIn, to form a flexible, resistive wire. Crimped, conductive hypodermic needles are located at each end of the elastomer tubing and provide a solid, conducting surface for external electrical connections. Heat-shrink tubing and silicone adhesive are used to secure the stainless steel needles to the silicone tubing while preventing leakage of the internal conductive fluid.

Sensors were fabricated with lengths of 114.3 mm and 495.3 mm. To fabricate the sensors, silicone tubing (0.51 mm ID × 0.94 mm OD, Shore 55A, McMaster-Carr) was first cut to the desired length. We prepared 30.2 mm lengths of hypodermic tubing by applying a heat gun to nominally 25.4 mm-long, blunt 23G Luer-lock syringe needles while manually twisting the stainless steel tubing out of the plastic needle housing. A sharp blade was used to scrape away excess

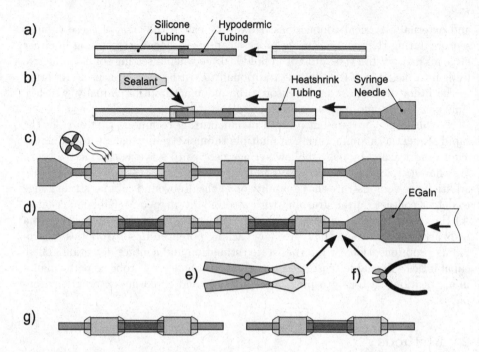

Fig. 1. The strain gauge presented in this work is simple to construct with a low part count. The sensors consisted of a conductive fluid inside an elastomer tube. a) For the construction of the strain gauge, conductive hypodermic tubing was first inserted into sections of silicone tubing that formed the body of the strain gauge. The hollow conductive tubing enabled the rapid manufacturing of multiple sensors in series. b) Sealant and heat shrink were applied to seal the joints between the hypodermic and elastomer tubing. Luer-lock syringe needles were inserted into the ends of the chain of tubes for later connection to a syringe. c) Excess sealant squeezed out after heat was applied to the heat-shrink tubing. The sealant was smoothed into a taper for a gradual transition in rigidity between the joint and the flexible, elastomer tubing. d) A conductive fluid, EGaIn, was injected into the chain of tubing until it reached the opposite end of the chain. e) Each length of the elastomer tubing was sealed from its neighbors in sequence by using a crimping tool on the hypodermic tubing. f) A cutting tool was used to pierce the crimped region of hypodermic tubing and to separate the EGaIn-filled tubes into distinct strain gauges. g) Additional crimping was performed on the ends of the hypodermic tubing for further sealing or on ferrules to attach wires to the ends of the strain gauge.

adhesive that remained on the outside surface of the hypodermic tubing after removal from the plastic needle housing.

Multiple lengths of silicone tubing could be chained together using hypodermic tubing for rapid sequential fabrication, with each length of silicone tubing forming a separate strain gauge (Fig. 1). Stainless steel hypodermic tubing was inserted with 6.4 mm of overlap into silicone tubing to form chains (Fig. 1a). Room-temperature-vulcanizing silicone sealant (Sil-Poxy, SmoothOn) was applied evenly to the external surfaces of overlapping hypodermic and silicone tubing (Fig. 1b). To mechanically secure the joints between hypodermic and silicone tubing, 12.7 mm-lengths of 1.6 mm-diameter heat-shrink tubing were immediately placed over the uncured sealant at each joint and briefly heated with a heat gun until shrunk (Fig. 1c). Any uncured sealant that squeezed out from underneath the heat-shrink during heating was manually formed into a smooth taper for a gradual transition in stiffness near each joint while taking care to leave a central portion of hypodermic tubing exposed for future electrical connection (Fig. 1 c). 23G Luer-lock syringe needles were inserted into the silicone tubing at either end of the chain and similarly sealed (Fig. 1b-d).

After the sealant had cured, liquid metal EGaIn was drawn into a syringe and injected into one of the Luer-lock needles until reaching the opposite end of the tubing chain (Fig. 1d). Then, approximately 5 mm at the center of each exposed hypodermic tube was crimped flat using a compound-action crimping tool, beginning with the syringe needle and proceeding in sequence to the opposite end of the tubing chain (Fig. 1e). The crimped regions of hypodermic tubing were cut using diagonal cutting pliers to separate the tubing chain into individual strain gauges (Fig. 1f). After separating the sensors, approximately 2 mm of hypodermic tubing at the ends of each strain gauge were re-crimped for improved sealing and then served as electrical leads (Fig. 1g). For connection to a sensor amplifier circuit, the leads of each strain gauge were attached to lengths of copper wire (24 AWG) using crimped stainless steel ferrules.

2.2   Sensor Characterization

Strain gauges were characterized by evaluating their change in resistance with respect to strain, measuring their mechanical hysteresis on a tensile testing machine, and estimating their electromechanical hysteresis when mounted on a soft actuator.

Resistance-Strain Response. Each sensor's change in resistance was measured with respect to strain by connecting the strain gauge to an LCR meter (Atrix MCR-5030) and manually extending the strain gauge. Shorter, 114.3 mm-long strain gauges were extended in increments of 10 mm up to 200 mm, corresponding to a strain of 175%. Longer, 495.3 mm-long strain gauges were extended in increments of 10 mm up to 350 mm, corresponding to a strain of 71%.

The theoretical resistance of the strain gauges was calculated while assuming a constant volume of conductive fluid [8]:

$$V_F = A_0 L_0 = AL \tag{1}$$

$$R = \frac{\rho L}{A} \tag{2}$$

$$R = \frac{L A_0}{L_0 A} R_0 = \frac{L^2}{L_0{}^2} R_0 = (1 + \varepsilon)^2 R_0 \tag{3}$$

where V_F is the volume of conductive fluid, A_0 and A are the initial and instantaneous fluid cross-section area (respectively), L_0 and L are the initial and instantaneous length of fluid (respectively), R_0 and R are the strain gauge's initial and instantaneous electrical resistance (respectively), ρ is the fluid's electrical resistivity, and ε is strain.

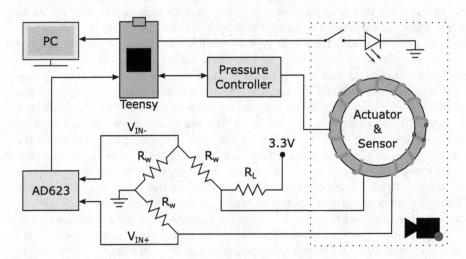

Fig. 2. Data logging setup for capturing the sensor signal from the strain gauge (thin grey lines), which is helically wrapped around a toroidal McKibben actuator (blue ring) during a test for electromechanical hysteresis. The strain gauge was connected to an amplified (AD623) Wheatstone bridge, and the amplified signal was recorded to a computer through a Teensy 4.0 microcontroller. A pressure controller received pressure setpoint values from the microcontroller and regulated the pressure in the McKibben actuator. The dotted rectangle indicates the region that was recorded by a video camera during hysteresis tests with a McKibben-mounted strain gauge. A manually-toggled switch and LED enabled synchronization between the video footage and the sensor data. Three fiducial markings on the actuator are used for tracking actuator strain in the video footage (orange dots). For mechanical hysteresis tests with the material testing system, the McKibben actuator and pressure controller are excluded from the data logging setup.

Mechanical Hysteresis. We evaluated the mechanical hysteresis of one 114.3 mm-long strain gauge and one 495.3 mm-long strain gauge in a material testing system (MTS Criterion Model 42, 50 N-load cell).

For the shorter 114.3 mm-long strain gauge, the crimped ends of the strain gauge were clamped by the testing system's fixed clamp and moving crosshead clamp. The maximum experimental crosshead extension was set to 114.3 mm, corresponding to 100% strain. For the longer 495.3 mm-long strain gauges, the testing system's maximum supported crosshead extension was insufficient to use

Table 1. Signal amplifier parameters for two different strain gauge lengths. The amplified Wheatstone bridge is shown in Fig. 2.

Parameter	Short Sensor	Long Sensor
Length (mm)	114.3	495.3
R_L (Ω)	$220 \pm 1\%$	$220 \pm 1\%$
R_W (Ω)	$1.0 \pm 1\%$	$1.62 \pm 1\%$
AD623 R_G (Ω)	$280 \pm 1\%$	$402 \pm 1\%$
AD623 Nominal Gain	358	250

the same clamping scheme as the shorter strain gauge. Instead, the 495.3 mm-long strain gauge was folded in half into an inverted U-shape that was 247.7 mm long. Both crimped ends were mounted in the testing system's fixed clamp, while the middle of the strain gauge was wrapped around a 10 mm-diameter disc magnet that was held in the moving crosshead clamp. The maximum experimental crosshead extension of the folded strain gauge was set to 247.7 mm, corresponding to a strain of 100%.

For both lengths of strain gauges, the MTS test program was set to sinusoidally cycle the strain gauges between 0% and 100% strain at 4 frequencies (0.25 Hz, 0.13 Hz, 0.063 Hz, and 0.031 Hz). Strain gauges were cycled for 4.5 periods within each frequency before proceeding to the next halved frequency. The crosshead returned to the position of 0 mm extension between frequencies. Load and extension data was logged to a text file at 100 Hz.

Electromechanical Hysteresis. To evaluate the sensor's electromechanical hysteresis in an applied setting, a strain gauge was mounted onto a McKibben actuator that was pressure cycled at multiple frequencies.

A toroidal McKibben actuator with a ~100 mm major diameter was fabricated using methods described by Dai et al. [3]. In brief, a latex balloon was cut to a length of ~280 mm and stretched over barbed reducer fittings (3.2 mm to 1.6 mm) at both ends. Braided mesh (9.5 mm, Flexo PET) was then pulled over the latex balloon and mechanically secured using a combination of Kevlar thread and cyanoacrylate adhesive. A 1.6 mm barbed T-fitting and two ~12 mm-long pieces of polyethylene tubing (1.6 mm ID × 3.2 mm OD, McMaster-Carr) were used to form the actuator into a toroid.

A 495.3 mm-long strain gauge was helically wrapped around the uninflated McKibben actuator, forming 13 complete turns around the toroid's cross-section and reaching from one of the actuator's barbed fittings to the other (Fig. 2). Spots of silicone adhesive were applied to tack together the strain gauge and the actuator at the barbed fittings and 12 additional, periodically spaced locations along the outer circumference of the toroid.

To record the analog electrical signal from the strain gauge, the strain gauge was plugged into an amplified Wheatstone bridge (AD623) with 24 AWG wire (Fig. 2). The amplified signal was then read by a microcontroller (Teensy 4.0) through an onboard 10-bit analog-to-digital converter (ADC) at a sampling frequency of 100 Hz and recorded to a text file on a PC through serial communication (PuTTY 0.70, 115200 Hz baud rate). Resistors for the Wheatstone bridge and amplifier gain were selected to prevent amplifier saturation at 100% strain (Table 1). The AD623 amplifier was setup with $+V_S = 3.3$ V, $-V_S = 0$ V, and $V_{REF} = +V_S/2 = 1.65$ V [1].

The Teensy microcontroller also controlled the pressure in the McKibben actuator through a pressure controller described in Dai et al. 2022 [3] while simultaneously logging the actuator's internal pressure signal (ELVH-030G-HAND-C-PSA4) to the same text file as the amplified strain gauge signal. The pressure controller received a sinusoidal pressure setpoint signal ranging from 0 to 69 kPa at 7 frequencies (1 Hz, 0.5 Hz, 0.25 Hz, 0.13 Hz, 0.063 Hz, 0.031 Hz, and 0.016 Hz). The actuator was cycled for 5 periods within each frequency before proceeding to the next halved frequency.

For calculating electromechanical hysteresis, the actuator's strain was estimated using computer vision to compare against the strain gauge's electrical signal. Video footage of the actuator and integrated strain gauge was recorded from a top-down view with the actuator resting on a tabletop surface (Canon EOS Rebel T7, 720p@60 Hz). For synchronizing the video footage and the microcontroller's data log, a button and LED were attached to the microcontroller and included in the frame of the video. By pushing the button, a Boolean flag was toggled in the data log and the LED simultaneously toggled on or off for reference in the video. The video's framerate of 60 Hz implies a maximum synchronization error of 16 ms. High-contrast, fiducial markings were created on the outside of the actuator using oil-based paint markers for easier tracking of actuator strain. The position data of three fiducial markings were tracked using Tracker 6.1.2 (Physlets) for estimating the toroidal actuator's strain along both the circumference and cross-sectional thickness.

Post-Processing Data Electromechanical hysteresis was evaluated by determining the relationship between strain measured by the video footage and strain measured by the strain gauge. Several data post-processing assumptions were made to determine the strain-strain relationship.

For the strain gauge, an empirically-derived relationship was used to convert between the amplified sensor voltage and strain values. The empirical relationship combined theoretically-derived output voltages from the amplified Wheatstone bridge, a theoretical relationship between strain and change in strain gauge resistance, and the experimentally-measured initial resistance of the strain gauge:

$$V_\varepsilon = G \left[\frac{R_W (R_W - R_\varepsilon)}{2 R_W (R_W + R_\varepsilon) + R_L (3 R_W + R_\varepsilon))} \right] V_P + V_{REF} \qquad (4)$$

$$\% \Delta R = \frac{R_\varepsilon}{R_0} - 1 = \frac{(1 + \varepsilon)^2 R_0}{R_0} - 1 = \varepsilon^2 + 2\varepsilon \qquad (5)$$

where V_ε is the amplified sensor voltage, G is the AD623 amplifier's gain, R_W is the resistance of Wheatstone bridge resistors (Fig. 2), R_ε is the strain gauge resistance, R_L is the resistance of an inline resistor to the Wheatstone bridge, $V_P = 3.3V$ is the voltage applied to the inline resistor, and $V_{REF} = 1.65V$ is the amplifier's reference voltage.

For the video footage, numerous assumptions were made to estimate the strain experienced by the strain gauge. Since the strain gauge was wrapped helically around the McKibben actuator, the strain gauge experienced a combination of strains from the expansion of the actuator's balloon cross-section as well as the contraction of the toroid circumference. The standard length of a helix can be calculated using:

$$L_H = n\sqrt{(p^2 + C^2)} \tag{6}$$

where L_H is the length of the helix, n is the number of turns, p is the helical pitch, and C is the helix's circumference.

From the three tracked points on the inner and outer diameter of the toroidal actuator (Fig. 2, orange dots), we calculated the pitch of the strain gauge helix as well as the cross-section thickness of the McKibben actuator.

The McKibben actuator's cross-section shape changes with inflation pressure (Fig. 3). At low pressures, the cross-section narrows due to the flatness of the actuator's braided mesh. As the actuator inflates, the cross-section becomes more circular. Therefore, we calculated the perimeter of the cross-section as a substitute for the helical circumference, C. We modeled the cross-section geometry using two circular arcs. The sum of arc lengths was equal to the perimeter of the helix. Arc lengths were calculated by finding the center point of the arc, then calculating the radius of the arc and the arc's central angle.

We placed the origin of our coordinate system at the center of the two circular arcs (Fig. 3a,b, white arrows). To find the center point of one of the circular arcs, we identified three points along the arc and applied the equation of a circle:

$$\begin{bmatrix} x_1 & y_1 \\ x_2 & y_2 \\ x_3 & y_3 \end{bmatrix} = \begin{bmatrix} 0 & \frac{h}{2} \\ \frac{t}{2} & 0 \\ 0 & -\frac{h}{2} \end{bmatrix} \tag{7}$$

$$r^2 = (x - x_C)^2 + (y - y_C)^2 \tag{8}$$

$$\begin{bmatrix} 2(x_1 - x_3) & 2(y_1 - y_3) \\ 2(x_1 - x_2) & 2(y_1 - y_2) \end{bmatrix} \begin{bmatrix} x_C \\ y_C \end{bmatrix} = \begin{bmatrix} x_1^2 - x_3^2 + y_1^2 - y_3^2 \\ x_1^2 - x_2^2 + y_1^2 - y_2^2 \end{bmatrix} \tag{9}$$

where h is the height of the actuator's cross-section, t is the thickness of the actuator's cross-section, r is the radius of the circular arc, and (x_C, y_C) is the center point of the arc. Then, the arc length and the actuator's cross-sectional perimeter were calculated:

$$s = r\theta \tag{10}$$

$$\theta = 2\arctan\left(\frac{y_1 - y_C}{x_1 - x_C}\right) \tag{11}$$

$$C = 2s \tag{12}$$

where s is the arc length, θ is the central angle, and C is the circumference or perimeter of the actuator's cross-section.

We measured thickness values, t, from the video footage and determined the height, h, using an empirically-derived relationship between t and h. To develop the empirical relationship between t and h, the actuator was inflated from 0 to 69 kPa in increments of 6.9 kPa, while t and h were measured manually using calipers. Then we fit a second-order curve to the data assuming units in millimeters (Fig. 3c):

$$h = 0.033t^2 - 0.367t + 15.7 \tag{13}$$

Near the actuator's fittings, the cross-section was constrained by the barbed fitting to be more circular. To estimate the strain gauge's strain near the barbed fittings, we applied another assumption that the cross-section geometry transitioned from a circular shape at the barbed fitting to the actuator's standard cross-section within the span of half a turn of the strain gauge's helix. For a full turn, the length of the strain gauge near the fittings was estimated by:

$$L_E = \sqrt{p^2 + \left(\frac{3C + \pi d}{4}\right)^2} \tag{14}$$

where L_E is the length of the strain gauge helix at the conical ends of the actuator and $d = 10$ mm is the fixed diameter of the actuator cross-section near the barbed fitting.

The full length of the strain gauge, with 11 standard turns and 2 conical end turns, was calculated by combining Eqs. 6 and 14:

$$L_\varepsilon = 11L_H + 2L_E \tag{15}$$

where L_ε is the full length of the strain gauge when wrapped around the actuator. This enabled us to estimate the strain seen by the strain sensor.

2.3   Contact Detection

To explore the contact detection capabilities of the strain sensor, we pressurized the toroidal McKibben actuator and monitored the strain gauge signal before and after placing a tennis ball (Penn) within the circumference of the actuator. The same experimental setup was used as with electromechanical hysteresis testing. First, the actuator's pressure controller received a sinusoidal control signal for 5 cycles between 0 to 69 kPa at 0.13 Hz while no objects were present within the actuator's circumference, to serve as contactless reference data. Next, a tennis ball was placed within the actuator's circumference. The actuator was cycled again for 5 cycles between 0 to 69 kPa at 0.13 Hz to collect contact detection data.

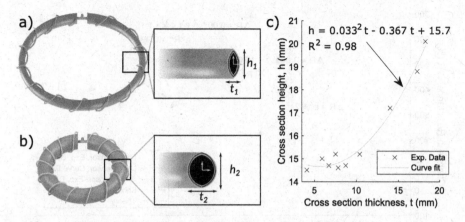

Fig. 3. The cross-section of the McKibben actuator changes shape depending on inflation pressure. a) At low pressure, the actuator's cross-section flattens, while b) at
high pressure, the actuator's cross-section becomes more circular. The perimeter of the
cross-section is modeled with two circular arcs (highlighted in red and blue). The coordinate system is represented by the white arrows. c) An empirical relationship between
t and h was established by fitting a second-order curve to experimental data. This
relationship was used to approximate the actuator height from thickness data taken
from video footage of the actuator.

3 Results

3.1 Strain and Resistance

The experimental resistance-strain responses of three 495.3 mm-long strain
gauges and two 114.3 mm-long strain gauges were found to be similar when compared to their theoretical quadratic responses (Fig. 4). Due to different starting
resistances, R_0, for different lengths of strain sensors, we normalized the data to
show % change in resistance. Second-order curves fit to the 495.3 mm-long strain
gauge data and the 114.3 mm-long strain gauge data have R^2 values of 0.992 and
0.998, respectively. Both fitted curves lie below the theoretical resistance-strain
relationship (Eq. 5), with the "Long" sensor data located closer to the theoretical
curve than the "Short" sensor data.

3.2 Mechanical Hysteresis

Both tested lengths of strain gauges exhibited mechanical stress-strain hysteresis
when loaded cyclically (Fig. 5a), with softening at intermediate strain values.
Data were post-processed with an exponential moving average ($w = 10$). Only
1 out of every 15 markers was plotted for clarity. At a cycling frequency of
0.031 Hz, the 114.3 mm-long sensor exhibited a higher peak stress of 713 kPa at
98.2% strain, compared to the 495.3 mm-long sensor's peak stress of 592 kPa at
98.2% strain.

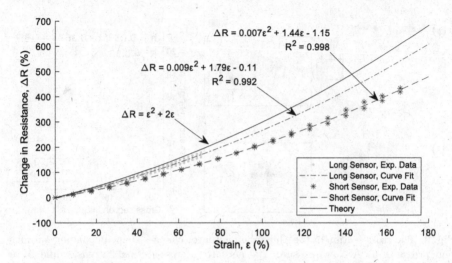

Fig. 4. Resistance response of two strain gauges with different lengths. The "Long" sensor measured 495.3 mm long and was extended up to 350 mm, corresponding to a strain of ∼71%. The "Short" sensor measured 114.3 mm long and was extended up to 200 mm, corresponding to a strain of ∼175%. The calculated theoretical resistance assumes a quadratic relationship between strain and resistance. Discrepancies between the experimental and theoretical results could be due to electrical contact resistance between the conductive fluid and the hypodermic tubing used in the sensor.

Due to limitations in the maximum travel speed of the MTS crosshead, the strain gauges did not experience the full range of cyclical motion for the higher cycling frequencies of 0.25 Hz and 0.13 Hz (Fig. 5b). As testing progressed from higher to lower cycling frequencies, the strain sensor visually exhibited slack when the crosshead returned to 0 mm extension between frequencies. The slack is evident in the data by examining the strains corresponding to 0 kPa stress. The strain gauge experienced 0 kPa stress at progressively higher strain values after each sequentially tested frequency.

3.3   Electromechanical Hysteresis

The strain gauge exhibited low electromechanical hysteresis, demonstrated by plotting the strain-strain response from both the strain gauge and video footage of the actuator (Fig. 6). The relationship is mostly linear with $R^2 = 0.993$ when evaluated using $y = x$. There is no distinct hysteresis loop visible in the figure. The strain calculated from the sensor signal deviates from the linear relationship between approximately 10% to 30% video data strain, with a peak mean deviation of 2.1% sensor signal strain at 20.6% video data strain.

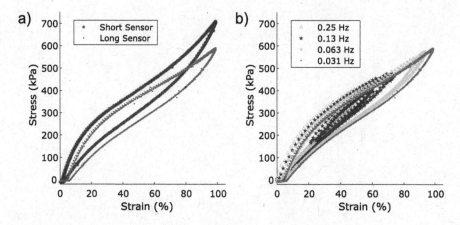

Fig. 5. Stress-strain hysteresis loops of strain gauges when cycled on a material testing system up to 100% strain. a) Both lengths of strain gauges exhibited similar hysteresis loops when cycled at a frequency of 0.031 Hz. The shorter, 114.3 mm-long sensor showed a higher peak stress than the longer, 495.3 mm-long sensor. b) Due to limitations of the testing system's crosshead speed, the strain gauges did not reach the full range of motion at higher frequencies of 0.25 Hz and 0.13 Hz. As the testing progressed from higher to lower frequencies, a 495.3 mm-long sensor's hysteresis loop shifted to the right, and the zero-stress crossing point corresponded to increasingly higher strain values, which suggests plastic deformation within the strain gauge.

3.4   Contact Detection

The strain sensor signal from the contact detection experiment shows a 1.00 V peak difference between the sensor data with and without contact (Fig. 7). The data presented were averaged over 5 cycles, using the 0 kPa pressure setpoint signal as a synchronizing reference. The peak pressure setpoint of 69 kPa was reached between 4–5 s, as expected from the 0.13 Hz pressure signal frequency. Due to the amplified Wheatstone bridge, an increase in resistance corresponds to a decrease in signal voltage. The sensor data without contact shows a minimum value of 1.37 V, corresponding to the highest inflation pressure in the actuator and the highest strain experienced by the strain gauge during contactless data collection. In contrast, the strain sensor voltage drops to a value of 0.37 V after contacting the ball, which is the saturation voltage of the signal amplifier and corresponds to a higher strain gauge resistance than in the contactless data.

4   Discussion

The strain sensor exhibits a resistance-strain response that follows a second-order curve fit, as expected by Eq. 5. We note that the fitted curves for both the 495.3 mm-long and 114.3 mm-long sensors lie below the quadratic relationship expected from theory (Fig. 4). This could be due to additional fixed-value

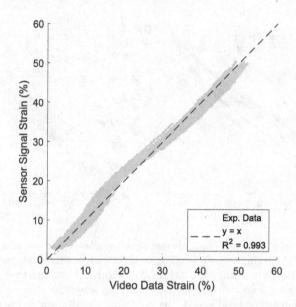

Fig. 6. The strain sensor did not exhibit noticeable strain-strain hysteresis when mounted on an actuator and cycled at varying frequencies. This suggests that any hysteresis in the integrated actuator-sensor system is dominated by the viscoelastic response of the McKibben actuator rather than by the sensor. In addition, the strain response measured by the sensor was nearly 1:1, with the strain calculated by a video imaging method. As a result, the strain gauge can be considered to provide quick and accurate feedback for sensing the state of the McKibben actuator. Discrepancies around 20–30% strain may be due to nonlinear effects of the McKibben actuator's geometry that require additional modeling when processing the video image data.

resistances within the strain gauge, such as contact resistances and the resistance of the stainless steel tubing, that were not a function of strain and were not modeled. The strain gauge resistance is composed of both fixed and strain-varying resistances. In an extreme, hypothetical case where the strain gauge was constructed from materials that do not exhibit any strain-varying resistance, we would expect to see a flat line with respect to strain. As the proportion of strain-varying resistance increases relative to fixed resistance, we expect the strain gauge's resistance-strain response to approach the curve described by Eq. 5. Supporting this hypothesis, we found that the longer 495.3 mm-long sensors are in closer proximity to the theoretical curve than the shorter 114.3 mm-long sensors. The longer sensors contain a greater proportion of elastomer tubing and conductive fluid than the shorter sensors and, therefore, a higher proportion of strain-varying to fixed resistance.

Regarding contact resistances within the strain gauge, we noted that the initial sensor resistance tended to be higher than expected immediately after fabrication, by up to multiple ohms. This discrepancy was rectified to the milliohm range by rapidly stretching and releasing the strain sensor. We hypothesize

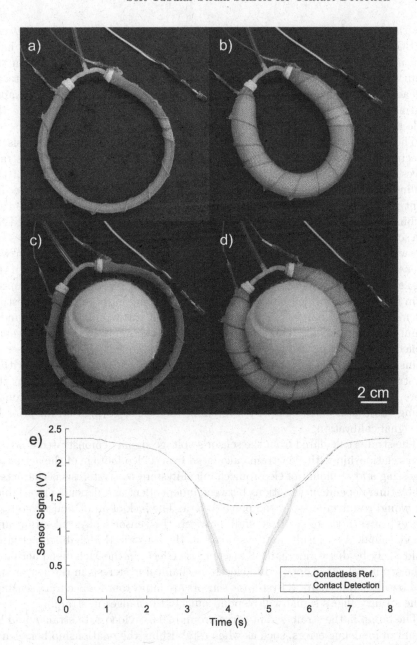

Fig. 7. The strain sensor was evaluated for contact detection capability by monitoring the sensor signal with and without contact. Contactless data was collected as the actuator was cycled between the a) deflated and b) inflated states while no object was present. Contact detection data was collected after c) placing a tennis ball within the actuator's circumference and d) pressurizing the actuator. e) The contact is observable through a sudden drop in the strain sensor's voltage signal. Lines indicate mean values, while shaded regions represent standard deviation.

that the high initial resistance could result from poor surface wetting between the EGaIn and the stainless steel hypodermic tubing. Surface wetting may have been improved by applying high acceleration to perturb the liquid within the strain sensor. In addition, gallium is known to form an oxide layer that can increase interfacial contact resistance [13]. In the future, hydrochloric acid vapor treatment could be explored during strain gauge fabrication to eliminate the oxide layer and reduce contact resistance.

The tested strain gauges exhibited mechanical stress-strain hysteresis as expected from their elastomer components. The non-Hookean stress-strain curves, with softening at intermediate strain values, are representative of the Mullins effect in viscoelastic materials [12]. When cycled at 0.031 Hz, the different peak stresses for the different lengths of strain gauges could be due to a combination of the Mullins effect and the different clamping methods used for each sensor length. As elastomers are exposed to higher peak strains and stresses, they will become softer at lower strain values. We note that the long sensor was softer than the short sensor at high strain values, which could be explained if the long sensor had experienced higher peak stress in prior testing. Since the longer strain gauges were formed into a U-shape for clamping into the material testing system, there was a portion of the strain gauge that was wrapped 180° around a 10 mm-diameter magnet. This wrapped portion of the strain gauge may have led to effective shortening of the strain sensor and, consequently, higher stresses or strains than expected for a given extension length. Slack that developed within the strain gauge during testing was likely due to plastic deformation. In the future, robotic applications that experience high strain should consider conditioning the sensor beforehand by stretching the sensor to high strain prior to any signal calibration.

The strains calculated from the sensor's voltage signal demonstrated a nearly linear relationship with the strain calculated from video footage of the actuator, suggesting a low amount of electromechanical hysteresis. Hysteresis is characterized by time-dependent variations between independent and dependent variables that would result in loops in the plotted data. The lack of an obvious hysteresis loop indicates little to no time shift between the sensor's physical strain and voltage signal. As a result, any hysteresis in the sensorized McKibben actuator would likely be due to mechanical viscoelastic effects in the McKibben actuator or the strain gauge, as opposed to electromechanical hysteresis in the sensor signal. Low electromechanical hysteresis sensors are important for accurate sensing, as the strain gauge's signal will respond quickly to changes in strain.

The bump in the strain-strain curve around 20.6% video data strain could be a result of modeling errors, such as when establishing the relationship between h and t (Fig. 3). We note that there is a nonlinear response in the actuator's cross-section dimensions with respect to pressure, which is indicated by the uneven intervals between collected data. While a second-order curve was fit to the data, future collection of cross-sectional dimensions at a higher resolution in t could result in a different fit, such as a piecewise linear function with a knee around $t = 10.4$ mm. We note that the scaling of the strain-strain relationship was sensitive to the assumptions made when post-processing the video data due to the effects of the assumptions on the strain gauge's calculated initial length. However, the assumptions did not affect trends in the data. We made no time-dependent assumptions that would result in a hysteresis loop if inaccurate.

During contact detection experiments, contact between the sensor and the tennis ball resulted in an abrupt change in sensor signal voltage as compared to the contactless signal data. As mentioned previously, the signal voltage decreases when the sensor resistance increases, due to the signal amplifier circuit. When the actuator and strain gauge touched the tennis ball, the ball pressed on the strain sensor's elastomer tubing and reduced the cross-sectional area of conductive fluid, resulting in higher resistance. The rapidly increased resistance during contact is responsible for the sudden drop in sensor signal voltage. The large 1.00 V contrast in signal voltage is desirable to distinguish contact events from false positives if used as a digital signal. Further experimentation to relate contact force and signal voltage could also enable high-resolution analog force sensing.

Integrating strain sensing with soft pneumatic actuators can provide additional sensing modalities for improved functionality in soft robots. In robots that solely monitor actuator pressure, state control may rely on open-loop control with predefined models that cannot robustly respond to disturbances. The addition of strain sensing as a second modality can help close the loop for robust control of pose with respect to both the robot and the external environment. Beyond measuring strain directly, strain sensors with contact detection capabilities can be used for proprioception between internal components, for orientation to environmental landmarks, and for applications including grasping and manipulation. The presented work demonstrates an easily fabricated strain gauge that can be used as a contact detection sensor to support these applications in the future. Since the strain gauge can be fabricated asynchronously from the fluidic actuator and without direct integration in the actuator's elastomer components, fatigue failures of elastomer elements can be easily repaired at low cost.

Further developments to the presented strain sensor will focus on reducing the contact resistance between the conductive fluid and the stainless steel leads or explore alternative materials for fabrication. In addition, characterizing the sensor's electromechanical hysteresis using automated data collection methods may help further quantify the sensor's signal response speed. We would also like to explore the integration of these sensors into an increased variety of actuators for internal proprioception in soft robots. As soft robots incorporate greater varieties of actuators, model-free integration of these sensors into robotic applications may become desirable to eliminate the sensor modeling and assumptions made in this paper.

5   Conclusion

The presented strain sensor design provides a possible solution for integrating strain sensing into existing soft robotic actuators. The simple manufacturing process of the strain gauge can enable rapid series production of several sensors. Characterization of these sensors showed expected resistance-strain and stress-strain responses when compared to engineering models. The low electromechanical hysteresis of these sensors suggests a sufficiently high response rate to changes in strain when mounted on a cyclically pressurized McKibben actuator. In addition to detecting changes in length, the sensor also displayed a high-contrast electrical signal for detecting contact between an actuator and a gripped ball. Further development of the sensor could provide a low-cost sensing solution for applications in soft robotic proprioception and manipulation.

Acknowledgements. The authors would like to thank Ashlee Liao for insightful feedback during manuscript editing.

References

1. Analog Devices: Single and Dual-Supply, Rail-to-Rail, Low Cost Instrumentation Amplifier, September 2020. rev. G
2. Cooper, C.B., et al.: Stretchable capacitive sensors of torsion, strain, and touch using double helix liquid metal fibers. Adv. Funct. Mater. **27**(20), 1605630 (2017). https://doi.org/10.1002/adfm.201605630
3. Dai, K., et al.: SLUGBOT, an aplysia-inspired robotic grasper for studying control. In: Biomimetic and Biohybrid Systems. Living Machines 2022. LNCS, vol. 13548, pp. 182–194. Springer, Cham (2022). https://doi.org/10.1007/978-3-031-20470-8_19
4. El-Atab, N., et al.: Soft actuators for soft robotic applications: a review. Adv. Intell. Syst. **2**(10), 2000128 (2020). https://doi.org/10.1002/aisy.202000128
5. Huang, X., et al.: Chasing biomimetic locomotion speeds: creating untethered soft robots with shape memory alloy actuators. Sci. Robot. **3**(25), eaau7557 (2018). https://doi.org/10.1126/scirobotics.aau7557
6. Kanno, R., Watanabe, S., Shimizu, K., Shintake, J.: Self-sensing McKibben artificial muscles embedded with dielectric elastomer sensor. IEEE Robot. Autom. Lett. **6**(4), 6274–6280 (2021). https://doi.org/10.1109/LRA.2021.3093276
7. Kellaris, N., Gopaluni Venkata, V., Smith, G.M., Mitchell, S.K., Keplinger, C.: Peano-hasel actuators: muscle-mimetic, electrohydraulic transducers that linearly contract on activation. Sci. Robot. **3**(14), eaar3276 (2018). https://doi.org/10.1126/scirobotics.aar3276
8. King, J.P., Valle, L.E., Pol, N., Park, Y.L.: Design, modeling, and control of pneumatic artificial muscles with integrated soft sensing. In: 2017 IEEE International Conference on Robotics and Automation (ICRA), pp. 4985–4990. IEEE (2017). https://doi.org/10.1109/ICRA.2017.7989580
9. Klute, G.K., Hannaford, B.: Fatigue characteristics of McKibben artificial muscle actuators. In: Proceedings. 1998 IEEE/RSJ International Conference on Intelligent Robots and Systems. Innovations in Theory, Practice and Applications (Cat. No. 98CH36190), vol. 3, pp. 1776–1781. IEEE (1998). https://doi.org/10.1109/IROS.1998.724854
10. Kothera, C.S., Jangid, M., Sirohi, J., Wereley, N.M.: Experimental characterization and static modeling of McKibben actuators. J. Mech. Des. **131**(9) (2009). https://doi.org/10.1115/1.3158982

11. Majidi, C.: Soft-matter engineering for soft robotics. Adv. Mater. Technol. **4**(2), 1800477 (2019). https://doi.org/10.1002/admt.201800477
12. Ogden, R.W., Roxburgh, D.G.: A pseudo-elastic model for the mullins effect in filled rubber. Proc. R. Soc. Lond. Ser. A Math. Phys. Eng. Sci. **455**(1988), 2861–2877 (1999). https://doi.org/10.1098/rspa.1999.0431
13. Ozutemiz, K.B., Wissman, J., Ozdoganlar, O.B., Majidi, C.: EGain-metal interfacing for liquid metal circuitry and microelectronics integration. Adv. Mater. Interfaces **5**(10), 1701596 (2018). https://doi.org/10.1002/admi.201701596
14. Piazza, A., Parker, A.: Highly elastic strain gage for low modulus materials. In: 2015 WRSGC Winter Test and Measurement Meeting. No. DFRC-E-DAA-TN22087 (2015)
15. Tondu, B.: Modelling of the McKibben artificial muscle: a review. J. Intell. Mater. Syst. Struct. **23**(3), 225–253 (2012). https://doi.org/10.1177/1045389X11435435
16. Wirekoh, J., Valle, L., Pol, N., Park, Y.L.: Sensorized, flat, pneumatic artificial muscle embedded with biomimetic microfluidic sensors for proprioceptive feedback. Soft Robot. **6**(6), 768–777 (2019). https://doi.org/10.1089/soro.2018.0110
17. Zhong, S., et al.: A contraction length feedback method for the McKibben pneumatic artificial muscle. Sens. Actuators A **334**, 113321 (2022). https://doi.org/10.1016/j.sna.2021.113321
18. Zhu, S., et al.: Ultrastretchable fibers with metallic conductivity using a liquid metal alloy core. Adv. Funct. Mater. **23**(18), 2308–2314 (2013). https://doi.org/10.1002/adfm.201202405

Bioderived Hygromorphic Twisted Actuator for Untethered Sustainable Systems

Reece Whatmore[1]([✉]), Emelia Keely[1], Zoe Lee[2], Adriane Minori[3], and Lining Yao[3]

[1] Department of Materials Science and Engineering, Carnegie Mellon University, Pittsburgh, PA 15218, USA
{rwhatmor,ekeely}@andrew.cmu.edu
[2] Industrial Design Department, Rhode Island School of Design, Providence, RI 02903, USA
zlee@risd.edu
[3] Human-Computer Interaction Institute, School of Computer Science, Carnegie Mellon University, Pittsburgh, PA 15218, USA
aminori@andrew.cmu.edu, liningy@cs.cmu.edu

Abstract. Environmentally friendly and hygromorphic actuators have gained increasing attention for energy harvesting, field robotics, seeding and biodegradable active structures and sensors. While recent works have used hygromorphic seeds as sources of bio-inspiration, it is challenging to engineer synthetic hygromorphic actuators with comparable stiffness, energy density, and reaction speed, and the processing of synthetic materials or need for external power sources inevitably increases fossil fuel consumption and waste production. In this paper, we harness an alternative bioderived design approach, utilizing the natural twisted body of the seed, *Hesperostipa Spartea*, itself as a sustainable and biodegradable hygromorphic twisting actuator that converts atmospheric water concentration into mechanical energy. Our self-powered twisted actuator is capable of providing twisting actuation with a load over 11,000 times its body mass. We further demonstrate the potential of modular biohybrid design to create untethered self-locking and crawling systems, powered solely by environmental stimuli. The ability to create biodegradable self-actuating systems with modular bioderived design presents opportunities to create biocompatible systems, improving sustainability in the field of soft robotics and beyond.

Keywords: bioderived and biohybrid design · morphing materials · active smart materials · hygromorphic motion · twisting actuator · sustainable robotics

1 Introduction

Nature provides endless sources of inspiration for designers and engineers. With climate change posing a threat to our society and planet, it is essential that we create sustainable systems that generate less harm to the natural world. One way to increase the compatibility between mechanical design and natural ecosystems is to create systems that are

Supplementary Information The online version contains supplementary material available at https://doi.org/10.1007/978-3-031-38857-6_17.

built of natural materials, tailored to harness renewable energy, and fully biodegrade. We can build further upon the principles of bioinspiration by using a bioderived design that harnesses organic materials in their natural form to create a fully biocompatible system.

One common source of self-powered actuation in nature is hygromorph. Moisture triggers a mechanical response in hygromorphic materials, causing materials such as wood and many seeds to morph with humidity changes in the atmosphere. Previous works have harnessed the hygromorphic ability of wood to enable untethered and self-sensing actuation as an inherently moisture-responsive material in architecture [1], design [2], robotics [3], and 3D printing [4, 5]. Other hygroscopically induced actuators have been made with biobased materials such as paper[6], thin wood laminates [7, 8], large wooden bilayers [9, 10], and 4D printing biobased composites [11, 12]. Additionally, other humidity-driven materials such as agarose [13] and polyethylene oxide films [14] have been used to create humidity-powered robotic locomotion.

Many natural seeds are hygromorphic, which have been presented as sources of bioinspiration for past works. In natural environments, oscillations in humidity and temperature conditions occur throughout the day and night transition cycle which stimulate the seeds' shape changes [15]. The self-powered motion and unique forms have inspired an array of bioinspired seed-actuators that have been used for motions such as microflier flight [16], self-drilling [17, 18] lifting [19], and coiling [20]. While these past works took the natural seeds as bio-inspirations, we propose an alternative bioderived approach, harnessing an organic seed itself as a sustainable natural actuator.

In this work, we investigate the porcupine grass seed, *Hesperostipa Spartea*, as an untethered self-sensing and powered actuator for potential robotic applications. The *Hesperostipa Spartea* is a species of perennial grass that is native to the Great Plains of North America [21]. It has a tightly twisted awn that generates torque to power its humidity-driven self-burial behavior [22]. We study their behavior to harness their twisted awn as natural and off-the-shelf actuators and to potentially enable other custom-made bioinspired actuators. We hypothesize that since the twisted bodies of the porcupine seed are tight and dense with respect to other coiled seeds (e.g., *Erodium*), we can harness a more advantageous time-response and actuation performance for soft and biohybrid robots. Furthermore, by leveraging the seed itself without post processing (e.g., chemical washing [17]), we maintain the integrity of the seed's strength and performance. To validate this hypothesis, we investigate the morphology and biomechanics of the seed, including its actuation strain, speed, and strength-to-weight ratio, and demonstrate its usability towards sustainable and biohybrid robotic applications (e.g., self-locking, crawling).

1.1 Background: *Hesperostipa Spartea*

The porcupine grass seed, *Hesperostipa Spartea*, is a hygro-responsive seed that harnesses humidity fluctuation for a self-burial motion [21]. The complete seed diaspore can be described in three distinct sections: the pointed tip (s1), extended awn (s2 and s3), and bent end (s4) (Fig. 1A, 1B). The sharply pointed tip consists of a hairy callus containing the seed embryo. The awn sprouts from the seed's tip in a twisted section that begins tightly twisted (s2) and transitions into looser twists (s3) as it approaches the bend. The end of the seed has a bent, untwisted portion (s4), sometimes with the double-bent structure. The twisted section provides the mechanical twisting of the seed and will be classified as the body of the seed throughout this paper. While the internal structure of the specific *Hesperostipa Spartea* seed has not been explored in detail, the internal structure holds similar to the *Stipa Epilosa* seed [23]. The structure of the seed can be described as a combination of two planes of lighter (p1) and darker (p2) shade, with the lightest shaded edge plane (e1) connecting these two, respectively (Fig. 1C, 1D). The internal structure of the two intertwined twisted bilayers allows for the reversibility of the twisting and untwisting of the segment as stimulated by humidity fluctuations (Fig. 1E). The basic kinetic shape change of the seed is a reversible humidity-driven untwisting and retwisting motion to provide mechanical energy for the seed's self-burial behavior. When the seed is exposed to humidity in the air or submerged in water, it transforms from its initial pre-twisted state to an untwisted, elongated state, by rotating in a clockwise direction, when viewed from above, with the seed tip downwards. The internal structure of the seed holds shape-memory, resulting in a repeatable motion. When the seed is fully untwisted and is exposed to a dry (low humidity) environment, or removed from high humidity conditions, it begins to retwist in a clockwise direction. When isolating the body of this seed, it can be mechanically viewed as a self-powered twisted actuator as a function of the humidity diffusion rate. The twisted body holds potential to be harvested for many applications beyond its natural burial behavior.

2   Biological Investigation

Porcupine grass seeds, *Hesperostipa Spartea,* were purchased online from Everwilde Farms. The seed's diameter was measured using a Carbon Fiber Composites Digital Caliper with a resolution of 0.1 mm. The seed mass was measured with a U.S. Solid Precision Balance with a resolution of 10–5 g. Seed characteristics including seed length and seed twist angles were conducted using ImageJ software with a pixel solution of 2532x1170. The seeds were placed in water and a humidity chamber to stimulate their untwisting motion, and the water and air temperatures were measured with a smart sensor infrared thermometer.

2.1   Analysis of *Hesperostipa Spartea* Geometry as a Hygroscopic Actuator

An analysis on the seed characteristics was conducted to understand the geometric parameters of the biological material. Due to the bioderived nature of our design, our ability to optimally construct a robotic system depends on our ability to both quantify and control the natural deviation within the seeds. We focused on quantifying the twisted body of the seed to understand its geometry and its resulting rotational shape changes. From this analysis, a method of harvesting with maximum consistency was developed to create a geometrically quantifiable twisted actuator.

The twist angle of the seed is defined as the angle from the seed's edge to its closest dark plane (Fig. 1F). When in its dry twisted state, the twist angle was quantified with a sample size of 13 natural *Hesperostipa Spartea* seeds (e.g., $n = 13$ for the following angle and twist number measurements). The complete seed has 14.15 ± 1.6 twists in its total length (complete extended awn), and the tightly twisting portion (s2) has an average of 10.84 ± 1.1 twists, resulting in an average of 3.90 ± 0.32 mm per seed twist. The average angle of the twists in the seed is 24.71 ± 1.95°. The twists in the region extruding from pointed tip (s2 in Fig. 1A) have the tightest and most consistent twist with an average angle of 22.60 ± 2.29°. At the opposing end of the awn (s3 in Fig. 1A), towards the bend, the twists become wider and hold more variation, with an average angle of 26.47 ± 2.82°. As a result of this variation in twisting angles, when harvesting the seeds as a twisting actuator, the seed length is limited to the section containing consistent tight twists (s2), on average a length of 42.11 ± 3.26 mm.

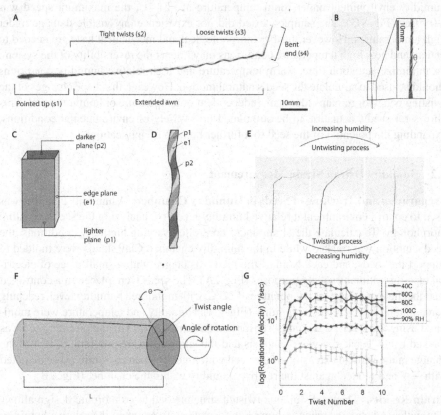

Fig. 1. Porcupine grass seed characteristics. (A) Anatomy of porcupine grass seed. (B) Porcupine grass seed with magnified image of tight twists near the pointed tip. (C) Schematic of seed planes. (D) Schematic of seed fully twisted, with the dark, edge, and light planes depicting the twists of the seed. (E) Twisting and untwisting process of seed at various times given an increase or decrease in humidity. (F) Cross-sectional schematic of seed demonstrating the angle of rotation of twists, and the twist angle of the seed. (G) Number of twists in a seed relative to the log scale of rotational velocity. Rotational velocity is the degree of untwisting per second given various temperatures of water and relative humidity levels. Data are means with standard deviations shown with error bars given n = 3 samples.

We additionally analyzed the rotational speed of the seed to further quantify actuation time. The speed of the seed's rotational actuation is a function of humidity level and temperature (Fig. 1G). Among the conditions tested, fastest actuation speeds occur under highest temperature and complete water submergence (i.e. in ~100 °C hot water) from the twisted to untwisted state. The rotational speed from the dehydrated to hydrated state was tested in a humidity chamber with 90% relative humidity, and in water at 40, 60, 80 and 100 °C temperatures. The maximum rotational speed in hot water submergence is much faster than when the seed is actuated under atmospheric humidity conditions (Fig. 1G). When transitioning from the twisted state to an untwisted state, the maximum speed in 100 °C hot water submergence was 90°/sec, while in a controlled 90% relative humidity environment under room temperature at ~21 °C, the maximum speed was 2.05°/sec (Fig. 1G). The samples tested did not experience any visible damage under high temperatures. However, further morphological and mechanical tests are needed to understand how high temperature conditions may impact the reversibility of the system. To minimize actuation time, warm temperature and high relative humidity conditions should be used to stimulate the seed's natural motion. However, the shape changes of the twisting behavior remains identical, independent of temperature or humidity level. This allows for seed's actuation to be stimulated in a variety of environmental conditions, expanding the potential of the seed to a further breadth of applications.

2.2 Humidity Driven Strain Measurement

Preparation and Tracking of Seeds in Humidity Chamber. A humidity chamber was used to control environmental relative humidity levels for analyzing the seed's twisting morphology. To calculate the strain under controlled varying humidity conditions, the seed's motion was tracked while in the humidity chamber. Clay stands were molded to support the seeds, and each bend of the seed was tagged with a small piece of electrical tape for optimal tracking purposes (Fig. 2A). The seeds were placed in a controlled chamber held at a constant temperature of 22°C, with monitored humidity level, reaching a maximum of 90% relative humidity (Fig. 2A). Humidity and temperature were monitored using the DHT-22 humidity sensor and Arduino UNO. The tag on each seed was tracked using Tracker, a video analysis and modeling software program, to record the change in the vertical extension of the seed with time. The percent strain was calculated with $\frac{l-l_0}{l_0}$ and plotted against the relative humidity within the chamber (Fig. 2B).

Strain Results. The seed's unique twisted structure and hygromorphic design allows it to withstand stresses when in humid atmospheres. To compare the relative humidity and strain of the seed, and thus, the deformation it can undergo, an experimental stress analysis was conducted. After a period of initial negative strain, the strain of the body increases with humidity, and reaches its maximum percent strain as the humidity in the chamber is standardized to 90% relative humidity (Fig. 2B). An increase in humidity causes elongation of the seed relative to its initial length: a humidity level of 90% results in a maximum strain of 25% of the seed's body. Before the 90% humidity level is reached, the seed undergoes a negative strain as a result of the end of the seed near the loosely twisted region bending while untwisting from a dehydrated to hydrated state. After upwards of 40 min, 90% humidity is reached, at which point the tighter twists near the pointed tip begin untwisting and elongating, creating an overall positive strain (Fig. 2B).

A strain analysis of the seed with the bend removed, portions s1-s3 of the seed, demonstrated a similar initial period of negative strain before elongation. A minimum percent strain of -7.34% ($\pm$ 3.95, n = 3) occurred due to the bending of the loosely twisted portion of the seed (s3) while transitioning from a dehydrated to hydrated state (Fig. 2Cii). The seed continues to untwist throughout the hydration process, reaching extension and resulting in a final maximum percent strain of 9.18% ($\pm$ 2.9, n = 3) (Fig. 2Civ). From these observations, we can hypothesize that the negative strain observed in the initial humidity strain test (Fig. 2B) is due to this bending of s3 compounded with further bending due to the weight of the tracking tag. The seed's tightly twisted portion (s2) shows no bending motion and therefore shows no period of negative strain. The tightly coiled region has a maximum percent strain of 15.25% ($\pm$ 1.36, n = 3) (Fig. 2D).

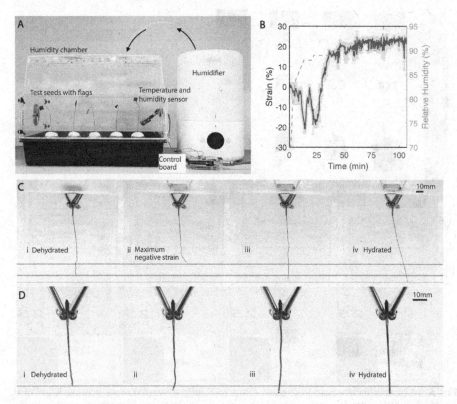

Fig. 2. (A) Experimental humidity chamber setup with tagged seeds that untwist from their initial dehydrated state to their final, untwisted hydrated state. (B) Percent strain of seed as relative humidity increases to 90%. Data are means with standard deviations shown in the shaded regions given n = 3 samples. (C) Time lapse photos of seeds untwisting in hot water, depicting the negative strain in a seed when loose and tight twists are present. (D) Time lapse photos of seeds untwisting in hot water, depicting the positive strain when the seed is cut so only tight twists are present in the seed.

2.3 Load Lifting Test

As a further investigation into the mechanical properties of the seed, a weight lifting analysis was conducted. The total lift distance and rotational speed as the seed transitioned from an initial untwisted state to a completely retwisted state was analyzed under varying loads (completed in a heated ~ 30–50 °C environment). To control variation in the organic structure, the bend (s4) was trimmed to 10 mm when in a dry state. Each seed was then fully untwisted in hot water, the pointed tip (s1) was removed, and all seeds were cut to a length of 60 mm. This process of controlled harvesting creates an optimized bioderived actuator. Four completely untwisted seeds were hung vertically with clips with four differing loads attached (0 g, 50 g, 100 g, 200 g) (Fig. 3A). Seeds were placed in a heated chamber and the distance each seed lifted its corresponding mass was measured.

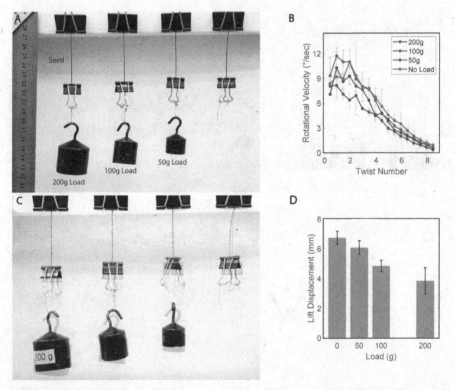

Fig. 3. (A) Experimental load lifting test setup with fully untwisted seeds bearing loads of 0, 50, 100 and 200 g. (B) The rotational velocity of the seed relative to its number of twists for the various loads lifted. Data are means and the error bars represent standard deviations given n = 3 samples. (C) Time lapse of seeds lifting their loads as they transition from hydrated to dehydrated states. (D) Lift displacement, calculated as the difference in height of the load as the seed twists from its initial hydrated state to its final twisted dehydrated state. Data are means and the error bars represent standard deviations given n = 3 samples.

The rotational velocity (°/sec) of the seed varied under load with the fastest rotation occurring under no load and slowest under the largest (e.g., 200 g load) (Fig. 3B). A 200 g load is over 11,700 times larger than its body mass (average seed mass is 0.017 ± 0.002 g, $n = 10$), demonstrating the ability for the seed to continue its twisting shape change and remain a functional twisting actuator under extremely large relative loads. The seeds were further demonstrated to translate their twisting motion to a load lifting actuation (Fig. 3C). There is an inverse relationship in the mass of the load and the distance of lift (Fig. 3D). The seed's ability to lift a load over 11,700 times its mass further demonstrates the remarkably powerful morphomechanics of the seed. Both the twisted actuation and lifting movements are powered solely by the seed's kinematic material properties under environmental stimuli. The lifting motion represents the ability to leverage the seed to create an organic self-powered and untethered system. Moreover, this lifting justifies the seed as a bioderived twisted muscle capable of providing both twisted actuation and lifting with extremely high relative loads.

3   Demonstrations of Harvesting *Hesperostipa Spartea* Seed as Hygromorphic Twisted Actuator

3.1   Interlocking Systems

Preparation and Execution of Seeds for Interlocking Test. To minimize variation, the length of each fully untwisted seed in the procedure was 80 mm in length. The dry seeds were placed in hot water until they fully untwisted, and were then cut to 80 mm, leaving the bend intact. Two seeds were placed on a platform with their bends facing towards each other, and their point ends supported by a 500 g weight. The seeds were positioned so they overlapped by 65mm, and a heater was positioned in front of them to accelerate the locking process (Fig. 4A). After the locking process, one end of the seed system was attached to a clip and hung vertically (Fig. 4B). A clip was attached to the other end of the system, and masses were hung incrementally, every 30 s. The maximum mass supported was that which caused the seeds to untwist.

Interlocking Demonstration. Through harnessing the natural kinetic motion of the seeds, we produced an intertwined two-seed interlocking system (Fig. 4C, 4D). The natural morphology of the seeds allows for untethered locking with response to environmental humidity change. During a wet to dry humidity cycle the system transitions from an unlocked to locked state, while a dry to wet state reversibly unlocks the system. The bioderived design of this system harnesses both the bent portion of the seed awn (s4) and the twisted body of the awn (s2 and s3). The natural bend in the end of the seeds provides optimal grasping to create a tight double twist (Fig. 4D). We controlled the geometric parameters of the length of the bend, length of the twisted body, and distance overlapped of the seed to create an efficient and consistent locking mechanism (Fig. 4A). With a 10 mm bend length (dry twisted state), 80 mm body (wet untwisted state), and 65 mm overlap (wet untwisted state), an average of 3.8 ($\pm$ 0.75, $n = 6$) intertwined twists were created (Fig. 4C, 4D). The resulting entwined two-seed system creates an environmentally stimulated reversible self-locking system. The lock was able to hold an average load of 113 g $\pm$ 20.7, $n = 6$ samples, over 3,400 times the mass of the two-seed system

(Fig. 4B). Beyond locking as a mechanical feature, this design demonstrates the modular potential of the bioderived twisted actuators. Through harnessing this interlocked design to create multi-actuator systems, future application opportunities may arise for moisture triggered docking mechanisms, self-entangled active structures, etc.

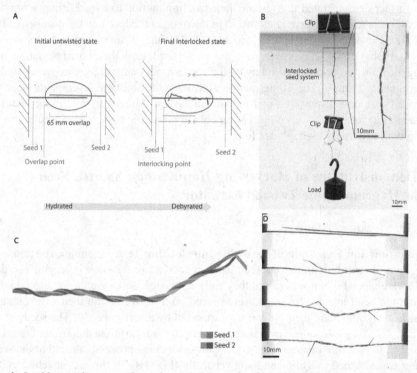

Fig. 4. Locking seed system schematics. (A) Schematic of seed interlocking experimental setup. Seeds overlap by 65 mm and interlock with increasing humidity. (B) Experimental setup for interlocked seed system load test. (C) Schematic of interlocking between two seeds. (D) Time lapse of two seeds locking together as humidity and temperature increase.

3.2 Biohybrid Crawling Design and Development

Design and Implementation. We harvested the tightly twisted body (s2) of the seed to create a biohybrid crawling robot. By controlling the geometry of the seed's body, a humidity-responsive twisted actuator that converts atmospheric water concentration into mechanical energy is achieved. The biohybrid structural design enables periodic crawling locomotion to occur. Through the addition of fixed circular "wheels", the crawling biohybrid design transfers the twisting motion of the seed's body into a rolling locomotion (Fig. 5A). The motion is driven solely by environmental stimuli and does not require any additional energy input, creating an untethered system.

The biohybrid design consists of a combination of laser cut wood wheels and porcupine grass seed bodies (Fig. 5B). Designs included both a single bioderived seed body glued to the center of two wheels (Fig. 5B, 5Ci, 5Ciii), as well as an altered modular design with two seeds acting as the body of the crawling structure (Fig. 5Cii). The wheels were attached to the seed bases using hot glue. In the modular design, the two seeds comprising the body were glued together before the wheels were attached. The crawling motion was conducted on a 150°C hot plate with a paper cover (Fig. 5D). Tracker video analysis and modeling software was used to quantify the path of locomotion. Figure 5E shows every 5 frames of 100x video, as used to quantify each point of motion.

Performance. The relatively large number of twists innate to the seed's tightly twisted structure allow the seed to "crawl" through a distinct, repeated motion. This results in increased actuation speed: by controlling the geometric parameters of the seed, the seed has repeated motion while under a single condition change (i.e. the robot completes multiple oscillations for each humidity cycle).

The seed's natural twisting movement thrusts the back wheel in a circumferential motion until it takes the place of the front wheel (Fig. 5A). This crawling motion occurs when stimulated by a change in environmental humidity conditions, and reaches optimal speed in a heated environment. While the conditions are held constant, the seed continues to crawl forward until the body reaches its full twisted state. Due to the diffusion-based mechanics of the rotation, the speed of locomotion decreases with the cycle of rotation (Fig. 5F). Each cycle of rotation is defined by the intercept of the displacement of wheel A and wheel B. There is an initialization time of approximately 2.22 min before the locomotion begins. The initial cycle has an average speed of 14.4 mm/min (0.361 BL/min), with a secondary speed of 10.8 mm/min (0.269 BL/min), and tertiary speed of 4.58 mm/min (0.064 BL/min) (n = 5). The biohybrid design allows the seed to travel in repeated linear motion while facing a single environmental change.

The biohybrid crawling robot has nearly circular step-motion. The circumferential motion of the rear wheel produces an average ratio of 0.45 between the length of the body of the natural harvested twisting actuator and the distance the system travels in one rotation (Fig. 5A). The relation between the length of the seed and the distance traveled mimics that of the radius and diameter of a circle, with mean deviation of less than 4% from a perfectly circular path (n = 5). The adapted biohybrid seed and wheel system generates geometric motion, regardless of the length of the body and diameter of the wheel. These parameters can be controlled to optimize the trajectory's path and speed.

Our biohybrid crawling design also supports a modular two-seed system. The multi-seed system (Fig. 5Cii) functions with the same locomotion trajectory as the single seed design, demonstrating the potential for further modulation of the crawling design. Due to the trajectory of the locomotion being circumferentially proportional to the body length (see Fig. 5A), modular design presents opportunities to further control the geometry and increase the overall speed of locomotion.

Considering the bioderived natural material of the twisted actuator, the results show a high level of consistency. The organic material has natural variation in the length of the body and the number of twists it contains. However, with controlled harvesting of the seed's body combined with the addition of biodegradable wood wheels, circular step-motion and overall linear motion is easily controlled and attainable.

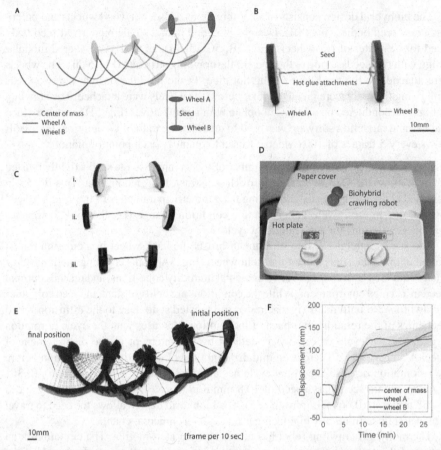

Fig. 5. Biohybrid crawling design. (A) Circumferential motion of the crawling system, with wheels A and B alternating motion, and the center of mass traveling approximately half of the distance of each wheel's path. (B) Image of biohybrid crawling design with dehydrated seed as the body. (C) Three biohybrid crawling systems with differing seed lengths and wheel sizes. (D) Experimental setup of the biohybrid crawling system. (E) Time lapse of the biohybrid crawling system and the alternating motion of wheels A and B, with frames at 10 s intervals of motion. (F) The distance each wheel and the center of mass travel with respect to time. The data are means and the standard deviation is shown in the shaded regions, given n = 5 samples.

4   Conclusion

Through harvesting the twisted body of the porcupine grass seeds, *Hesperostipa Spartea*, we produce a bioderived hygromorphic twisted actuator that converts atmospheric water concentration into mechanical energy. Biohybrid design further creates the potential for translating the seed's natural self-burial motion into untethered, self-powered soft robotic applications. With rotational velocity dependent on environmental relative humidity and temperature, a maximum rotation of 90°/sec can be achieved in submergence of 100°C water. The seed is able to function as a twisted actuator, producing rotational motion and load lifting, under large relative loads over 11,000 times its body mass. The unique twisted body of the seed allows for natural locking, and when this is harnessed, the interlocked seed system can withstand a mass 3,600 times its own. By utilizing biohybrid design to further leverage the twisting actuation of the seed, a crawling system can be constructed, with a forward locomotion rate of 14.4 mm/min. The guiding principles of sustainability demand that the future of robotics must be biodegradable after their life span, and our bioderived hygromorphic twisted actuator has the ability to meet these demands. We expect that through future research, our bioderived actuator will be embedded into more complex robotic systems, providing a sustainable solution to the field of soft robotics.

Acknowledgements. This work was supported by National Science Foundation Grants Career IIS-2047912 and IIS-2017008.

References

1. Holstov, A., Bridgens, B., Farmer, G.: Hygromorphic materials for sustainable responsive architecture. Constr. Build. Mater. **98**, 570–582 (2015)
2. Reyssat, E., Mahadevan, L.: Hygromorphs: from pine cones to biomimetic bilayers. J. R. Soc. Interface **6**(39), 951–957 (2009)
3. Kay, R., Nitiema, K., Correa, D.: The bio-inspired design of a self-propelling robot driven by changes in humidity, Berlin, Germany, pp. 233–242 (2020)
4. Krapež Tomec, D., Straže, A., Haider, A., Kariž, M.: Hygromorphic response dynamics of 3D-printed wood-PLA composite bilayer actuators. Polymers **13**(19), 3209 (2021)
5. Le Duigou, A., Castro, M., Bevan, R., Martin, N.: 3D printing of wood fibre biocomposites: from mechanical to actuation functionality. Mater. Des. **96**, 106–114 (2016)
6. Poppinga, S., Schenck, P., Speck, O., Speck, T., Bruchmann, B., Masselter, T.: Self-actuated paper and wood models: low-cost handcrafted biomimetic compliant systems for research and teaching. Biomimetics **6**(3), 42 (2021)
7. Reichert, S., Menges, A., Correa, D.: Meteorosensitive architecture: biomimetic building skins based on materially embedded and hygroscopically enabled responsiveness. Comput. Aided Des. **60**, 50–69 (2015)
8. Menges, A., Reichert, S.: Material capacity: embedded responsiveness. Archit. Design **82**(2), 52–59 (2012)
9. Wood, D.M., Correa, D., Krieg, O.D., Menges, A.: Material computation—4D timber construction: towards building-scale hygroscopic actuated, self-constructing timber surfaces. Int. J. Archit. Comput. **14**(1), 49–62 (2016)
10. Rüggeberg, M., Burgert, I.: Bio-inspired wooden actuators for large scale applications. PLoS ONE **10**(4), e0120718 (2015)
11. Tahouni, Y., et al.: Programming sequential motion steps in 4D-printed hygromorphs by architected mesostructure and differential hygro-responsiveness. Bioinspir. Biomim. **16**(5), 055002 (2021)
12. Le Duigou, A., Correa, D.: 4D printing of natural fiber composite. In: Smart Materials in Additive Manufacturing, Volume 1 : 4D Printing Principles and Fabrication, pp. 297–333. Elsevier (2022)
13. Fu, L., et al.: A humidity-powered soft robot with fast rolling locomotion. Research, **2022**, 2022/9832901 (2022)

14. Shin, B., et al.: Hygrobot: a self-locomotive ratcheted actuator powered by environmental humidity. Sci. Robot. **3**(14), eaar2629 (2018)
15. Burgert, I., Fratzl, P.: Actuation systems in plants as prototypes for bioinspired devices. Phil. Trans. R. Soc. A. **367**(1893), 1541–1557 (2009)
16. Kim, B.H., et al.: Three-dimensional electronic microfliers inspired by wind-dispersed seeds. Nature **597**(7877), 503–510 (2021)
17. Luo, D., et al.: Autonomous self-burying seed carriers for aerial seeding. Nature **614**(7948), 463–470 (2023)
18. Fiorello, I., Margheri, L., Filippeschi, C., and Mazzolai, B.: 3D micromolding of seed-like probes for self-burying soft robots. 2022 IEEE 5th International Conference on Soft Robotics (RoboSoft), pp. 255–260. IEEE, Edinburgh (2022)
19. Cecchini, L., Mariani, S., Ronzan, M., Mondini, A., Pugno, N.M., Mazzolai, B.: 4D printing of humidity-driven seed inspired soft robots. Adv. Sci. **10**(9), 2205146 (2023)
20. Geer, R., Iannucci, S., Li, S.: Pneumatic coiling actuator inspired by the Awns of Erodium Cicutarium. Front. Robot. AI **7**, 17 (2020)
21. Molano-Flores, B.: Diaspore morphometrics and self-burial in Hesperostipa Spartea from loam and sandy soils. J. Torrey Bot. Soc. **139**(1), 56–62 (2012)
22. Jung, W., Kim, W., Kim, H.-Y.: Self-burial mechanics of hygroscopically responsive Awns. Integr. Comp. Biol. **54**(6), 1034–1042 (2014)
23. Yanez, A., Desta, I., Commins, P., Magzoub, M., Naumov, P.: Morphokinematics of the hygroactuation of feather grass Awns. Adv. Biosys. **2**(7), 1800007 (2018)

Bioinspiration Under Water

Underactuated Robotic Fish Control: Maneuverability and Adaptability Through Proprioceptive Feedback

Gianluca Manduca[1,2]([✉]) [iD], Gaspare Santaera[1,2] [iD], Paolo Dario[1,2] [iD],
Cesare Stefanini[1,2] [iD], and Donato Romano[1,2] [iD]

[1] The BioRobotics Institute, Scuola Superiore Sant'Anna,
Viale R. Piaggio 34, 56025 Pontedera, PI, Italy
{gianluca.manduca,gaspare.santaera,paolo.dario,
cesare.stefanini,donato.romano}@santannapisa.it
[2] Department of Excellence in Robotics & A.I., Scuola Superiore Sant'Anna,
Piazza Martiri della Libertà, 33, 56127 Pisa, Italy

Abstract. Bioinspired robotics is a promising technology for minimizing environmental disruption during underwater inspection, exploration, and monitoring. In this research, we propose a control strategy for an underactuated robotic fish that mimics the oscillatory movement of a real fish's tail using only one DC motor. Our control strategy is bioinspired to Central Pattern Generators (CPGs) and integrates proprioceptive sensory feedback. Specifically, we introduced the angular position of the tail as an input control variable to integrate a feedback into CPG circuits. This makes the controller adaptive to changes in the tail structure, weight, or the environment in which the robotic fish swims, allowing it to change its swimming speed and steering performance. Our robotic fish can swim at a speed between 0.18 and 0.26 body lengths per second (BL/s), with a tail beating frequency between 1.7 and 2.3 Hz. It can also vary its steering angular speed in the range of 0.08 rad/s, with a relative change in the curvature radius of 0.25 m. With modifications to the modular design, we can further improve the speed and steering performance while maintaining the developed control strategy. This research highlights the potential of bioinspired robotics to address pressing environmental challenges while improving solutions efficiency, reliability and reducing development costs.

Keywords: Biorobotics · Biomimetics · Underwater robotics · Fish robot · Proprioceptive control · Environmental robotics

1 Introduction

Underwater environments exploration and monitoring are crucial applications for robotics, as highlighted by research in [1,2]. Drawing inspiration from the

This research was carried out in the framework of the EU H2020-MSCA-RISE-2018 ECOBOTICS. SEA - Bio-inspired Technologies for a Sustainable Marine Ecosystem [824043].

graceful and efficient movements of aquatic species, researchers aim at developing robotic solutions that can navigate with agility in complex underwater areas. Moreover, the use of bioinspired robots can mitigate the disturbance to underwater ecosystems, while also potentially improving animal farming conditions, preserving wildlife, and aiding in the control of animal populations in agriculture, as discussed in [3,4].

The rich underwater biodiversity has inspired the design and control strategies of numerous marine robots, as highlighted in [5]. Among various locomotion strategies used in aquatic environments, carangiform and subcarangiform swimmers are capable of achieving high speeds, albeit at the cost of reduced maneuverability compared to anguilliform swimmers, which have more degrees of freedom.

Underactuated mechanisms can provide robust and reliable solutions for robotic systems. El Daou et al. [6] developed a compliant body subcarangiform robot with a linked fin, while [7] used an active wire-driven body and a passive compliant body. Zhong et al. [8] also used a wire-driven mechanism to achieve high-speed swimming, and a two-joint-centred compliant tail was employed for maneuverability in [9]. Alternatively, hydraulic actuation was utilized in the robot proposed in [10]. Moreover, magnetic actuation is rapidly gaining popularity in the field of robotics due to its simplicity, robustness, and reliability. Magnetic actuation allows for the separation of the fish tail's moving parts in contact with water from the electronic components, thereby improving waterproofing and reducing the risk of motor overload in the event that the tail cannot move. This makes magnetic actuation an ideal choice for designing underwater robots that require enhanced durability and resilience in challenging environments. Previous studies have investigated magnetic actuation for multi-link actuated [11] and underactuated [12] robots.

However, bioinspiration is not limited to thrust generation; control strategy can also benefit from it. Animals manage locomotion through Central Pattern Generators (CPGs) [13,14]. These neural networks provide feedforward rhythmic activity. The inspiration from CPGs in the control strategy of underwater robots has been proposed in several studies [15–17]. This approach is usually used to synchronize different actuators in robots. However, CPG-based control has been shown to guarantee multi-mode swimming even for underactuated solutions [18,19]. Proprioception refers to the perception and awareness of the body's position, movement, and orientation in space, which is provided by sensory receptors located in the muscles, joints, and tendons [20,21]. The evolution of proprioceptive sense in biological systems allows for adaptive management of rhythmic activity [22,23]. This concept has been applied to bioinspired underwater robots through the use of feedback control strategies that incorporate information from proprioceptive sensors [24,25]. In the study [24], it was demonstrated, by means of a robotic fish with multi-joint actuation, that fishes are able to save energy by means of proprioceptive feedback. A control strategy with proprioceptive feedback for an underactuated robotic fish has been proposed in [25].

Our research focuses on developing a novel control strategy based on proprioceptive feedback for an underactuated robotic fish inspired to pelagic fishes. The proposed robot features subcarangiform locomotion and a non-blocking actuation mechanism that generates a tail swing through the interaction of magnets and a coupling of vertebrae via a wire system, all driven by an oscillating movement of a single DC motor. In this updated version of the robot proposed in [12], we have incorporated an electronic control apparatus and changed the actuation system from a one-way motor movement to a back-and-forth solution. The updated robot can not only vary its swimming speed but also its direction thanks to the integration of a bioinspired control strategy that enhances the robots maneuverability and allows for adaptation to different environments and loads on the tail.

2   Materials and Methods

2.1   Modelling of the Travelling Wave

The bioinspired robotic fish developed takes pelagic fishes as a biological reference, and it generates the thrust by bending its body into a propulsive wave that extends back to its caudal fin. Figure 1 shows the artifact structure, the working principle of the actuation system, and the reference systems. The body and/or caudal fin (BCF) locomotion is typical of most fish in nature and can be described as an amplitude-modulated traveling wave [26,27]. As proposed by [28], the following equation can model the travelling wave in the case of carangiform robotic fish:

$$y_t(x,t) = (c_1 x_t + c_2 x_t^2) \sin (k x_t - \omega t), \tag{1}$$

Equation 1 describes a body wave traveling from head to tail in a body-fixed coordinate system with the abscissa positive towards the tail. y_t and x_t are the sideward and axial displacement, respectively, in the coordinate system $\{S_t\}$ presented in Fig. 1(b), while t denotes the time. $k = 2\pi/\lambda$ is the wave number, λ represents the wavelength, and ω is the wave frequency. c_1 and c_2 are the wave amplitude's linear and quadratic coefficients, respectively. The last two parameters can be adjusted to achieve the desired BCF swimming mode. We remind to the previous work for a more comprehensive description [12].

2.2   Structure and Mechanism

The robotic fish comprises a water-resistant head and an oscillating mechanism that is exposed to water, as shown in Fig. 1(a). The head contains all the electronics, while the oscillating mechanism is composed of a peduncle, three segments, two hinges, and a final caudal fin inserted into the final segment. The wire mechanism connects the three segments to the head, see Fig. 1(c). The motor, located in the head, oscillates a plastic disc that contains four permanent magnets (disc magnet). The magnets' arrangement and orientation divide the

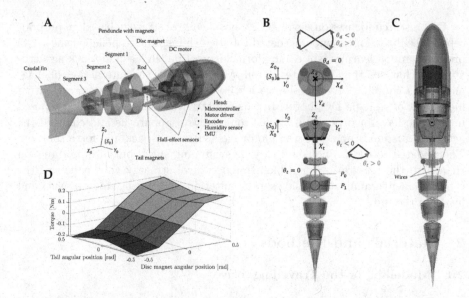

Fig. 1. Robotic fish design: (**a**) Structure representation with the related components description. (**b**) Reference coordinate systems considered. (**c**) Visual representation of the wire system. (**d**) Torque exerted on the tail by the magnetic coupling between disc magnet and oscillating arm magnets according to different disc magnet/tail configurations.

disc magnet into two areas with different polarities. Two magnets on the peduncle face the disc side with the same polarity. The contactless mechanical power transmission between the disc magnet and the peduncle magnets results from the attractive/repulsive forces. There is no passive actuation, and all segments are linked by wires. When the magnets on the disc attract one of the peduncle magnets, the other is repelled, causing the oscillating rod to bend to the attracted magnets' side while the tail tip points to the repelled magnet's side. See Fig. 2 for a visual representation of the actuation mechanism. Because there is no mechanical connection between the motor shaft and the oscillating arm, the system is non-blocking and prevents the DC motor and the entire structure from overloading. If the fish tail were to become stuck, it would remain in a fixed position while the motor continued running smoothly, breaking the magnetic coupling.

The current robotic design represents an evolution of a prior prototype developed at the BioRobotics Institute of Scuola Superiore Sant'Anna (Pisa, Italy) [12], with several significant changes. While the previous version of the robot validated the non-blocking actuation system with a single DC motor and excluded any electronic components from the body, the present version increased the robot's size. The distance between the two ends of the body now measures 400 mm with a weight of 875 g, as opposed to the prior version that measured only 179 mm in length and weighed 77 g. The current design integrates a motor driver,

Fig. 2. Visual representation of the actuation mechanism.

a microcontroller, and a sensor apparatus that includes an optical encoder, Hall effect sensors, an inertial measurement unit (IMU), and a humidity sensor. The current design also features different magnets and a motor with back-and-forth actuation, in contrast to the previous version that used a continuous unidirectional motor rotation.

The position of the disc magnet θ_d determines the magnetic force exerted on the tail. The force values have been empirically measured with different disc magnet/tail configurations through a dynamometer placed in P_0 Fig. 1(b). Figure 1(d) shows the results converted into torque values. When $\theta_d = 0$ rad, neutral position, the attraction/repulsive forces exerted by the disc magnet on the tail are zero. An oscillation of the disc magnet around the neutral position generates an oscillation of the tail. When $\theta_d = \pm 0.52$ rad, the interaction forces between disc magnet and tail are maximal.

The optical encoder in the head, coupled with the electric motor, provides the shaft's relative position, speed, and acceleration. An Hall effect sensor, measures the magnetic field of the disc magnet, determining its absolute position during an initial setting phase. Another bipolar Hall effect sensor measures the magnetic field of two magnets placed on the tail rod, see Fig. 1. The magnets face with different polarities on the sensor. During tail oscillation, the bipolar Hall effect sensor thus measures an oscillation of the magnetic field. The curve relating the tail angular position and the sensor measurements has been characterized by interpolation through the Matlab software Curve Fitting Tool. Different functions have been evaluated. A second-degree polynomial had better fit the extrapolated data by considering two different sets of parameters according to the θ_t angle sign.

2.3 Control Strategy

By generating a rhythmic activity of the disc magnet, it is possible to obtain in response a tail oscillation, similar to how locomotion is handled by CPGs [13].

CPGs determine the appropriate set of activation of the muscles without requiring feedback from the sensors. Motion management, in this sense, resorts to a feed-forward control, thus ensuring the exact torque to achieve goal-directed motion at certain speeds [14, 29]. Since our robotic fish features a non-mechanically coupled system, a feed-forward control approach would not be suitable for various environments conditions and could be challenging to implement. This is because the oscillation frequency and amplitude would need to be calibrated taking into account the interaction forces that depend on the environment in which the robotic fish swims. Failure to accurately calibrate these parameters could cause a decoupling of the actuation system, resulting in undesired movements. Therefore, a more adaptable and effective solution is to use a feedback control approach, such as our bioinspired control strategy that incorporates proprioceptive feedback and enables the robot to adapt to different environment conditions and loads. For this reason, as also proposed in [25], oscillatory action is integrated with proprioceptive sensory feedback.

We therefore proposed a parameterized control law that receives as input the position of the tail as proprioceptive feedback. The disc magnet configuration determines the torque exerted on the fishtail which is the control action considered. The following equation expresses the proposed control low, which is composed of three contributions:

$$\tau_t(\hat{\theta}_t) = \tau_{t,1}(\hat{\theta}_t) + \tau_{t,2}(\hat{\theta}_t) + \tau_s(\hat{\theta}_t), \tag{2}$$

where

$$\tau_{t,1}(\hat{\theta}_t) = k_1 sign(\dot{\hat{\theta}}_t)(1 - |\hat{\theta}_t|), \tag{3}$$

$$\tau_{t,2}(\hat{\theta}_t) = -k_2 \hat{\theta}_t, \tag{4}$$

$$\tau_s(\hat{\theta}_t) = k_s(1 - |\hat{\theta}_t|). \tag{5}$$

$\hat{\theta}_t$ is the tail angle θ_t divided by its maximum value resulting in $\hat{\theta}_t \in [-1.1]$. $\tau_{t,1}(\hat{\theta}_t)$ generates a torque contribution that varies its sign according to the direction of the tailbeat, with maximum and minimum peaks at $\hat{\theta}_t = 0$. It becomes null when the tail reaches the limit switches ($\hat{\theta}_t = \pm 1$). $\tau_{t,2}(\hat{\theta}_t)$ opposes $\tau_{t,1}(\hat{\theta}_t)$ to guarantee a call-back to the tail when reaching the limit switches. Unlike $\tau_{t,1}(\hat{\theta}_t)$, it has maximum and minimum peaks when $\hat{\theta}_t = \pm 1$ and vice versa it cancels at $\hat{\theta}_t = 0$. $\tau_s(\hat{\theta}_t)$ instead is the steering contribution. It generates an asymmetry in $\tau_{t,1}(\hat{\theta}_t)$, increasing the value towards one direction and decreasing towards the other. The control law is therefore:

$$\tau_t(\hat{\theta}_t) = (k_1 sign(\dot{\hat{\theta}}_t) + k_s)(1 - |\hat{\theta}_t|) - k_2 \hat{\theta}_t, \tag{6}$$

and it is governed by three parameters k_1, k_2 and k_s. k_1 is a positive parameter. It varies the $\tau_{t,1}(\hat{\theta}_t)$ and thus the torque exerted on the tail during the beat with a consequent increase in oscillation frequency. k_2 is also a positive parameter and determines the value of torque that the tail receives at the limit switches to oppose the motion and change direction of the beat. k_2 must always be less

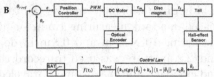

Fig. 3. General description of the bioinspired approach (**a**) and block diagram of the system (**b**).

than k_1, otherwise the control would impose a decrease in torque during the tail restart. The sign of k_s determines the direction of curvature. Its value, on the other hand, varies the asymmetry between one direction of tail beating and the opposite one. Since k_s diminishes the k_1 effect in one direction while augmenting it in the opposite one, it must not diminish k_1 to such an extent that it becomes less than k_2 for the same reasons explained above. The following system collects the constraints to which the three parameters are subject:

$$\begin{cases} k_1, k_2 > 0 \\ k_1 > k_2 \\ (k_1 - |k_s|) > k_2. \end{cases} \tag{7}$$

We approximated the relation between the torque exerted on the fishtail and the disc magnet angular position with the following linear function:

$$\theta_d = k_{ln}\tau_t(\hat{\theta}_t). \tag{8}$$

θ_d is the angular position of the disc magnet (rad) according to the coordinate system $\{S_t\}$ in Fig. 1(b). k_{ln} is a parameter that converts the desired torque into the disc magnet position, and it is related to the angular operating region of the disc magnet and the maximum torque allowed by the system. If the normalised torque value is considered, the control law can be generalised. At this point, the choice of k_{ln} depends solely on the maximum oscillation range of the disc magnet. This parameter is structural and depends on the spacing of the magnets. Therefore k_{ln} must equal this value, which, as mentioned in the previous subsection, corresponds to 0.52. At a maximum torque value $(\tau_t(\hat{\theta}_t) = 1)$, the position of the disc magnet will therefore correspond to $\theta_d = 0.52\,\text{rad}$. Conversely, at a minimum torque value $(\tau_t(\hat{\theta}_t) = -1)$, θ_d will equal $-0.52\,\text{rad}$. The overall strategy reduces to position control of the disc magnet. The reference position tracking relies on a PID controller. A Pulse Width Modulation (PWM) strategy is adopted. Figure 3(b) shows the block scheme of the entire system. The saturation is considered to prevent the disc magnet from going beyond its operating range and nullifying the control strategy.

2.4   Experimental Set-Up and Performance Assessment

The control strategy was validated by conducting experiments on the robot both in air and underwater. Initially, the robot was tested in air, where its body was held in place while allowing its tail to swing freely. Subsequently, the robot was placed in a tank measuring 1m in length and 0.5 m in height, and then in a pool measuring 10×5 m and 0.8 m in depth. A camera with a 12 MP resolution and/2.2 aperture was used to record the predetermined trajectories (rectilinear and circular), and the distances traveled were extrapolated using post-processing analysis. Travel times of a predefined stretch were collected to determine the speed, and data on the position of the disc magnet and tail were saved in the robot's internal memory for later analysis. The controller's adaptability to different conditions and the possibility of varying swimming performance in relation to the control law's parameters were evaluated to assess the results.

3   Experimental Results

The PID controller was tuned using the Ziegler-Nichols method ($k_p = 0.15$, $k_d = 0.1$, and $k_i = 0$). Figure 4(a) shows the tail beating oscillation in relation with the disc magnet one for a given set of parameters ($k_1 = 1$, $k_2 = 0.4$, $k_s = 0$) considering the fish robot stuck in water. Just as defined by the control law, the maximum and minimum values of the angular position of the disc magnet correspond to the moment when the position of the tail is close to zero. The contribution of non-zero k_2, allows the disc magnet, not to be in the neutral position when the tail reaches the limit switches. The call-back contribution thus generated, allows the tail not to stall and generate a continuous oscillation. With the same parameters, Fig. 4(b) presents the change in tail frequency according to different environmental and load conditions. Frequencies were obtained with *plomb* Matlab function by considering the maximum peak of the periodigram. The results compare the control considering the robot first in air and then in water. In the latter case, two different weights (75 and 140 g) were then added to the first tail segment, 0.1 m from its axis of rotation. Without the integration of proprioceptive feedback, the frequency would have remained the same for all cases considered. The amplitude of oscillation of the tail would decrease as the load on the tail increases. The control would therefore lose the coupling between the disc magnet and the tail. A feed-forward solution would require a calibration of parameters for each presented condition. The strategy developed in this work results instead adaptive to changes in shape, the weight of the tail, or liquid density in which the robotic fish swims, thanks to proprioceptive feedback.

Instead, a change in controller parameters generates a change in swimming performance as presented in Fig. 5. In the following, the swimming speed of the robot will be indicated in body lengths per second (BL/s). Varying k_1 and maintaining the remaining parameters fixed, as discussed in the previous section, we expect a change in the tail beating frequency reflecting on a change in the swimming speed. Figure 5(a) shows the velocity value of the robotic fish and the corresponding value of the tailbeat frequency, as k_1 changes, with $k_s = 0$ and $k_2 = 0.4$ fixed. Results prove the hypothesis assumed. The tail beating frequency varies between 1.7 Hz and 2.3 Hz. The measured swimming speed values change with the same trend between 0.18 BL/s and 0.26 BL/s. Subsequently,

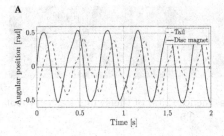 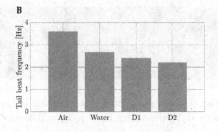

Fig. 4. Control strategy validation in nominal condition ($k_1 = 1$, $k_2 = 0.4$, and $k_s = 0$) with the robotic fish stuck: (**a**) Phase shift between the angular position of the tail and the disc magnet (test in water). (**b**) Tail beat change in frequency according to different environments (air - water) and different loads applied to the tail (D1 = 75 g, D2 = 140 g, water tests).

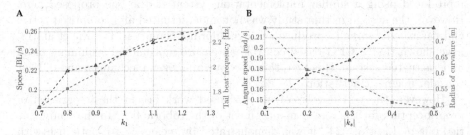

Fig. 5. Robotic fish performances according to the control parameters choice: (**a**) Change in tail beat frequency (red line) and the related robotic fish body speed (blue line) considering different values of k_1 with $k_2 = 0.4$, and $k_s = 0$, fixed. (**b**) Angular radius (red line) and speed (blue line) varying the steering parameter k_s with $k_1 = 1$, and $k_2 = 0.4$, fixed.

the possibility of changing curvature direction and performance was investigated. Figure 5(b) shows the steering performance in terms of angular velocity and angle of curvature as k_s varies, keeping $k_1 = 1$, and $k_2 = 0.4$. The robotic fish can vary the steering angular speed in the range of 0.08 rad/s with a relative change in the curvature radius of 0.25 m. Figure 6 presents a visual representation of the experimental results, showcasing the abilities of the developed control strategy. The trajectory of the robotic fish follows a circular path, demonstrating the effectiveness of the control parameters chosen to guide the fish's movement. Considering the curves empirically obtained, the robotic fish developed, according to the bioinspired control strategy proposed, shows a range of maneuverability despite its underactuated design.

4   Discussion

This study presents a novel bioinspired control approach for an underactuated robotic fish whose mechanical design was previously described [12].

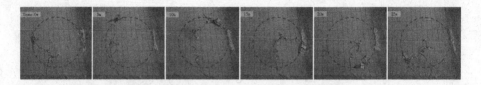

Fig. 6. Swimming pool experiments: Image sequence (25 s) of the swimming fish robot with the parameters $k_1 = 1$, $k_2 = 0.4$, and $k_s = -0.5$.

The control strategy proposed in this study manages the rhythmic movement of the robotic fish's tail in a manner similar to that of CPGs. Previous literature has utilized CPGs to coordinate numerous actuators for oscillatory movements [15–17]. In another investigation, a lamprey-like robotic fish was reproduced using a similar implementation system to the one proposed here. However, the system in that study was not underactuated and comprised active and passive vertebrae to produce an anguilliform locomotion [11]. Xie et al. [18] have shown that a CPG-based control can ensure multimodal swimming of an underactuated system. However, they used a wire-driven mechanism and did not consider magnetic actuation.

However, the real novelty of our proposed work lies in the integration of proprioception for the motor management of the robotic fish. In the study carried out by Li et al. [24], it was demonstrated by means of a robotic fish with multi-joint actuation that fishes are able to save energy by means of proprioceptive feedback. The researchers considered a CPG controller that adjusts the body undulation of the robot after receiving feedback from the proprioceptive sensing signal. They considered the force or force-related signals as the proprioceptive signal from the caudal fin, decoded via reinforcement learning. Sánchez-Rodríguez et al. [25] integrated the information from the proprioceptive sensors to moderate the tail deformation in an underactuated solution. An actuation based on mechanical coupling and a force sensor was considered. In contrast, we proposed this approach on a non-blocking type of actuation, considering the tail position information as proprioceptive feedback. This solution, through the proposed parameterized control law, is thus able to adapt the rhythmic activity of the tail according to the environment in which the robotic fish swims and the load supported. Furthermore, the variation of control law parameters enables the robot's manoeuvrability. This study opens the door to an integration of exteroceptive sensors for autonomous swimming.

The robot proposed in this work, in accordance with the control strategy developed, proved to be able to vary the swimming speed by 0.08 BL/s reaching a maximum speed of 0.26 BL/s with a relative tail-beat frequency of 2.3 Hz. The swimming performance has clear margins for improvement when compared with other works, such as [7] in which speeds of 2.02 BL/s at a tail-beat frequency of 5.46 Hz are achieved. In fact, the intention of the work was to propose and validate a control strategy that would make a previously proposed implementation system effective. The work was therefore not focused on swimming performance.

In comparison with the previous version, the speed decreased by 0.47 BL/s. However, several factors must be considered in the comparison. Firstly, the reduced size of the first version of the robot, which weigthed 77 g compared to the 875 g of the one proposed in this work, having a larger volume for the insertion of electronic components. Secondly, the maximum tailbeat frequency reached by the first version was higher (3.25 Hz). This aspect is related to the sizing of the magnets. By introducing magnets with a higher attractive/repulsive force, better performance can be achieved. Furthermore, the modular design allows performance improvements to be investigated secondarily. Different designs can be integrated and compared while maintaining the same control strategy.

The successful steering of the robot was achieved by utilizing an asymmetric tail-beat, which was inspired by natural behavior [30,31]. Meurer et al. [32] also employed a similar mechanism in a compliant robotic fish using a nonlinear controller, but with a mechanically coupled actuation system and without considering proprioception. On the other hand, classical approaches for steady turning maneuvers involve changing the center of oscillation of the robot's tail, which require large tail deflections to be effective [33,34]. However, the robot presented in this study has relatively small tail segments with space in between them. The results showed a change in angular velocity of 0.08 rad/s with a respective change in curvature angle of 0.25 m. To improve these results, a larger lateral tail surface and reducing the spaces between the vertebrae could be considered. Future studies could also involve incorporating a strategy based on changing the center of oscillation of the tail for comparison.

The control strategy developed in this work manages the rhythmic activity of the robotic fish's tail in a way that resembles how CPGs control the activation of muscles. This allows the strategy to adapt to changes in the tail's structure, weight, or environment through proprioceptive feedback. The system's speed and steering performances could be improved by making design changes to the modular structure while maintaining the control strategy. The underactuated solution provides the benefits of increased reliability and energy savings. Future investigations will focus on evaluating the energy consumption of the proposed platform, exploring different approaches to swimming deeper, and integrating exteroceptive sensors like cameras to enable autonomous swimming. This robotic platform could be used for non-invasive environmental monitoring operations and animal/robot interactions within the marine ecosystem.

Acknowledgements. The authors are grateful to the communal swimming pool of Pontedera staff for having made available their own spaces to do the experiments. The authors also thank Ms. Gloria Bianco and Mr. Raffaele Picichè for their assistance during the tests and their graphic support and Mr. Godfried Jansen Van Vuuren and Dr. Marco Miraglia for their technical support during the design and development of the robotic artifact.

References

1. Mayer, L., et al.: The Nippon Foundation-GEBCO seabed 2030 project: the quest to see the world's oceans completely mapped by 2030. Geosciences **8**(2), 63 (2018)
2. Halpern, B.S., et al.: Recent pace of change in human impact on the world's ocean. Sci. Rep. **9**(1), 1–8 (2019)
3. Ryuh, Y.S., Yang, G.H., Liu, J., Hu, H.: A school of robotic fish for mariculture monitoring in the sea coast. J. Bionic Eng. **12**(1), 37–46 (2015)
4. Kruusmaa, M., Gkliva, R., Tuhtan, J.A., Tuvikene, A., Alfredsen, J.A.: Salmon behavioural response to robots in an aquaculture sea cage. R. Soc. Open Sci. **7**(3), 191220 (2020)
5. Li, Y., et al.: A comprehensive review on fish-inspired robots. Int. J. Adv. Rob. Syst. **19**(3), 17298806221103708 (2022)
6. El Daou, H., Salumäe, T., Toming, G., Kruusmaa, M.: A bio-inspired compliant robotic fish: design and experiments. In: 2012 IEEE International Conference on Robotics and Automation, pp. 5340–5345. IEEE, May 2012
7. van den Berg, S.C., Scharff, R.B.N., Rusák, Z., Wu, J.: Biomimetic design of a soft robotic fish for high speed locomotion. In: Living Machines 2020. LNCS (LNAI), vol. 12413, pp. 366–377. Springer, Cham (2020). https://doi.org/10.1007/978-3-030-64313-3_35
8. Zhong, Y., Li, Z., Du, R.: A novel robot fish with wire-driven active body and compliant tail. IEEE/ASME Trans. Mechatron. **22**(4), 1633–1643 (2017)
9. Yu, J., Zhang, C., Liu, L.: Design and control of a single-motor-actuated robotic fish capable of fast swimming and maneuverability. IEEE/ASME Trans. Mechatron. **21**(3), 1711–1719 (2016)
10. Katzschmann, R.K., Marchese, A.D., Rus, D.: Hydraulic autonomous soft robotic fish for 3D swimming. In: Hsieh, M.A., Khatib, O., Kumar, V. (eds.) Experimental Robotics. STAR, vol. 109, pp. 405–420. Springer, Cham (2016). https://doi.org/10.1007/978-3-319-23778-7_27
11. Stefanini, C., et al.: A mechanism for biomimetic actuation in lamprey-like robots. In: The First IEEE/RAS-EMBS International Conference on Biomedical Robotics and Biomechatronics, 2006. BioRob 2006, pp. 579–584. IEEE, February 2006
12. Romano, D., Wahi, A., Miraglia, M., Stefanini, C.: Development of a novel under-actuated robotic fish with magnetic transmission system. Machines **10**(9), 755 (2022)
13. Grillner, S.: The motor infrastructure: from ion channels to neuronal networks. Nat. Rev. Neurosci. **4**(7), 573–586 (2003)
14. Grillner, S.: Biological pattern generation: the cellular and computational logic of networks in motion. Neuron **52**(5), 751–766 (2006)
15. Zhao, W., Hu, Y., Zhang, L., Wang, L.: Design and CPG-based control of biomimetic robotic fish. IET Control Theory Appl. **3**(3), 281–293 (2009)
16. Stefanini, C., et al.: A novel autonomous, bioinspired swimming robot developed by neuroscientists and bioengineers. Bioinspiration Biomim. **7**(2), 025001 (2012)
17. Thandiackal, R., et al.: Emergence of robust self-organized undulatory swimming based on local hydrodynamic force sensing. Sci. Robot. **6**(57), eabf6354 (2021)
18. Xie, F., Zhong, Y., Du, R., Li, Z.: Central pattern generator (CPG) control of a biomimetic robot fish for multimodal swimming. J. Bionic Eng. **16**, 222–234 (2019)
19. Chen, J., Yin, B., Wang, C., Xie, F., Du, R., Zhong, Y.: Bioinspired closed-loop CPG-based control of a robot fish for obstacle avoidance and direction tracking. J. Bionic Eng. **18**, 171–183 (2021)

20. Tuthill, J.C., Azim, E.: Proprioception. Curr. Biol. **28**(5), R194–R203 (2018)
21. Laskowski, E.R., Newcomer-Aney, K., Smith, J.: Proprioception. Phys. Med. Rehabil. Clin. N. Am. **11**(2), 323–340 (2000)
22. Pearson, K.G.: Proprioceptive regulation of locomotion. Curr. Opin. Neurobiol. **5**(6), 786–791 (1995)
23. Ryczko, D., Simon, A., Ijspeert, A.J.: Walking with salamanders: from molecules to biorobotics. Trends Neurosci. **43**(11), 916–930 (2020)
24. Li, L., Liu, D., Deng, J., Lutz, M.J., Xie, G.: Fish can save energy via proprioceptive sensing. Bioinspiration Biomim. **16**(5), 056013 (2021)
25. Sánchez-Rodríguez, J., Celestini, F., Raufaste, C., Argentina, M.: Proprioceptive mechanism for bioinspired fish swimming. Phys. Rev. Lett. **126**(23), 234501 (2021)
26. Sfakiotakis, M., Lane, D.M., Davies, J.B.C.: Review of fish swimming modes for aquatic locomotion. IEEE J. Oceanic Eng. **24**(2), 237–252 (1999)
27. Blake, R.W.: Fish functional design and swimming performance. J. Fish Biol. **65**(5), 1193–1222 (2004)
28. Barrett, D.S., Triantafyllou, M.S., Yue, D.K.P., Grosenbaugh, M.A., Wolfgang, M.: Drag reduction in fish-like locomotion. J. Fluid Mech. **392**, 183–212 (1999)
29. Yu, J., Tan, M., Chen, J., Zhang, J.: A survey on CPG-inspired control models and system implementation. IEEE Trans. Neural Netw. Learn. Syst. **25**(3), 441–456 (2013)
30. Gray, J.: Directional control of fish movement. Proc. R. Soc. Lond. Ser. B Contain. Pap. Biol. Character **113**(781), 115–125 (1933)
31. Webb, P.W., Fairchild, A.G.: Performance and maneuverability of three species of teleostean fishes. Can. J. Zool. **79**(10), 1866–1877 (2001)
32. Meurer, C., Simha, A., Kotta, Ü., Kruusmaa, M.: Nonlinear orientation controller for a compliant robotic fish based on asymmetric actuation. In: 2019 International Conference on Robotics and Automation (ICRA), pp. 4688–4694. IEEE, May 2019
33. Hu, Q., Hedgepeth, D.R., Xu, L., Tan, X.: A framework for modeling steady turning of robotic fish. In: 2009 IEEE International Conference on Robotics and Automation, pp. 2669–2674. IEEE, May 2009
34. Tan, X., Carpenter, M., Thon, J., Alequin-Ramos, F.: Analytical modeling and experimental studies of robotic fish turning. In: 2010 IEEE International Conference on Robotics and Automation, pp. 102–108. IEEE, May 2010

Design and Performance of a Cownose Ray-Inspired Robot for Underwater Exploration

Giovanni Bianchi[✉][iD], Lorenzo Maffi, Michele Tealdi,
and Simone Cinquemani[iD]

Dipartimento di Meccanica, Politecnico di Milano, Via La Masa 1, 20156 Milan, Italy
giovanni.bianchi@polimi.it

Abstract. This paper describes the design and experiments of a bioinspired robot imitating the swimming behavior of cownose rays. These creatures propel themselves by moving their flat and large pectoral fins, which generate a wave that pushes back the surrounding water, generating thrust through momentum conservation. The robot mimicking this motion features a stiff central body, which houses motors, batteries, and electronics and is equipped with flexible pectoral fins crafted from silicone rubber. Each fin is driven by a servomotor that propels a link inside the leading edge, allowing the wave motion to be recreated through the flexibility of the fins. To enhance maneuverability, two small, rigid caudal fins have also been added. The robot was designed, constructed, and tested, and the results indicated that the locomotion principle was effective, as the robot was capable of forward propulsion, left and right turns, and floating and diving maneuvers.

Keywords: Bioinspired Robot · Swimming Locomotion · Autonomous Underwater Vehicle · Cownose Ray · Batoid Fishes · Flexible Fins

1 Introduction

The development of autonomous underwater vehicles (AUVs) is a thriving area of research, owing to their numerous applications, ranging from environmental monitoring and submarine exploration to aquatic farming and infrastructure maintenance [31]. These tasks entail prolonged underwater operation, maneuvering in confined spaces, and minimal disturbance to marine life. Traditional AUVs, which rely on helical thrusters for propulsion, fail to meet fish in terms of energy efficiency and maneuverability [31]. Therefore, the fish's propulsion mechanisms offer a source of inspiration for developing novel AUV propulsion systems that comply with these requirements.

Fish and cetaceans showcase a diverse range of swimming techniques, broadly classified into two categories: Body-Caudal Fin (BCF) swimming and Median

Paired Fin (MPF) swimming [31,32]. The majority of fish use BCF swimming, which involves an undulating motion of the caudal fin and part of the body. In contrast, MPF swimming is characterized by the deformation of the pectoral or dorsal and anal fins, creating a traveling wave that propels water backward and generates thrust through momentum conservation. BCF swimmers possess high cruise speeds and acceleration bursts, while MPF locomotion excels in maneuverability and stability [31,32]. Mantas and rays fall under the latter category, as they swim by flapping their large, triangular fins, which is considered one of the most energy-efficient and maneuverable swimming techniques [14]. In addition, unlike helical propellers, these fins do not disturb marine life, making them ideal for environmental monitoring and observing marine habitats [20].

Fish belonging to the Batoidea order have flattened bodies that are wider dorsoventrally and have large pectoral fins that are fused to their head, forming disc or diamond-like shapes [29]. The motion of the fins involves the propagation of two waves, one in the chordwise direction (from head to tail) and the other in the spanwise direction (from fin root to fin tip). The primary thrust is generated by the chordwise traveling wave, which pushes the water backward, while the spanwise wave is caused by the fin's flexibility, delaying the motion of the fin tip and enhancing hydrodynamics [14]. Additionally, the spanwise wave reduces the vertical force and pitching moment, which stabilizes locomotion [19]. Fish movements can be categorized into two groups based on the ratio of body length (L) to the wavelength (λ) of the chordwise wave. If the L/λ ratio is greater than 0.5, the motion is oscillatory, while a ratio less than 0.5 is undulatory [29]. Smaller undulatory species typically live near the seabed and lack speed but have high maneuverability to turn with a null curvature radius [16]. Larger oscillatory species, on the other hand, can swim at high speeds for an extended time in pelagic environments [29]. Batoidea species range from completely undulatory to completely oscillatory swimming, with cownose rays (*Rhinoptera bonasus*, Mitchill, 1815) lying in the middle of this continuum, displaying a good trade-off between speed and maneuverability. Cownose rays have a L/λ ratio of 0.4, flap their fins at 1 Hz, and cruise at approximately 1.2 m/s [30].

The characteristics of the swimming techniques of mantas and rays have served as a source of inspiration for the development of numerous biomimetic robots. Replicating the intricate movements involved in this type of locomotion has posed a significant challenge, leading to the exploration of various solutions.

Soft actuators are being used to move robots, which allows for more flexibility and distributed actuation in the fins, similar to fish movement. While this technology provides good swimming performance in terms of speed and maneuverability, it is typically limited to robots of small dimensions [21].

The majority of biomimetic robots use traditional motors and joints for actuation, and some of them use three or more independent mechanisms for each fin, actuated with a phase delay to replicate the traveling wave [4,12,17,18,22,23,25, 35]. These mechanisms accurately reproduce the curvature of the fin, providing excellent maneuverability. However, this actuation strategy imposes limitations on the fin's shape and material, which must be highly stretchable to mount many actuators on it. The Novel Robotic Manta Ray uses eight Soft Fluidic Actuators of different cross-sections and lengths to reproduce the traveling wave, exploiting the viscosity-induced resistance effects in different actuators [33]. Robotic devices that employ multiple motors for actuating fins are often characterized by exceptional maneuverability. This is mainly due to their capability of controlling the traveling wave's velocity and direction, which allows them to execute turns with zero curvature radius and, in some cases, swim in reverse. Nevertheless, attaching numerous actuators to the fin poses specific constraints on the material and shape of the structure, necessitating a highly stretchable design.

Some biomimetic robots use a different approach to model the oscillatory movement of fins by combining a flapping movement and a pitching rotation of the fin properly phased. This approach is possible for the cownose ray because its body length is approximately 0.4 times the wavelength [29]. Such robots have only two degrees of freedom per fin, and only two motors are required for actuation, one for flapping and one for pitching [13,24,36]. This approach is simple yet effective in generating thrust, but it can only reproduce motions with large wavelengths. The fins of the robots in this category are composed of flexible ribs mounted on a flexible shaft and covered by an elastic skin, allowing for large amplitude fin deflection. The Bionic Robot Fish [9] and the Bionic Pectoral Fin [34] use an articulated mechanism composed of sliding rods and spherical joints to achieve flapping and pitching movements, accurately reproducing the fin's shape.

Finally, some robots use a single actuator to move each pectoral fin, allowing the fin's flexibility to create a passive traveling wave. The body of these robots is divided into four modules, with only the first directly moved by an actuator, while the others are free to move and generate the traveling wave. Robo-Ray II and Robo-Ray III both use silicone rubber fins actuated by pneumatic artificial muscles or thin rubber sheets, respectively [6]. Similarly, the MantaDroid [11] and Manta Ray Robot [15] have fins made of thin films of PVC, and the Robotic Cownose Ray has fins made of ionic polymer-metal composite actuated by servomotors or a crank-rocker mechanism [10]. This design has several advantages, including simplicity, as no articulated mechanisms are needed within the fin, and higher energy efficiency due to the detached and more flexible fin with a larger angle of attack [1]. Although maneuverability is reduced compared to other designs, small radius turns, and high angular velocities can still be achieved.

The robot described in this paper takes inspiration from the cownose ray and has a central rigid body with flexible silicone rubber fins. Each fin is driven by a servomotor that operates a link in the leading edge, and the traveling wave is generated through the passive deformation of the fin. An important innovative aspect of the fin design is that the cross-section of the fins is a biomimetic profile that was chosen to maximize thrust. Thus, even though the fins are detached from the central body, unlike for the real cownose ray, the aspects related to propulsion are replicated very closely. Additionally, a novel aspect of this robot is its tail which functions as a rudder actuated by two servomotors for maneuvering purposes. This kind of caudal fin is not present in the cownose ray, but it was added to the robot to improve maneuverability overcoming the limitations brought by the single-actuator fin design.

The main aim of this research is to showcase the advantages of this propulsion mechanism, which the article mainly focuses on related aspects of fin design and swimming performance characterization. The fins designed for the robot accurately reproduce the shape and dynamics of cownose ray fins, allowing the robot to swim at high speed and with high maneuverability despite its simple design.

The paper is divided into four sections: Sect. 2 explains the robot's design, Sect. 3 discusses the experimental results, and Sect. 4 provides the conclusions and discussion.

2   Fin Design

2.1   Cownose Ray Geometry and Fin Kinematics

Batoid fishes have a flat, wide body shape that can be approximated as a NACA 0020 symmetric airfoil when viewed in cross-section [4]. To accurately model the locomotion of the cownose ray, researchers have analyzed the fish's skeletal structure and fin motion. Russo *et al.* developed a biomechanical model that reconstructed the fin's deformed shape at each time step [30]. The fin's cartilaginous structure consists of multiple small radial segments connected with rotational joints. The angle θ of each segment in relation to the horizontal plane is determined through this analysis according to Eq. 1.

$$\theta(s,t) = \theta_{max}s\sin\left(\phi x + \psi s - \omega t\right) + \delta s \qquad (1)$$

where θ_{max} is the angle at the fin tip, s is the distance of the cartilage segment from the fin root, x is the position from the leading edge, as shown in Fig. 1, ϕ is the chordwise wave number divided by the fish body length, ψ is the spanwise wave number divided by the fin span, ω is the circular frequency of fin flapping, and δ is the mean value of the angle θ during a flapping cycle. The wave numbers ϕ and ψ are defined as:

$$\phi = \frac{2\pi}{\lambda_x} \qquad \psi = \frac{2\pi}{\lambda_s} \qquad (2)$$

where λ_x is the wavelength in a longitudinal direction, whereas λ_s is the wavelength along the fin span. Due to the cownose ray fin's flexibility and the fact that it is made up of numerous small segments and joints, it is possible to view the motion of the fin as a smooth deformation without sacrificing accuracy in its geometry [2,30]. As a result, Eq. 1 can be utilized to describe the full range of motions that the fin can perform.

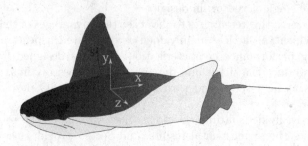

Fig. 1. Representation of a cownose ray with the reference system adopted in Eq. 1.

In order to replicate the locomotion of a fin accurately, the central body needs to be rigid and have a hydrodynamic shape. Conversely, the fins should be highly flexible and exhibit both spanwise and chordwise traveling waves. To achieve this, the leading edge of the fin should be actuated while allowing the fin tip and trailing edge to deform freely.

2.2 Bioinspired Fin Realization

The shape of the pectoral fins on the robot imitates the form of a cownose ray's fins found in literature [4,5]. The contour was scaled to the robot's chord length and closely matches that of a real ray, as depicted in Fig. 2a. The fins' cross-section mimics a biomimetic profile, thicker near the leading edge and thinner towards the trailing edge, resulting in a flat surface at the end. This design generates more thrust in the cownose ray's frequency range than a symmetric NACA profile [27]. The leading edge also tapers towards the fin tip. Figure 2 shows the outer surface of the fin, which is obtained by combining the external contour and cross-section.

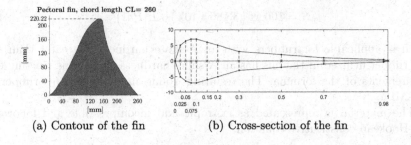

(a) Contour of the fin   (b) Cross-section of the fin

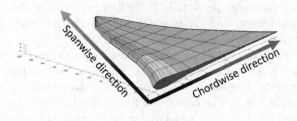

(c) Model of the fin

Fig. 2. Fin geometry reconstruction.

The fin is composed of silicone rubber material, and an aluminum stick is added to the motor bracket to stiffen the leading edge. To produce the fins, liquid silicone rubber is poured into 3D-printed molds and vulcanized at room temperature.

To ensure that the fins' stiffness is appropriately adjusted, the first natural frequency should be around 1 Hz, which is in the range of feasible large-amplitude movements with the selected motors. The calculation of the underwater vibration modes' accurate values is highly complex and beyond the scope of this research. However, to assess whether the fins deform as intended during water movement, a simplified approach can be utilized. This approach involves the use of a constant ratio called Λ between the natural frequencies of a body in water and in the empty space, which can be calculated as the square root of the ratio of modal mass to the sum of modal mass and added water mass (m_w). This ratio varies with different vibration modes, with a value of approximately 0.6 for the first natural frequency, and tends towards 1 as the frequency approaches infinity [8]. Assuming this approach is valid for the large fin deformations, the first natural frequency out of the water can be calculated and then multiplied by this scale factor to obtain the natural frequency underwater.

The fins are composed of silicone rubber with a density of 1170 kg/m^3 and a Young modulus, E, determined via an empirical formula cited in [3]. The formula used is as follows:

$$S = 100\mathrm{erf}\left(3.186 * 10^{-4}\sqrt{E[Pa]}\right),\tag{3}$$

which is applicable for rubbers with an A-shore hardness S greater than 40. The rubber utilized in the fins has an A-shore hardness of 45, thus meeting the requirements of the formula. The resulting Young modulus for this rubber is 1.76 MPa.

The material is represented as isotropic and incompressible and follows a Neo-Hookean constitutive equation:

$$W = C_1\left(\bar{I}_1 - 3\right),\tag{4}$$

where W is the strain energy density, $\bar{I}_1$ is the first invariant of the left Cauchy-Green deformation tensor, and C_1 is a constant of the material. For silicone rubber, C_1 is equal to 1.3078 MPa, as specified in [26].

To verify the accuracy of the computed Young modulus and constitutive law, a static simulation was conducted on the fin. The only load applied during the simulation was gravity. The results were compared with experimental measurements, as depicted in Fig. 3. The calculated fin tip displacement was 128.7 mm, while the measured displacement was 123.7 mm. It can be observed that there is a negligible difference between the two results.

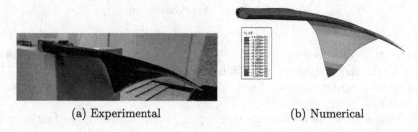

(a) Experimental   (b) Numerical

Fig. 3. Comparison of experimental measurements and FEA simulation results for fin tip displacement.

The frequency response of the fin is evaluated through a two-step process. Initially, a linearized frequency analysis is conducted to provide an approximate value for the first natural frequency. Subsequently, dynamic simulations are performed using an implicit solver by applying a sinusoidal motion to the aluminum stick and calculating the resulting fin deformation. These simulations are conducted at various frequencies in close proximity to the natural frequency determined from the initial linearized step. The objective of these simulations is to determine the frequency at which the trailing edge displacement is at its maximum. This frequency is found to be 1.35 Hz, indicating that the first natural frequency underwater is 0.8 Hz. Thus, the motors selected for use are capable of driving the fins at their resonance frequency with a peak-to-peak amplitude exceeding 90°.

Then, the behavior of the fin underwater is monitored in a compact tank, where an aluminum frame supports the fin and motor. The motor produces a sinusoidal motion of 45°, and Fig. 4 displays the corresponding movement of the fin. This test is repeated, varying the frequency of fin movement to evaluate the fin deformation underwater and understand which is the frequency of actuation that guarantees the maximum displacement of the trailing edge and, as a consequence, the highest thrust.

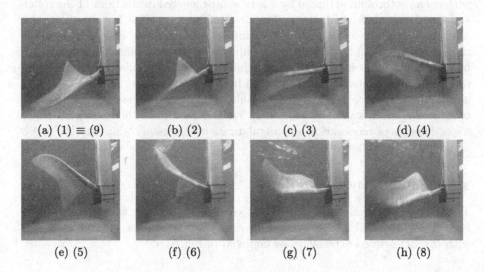

(a) (1) ≡ (9)   (b) (2)   (c) (3)   (d) (4)

(e) (5)   (f) (6)   (g) (7)   (h) (8)

Fig. 4. Underwater movement of the fin at 0.8 Hz.

When the fin moves at its resonance frequency (0.8 Hz), its tip at the end of the leading edge deforms in a manner similar to that of a biological reference. This movement of the fin causes water to move backward, generating a noticeable thrust force on the aluminum structure. However, the fin has certain limitations that could be addressed to improve its design in the future. Notably, the tip of the fin's trailing edge does not contribute to thrust generation. This can be observed in frame (2), where it remains elevated as the stick moves upwards, and vice versa in frame (6). In the subsequent frames (3) and (7), the movement of the stick reverses the deformation of the fin's base, and when the stick is stationary at the peak position (frames 5 and 9), the tip is again in the opposite phase. This behavior arises from the low stiffness of the fin's base. The fin lacks sufficient elastic potential energy to move the water and restore its shape, resulting in passive deformation under the influence of water resistance. To improve the fin's performance, the stiffness of its base could be increased to enable it to move more water and generate greater thrust.

The fin movement has been qualitatively compared with the observations of a swimming cownose ray by Cai et al. [7], and the motion of the realized fin shows a substantial similarity. In future work, the movement of the fin will be measured more accurately to get the precise trajectory of some reference points in order to make it possible to compare the obtained movement with the fin motion of a real cownose ray.

3   Mechanical Design of the Robot

The robot's central body and its fins are designed independently of each other, with each pectoral fin actuated by a servomotor located in the front of the robot and the motor shaft easily accessible for changing fins. This feature allows the robot to be used as a test platform for future research on fin efficiency. In addition, the robot is equipped with two caudal fins that are actuated independently by servomotors to control pitching rotation and ensure locomotion stability. The robot is neutrally buoyant and balanced by adding ballasts to its mass. The fins are required to move at a frequency of about 1 Hz with a maximum amplitude of ±45°, requiring a velocity of at least 5 rad/s. To control the robot's attitude, measurements of acceleration and angular rate are necessary; thus, an IMU must be added to the robot.

3.1   Central Body Design

The robot's electronic components are contained within a waterproof central body that has an IP68 rating. The central body comprises a waterproof box with two 3D-printed extensions, as depicted in Fig. 5.

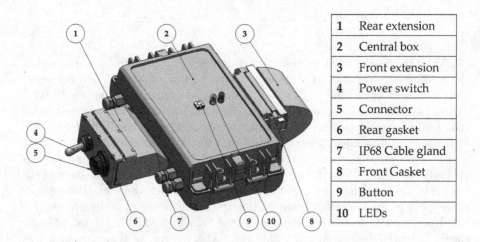

1	Rear extension
2	Central box
3	Front extension
4	Power switch
5	Connector
6	Rear gasket
7	IP68 Cable gland
8	Front Gasket
9	Button
10	LEDs

Fig. 5. CAD model of the robot's central body.

The waterproof box of the robot is fitted with two 3D-printed extensions, one at the rear and the other at the front. The dimensions of the box are 80 mm × 150 mm × 60 mm, and it houses all the electronic components that are stacked between plastic layers inside it. The bottom of the box accommodates two LiPo batteries, which are connected in series, and have a nominal voltage of 3.7 V, and a capacity of 1200 mAh, with a discharge rate of 15C. The Arduino Due electronic board is positioned above the batteries, while the top level of the box houses all the sensors and accessories required to control the robot and interact with it. The Inertial Measurement Unit (IMU) comprises a 3-axes accelerometer, a 3-axes gyroscope, and a 3-axes magnetometer and is used to reconstruct the robot's orientation in space. The Wi-Fi module allows communication of data and changing of control parameters without accessing the board or the connector, which are sealed to avoid water leakage inside the box. The SD-card module stores the navigation data, and the ammeter monitors the current delivered by the batteries and the power consumed by the robot during the testing phase.

The rear extension of the box houses a switch and an IP68-rated seven-pin connector used to recharge and balance the batteries and connect to the electronic board. On the other hand, the front extension contains a camera module OV7670, which captures images from the robot's point of view while swimming, with no role in controlling the robot's movement. The box is mounted on a chassis made of a 2 mm thick aluminum sheet that is cut and bent appropriately, with holes and flaps to mount the box and the servomotors, as illustrated in Fig. 6.

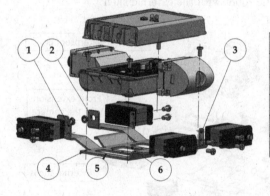

1	Rear motor mounting holes
2	Caudal fin bearings holes
3	Front motor mounting holes
4	Central box mounting holes
5	Cover mounting holes
6	Extra holes for ballast

Fig. 6. Exploded view of the assembly highlighting the components on the chassis.

The servomotors need to be waterproof since they are placed outside the box and in direct contact with water. To fulfill this requirement, IP68 rated digital brushless servomotors PowerHD 40 have been chosen. These motors have a stall torque of 3.9 Nm and a nominal speed of 12.4 rad/s when powered at 7.4 V. To improve the robot's hydrodynamics, a 3D-printed external shell has been added to the central body. For this robot, a NACA 0020 profile has been selected to approximate the cownose ray's body, and it has been used to make the surface smooth and the shape more streamlined. The central body's thickness remains constant throughout its width. The caudal fins are rigid and follow the shape of the NACA 0020 profile from the central body tapering towards the trailing edge. Each caudal fin is attached to the servomotor using a bracket and supported on the other side by a bearing mounted on the chassis. The caudal fins can rotate at an angle of ±45°.

Figure 7 shows a CAD model and an exploded view of the robot assembly.

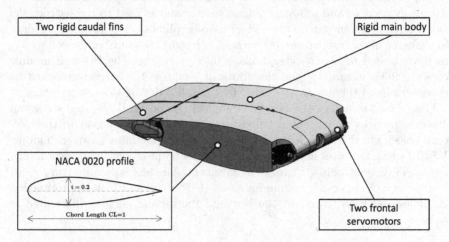

(a) CAD model of the robot with the external shell

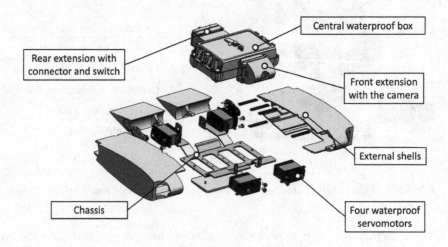

(b) Exploded view of the robot

Fig. 7. CAD model of the robot.

3.2   Robot Assembly

The construction and assembly of the robot are depicted in Fig. 8.

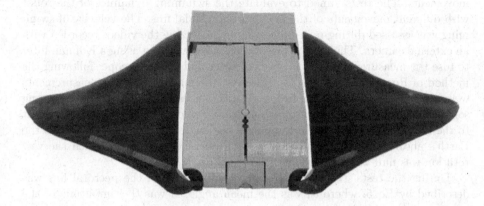

Fig. 8. Assembly of the robot.

The robot has a total length of 260 mm, a full width of 620 mm (including the fins), and a maximum thickness of 78 mm. Ballasts were added between the central body and the external shell to achieve neutral buoyancy, resulting in a total mass of 1.86 kg. To prevent pitch or roll rotations when the robot is still, the ballasts were positioned to align the center of mass with the center of buoyancy. The robot's buoyancy is not actively controlled, but it remains at the same depth when still since it does not receive any hydrostatic force. To move the robot up or down, asymmetric fin movements are employed, which will be explained in the following section.

3.3   Robot Control

The user inputs the kinematic parameters and the desired motion type, which can be rectilinear or a type of maneuver, via Wi-Fi while the robot is out of the water. This information is then stored in the SD-card memory, which the MCU reads during startup. Afterward, a motion law is generated for each motor based on the previously communicated kinematic parameters and is executed by the servomotors. During the initial testing phase, the pectoral fin motors follow a sinusoidal motion law with a non-zero mean value, whereas the caudal fins remain stationary at the desired angle. The gyroscope and accelerometer readings are saved on the SD card for post-processing and are also used for real-time estimation of the robot's orientation.

4   Experimental Results

The swimming performance of the robot was assessed underwater using a camera to capture the deformation of the fins and forward motion. The main movement of the robot while swimming was the flapping of the pectoral fins, which generated the thrust and moments necessary for maneuvering. On the other hand, the caudal fins were used for correcting the robot's orientation with only small movements. The tests aimed to evaluate the swimming dynamics of the robot with different movements of the pectoral and caudal fins. The velocity of swimming was assessed during post-processing by analyzing the videos recorded with an external camera. The robot's orientation was computed using a Kalman filter to fuse the measurements of the accelerometer and the gyroscope, following the method of Roetemberg et al. [28]. However, the magnetometer's measurements were not included in the sensor fusion algorithm because it was affected by strong soft-iron effects from the electronic board and cables that bring electric current to the motors. As a result, the computed yaw angle was not with respect to the Earth's absolute reference system but to a reference system in which the yaw rotation was null when the robot was turned on.

During the tests, the rotation of the leading edge of the pectoral fins was described by Eq. 5, where θ_0 was the mean angle, A was the amplitude of the motion, and f was the frequency.

$$\theta(t) = \theta_0 + A \sin (2\pi f t) \tag{5}$$

4.1 Rectilinear Motion

Regarding rectilinear motion, a sequence of photograms of the robot's rectilinear movement was shown in Fig. 9. The pectoral fins were flapping with an amplitude of 20° and a frequency from 0.5 Hz to 1 Hz, while the caudal fins remained still. The robot moved along a rectilinear trajectory with an average velocity of 0.15 m/s, corresponding to 0.6 BL/s at 0.5 Hz. At 1 Hz, the robot could reach a velocity of 0.4 m/s, corresponding to 1.5 BL/s. However, these values did not result from direct velocity measurement but from the average speed obtained by measuring the elapsed time and the distance traveled for each test.

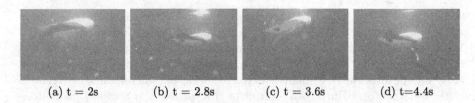

(a) t = 2s   (b) t = 2.8s   (c) t = 3.6s   (d) t=4.4s

Fig. 9. Rectilinear swimming - f = 0.5 Hz - A = 20°.

During rectilinear forward swimming, the robot underwent a slight rotation about the pitch axis because the fins generated alternate pitching moments that caused a periodic pitching rotation. The frequency of pitching rotation was the same as the frequency of fin motion, and the average amplitude of this rotation was 24° at 0.5 Hz and 16° at 1 Hz. The oscillations about the roll axis were minor and were caused by small asymmetries between the movements of the left and right fins, as shown in Fig. 10.

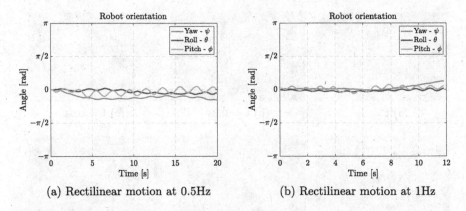

(a) Rectilinear motion at 0.5Hz   (b) Rectilinear motion at 1Hz

Fig. 10. Euler's angles during rectilinear motion at different fin motion frequencies.

4.2 Floating and Diving Maneuvers

When the movement of the fin is balanced across the horizontal plane, the robot will follow a level trajectory. Conversely, if the fin movement is imbalanced, it will generate a pitching moment, which allows for diving or floating maneuvers. The robot will move downwards when the average angle of the fin with respect to the horizontal plane is positive, as depicted in Fig. 11, while it will move upwards when the mean angle is negative, as illustrated in Fig. 12. In both experiments, the flapping frequency of the fin is 1 Hz, the amplitude is 20°, and the asymmetry is ±22.5°.

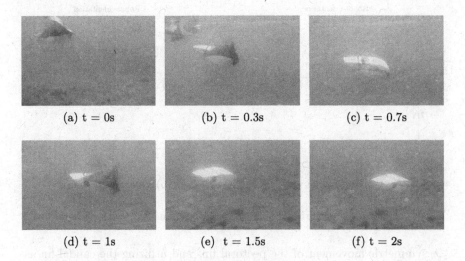

(a) t = 0s   (b) t = 0.3s   (c) t = 0.7s

(d) t = 1s   (e) t = 1.5s   (f) t = 2s

Fig. 11. Downward swimming - f = 1 Hz - θ_0 = +22.5° - A = 20°.

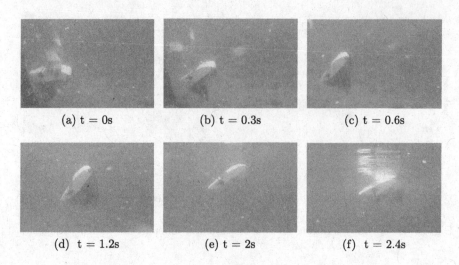

(a) t = 0s   (b) t = 0.3s   (c) t = 0.6s

(d) t = 1.2s   (e) t = 2s   (f) t = 2.4s

Fig. 12. Upward swimming - $f = 1\,\text{Hz}$ - $\theta_0 = -22.5°$ - A = 20°.

Figure 13 shows the Euler's angles of the robot while performing floating and diving maneuvers. The robot exhibits a significant pitch rotation of 45° while descending and 65° while ascending. This dissimilarity is attributable to the unbalanced mass distribution between the robot's front and rear, making it more effortless to pitch upward than downward. Additionally, the fin's motion produced slight oscillations about the pitch axis, similar to those observed during rectilinear swimming.

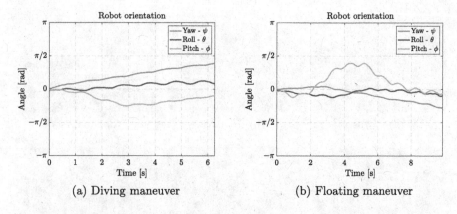

(a) Diving maneuver   (b) Floating maneuver

Fig. 13. Euler's angles during diving and floating maneuvers with pectoral fins.

A symmetric movement of the pectoral fins and utilizing the caudal fin as a rudder can also allow for floating and diving maneuvers. Figure 14 demonstrates an upward ascending maneuver achieved by rotating the caudal fins 45° upwards. Similarly, a descending maneuver can be performed by rotating the caudal fins downwards at the same angle.

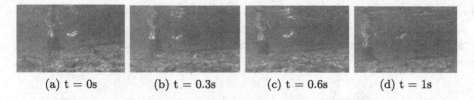

(a) t = 0s   (b) t = 0.3s   (c) t = 0.6s   (d) t = 1s

Fig. 14. Upward swimming - f = 1 Hz - $\theta_0 = 0°$ - A = $20°$ - $\theta_c = +45°$.

Figure 15 illustrates the variation in the pitch angle of the robot as the caudal fins are rotated at different angles during this maneuver.

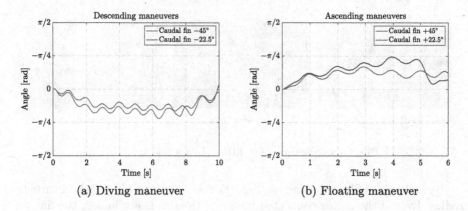

(a) Diving maneuver   (b) Floating maneuver

Fig. 15. Pitch angle during diving and floating maneuvers with caudal fins.

The top pitch angle achieved during upward motion is 52.7°, while during downward motion, it is −39.5°. Again, the pitch angle is larger for floating maneuvers than for diving maneuvers, indicating that a slight imbalance in robot mass is responsible for this difference.

Comparing Fig. 13 and Fig. 15, it is clear that maneuvering with the pectoral fins results in better performance. This technique generates a greater pitch angle, allowing the robot to move upward or downward more quickly. However, using the pectoral fins requires setting a mean value for the fin motion, which limits the stroke and amplitude of the fin oscillation, producing a smaller thrust that slows down the robot. Therefore, using the caudal fins is more practical for these maneuvers unless a rapid height variation is necessary. In that case, a combination of both fin pairs can be used to achieve an even higher pitch angle.

4.3 Left/Right Turning Maneuvers

To initiate a turn to either side, the robot adjusts the amplitude of motion of the two pectoral fins in an asymmetric manner, resulting in a smaller radius of curvature as the amplitude difference between the fins increases. Figure 16 and 17 demonstrate a right turn executed with the left pectoral fin flapping at 20° amplitude and the right pectoral fin flapping at 10° amplitude in Fig. 16, and 0° amplitude in Fig. 17.

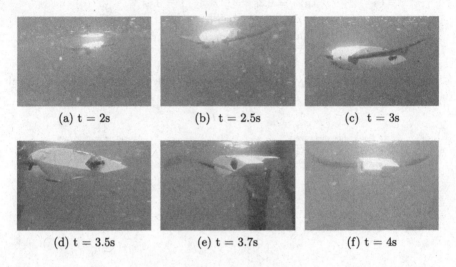

(a) t = 2s   (b) t = 2.5s   (c) t = 3s

(d) t = 3.5s   (e) t = 3.7s   (f) t = 4s

Fig. 16. Right turn - f = 1 Hz - $A_l = 20°$ - $A_r = 10°$.

By activating only one of the two fins, the robot can generate a tighter turning radius. Even if the motor connected to one of the fins is not in use, the fin can still be moved by the robot's periodic pitch and roll movements, causing it to bend and create a wave that travels through the water due to the interaction between the fin and the water.

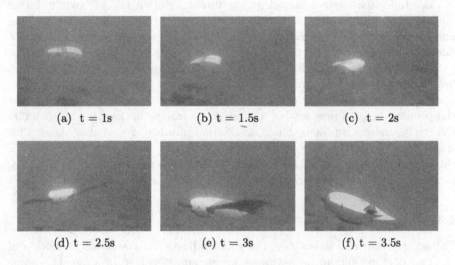

(a) t = 1s   (b) t = 1.5s   (c) t = 2s

(d) t = 2.5s   (e) t = 3s   (f) t = 3.5s

Fig. 17. Right turn - f = 1 Hz - $A_l = 20°$ - $A_r = 0°$.

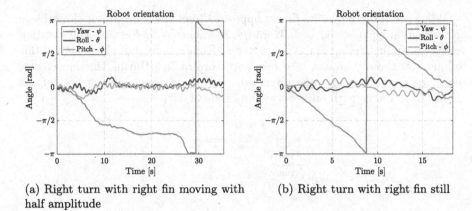

(a) Right turn with right fin moving with half amplitude

(b) Right turn with right fin still

Fig. 18. Euler's angles during right turns.

Figure 18 illustrates the Euler's angles observed during right-turning maneuvers. When the robot turns right with one fin stationary, the angular velocity around the yaw axis is 0.36 rad/s. However, if the right fin moves with half the amplitude of the left fin, the average angular velocity reduces to 0.12 rad/s. During a turn where both fins move, the robot also swims forward, resulting in a more complicated interaction between the fins and the surrounding water, which causes the robot to drift laterally. Similar to rectilinear swimming, oscillations around the pitch axis occur during turning, and the asymmetry between the left and right fins produces an oscillation around the roll axis with an average amplitude of 15°.

By moving both fins with opposite amplitudes, a zero curvature radius can be achieved, as depicted in Fig. 19. In this scenario, the left fin has an amplitude A of 20°, and the right fin has an amplitude of −20°, resulting in no net turning motion.

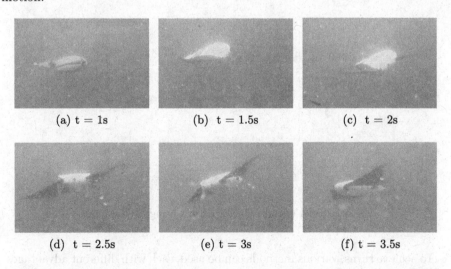

(a) t = 1s   (b) t = 1.5s   (c) t = 2s

(d) t = 2.5s   (e) t = 3s   (f) t = 3.5s

Fig. 19. Small curvature radius right turn - f = 1 Hz - $A_l = 20°$ - $A_r = −20°$.

When the robot moves its fins in opposite directions to rotate, it can achieve an average angular speed of 0.32 rad/s, as depicted in Fig. 20. The rotation velocity is similar to that of the maneuver with one still fin, but the benefit of this technique is the attainment of a zero curvature radius. During this movement, the robot oscillates about the pitch axis, and there are significant oscillations about the roll axis, with an average amplitude of 33°.

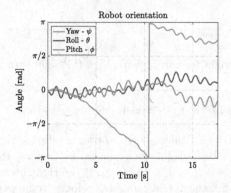

Fig. 20. Euler's angles during a turn with null curvature radius.

Ultimately, utilizing the caudal fins is also an option for executing turns in either direction. This is achievable since the asymmetrical rotation of the caudal fins induces a roll moment, causing the robot to steer. Figure 21 demonstrates this concept, depicting the Euler angles for a right turn accomplished by rotating the left caudal fin to +45° and the right caudal fin to −45°.

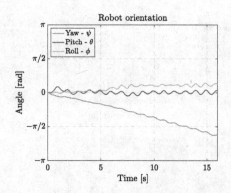

Fig. 21. Euler's angles during a turn using caudal fins.

To achieve turns, various methods can be used, each with different advantages and disadvantages. Figure 22 provides a comparison of all the possible ways to turn. It can be seen that the fastest turn is obtained by keeping one fin still and moving the other at high amplitude, while a slightly slower turn can be achieved by moving fins in counter-phase. An intermediate turn speed can be achieved by using just one of the caudal fins, while a very slow turn is possible if both caudal fins are rotated in opposite directions or if the pectoral fins move with a slight amplitude difference.

However, using pectoral fins for maneuvering reduces the amplitude of the movement of one or both fins resulting in a lower thrust generation. Thus, it is better to use caudal fins for maneuvering and pectoral fins for propulsion. Nonetheless, if a sharp turn is required, an asymmetric movement of the pectoral fins can be used to increase the angular speed and reduce the turning radius. It is important to note that the use of caudal fins for turning is slow compared to other methods, but it is possible to achieve a higher angular speed if one fin is rotated by $\pm45°$ and the other by $0°$.

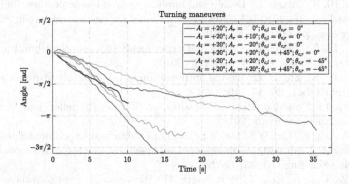

Fig. 22. Comparison of the yaw angle obtained with all the possible turning maneuvers.

5   Conclusion

The present study describes the development of a biomimetic robot inspired by cownose rays, which swim by flapping their pectoral fins, giving them excellent maneuverability and efficiency. The fins of the robot are designed to mimic the natural counterpart's shape and movement, generating a traveling wave that produces thrust by pushing water backward. A servomotor actuates the leading edge of the robot's pectoral fins, while the passive generation of the traveling wave allows for greater fin flexibility by detaching the trailing edge from the central body. Experimental tests have shown that this design effectively generates propulsive thrust, allowing the robot to reach a velocity of 0.4 m/s when the fins move at 1 Hz, which is comparable to other batoid robots' performances. Moreover, the robot's maneuverability was assessed, and it was found that it could perform floating and diving maneuvers and turns by moving the caudal and pectoral fins. The robot's simplicity in fin actuation and the small number of actuators used did not compromise its excellent maneuverability, which can generate high propulsive force and move in all directions with great agility. Future work will focus on implementing a control algorithm to follow a trajectory and maintain a constant orientation.

References

1. Arastehfar, S., Chew, C.: Effects of root chord movement on thrust generation of oscillatory pectoral fins. Bioinspir. Biomimet. **16**, 036009 (2021)
2. Bianchi, G., Cinquemani, S., Schito, P., Resta, F.: A numerical model for the analysis of the locomotion of a cownose ray. J. Fluids Eng. **144**(031203) (2022)
3. British Standard 903: Methods of testing vulcanised rubber - Part 19 (1957)
4. Cai, Y., Bi, S., Li, G., Hildre, H., Zhang, H.: From natural complexity to biomimetic simplification. The realization of bionic fish inspired by the cownose ray. IEEE Robot. Autom. Mag. **26**, 27–38 (2018)
5. Cai, Y., Bi, S., Zhang, L.: Design and implication of a bionic pectoral fin imitating cow-nosed ray. In: 2010 IEEE/RSJ International Conference on Intelligent Robots and Systems, pp. 3525–3529 (2010)
6. Cai, Y., Bi, S., Zheng, L.: Design and experiments of a robotic fish imitating cownosed ray. J. Bionic Eng. **7**, 120–126 (2010)
7. Cai, Y., Bi, S., Zheng, L.: Design optimization of a bionic fish with multi-joint fin rays. Adv. Robot. **26**, 177–196 (2012)
8. Carlton, J.: Propeller Blade Vibration in Marine Propeller and Propulsion. Butterworth-Heinemann (2012)
9. Chen, L., Bi, S., Cai, Y., Cao, Y., Pan, G.: Design and experimental research on a bionic robot fish with tri-dimensional soft pectoral fins inspired by cownose ray. J. Marine Sci. Eng. **10**, 537 (2022)
10. Chen, Z., Um, T., Zhu, J., Bart-Smith, H.: Bio-inspired robotic cownose ray propelled by electroactive polymer pectoral fin. In: ASME 2011 International Mechanical Engineering Congress & Exposition, pp. 1–8 (2011)
11. Chew, C., Lim, Q., Yeo, K.S.: Development of propulsion mechanism for robot manta ray. In: 2015 IEEE Conference on Robotics and Biomimetics, pp. 1918–1923 (2015)
12. Chi, W., Low, K.: Review and fin structure design for robotic manta ray (roman IV). J. Robot. Mechatron. **24**(4), 621–628 (2012)
13. Evologics: Boss Project. Manta ray AUV. Techincal report (2017). https://evologics.de/projects/boss
14. Fish, F., Schreiber, C., Moored, K., Liu, G., Dong, H., Bart-Smith, H.: Hydrodynamic performance of aquatic flapping: efficiency of underwater flight in the manta (2016)
15. Gao, J., Bi, S., Xu, Y., Liu, C.: Development and design of a robotic manta ray featuring flexible pectoral fins. In: 2007 IEEE International Conference on Robotics and Biomimetics, pp. 519–523 (2007)
16. Hall, K., Hundt, P.J., Swenson, J., Summers, A., Crow, K.: The evolution of underwater flight: the redistribution of pectoral fin rays in manta rays and their relatives (myliobatidae). J. Morphol. **279**, 1155–1170 (2018)
17. Hao, Y., Cao, Y., Cao, Y., Huang, Q., Pan, G.: Course control of a manta robot based on amplitude and phase differences. J. Marine Sci. Eng. **10**(2), 285 (2022)

18. He, J., Cao, Y., Huang, Q., Cao, Y., Tu, C., Pan, G.: A new type of bionic manta ray robot. In: Global Oceans 2020: Singapore, U.S. Gulf Coast (2020)
19. He, J., Cao, Y., Huang, Q., Pan, G., Dong, X., Cao, Y.: Effects of bionic pectoral fin rays' spanwise flexibility on forwarding propulsion performance. J. Marine Sci. Eng. **10**, 783 (2022)
20. Katzschmann, R., Preto, J.D., Curdy, R.M., Rus, D.: Exploration of underwater life with an acoustically controlled soft robotic fish. Sci. Robot. **3**(16), eaar3449 (2018)
21. Li, T., et al.: Fast-moving soft electronic fish. Sci. Adv. **3**, e1602045 (2017)
22. Liu, G., Ren, Y., Zhu, J., Bart-Smith, H., Dong, H.: Thrust producing mechanisms in ray-inspired underwater vehicle propulsion. Theor. Appl. Mech. Lett. **5**, 54–57 (2015)
23. Low, K., Zhou, C., Seet, G.: Improvement and testing of a robotic manta ray (roman-III). In: The 2011 IEEE International Conference on Robotics and Biomimetics, pp. 1730–1735 (2011)
24. Ma, H., Cai, Y., Wang, Y., Bi, S., Gong, Z.: A biomimetic cownose ray robot fish with oscillating and chordwise twisting flexible pectoral fins. Industr. Rob.: Int. J. **42**(3), 214–221 (2015)
25. Meng, Y., Wu, Z., Donng, H., Wang, J., Yu, J.: Toward a novel robotic manta with unique pectoral fins. IEEE Trans. Syst. Man Cybern.: Syst. **1**, 1–11 (2020)
26. Noor, S.N.A.M., Mahmud, J.: Modelling and computation of silicone rubber deformation constitutive equation. In: 2015 5th International Conference on Communication Systems and Network Technologies, pp. 1323–1326 (2015)
27. Riggs, P., Bowyer, A., Vincent, J.: Advantages of a biomimetic stiffness profile in pitching flexible fin propulsion. J. Bionic Eng. **7**(2), 113–119 (2010)
28. Roetemberg, D., Luinge, H., Baten, C., Veltink, P.: Compensation of magnetic disturbance improves inertial and magnetic sensing of human body segment orientation. IEEE Trans. Neural Syst. Rehabil. Eng. **13**(3), 395–405 (2005)
29. Rosemberger, L.: Pectoral fin locomotion in batoid fishes: undulation versus oscillation. J. Exp. Biol. **204**, 379–394 (2001)
30. Russo, R., Blemker, S., Fish, F., Bart-Smith, H.: Biomechanical model of batoid (skates and rays) pectoral fins predicts the influence of skeletal structure on fin kinematics: implications for bio-inspired design. Bioinspir. Biomimet. **10**, 046002 (2015)
31. Salazar, R., Fuentes, V., Abdelkefi, A.: Classification of biological and bioinspired aquatic systems: a review. Ocean Eng. **148**, 75–114 (2018)
32. Sfakiotakis, M., Lane, D., Davies, J.: Review of fish swimming modes for aquatic locomotion. IEEE J. Oceanic Eng. **24**(2), 237–252 (1999)
33. Sun, Y., Wu, L., Wang, H., Althoefer, K., Qi, P.: The validation of viscosity induced chord-wise undulation on soft fin array towards a novel robotic manta ray. In: 2022 IEEE 5th International Conference on Soft Robotics (RoboSoft), pp. 673–680 (2022)
34. Xing, C., Cao, Y., Cao, Y., Pan, G., Huang, Q.: Asymmetrical oscillating morphology hydrodynamic performance of a novel bionic pectoral fin. J. Marine Sci. Eng. **10**, 289 (2022)
35. Zhang, D., Pan, G., Cao, Y., Huang, Q., Cao, Y.: A novel integrated gliding and flapping propulsion biomimetic manta-ray robot. J. Marine Sci. Eng. **10**, 924 (2022)
36. Zhang, Y., Wang, S., Wang, X., Geng, Y.: Design and control of bionic manta ray robot with flexible pectoral fin. In: IEEE 14th International Conference on Control and Automation (ICCA), pp. 1034–1039 (2018)

Sucker Attachment and Detachment Patterns in *Octopus Vulgaris*

Janina Leonie Röckner[1,2] ⓘ, Mariana Díaz Arellano[3], and Letizia Zullo[4(✉)] ⓘ

[1] Center for Micro-BioRobotics and Center for Synaptic Neuroscience and Technology (NSYN), Genova, Italy
janina.rockner@iit.it
[2] University of Genova, Genova, Italy
[3] Université Côte d'Azur, Nice, France
mariana.diazare@gmail.com
[4] IRCSS Ospedale Policlinico San Martino, Genova, Italy
letizia.zullo@hsanmartino.it

Abstract. *Octopus vulgaris* has become an important model for motor control studies in soft robotics, due to its highly developed neural system and complexity in motion. For the past ten years, research on octopus arm motor system has provided advancements in understanding the control system of these hyper-redundant and flexible structures with further implementation in the field of soft robotics. In this work, we performed a correlation study of the sucker size and structure with their pattern of "attachment and detachment" using morphological and in-vivo behavior observational approaches.

Three main patterns of sucker attachment and detachment were identified and coded as 'Contraction Attachment/Detachment' (CA/CD), 'Orientation-Contraction Attachment' (OCA), and 'Wave-Like Attachment/Detachment' (WLA/WLD). The first two were more frequently used in attachment and the third one in detachment. Suckers involved in these motions showed a similar morphology and no correlation between the use of a specific strategy and their size was found.

We interestingly found indications of a possible association between the sucker strategy of attachment/detachment and overall arm movement. This suggests that the control of the sucker motion pattern may be linked to the suckers' functional use and interpreted within the framework of the animal behavior.

Keywords: Sucker · Octopus · Attachment · Detachment · Soft robotics · Behavior · Motion · Neural control

1 Introduction

Cephalopods have intrigued humanity since ancient times and have been part of various mythologies. They have inspired art, gastronomy, and science [1]. Octopuses play an important role in ecology as they are able to adapt to a changing environment, allowing them to live in very diverse marine ecosystems, from the shore to the deep sea. We

F. Meder et al. (Eds.): Living Machines 2023, LNAI 14157, pp. 266–280, 2023.
https://doi.org/10.1007/978-3-031-38857-6_20

can find studies on these animals in different scientific fields, such as ethology, physiology, regenerative sciences, genetics, and lately, soft robotics. Moreover, due to their soft but dynamic body, camouflage abilities, and high cognitive capacities, octopuses have especially prompted studies aiming at translating their biological features into the development of new technologies [2, 3].

Octopus's arms are special structures that can both sense objects within the environment and manipulate them through complex deformations and motions. Arm movements can be categorized into basic motions, including elongation, shortening, bending, and twisting, and complex motion-like crawling, walking, and fetching (the motion used by the animal to bring food directly to the mouth) [4–11]. Several of these complex motions require tight integration between motor commands delivered from the central nervous system to the arm and inputs (chemical and mechanical) from the arms and suckers. Some of these behaviors are even carried out by arms that are isolated from the rest of the body [12, 13]. However, sensory responses from the suckers appear to be an integral part of the construction of complex behaviors [14–16].

Studying these aspects of peripheral control of sucker behaviors will have a direct translation into the field of soft bio-robotics as it may provide important insights into both the construction and activation of artificial suckers [17–19] while leveraging their control architecture.

1.1 Octopus's Arm

Arm Morphology

The ability of the arms to coordinate their motion and perform complex tasks is due to a fine communication between the central nervous system in the brain (CNS) and the eight arms' peripheral nervous system (PNS) (Fig. 1, [20]). Each arm contains around 3 million motor neurons [4]. The CNS issues motor commands to the nervous system of the arm and integrates sensory information from the PNS to control arm movement and possibly to learn about the environment [21]. The arms and the CNS are connected by the axial nerve cord (ANC) which is composed of two cerebro-brachial tracts and a chain of ganglia organized in a medullary cord (MC). The ANC thus allows the exchange of information from the brain to the arm and vice versa. Motor control neurons located in the brain do not control muscles directly but rather send most of their efferences to motor neurons in the MC. These, in turn, control a rather narrow area of the intrinsic musculature of the arm [16]. The overall complexity of the motor control system organization and the octopus's arm coordination ability is, to a large extent, still unanswered.

As an example, there is no indication of the arrangement of motor neurons in the MC controlling different muscle types, and we do not know how motor neurons are activated to generate motor components like stiffening or shortening, involving the coordinated activation of more than one muscle type at a time [22]. In addition, several arm motions require not only the activation of a motor program but also the integration of sensory information from the arms' suckers detecting both chemical and mechanical inputs. Fetching behavior and the sucker reflex response are two prominent examples [13, 23].

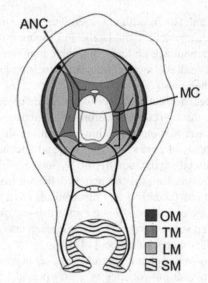

Fig. 1. *Octopus vulgaris* transverse arm section showing the axial nerve cord (ANC) including the medullary cord (MC) and the four different muscles: the oblique muscle (OM), the transverse muscle (TM), the longitudinal muscle (LM) and the sucker muscle (SM). Modified from [20].

1.2   Octopus's Sucker

Sucker Morphology

Each arm of *Octopus vulgaris* has around 200–300 suckers that allow it to hold and manipulate objects and detect chemical/mechanical stimuli from the environment. The suckers of the arm do not have the same dimensions. In particular, they increase in size outward from the mouth, reach their maximum at the middle arm's portion, and then decrease in size toward the arm's tips in both males and females [24].

Suckers are made of two main chambers: the infundibulum, the external chamber that seals the objects in contact, and the acetabulum, the inner chamber used to apply negative pressure and generate a suction effect [18]. An intermediate muscular part of the sucker, known as the sphincter, links together the acetabulum and the infundibulum (Fig. 2). The sucker's receptor cells have been categorized based on their morphology, position along the sucker's cuticle and physiological responses [25, 26]. Described as the thick cuticle, the internal part of the infundibulum holds a non-continuous "tooth-shaped" structured layer referred to as the pyramids, containing receptors with either a mechanical or a chemical function [25].

Sucker Use

Suckers are structures involved in many animals' behavior. As an example, they are used in locomotion, object manipulation, cleaning maneuvers, and several others [27]. Also, the suckers have a short-distance chemical recognition function based on the "touch-taste" characteristic which allows them to discriminate prey [28] and other chemicals found in the environment. Mechanoreceptors, on the other hand, are also an integral part

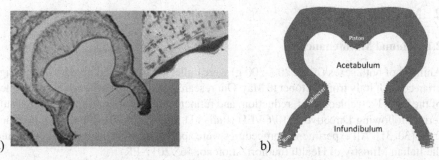

Fig. 2. (a) Longitudinal section of a sucker stained with Nissl. Pyramids are visible at the sphincter and infundibulum (red arrows; *inset*: a close up of two pyramids). (b) Schematic representation of a sucker with the two main chambers (acetabulum and infundibulum) and the three main structural elements: piston, sphincter and rim. The pyramidal structures (in red) the free receptor clusters (in yellow) are differently distributed on the sucker internal and external surface.

of the sucker sensory system and they are used to detect texture [26]. The touch-taste system is known for its use in foraging behavior and environmental exploration.

Suckers' chemoreceptors have also been shown to play a role in avoiding arm self-attachment. It has been observed that an amputated arm does not stick to another arm or to a surface containing the same animal skin extract. This is explained by the presence of an inhibitory compound on the arm's skin surface that, once perceived from the sucker chemoreceptors, prevents sucker attachment. This mechanism might represent an efficient fully-autonomous system to avoid arm self-entangling, a phenomenon never observed in freely behaving animals [29].

Based on the task performed, the animal might need to provide a different control over the sucker attachment/detachment. As an example, during walking or crawling over the sea floor, the animal might not need the sucker to attach strongly to the substrate, but rather to perform a fast attachment and detachment or to function exclusively as passive elements. Another example is the use of suckers in exploratory actions like arm probing. Here, the suckers can loosely attach to stones and objects on the sea floor but can also hold them strongly or manipulate them for longer. In behavior-like fetching, the situation is again different as the suckers need to hold firmly the piece of food that will be brought to the animal's mouth. This requires a continuous strong attachment of the sucker to the object while performing a stereotyped arm reconfiguration [11].

The aim of this study is to investigate these fundamental aspects of the sucker functioning, including (i) the attachment and detachment pattern and (ii) the sucker size and structure.

2   Method

2.1   Animal Maintenance

Animals of both sexes (mass 200–300 g) were collected from local anglers on the Ligurian coast of Italy from October to May. Our research conformed to the ethical principles of the three Rs (replacement, reduction, and refinement) and of minimizing animal suffering, following Directive 2010/63/EU (Italian D. Lgs. n. 26/2014) and the guidelines from [30, 31]. All experimental procedures were approved by the institutional board and the Italian Ministry of Health (authorization no. 465/2017-PR).

After capture, the animals were placed in 80 × 50 × 45 cm aquarium tanks filled with artificial seawater (Tropic Marine) and enriched with sand substrate and clay pot dens. The temperature was maintained constant at 17 °C, corresponding to the average temperature at the collection site, and continuously circulated through a biological filter system. Oxygenation was ensured using a dedicated aeration system, and all relevant water chemical/physical parameters were checked daily. Animals were allowed to adapt for at least 5 days before the experiments. They were inspected daily and fed shrimp 3 times per week. Three *Octopus vulgaris* Cuvier 1797 specimens were used in this study.

2.2   Video Recordings

Video footage was recorded using a high-speed camera (Huawei Nova 5T) mounted on a tripod and placed in front of the specimens' tank. Three sequences of the one animal's arm motion and crawling over the tank's vertical glass surface were selected over the entire video recorded and further analyzed. Within the first seconds of each recording, a scale bar was held against the glass tank for later analysis of the sucker's cup diameter. Suckers' attachments and detachments were acquired at 120 frames per second (fps).

2.3   Video Analysis

Videos were analyzed using the interactive zoom and frame-by-frame function of the software VLC player (VideoLAN, 1996). For comparative reasons, only suckers from the middle section of the arm length were analyzed.

Suckers can attach to surfaces using a range of forces. Here we could distinguish three types of attachment (loose, medium, and strong) based on the amount of resistance observed over the arm movement (inferred from the overall motion pattern, see below for a description). The presence of attachment from neighboring suckers, the overall arm movement, and the suckers' diameter were also described.

2.4   Morphology

Two animals were anesthetized with 3.5% MgCl2 seawater and three short segments were cut from the arm's medial portion. Arm samples were fixed overnight in 4% paraformaldehyde (PFA) in artificial seawater (ASW: NaCl 460 mmol l^{-1}, KCl 10 mmol l^{-1}, MgCl2 55 mmol l^{-1}, CaCl2 11 mmol l^{-1}, Hepes 10 mmol l^{-1}, glucose 10 mmol l^{-1}; pH 7.6), cryopreserved in 30% sucrose overnight, embedded in OCT

(Tissue-Tek®, VWR) using standard procedures (for details, see [32, 33]). Samples used for histology were sectioned into 20 μm sections, treated with standard Nissl staining and mounted on coverslips using DPX mount (for details, see [32, 33]). Images of the stained sections were acquired in a bright field using an upright microscope (Nikon Eclipse Ni) and processed using ImageJ software.

Samples for immunofluorescence were sliced at 200 μm at the cryostat (MC5050 Cryostat Microtome), immuno-stained using anti-acetylated tubulin diluted 1:500 (Sigma-Aldrich®, Darmstadt, Germany) as primary antibody and mouse Alexa 488 diluted 1:500 (ThermoFisher®, Waltham, Massachusetts, United States) as secondary antibody, plus Hoechst dye diluted 1:1000 (Sigma-Aldrich®, Darmstadt, Germany). Pyramids were observed under the confocal microscope (SP8, Leica microsystem GmbH, Wetzlar, Germany) and the distribution of cell receptors in the pyramid on the Acetabulum, Infundibulum, and Sphincter was described. The aim was to observe the receptor cells and compare their structure and shape with those described in previous works [25, 26].

2.5 Statistical Analysis

To test the relationship between the suckers' diameter and the pattern of attachment and detachment observed, a Kruskal-Wallis test and a pairwise Wilcox test for post hoc analysis were performed using RStudio Version 2023.03.0 [34].

3 Results

3.1 Sucker Attachment and Detachment Patterns

52 attachment and detachment video-recorded motions of 16 different suckers from three different arms were analyzed (See Table 1).

The following parameters were measured during attachment or detachment: sucker position in each row, attachment strength, attachment and detachment strategies, behavior of neighboring suckers, behavior of the arm, and sucker diameter. From video footage, we identified two different strategies of attachment: the 'Wave-Like Attachment' (WLA) and the 'Whole-Cup Attachment'.

WLA is achieved when the sucker touches the glass surface with one edge of the sucker rim and then places the complete cup stepwise. This creates a wave-like motion of the entire sucker rim surface over the glass (Fig. 3; WLA).

In 'Whole-Cup Attachment' the entire rim of the sucker is immediately attached to the surface. Whole-cup attachments were further subdivided into 'Contraction Attachment' (CA) and 'Orientation-Contraction Attachment' (OCA). In CA, the sucker cup already faces the glass surface for immediate placing and thus immediately attaches using the entire rim. In OCA, suckers and their neighboring suckers do not initially face the glass. They start turning, either simultaneously or one by one, to the glass surface and adjust their position with a small forward movement, to allow immediate whole-cup attachment (Fig. 3, OCA).

Similar to attachment, detachment strategies can be sorted into two major groups: 'Wave-Like Detachment' (WLD) and immediate detachment through 'Contraction

Table 1. Video footage observations of single octopus suckers

Videos	Type of attachment	Type	Strategy	Behaviors of neighboring suckers	Behavior of the arm	Diameter (mm)
1	Loose	Detachment	WLD	One attached	Steady	3.00
1	Loose	Detachment	WLD	One attached	Steady	2.60
1	Loose	Attachment	OCA	Both attached	Steady	3.00
1	Loose	Attachment	OCA	Both attached	Steady	2.60
1	Medium	Detachment	WLD	Both attached	Steady	3.70
1	Loose	Detachment	WLD	One attached	Steady	2.60
1	Strong	Detachment	WLD	None attached	Steady	3.50
1	Loose	Detachment	WLD	One attached	Steady	3.00
1	Medium	Detachment	WLD	One attached	Pull-Stop-Release	3.30
1	Strong	Detachment	CD	None attached	Pull-Release	3.00
2	Loose	Detachment	WLD	Both attached	Pull-Release	5.60
2	Loose	Detachment	WLD	None attached	Pull-Release	5.60
2	Medium	Detachment	WLD	One attached	Pull-Release	5.50
2	Medium	Detachment	WLD	None attached	Pull-Release	4.90
2	Medium	Detachment	WLD	None attached	Pull-Release	5.40
2	Medium	Detachment	WLD	None attached	Pull-Release	5.10
2	Loose	Attachment	OCA	None attached	Steady	5.50
2	Loose	Attachment	OCA	One attached	Steady	5.40
2	Loose	Detachment	CD	One attached	Steady	5.40
2	Loose	Detachment	CD	None attached	Steady	5.50
2	Strong	Attachment	CA	None attached	Steady	5.50
2	Strong	Detachment	WLD	None attached	Pull-Release	5.50
2	Strong	Attachment	OCA	None attached	Steady	5.50
2	Strong	Detachment	WLD	One attached	Pull-Release	5.50
2	Loose	Attachment	OCA	None attached	Steady	5.50
2	Strong	Attachment	OCA	None attached	Steady	5.40
2	Strong	Attachment	OCA	None attached	Steady	4.90
2	Strong	Detachment	CD	One attached	Pull-Release	4.90
2	Strong	Detachment	CD	One attached	Release-Pull	5.40
2	Loose	Detachment	WLD	None attached	Pull-Release	5.50
3	Strong	Detachment	WLD	One attached	Pull-Release	4.20
3	Strong	Detachment	WLD	None attached	Pull-Release	4.40
3	Strong	Detachment	CD	One attached	Pull-Stop-Release	5.00
3	Loose	Detachment	CD	None attached	Pull-Release	5.00
3	Medium	Attachment	WLA	None attached	Move-Attach	5.00
3	Medium	Attachment	WLA	None attached	Move-Attach	5.00
3	Medium	Detachment	WLD	One attached	Pull-Release	5.00
3	Medium	Detachment	WLD	None attached	Pull-Release	5.00
3	Strong	Attachment	CA	None attached	Move-Attach	4.40
3	Strong	Detachment	WLD	One attached	Pull-Release	4.40
3	Strong	Attachment	CA	Both attached	Steady	4.20
3	Loose	Attachment	CA	One attached	Steady	4.40
3	Medium	Attachment	OCA	One attached	Steady	5.00
3	Strong	Attachment	OCA	One attached	Steady	5.00
3	Medium	Detachment	WLD	Both attached	Pull-Release	4.20
3	Strong	Detachment	WLD	One attached	Pull-Release	4.40
3	Strong	Detachment	CD	One attached	Pull-Stop-Release	5.00
3	Medium	Detachment	WLD	One attached	Pull-Release	5.00
3	Strong	Attachment	WLA	None attached	Move-Attach	5.00
3	Medium	Attachment	OCA	One attached	Steady	5.00
3	Strong	Detachment	WLD	One attached	Pull-Stop-Release	5.00
3	Medium	Detachment	WLD	None attached	Pull-Release	5.00

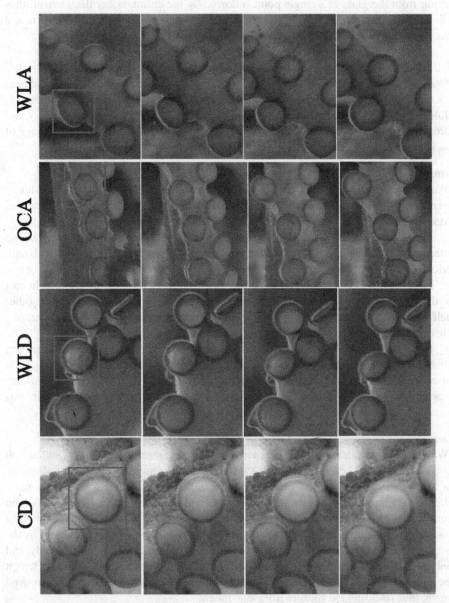

Fig. 3. Sucker strategies showing 'Wave-Like Attachment' (WLA), 'Orientation-Contraction Attachment' (OCA), 'Wave-Like Detachment' (WLD) and 'Contraction Detachment''(CD) within a timeframe of 1 s.

Detachment' (CD). In WLD the sucker cup is either detached step-by-step from the surface or all at once (Fig. 3, WLD). In both cases, detachment is initiated by the rim lifting from the glass at a single point followed by the entire sucker detachment, thus allowing the pressure to be released. In the CD strategy, the sucker rim contracts and detaches immediately from the glass surface (Fig. 3, CD).

Additionally, we identified three different types of attachment: 'Strong', 'Medium', and 'Loose'. Sucker attachments that resisted arm movements were labeled as 'Strong'. Attachments that were released with arm movement were considered 'Medium'. Suckers that were detaching without any obvious arm movement involved were labeled as 'Loose'. No obvious correlation was found between sucker identity and strategy and strength of attachment or detachment. However, more observations on a wider range of sucker sizes and positions along the arm are needed to fully assess this point.

Attachment

'Wave-Like Attachment' (WLA) was observed in 3/18 cases and 'Whole-Cup Attachment' in 15/18 cases. The latter was further divided into two categories: 'Contraction Attachment' (4/15; CA) and 'Orientation-Contraction Attachment' (11/15; OCA).

In 2/3 cases, WLA resulted in a medium attachment, and in 1/3 cases in a strong attachment. In all WLA, no attachment of the neighboring suckers was observed, and, prior to attachment, the arm was in motion.

In 1/4 cases, CA resulted in a loose and in 3/4 cases in a strong attachment. In half of the cases this strategy was used, no neighboring suckers were attached. In the other half of the cases, either one or both neighboring suckers were attached. In all but one observation, the arm was moving prior to attachment.

In 5/11 cases, OCA resulted in a loose attachment, in about 2/11 cases in a medium attachment, and in 4/11 cases in a strong attachment. Regarding the neighboring suckers, in most of the cases (5/11) no neighboring sucker was attached. In 4/11 cases one sucker was attached and in 2/5 cases both suckers were attached. In all cases, the arm was steady.

Detachment

'Wave-Like Detachment' was observed in 26/34 cases, (Table 1, WLD) and 'Contraction Detachment' in 8/34 cases (CD). WLD was used in 7/26 cases from a loose attachment, in 11/26 cases from a medium attachment, and in 8/26 cases from a strong attachment. Half of the time (13/26), one neighboring sucker was also attached. In 10/26 cases of the detachments, no neighboring sucker was attached. In only 3/26 cases, both neighboring suckers were attached. In 18/26 cases, the arm was moving and WLD was induced by the overall arm motion (Pull-Release behavior). In about 6/26 cases, the arm was steady, and only in 2/26 cases, we observed an interesting sequence of Pull-Stop-Release, in which the arm first pulled the sucker and, upon sucker resistance, stopped and then moved again, thus releasing the suckers from attachment.

The remaining detachments are achieved through the CD strategy of releasing the sucker from either a loose (3/8) or a strong (5/8) attachment. In most cases (5/8) a single neighboring sucker was attached and in the remaining ones (3/8) there was no other sucker attached. In the majority of the cases (3/8), the arm was moving while the sucker detached (Pull-Release behavior). In 2/8 cases, we observed the Pull-Stop-Release schema described above. In a single case, we observed the sucker contracting its cup and releasing the attachment right before the arm moved. In 2/8 of the cases, the sucker was detaching without the arm moving before or shortly after.

3.2 Morphology

Morphometric Measurements

The average diameter of the sucker that was included in the video analysis was 4.6 ± 0.9 mm. A detailed list of measurements of all the suckers included in the video analysis is reported in Table 1. No correlation was found between sucker diameter and attachment (Fig. 4a; attachment, n = 18, Kruskal-Wallis, p > 0.05) and detachment (Fig. 4b; detachment, n = 34, Kruskal-Wallis, p > 0.05) trategies or type of attachment (Fig. 4c; attachment, n = 18, Kruskal-Wallis, p > 0.05).

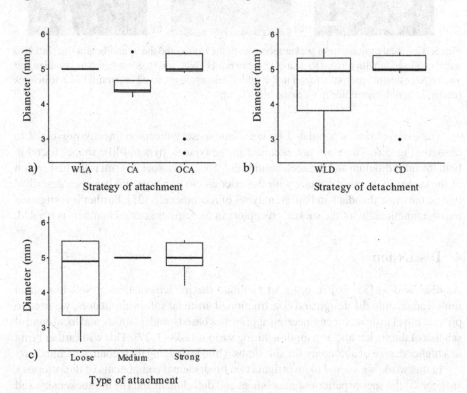

Fig. 4. Relation between sucker diameter and the strategy of (a) attachment (n = 18, Kruskal-Wallis, p > 0.05) or (b) detachment (n = 34, Kruskal-Wallis, p > 0.05) and (c) type of attachment (n = 18, Kruskal-Wallis, p > 0.05).

Histology

Nissl staining was used to visualize the distribution of the pyramid-like structures and receptors of the sucker's surface (Fig. 5a). The pyramids tend to be evenly spread throughout the infundibulum while they are concentrated at the center of the acetabulum, in correspondence with the protuberance used to seal the chamber in the sucker attachment phase (Fig. 5a, b) [27]. This interesting observation points to the possible functional specialization of the acetabular mechanoreceptors in the detection of pressure changes.

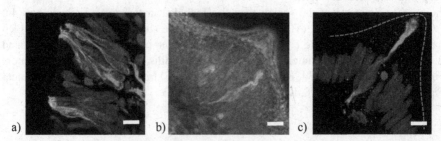

Fig. 5. Confocal projections of sucker receptors of the rim (a) and the infundibulum (b,c) labelled with acetylated tubulin (green) to visualize nerve projections, and Hoechst (blue) to visualize cell nuclei. Note that the receptors found in the infundibulum are enclosed in pyramid-like structures (encircled in red dashed line in c). Scale bar 10 μm.

The external rim is populated by abundant sensory receptors mostly organized in clusters (Fig. 5a). These are not enclosed in the typical 'pyramid-like shape' found in both the infundibulum and the acetabulum (Fig. 5b, c). The sucker's rim is the first region of the sucker that gets in contact with the external environment and has been described to bear the most abundant and different types of receptor cells [25]. Further investigation into the functionality of the sucker's receptors in the various sucker chambers is needed.

4   Discussion

As discussed in [35, 36] in order to facilitate the implementation of soft biological limb features into the design and construction of artificial soft manipulators, we need to provide novel insights for engineering approaches based on adaptability and local control schema of the sucker and arm motion during various tasks [1, 17]. This will further bring to a higher degree of autonomy for soft limbs while leveraging their control architecture.

In this work, we started to investigate two fundamental components of the octopus's suckers: (i) the sucker pattern of attachment and detachment and (ii) the sucker size and structure.

Suckers are used in a variety of behaviors and the control of their attachment/detachment is a field yet to be explored. It is known that suckers can be controlled locally at the level of the arm's peripheral nervous system and can autonomously react to both mechanical and chemical stimuli producing complex stereotyped motions like the sucker reflex arch [13]. We also know that some of the information from the suckers are sent to a higher center of computation in the central brain that, based on that, can deliver motor inputs back to the arms. The extent to which the peripheral and central nervous systems are involved in the control of suckers may determine the sucker motion pattern used in various behaviors.

Here we started investigating this issue by performing behavioral observations and video analyses of suckers' attachment/detachment patterns during octopus spontaneous crawling and probing motion over a vertical glass surface. We identified three main mechanisms of sucker attachment: 'Wave-Like Attachment' (WLA), Contraction Attachment (CA), and Orientation-Contraction Attachment (OCA). The most frequently used strategy is the contraction attachment (CA) where the cup is first placed before applying the suction. CA are often accompanied by steady arms and the attachment of the sucker is generally strong. This strategy may be most likely used to support the arm and the animal's attachment to surfaces.

Suckers can also employ strategies that do not provide a strong and stable anchoring of the arm to the surface like the OCA with loose attachment. In this case, the attachment can be restricted to a single sucker without the support of neighboring suckers. Hence, the sucker can attach and detach quite quickly and easily follow the whole arm movement. This strategy might be used in pure explorative behavior when the animal wants to retrieve information (sent either peripherally or centrally) about the probed surfaces. This information could be used, for example, to recruit additional suckers in the exploration or to continue probing with a single sucker.

Interestingly, the most frequent attachment method observed when arms are in motion, and no neighboring suckers are attached, is the WLA. The WLA might help to fully attach the cup in the direction of the moving arm and to support the exploratory behavior.

We also noticed that suckers could attach using various strengths. This might a have functionally relevant explanation. In loose attachment, only the sucker's rim (the region richest in sensory receptors [25]) seems to be in contact with the surface. In medium and in strong attachments a larger portion of the sucker's inner surface (the infundibulum) gets in closer contact with the surface and the protuberance of the acetabulum is pressed over the sphincter. In this configuration, the internal negative pressure increases, and a stronger attachment [27, 37]. Loose attachments might be mostly used in purely exploratory actions when a strong attachment is not needed. Only upon sensing a 'potentially interesting' target, the sucker might initiate a stronger attachment.

Our results are even more interesting when interpreted in light of the morphological analysis of the sucker receptor distribution. Indeed, we showed that the distribution of the pyramids and consequently of the receptors is not homogeneous on the sucker surface. In particular, we noticed that pyramids tend to be evenly spread throughout the infundibulum while in the acetabulum, they are concentrated only at the center of the acetabular surface, in correspondence with the protuberance [25]. As the protuberance is used to seal the chamber in the sucker attachment phase, it is possible that acetabular receptors are specialized in the detection of pressure changes and that of the rim surface in the exploration of the environment. This point deserves further investigation.

Following attachment, the sucker detaches from the surface using two main strategies: 'Wave-Like Detachment' (WLD) and 'Contraction Detachment' (CD). The most frequent pattern observed was the WLD. Most of the time, detachment seems to be induced indirectly by the moving arm that pulls the sucker away from the surface. Whether this is caused by the pulling mechanical force or by a neural signal inducing muscle cup contraction/relaxation and concomitant sucker release from the surface, will be further investigated. However, it has been observed in lab environments that, under certain circumstances, animals can lose their suckers if a strong attachment is not released upon arm pulling. Interestingly this has been observed more often in partially decerebrated animals (personal observation).

This may suggest that suction release and arm movement can be controlled synchronously or asynchronously by different compartments of the nervous system based on the animal's behavioral context.

To further investigate these issues, the next steps will be to (1) identify the motion pattern during sucker exposure to various types of mechanical deformation and (2) analyze the neural responses underlying the sucker's mechanical deformation. This information will be further translated into the soft-robotic field for the integration of a control command loop able to autonomously activate mechanical responses in artificial sensorized suckers.

Acknowledgments. We thank the local anglers of Santa Margherita Ligure for providing us with wild-caught animals and the animal care and maintenance facility of the IRCCS, San Martino Hospital of Genoa. This work was supported by the Office of Naval Research (N0001421-1-2516 and N00014-23-1-2083 to L.Z.).

References

1. Nakajima, R., Shigeno, S., Zullo, L., De Sio, F., Schmidt, M.R.: Cephalopods between science, art, and engineering: a contemporary synthesis. Front. Commun. (Lausanne) **3** (2018). https://doi.org/10.3389/fcomm.2018.00020
2. Laschi, C., Cianchetti, M., Mazzolai, B., Margheri, L., Follador, M., Dario, P.: Soft robot arm inspired by the octopus. Adv. Robot. **26**(7), 709–727 (2012). https://doi.org/10.1163/156855312X626343
3. Laschi, C., Mazzolai, B., Cianchetti, M.: Soft robotics: technologies and systems pushing the boundaries of robot abilities. Sci. Robot. **1**, 1–11 (2016). https://doi.org/10.1126/scirobotics.aah3690
4. Levy, G., Hochner, B.: Embodied organization of octopus vulgaris morphology, vision, and locomotion. Front. Physiol. **8**(Mar), 1–5 (2017). https://doi.org/10.3389/fphys.2017.00164
5. Nesher, N., Levy, G., Zullo, L., Hochner, B.: Octopus motor control. In: Oxford Research Encyclopedia of Neuroscience. Oxford University Press (2020).https://doi.org/10.1093/acrefore/9780190264086.013.283
6. Wells, M.J., Wells, J.: The function of the brain of octopus in tactile discrimination. J. Exp. Biol. **34**(1), 131–142 (1957). https://doi.org/10.1242/jeb.34.1.131
7. Kennedy, E.B.L., Buresch, K.C., Boinapally, P., Hanlon, R.T.: Octopus arms exhibit exceptional flexibility. Sci. Rep. **10**(1), 1 (2020). https://doi.org/10.1038/s41598-020-77873-7
8. Hanassy, S., Botvinnik, A., Flash, T., Hochner, B.: Stereotypical reaching movements of the octopus involve both bend propagation and arm elongation. Bioinspir. Biomim. **10**(3), (2015). https://doi.org/10.1088/1748-3190/10/3/035001
9. Levy, G., Flash, T., Hochner, B.: Arm coordination in octopus crawling involves unique motor control strategies. Curr. Biol. **25**(9), 1195–1200 (2015). https://doi.org/10.1016/j.cub.2015.02.064

10. Richter, J.N., Hochner, B., Kuba, M.J.: Octopus arm movements under constrained conditions: adaptation, modification and plasticity of motor primitives. J. Exp. Biol. **218**(7), 1069–1076 (2015). https://doi.org/10.1242/jeb.115915

11. Sumbre, G., Fiorito, G., Flash, T., Hochner, B.: Octopuses use a human-like strategy to control precise point-to-point arm movements. Curr. Biol. **16**(8), 767–772 (2006). https://doi.org/10.1016/j.cub.2006.02.069

12. Sumbre, G., Gutfreund, Y., Fiorito, G., Flash, T., Hochner, B.: Control of octopus arm extension by a peripheral motor program. Science (1979) **293**(5536), 1845–1848 (2001). https://doi.org/10.1126/science.1060976

13. Fraser Rowell, C.H.: Excitatory and inhibitory pathways in the arm of octopus. J. Exp. Biol. **40**(2), 257–270 (1963). https://doi.org/10.1242/jeb.40.2.257

14. Gutfreund, Y., Flash, T., Yarom, Y., Fiorito, G., Segev, I., Hochner, B.: Organization of octopus arm movements: a model system for studying the control of flexible arms. J. Neurosci. **16**(22), 7297–7307 (1996). https://doi.org/10.1523/jneurosci.16-22-07297.1996

15. Gutfreund, Y.: Patterns of arm muscle activation involved in octopus reaching movements. J. Neurosci. **18**(15), 5976–5987 (1998). https://doi.org/10.1523/jneurosci.18-15-05976.1998

16. Gutfreund, Y., Matzner, H., Flash, T., Hochner, B.: Patterns of motor activity in the isolated nerve cord of the octopus arm. Biol. Bull. **211**(3), 212–222 (2006)

17. Kang, R., Guglielmino, E., Zullo, L., Branson, D.T., Godage, I., Caldwell, D.G.: Embodiment design of soft continuum robots. Adv. Mech. Eng. **8**(4), 1–13 (2016). https://doi.org/10.1177/1687814016643302

18. Grasso, F.W., Setlur, P.: Inspiration, simulation and design for smart robot manipulators from the sucker actuation mechanism of cephalopods. Bioinspir. Biomim. **2**(4), 170–181 (2007). https://doi.org/10.1088/1748-3182/2/4/S06

19. Zullo, L., Chiappalone, M., Martinoia, S., Benfenati, F.: A 'spike-based' grammar underlies directional modification in network connectivity: effect on bursting activity and implications for bio-hybrids systems. PLoS One **7**(11), 2012. https://doi.org/10.1371/journal.pone.0049299

20. Bellier, J.-P., Xie, Y., Farouk, S.M., Sakaue, Y., Tooyama, I., Kimura, H.: Immunohistochemical and biochemical evidence for the presence of serotonin-containing neurons and nerve fibers in the octopus arm. Brain Struct. Funct. **222**(7), 3043–3061 (2017). https://doi.org/10.1007/s00429-017-1385-3

21. Gutnick, T., Zullo, L., Hochner, B., Kuba, M.J.: Use of peripheral sensory information for central nervous control of arm movement by octopus vulgaris. Curr. Biol. **30**(21), 4322-4327.e3 (2020). https://doi.org/10.1016/j.cub.2020.08.037

22. Zullo, L., Imperadore, P.: Regeneration and healing. In: Gestal, C., Pascual, S., Guerra, Á., Fiorito, G., Vieites, J.M. (eds.) Handbook of Pathogens and Diseases in Cephalopods, pp. 193–199. Springer, Cham (2019). https://doi.org/10.1007/978-3-030-11330-8_14

23. Sumbre, G., Fiorito, G., Flash, T., Hochner, B.: Motor control of flexible octopus arms. Nature **433**(7026), 09 February 2005. https://doi.org/10.1038/nature03372

24. Tramacere, F., Beccai, L., Kuba, M.J., Mazzolai, B.: Octopus Suckers Identification Code (OSIC). Mar. Freshw. Behav. Physiol. **46**(6), 447–453 (2013). https://doi.org/10.1080/10236244.2013.856586

25. Graziadei, P.P.C., Gagne, H.T.: Sensory innervation in the rim of the octopus sucker. J. Morphol. **150**(3), 639–679 (1976). https://doi.org/10.1002/jmor.1051500304

26. van Giesen, L., Kilian, P.B., Allard, C.A.H., Bellono, N.W.: Molecular basis of chemotactile sensation in octopus. Cell **183**(3), 594-604.e14 (2020). https://doi.org/10.1016/j.cell.2020.09.008

27. Packard, A.: The skin of cephalopods (coleoids): general and special adaptations. In: Form and Function, pp. 37–67. Elsevier (1988). https://doi.org/10.1016/b978-0-12-751411-6.50010-2

28. Buresch, K.C., et al.: Contact chemoreception in multi-modal sensing of prey by Octopus. J. Comp. Physiol. A Neuroethol. Sens. Neural. Behav. Physiol. **208**(3), 435–442 (2022). https://doi.org/10.1007/s00359-022-01549-y

29. Nesher, N., Levy, G., Grasso, F.W., Hochner, B.: Self-recognition mechanism between skin and suckers prevents octopus arms from interfering with each other. Curr. Biol. **24**(11), 1271–1275 (2014). https://doi.org/10.1016/j.cub.2014.04.024

30. Fiorito, G., et al.: Guidelines for the care and welfare of cephalopods in research – a consensus based on an initiative by CephRes, FELASA and the Boyd Group. Lab. Anim. **49**, 1–90 (2015). https://doi.org/10.1177/0023677215580006

31. Fiorito, G., et al.: Cephalopods in neuroscience: regulations, research and the 3Rs. Invertebr. Neurosci. **14**(1), 13–36 (2013). https://doi.org/10.1007/s10158-013-0165-x

32. Fossati, S., Benfenati, F., Zullo, L.: Morphological characterization of the octopus vulgaris arm. Vie et Milieu **61**(4), 191–195 (2011)

33. Maiole, F., Tedeschi, G., Candiani, S., Maragliano, L., Benfenati, F., Zullo, L.: Synapsins are expressed at neuronal and non-neuronal locations in Octopus vulgaris. Sci. Rep. **9**(1), 1–13 (2019). https://doi.org/10.1038/s41598-019-51899-y

34. R Core Team: R: language and environment for statistical computing. R Foundation for Statistical Computing, Vienna, Austria (2021). https://www.r-project.org/

35. Pfeifer, R., Lungarella, M., Iida, F.: Self-organization, embodiment, and biologically inspired robotics. Science (1979) **318**(5853), 1088–1093 (2007). https://doi.org/10.1126/science.1145803

36. Pfeifer, R., Iida, F., Lungarella, M.: Cognition from the bottom up: on biological inspiration, body morphology, and soft materials. Trends Cogn. Sci. **18**(8), 404–413 (2014). https://doi.org/10.1016/j.tics.2014.04.004

37. Tramacere, F., Beccai, L., Kuba, M., Gozzi, A., Bifone, A., Mazzolai, B.: The morphology and adhesion mechanism of octopus vulgaris suckers. PLoS One **8**(6), June 2013. https://doi.org/10.1371/journal.pone.0065074

Understanding Preload Force for Grasping Objects with Different Stiffness Using Sensorized Suction Cups

Ebrahim Shahabi[1,2]([✉]) [iD], Francesco Visentin[3] [iD], Alessio Mondini[2] [iD],
and Barbra Mazzolai[2]([✉]) [iD]

[1] Biorobotics Institute, Scuola Superiore Sant'Anna, 56025 Pontedera, PI, Italy
Ebrahim.shahabishalghouni@iit.it
[2] Bioinspired Soft Robotics Lab, Istituto Italiano di Tecnologia, 16163 Genova, GE, Italy
Barbara.mazzolai@iit.it
[3] Università degli Studi di Verona, 37134 Verona, VR, Italy

Abstract. The ability to grasp objects of varying stiffness is a crucial skill for robotic manipulators to perform tasks in real environments. Sensorized suction cups have been shown to be effective in grasping objects with different stiffness by measuring the preload force applied to the object. In this study, we investigate the effect of preload force on grasping objects with different stiffness using sensorized suction cups. We conducted experiments using sensorized suction cups to measure the preload force applied to objects of varying stiffness. Results show that the preload force depends on the type of material, and it increases with the increase of the stiffness of the object. Those findings provide valuable insights into the design of robotic manipulators that can effectively grasp objects with different stiffness using sensorized suction cups.

Keywords: Sensorized Suction Cup · Preload Force · Grasping Object

1 Introduction

Robotic arms are often used to grasp and handle objects with the help of an end-effector for transporting and/or manipulating them. In general, end-effectors can be divided in four categories: a first category that contains end-effectors with an hand or finger-like shape; a second one in which they are shaped like suction cups or bellows; a third one that consists in end-effectors shaped like hooks or hackles; and a last one that is related to the interconnection between materials [1–6]. Most of these end-effectors are used in highly structured environments, such as factories, and they can be equipped with dedicated technological solutions to provide optimal grasping of a specific set of objects. However, to operate in more dynamic environments, the end-effector should be endowed with feedback capabilities that can guide the correct picking of the object.

Nature has inspired many innovative designs, including grippers [7]. Octopuses are known for their incredible ability to manipulate objects with their eight arms [8], which are lined with suction cups [9]. These suction cups work by creating a vacuum that allows the octopus to grip onto surfaces and objects with great force [10].

F. Meder et al. (Eds.): Living Machines 2023, LNAI 14157, pp. 281–288, 2023.
https://doi.org/10.1007/978-3-031-38857-6_21

Scientists have developed a gripper that mimics the structure and function of octopus suction cups [11]. The gripper is made up of soft, flexible material with small, suction cup-like structures that can adhere to surfaces through vacuum pressure [12, 13]. One advantage of the octopus-inspired gripper is its ability to conform to the shape of different objects, allowing for a more secure grip. Additionally, the soft and flexible material used in the gripper reduces the risk of damage to delicate objects during handling. Suction cups have a simple structure and the ability to be used in combination with a vacuum to catch objects with different surfaces and shapes, which gives more flexibility and simplified control in handling different objects than the use of finger-based grippers [14].

Visual and tactile force sensors have been used to understand the contact with objects [12, 13, 15]. The use of tactile sensors can help in reducing the computational needs, however, there are some challenges to using embedded tactile sensors instead of external visual sensors. For example, they need to be miniaturized and embeddable in the sucker and be able to provide good accuracy and sensitivity, to detect contact between the suction cup and the object which is mandatory information for activating/deactivating the vacuum [12, 16]. At the same time, they need to be thin and soft to not affect the softness of the rim and the suction capabilities.

In a common passive suction cup, a preload is necessary to squeeze out the air inside the cup and attach it to the substrate. Also actuated suction cups need a preload to help in creating a seal between the suction cup and the object, which allows the suction cup to generate a vacuum when a pump is activated. Knowing the preload force of the suction cup is crucial to apply the force necessary to seal the rim, without exceeding it, in order not to risk damaging the object to be gripped. Materials and textures of the suction cup affect the preload force. Softer and more flexible ones, such as silicone, can better conform to the surface of the object, thereby improving the seal at lower preload forces.

The integration of tactile sensors in robotic manipulators can optimize the preload force for objects of different shapes and textures. This adaptive mechanism enhances the grasping process's overall effectiveness and reduces the risk of damaging the object due to excessive force. By measuring the pressure distribution between the suction cup and the object, tactile sensors can adjust the preload force in real time. This approach can ensure that the suction cup always grips the object with the appropriate amount of force, improving the performance of robotic manipulators in handling objects of diverse shapes and textures.

This study presents a new design and manufacturing process for creating an artificial suction cup with embedded sensing capabilities. The suction cup uses resistive material for sensing and can detect object contact. Machine learning techniques are used to determine the minimum force required for grasping objects with varying stiffness in both air and water. These findings suggest potential practical applications for the system in unstructured industrial settings where visual sensors are not feasible.

The paper is structured as follows. The design and the manufacturing process of the sucker and the sensors, and their working principles are presented in Sect. 2. Section 3 presents the approach used to identify and predict the minimum preload force for grasping objects with different stiffness in the air and under water. Conclusions and future work are then presented in Sect. 4.

2 Materials and Methods

2.1 Design and Fabrication

The body of an octopus is completely soft, and this characteristic provides the animal with peculiar abilities, such as the ability to compress, change its shape, and vary its stiffness, just to mention some of them. Moreover, with its suckers, the octopus is able to explore the environment, grasp objects and manipulate them with high accuracy. Inspired by this property, we designed an artificial suction cup that resembles natural suckers.

The manufacturing process for the suction cup is analogous to that demonstrated in our previous paper [12]. Briefly begins with designing the molds using 3D CAD software (Solid Works 2019, Das-sault Systems Solid Works Corp, USA) and then 3D printing (Prusa MK3S +, filament diameter 1.75 mm, nozzle diameter 0.4 mm) them using PLA filament. The molds consist of two parts, with the first part used to cast the upper part of the sucker body containing microfluidic channels for strain sensors, and the second part used to protect the channels. Polydimethylsiloxane (PDMS) is poured into the mold and degassed before curing, after which a Kapton sheet is laser-cut (VersaLaser VLS 3.50, Universal Laser Systems) and used as a mask to guide the placement of sensors. The conductive material is then injected into the microfluidic channels and the sucker is sealed with a second layer of Dragon Skin 10 (Smooth-on). The process is depicted in Fig. 1A, with a schematic of the final sucker shown in Fig. 1B.

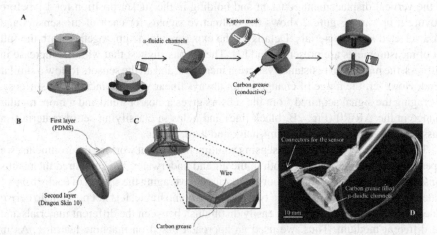

Fig. 1. Manufacturing process. (A) The suction cup is cast in two steps. The first mold is used to cast the top part of the sucker and to create micro-fluidic channels to host the conductive carbon grease. Once cured, a Kapton mask is placed on the internal part of the artificial infundibulum to improve the deposition of the conductive material. An additional protective layer is then cast over the artificial infundibulum to seal the conductive material from the external environment. (B) A schematic overview of the developed sucker. In this work we used the PDMS (Sylgard 184) for top layer and Dragon Skin 10 (Smooth-On) for bottom layer, however, any material can be used in the process. (C) A schematic overview of how the conductive grease is connected to the read-out electronics. (D) The final developed sensorized artificial sucker. The wires that exit from the rear part of the sucker are further covered with a layer of Sil-Poxy (Smooth-On) to guarantee sealing and avoid contamination of the conductive carbon grease.

The proposed sensors are conductive strain sensors using carbon conductive grease. Thin electric wires (Figure C) are introduced into the sucker from its top part to connect with an external read-out board, which reads the change in resistivity due to an applied force in the artificial infundibulum. Each channel has a cross-section of 600 μm, and the resulting sensor elements have a resistance in the range of 100–200 kΩ. A final version of the artificial sucker is presented in Fig. 1D. The process is shown with more details in [12].

3 Results and Discussion

3.1 Material Classification

An initial set of tests have been carried out to determine the capability of the system in detecting different shore hardness (range 0010 to D50) so that different materials could be classified. For each material, we 3D-printed or cast a cube 50 x 50 x 25 mm^3 (average weight is 65 g) which we used to acquire the signals from the sensorized sucker. The data is based solely on preload and does not consider vertical displacement. The primary focus here is to detect the necessary amount of force/pressure required to secure the connection between the suction cup and an object. We first applied a vertical displacement of 2 mm on the sucker when in contact with one of the selected materials, and we recorded the corresponding resistance variation. We repeated each test 15 times keeping the speed of the vertical displacement constant and holding in the sucker position for 1 s before moving it upward. Figure 2 shows the distinctive signals for each of the sensors and for a selected set of materials. Details on the experimental setup, together with the full set of measurements are presented in [12]. The graphs suggest that with the increase in stiffness, the maximum resistance variation increases, and all the sensors follow a similar trend. However, the range of change is not always linear with the increase in stiffness. Averaging the signal acquired from the sensors gives a clearer trend and a more regular change in the ΔR\R0 (Fig. 2B, black line) and helps in classifying set of materials in classes such as soft, semi-soft, semi-hard, and hard.

To assess the reliability of our sensing solution in different working environments, we repeated the same experiments both in the air and underwater. We compared the results considering the clustering in the four categories by averaging the signals of each group of materials. Even if the signals in the two media are comparable, it is not possible to derive a clear, identification threshold to easily distinguish between the different materials and the different medium. Thus, we used an approach based on machine learning. As in [12] we used a multilayer perceptron neural network consisting of an input layer with a size equal to the feature vector (195 values), two hidden layers that having ten and six neurons, respectively, and an output layer containing one neuron per result considered (4 classes as described above). The network was trained using 120 samples and tested

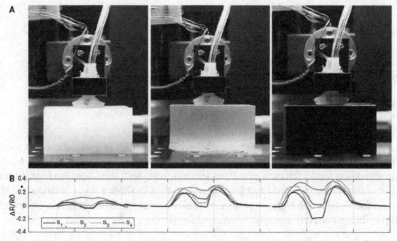

Fig. 2. Material characterization based on the sensor readings. (**A**) Three examples of material tested (ordered from left to right, from the softest to the hardest). (**B**) Individual strain sensor readings (colored lines) for each of the tested materials. On top (black line) the average of the signals, which capture computed the common trend of the four strain sensors.

with a set of more than 2400 samples. Results showed comparable results both in air and in water providing a mean accuracy of 97.5% and 97.1% in air and water, respectively.

3.2 Optimal Suction Force

After obtaining the results of the material classification, we proceeded to assess the efficacy of the artificial sucker by conducting tests to determine the minimum force necessary for proper adhesion to the material, ensuring complete sealing before activating the vacuum and subsequently grasping the object. Regarding the preload force test, we connected the artificial sucker to a load cell positioned on a vertical linear stage. Subsequently, we meticulously measured the minimum force required for the sucker to adhere to each arterial under various scenarios. This facilitates streamlined control implementation for activating the pump. However, since the force regression is dependent on the material (Fig. 3), to properly evaluate the measured force, we cannot use a unified model, instead, we need to first identify the material, using the previously described approach, and then select the correct model.

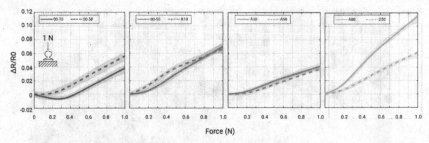

Fig. 3. We expanded the sensing capabilities by performing a set of preload measurements in which we wanted to evaluate the relationship between the measured force and the voltage readings. Here, the regression model for each of the classes (soft, semi-soft, semi-hard, and hard) for each of the application scenarios considered (air and water). Results show a linear behavior for all the cases except for 00-10 which high compliance increases the error in the linear fitting. Nevertheless, it is still possible to correctly identify the reaction force.

Therefore, we have defined a specific protocol to evaluate the performance of the active, sensorized sucker, which follows these steps: i) the sucker is moved downwards towards the material, ii) once it touches the block surface, it is moved downward for an additional 2 mm, the acquired data is then used to iii) identify the material class and the material itself. Afterward, iv) the sucker is moved upwards of 2 mm and then again downwards until the required force for the identified material is achieved. This is done by evaluating in run-time the applied force using the sensors readings. When the minimum force to properly adhere to the material is achieved, v) the vacuum pump is activated, and the slider is moved upwards. The maximum force that can be exerted on the sucker is 1.3 N, beyond which the infundibulum becomes completely flat. According to that, we systematically applied a pre-load force from 0 to 1 N to the sucker and when reached, we manually activated the connected vacuum pump (Fig. 4A). Materials in air and water share similar results, especially for ones with lower stiffness. The adhesion force still holds the object in mid-air, and it disappears just after the release of the vacuum forcing the object to automatically detach from the sucker and fall into the container. Figure 4B shows the run-time plot of the acquired relative resistivity, the computed force using the material-specific model, and the status of the vacuum pump (i.e., on or off) for two materials either in the air or the water scenario. Results show the effectiveness of the proposed artificial sucker and the reliability of the method used to blindly identify different materials and successfully grab them.

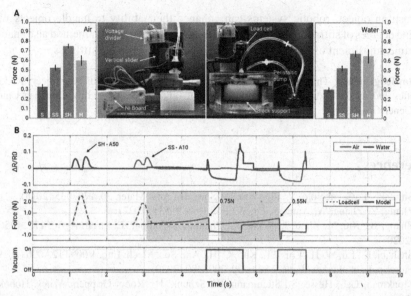

Fig. 4. (**A**) Minimum force required to provide a proper adhesion to the object before activating the vacuum in air (left) and water (right). Between the graphs, the experimental setup with all the components used. The loadcell is only depicted to provide completeness to the whole picture but was not used in this experimental protocol. (**B**) Run-time measurements of the sensors (averaged between the four sensors), the measured force from the loadcell (dashed line) and the computed force measured using the regression model (solid line), and the activation of the vacuum pump. In the first row, the highlighted portion of the plots indicates the data used for classification, while in the second row the data used to estimate the threshold on the force readings above which the vacuum pump is activated.

4 Conclusion

In conclusion, our method for understanding preload force in the air and underwater for grasping objects with different stiffness using sensorized suction cups provides a valuable tool for robotic systems. In order to accomplish this, we first tested the suction cup with objects of differing stiffnesses under different forces (the force started from 0.1 N to 1N). In the next step, we determined the minimum force necessary to grip objects with varying stiffnesses. Then we used machine learning (regression) to determine the relationship between the amount of incoming force and the output signal from the suction cup, which can help to understand the minimum force for grasping the object regarding the output signal and overcoming the issue of the nonlinear fitting of the signals. In the end, we tested the system for recognizing the stiffness of the object and activated the pump after passing the minimum force.

In fact, achieving complete contact becomes challenging when the objects have different stiffness levels, and the suction cup is linearly displaced toward the surface. When this situation arises, the softness of the suction cup, in conjunction with the vacuum, facilitates perfect adhesion. However, if this condition is not met, the suction cup fails to grip the object. By precisely determining the optimal preload force required to grasp an object, robotic systems can enhance their ability to handle objects with varying degrees of stiffness and adapt to environmental changes. Our method also enables real-time adjustment of the grip force based on changes in object stiffness.

Acknowledgements. This work was carried out within the framework of the project "RAISE-Robotics and AI for Socio-economic Empowerment" and was supported by European Union-NextGenerationEU.

References

1. Shintake, J., Cacucciolo, V., Floreano, D., Shea, H.: Adv. Mater. **30**, 1707035 (2018)
2. Zhang, Y., Zhang, W., Yang, J., Pu, W.: Soft Rob. **9**, 531 (2022)
3. Zhang, B., Xie, Y., Zhou, J., Wang, K., Zhang, Z.: Comput. Electron. Agric. **177**, 105694 (2020)
4. Shahabi, E., Lu, W.-H., Lin, P.T., Kuo, C.-H.: Am. Soc. Mech. Eng. V009T12A006 (2019)
5. Fiorello, I., et al.: Adv. Func. Mater. **30**, 2003380 (2020)
6. Monkman, G.J., Hesse, S., Steinmann, R., Schunk, H.: Robot Grippers. Wiley, Hoboken (2007)
7. Hughes, J., Culha, U., Giardina, F., Guenther, F., Rosendo, A., Iida, F.: Front. Robot. AI **3**, 69 (2016)
8. Gutfreund, Y., Flash, T., Yarom, Y., Fiorito, G., Segev, I., Hochner, B.: J. Neurosci. **16**, 7297 (1996)
9. Tramacere, F., Follador, M., Pugno, N., Mazzolai, B.: Bioinspir. Biomim. **10**, 035004 (2015)
10. Follador, M., Tramacere, F., Mazzolai, B.: Bioinspir. Biomim. **9**, 046002 (2014)
11. Tramacere, F., Beccai, L., Kuba, M., Gozzi, A., Bifone, A., Mazzolai, B.: PLoS ONE **8**, e65074 (2013)
12. Shahabi, E., Visentin, F., Mondini, A., Mazzolai, B.: Adv. Intell. Syst. **5**, 2200201 (2023)
13. Huh, T.M., et al.: IEEE, pp. 1786–1793 (2021)
14. Mazzolai, B., et al.: Adv. Intell. Syst. **1**, 1900041 (2019)
15. Aoyagi, S., Suzuki, M., Morita, T., Takahashi, T., Takise, H.: IEEE/ASME Trans. Mechatron. **25**, 2501 (2020)
16. Frey, S.T., et al.: Sci. Adv. **8**, eabq1905 (2022)

Development, Modeling, and Testing of a Passive Compliant Bistable Undulatory Robot

Anson Kwan[1]([⊠]) and Daniel Aukes[2]

[1] Ira A. Fulton School of Engineering, Arizona State University, Mesa, AZ 85212, USA
akwan2@asu.edu
[2] School of Manufacturing Systems and Networks, Arizona State University, Mesa, AZ 85212, USA

Abstract. This proposed device uses a single actuator to transition a bistable constrained compliant beam to generate undulatory motion. Undulatory locomotion is a unique form of swimming that generates thrust through the propagation of a wave through a fish's body. This paper draws inspiration from Anguilliformes and discusses the kinematics and dynamics of wave propagation of a bistable underwater robot. Thrust generation is explored through modeling and experimentation of the length constraint to better understand the device. This paper validates the theoretical spine behavior through experimentation and provides a path forward for future development in device optimization for various applications. Previous work developed devices that utilized either paired soft actuators or multiple redundant classical actuators that resulted in a complex prototype with intricate controls. Our work contrasts with prior work in that it aims to achieve undulatory motion through passive actuation from a single actively driven point which simplifies the control. Through this work, the goal is to further explore low-cost soft robotics via bistable mechanisms, continuum material properties, and simplified modeling practices.

Keywords: Bistable Mechanism · Compliant Material · Anguilliform · Simulation · Bioinspired

1 Introduction

This paper presents a novel, passive, and compliant material system that uses a single actuator accompanied by a rigid length constraint to generate motion inspired by eels. The motivation of our paper is to explore how bistable devices (see Fig. 2) can generate complex motion from simple input signals via careful selection of material properties, beam geometry, and geometric constraints. From this, exploring undulatory swimming is a natural progression, due to its elegant wave propagation dynamics [1]. Our proposed

---

Supplementary Information The online version contains supplementary material available at https://doi.org/10.1007/978-3-031-38857-6_22.

device utilizes the tuned dynamics of a compliant material arranged in a bistable config-uration so that when engaged it forces the material to transition between stable states. This generates a wave that propagates along its length, facilitating a swimming gait reminiscent of anguilliform swimmers (see Fig. 2). A pseudo rigid body (PRB) approxi-mation of a flexible material is used to provide a framework for device optimization and design. The model is validated against an experimental prototype to ensure an accurate analytical model is used for future optimization.

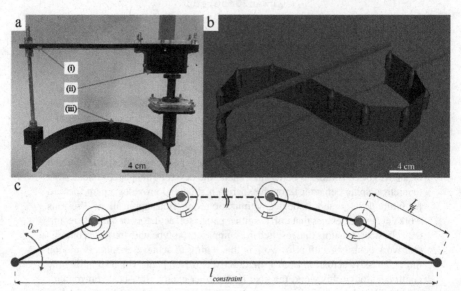

Fig. 1 (a) Manufactured prototype of proposed design comprised of the (i) length constraint mechanism, (ii) Dynamixel Servo, and (iii) fiberglass beam. (b) Orthonormal view of ten-link (gray) PRB connected by hinge joints (red dot). The model was designed so that each link was one tenth of the overall length of the spine and connected to the length constraint (blue). (c) Pseudo-rigid body of n-link (black line) approximation of compliant material. Each joint has a single degree of freedom with a torsional spring (spiral) and rotational damper (dashpot). The length constraint (blue) was then derived as a rigid body that connected each end of the spine by a zero-friction pin joint (blue dot). The angle ϑ_{act} of the head drives the position and state of the device (green arrow) (Color figure online)

Eels and other body caudal fin (BCF) fish demonstrate 'pure' anguilliform loco-motion by way of lateral compression; the compression and release of muscular forces propagate a wave down their spine, which travels along their flexible bodies to create thrust [2, 3]. Undulatory locomotion demonstrates outstanding hydromechanical effi-ciency by generating substantial amounts of momentum via the timed storage and release of energy [2, 4]. The release of potential energy through a wave to generate momentum by pushing against water has also inspired roboticists to explore and develop undula-tory devices [4]. In the past decade, research has focused on bio-inspired, undulatory swimmers, utilizing both soft bodies and classical rigid mechanics to understand this hydrodynamic effect [4–7]. For these devices, the timing of actuators mounted in series along the body not only limits the adaptability of many prototypes but impedes our ability to mimic nature. In recent years, the push towards simplified robots which utilize soft or compliant materials has enabled new developments in bio-inspired swimming devices, which take advantage of material properties, curvature, and asymmetric system stiffness [8–12]. Previous bistable undulatory devices focused on snap-through buckling effects to generate momentum [13]

In contrast with the work above, we propose using geometric constraints alongside bending, compliant beams to create a bistable, dynamic system to develop undulatory locomotion. This study fits under the umbrella of a new class of devices we call "Soft, Curved, Reconfigurable, Anisotropic Mechanisms" (SCRAMs), which we have previously studied in the context of buckling beams [10], pinched tubes [11], and twisted beams [12]. The novelty of this device is highlighted by its simple control, high degree of tunability, and continuous beam deformation due to continuum material and fluidic interaction. A prototype of our device has been simulated and validated experimentally. The model employed is based on a rigid-body approximation of a flexible material; it utilizes estimated environmental forces to help understand locomotion performance in water. The prototype and experimental results both validate the parameterization of the physics-based model and demonstrate several design variables that play a key role in influencing performance.

The rest of this paper is laid out in the following order. In the second section, we describe the approach and methodology of how the proposed device was modeled and experimentally validated. The third section discusses the experimental results and analysis. The fourth section outlines our conclusions on the research and impacts of this concept for future work.

2   Approach and Methodology

The following sections outline our intent and procedure for modeling, prototyping, and simulation of the proposed device.

2.1   Analytical Model

The proposed model is shown in Fig. 1. At the top half of the frame, we see a continuum material whose length is constrained by a rigid element of length '$l_{constraint}$' (see Fig. 1). The approximated pseudo-rigid-body (PRB) model is shown in Fig. 1c with n rigid links connected by a series of hinge joints (shown in red). Other methods of modeling flexible materials utilize shell theory or fabric mechanics, which can generate higher fidelity results, but must often make compromises with the fluidic models to balance computational time [14]. In previous work, forward momentum is generated by the body pushing against the fluid which requires modeling of the environment and the device body [4–7]. Therefore, the interactions between the flexible material and the environment are critical to understanding the proposed device and such methods were not appropriate. Therefore, a PRB model was used due to its success in approximating undulatory motion in a fluid [15].

In the proposed model, a torsion spring and damper are added to each joint to represent the stiffness and damping of the selected flexible material (see Fig. 1c). The model dynamics are characterized such that each link's inertia comprises the system inertia and the hydrodynamic forces are applied to the center of mass of each link. The number of links selected was determined by balancing the need for fast and accurate computation to use the model for model fitting and optimization; this is discussed further in the paper. The flexible beam is called the spine and the rigid length element is called the length constraint. The length constraint is applied to the continuum material, such that its natural configuration is in one of two "C" shapes, facing either left or right, highlighting the bistable nature of the system (see Fig. 2b).

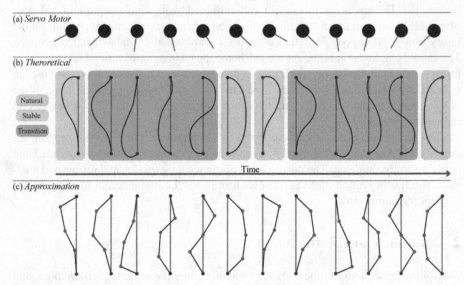

Fig. 2 (a) Servo motor control input positions at correlated positions of theoretical and approximated gait. Control input depicts a single period of a sinusoidal waveform that represents a single gait cycle of the device. (b) Theoretical representation of the proposed device in different transition phases between bistable natural states (highlighted green) over time (green arrow). The stable configurations (highlighted orange) are the starting states of the gait cycle and the transition phases (highlighted red) promote wave propagation. The blue lines represent the length constraint that forces the geometric configuration. (c) The approximated representation is a visualization of how we model the phases of the proposed device using PRB. The red dots represent the approximated joints that estimate the material property of the spine (Color figure online)

Our intent is to use this model to analyze the dynamics of the device as it transitions between bi-stable states. Analyzing the two stable states is critical because it is the continuous transition between each that generates the forward thrust of the device (see Fig. 2). The excitation for the device to transition between stable equilibrium depends on the material's internal stiffness characteristics and the length of the geometric constraint. We use the model generated in simulation to understand how the material, beam geometry, and length constraint affects the performance of the device in water. To build

the designed model (see Fig. 1), we selected MuJoCo[1] because it has been developed
with the intent for model-based optimizations, which was critical for the design process
of the mechanism [16].

2.2 Design Process

Based on assumptions of the physical environment, design decisions need to be made
before characterizing the model and manufacturing the prototype. The primary assumption for the system is that the device will operate in water and is constrained to operate
within planar motion to match our physical experiment's limited workspace, which is discussed later in this section. Therefore, it is critical that the material selected for the spine
has material properties that match this environment. Namely, matching the impedance
of the material to the environment is critical in maximizing performance. A composite
fiberglass sheet was selected for its low damping and high stiffness to maximize the time
spent in transition between stable states since this is responsible for propagating a wave
in the spine to generate thrust. These characteristics were critical to ensure the spine
was responsive to excitation and to maximize the amount of energy transferred to the
environment.

a   b

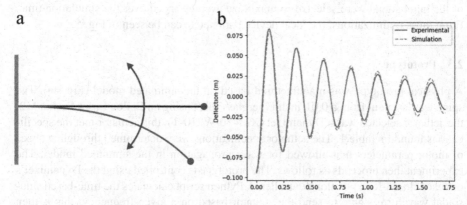

Fig. 3 (a) Visualization of beam deflection test where one side of the beam was fixed (gray)
and started with an initial deflection (red) and let it come to rest to its natural state (black)
with a reflective tracker (blue) to collect tip position information. (b) Results of the simulated and
experimental deflection test of the 0.01-inch Fiberglass sheet. The estimated stiffness and damping
constants were found using the pseudo rigid body model and optimized joint parameters through
Python library, SciPy minimize function (Color figure online)

To model the fiberglass sheet, a deflection test was conducted to parameterize the
estimated torsion spring and damping constants for the approximated flexible material.
To calculate these values, we conducted a beam deflection experiment, where the tip
of a 170 × 40 mm fiberglass beam was elastically deformed and released, coming then

---

[1] MuJoCo, DeepMind Technologies Limited. MuJoCo is an open source, full-featured rigid body
physics simulator.

to rest. The tip of the deflected beam was tracked using an OptiTrack motion capture system at 360 fps. An equivalent model was then created in the MuJoCo simulator and the SciPy library[2] was used to fit the simulated tip data to the collected experimental data (see Fig. 3). To prevent the inherent viscoelastic hysteresis of the material from dominating model parameters, the experimental data was truncated at the point where the amplitude of the initial displacement attenuates to 80%. For a small displacement, viscoelasticity causes a flexible material to creep over an extended period to reach its final neutral position [17]. The included creep data would reflect a higher estimated damping constant because the material's shift in trajectory reflects energy absorbed over longer time periods. Based on the fitted data, a torsional stiffness and damping constant were found and implemented as joint parameters for the selected fiberglass sheet (see Table 1).

After parameterization of the spine, further optimizations were run to maximize the speed of the actuated system. In dynamics, there is a strong influence of excitation frequency on the system behavior [18]. However, due to the limitations of the actuator, it was not possible to conduct a frequency sweep to find the resonance frequency of the device. Therefore, the frequency of the actuator and the length of the spine were kept constant during the optimization because of the actuator limitations and the size of the experimental tank, respectively. The length of the constrained beam and the amplitude of the input signal were selected to maximize average speed over the simulation time. From those optimizations, the ideal device parameters can be seen in Fig. 5.

2.3 Prototype

A physical prototype was manufactured based on the simulated model (Fig. 4a). The spine was laser cut from a 0.01-inch Fiberglass sheet using an Epilog Laser Fusion M2; the actuator selected was a Dynamixel (XM430-W210-T); this actuator met the specifications found in Table 1. The actuator specifications were determined through analysis of motor parameters that allowed for wave propagation in the simulated model. The experiment then proceeds as follows. The prototype is controlled using the Dynamixel's onboard closed-loop position controller. A Python script calculates the time-based sinusoidal waveform signal to send the actuator based on a given frequency; this is then transmitted via UART to a Dynamixel OpenCM 9.04 Type-C Module that connects to the servo (see Fig. 4b). The servo driver then returns the current position and status of the actuator to receive the next command.

2.4 Experimental Setup

To validate the model and design optimization discussed previously, the prototype was run in a water tank to compare against simulated results. The simulation was run under ideal conditions to observe the behavior of the device in water. This meant that buoyancy,

---

[2] A bound-constrained scipy.optimize.minimize() function was used for all optimizations. Implementation was done to minimize a scalar square error through adjusting parameters of the simulation model. Bounds of parameters were selected through physical limitations of the system.

Table 1 Parameters of Device and Simulation

Parameter	Value
Spine Length	400 mm
Spine Height	40 mm
Material Thickness	0.01 in
Optimized System Energy Loss	0.090685951
Torsional Stiffness Constant (k)	0.8764 N·m/rad
Torsional Damping Constant (C)	$4.511 \cdot 10^{-4}$ N·m·s/rad
Servo Amplitude	115°
Frequency	0.5 Hz
Material Density	1235 kg/m^3
Environment Density	1000 kg/m^3
Environment Viscosity	0.0009 Pa·s

hydrodynamic forces generated from turbulence, and environmental factors such as wind were not considered. To minimize discrepancies, the prototype was tested in an enclosed tank ($4 \times 2 \times 2$ ft) with a low-friction gantry system that permits x and y-axis motion over the surface of the water but restricts motion corresponding to the vehicle's depth (see Fig. 4b). This allowed the device to be suspended in water at a fixed height, to limit the effects of buoyancy.

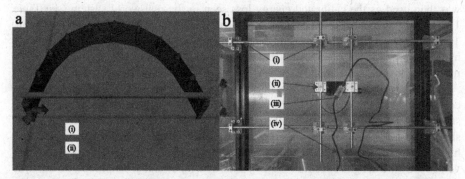

Fig. 4 (a) Snapshot of rendered model in Mujoco with added global movement in the (i) x and (ii) y-axis to represent the experimental gantry system. (b) Experimental setup for conducting a planar swimming test. Experimental testing consisted of (i) planar gantry mechanism using low friction linear bearings, (ii) device attachment point with red tracking dots, (iii) onboard Dynamixel OpenCM 9.04 Type-C servo driver transmitting position information to a computer via data-cable, and (iv) power cable to supply 12VDC 1A power to actuator

To ensure that the model can be validated for real-world applications, data was collected during the experiments. The tests were recorded at 60 frames per second and imported into motion tracking software[3] to interpret position data of the trackers (see Fig. 4b). The positions were collected at the front of the device. Reflections on the water's surface made additional marker placement difficult and therefore visual correlation was used to verify the wave propagation between the simulation and prototype. These results were then validated by the device's average velocities.

3 Results

To validate the simulation to the prototype, additional post-processing of the data and calibration of the model to the experimental setup was required. To minimize interference of the water tank on the device, the experimental data was truncated. As the prototype reached the end of the tank, the turbulence created from the wave propagation bounced off the walls of the tank and reflected towards the device. This resulted in a portion of the generated thrust to be negated from these disturbances. The experimental data was thus truncated to the initial 4.5 s of each test to minimize the differences due to the build-up of wave-based disturbances.

There are several discrepancies in the experimental setup that the simulation does not account for. This includes real-world wall effects observed due to the tank size and material property nonlinearities, as well as friction and inertial effects observed in the gantry system (see Fig. 4b). Therefore, the simulation was calibrated to consolidate discrepancies observed in the experiments. By tuning the x and y-axis friction constants of the simulated gantry system, the model speed was fitted to the average velocity across multiple length-constraint experimental tests (see Fig. 4a). The calibration was conducted by fitting the simulation average velocity to the experimental velocities at each length constraint. The average friction coefficient across all the length constraints was then used as the calibrated energy loss seen in the real-world system (see Table 1). The calibrated simulation compared to the experimental data can be seen in Fig. 5b. The differences in the calibrated model and prototype are likely due to the simplified hydrodynamic model. The benefits and tradeoffs of this approach are further discussed in the conclusions section of this paper.

Despite the discrepancy in overall device speed, the model can accurately suggest correlations between parameters and outputs. Multiple tests over a range of length con- straints were conducted to validate the model for the physical device. As seen in Fig. 5b, shortening the length constraints in both simulation and experiments correlates to a higher average device speed. Additionally, the model was configured for maximum velocity with a length constraint of 200 mm and input signal amplitude of 80° was determined as the minimum to initiate bistable transitions. This is reflected in the aver- age speeds from the tests conducted at this length constraint (see Fig. 5b). However, the amplitude value discovered in simulation did not successfully initiate a transition between stable states in the prototype. A higher amplitude was thus needed to generate successful wave propagation in the prototype. This is most likely due to differences between the PRB model and the real behavior of the fiberglass sheet. To accurately compare the simulations and experiments, the input signal amplitude was matched to

---

[3] Tracker: *Video Analysis and Modeling Tool.*

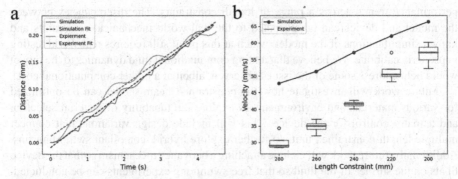

Fig. 5 (a) Example plot of position (in the direction of motion) versus time for calibrated simulated model (blue) and experimental prototype (red). The simulation was calculated at the same parameters for the respective experiment. In this plot the length constraint was 220 mm, and the signal input amplitude was 115°. Both data sets were then fitted to a linear regression model (dashed lines) to approximate the average speed of the device. (b) Trend of calibrated simulation (blue) and device speeds (red) as a function of different length constraints. For each length constraint, the experiment was run four times, and an average velocity (red line) was calculated using linear regression. The box plots are defined such that the horizontal line represents the median and the box bounds are the upper and lower quartiles. Outliers in the data set are represented as circles (Color figure online)

the experimentally used input signal. Overall, there is a qualitative similarity between the model and device that suggests that the simulation results provide evidence towards a validated prototype.

From the experiments with the prototype, it was observed that material selection in relation to the working environment is critical. In the case of water, a softer material is necessary to slow down wave propagation in our prototype to allow for the spine to transition between stable states. If a stiffer material or shorter spine is used, this results in faster snapping and less-effective thrust generation. This implies that the continuous transition between stable states is critical and minimizing the time spent in the natural configuration of the device produces more continuous thrust. This can be seen in the oscillatory behavior visible in Fig. 5a. The discrepancies between simulation and experimental oscillations can be attributed to the model discrepancies discussed above.

4 Conclusion

In this paper, we modeled and characterized a compliant bistable undulatory robot. An analytical model was generated using geometric approximation of the compliant material to parameterize the variables critical to wave propagation and thrust generation. We selected and experimentally identified the material properties of a fiberglass sheet to estimate the stiffness and damping of a hinge joint with a damper and torsion spring. A prototype of the device was manufactured, and experiments were conducted to validate the simulated model at various length constraints. While there were clear differences in velocity between the simulations and tests, the model and prototype both showed similar performance trends across a range of length constraints. The discrepancies between the model and device can be attributed to the real-world mechanical constraints and known simplifications of the model, which at this point still requires real-world testing to properly calibrate. We believe that adding computational fluid dynamics to the model would help address some of the issues observed, albeit at a higher computational cost.

Future work will investigate how the constrained beam model can be optimized for various materials and environments to explore the tunability of material selection and actuator control for the device. This will include design variations that connect multiple length-constrained units to further explore hybrid, compliant swimming fins. Additionally, future work will include attaching a buoyancy mechanism so that the device floats on the surface of the fluid so that free swimming experiments can be conducted. Furthermore, using a higher fidelity fluidic model would allow for analysis on the device's resonance frequency which would allow for increased efficiency of device. By taking advantage of continuum materials, it is possible to lower manufacturing time of soft robots and allows for high adaptability for these devices. This paper aims to present preliminary work within the field of soft robotics on exploring low cost, bistable systems that can be modeled via a simplified physics-based approach.

Funding.. This work is supported by the National Science Foundation (NSF) Grant No. 1935324.

References

1. Lighthill, M.J.: Aquatic animal propulsion of high hydromechanical efficiency. J. Fluid Mech. **44**(02), 265 (1970)
2. Lauder, G.V., Tytell, E.D.: Hydrodynamics of undulatory propulsion. Fish Physiol. **23**, 425–468 (2005)
3. Tytell, E.D., Lauder, G.V.: The hydrodynamics of eel swimming. J. Exp. Biol. **207**(11), 1825–1841 (2004)
4. Feng, H., Sun, Y., Todd, P.A., Lee, H.P.: Body wave generation for anguilliform locomotion using a fiber-reinforced soft fluidic elastomer actuator array toward the development of the EEL-inspired underwater soft robot. Soft Robotics **7**(2), 233–250 (2020)
5. Nguyen, D.Q., Ho, V.A.: Kinematic evaluation of a series of soft actuators in designing an eel-inspired robot. In: 2020 IEEE/SICE International Symposium on System Integration (SII), pp. 1288–1293, January 2020
6. Fremerey, M., Fischheiter, L., Mämpel, J., Witte, H.: Locomotion study of a single actuated, modular swimming robot. WIT Trans. Ecol. Environ. (2010)
7. Chen, D., Wu, Z., Dong, H., Tan, M., Yu, J.: Exploration of swimming performance for a biomimetic multi-joint robotic fish with a compliant passive joint. Bioinspiration Biomimetics **16**(2), 026007 (2020)
8. Xu, Y., Hu, J., Song, J., Xie, F., Zuo, Q., He, K.: A novel multiple synchronous compliant and passive propeller inspired by loons for swimming robot. In: 2022 IEEE International Conference on Robotics and Biomimetics (ROBIO) (2022)
9. Sharifzadeh, M., Jiang, Y., Aukes, D.M.: Reconfigurable curved beams for selectable swimming gaits in an underwater robot. IEEE Robot. Autom. Lett. **6**(2), 3437–3444 (2021)
10. Sharifzadeh, M., Aukes, D.M.: Curvature-induced buckling for flapping-wing vehicles. IEEE/ASME Trans. Mechatron. **26**(1), 503–514 (2021)

11. Jiang, Y., Sharifzadeh, M., Aukes, D.M.: Shape change propagation through soft curved materials for dynamically-tuned paddling robots. 2021 IEEE 4th International Conference on Soft Robotics (RoboSoft) (2021)
12. Jiang, Y., Chen, F., Aukes, D.M.: Tunable dynamic walking via soft twisted beam vibration. IEEE Robot. Autom. Lett. **8**(4), 1967–1974 (2023). https://doi.org/10.1109/LRA.2023.324 4716
13. Ta, T.D., Umedachi, T., Kawahara, Y.: A multigait stringy robot with bi-stable soft-bodied structures in multiple viscous environments. In: 2020 IEEE/RSJ International Conference on Intelligent Robots and Systems (IROS) (2020).https://doi.org/10.1109/iros45743.2020.934 1059
14. Chen, B., Govindaraj, M.: A physically based model of fabric drape using flexible shell theory. Text. Res. J. **65**(6), 324–330 (1995)
15. Melsaac, K.A., Ostrowski, J.P.: A geometric approach to anguilliform locomotion: modeling of an underwater eel robot. In: Proceedings 1999 IEEE International Conference on Robotics and Automation (Cat. No.99CH36288C) (1999)
16. Todorov, E., Erez, T., Tassa, Y.: MuJoCo: a physics engine for model-based control. In: IEEE/RSJ International Conference on Intelligent Robots and Systems (IROS), pp. 5026–5033 (2012)
17. Mei, S., Wang, Y.: Viscoelasticity: a new perspective on correlation between concrete creep and damping. Constr. Build. Mater. **265**, 120557 (2020)
18. Wang, X., Alben, S.: Dynamics and locomotion of flexible foils in a frictional environment. Proc. R. Soc. A: Math. Phys. Eng. Sci. **474**(2209), 20170503 (2018). https://doi.org/10.1098/rspa.2017.0503

Synthetic Nervous System Control of a Bioinspired Soft Grasper for Pick-and-Place Manipulation

Ravesh Sukhnandan[1]([✉]) [iD], Yanjun Li[4] [iD], Yu Wang[1], Anaya Bhammar[1], Kevin Dai[1] [iD], Michael Bennington[1] [iD], Hillel J. Chiel[5,6,7] [iD], Roger D. Quinn[4] [iD], and Victoria A. Webster-Wood[1,2,3]([✉]) [iD]

[1] Department of Mechanical Engineering, Carnegie Mellon University, Pittsburgh, PA, USA
[2] Department of Biomedical Engineering, Carnegie Mellon University, Pittsburgh, PA, USA
[3] McGowan Institute for Regenerative Medicine, Carnegie Mellon University, Pittsburgh, PA, USA
[4] Department of Mechanical Engineering, Case Western Reserve University, Cleveland, OH, USA
[5] Department of Biology, Case Western Reserve University, Cleveland, OH, USA
[6] Department of Neurosciences, Case Western Reserve University, Cleveland, OH, USA
[7] Department of Biomedical Engineering, Case Western Reserve University, Cleveland, OH, USA
vwebster@andrew.cmu.edu

Abstract. Manipulation of objects of variable size, shape and surface properties remains a challenging problem in robotics. In this paper, we present the design of a soft, pneumatically variable contact stiffness grasper and the training of a sparse, bioinspired neural network controller for pick-and-place manipulation. Both the soft grasper and the neural network controller are inspired by the sea slug *Aplysia californica*. The compliant nature of the grasper is beneficial for maintaining rich contact with objects, which simplifies the control problem. Adopting biologically inspired neural dynamics and network structure has the further advantage of building neural network controllers that are robust and efficient for real-time control. To verify the effectiveness of our bio-inspired approach for object grasping and manipulation, we developed a simulation environment that reflects the compliance between the soft grasper and the object. We demonstrate that when integrated with the neural network controller, the grasper successfully completed the pick-and-place task in simulation. With minimal tuning, the controller was

This work was supported in part by the National Science Foundation (NSF) grant no. FRR-2138873 and by a GEM fellowship. Any opinions, findings, and conclusions or recommendations expressed in this material are those of the authors and do not necessarily reflect the views of the NSF.
R. Sukhnandan and Y. Li—These authors contributed equally to the work.

F. Meder et al. (Eds.): Living Machines 2023, LNAI 14157, pp. 300–321, 2023.
https://doi.org/10.1007/978-3-031-38857-6_23

then successfully transferred to the physical soft grasping platform and was able to successfully pick-and-place objects of various size and mass, up to a maximum tested mass of 706 g. The bio-inspired approach to both the morphology and the control of the soft-grasper presented here thus represents an exciting first step toward the robust adaptive manipulation of a broad class of objects.

Keywords: Soft robotics · Robotic Manipulation · Synthetic Nervous Systems · *Aplysia*

1   Introduction

In the pursuit of robotic manipulators that can replicate the dexterity and sensitivity of prehensile appendages found in nature, roboticists have increasingly incorporated soft materials and compliant structures in their designs [1,21,27]. Soft graspers offer advantages that make them attractive options for the manipulation of objects in challenging environments, such as in agriculture. Some fruit, fungi, and vegetables are often soft, slippery, and fragile [37]. Soft graspers and compliant structures can solve contact problems encountered in the manipulation of such objects morphologically by conforming to the surface of the object [27]. Moreover, unlike point contact between rigid bodies, compliant structures have the ability to conform to the grasped object, which increases the contact area and the frictional forces and torques that can be applied to keep the object stable [2].

Prehensile appendages like tentacles [1] and soft fingertips [22] often serve as a direct source of inspiration for the morphology of their soft robotic counterparts [27]. However, soft structures possess many degrees of freedom, which make predicting how these structures will deform computationally expensive. The computational cost is further compounded when the objects being grasped are soft or irregular. Hence, the real-time control of soft robotic grasping and manipulation systems remains a challenge [33]. However, many natural organisms are capable of similar real-time control to execute such complicated manipulation tasks.

One organism that is adept at grasping and manipulating a wide variety of objects, including small, fragile, and slippery objects in real-world settings using a soft grasper is the sea slug *Aplysia californica*. *Aplysia* regularly manipulates seaweeds of a wide range of geometries and stiffness and adapts to mechanical loads in the environment. Furthermore, *Aplysia* possesses a tractable nervous system that has facilitated the creation of detailed neuromechanical models of its soft grasper and neural controller [34]. This detailed understanding of both the biomechanics and neural controller of *Aplysia* has been used to create soft robots that can capture the major kinematics of *Aplysia*'s feeding behavior [5,21]. Abstracting key features from *Aplysia*'s feeding mechanisms for engineering applications may help to bridge the gap between the manipulation benefits inherent to soft graspers and the difficulty in controlling such structures.

Adapting the advantages of *Aplysia*'s soft grasper for engineering applications requires the adoption of principles from both the grasper's morphology and control. *Aplysia*'s soft grasper can conform to the shape of a grasped object by enveloping it within the soft grasper and modulating the shape of its lumen [14]. Through active modulation of closing force in the musculature of the grasper [10], it can tune the contact stiffness of the grasper to maintain a secure hold of the object. To mimic the modulatory characteristics of the *Aplysia* grasper in soft robots, a combination of grasper morphology and material properties can be exploited to achieve tunable stiffness. Methods to modulate contact stiffness through thermally actuated polymers and metals [3,24], dielectric elastomers (DEA) [28] and dielectric liquids [36], and variable fluidic pressure [16,22,29] have previously been used by soft roboticists, but gaps remain. For example, thermally actuated methods can achieve order of magnitude changes in stiffness but can require timescales on the order of minutes to do so [24]. Dielectric elastomer and dielectric liquid based graspers have the advantage of direct interfacing with electrical control systems. However, they require operating voltages on the order of kilovolts (kV) [28,36] which needs specialized circuitry and handling [20]. Fluidic actuated graspers can achieve tunable stiffness by modulating pressure, while simultaneously providing feedback of contact pressure [22] and geometry [16,29]. The graspers presented in [16,29] and [22] achieve tunable stiffness with feedback of contact by modulating and monitoring pressure in an elastic enclosure. However, these graspers adopt a parallel jaw configuration which limits their ability to spatially tune stiffness and maximize the surface area in contact with the target object. Although other fluidic graspers have been reported that can provide a greater contact area with the object using stochastic tentacle-like appendages [1] or a fluidic toroid [25], they do not explicitly provide the ability to spatially tune contact stiffness and sense changes in contact state along the grasping surface.

In addition to the compliance and tunable materials of *Aplysia*'s feeding apparatus, the controller for *Aplysia*'s soft grasper demonstrates real-time control of feeding behavior that adapts to the environment. The controller exhibits a hierarchical control architecture that is composed of command and interneurons that creates emergent adaptability based on sensory feedback [34]. To create a similar, real-time controller for our *Aplysia*-inspired soft grasper, we implemented a Synthetic Nervous System (SNS) controller. SNSs incorporate the dynamics of real neurons and can be designed to perform basic arithmetic operations efficiently, which makes them a promising approach for the control of real-time robotic systems [9,31,32]. Furthermore, SNSs can be designed to replicate a hierarchical control architecture, inspired by that found in *Aplysia* [18]. We have previously demonstrated that an SNS tuned in simulation can successfully control a Cartesian gantry robot for a real-time pick-and-place manipulation task [18]. However, SNSs have not been previously used to control a soft grasper in a manipulation task. SNSs' ability to robustly and efficiently perform computations in real-time [18] makes it particularly attractive for the real-time control of a soft grasper for manipulating objects of various sizes, shapes, and surface properties.

To address the need for real-time control of soft robotic graspers for pick-and-place manipulation, in this work, we present the design, manufacturing, and characterization of a bio-inspired soft grasper based on the abstraction of key features from the feeding mechanism of *Aplysia californica*. The grasper's morphology was inspired by the conformable grasping surface of *Aplysia*, and was able to envelop grasped objects via pneumatic soft actuators that contract radially. Spatial tuning of contact stiffness was achieved by soft jaws with pneumatically variable contact stiffness, which also simultaneously provide contact feedback via monitoring of abrupt pressure changes. We then show that an SNS controller inspired by the hierarchical structure of the *Aplysia* feeding control circuitry can be first tuned in simulation and then transferred to the physical soft robotic grasper to perform pick-and-place manipulation, with limited additional tuning. The physical grasper qualitatively replicated the key dynamics of the simulated grasper. Without any additional tuning of the controller, the soft grasper with SNS control was able to pick up objects of varying size, shape, and mass. This work lays the foundation for a soft grasper platform that can adaptively change its control and actuation to robustly manipulate objects of various shape and surface properties. Such a grasping platform may be particularly useful in an agricultural environment where the ability to simultaneously modulate and sense contact pressure can aid in the manipulation of soft, fragile, and slippery objects.

2   Methods

2.1   Bioinspired Soft Grasper

Assembly and Characterization of Closure Artificial Muscle. To achieve circumferential contraction of the closure muscle, two layers of McKibben actuators are placed in a fabric sleeve (80% Nylon, 20% Spandex). Each layer of actuators was composed of two McKibben actuators fabricated using methods previously described by Dai et al. [5], each 245 mm long, connected via 1.6 mm (1/16 in.) inner diameter (ID) tubing. To maintain a cylindrical shape, the layers of McKibbens were offset by 90° (Fig. 1A). This 90° offset minimized the strain on the tubing connections between the McKibben actuators, which otherwise had a tendency to buckle when pressurized. This buckling would cause the closure muscle to lose its circular shape if only one actuator layer was used.

When actuated, these McKibben's exhibited approximately 25% contraction from their original length. For a closure muscle of circumferential length of 490 mm, we would expect to see a change of radius of the circular area of the actuator from 46.5 mm when fully deflated to 19.5 mm when fully inflated, for a total radial change of 27 mm (Fig. 1A). To characterize the contraction of the fabricated closure muscle, the pressure applied to the muscle was increased from 0 to 12 psig at increasing intervals of 0.5 psig. At every pressure point, the system was pneumatically inflated in a twenty-second period, and three measurements of the diameter of the muscle were taken on the inner wall of the closure muscle with a 1-mm resolution ruler.

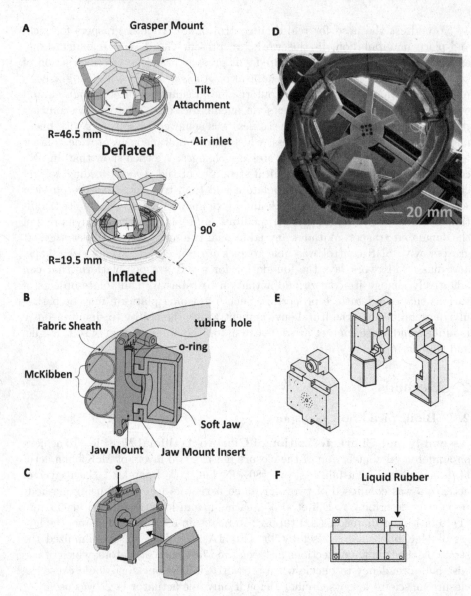

Fig. 1. A. Schematic of grasper in the uninflated and inflated states. Design values for the radii of the enclosed grasping area are shown. **B** Cross-section of the soft grasper. Air tightness was kept via the flange of the soft jaw. **C** Exploded view of soft jaw assembly. **D** Fabricated Grasper (underside view). The soft grasper without the tilt attachments weighed 143 g. The total radial contraction of the manufactured grasper was 19 mm. **E** Mold used to create the soft jaw. **F** After the mold was assembled, the liquid urethane elastomer was injected via a syringe.

Assembly and Characterization of Soft Jaws With Tunable Stiffness.

While the closure muscle became increasingly stiff with applied pressure, this change was coupled with a decrease in diameter. Moreover, it was not possible to spatially tune the contact stiffness of the closure actuator. To be able to tune the contact stiffness spatially and to decouple the contact stiffness from the positional state of the closure muscle, soft deformable jaws were designed and affixed to the inner diameter of the closure muscle (Fig. 1). The stiffness of these jaws could be varied pneumatically, such that increasing the air pressure to the internal cavity of a jaw increased its effective stiffness.

To fabricate the jaws, an injection molding technique was used. A four-piece mold was 3D printed on a Prusa MK3S+ out of Hatchbox PRO+ polylactic acid filament (PLA) and sprayed with mold release (Mann). Then, a liquid ure-thane rubber was mixed according to the manufacturer's instructions (Smooth-On Vytaflex 30A) and was placed in a vacuum chamber @ −100 kPa for 20 min to remove bubbles introduced during mixing. The four-piece mold was then assembled (Fig. 1E), and the liquid rubber was injected into the inlet with a syringe (Fig. 1F). The liquid rubber was left for 24 h at room temperature to cure. After curing, the mold was disassembled, and the soft jaw was removed from the core. Smooth-on Vytaflex 30A was chosen in part because of its ability to withstand up to 1000% strain, which facilitates not only high deformations during grasping but also removal from the mold during fabrication.

To enable a modular design where soft jaws of different sizes, geometries, and material properties could be used, the jaw mounts were attached to the soft grasper, and a removable attachment insert was used to fasten the flange of the soft jaws to the jaw mount using four M2 screws. The mount and insert were 3D printed on an Asiga Freeform PICO2 using a 79D shore hardness resin (PlasCLEAR) with 0.1 mm layer height. The mount included routing channels for the air inlet, which was attached to the pressure controller with a 3.2 mm (1/8 in.) outer diameter (OD) and 1.6 mm (1/16 in.) inner diameter (ID) tube. To ensure airtightness between the mount and the air inlet, a 4.5 mm OD, 2.5 mm ID, 1 mm thick rubber O-ring (McMaster-Carr) was placed

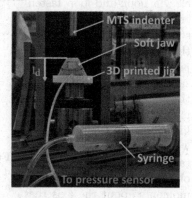

Fig. 2. Experimental setup to characterize the soft jaw stiffness as a function of indentation depth and pressure.

in a slot in the inlet tube pathway. The flange of the soft jaw was slightly oversized for the cavity formed between the mount and the insert (Fig. 1B–C), which aided in making an airtight seal when tightened with the M2 screws. To further prevent air leaks at the boundary of the soft jaw and the jaw mount, Loctite SI5011 Silicone RTV sealant was applied around the boundary before final assembly.

To characterize the stiffness of the jaws, the soft jaw and mount assembly were placed in a 3D printed jig on an MTS Criterion 42 electromechanical load testing system (Fig. 2). A syringe was connected to the air inlet of the jaw, with a 30 psig pressure gauge (ELVH-030G-HAND-C-PSA4) used to monitor the pressure. To achieve a given pressure setpoint, a caulking gun (Albion B12 26:1) was used to actuate the syringe and hold it in place. Then, the MTS indenter (diameter 12.7 mm) was lowered at a speed of 2 mm/s up to a maximum indentation depth of 5 mm. Pressure setpoints of 0, 0.1, 0.2, 0.3, 0.4, 0.5, 0.6, 0.7, 1.0, 1.5, 1.8, and 2.5 psig were tested, with each setpoint experiment repeated three times. The zero indentation depth for all pressure setpoints was set at the height of the soft jaw when it was uninflated, i.e. the pressure was 0 psig. An empirical model of the measured reaction force as a function of indentation depth and the applied pressure was then fitted for use in the simulation of the soft grasper.

Assembly of Complete Soft Grasper. To assemble the complete soft grasper for pick-and-place manipulation, the soft jaws were first connected to the closure muscle via hook-and-loop fasteners and secured in place via stitches with Kevlar thread through inserts placed in the jaw holder. This was necessary to prevent the jaws from tilting around the closure muscle when it attempted to lift objects. Rigid graspers with only two frictional contact points with the grasped objects often cannot resist moments about the axis that join the contacts [19]. A minimum of three contact points greatly improves the ability to resist external forces and

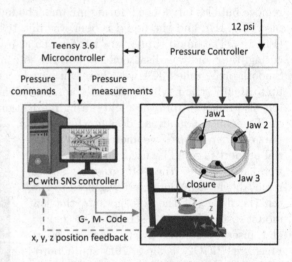

Fig. 3. Block diagram of the robotic system to demonstrate real-time control of the soft grasper for a pick-and-place task. Geometry (G-) and Machine (M-) Code which contains the position commands for the gantry are used to communicate between the computer and the gantry. PC Icon from Biorender.com.

torques applied to the grasped object and establish force closure [19]. To improve the stability of the grasped object, three soft jaws were attached to the closure muscle spaced 120° apart. Note that the design could accommodate a total of 6 jaws spaced 60° apart if there is a need for greater contact force or finer tuning of spatial stiffness. The soft grasper was then connected to a gantry via a 3D printed mount, with 3D printed tilt attachments that rotate to allow the closure muscle to contract and relax (Fig. 1A). The gantry was built using a Creality CR-10 S5 3D printer whose firmware was modified to accept M-code commands to control the grasper's position and report its current positional state [18].

2.2 Simulation Environment

To facilitate the design of a controller for real-time pick-and-place tasks in the soft grasper, a simulation of the soft grasper's mechanics was implemented in PyBullet (Fig. 7) [4]. The simulation uses a gantry system for spatial positioning of the grasper as described in our prior work [18]. The mechanics of the closure muscle were simulated as linear motor-powered prismatic joints along which each jaw can slide. To take advantage of PyBullet's fast computation for rapid controller tuning, the soft jaws were represented as rigid bodies with a contact stiffness that varied with applied pressure in accordance with the experimentally characterized soft jaw stiffness. To simulate a pick-and-place task, a 1 kg cube of size (39, 39, 34.5) mm was placed at the initial position ([0, 0, −0.315] m). The target position for the pick-and-place operation was [0.15, 0.15, −0.335] m. The coefficient of friction between the object and the soft grasper was set as 0.75, which is a typical value of the static coefficient of friction between rubber and other materials [26]. Note that the target position (x_t, y_t, z_t) and object position (x_o, y_o, z_o) are fixed parameters. The pick-and-place of random target and object positions are not addressed in this work but may be accomplished in the future through the use of vision or tactile feedback from the robot.

2.3 Controller Design and Tuning

Synthetic Nervous Systems. To control the soft grasper for pick-and-place manipulation tasks, we developed a bio-inspired neural network controller using the Synthetic Nervous System (SNS) approach. Synthetic Nervous Systems (Fig. 4A) are neural network models inspired by the biophysics of neurons [30,31]. This approach treats synaptic inputs to a neuron as conductance changes while simplifying the function of the neuron's axon as a nonlinear relationship between the membrane potential and neural activity. This representation endows a model neural network with the necessary inductive bias to conduct nonlinear operations with low computational complexity [7,11,15]. The dynamics of the ith neuron in an SNS can be described as the following ordinary differential equations [31]:

$$C_{\mathrm{m},i}\frac{dU_i}{dt} = g_{\mathrm{m},i}(E_{\mathrm{r},i} - U_i) + \sum_j g_{ij}y_j(E_{ij} - U_i) + I_i \qquad (1)$$

$$y_i = \phi_i(U_i) = \frac{\min(\max(U_i, E_{\mathrm{lo},i}), E_{\mathrm{hi},i})}{E_{\mathrm{hi},i} - E_{\mathrm{lo},i}} \qquad (2)$$

where Eq. 2 represents a piecewise-linear relationship between membrane potential U_i and neural activity y_i, with $E_{\mathrm{lo},i}$ and $E_{\mathrm{hi},i}$ the lower and upper limit of the activation function ϕ_i, respectively. In Eq. 1, $C_{\mathrm{m},i}$, $g_{\mathrm{m},i}$, and $E_{\mathrm{r},i}$ are the membrane capacitance, leak conductance, and resting potential of the neuron, respectively. The summation term is the net synaptic current, where the product of maximal conductance of the jth synapse g_{ij} and the corresponding presynaptic neural activity y_j defines the synaptic conductance, and E_{ij} is the reversal potential of the synapse. I_i represents external stimuli or bias current.

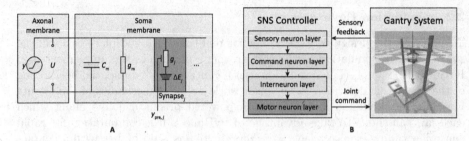

Fig. 4. A Schematic of non-spiking, single-compartment neurons in Synthetic Nervous Systems (U: membrane potential, y: neural activity, C_m: membrane capacitance, G_m: leak conductance, g: maximal synaptic conductance, ΔE: reversal potential, y_pre: presynaptic neural activity) and **B** a bio-inspired SNS controller for the pick-and-place control of the soft grasper. In SNSs, neurons are represented by single-compartment units with conductance-based inputs and rated outputs. All neurons in our neural network controller are modeled in the SNS framework. The hierarchical structure of the controller was inspired by the nervous system of *Aplysia*.

After determining the specific network structure, the parameters in an SNS must be set appropriately to accomplish the assigned tasks of each pathway. The use of Functional Subnetworks (FSNs) [8,31] is an analytical approach to solving the parameter-tuning problem in SNSs. By deriving the constraints that govern the network behaviors, an SNS user can design static networks for elementary mathematical operations and dynamic networks for differentiation and integration. However, the analytical nature of FSNs limits their application in constructing complex networks and pathways implementing highly nonlinear operations. A more systematic way to tune the SNS parameters is using supervised learning methods. We can discretize Eq. 2 by a semi-implicit method [17] and express the governing differential equations of n neurons as a recurrent neural network (RNN) model in machine learning [18]

$$\hat{\tau}_t = \frac{\tau}{1 + V\phi(h_{t-1})} \tag{3}$$

$$z_t = \frac{\Delta}{\hat{\tau}_t + \Delta} \tag{4}$$

$$\hat{h}_t = \frac{b + W\phi(h_{t-1})}{1 + V\phi(h_{t-1})} \tag{5}$$

$$h_t = (1 - z_t) \odot h_{t-1} + z_t \odot \hat{h}_t \tag{6}$$

where t is the current time and Δ is the time step. h_t denotes the state vector $[U_1, \cdots, U_n]^\top$. z_t and h_t are two intermediate variables defined in Eq. 4 and Eq. 5, respectively. $\tau = [\tau_1, \cdots, \tau_n]^\top$ is the time constant vector with $\tau_i = C_{\mathrm{m},i}/g_{\mathrm{m},i}$ representing the time constant of ith neuron, while τ_t defined in Eq. 3 is the effective time constant vector. The weight matrix $W = (w_{ij})$ and conductance matrix $V = (v_{ij})$ are two $n \times n$ matrices with $w_{ij} = g_{i,j}E_{ij}/g_{\mathrm{m},i}$

and $V_{ij} = g_{i,j}/g_{m,i}$ representing the normalized synaptic weight and synaptic conductance from the jth neuron to the ith neuron, respectively. $\odot$ denotes element-wise product. We can then formulate the parameter tuning problems of SNSs as machine learning tasks such as function approximation or time series prediction and adopt methods like backpropagation through time (BPTT) [35] to effectively calculate the gradient and optimize the parameters τ, W, V, E_{hi}, and E_{lo}. Due to the conductance-based synapses, the activities of presynaptic neurons exist in both the numerator and denominator of Eq. 5. This rational function, as an additional source of nonlinear computation besides the activation function ϕ, increases the expressive power of SNSs [7], allowing users to design compact and interpretable controllers with sparse synaptic connections. In [18], it is demonstrated that compact SNSs have superior performance to classical neural network models such as multilayer perceptrons (MLPs) in terms of implementing nonlinear arithmetic operations that are essential for robotic control. Furthermore, bio-inspired neural network models can exploit the temporal nature of the task, enabling them to filter out transient disturbances and provide superior noise resiliency, compared to feedforward models [17].

An SNS Controller for the Soft Grasper. Using SNSs, we designed a soft grasper controller to implement pick-and-place manipulation. The structure of the neural network controller (Fig. 4B) was inspired by the nervous system of *Aplysia*. *Aplysia* can achieve robust and multifunctional feeding control based on a relatively small number of neurons [6,34]. Its command-like cerebral-buccal interneurons in the cerebral ganglion receive afferent feedback from sensory neurons. They coordinate behaviors by mediating the buccal interneurons in the buccal ganglion [12]. The buccal interneurons, in turn, mediate motor neurons to generate features that are fundamental for the selected feeding behavior [13]. Our grasper controller used a similar structure. The sensory neuron layer (Fig. 5A) received the grasper position (x_g, y_g, z_g), object position (x_o, y_o, z_o), target position (x_t, y_t, z_t), and contact force (F_1, F_2, F_3) between the three jaws and the object. [1] The output neurons of this layer detected whether the distance between the grasper and the object/target $(\Delta o/\Delta t)$ was greater than a relatively large threshold $(th_1 = 8\,cm)$ or a relatively small threshold $(th_2 = 1\,cm)$. Two model neurons were included in the controller to detect whether a stable contact had been established (all forces were greater than a large threshold $th_{F,1} = 15\,N$) or discarded (any force was greater than a small threshold $th_{F,1} = 0.5\,N$). The command neuron layer (Fig. 5B) contained 8 neurons, each representing a critical behavior in the pick-and-place task. The excitation of a neuron led to the generation of the corresponding behavior. Synapses from the sensory layer ensured the behaviors could be executed in sequence. Neurons in the interneuron layer (Fig. 5C) were implemented with synaptic connections to motor neurons (Fig. 5D), which defined four necessary motion primitives in the pick-and-

---

[1] Although we can achieve variable stiffness through active pressure control, we set the pressure applied to the soft jaws as a constant in this work. The regulation of the stiffness is treated as future work (see Sect. 4)

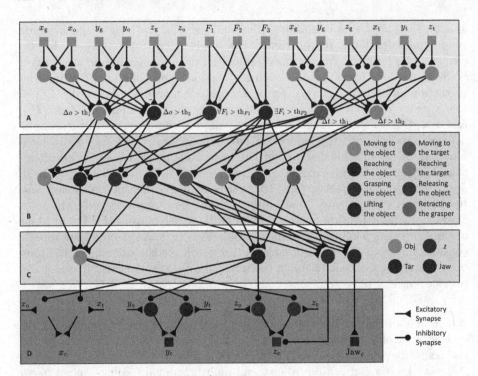

Fig. 5. A Neurons and synaptic connections in the sensory neuron layer, **B** command neuron layer, **C** interneuron layer, **D** and motor neuron layer of the soft grasper controller. Neurons in the interneuron layer represent four different motion primitives, namely moving to the object (Obj), moving to the target (Tar), lifting the grasper (Δz) up, and closing the jaw (Jaw). The activities of motor neurons represent the joint commands sent to the gantry system (grasper position (x_c, y_c, z_c) and radial contraction of the grasper Jaw_c). A command neuron will be activated if all of its excitatory neurons are firing while inhibitory neurons are silent. In contrast, an interneuron will be activated if any of its excitatory neurons are firing.

place control. By selectively exciting the interneurons, a command neuron can accomplish its behavioral coordination function. For example, the reaching-the-object command neuron excites the moving-to-the-object (Obj) interneuron. In contrast, the reaching-the-target command neuron excites the moving-to-target (Tar) and closing-the-jaw (Jaw) interneurons.

To find appropriate parameters for the SNS controller, we built the neural network model in Pytorch (version 2.1.0, Python version 3.9.16) [23] and used the supervised learning paradigm introduced in the previous Subsect. 2.3 to train the controller in an offline and layer-wise manner. The learning was formulated as a time sequence prediction task. The training set for each layer contained 10000 training examples. Each training example included randomly sampled constant series as layer inputs and the desired layer outputs specified in Fig. 5 as label series. Specifications of the SNS training are summarized in Table 1.

Table 1. The training parameters of the soft grasper controller.

Training parameters	Value
Time step	0.1 s
Number of training examples	10000
Window size	50
Batch size	200
Training epoch	50
Training method	BPTT
Optimizer	Adam
Performance	Mean squared error (MSE)

2.4 Testing SNS Control on the Soft Grasper Platform

To demonstrate the effectiveness of the controller in performing a pick-and-place task with the soft grasper, the soft grasper was mounted to a customized gantry, and the pressure of the pneumatic components was controlled by a pressure regulator (Fig. 3). The gantry and the pressure regulator were previously presented in [18] and [5], respectively. The pressurization of the closure muscle and each of the three soft jaws was independently controlled by the pressure controller which received pressure commands from and sent pressure sensor readings to the host PC in real-time. Communication with both the pressure regulator and the gantry occurred over separate serial ports at 115200 Baud-rate.

In accordance with the controller tuned in simulation, at the start of a pick-and-place test, each of the jaws was inflated to a pressure of 1 psig. Once all the jaws were within 0.050 psig of this threshold, the inlet and outlet valves for the corresponding ports on the pressure regulator were kept closed for the duration of the experiment to maintain a constant volume of air within the jaws. The controller sent position commands for the x-y-z axes of the gantry and sent the pressure command corresponding to the desired radial change of the closure muscle to the pressure regulator. The pressure readings of the closure muscle and each of the soft jaws were reported by the pressure regulator and logged on the host PC. Changes in the measured pressure at each of the jaws were used as a proxy for contact force measurement. For compatibility with the SNS controller thresholds, force feedback presented to the SNS was calculated as follows. The change in pressure (measured in psig) from the 1 psig setpoint was scaled by a factor of 5 if the difference was greater than 0.2 psig; otherwise, the force for that jaw was set to 0. The 0.2 psig threshold was manually tuned to prevent false triggering of a state change from sensor noise. The scale factor of 5 was manually tuned so that when secure contact with an object was initiated, it would trigger a change in state from Phase III (close grasper) to Phase IV (lift object).

3   Results and Discussion

3.1   Force vs. Pressure Characterization for Soft Jaw

The soft deformable jaws demonstrated increased reaction force as a function of both indentation distance and pressure applied to the internal cavity of the jaws (Fig. 6A). The following nonlinear empirical model was fitted to the data using MATLAB's `fitnlm` routine:

$$F_R[N] = (0.0416 + 0.505P_J^{1.0647})(0.179^{2P_J} l_d^2 + 0.891^{P_J} l_d + 5.4641) \qquad (7)$$

where F_R is the reaction force in N, l_d is the indentation depth in mm and P_J is the pressure applied to the jaw in psig.

Similar to the increase in reaction force with increased pneumatic pressure applied to the jaw at a given indentation depth, there was also an increase in stiffness. This was reflected in the empirical model by differentiating F_R (Eq. 7) with respect to l_d:

$$k_{eff}[N/mm] = \frac{\partial F_R}{\partial l_d} = (0.0416 + 0.505P_J^{1.0647})(0.891^{P_J} + 0.3581^{2P_J} l_d) \qquad (8)$$

where k_{eff} is the stiffness in N/mm.

At pressures beyond atmospheric (i.e. greater than 0 psig), there was a non-zero force present at 0 indentation depth. This was because the faces of the soft jaw bulged outward when pressurized. This increase in the effective size of the jaw has the potential benefit of allowing the grasping of smaller objects than was initially designed for by decreasing the radius of the space enclosed by the jaws when the closure muscle is fully activated (19.5 mm, Fig. 1). However, this increase in the size of the jaw was coupled with an increase in both force and stiffness and may not be appropriate in all grasping applications, particularly for very small and fragile objects. Future work will look at ways to limit the deflection of the jaw surface during inflation, such as using selective fiber reinforcements.

While the empirical model captures the change in contact force as a function of pressure and indentation depth, it does not capture the time-varying dynamics of the soft jaw. Including the dynamics introduced by the viscoelasticity of the elastomeric materials and inflation of the soft jaw will be important for real-time control of the grasper's mechanical properties. Future work will characterize such dynamics through both experiment and simulation using finite-element-based methods.

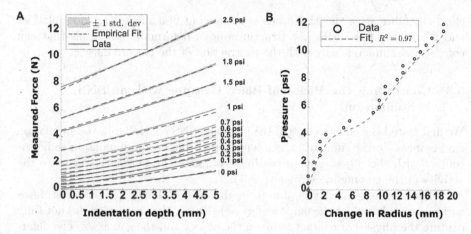

Fig. 6. A Reaction force and stiffness increase with increased pressure applied to the internal cavity of the jaw. Indentation depth was measured relative to the height of the jaw in the 0 psig state. **B** Pressure required to achieve a given change in the radius of the closure muscle. To achieve changes larger than a few mm, pressures beyond 5 psig were required. At 12 psig, the closure muscle reached the limit of its contraction.

3.2 Mapping Input Pressure to Radial Contraction in the Closure Muscle

The closure muscle showed a non-linearly monotonic decrease in radius as pressure was increased (Fig. 6B). The pressure required to achieve a given change in radius was captured by the following 6th-order polynomial fit to the data:

$$P_C[psig] = 3.03 \times 10^{-6} \Delta r^6 - 1.26 \times 10^{-4} \Delta r^5 + 9.37 \times 10^{-4} \Delta r^4$$
$$+ \; 0.0217 \Delta r^3 - 0.364 \Delta r^2 + 2.075 \Delta r \tag{9}$$

where P_C is the pressure applied to the closure muscle in psig and Δr is the decrease in radius in mm. Decreases in the radius from the uninflated closure muscle state are considered positive.

The closure muscle contracted only a few mm for pressures below 5 psig, with most of the contraction occurring between 5–11 psig. At pressures beyond 12 psi, there was no noticeable reduction in the radius of the grasper. This is consistent with the previously observed behavior of these types of McKibben actuator rings [5], where although the inner latex bladder increases in diameter for pressures below 5 psig, it is not yet in contact with the over-expanded mesh, and so little contraction occurs. The maximum achievable decrease in radius of 19 mm was lower than the expected 27 mm. This may be caused by two factors: 1) the tubing used to connect the two McKibben actuators in the same layer of the closure muscle reduces the effective length of the McKibben and doesn't contribute to contraction, and 2) The rigid jaw supports that were sewn into the closure muscle served as constraints that prevented those regions from contracting. Future iterations of the soft grasper should attempt to mitigate these effects by fabricating the McKibben actuators out of a single long latex bladder and fabricating the entire jaw structure out of deformable materials that can compress circumferentially with the contraction of the closure muscle.

3.3 Controlling the Pick-and-Place Grasper with an SNS in Simulation

We first tested the effectiveness of the proposed SNS controller in the simulation environment. In the simulation, the soft grasper model could maintain sufficient contact with the object and successfully complete the task in response to the activity of the command neurons (Fig. 7).

While the simulation was able to modulate the change in contact stiffness with pressure based on the empirical model (Eq. 8), the simulation did not fully capture the physics of contact between the object and the soft jaws. The deformation of the soft jaws around the grasped object was not captured by the simulation because of the use of rigid bodies to represent the jaws. Future work will address the limitations of the current simulation environment by using finite element-based methods (FEA) to capture the physics of the interaction more accurately.

3.4 Controller Validation on Physical Robot w/grasper

The controller tuned in the simulation environment was then used to control the physical gantry and soft robot (Fig. 3). To approximate the position control used in the simulation for use with the physical closure muscle, the experimentally determined relationship between change in radius and input pressure was used (Eq. 9). With no further tuning of the controller thresholds and appropriate scaling of the change in contact pressure of the jaw as a proxy for contact force, the grasper successfully executed all nine phases of SNS control (Fig. 8A). In addition, the grasper successfully completed the pick-and-place operation on a variety of different object shapes and masses, up to a maximum tested weight of 706 g (Fig. 8B). No additional tuning of the SNS controller was required to account for the different shapes and masses of the objects grasped.

While there was a potential risk of damage to the grasper or the grasped object because the dimensions of the object were not accounted for in the control, the compliance of the soft jaws and the closure muscle made it not likely to damage the objects grasped in this work. To grasp fragile objects in the future however, it will be important to actively control the radial opening of the grasper to enclose the object without damaging it by providing feedback of shape information. Methods for achieving such feedback include vision-based methods, or processing the spatial contact information provided by the change of pressure in each of the jaws. Currently, the controller does not reason about the change in pressure in each jaw individually to extract shape information about the object, but this could be explored in the future. As the internal radius of the closure muscle is on the order of centimeters (design target: 19 mm, measured: 27 mm) when fully inflated, the grasper was incapable of grasping very thin objects. In

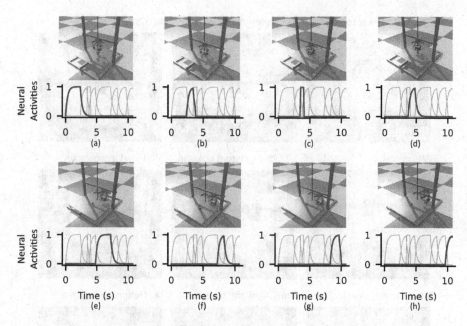

Fig. 7. Different phases of the pick-and-place manipulation and the activities of the working command neurons. The top figure represents the simulation environment and the bottom figure indicates the temporal activity of the command neuron from Fig. 5B that is active in that phase (bold blue line). **A** Moving to the object. **B** Reaching the object. **C** Grasping the object. **D** Lifting the object. **E** Moving to the target. **F** Reaching the target. **G** Releasing the object. **H** Retracting the grasper. (Color figure online)

contrast, *Aplysia* excels at tearing and ingesting thin objects such as seaweed using the closure of the feeding apparatus' internal grasper that can protract to grasp the seaweed and retract to ingest the seaweed [14]. Future versions of this bio-inspired soft grasper will incorporate similar structures to grasp a larger range of objects.

The physical robotic system replicated key features of the dynamics of the SNS-controlled simulation (Fig. 9A–C). The pressurization of the grasper (Fig. 9B right plot) began when the commanded radial position increased at the start of Phase III (Close Grasper). The transition from Phase III to Phase IV (Lift Object) corresponded to an increase in contact pressure in all three jaws as the grasper closed around the object (Fig. 9C). When the object was released in Phase VII and the grasper began to move up in Phase VIII, there was a corresponding decrease in contact pressure that tracked with the decrease in contact force seen in the simulation (Fig. 9C). The kinematics of the gantry to which the grasper was attached also demonstrated qualitatively similar behavior to the simulation (Fig. 9A), which aligns with our prior observations of transferring SNS-controllers of the gantry from simulation to the physical platform [18].

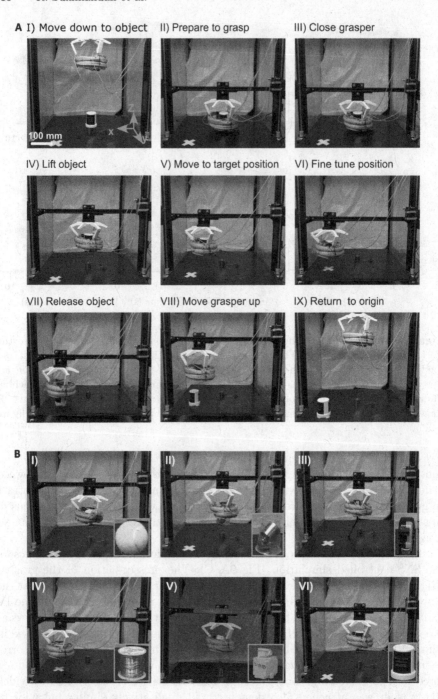

Fig. 8. A Phases of Grasper Motion. **B** Under SNS control, the grasper can successfully grasp and manipulate a wide range of common household and laboratory objects (Inset image shows objects). Masses of objects tested include I) 58 g, II) 706 g, III) 328 g, IV) 497 g, V) 62 g, VI) 62.9 g.

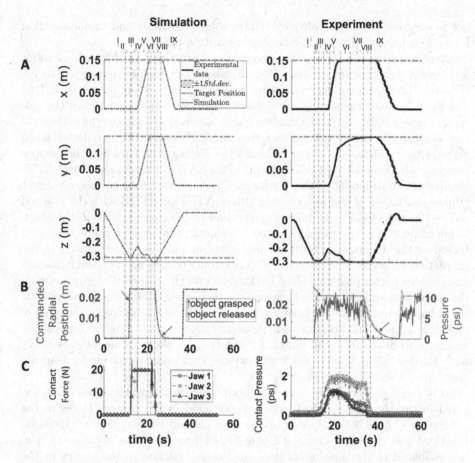

Fig. 9. A–C Comparison of simulation (left) vs. experimental (right) kinematics, pressures, and forces. All data shown were from three pick-and-place trials of object VI in Fig. 8. **A** Kinematics of the grasper position in the x, y and z axes. Phases of the SNS control (I through IX) are indicated at the top. The kinematics of the actual robotics system followed a similar shape to the experimental protocol but took longer to execute phases VI–IX. **B** Commanded radial position. In the physical grasper, the measured pressure (right) followed the general trend of the commanded radial position. **C** Pressure increased upon making contact with the object (right), which corresponds to the increased contact force seen in simulation (Phases III–IV). Pressure decreased in the jaws when the object was released (Phases VII–IX).

While the grasper was able to execute each phase of the pick-and-place task successfully, it should be noted that there were deviations in the physical grasper robot's dynamics when compared to the expected simulation results. The physical gantry robot took 51.2 s to complete the pick-and-place task compared to 37.1 s in the simulation. A large portion of this discrepancy was due to phases VII–VIII, where the gantry moved very slowly as it approached its target so as not to overshoot it. In the physical gantry robot, hardware and communication limitations prevented rapid fine-tuning of position [18].

Another noticeable difference between the simulation and the physical robot was seen when grasping smaller objects, where the grasper attempted to lift (Phase IV) before the grasper's closure muscle had completely pressurized. This was likely because the simulation did not incorporate the dynamics of the closure muscle's inflation (and deflation) and assumed the closure muscle could respond instantaneously to a position command. This was likewise reflected when attempting to release the object (Phase VII). During object release, the grasper incompletely depressurized before lifting (Phase VIII), causing the object to lift slightly before dropping to the platform. This increased time to create contact (Phase II–Phase IV) and lose contact (Phase VII–Phase VIII) with the grasped object was reflected in the different rise times of the contact force in the simulation compared to the contact pressure in the physical grasper robot (Fig. 9C). Including the dynamics of both the jaw inflation and the closure muscle in the simulation will allow us to tune the SNS controller to account for these dynamics and achieve better pick-and-place performance in the future. The gap between the simulation and the physical grasper can be further minimized by incorporating online learning of the parameters of the SNS. While the controller operated in real-time as the transition from one phase to another was dependent on position and force feedback from the physical robot (Fig. 5), the parameters of the SNS were learned offline. Future work will explore such online methods for learning and tuning the SNS parameters.

It was also observed that there was asymmetry in the contact pressures measured in the three jaws, which was not exhibited in the contact forces in the simulation (Fig. 9C). While two of the jaws showed similar pressure changes, the third jaw exhibited about 0.4 psig higher pressure. This asymmetry may be attributed to the misalignment of the grasper relative to the gantry or the misalignment of the center of the object relative to the center of the grasper. Future iterations of the grasper will replace the tilt attachments (Fig. 1A), which are currently 3D printed, with McKibben actuators to allow active tilting of the closure muscle, which may lead to more even contact pressure distributions.

4   Conclusions

In this work, we have demonstrated that an SNS-controlled *Aplysia*-inspired soft robot grasper can successfully pick-and-place objects of varying mass and size (Fig. 8). Inspired by *Aplysia*'s ability to modulate grasp force and conform to the shape of the grasped object, we presented the design and manufacture of a SNS-controlled soft grasper capable of closing around the target object. The grasper successfully modulated contact stiffness while providing simultaneous feedback of contact using pneumatic soft actuators (Fig. 1). To our knowledge, this is the first time the Synthetic Nervous System approach has been adapted for soft robotic grasping and manipulation.

Future work will aim to expand the adaptability of the soft grasping platform by improving the physical grasper, controller and simulation. To improve the fidelity of the simulation to the physical robot, the temporal dynamics of the closure muscles and the soft jaws will be included in the simulation. In addition, the positions of the object and target locations are currently fixed and the parameters of the SNS are tuned offline. To improve the flexibility of the grasper robot, future work will explore real-time feedback of the object and target position and online methods for learning the SNS parameters at run-time. The tunable stiffness of the soft jaws was not exploited during the pick-and-place tasks. Future work will explore the benefits of tunable stiffness to real-time manipulation tasks, particularly for soft and fragile objects.

The ability of this soft grasper platform to successfully manipulate objects of variable size and mass in real-time with limited tuning of the controller is exciting because it demonstrates that a soft grasper can combine the benefits of compliant surfaces inherent to soft robotic graspers with the efficient and robust computational advantages of the SNS. In addition, the SNS is capable of emergent dynamics that we will continue to explore in future work. For instance, in limited trials, it was observed in both simulations and on the physical grasper that the SNS controller had the ability to correct some grasping mistakes. Further development of the platform will attempt to exploit this emergent feature for use in the robust grasping of fragile and slippery objects, which may be particularly important in agricultural and industrial applications.

Acknowledgements. The authors would like to thank Ashlee Liao, Saul Schaffer, and Avery Williamson for their helpful comments in editing this manuscript.

References

1. Becker, K., et al.: Active entanglement enables stochastic, topological grasping. Proc. Natl. Acad. Sci. **119**(42), e2209819119 (2022)
2. Ciocarlie, M., Miller, A., Allen, P.: Grasp analysis using deformable fingers. In: 2005 IEEE/RSJ International Conference on Intelligent Robots and Systems, pp. 4122–4128, August 2005. ISSN: 2153-0866
3. Coulson, R., Stabile, C.J., Turner, K.T., Majidi, C.: Versatile soft robot gripper enabled by stiffness and adhesion tuning via thermoplastic composite. Soft Robot. **9**(2), 189–200 (2022)
4. Coumans, E., Bai, Y.: Pybullet, a python module for physics simulation for games, robotics and machine learning (2016)
5. Dai, K., et al.: SLUGBOT, an *Aplysia*-inspired robotic grasper for studying control. In: Hunt, A., et al. (eds.) Biomimetic and Biohybrid Systems. LNAI, vol. 13548, pp. 182–194. Springer, Cham (2022). https://doi.org/10.1007/978-3-031-20470-8_19
6. Gill, J.P., Chiel, H.J.: Rapid adaptation to changing mechanical load by ordered recruitment of identified motor neurons. eNeuro **7**(3) (2020). ENEURO.0016-20.2020
7. Hasani, R., Lechner, M., Amini, A., Rus, D., Grosu, R.: Liquid time-constant networks. In: Proceedings of the AAAI Conference on Artificial Intelligence, vol. 35, pp. 7657–7666 (2021)

8. Hilts, W.W., Szczecinski, N.S., Quinn, R.D., Hunt, A.J.: A dynamic neural network designed using analytical methods produces dynamic control properties similar to an analogous classical controller. IEEE Control Syst. Lett. **3**(2), 320–325 (2018)
9. Hunt, A., Szczecinski, N., Quinn, R.: Development and training of a neural controller for hind leg walking in a dog robot. Front. Neurorobot. **11**, 18 (2017)
10. Hurwitz, I., Susswein, A.J.: Adaptation of feeding sequences in *Aplysia oculifera* to changes in the load and width of food. J. Exp. Biol. **166**(1), 215–235 (1992)
11. Jayakumar, S.M., et al.: Multiplicative interactions and where to find them. In: 8th International Conference on Learning Representations, ICLR 2020, Addis Ababa, Ethiopia, 26–30 April 2020. OpenReview.net (2020)
12. Jing, J., Weiss, K.R.: Neural mechanisms of motor program switching in *Aplysia*. J. Neurosci. **21**(18), 7349–7362 (2001)
13. Jing, J., Weiss, K.R.: Generation of variants of a motor act in a modular and hierarchical motor network. Curr. Biol. **15**(19), 1712–1721 (2005)
14. Kehl, C.E., et al.: Soft-surface grasping: radular opening in *Aplysia californica*. J. Exp. Biol. **222**(16), jeb191254 (2019)
15. Koch, C.: Biophysics of Computation: Information Processing in Single Neurons. Oxford University Press, Oxford (1998)
16. Kuppuswamy, N., Alspach, A., Uttamchandani, A., Creasey, S., Ikeda, T., Tedrake, R.: Soft-bubble grippers for robust and perceptive manipulation. In: 2020 IEEE/RSJ International Conference on Intelligent Robots and Systems (IROS), pp. 9917–9924 (2020)
17. Lechner, M., Hasani, R., Amini, A., Henzinger, T.A., Rus, D., Grosu, R.: Neural circuit policies enabling auditable autonomy. Nat. Mach. Intell. **2**(10), 642–652 (2020)
18. Li, Y., Sukhnandan, R., Gill, J.P., Chiel, H.J., Webster-Wood, V., Quinn, R.D: A bioinspired synthetic nervous system controller for pick-and-place manipulation. In 2023 IEEE International Conference on Robotics and Automation (ICRA), pp. 8047–8053 (2023)
19. Lynch, K.M., Park, F.C.: Modern Robotics: Mechanics, Planning, and Control. Cambridge University Press, Cambridge (2017)
20. Majidi, C.: Soft-matter engineering for soft robotics. Adv. Mater. Technol. **4**(2), 1800477 (2019)
21. Mangan, E.V., Kingsley, D.A., Quinn, R.D., Sutton, G.P., Mansour, J.M., Chiel, H.J.: A biologically inspired gripping device. Ind. Robot. **32**(1), 49–54 (2005)
22. Nishimura, T., Suzuki, Y., Tsuji, T., Watanabe, T.: Fluid pressure monitoring-based strategy for delicate grasping of fragile objects by a robotic hand with fluid fingertips. Sensors **19**(4), 782 (2019)
23. Paszke, A., et al.: PyTorch: an imperative style, high-performance deep learning library. In: Advances in Neural Information Processing Systems, vol. 32, pp. 8024–8035. Curran Associates, Inc. (2019)
24. Peters, J., et al.: Actuation and stiffening in fluid-driven soft robots using low-melting-point material. In: 2019 IEEE/RSJ International Conference on Intelligent Robots and Systems (IROS), Macau, China, pp. 4692–4698. IEEE, November 2019
25. Root, S.E., et al.: Bio-inspired design of soft mechanisms using a toroidal hydrostat. Cell Rep. Phys. Sci. **2**(9), 100572 (2021)
26. Roth, F.L., Driscoll, R.L., Holt, W.L.: Frictional properties of rubber. Rubber Chem. Technol. **16**(1), 155–177 (1943). https://doi.org/10.5254/1.3540095
27. Shintake, J., Cacucciolo, V., Floreano, D., Shea, H.: Soft robotic grippers. Adv. Mater. **30**(29), 1707035 (2018)

28. Shintake, J., Schubert, B., Rosset, S., Shea, H., Floreano, D.: Variable stiffness actuator for soft robotics using dielectric elastomer and low-melting-point alloy. In: 2015 IEEE/RSJ International Conference on Intelligent Robots and Systems (IROS), pp. 1097–1102, September 2015
29. Suh, H.T., Kuppuswamy, N., Pang, T., Mitiguy, P., Alspach, A., Tedrake, R.: SEED: series elastic end effectors in 6D for visuotactile tool use. In: 2022 IEEE/RSJ International Conference on Intelligent Robots and Systems (IROS), pp. 4684–4691 (2022)
30. Szczecinski, N.S., Hunt, A.J., Quinn, R.D.: Design process and tools for dynamic neuromechanical models and robot controllers. Biol. Cybern. **111**(1), 105–127 (2017). https://doi.org/10.1007/s00422-017-0711-4
31. Szczecinski, N.S., Hunt, A.J., Quinn, R.D.: A functional subnetwork approach to designing synthetic nervous systems that control legged robot locomotion. Front. Neurorobot. **11**, 37 (2017)
32. Szczecinski, N.S., Quinn, R.D.: Template for the neural control of directed stepping generalized to all legs of MantisBot. Bioinspiration Biomimetics **12**(4), 045001 (2017)
33. Wang, J., Chortos, A.: Control strategies for soft robot systems. Adv. Intell. Syst. **4**(5), 2100165 (2022)
34. Webster-wood, V.A., Gill, J.P., Thomas, P.J., Chiel, H.J.: Control for multifunctionality: bioinspired control based on feeding in *Aplysia californica*. Biol. Cybern. **114**(6), 557–588 (2020). https://doi.org/10.1007/s00422-020-00851-9
35. Werbos, P.: Backpropagation through time: what it does and how to do it. Proc. IEEE **78**(10), 1550–1560 (1990)
36. Yoder, Z., Macari, D., Kleinwaks, G., Schmidt, I., Acome, E., Keplinger, C.: A soft, fast and versatile electrohydraulic gripper with capacitive object size detection. Adv. Funct. Mater. **33**(3), 2209080 (2022)
37. Zhang, B., Xie, Y., Zhou, J., Wang, K., Zhang, Z.: State-of-the-art robotic grippers, grasping and control strategies, as well as their applications in agricultural robots: a review. Comput. Electron. Agric. **177**, 105694 (2020)

Invertebrate Locomotion and Perception Mechanisms and Thereof Inspired Systems

Fly H1-Cell Distance Estimation in a Monocular Virtual Reality Environment

Jiaqi V. Huang[(✉)] [iD] and Holger G. Krapp[iD]

Imperial College London, London SW7 2AZ, UK
j.huang09@imperial.ac.uk

Abstract. The ability of animals and robots to move through a given environment without colliding with any obstacles requires a robust distance estimation mechanism. Previous electrophysiological studies and work using a biohybrid fly-robot-interface (FRI) suggest that fly directional-selective interneurons may be involved in the neural control of collision-avoidance behaviour. We have set up a virtual reality (FlyVR) environment and studied the blowfly's H1-cell, an interneuron analyzing visual wide-field motion, to access its distance-dependent responses that was discovered using the FRI. The results gathered under open-loop FlyVR conditions are in qualitative agreement with open- and closed-loop data obtained on the FRI. They suggest that the capability of flies to estimate distance may depend on the animal's specific movement trajectory in combination with the receptive field properties of the H1-cell. Our findings in the fly motion vision pathway may inform the design of energy-efficient collision avoidance strategies for autonomous robotic systems.

Keywords: H1-cell · virtual reality · distance estimation · blowfly

1 Introduction

While mobile engineered systems can rely on a variety of sensors for distance estimation, including sonar, Lidar or other laser-based range finders which output absolute values, most animals and humans rely on visual mechanisms for relative distance information. Besides echolocation in bats and whales [1] as well as electrolocation in weakly electric fish and some mammals [2, 3], vision is the dominant modality to gauge proximity. Animals with binocular overlap or converging eye movements may use stereo vision or neural actuation commands when accommodating their focal planes [4, 5]. Others by and large use optic flow, or motion parallax, which provides a viable way to interpret the 3-d layout of the environment [6, 7]. Especially highly manoeuvrable flying insects depend heavily on optic flow-based, and thus motion-dependent distance estimation. Formally, this requires knowledge of image velocity and flight speed [8, 9]. Insect motion vision, however, is mostly provided by elementary movement detectors which output a signal that is a non-linear function of temporal frequency, also depending on the spatial frequency distribution of image contrasts in the environment [10–13]. Except for a few studies in bees which suggest the existence of neurons with partially linear

F. Meder et al. (Eds.): Living Machines 2023, LNAI 14157, pp. 325–337, 2023.
https://doi.org/10.1007/978-3-031-38857-6_24

input-output characteristics in the velocity domain [14], possibly fed by gradient motion detectors [15], the functional structure of most other motion detectors does not permit the estimation of absolute distance.

Interestingly, flies have been shown to exploit optic flow for state estimation in the context of flight and gaze control [16, 17]. They have evolved a network of individually identifiable interneurons which are tuned to process optic flow fields generated during specific self-motions [18, 19]. These wide-field neurons are located in an anatomical structure of the fly optic lobes called lobula plate and are hence generally referred to as lobula plate tangential cells, LPTCs [20]. LPTCs receive input from local elementary movement detectors which results in temporal frequency dependent response to directional visual motion [21, 22]. Earlier studies suggested that some LPTCs, specifically HS-cells that respond preferentially to horizontal front-to-back motion, may be involved in distance estimation during translational movements of the fly [23].

Another identified LPTC, the H1-cell, has been used as a motion vision sensor on a bio-hybrid fly robotic interface (FRI) that was shown to avoid collisions with the wall of an experimental arena [24]. In this system, the spiking activity of the H1-cell was used to estimate wall distance and, whenever exceeding a set threshold activity, induced a collision avoidance manoeuvre of the FRI [24–27]. Due to the H1-cell's preference for back-to-front motion, the FRI was forced to move on an oscillatory trajectory, i.e. turns towards and away from the wall alternatively, increased and decreased the cell's spike rate, respectively. The closer the FRI approached the wall the higher the spike rate increase. A crucial parameter for this collision avoidance behaviour to emerge was the turning radius of the FRI.

Systematic open- and closed loop experiments revealed that smaller turning radii of the FRI resulted in a higher dynamic output range of the H1-cell spike rate that was inversely proportional to wall distance (Fig. 3). Although convenient from the robotic control perspective, the interpretation of the observed results was not straight forward when considering the response properties of elementary movement detectors (EMDs). For instance, with increasing turning radii, the dynamic output range of the H1-cell decreased, became independent of wall distance and – for the largest turning radii – was inverted (Fig. 3).

Previous studies suggested that the compound dependence of the H1-cell response on the FRI turning radius and wall distance may be explained by the cell's receptive field organization in combination with the optic flow generated during the oscillatory FRI trajectory [27]. Model simulations suggest that the oscillations induced optic flow vectors, in which parts of the H1-cell receptive field align with its local motion preferences, increasing the spike rate. In other areas, optic flow vectors are oriented in the opposite direction, inhibiting the cell's response ([24] Fig. 6). The ratio of excitation and inhibition at different turning radii and wall distance dynamically changes along the FRI's oscillatory trajectory.

Although experimental data obtained with the FRI describe the dependence of the H1-cell responses on turning radius and wall distance, it was still not possible to identify and characterize the underlying processing at the mechanistic level. This is partially due to methodological challenges as the spike rate of the H1-cell when studied on the FRI operating in an experimental arena is likely to be affected by other sensory modalities and the exact visual input parameters to the motion vision pathway are difficult to control and quantify.

To systematically study the neuronal processing of visual motion that results in distance-dependent responses, we set up a virtual reality (FlyVR) environment. FlyVR provides unilateral input to the eye of a stationary fly positioned in front of a high-speed computer monitor, while recording the neural responses of the H1-cell. The system will ultimately provide us with full control and knowledge of relevant visual and kinematic input parameters while designing specific stimuli that can be used to analyse the cell's integration properties. The final objective of this project is to obtain a mechanistic understanding of the emergence of distance-dependent response of the H1-cell.

Here we present the pilot version of the FlyVR system we have developed and the results of our first open-loop validation experiments, which are compared with the data previously accumulated using the FRI. We will also discuss the results including a preliminary interpretation and outline further steps to identify neural processing strategies to obtain distance estimates using elementary movement detectors.

2 Methods

2.1 Fly Virtual Reality (FlyVR) Setup

Hardware components of the FlyVR include a high-speed computer screen (360 fps FHD display) of a "Razer Blade 15 Advanced" gaming laptop computer, with Intel Core i7-10875H, Nvidia GeForce RTX 3070 and 16GB RAM. The brightness of the monitor was set to medium (white: 114.77 cd/m^2, black: 0.11 cd/ m^2, Michelson contrast = $(114.77-0.11)/(114.77 + 0.11) = 99.81\%$). The computer was streaming visual stimuli at maximum frame rate to the computer screen, which were programmed in Python, using the OpenGL Shading Language (GLSL 3.30 spec) for rendering.

The FlyVR was composed of a wall with a vertical black and white grating pattern on one side and a pure black screen on the other, located in an arena with black background. A virtual camera was moving on a circular path in front of the wall, with turning radius and wall distance as controlled parameters, to approximate the experimental conditions used by Huang and Krapp [27] in earlier FRI studies (Fig. 1). The turning centre of the circular trajectory was in front of the patterned wall for turning radii of 5, 10, 15, 20, 25 cm, with distances between the fly and wall assuming values of 10, 15, 20, 25, 30 cm.

To reproduce the FRI kinematics applied by Huang and Krapp [27], we chose the distance between the two wheels of a virtual FRI to be 10 cm, resulting in a robot radius $R_r = 5$ cm and set the maximum robot wheel speed to a value as an upper limit. Specific parameters applied during the experiments are given in Table 1 and were computed by the equations:

$$\omega = \frac{V_{low}}{R_t - R_r} = \frac{V_{robot}}{R_t} = \frac{V_{high}}{R_t + R_r} \qquad (1)$$

where R_r is the radius of the robot, the R_t is the turning radius and V_{robot} is the ground speed of the virtual FRI robot moving along the circular path. V_{high} is the ground speed of the robot wheel with a higher speed. V_{low} is the lower ground speed of the robot wheel and ω is the angular velocity of the robot moving around the turning centre.

Table 1. Values of turning radii and velocities in the Fly Virtual Reality

R_t (cm)	5	10	15	20	25
ω (rad/s)	3	2	1.5	1.2	1
V_{robot} (cm/s)	15	20	22.5	24	25
V_{high} (cm/s)	30	30	30	30	30
V_{low} (cm/s)	0	10	15	18	20

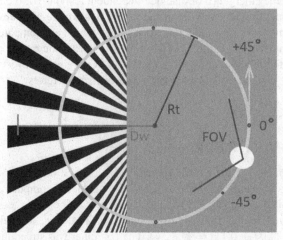

Fig. 1. The trajectory of the virtual camera (white dot) in the FlyVR environment (top view, with perspective), was moving in counter clockwise direction (yellow arrow). The lateral field of view (FOV) was covering around 120°. The purple and green lines indicate the turning radius (Rt) and the wall distance (Dw), respectively, defined in the VR software. (Note: The background colour was set to grey for illustration and test, it was black during the experiment. A video link for verifying the FOV control: https://youtu.be/bhb8ZSWtOR8, where the four boundaries of the FOV are labelled by four red dots (Color Figure Online).)

Given five different turning radii and wall distances, there were 25 parameter combinations. The response of the H1-cell to each of those 25 parameter combinations were logged over 16 s, including several completed circular trajectories in the VR arena. The overall recording time was ~25*16/60 = 6.66 min for one animal. Our results are based on experiments in 5 different animals.

2.2 Fly Preparation

We used blowflies, *Calliphora vicina*, in our experiments, which were bred in an environmental chamber with 20–25 degree Celsius, 50–60% relative humidity, at a 12-h-day-12-h-night cycle. Flies were chosen when their age was between 4 to 11 days. The preparation has been described in previous publications (e.g. [13, 27]). In brief: Before mounting the fly onto a dedicated holder, its legs and proboscis were removed and all open wounds as well as the wing hinges were covered by beeswax. The deep pseudopupil method [28] was used to adjust the head orientation of the blowfly. Afterwards, the animal's head was fixed to the fly holder. Then the thorax was pushed down and also waxed to the fly holder so that a space was created between the back of the head and the thorax. The cuticle on the back of the head was cut open to access the visual neuropil. Muscle tissue, fat and air sacks were removed to expose the lobula plate. The dissection was performed under optical magnification using a stereo microscope (OPMI 1-F, Zeiss©). Ringer solution was added to the opening in the head capsule to prevent tissue desiccation (for recipe see e.g. [29]), whenever needed.

The H1-cell responses were extracellularly recorded using sharp tungsten electrodes (of ~3 MΩ impedance, product code: UEWSHGSE3N1M, FHC Inc., Bowdoin, ME, USA). The signal-to-noise-ratio (SNR) was never <2:1 before the experimental protocol was started. The SNR was defined by the peak amplitude of the action potentials divided by the largest peak amplitudes in the background noise (e.g. electrical noise and action potentials from other cells). The instantaneous spike rate was computed based on the inverse of the inter-spike-intervals (ISIs).

2.3 Electrophysiology

Blowflies were centered in front of the high-speed computer screen where the longitudinal body axis of the animal was in parallel with the computer screen. The distance from the fly to the screen (97 mm) was half of the height of the screen (194 mm), to guarantee coverage of the sensitive areas within the H1-cell receptive field ±45° in elevation with respect to the eye equator at 0° elevation [23]. The aspect ratio of the screen was 16:9, the azimuth coverage of the screen was around ±60°. This distance from fly to the screen made sure the average screen pixel resolution (90°/1080 = 0.083°) was ~2 orders of magnitude finer than the fly's smallest interommatidial angle of 1.1° [27], which corresponds to the spatial sampling base of neighbouring inputs to the motion detection circuits.

We used a data acquisition board (NIDAQ USB-6211) that was recording two analog input channels at 20 kHz sampling frequency: (i) the extracellular H1-cell response and (ii) the output of a photodiode, which was attached to the computer screen providing a sync signal. The sync was set ON when the virtual robot was moving from −45° to 45° along the circular trajectory and was set OFF during the rest of movement. We define 0° as the starting point of the trajectory, where body axis of the fly was in parallel to the virtual wall (Fig. 1).

A video showing a test run of an experiment using the FlyVR can be found at: https://youtu.be/j6y0zo_f10o.

3   Results

To test the viability of the FlyVR system for systematic studies of the neural mechanisms underlying distance estimation we recorded the responses of the H1-cell under conditions simulating previous FRI experiments. This included the choice of turning radii and wall distances as described in the Methods section and the analysis of the recorded H1-cell activities within time windows suitable for a comparison of the two data sets.

Figure 2 shows an example of the raw data and initial analysis results obtained with the FlyVR system for a turning radius of 5 cm and a distance of the mean fly trajectory of 15 cm to the wall in the virtual environment. The H1-cell spike rate gradually increased while the visual stimulus was projected onto the less sensitive part of the caudolateral receptive field of the cells. When moving out of the most sensitive part of the frontolateral receptive field, the spike rate dropped more suddenly. To compare the FlyVR data to the FRI robot data, the response of the stimulus was selected from the rising edge of the sync signal of the stimulus until twice the length of the stimulus period, to compensate the stopping distance of the brake because of the high robotic momentum in the FRI setup. (Fig. 2).

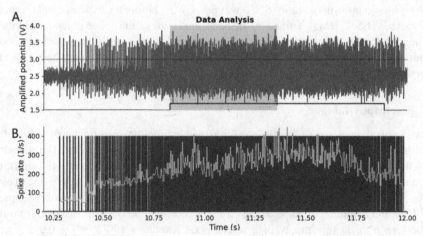

Fig. 2. Example recording trace and spike rate estimation of the H1-cell activity obtained using the FlyVR system. (**A**) The extracellularly recorded raw signal (green) plotted as a function of time. H1-cell spikes were detected when their peak value exceeded a voltage threshold of 3V (red horizontal line). The pink marking indicates the time period during which the fly's body orientation changes from −45 to +45° relative to the patterned wall when moving along a circular trajectory in the FlyVR environment. The shallow black step below the recording trace shows the time interval over which the average spike rate was computed, which was twice the length of the period of the visual stimulus in the pink period. (**B**) Detected spikes (blue) and the instantaneous spike rate (yellow) of the H1-cell und FlyVR stimulation. (Stimulus parameters: Rt = 5cm, Dw = 15cm) (Color figure online)

The mean spike rates of the H1-cells at different turning radii (Rt) and wall distances (Dw) were studied in five flies (N = 5). To obtain averages across experiments in different animals for each parameter combination we computed the mean spike rates and the standard error of the mean (SEM) obtained during the stimulus intervals. The results are compared with those obtained using the FRI in Fig. 3.

We could see from the comparison (Fig. 3) of the FlyVR and FRI results that the Rt has similar effects on the H1-cell wall-distance dependence. In particular at small wall distances (e.g. Dw = 10cm), the modulations of the H1-cell responses on the FlyVR (Fig. 3A) followed the same trend as the modulation on the robot platform (Fig. 3B).

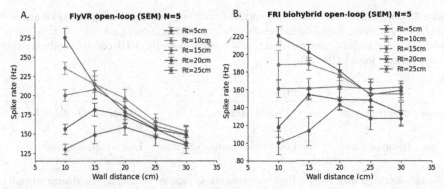

Fig. 3. Average H1-cell spike rate as a function of wall distance for different turning radii (*Rt*) (**A**) Data obtained with the FlyVR system under open-loop condition (N = 5). (**B**) Data obtained with the FRI under open-loop condition (N = 5). (Note: the different y-axis ranges in (A) and (B). Error bars represent SEM. B: Modified from [27].)

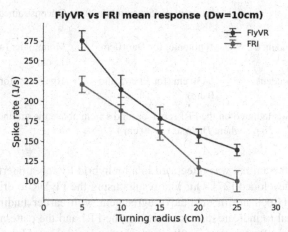

Fig. 4. Comparison of the modulation of H1-cell responses in FlyVR and FRI. Error bars represent SEM.

If we re-plot the modulation curves from FRI and FlyVR of the H1-cell responses at $Dw = 10$ cm on top of each other (Fig. 4), we could see that although the spike rates were different, they were shown as two lines nearly in parallel to each other. The differences between the maximum rate (at Rt = 5 cm) and minimum rate (at Rt = 25 cm) were similar, both ~125 Hz. The plots were both almost linear relationships between response and *Rt*, with similar slopes and different offsets (at $Dw = 10$ cm).

4   Discussion

Here we have tested a virtual reality-based stimulation system (FlyVR) developed to study neural mechanisms that contribute to visual distance estimation in the fly motion vision pathway. The system was designed to approximate the dynamics of visual stimuli

Table 2. Comparison of H1-cell responses under open-loop conditions using the FlyVR and FRI experimental regimes. Experimental results were obtained for 5 flies each. Rt = turning radius, Dw = wall distance, pd = preferred direction = > excitatory input to H1-cell, nd = null-direction = > inhibitory input to H1-cell.

	FlyVR	FRI
Dynamic output range	125–275 [spikes/s] = 150 [spikes/s]	100–220 [spikes/s] = 120 [spikes/s]
Light adaptation state	Low - visual grating ~57 cd/m^2	Low – patterned wall ~9 cd/m^2
Motion adaptation state	High – continuous pd motion	Neutral – alternating pd and nd motion
Pattern contrast	99.8%	84.0%
Pattern elevation at Dw(min)	>±45°	>±45°
Pattern elevation at Dw(max)	>±45°	from $-26.6°$ to >+45° (*)
Field of view	elevation: ± 45°; azimuth 30° - 150°	Unconstrained
Range of Rt-dependence	Monotonic; for Dw 10cm	Monotonic; for Dw 10 and 15 cm
Range of Dw-dependence	10–30 cm (for Rt = 5 and 10 cm)	10–25 cm (for Rt = 5 cm)

(*. Note: The fly was tethered on the FRI robot, around 15 cm above the ground level, in which case arctan(15/30) = 26.6°, where Dw(max) = 30 cm.)

generated when the animal was integrated in a biohybrid fly robot interface (FRI) that was previously developed [27]. Our first results using the FlyVR to drive the spiking activity of the H1-cell are in qualitative agreement with earlier findings suggesting the cell's potential to indicate distance between the FRI and the patterned walls of an experimental arena. Both sets of results were obtained under open loop conditions but using fundamentally different stimulation regimes: a virtual reality environment rendered on a computer screen versus a real-world experimental arena.

Despite the observation that the H1-cell spike rate as a function of wall distance depends on the turning radius, Rt, of the FRI in both the VR and real-world environments, we found some conspicuous differences between the results obtained under the two experimental regimes which will be discussed the following.

4.1 Differences in the Absolute Spike Rate

Despite our efforts to capture the experimental condition of previous FRI studies in the FlyVR environment, there are a few methodological differences between the settings. While the parameters of interest, i.e. turning radius and wall distance, were controlled sufficiently well as were the stimulus dynamics, other parameters which may have affect the motion vision pathway were slightly different. These include the mean light intensity, pattern contrast and the direction of visual motion throughout the experiments as well as the stimulus pattern size in relation to the animal's field of view and the H1-cell's receptive field organization (cf. Table 2). Photoreceptor responses are known to adapt to the mean light intensity to avoid output saturation over several orders of magnitude [30]. Although different by about a factor of 5, the mean light intensity of the stimulus patterns used under either experimental regime was within the same order of magnitude and is therefore unlikely to have had a significant impact on the results. For a similar reason we are confident that the slight pattern contrast difference during the FlyVR and FRI experiments had no differential effect on the H1-cell responses. Previous studies suggest that pattern contrasts >40%, which was given for both regimes, drive the input elements to the motion vision pathway into saturation [31]. The differences in the directional motion stimulus throughout the experiments, however may have caused some differences in the motion adaptation state of the H1-cell [32]. While directional motion in the same (preferred) direction of the cell during the FlyVR experiments has most likely adapted the responses of the cell, the alternating stimulation in the preferred and anti-preferred direction of the H1-cell may have prevented motion adaption to kick in. We will discuss below how motion adaptation might have affected the cell's spike rate as well as the differences in stimulus pattern size between the FlyVR and FRI experiments.

There are several differences between the two setups which could have affected the H1-cell response under the different regimes, including: (1) virtual vs real world trajectories, (2) Field of view (FOV), (3) bandwidth and noise, and (4) contributions of other sensory systems than vision.

Firstly, the fly trajectories were different. In the FlyVR setup, the trajectories were along circular paths of different turning radii. Along these trajectories, the H1-cell was repeatedly stimulated with pattern motion mostly in its preferred direction (pd) which induced excitation in the cell, or subjected to a stationary black screen. While in the FRI experiments, the trajectory was an oscillatory forward movement, which alternatingly excited and inhibited the H1-cell due to motion in its pd and opposite null-direction (nd). For future experiments, we will implement more advanced 3D rendering, e.g. by using the Unity engine to program more complex visual stimuli that (i) enable a more direct comparison of data obtained under different regimes, and (ii) are suitable for designing appropriate analytical motion stimuli.

Secondly, the fields of view (FOV) were different. In the FlyVR system, the blowfly's FOV was limited to ±60° (in azimuth). While on the robotic system, the field of view was basically unconstrained, covering an azimuth range from −15° to +150° [23] which roughly corresponds to the horizontal extend of the H1-cell receptive field. We believe that the wall-distance related modulations of the neural response were induced on the lateral side of the animal, according to the model (Fig, 5), regardless the interommatidial angles at the anterior side of the retina, which are normally smaller, higher spatial resolution, bigger corneal lens diameters and high-performance photoreceptors (in male flies) [33]. Because the frontal part of the compound eye receives no optic flow from the screen, the neural response might be different.

Thirdly, the bandwidth and noise of the visual stimulus was different. In the FlyVR system, although the FHD screen was a low pass filter for the representation of the virtual world, the pixel resolution of the monitor was >2 orders of magnitude higher than the smallest interommatidial angle. The difference should be small. But there could be noises from the real-world visual stimulus, such as the flatness/homogeneity of the printed pattern, as well as the distribution of the amount of the ink, and the distribution of the reflections of the ink, the homogeneity of the light emission from the LED light bulbs. The bandwidth and noise would be causing randomness on the input of the elementary motion detector (EMD). To minimize this randomness, in future experiments, a back projected (to avoid shadows) visual stimulus in a real-world robot arena could be an upgrade of the apparatus for a more detailed control of parameters.

Those additional sensory modalities may affect the H1-cell responses, like in the V1-cell [34]. Previous research has also found that the spike rate of the blowfly H1-cells could be doubled by the octopamine release when changing the mode of locomotion from still to locomoting [35]. We observed minimum differences between the H1-cell responses measured during slow movements of the FRI and equivalently small visual image shifts under FlyVR stimulation. This finding suggests that in the small dynamic range the H1- responses are mainly driven by visual input. In future experiments we will increase the dynamic input range, stimulating mechanosensory modalities, e.g. the gyroscopic hal- teres sensing angular rates [16] and the antennae measuring sensing airspeed, to assess the impact of non-visual modalities on the activity of the H1-cell.

4.2   Modelling as a Complementary Approach to the Experimental Studies

Modelling enables predictions that can be experimentally tested in the FlyVR environment, where it is possible to generate 'unnatural stimuli' that help to understand how excitatory and inhibitory inputs are combined at the level of the H1-cell.

One model that might explain the relationship between the H1-cell response, wall-distance and turning radius was proposed in a previous research [24] (Fig. 5). It suggests that given a fixed wall distance, additional wall patterns would be creating optic flows in the cell's preferred direction (pd), when the turning radius is small. (In an extreme case, when the tuning radius is zero, all optic flow would be in the cell's preferred direction.) At bigger turning radii, the wall patterns induce a high level of inhibitory null directions (nd) motion, reducing any excitatory responses.

The proportion of the optic flows in the preferred directions and in the null directions which captured by the retinal input of the H1-cell was impacted by the wall distance. Hence, the responses of the H1-cell could be used to estimate the wall distance if the turning radius is given. Strategically, two methods could be used to measure the distance of the wall. The first method is using a small turning radius all the time. Because of the monotonic relationship between the spike rate and wall distance within the linear range of the wall distance, the response of the H1-cell decreases due to the increment of the distance, the wall distance could be estimated by the spike rate. The second method is using the difference of the spike rates at two consecutive different turning radii, for example a small saccade was performed right after a long arch of flight, a sudden increasing of the spike rate would indicate that the wall distance is small.

Although the two methods could both estimate the wall distance, the overall strategic energy consumptions could be different. The smaller the turning radius of the circular locomotion, the higher resolution of distance estimation the insect could get. But it also means that the insect needs more frequent leftwards and rightwards yaw switching during the flight, which consumes more energy. On the contrary, if an insect is flying

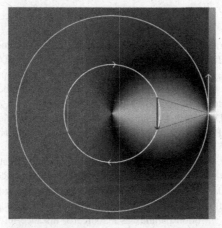

Fig. 5. The model of the distance estimation for the H1-cell (top view). The yellow vector indicates the movement direction of the insect, the yellow circle shows the trajectory. The white circle indicates the equivalent optic flow which is created by the counter rotation of an object/pattern edge, while the insect is observing the environment from its ego coordinate. The green arrow is the projection of a preferred direction optic flow, generated by a moving object further than the turning centre. The blue arrow is the projection of a null direction optic flow, generated by a moving object closer than the turning centre. (Color figure online) (Modified from previous research [24])

in a circular trajectory with a big turning radius, it saves energy in the flight maneuver, but the resolution of the distance estimation would be reduced. By combining the big and small turning radii, both the resolution of the distance estimation and the energy consumption can be balanced.

Although OpenGL is a powerful tool to speed up the rendering process and create virtual environment arbitrarily, it takes a long time to programme from scratch, to allocate the dimensions and positions of every virtual object, as well as to test the moving trajectories of the virtual camera. Utilizing a 3D engine (e.g. the Unity Engine) could be the next step to construct the virtual experimental arena and setup the experimental parameters with more confidence and less inconvenience.

5   Conclusion

From the recording of the responses of an H1-cell in the FlyVR system, we could reproduce the modulation of the neural responses of the H1-cell which were observed using the FRI. Distance-dependent H1-responses do not require inputs from both eyes and can be studied in animals that receive only motion vision input.

The FlyVR system in combination with modelling and further, refined experimental stimuli will be a powerful tool to understand the neural mechanisms underlying visual distance-estimation in flies and potentially other small animal model systems.

Acknowledgments. Thanks for the discussion and feedback from Ben Campbell, Yinjie Yang, Jack Supple. This work was partially supported by US AFOSR/EOARD grant [FA8655-22-1-7030] (HGK).

References

1. Madsen, P.T., Surlykke, A.: Functional convergence in bat and toothed whale biosonars. Physiology **28**, 276–283 (2013). https://doi.org/10.1152/physiol.00008.2013
2. Shieh, K.-T., Wilson, W., Winslow, M., McBRIDE, D.W., Jr., Hopkins, C.D.: Short-range orientation in electric fish: an experimental study of passive electrolocation. J. Exp. Biol. **199**, 2383–2393 (1996). https://doi.org/10.1242/jeb.199.11.2383
3. Czech-Damal, N.U., Dehnhardt, G., Manger, P., Hanke, W.: Passive electroreception in aquatic mammals. J. Comp. Physiol. A. **199**, 555–563 (2013). https://doi.org/10.1007/s00359-012-0780-8
4. Nityananda, V., Read, J.C.A.: Stereopsis in animals: evolution, function and mechanisms. J. Exp. Biol. **220**, 2502–2512 (2017). https://doi.org/10.1242/jeb.143883
5. Read, J.C.A.: Binocular vision and stereopsis across the animal kingdom. Ann. Rev. Vis. Sci. **7**, 389–415 (2021). https://doi.org/10.1146/annurev-vision-093019-113212
6. Kral, K., Poteser, M.: Motion parallax as a source of distance information in locusts and mantids. J. Insect. Behav. **10**, 145–163 (1997). https://doi.org/10.1007/BF02765480
7. Koenderink, J.J., van Doorn, A.J.: Facts on optic flow. Biol. Cybern. **56**, 247–254 (1987). https://doi.org/10.1007/BF00365219
8. Kern, R., Boeddeker, N., Dittmar, L., Egelhaaf, M.: Blowfly flight characteristics are shaped by environmental features and controlled by optic flow information. J. Exp Biol. **215**, 2501–2514 (2012). https://doi.org/10.1242/jeb.061713
9. Serres, J.R., Ruffier, F.: Optic flow-based collision-free strategies: from insects to robots. Arthropod Struct. Dev. **46**, 703–717 (2017). https://doi.org/10.1016/j.asd.2017.06.003
10. Buchner, E.: Elementary movement detectors in an insect visual system. Biol. Cybernetics. **24**, 85–101 (1976). https://doi.org/10.1007/BF00360648
11. Hassenstein, B., Reichardt, W.: Systemtheoretische Analyse der Zeit-, Reihenfolgen- und Vorzeichenauswertung bei der Bewegungsperzeption des Rüsselkäfers Chlorophanus. Zeitschrift für Naturforschung B. **11**, 513–524 (1956). https://doi.org/10.1515/znb-1956-9-1004
12. O'Carroll, D.C., Bidweii, N.J., Laughlin, S.B., Warrant, E.J.: Insect motion detectors matched to visual ecology. Nature **382**, 63–66 (1996). https://doi.org/10.1038/382063a0
13. Huang, J.V., Krapp, H.G.: Miniaturized electrophysiology platform for fly-robot interface to study multisensory integration. In: Lepora, N.F., Mura, A., Krapp, H.G., Verschure, P.F.M.J., Prescott, T.J. (eds.) Living Machines 2013. LNCS (LNAI), vol. 8064, pp. 119–130. Springer, Heidelberg (2013). https://doi.org/10.1007/978-3-642-39802-5_11
14. Srinivasan, M.V., Zhang, S.W., Lehrer, M., Collett, T.S.: Honeybee navigation en route to the goal: visual flight control and odometry. J. Exp. Biol. **199**, 237–244 (1996). https://doi.org/10.1242/jeb.199.1.237
15. Srinivasan, M.V., Poteser, M., Kral, K.: Motion detection in insect orientation and navigation. Vision. Res. **39**, 2749–2766 (1999). https://doi.org/10.1016/S0042-6989(99)00002-4
16. Hengstenberg, R.: Roll-stabilization during flight of the blowfly's head and body by mechanical and visual cues. In: Varjú, P.D., Schnitzler, P.H.-U. (eds.) Localization and Orientation in Biology and Engineering, pp. 121–134. Springer, Heidelberg (1984). https://doi.org/10.1007/978-3-642-69308-3_25
17. Schilstra, C., van Hateren, J.H.: Stabilizing gaze in flying blowflies. Nature **395**, 654 (1998). https://doi.org/10.1038/27114
18. Krapp, H.G., Taylor, G.K., Sean Humbert, J.: The mode-sensing hypothesis: matching sensors, actuators and flight dynamics. In: Barth, F.G., Humphrey, J.A.C., Srinivasan, M.V. (eds.) Frontiers in Sensing, pp. 101–114. Springer, Vienna (2012). https://doi.org/10.1007/978-3-211-99749-9_7

19. Krapp, H.G., Hengstenberg, R.: Estimation of self-motion by optic flow processing in single visual interneurons. Nature **384**, 463–466 (1996). https://doi.org/10.1038/384463a0

20. Hausen, K.: Functional characterization and anatomical identification of motion sensitive neurons in the Lobula plate of the blowfly Calliphora erythrocephala. Zeitschrift für Naturforschung C. **31**, 629–634 (1976). https://doi.org/10.1515/znc-1976-9-1001

21. Krapp, H.G., Hengstenberg, R.: A fast stimulus procedure to determine local receptive field properties of motion-sensitive visual interneurons. Vision. Res. **37**, 225–234 (1997). https://doi.org/10.1016/S0042-6989(96)00114-9

22. Borst, A., Haag, J., Mauss, A.S.: How fly neurons compute the direction of visual motion. J. Comp. Physiol. A. **206**(2), 109–124 (2019). https://doi.org/10.1007/s00359-019-01375-9

23. Krapp, H.G., Hengstenberg, R., Egelhaaf, M.: Binocular contributions to optic flow processing in the fly visual system. J. Neurophysiol. **85**, 724–734 (2001)

24. Huang, J.V., Wang, Y., Krapp, H.G.: Wall following in a semi-closed-loop fly-robotic interface. In: Lepora, N.F.F., Mura, A., Mangan, M., Verschure, P.F.M.J.F.M.J., Desmulliez, M., Prescott, T.J.J. (eds.) Living Machines 2016. LNCS (LNAI), vol. 9793, pp. 85–96. Springer, Cham (2016). https://doi.org/10.1007/978-3-319-42417-0_9

25. Huang, J.V., Wei, Y., Krapp, H.G.: A biohybrid fly-robot interface system that performs active collision avoidance. Bioinspir. Biomim. **14**, 065001 (2019). https://doi.org/10.1088/1748-3190/ab3b23

26. Huang, J.V., Wei, Y., Krapp, H.G.: Active collision free closed-loop control of a biohybrid fly-robot interface. In: Vouloutsi, V., et al. (eds.) Living Machines 2018. LNCS (LNAI), vol. 10928, pp. 213–222. Springer, Cham (2018). https://doi.org/10.1007/978-3-319-95972-6_22

27. Huang, J.V., Krapp, H.G.: Neuronal distance estimation by a fly-robot interface. In: Mangan, M., Cutkosky, M., Mura, A., Verschure, P.F.M.J., Prescott, T., Lepora, N. (eds.) Living Machines 2017. LNCS (LNAI), vol. 10384, pp. 204–215. Springer, Cham (2017). https://doi.org/10.1007/978-3-319-63537-8_18

28. Franceschini, N.: Pupil and pseudopupil in the compound eye of drosophila. In: Wehner, R. (ed.) Information Processing in the Visual Systems of Anthropods, pp. 75–82. Springer, Heidelberg (1972). https://doi.org/10.1007/978-3-642-65477-0_10

29. Karmeier, K., Tabor, R., Egelhaaf, M., Krapp, H.G.: Early visual experience and the receptive-field organization of optic flow processing interneurons in the fly motion pathway. Vis. Neurosci. **18**, 1–8 (2001)

30. Laughlin, S.B., Hardie, R.C.: Common strategies for light adaptation in the peripheral visual systems of fly and dragonfly. J. Comp. Physiol. **128**, 319–340 (1978). https://doi.org/10.1007/BF00657606

31. Egelhaaf, M., Borst, A.: Transient and steady-state response properties of movement detectors. J. Opt. Soc. Am. A, JOSAA. **6**, 116–127 (1989). https://doi.org/10.1364/JOSAA.6.000116

32. Harris, R.A., O'Carroll, D.C., Laughlin, S.B.: Contrast gain reduction in fly motion adaptation. Neuron **28**, 595–606 (2000). https://doi.org/10.1016/S0896-6273(00)00136-7

33. Burton, B.G., Laughlin, S.B.: Neural images of pursuit targets in the photoreceptor arrays of male and female houseflies Musca domestica. J. Exp. Biol. **206**, 3963–3977 (2003). https://doi.org/10.1242/jeb.00600

34. Parsons, M.M., Krapp, H.G., Laughlin, S.B.: A motion-sensitive neurone responds to signals from the two visual systems of the blowfly, the compound eyes and ocelli. J. Exp. Biol. **209**, 4464–4474 (2006). https://doi.org/10.1242/jeb.02560

35. Longden, K.D., Krapp, H.G.: Octopaminergic modulation of temporal frequency coding in an identified optic flow-processing interneuron. Front. Syst. Neurosci. **4**, 153 (2010). https://doi.org/10.3389/fnsys.2010.00153

A Dynamic Simulation of a Compliant Worm Robot Amenable to Neural Control

Shane Riddle[✉][iD], Clayton Jackson[iD], Kathryn A. Daltorio[iD],
and Roger D. Quinn[iD]

Department of Mechanical and Aerospace Engineering, Case Western Reserve
University, Cleveland, OH 44106, USA
shane.riddle@case.edu

Abstract. This paper details the development and validation of a
dynamic 3D compliant worm-like robot model controlled by a Synthetic Nervous System (SNS). The model was built and simulated in the
physics engine Mujoco which is able to approximate soft bodied dynamics
and generate contact, gravitational, frictional, and internal forces. These
capabilities allow the model to realistically simulate the movements and
dynamic behavior of a physical soft-bodied worm-robot. For validation,
the results of this simulation were compared to data gathered from a
physical worm robot and found to closely match key behaviors such as
deformation propagation along the compliant structure and actuator efficiency losses in the middle segments. The SNS controller was previously
developed for a simple 2D kinematic model and has been successfully
implemented on this 3D model with little alteration. It uses coupled
oscillators to generate coordinated actuator control signals and induce
peristaltic locomotion. This model will be useful for analyzing dynamic
effects during peristaltic locomotion like contact forces and slip as well as
developing and improving control algorithms that avoid unwanted slip.

Keywords: 3D Model · Compliant Structure · Mujoco · Synthetic
Nervous System · Peristalsis · Worm Robot

1 Introduction

Soft robots are desirable for their efficacy in environments and tasks unsuitable
for rigid body robots. Earthworm-inspired robots are a prime example of this.
Their soft bodied locomotion lends itself well to squeezing through constrained
spaces such as pipes and tunnels that are impassable for rigid bodied robots [3,
13]. They can also be useful in medical procedures, like endoscopy, for which
rigid structures are undesirable [15]. The compliance that makes these worm-like
robots so useful also makes them difficult to model accurately. While materials
engineering and manufacturing methods continue to advance, easing the design

This work was supported by NSF PIRE Award 1743475 and NSF DBI 2015317 as part
of the SF/CIHR/DFG/FRQ/UKRI-MRC Next Generation Networks for Neuroscience
Program.

and fabrication process, so too have the modeling methods used to simulate these increasingly complex soft bodied structures and mechanisms [20].

There are many approaches to modeling and simulating soft robots each with their own set of advantages and trade-offs. Some focus on modeling flexible deformation analytically [21]. Others use finite element methods (FEM) to characterize the behavior of more complex mechanisms [4]. To perform dynamics analysis and controller development, the model in this paper uses a physics engine. Physics engines are frequently employed for rigid body robot modeling but some can also model soft body dynamics by approximating compliant structures using many discrete rigid bodies [27]. The rigid bodies are connected via joints with flexural and torsional stiffness and allow for bending and twisting movements within the structure. These approximations allow for dynamic computational efficiency but with less precision than FEM models. Reduced precision is not necessarily a detriment so long as the accuracy of the results can be validated externally. For example, we validate the model presented in this paper by comparing our results to those from a physical robot.

Peristaltic locomotion relies on geometric coupling between segment diameter and segment length [7,26]. As a segment's diameter contracts, its length increases and vice versa. Earthworms take advantage of their hydrostatic skeletons to accomplish this. Their bodies maintain a constant volume so a change in one dimension necessitates a change in another. Many worm-like robots [13,22,28] and models [3,8,19] utilize a two dimensional geometric approximation consisting of rhombus structures with coupled height and length. None of these models, however, accurately portray both the soft bodied dynamics and three dimensional range of motion that the physical robots exhibit. While the previous models have been used to analyze behaviors like slip, turning, and reaction to perturbations and contact surface irregularities, further refinements of the model and expansion to 3D space will improve understanding of these phenomena.

This paper details the development of a three dimensional compliant worm-like robot model compatible with a Synthetic Nervous System (SNS) controller. The SNS used to control this model was developed for and implemented on a two dimensional simulated worm robot we introduced previously [19]. An SNS is a dynamical neural network comprised of computational models of neurons and synapses which have been implemented as controllers for many biologically inspired robots [5,8,9,13,24,25]. This SNS uses coupled central-pattern generators (CPGs), oscillators thought to control many rhythmic behaviors in animals [16], to produce a peristaltic wave-form. The wave coordinates segment muscle contraction cycles, facilitating locomotion [10,31].

The model reported in this paper is designed to emulate the worm-like robot presented by Wang [28], which uses the rhombus segment approximation. The model is built in the physics engine Mujoco, a platform oriented towards robotics and biomechanics research. Mujoco was selected for three reasons: it easily interfaces with the SNS bio-inspired control signals, it is capable of approximating soft bodied dynamics, and it can simulate ground reaction, gravitational, elastic, and friction forces [27]. The resulting simulation captures more realistic robot motions, including deformation propagation whereby actuating segments can deform nearby segments. Deformation propagation is modeled more accurately here than in previous models [3,8,12,19].

2 Methods

2.1 2D Worm Models

Many worm-like robot models use a two dimensional segment approximation. As found in Daltorio et al. [3] (Fig. 1b) and later in our previous work [19] (Fig. 1a) these models can exist in a 2D plane with segments consisting of rigid side lengths with hinge jointed vertices. Contraction of the segment occurs when an actuator pulls two opposing vertices inward, thus pushing the remaining vertices outwards. A spring connecting the outward displaced vertices provides tension to return them to the original position, thus re-expanding the segment. The geometric relationship governing this coupling is $l^2 + w^2 = 4l_s^2$ where (w) and (l) are rhombus height and length and (l_s) is the given side length.

While both models use rigid side lengths for the rhombi, the Daltorio model incorporates torsional springs at the joints to resist differences in neighboring segment heights. This mimics behavior exhibited in continuous mesh worm-like robots where structural compliance causes the deformation of one segment to propagate to its surrounding elements. A similar model presented in Boxerbaum et al. [1] (Fig. 1c) also implements torsion springs but places them in the middle of the otherwise rigid rhombus side lengths to mimic the compliance within the segment structure rather than between segments.

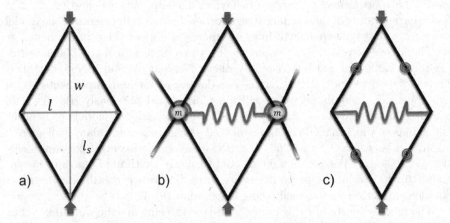

Fig. 1. Three previously reported models for 2D worm segments: a) Riddle et al. [19], b) Daltorio et al. [3], c) Boxerbaum et al. [1]. The blue arrows represent contractile actuator forces and the orange objects represent linear and torsional springs.

While useful in their own right all of these models, to varying degrees, suffer from oversimplification. Our previous model [19] was capable of peristalsis but was purely kinematic, neglecting all forces as its purpose was only to validate the control system presented in that work. The Daltorio model simulates sagittal plane dynamics but neglects gravity, focusing instead on the larger forces provided by contact with pipe walls which limits it to such environments [14]. The Boxerbaum model also simulates 2D dynamics but neglects ground contact forces. Importantly, none of these captures the behavior of the compliant structure between actuated segments. Some worm-like robots such as MIT's meshworm [22] are made of a continuous mesh. They do not actuate every adjacent rhombus but instead rely on the mechanical advantage of deformation propagation along the structure (Fig. 2). To model this behavior and more accurately simulate gravitational and contact force effects, a 3D model is needed.

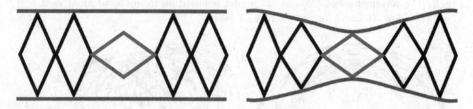

Fig. 2. Visualization of segment contraction with deformation propagation (right) and without (left). The contracting segment is orange and unactuated segments are black. (Color figure online)

2.2   3D Compliant Worm Model

Modeling a 3D robot using a physics engine has many advantages. A 2D approximation is most often implemented in physical worm robots by wrapping a mesh of rhombuses into a cylindrical tube, expanding it to 3D space [1,13,22,28]. Huang et al. [8] analytically modeled the kinematics of a 3D worm-like robot in this fashion previously but utilized rigid side lengths and did not incorporate forces. Analytically deriving these forces is a difficult task, however, a physics engine can predict these. Assuming the model closely behaves like the robot, a physics engine is capable of simulating the forces without requiring an analytical derivation. This is useful for examining dynamic phenomena in complex three dimensional structures like sagging due to gravity and slip which is an important factor in peristaltic locomotion and has been the subject of many studies [3,12,28,30,32].

The 3D model described in this paper was designed to mimic the worm-like robot presented in Wang's dissertation [28] (Fig. 3). The physical robot's rhombus mesh was constructed from 12 polyethylene tubes wrapped helically in both clockwise and counterclockwise directions and pinned at the intersection points to create rotating joints. The joints serve as anchor points both for the elastic springs and for eyelets through which actuator cables were threaded.

Fig. 3. The physical robot [28] the 3D model is based on from the a) axial view and b) sagittal view. Robot images provided by Wang.

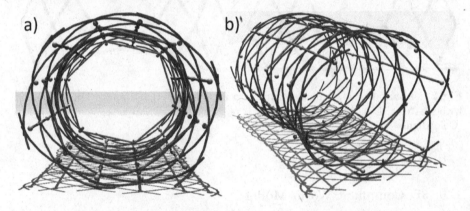

Fig. 4. Rendering of the model in Mujoco from the a) axial view and b) isometric view. The blue lines are the flexible cables used for the robot's structure. The circumferential red rings represent contractile muscle actuators. The axially oriented red lines are tendon springs. The spheres are visual markers for the joints holding everything together. (Color figure online)

The cables attach to spool wheels mounted to servo motors. When the actuators rotate, the cables are spooled in or out to shrink or expand the segment diameter, akin to the circumferential muscles found in a real worm. The number of actuated segments is defined by the number of actuator cables. The Wang robot is capable of turning so it has two motors per segment but for straight line locomotion only one motor per segment is required.

Soft Structure: The physics engine Mujoco was chosen for this task as it was designed specifically to facilitate robotics and biomechanics research [27]. The model was built by generating twelve sets of coordinates forming helical paths which follow the shapes of the polyethylene tubing in the physical robot's resting state. Flexible cable composite objects were then defined in Mujoco overlayed on these paths. As in the physical robot, half of these twist clockwise and half twist counterclockwise with joints defined at the intersection points, thus forming the cylindrical rhombus mesh seen in Fig. 4. Mujoco models composite cable objects by discretizing them into smaller rigid body capsules connected end-to-end with flexible joints that allow for deformation of the structure. There are three such capsule discretizations per each side length of the rhombuses in this model. The coordinates and properties defining the structure and its compliant behavior are assembled in an XML file which Mujoco is able to read into the physics engine for both computation and rendering. A MATLAB code, available at https:// github.com/sriddle97/SNS-Controlled-Peristalsis.git, was used to automate the XML generation given the desired dimensions (m), number of helixes (must be even and ≥6), and number of discretizations per rhombus side length.

We used a number of methods to set material and stiffness properties in the Mujoco model. The "bend" and "twist" properties of the cable object correlate to the Young's and shear Moduli of the cable material, respectively, and dictate the degree of flexibility the structure exhibits. As such we set the "bend" and "twist" properties to their respective moduli for polyethelyene (approximately 0.3 GPa and 0.2 GPa). To ensure the model and the physical robot have the same mass, the density was also set to that of polyethylene (940 kg m^{-3}) and the cable thickness was set to match the cross-sectional area of the tubing, a necessary adjustment as Mujoco does not have an option to model hollow tubes directly. The cross sectional area for the tubing was found to be 1.7×10^{-5} m^2 which equates to a radius of about 0.002 m for a solid circular cross section. It should be noted that Mujoco does not inherently define default units of measurement. Instead, it allows the user to define the units through the scale of their inputs. To ensure a consistent unit system for the simulated environment we define all physical properties using standard SI units (kg, m, s, N, Pa) and verified that resulting units of force were in Newtons (N).

Actuation: As a biomechanics oriented physics engine, Mujoco is capable of dynamically modeling muscles and tendons. Passive tendon objects, serving the same purpose as the elastic springs in the Wang robot, were attached to the model structure at joints running in the axial direction. These tendons are initialized such that their unstretched lengths coincide with the fully expanded resting state of the structure. Since the tendons only provide force in tension, this prevents them from expanding the model diameter beyond the physical robot's mechanical limitations. The spring stiffness coefficient for these tendons was set to 19.9N/m to match those of the physical robot.

Rather than directly modeling servo motors, we took advantage of Mujoco's built-in muscle actuators to provide contraction. Mujoco models these muscles as abstract force generators attached to fixed-length tendons. The muscle actuator behavior is dictated by a force-length-velocity function commonly reported in biomechanics literature [27]. The exact function used by Mujoco can be found in the FLV.m MATLAB file provided in Mujoco's documentation and is visualized in Fig. 5. The function requires the muscle's maximum and minimum lengths (l_{max}, l_{min}), the maximum shortening velocity at which the muscle force drops to zero (v_{max}), the passive force generated at the muscle's maximum length $(f_{p,max})$, and the active force generated at saturated lengthening velocity $(f_{v,max})$. The muscles in our model use the default values Mujoco sets for these parameters except for the minimum length $(l_{max} = 1.6, v_{max} = 1.5, f_{p,max} = 1.3, f_{v,max} = 1.2)$. l_{min} was increased from the default 0.5 to 0.58 to avoid over-contraction of the mesh.

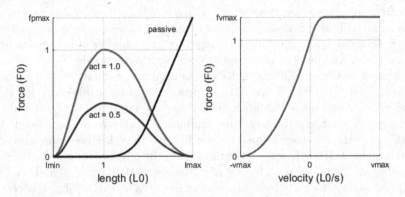

Fig. 5. Visual of the Force-Length-Velocity relationship (Eq. 1) Mujoco uses to model muscle actuator forces [27].

The forces are relative to the peak muscle activation force at zero velocity (F_0) and the lengths are relative to l_0, the length where F_0 is generated. Both l_0 and F_0 are calculated automatically by the model compiler using the parameter values defined above. The compiler also has a scaling factor with which the user can manually adjust F_0 if needed. The actuator forces generated within the physics engine are determined using the function in Eq. 1. Here, the muscle activation signal $act(U)$ is a function of the corresponding CPG neuron membrane potentials. The muscle activation varies from 0 (deactivated) to 1 (fully activated) via a monotonic and saturating sigmoid as detailed in Sect. 2.3.

$$\text{actuator\_force} = -\text{FLV}(l, v, act(U)) * F_0 \tag{1}$$

The automatically generated F_0 did not provide enough force to contract the segment so a scaling factor of 550,000 was included. This may seem high but the actuators generated forces up to 2.5 N at this scale. This is in line with the amount of force required to displace six 19.9 N/m tendon springs (the number of tendons per segment) approximately 2–3 cm, which is sufficient for appreciable segment contraction in this model.

Sensing: Mechanoreceptors and sensory neurons provide animal nervous systems with proprioceptive feedback to mediate locomotion. Worms have sensory neurons that perceive muscle stretch and are used to control their muscle contractions during peristalsis and steering [29]. Here, these sensory neurons are approximated with mechanical stretch sensors. The stretch sensors feed the segment length data into the controller where it is used to coordinate actuation and propagate the peristaltic wave down the body. This approach is used on both the Wang robot and in our previous work where they give the SNS positional feedback from the 2D model. The data packet Mujoco outputs at each timestep of the simulation contains the tendon lengths which can be exported to the SNS controller where they are used to generate input signals for the next time step.

2.3   Synthetic Nervous System Controller

The SNS controller used in this work, seen in Fig. 6, is nearly identical to that presented in our previous paper [19].

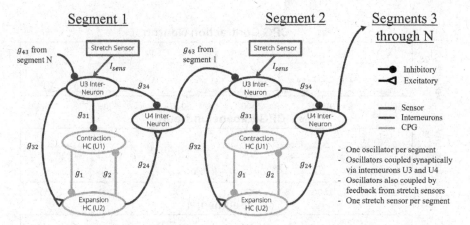

Fig. 6. Worm robot Synthetic Nervous System control network diagram (Fig. 2 of [19]).

The only substantial difference is that the network code was ported from MAT-LAB to python for Mujoco compatibility and reformatted using the SNS-Toolbox package developed by Nourse et al. [18]. SNS-Toolbox simplified the network building and Mujoco interfacing processes and will reduce the effort required to alter the controller for future work. As before, each segment's contraction cycle is controlled by a half-center oscillator CPG [2,23]. The time dynamics enabled by the Hodgkin-Huxley fast transient sodium currents and mutual inhibition cause the neurons to flip between excited and inhibited states in a catch-and-release type manner [6]. The membrane potential of each half-center neuron is fed into the function shown in Eq. (2) to generate the muscle activation signal used in Eq. (1):

$$act = 1/(1 + e^{-0.35*(U_{exp}-U_{con})}) \qquad (2)$$

Our previous 2D model had linear actuators that operated with position control. A piecewise linear sigmoid function, not unlike Eq. (2), mapped the neuron potentials to position targets and a simple proportional controller dictated the actuator speed accordingly. The 3D model employs muscle actuators controlled by the force-length-velocity function in Eq. (1), so while the actuation command signal is similar, the actuation itself is much more bio-plausible than the position control. Regardless the end result is the same. When the contraction neuron potential is higher, the signal sent to the actuator tells it to contract the segment. Likewise, a higher expansion neuron potential signals for segment expansion. Interneurons and stretch sensors couple the CPGs from one segment to the next to coordinate the peristaltic wave propagation. For more details on the SNS controller, please refer to our previous publication [19].

3   Results

For a direct comparison to the previous 2D simulation results, the Mujoco model presented here is composed of 3 segments (N = 3). In practice this can

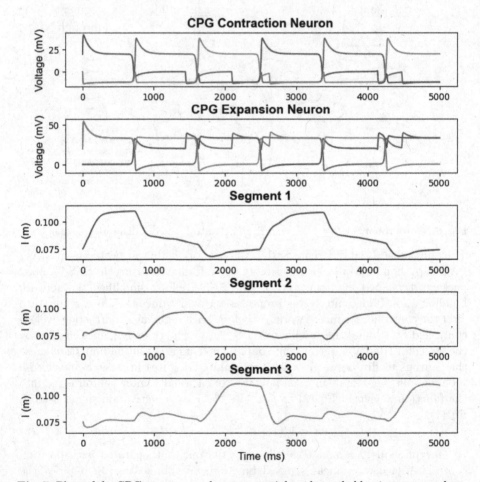

Fig. 7. Plots of the CPG neuron membrane potentials, color coded by segment number, and stretch sensor length readings for the 3 segment 3D model.

be expanded to any number $N \geq 3$ but does become more computationally expensive the larger the model gets. For reference, running this model for 5000 time steps took 3.5 min on a high-end, consumer grade computer. Rather than having actuators defined at every axially adjacent rhombus, one rhombus was left between each muscle ring. This was done to demonstrate that the structural deformation propagation can extend beyond directly neighboring rhombuses. Running the simulation for 5 s with 1 ms time steps produced the data plotted in Fig. 7. A video of this simulation as well as the code required to run it are available at https://github.com/sriddle97/SNS-Controlled-Peristalsis.git.

The results show that the controller generates peristaltic behavior as it did in the 2D model (see Fig. 4 in [19] for comparative data). The stretch sensor readings indicate lengthening of the segment when the contraction neuron is excited and shortening when the CPG flips and the expansion neuron is excited, as expected. Segments 1 and 3 experienced a maximum elongation of 4.20 cm and 4.02 cm respectively, a mere 4.45% difference. Segment 2, however, experienced a maximum elongation of just 2.55 cm, 39.4% less than that of Segment 1.

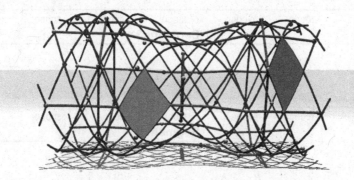

Fig. 8. The compliant worm model with the second segment contracted at t = 1500 ms. The green rhombus shows deformation propagating to a nearby unactuated segment. The pink rhombus indicates a segment sufficiently far from the contracted segment to remain relatively unaffected.

4   Discussion

The key difference between the 2D model data [19] and the 3D model data here lies in the stretch sensor length readings. The purely kinematic 2D model produced very smooth, idealized length changes that do not capture deformation caused by nearby segment actuation. On the other hand, the 3D model does capture the deformation propagation of the mesh, even when actuated rhombuses are not directly adjacent. This can be seen in the length plot data of Fig. 7 and is visualized with a rendering of the model during contraction in Fig. 8. When Segment 1 contracts, the length of Segment 2 also increases slightly and both

Segments 1 and 3 have elevated length readings when Segment 2 contracts since it neighbors both. This behavior closely emulates that exhibited by the Wang robot in their length readings seen in Fig. 9 (data provided by the authors [28]). The physical robot has two stretch sensors per segment to measure asymmetric contraction during turning.

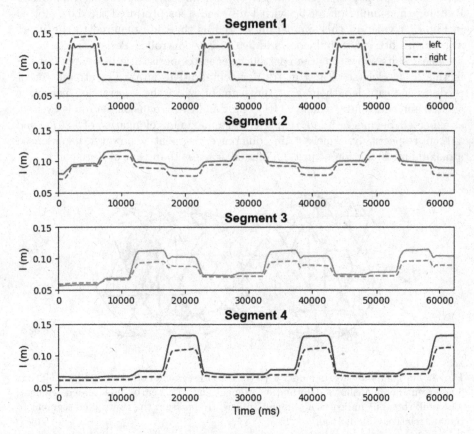

Fig. 9. Stretch sensor length readings from the physical robot during straight-line locomotion, provided by Wang [28]. The solid and dotted lines are for sensors on the left and right side of the robot, respectively.

It should be noted that Segment 2's smaller length change is due to contact frictional forces and its central location along the worm. While all segments experience losses from friction in the joints, Segment 2, unlike Segments 1 and 3, must push against the rest of the worm body in both directions in order to contract. Thus, it is reasonable to conclude that this energy loss is the result of the surrounding segments slipping along the ground as Segment 2 pushes them outward. In this simulation the robot model moves along flat ground, not inside a pipe, so ground contact forces are produced by gravitational effects.

If the model contained more segments the reduced efficiency would be present in all interior segments $(2, N-1)$. These observations are all supported by the Wang robot length data in Fig. 9 which also exhibits decreased lengthening in Segments 2 and 3 of their four segment robot $(N=4)$ while locomoting across flat ground with a non-zero coefficient of friction. The averages of the left and right sensor readings for each segment were used to compare maximum length changes to those of the 3D model. The average maximum length change of the physical robot's Segments 1–4, respectively, were 6.15 cm, 3.82 cm, 4.78 cm, and 5.98 cm. Just as in the model, the first segment elongates the most, there is a small difference between the first and last segment elongations (2.75%), and the middle segments elongate much less than Segment 1 (37.8% decrease for Segment 2, 22.2% for Segment 3).

5 Conclusions and Future Work

The primary purpose of this paper is to report the development of a 3D compliant worm-like robot model and show it is capable of accurately simulating soft bodied dynamics. The quantitative results in Fig. 7 substantiate these claims as our modeled data is comparable to that recorded from the Wang physical robot shown in Fig. 9 [28]. The qualitative evidence also supports this, as the snapshot in Fig. 8 and the video found at the linked Github page show behavior that visually matches the physical robot motion. A secondary purpose of this work was to show that the SNS developed in our previous publication could be applied to a more realistic robot model with little to no changes as we claimed [19]. Since the controller instigated peristaltic behavior in this much more realistic model, this work confirms that hypothesis.

Now that we have a model that simulates soft worm robot dynamics more realistically, we can use it to develop improved control systems. While peristaltic wave-forms were achieved, the parameters were not fine-tuned to produce appreciable directional locomotion in the simulated environment. As such the model, as presented in this paper, was only capable of achieving negligibly small speeds. This is largely due to unoptimized friction coefficients (Mujoco's default friction coefficient $\mu = 1$ was used) and a small number of segments, both of which impact locomotive efficiency [13]. As mentioned earlier, friction and slip play a large roll in peristaltic locomotion and the SNS controller, in its current state, was not designed to account for these since the initial 2D kinematic model did not simulate them. Furthermore, the tendon length data used for the approximated stretch sensor readings were somewhat idealized in that they did not include noise. Noise is present in nearly all sensor readings and must be mitigated when applying any control algorithm to a physical robot. Accounting for noise should be as simple as adjusting the stretch sensor signal threshold in the SNS controller but this remains to be validated.

Future work will focus on adjusting the controller to accommodate sensor noise and improve straight-line motion. This will likely involve adding contact pressure sensors to sense the normal forces along the underside of the worm model. The combination of pressure and stretch sensors has been shown by Wang to provide reasonably reliable slip detection in soft worm robots [28]. We also plan to add more functionality to the SNS control system, namely adaptive peristaltic gaits. Nourse et al. [17] proposed an adaptive frequency CPG model which can increase and decrease oscillation rates in response to manual, neural, or sensory stimuli. In another paper, Ijspeert et al. [11] present a network of connected descending CPGs which exhibited the ability to transition a salamander robot's gait from walking to swimming by changing only the drive input. These works indicate that it should be feasible to implement an adaptive CPG in the SNS to enable adaptive locomotion in a worm robot. Such functionality would allow it to react to changes in its environment, such as the narrowing of a pipe, by increasing the peristaltic wave speed or even changing waveforms altogether.

Acknowledgements. We would like to thank Yifan Wang, Mingyi Wang, and Natasha Rouse for providing the sensor data from their physical worm robot and allowing us to use it in this publication for comparison to our 3D model [28].

References

1. Boxerbaum, A.S., Shaw, K.M., Chiel, H.J., Quinn, R.D.: Continuous wave peristaltic motion in a robot. Int. J. Robot. Res. **31**(3), 302–318 (2012)
2. Brown, T.G.: On the nature of the fundamental activity of the nervous centres; together with an analysis of the conditioning of rhythmic activity in progression, and a theory of the evolution of function in the nervous system. J. Physiol. **48**(1), 18–46 (1914)
3. Daltorio, K.A., Boxerbaum, A.S., Horchler, A.D., Shaw, K.M., Chiel, H.J., Quinn, R.D.: Efficient worm-like locomotion: slip and control of soft-bodied peristaltic robots. Bioinspiration Biomimetics **8**(3), 035003 (2013)
4. Duriez, C.: Control of elastic soft robots based on real-time finite element method. In: 2013 IEEE International Conference on Robotics and Automation, pp. 3982–3987 (2013)
5. Goldsmith, C.A., Szczecinski, N.S., Quinn, R.D.: Neurodynamic modeling of the fruit fly drosophila melanogaster. Bioinspiration Biomimetics **15**(6), 065003 (2020)
6. Hodgkin, A.L., Huxley, A.F.: A quantitative description of membrane current and its application to conduction and excitation in nerve. J. Physiol. **117**(4), 500–544 (1952)
7. Horchler, A.D., et al.: Peristaltic locomotion of a modular mesh-based worm robot: precision, compliance, and friction. Soft Rob. **2**(4), 135–145 (2015)
8. Huang, Y., Kandhari, A., Chiel, H.J., Quinn, R.D., Daltorio, K.A.: Mathematical modeling to improve control of mesh body for peristaltic locomotion. In: Mangan, M., Cutkosky, M., Mura, A., Verschure, P.F.M.J., Prescott, T., Lepora, N. (eds.) Living Machines 2017. LNCS (LNAI), vol. 10384, pp. 193–203. Springer, Cham (2017). https://doi.org/10.1007/978-3-319-63537-8_17
9. Hunt, A., Szczecinski, N., Quinn, R.: Development and training of a neural controller for hind leg walking in a dog robot. Front. Neurorobot. **11**, 18 (2017)
10. Ijspeert, A.J.: Central pattern generators for locomotion control in animals and robots: a review. Neural Netw. **21**(4), 642–653 (2008). Robotics and Neuroscience

11. Ijspeert, A.J., Crespi, A., Ryczko, D., Cabelguen, J.M.: From swimming to walking with a salamander robot driven by a spinal cord model. Science **315**(5817), 1416–1420 (2007)
12. Kandhari, A., Wang, Y., Chiel, H.J., Daltorio, K.A.: Turning in worm-like robots: the geometry of slip elimination suggests nonperiodic waves. Soft Rob. **6**(4), 560–577 (2019)
13. Kandhari, A., Wang, Y., Chiel, H.J., Quinn, R.D., Daltorio, K.A.: An analysis of peristaltic locomotion for maximizing velocity or minimizing cost of transport of earthworm-like robots. Soft Rob. **8**(4), 485–505 (2021)
14. Keudel, M., Schrader, S.: Axial and radial pressure exerted by earthworms of different ecological groups. Biol. Fertil. Soils **29**(3), 262–269 (1999)
15. Kim, B., Young, H., Hyeon, J., Park, J.O.: Inchworm-like colonoscopic robot with hollow body and steering device. JSME Int. J. Ser. C Mech. Syst. Mach. Elements Manuf. **49**, 205–212 (2006)
16. Marder, E., Bucher, D.: Central pattern generators and the control of rhythmic movements. Curr. Biol. **11**(23), R986–R996 (2001)
17. Nourse, W., Quinn, R.D., Szczecinski, N.S.: An adaptive frequency central pattern generator for synthetic nervous systems. In: Vouloutsi, V., et al. (eds.) Living Machines 2018. LNCS (LNAI), vol. 10928, pp. 361–364. Springer, Cham (2018). https://doi.org/10.1007/978-3-319-95972-6_38
18. Nourse, W.R.P., Szczecinski, N.S., Quinn, R.D.: SNS-toolbox: a tool for efficient simulation of synthetic nervous systems. In: Hunt, A., et al. (eds.) Biomimetic and Biohybrid Systems. Living Machines 2022. LNCS, vol. 13548, pp. 32–43. Springer, Cham (2022). https://doi.org/10.1007/978-3-031-20470-8_4
19. Riddle, S., Nourse, W.R.P., Yu, Z., Thomas, P.J., Quinn, R.D.: A synthetic nervous system with coupled oscillators controls peristaltic locomotion. In: Hunt, A., et al. (eds.) Biomimetic and Biohybrid Systems. Living Machines 2022. LNCS, vol. 13548, pp. 249–261. Springer, Cham (2022). https://doi.org/10.1007/978-3-031-20470-8_25
20. Schmitt, F., Piccin, O., Barbé, L., Bayle, B.: Soft robots manufacturing: a review. Front. Robot. AI **5**, 84 (2018)
21. Sen, S., Awtar, S.: A closed-form nonlinear model for the constraint characteristics of symmetric spatial beams. J. Mech. Des. **135**(3) (2013)
22. Seok, S., Onal, C.D., Cho, K.J., Wood, R.J., Rus, D., Kim, S.: Meshworm: a peristaltic soft robot with antagonistic nickel titanium coil actuators. IEEE/ASME Trans. Mechatron. **18**(5), 1485–1497 (2013)
23. Szczecinski, N.S., Hunt, A.J., Quinn, R.D.: Design process and tools for dynamic neuromechanical models and robot controllers. Biol. Cybern. **111**(1), 105–127 (2017)
24. Szczecinski, N.S., Hunt, A.J., Quinn, R.D.: A functional subnetwork approach to designing synthetic nervous systems that control legged robot locomotion. Front. Neurorobot. **11**, 37 (2017)
25. Szczecinski, N.S., Quinn, R.D.: Template for the neural control of directed stepping generalized to all legs of MantisBot. Bioinspiration Biomimetics **12**(4), 045001 (2017)
26. Tanaka, Y., Ito, K., Nakagaki, T., Kobayashi, R.: Mechanics of peristaltic locomotion and role of anchoring. J. R. Soc. Interface **9**(67), 222–233 (2012)
27. Todorov, E., Erez, T., Tassa, Y.: MuJoCo: a physics engine for model-based control. In: 2012 IEEE/RSJ International Conference on Intelligent Robots and Systems, pp. 5026–5033. IEEE (2012)

28. Wang, Y.: Preparing worm-like robots for unknown environments: perception and path planning. In: CWRU Dissertation (2022)
29. Yeon, J., et al.: A sensory-motor neuron type mediates proprioceptive coordination of steering in C. elegans via two TRPC channels. PLoS Biol. **16**(6) (2018)
30. Zarrouk, D., Sharf, I., Shoham, M.: Analysis of earthworm-like robotic locomotion on compliant surfaces. In: 2010 IEEE International Conference on Robotics and Automation, pp. 1574–1579 (2010)
31. Zhou, Q., Xu, J., Fang, H.: A CPG-based versatile control framework for metameric earthworm-like robotic locomotion. Adv. Sci. **n/a**(n/a), 2206336 (2023)
32. Zimmermann, K., Zeidis, I.: Worm-like locomotion as a problem of nonlinear dynamics. J. Theor. Appl. Mech. **45**, 179–187 (2007)

Inchworm Locomotive Soft Robots Actuated by a Single Pneumatic Line

Hyeongseok Kang[1,2] (iD), Bohyun Hwang[1] (iD), and Byungkyu Kim[1,2](✉) (iD)

[1] Department of Smart Air Mobility, Korea Aerospace University,
10540 Goyang, Republic of Korea
bkim@kau.ac.kr
[2] School of Aerospace and Mechanical Engineering, Korea Aerospace
University, 10540 Goyang, Republic of Korea

Abstract. Constitutive hyperelastic materials are highly useful in achieving both large deformation and compliant interaction with the environment. Due to these promising mechanical characteristics, soft robotics is an attractive research topic that explore possibilities to mimic creatures in nature for real-world applications. Nonetheless, the implementation of the higher motion primitives capable of multiple degrees of freedom remains an open challenge due to the complexity in control and modeling. In this view, this work presents preliminary results on an inchworm-like soft robot actuated by only one pneumatic line. Similar to an inchworm in nature, our robot can generate the gait by controlling the airflow in the robot body through the solenoid valve. The monolithic soft body integrated with the suction cup enables to improve mechanical functionalities. Conclusively, our design strategies allowed the robot to maneuver at an inclined track of 20° with a linear velocity of 0.2 mm/s.

Keywords: Inchworm locomotion · Suction cup · Bioinspiration

1 Introduction

In the last decade, soft robots have shown strong potentials, in mimicking the inherent characteristics of creatures in nature, and/or in addressing open challenges that today's rigid bodies robots cannot achieve [1–3]. These unprecedented achievements are mainly due to undeniable usefulness of constitutive hyperelastic materials, i.e., high deformability, compliance, customizability, etc. [4]. Indeed, robots made of soft materials can exhibit versatile and dexterous movements while performing highly safe and compliant interaction with the environment [5]. Furthermore, based on understanding of natural organisms, pioneered studies explored new possibilities that can allow the machines to explore different environment while generating movements by accommodating unique principles into the designs [6, 7].

In general, to achieve the higher motion primitives capable of multiple degrees of freedom, the complexity in computation for a model and control becomes significant.

F. Meder et al. (Eds.): Living Machines 2023, LNAI 14157, pp. 353–363, 2023.
https://doi.org/10.1007/978-3-031-38857-6_26

Thus, it is noted that compromising desired motion principles inspired by nature, design strategies, and methodologies to allow for model-based control is a vital aspect. Here, the pivotal question posed through this work: how to simplify the inchworm inspired mechanisms, making it more deformable and dexterous while ensuring bioinspired principles.

Inchworms, also known as caterpillars, achieve the movement via a distinctive traveling wave [8]. Specifically, to move forward, the inchworm anchors on the ground through its back legs and then stretches its body forward. It then extends its front legs to anchor itself again and releases its back legs to contract its body. The inchworm repeats this sequence of locomotion to slowly and steadily advance along the contact surface [9].

In literature, various studies have presented inchworm like locomotion using different mechanisms, materials, and control strategies [10–13]. Up to date, mimicking longitudinal fibers has been mainly addressed by using shape memory alloy (SMA) or polymer. Also, pneumatic driven actuators capable of axial or bending movements have been explored. As an alternative strategy motorless or tetherless magnetic driven approaches are being researched.

As regards the SMA actuation, Wang et al., presented an inchworm-inspired robot with a soft-bodied made of smart soft composite (i.e., shape memory alloy wire and soft polymer). This robot maneuvered by controlling the abdominal contraction of SMA wires, and achieved a linear speed of 3.6 mm/s [14]. Xie et al., presented a pneumatic driven soft robot capable of inchworm like locomotion, by winding the inextensible fiber along the elastomeric body, and they demonstrated a speed robot up to 6.67 mm/s [15]. Meanwhile, Joyee et al., introduced a new type of inchworm-inspired soft robot using magnetic actuation. This motorless approach enabled the tetherless biomimetic soft robots, and demonstrated a linear locomotion at a speed of 1.67 mm/s with a locomotion efficiency of 93.28% [16].

In light of these, a comprehensive finding among different actuators relies on the control strategies. More specifically, the SMA wire is useful to implement the axial stroke without complex computational resources, while at the cooling phase it needs a recovery time which may delay overall stoke time [17]. In the meantime, the magnetic driven actuations are also highly useful to allow the robot to maneuver at confined space while achieving lightweight, noise free, and high deformability [16]. However, the presence of the permanent magnet might induce uniform distribution of the mass, interfering overall gaits. In particular, their uses are limited by given environment, e.g., with non-ferromagnetic materials. On the other hand, pneumatic actuators ensure a fast speed while producing large deformations, but it generally needs three chambers (i.e., front, mid-, and rear) allowing for independent control, which results in high complexity in control. In addition to this, employing adequate mechanisms/materials that create friction is important to accomplish reliable gait while ensuring efficiency.

In our previous studies [18, 19], we developed an inchworm like robot composed of a flexible material (i.e., spring) and a single pneumatic line. By employing a novel design principle, each chamber (i.e., rear and front) had different size of holes (like nozzle), gradually propagating the airflow from the rear to the front. Even though our approaches were remarkable to accomplish a simplified control in mimicking inchworm like locomotion, it does not ensure compliant interaction with the environment like an inchworm does in nature. In particular, since deformations in radial at the rear and front chamber were limited by the flexible material, the robot undergoes slippage, resulting in complete gain failure and cannot maneuver different environment, e.g., pipeline having different diameter, mainly due to less deformability.

With these in mind, the primary objective of this robot is to achieve high maneuverability through an adequate friction force enough to support the traction force and the weight of robot, and to accomplish inchworm like locomotion with simplified control. Helping to reduce complexity in control. Moreover, reducing the number of pneumatic lines is possible. This way, lightweight is attributed, and drag forces that impede locomotion can be avoided. To aim these, this work focuses on more advanced inchworm like robot made of constitutive hyperelastic materials and demonstrates high speed gait locomotion.

2 Materials and Methods

2.1 Concept Design

Figure 1 shows a concept design of inchworm locomotive soft robots, which consists of front and rear clamping balloons, air tube, and elongation modules that feature convoluted skin (like bellow) together with O-rings interfaced at each convolution. Each clamping balloons have suction cups with a particular pattern.

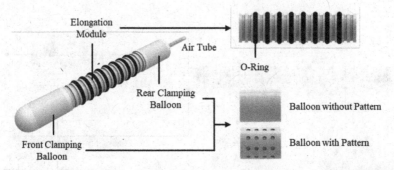

Fig. 1. Concept design of inchworm locomotive robots actuated by a single pneumatic line.

2.2 Working Principle

As depicted in Fig. 2, the inchworm locomotion is achieved by a single pneumatic line. As the positive pressure imposes (Valve ON), the rear clamping balloon is inflated in radial, leading the rear part of the robot to be fixed support. Once the inner pressure of the rear clamping balloon triggers the air flow to the elongation module, the elongation module exhibits purely axial strain (mainly tensile strain). Meanwhile, once the inner pressure triggers the air flows to the front clamping balloon, the front clamping balloon expands radially, and the peak stroke is identified.

To complete a cycle, the pressure applied to the entire body of the robot is deflated by releasing the valve (Valve OFF). The inner pressures at each module are passively released down to atmospheric pressure (P_{atm}) mainly due to the restored energy at elastomeric materials.

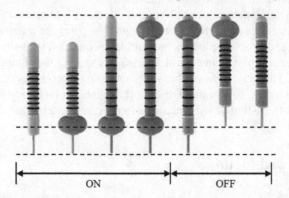

Fig. 2. Working principle of the inchworm locomotive robots.

Mathematical Analysis. To understand better on the working principle, we introduce a theoretical approach, based on a free body diagram (see Fig. 3.)

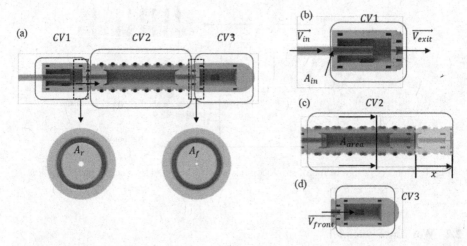

Fig. 3. (a) Freebody diagram of the airflow, at (b) the rear clamping balloon, (c) the elongation module, and (d) the front clamping balloon, respectively.

Given that the mass flow rate is preserved in control volume (CV1) and that the the air density is constant, the relation of the area ratio and the velocity ratio at the rear clamping balloon is written, as follows:

$$\frac{A_{in}}{A_r} = \frac{\overrightarrow{V_{exit}}}{\overrightarrow{V_{in}}} \tag{1}$$

Thus, it is noted that the larger the area ratio of the rear clamping balloon and the elongation module, the larger the velocity ratio. Once the pressure of the rear clamping balloon increases up to P_2, then the air flow rate in control volume (CV2) can be written by:

$$\frac{\partial}{\partial t} \int_{CV2} \rho dV = \rho A_r \overrightarrow{V_{exit}} \tag{2}$$

Here, assuming that the overall volume of the elongation module can be approximated to cylinder ($A_{area}x$), then the air flow rate in CV2 corresponds to the flow rate at the inlet ($A_{in}\overrightarrow{V_{in}}$), which can be represented by:

$$\frac{\partial}{\partial t} \int_{CV2} \rho dV = \frac{\rho A_{in} \overrightarrow{V_{in}}}{A_{area}x} = \frac{\rho Q_{in}}{A_{area}x} \tag{3}$$

By applying the ideal gas equation ($P = \rho RT$), the Eq. (3) can be rewritten by:

$$\frac{\partial P}{\partial t} = \frac{P_{in}Q_{in}}{A_{area}x} \tag{4}$$

Therefore, the inner (gauge) pressure at the elongation module (P_{elong}) is equivalent to the following:

$$P_{elong} = \frac{P_{in}Q_{in}t}{A_{area}x} \tag{5}$$

Finally, in the control volume of the front balloon module, the relation of the area ratio and velocity ratio can be obtained from Eq. (1), as follows:

$$\frac{A_f}{A_r} = \frac{\overrightarrow{V_{front}}}{\overrightarrow{V_{exit}}} \tag{6}$$

Furthermore, when the front/rear balloons are inflated and attached to the wall, an adhesion force is generated by the suction force of the suction cups configured on the balloons (Fig. 4(a)). The suction force is derived as follows (Fig. 4(b)) [20]:

$$F = P\left(1 - \frac{V_{min}}{V_0}\right)A \tag{7}$$

where P is the atmospheric pressure, V_{min} is the volume of inside the suction cup at null, V_0 is the volume of the inside the suction cup before detachment, and A is the base area of suction cup.

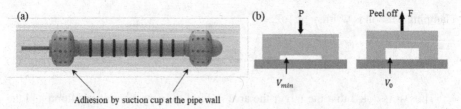

Fig. 4. (a) Adhesion by suction cup when the balloon is inflated and anchoring the pipe (b) Concept of adhesion by suction cup.

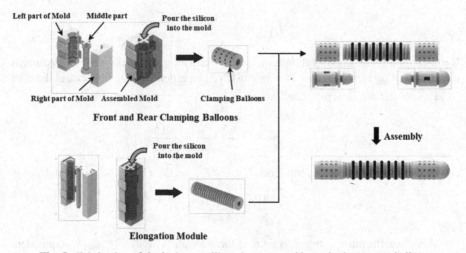

Fig. 5. Fabrication of the inchworm like robot actuated by a single pneumatic line.

2.3 Fabrication

The fabrication process of the robot is depicted in Fig. 5.

The entire body of the robot is made of the elastomeric material (EcoFlex™ 30, Smooth-On Inc., Macungie, PA, USA). To fabricate the rear and front clamping balloons and the elongation module, we used 3D printed molds made of a polyacrylate (PLA) material. Part A and B of the EcoFlex were manually mixed with a weight ratio of 1:1 and degassed by vacuum chamber. Then, the mixed liquid silicone was poured into the molds, and cured them for 30 min at 60 °C. The backbone structures were used to ensure desired areas of both clamping balloons, which were obtained by 3D printing (Objet24, STRATASYS, Minneapolis, USA). The bellow skin was fabricated through molding and casting. To ensure structure stability, O-rings with a diameter of 16 mm and 2.5 mm thickness were mechanically interfaced at each convolution profile. Then, all components (i.e., both clamping balloons, bellow skin, and backbones) were bonded together by brushing silicone adhesive (SIL-Poxy® adhesive, Smooth-On Inc., Macungie, PA, USA). Then, finally the silicone tube having 3.5 mm in diameter was interfaced at the rear clamping balloon.

2.4 Experimental Setups

To demonstrate our robot, the experimental setup was built, as depicted in Fig. 6. A binary control (On/Off) was applied by solenoid valves (DC12V) and relay modules (JQC-3FF-S-H, Tongling Electric Appliances Co., China). Due to this, pressure control (i.e., imposing and releasing the pressure) was achieved, respectively. A control program was developed for generating digital signal through an Arduino board (Arduino UNO, ARDUINO, Italy). An acrylic pipe having 30 mm in diameter and 600 mm in length was used to demonstrate the mechanical performance of the robot.

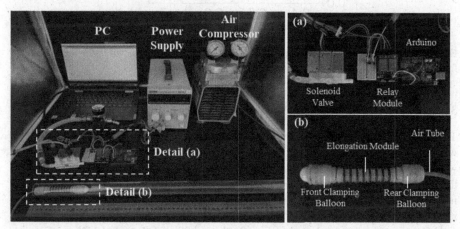

Fig. 6. Experimental setups consist of laptop, power supply, and air compressor, together with Arduino, Solenoid valve, and relay module at detailed view (a), and fabricated inchworm like soft robot actuated by a single pneumatic line at detailed view (b), respectively.

3 Results and Discussion

3.1 Operational Frequency

The velocity of the robot is varied by the injection and emission time. We identified that the balloons were not inflated sufficiently, in the case of a short injection and emission times less than 0.4 s. For this reason, the locomotion is unlikely to occur because the robot is not able to form the supports. Therefore, it is worth to noting that the injection and emission times of 0.4 s are the threshold that determines whether the robot can generate locomotion. With this in mind, we varied the injection and emission times ranging from 0.4 s to 0.7 s, with steps of 0.1 s. Overall, as the injection and emission times increase, the velocity of the robot decreases (see Fig. 7). The velocity of the robot is up to 1.6 mm/s (std. 0.15) when both the injection and emission times are 0.4 s. However, the velocity of the robot reduces down to 0.4 mm/s, when the injection and emission times are larger than 0.7 s.

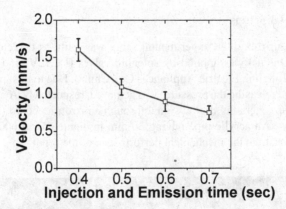

Fig. 7. The relationship of the velocity of the robot versus injection and emission times, ranging from 0.4 to 0.7 s, with steps of 0.1 s.

3.2 The Velocity of the Robot Versus the Presence of the Suction Cup

The presence of the suction cup improved the mechanical performance of the robot, when it maneuvered at inclined track. Indeed, as shown in Fig. 8., the robot with and without suction cup showed the same performance (R: 0.51 mm/s, RwS: 0.5 mm/s) at the normal (slope = 0°) track. The robot without suction cup did not maneuver at the inclined track (more than 15°), while the robot with suction maneuvered when the slop reached to 20°.

More specifically, as plotted in Fig. 9., the velocity of the robot with suction cup decreased down to 0.2 mm/s, as the slope increased. When the slope is at 10°, the difference of the mean velocities between the robot with and without suction cup was 0.2 mm/s, and it is noted that the presence of the suction cup significantly influences to the velocity of the robot when it maneuvers at inclined track.

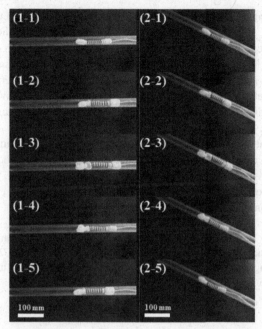

Fig. 8. Sequential photographs showing inchworm like locomotion with steps of 0.2 s. (1–1) to (1–5) and (2–1) to (2–5) show the locomotion when the slop is at 0° and at 20°, respectively.

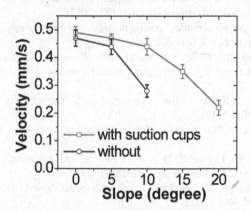

Fig. 9. The relationship of the velocity of the robot versus different slope angle from 0 to 20°, with steps of 5° (pink and bule colored line indicate the robot with and without suction cup, respectively).

4 Conclusion

This work highlights that the inchworm like soft robot is capable of a fast locomotion at 1.6 mm/s when the injection and emission times are 0.4 s. The sizes (in diameter) of two holes were selected to 0.6 mm (A_r at the rear clamping balloon) and 1.2 mm (A_f

at the front clamping balloon), respectively. This difference between two areas induces different velocities, making the airflow to gradually propagate from the rear to the front. Overall, the robot can perform inchworm like locomotion. Compared to our previous studies [18, 19], it is worth noting that the robot allows for highly safe and compliant interaction with environment due to the constitutive hyperelastic material. Moreover, the suction cups integrated at both the rear and front clamping balloons avoid slippages that could possibly occur during movement while allowing the robot to maneuver at inclined track that the gravity fluences.

We envision that this preliminary work lays a groundwork for optimization, allowing the robot to maneuver at different environments (i.e., not only rigid bodied pipe, but also soft bodied pipe having much complex track) with fast velocity. Also, it will be possible to develop and incorporate a steering mechanism so that the robot can achieve better mechanical functionalities.

Acknowledgement. This work has supported by the National Research Foundation of Korea(NRF) grant funded by the Korea government(MSIT) (No. 2021R1A2C2010903) and BK21 FOUR program through the National Research Foundation of Korea (NRF) funded by the Korean government (grant number: 5199990714521).

References

1. Laschi, C., Cianchetti, M., Mazzolai, B., Margheri, L., Follador, M., Dario, P.: Soft robot arm inspired by the octopus. Adv. Robot. **26**, 709–727 (2012)
2. Zhang, J., et al.: A preprogrammable continuum robot inspired by elephant trunk for dexterous manipulation. Soft Robot. **3**, 636–646 (2023)
3. Crooks, W., Vukasin, G., O'Sullivan, M., Messner, W., Rogers, C.: Fin ray® effect inspired soft robotic gripper: from the robosoft grand challenge toward optimization. Front. Robot. AI **3**, 70 (2016)
4. Chubb, K., Berry, D., Burke, T.: Towards an ontology for soft robots: what is soft? Bioinspir. Biomim. **14**, 063001 (2019)
5. Rus, D., Tolley, M.T.: Design, fabrication and control of soft robots. Nature **521**, 467–475 (2015)
6. Coyle, S., Majidi, C., LeDuc, P., Hsia, K.J.: Bio-inspired soft robotics: material selection, actuation, and design. Extreme Mech. Lett. **22**, 51–59 (2018)
7. Yang, Y., He, Z., Jiao, P., Ren, H.: Bioinspired soft robotics: how do we learn from creatures? IEEE Rev. Biomed. Eng. (2022)
8. Yamamoto, T., Konyo, M., Tadakuma, K., Tadokoro, S.: High-speed sliding-inchworm motion mechanism with expansion-type pneumatic hollow-shaft actuators for in-pipe inspections. Mechatronics **56**, 101–114 (2018)
9. Plaut, R.H.: Mathematical model of inchworm locomotion. Int. J. Non-Linear Mech. **76**, 56–63 (2015)
10. Gao, J., Yan, G.: Locomotion analysis of an inchworm-like capsule robot in the intestinal tract. IEEE Trans. Biomed. Eng. **63**, 300–310 (2015)
11. Lee, D., Kim, S., Park, Y.-L., Wood, R.J.: 2011 IEEE International Conference on Robotics and Automation, pp. 3197–3204 (IEEE)
12. Wang, X., Meng, M.Q.-h.: 2006 IEEE/RSJ International Conference on Intelligent Robots and Systems, pp. 1267–1272 (IEEE)

13. Duggan, T., Horowitz, L., Ulug, A., Baker, E., Petersen, K.: 2019 2nd IEEE International Conference on Soft Robotics (RoboSoft), pp. 200–205 (IEEE)
14. Wang, W., Lee, J.-Y., Rodrigue, H., Song, S.-H., Chu, W.-S., Ahn, S.-H.: Locomotion of inchworm-inspired robot made of smart soft composite (SSC). Bioinspir. Biomim. **9**, 046006 (2014)
15. Xie, R., Su, M., Zhang, Y., Li, M., Zhu, H., Guan, Y.: 2018 IEEE International Conference on Robotics and Automation (ICRA), pp. 3448–3453 (IEEE)
16. Joyee, E.B., Pan, Y.: A fully three-dimensional printed inchworm-inspired soft robot with magnetic actuation. Soft Rob. **6**, 333–345 (2019)
17. Menciassi, A., Gorini, S., Pernorio, G., Dario, P.: IEEE International Conference on Robotics and Automation, Proceedings. ICRA'04, pp. 3282–3287. IEEE (2004)
18. Lim, J., Park, H., Moon, S., Kim, B.: 2007 IEEE International Conference on Robotics and Biomimetics (ROBIO), pp. 330–335. IEEE (2007)
19. Lim, J., Park, H., An, J., Hong, Y.-S., Kim, B., Yi, B.-J.: One pneumatic line based inchworm-like micro robot for half-inch pipe inspection. Mechatronics **18**, 315–322 (2008)
20. Thanh-Vinh, N., Takahashi, H., Kan, T., Noda, K., Matsumoto, K., Shimoyama, I.: 2011 IEEE 24th International Conference on Micro Electro Mechanical Systems, pp. 284–287. IEEE (2011)

A Synthetic Nervous System for on and Off Motion Detection Inspired by the *Drosophila melanogaster* Optic Lobe

William R. P. Nourse[1]([✉]) [iD], Nicholas S. Szczecinski[2][iD], and Roger D. Quinn[3][iD]

[1] Department of Electrical, Computer, and Systems Engineering,
Case Western Reserve University, Cleveland, OH 44106, USA
nourse@case.edu
[2] Department of Mechanical and Aerospace Engineering, West Virginia University,
Morgantown, WV 26506, USA
[3] Department of Mechanical and Aerospace Engineering, Case Western Reserve
University, Cleveland, OH 44106, USA

Abstract. In this work, we design and simulate a synthetic nervous system which is capable of computing optic flow throughout a visual field, inspired by recent advances in the neural anatomy of *Drosophila melanogaster* found through connectomics. We present methods for tuning the network for desired stimuli, and benchmark its temporal properties and capability for directional selectivity. This network acts as a stepping point towards visual locomotion control in a hexapod robot inspired by the anatomy of *Drosophila*.

Keywords: Motion Vision · Optic Flow · Synthetic Nervous System

1 Introduction

A continuing goal in the robotics community is to develop robots with the dynamic capabilities and resilience of animals. A particular focus is on adding the influence of visual information to improve the adaptability of robotic systems [4,37]. A promising approach is to design robotic controllers using neuromorphic networks of neurons with biologically inspired dynamics [3], also known as synthetic nervous systems (SNS) [13,18,31].

Much is known about the circuitry within the *Drosophila melanogaster* optic lobe, making it a convenient inspiration for robotic vision systems. For visual motion processing in particular, the *Drosophila* nervous system contains many of the same logical elements as that of mammals and vertebrates [8], but does so with three orders of magnitude fewer neurons in the visual system [6,22]. An

This work was funded by National Science Foundation (NSF) RI 1704436, as well as by NSF DBI 2015317 as part of the NSF/CIHR/DFG/FRQ/UKRI-MRC Next Generation Networks for Neuroscience Program.

F. Meder et al. (Eds.): Living Machines 2023, LNAI 14157, pp. 364–380, 2023.
https://doi.org/10.1007/978-3-031-38857-6_27

additional advantage of *Drosophila* over other model organisms is that extensive work has been done in recent years to create a full connectome of their brains [26, 36], and the visual system in particular has been extensively studied [28, 29, 33].

The motion vision pathway is extremely important for adaptive behavior in *Drosophila*, aiding in estimation of body motion and enabling rapid response to oncoming threats [1, 9, 12]. The structure is well documented, see Fig. 1 for a visual representation and refer to [6] for a more thorough review. Within the *Drosophila* optic lobe, retinal and lamina cells convert changes in light intensity into information used in the rest of the network. Of particular relevance to the motion vision system are cells L1-L3, which perform spatiotemporal filtering of input stimuli and separate information flow into two pathways: an On pathway for encoding increases in brightness, and an Off pathway for encoding decreases in brightness [28, 33]. From there, the transformed visual information is further filtered in the medulla into a bank of unique filters (Mi1, Tm3, Mi4, Mi9 for the On pathway; Tm1, Tm2, Tm4, Tm9 for the Off pathway), each with slightly different spatiotemporal characteristics [2, 11]. These are then combined nonlinearly (along with the wide amacrine cell CT1 [24]) onto the elementary motion detector (EMD) cells T4 and T5, and the resulting combination generates directional selectivity for each point in the visual field [29] which can then be spatially integrated for more complex behavior [6].

Previous work has adapted this circuitry to robotics [4] and SNS networks [27], but these studies were performed before the wide breadth and depth of connectivity information from connectomic analysis for *Drosophila* became available. In this work, we design an SNS network which measures optic flow for both rising and falling brightness levels, using inspiration from the current body of knowledge about connectivity and activity within the *Drosophila* optic lobe [6, 29]. As there is less known about the exact operation of the Off EMD, we make some design-based decisions in its construction. Using the capabilities of this network, we plan future visual control of motion onboard the bio-inspired robot *Drosophibot* [13].

2   Network Components

2.1   Neural and Synaptic Models

As this work is primarily focused on designing general network behavior instead of exactly reproducing neural recordings, all neurons in the network are simulated as non-spiking leaky integrators following [31], where the neural state U is updated as

$$\tau \cdot \dot{U} = -U + S + B + I, \tag{1}$$

where τ is the neural time constant, I is any external input, and B is a constant bias term. S is the synaptic input from any presynaptic neurons in the network,

$$S = \sum_{n}^{N} G_{syn,n}\left(U_n\right) \cdot \left(E_{syn,n} - U\right), \tag{2}$$

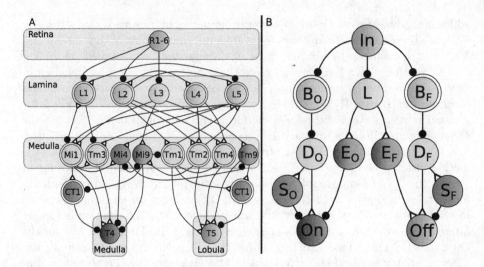

Fig. 1. A: A circuit diagram of a single column within the *Drosophila* motion vision pathway, adapted from [6,29]. **B:** Reduced diagram used in this work. Node colors in both diagrams are chosen to highlight their common functional roles. Single circles designate neurons which behave as a low-pass filter, double circles indicate a band-pass filter. Dark closed circles indicate inhibitory synapses, open triangles indicate excitatory synapses. In panel **B**, D and S neurons approximate band-pass behavior by filtering the responses of the B neurons, for reduced computational complexity.

with U_n denoting a presynaptic neuron, and $E_{syn,n}$ denoting the synaptic reversal potential. In this work, all excitatory synapses have $E_{ex} = 5R$, $E_{in} = -2R$ for inhibitory synapses, and specific modulatory synapses have a reversal potential of $E_{mod} = -0.1R$, where R is the primary range of neural activity in the network. For numerical simplicity, $R = 1$ in this work so that most neurons communicate when their state is between 0 and 1, with the exception of the synapse between neurons B_F and D_F. E_{ex} has an effect roughly analogous to cholinergic synapses in *Drosophila*, E_{in} to GABAergic synapses, and E_{mod} to glutamatergic synapses. $G_{syn,n}(U_n)$ is a monotonic function which describes the incoming synaptic conductance such that $G_{syn,n}(U_n) \in [0, g_{max,n}]$ where $g_{max,n}$ is the upper bound. In this work, we define G_{syn} as

$$G_{syn,n} = g_{max,n} \cdot max\left(0, min\left(\frac{U_n - \theta_{lo}}{\theta_{hi} - \theta_{lo}}, 1\right)\right), \qquad (3)$$

where θ_{lo} and θ_{hi} are the lower and upper threshold states of synaptic activity. For most synapses in the network, we set $\theta_{lo} = 0$, and $\theta_{hi} = R$. For the synapse between neurons B_F and D_F, we set $\theta_{lo} = R$, and $\theta_{hi} = 2R$.

Steady State Formulation. For some design sections, we required solving for the steady state of the neuron given steady inputs. As in [31], the steady-state response U^* is

$$U^* = \frac{\sum_n^N g_{max,n} \frac{U_n^*}{R} \cdot E_{syn,n} + B + I}{1 + \sum_n^N g_{max,n} \frac{U_n^*}{R}}. \tag{4}$$

Synaptic Pathway Designs. When connecting components of our network, different pathways are tuned analytically based on their functional role. One common example is signal transmission, where the desired steady-state value (see Eq. 4) of the postsynaptic neuron U^* is the steady-state voltage of the presynaptic neuron multiplied by a transmission gain K. From [31], this can be solved as

$$g_{max} = \frac{K \cdot R}{E_{syn} - K \cdot R}, \tag{5}$$

where E_{syn} is E_{ex} for excitatory synapses, and E_{in} for inhibitory synapses.

Another formulation which is used throughout this work comes from setting a target state T of the postsynaptic neuron, given a presynaptic steady-state and the presence of other external or synaptic currents to the postsynaptic neuron. This is derived from Eq. 4 and written as

$$g_{max} = \frac{R \cdot (B - T)}{U_{pre}^* \cdot (T - E_{syn})}. \tag{6}$$

Finally, in some instances it is desirable for a presynaptic neuron to modulate the sensitivity of a postsynaptic neuron to external and synaptic inputs. For this we follow the derivation in [31], and use the modulatory reversal potential E_{mod} and set the synaptic conductance as

$$g_{max} = \delta - 1, \tag{7}$$

where the desired behavior is such that U^* is divided by δ when $U_{pre}^* = R$. This form of synapse is used within the On pathway between E_O and On.

2.2 Neural Filters

Most neurons within the *Drosophila* motion vision pathway behave temporally as either low or band-pass filters [6], and here we describe our methodology in designing our network to behave accordingly. The process to tune our neurons as low-pass filters is straightforward, as the leaky integrator is itself a low-pass filter with a cutoff frequency (where the gain is -3dB) defined as $f_c = \frac{1}{2\pi\tau}$.

Common methods for implementing a neuron with band-pass temporal behavior typically involve adding a second dynamic variable to the neuron model [19], such as a voltage-gated ion channel [30] or adaptive spiking threshold [32,34]. Inspired by the differentiation network in [31], we implement band-pass filters in our network using a subnetwork of four non-spiking leaky integrators instead of adding a new, more complex neural model. While this adds more neurons to the network, we do this to reduce the computational complexity of our system in anticipation of running it on embedded hardware. For a visual representation, please see Fig. 2.

A   B

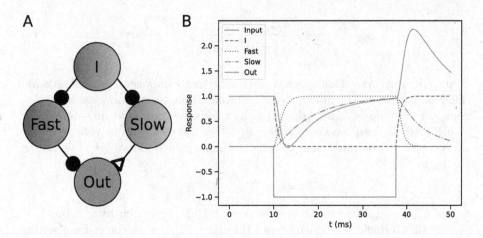

Fig. 2. A: Circuit diagram of a band-pass subnetwork. Two neurons are tuned as low-pass filters with different cutoff frequencies, and are subtracted to produce a band-pass response. **B:** Response of each neuron within the subnetwork when subjected to a time-varying input.

This network is designed as follows. Inputs to the subnetwork enter as a synaptic input for neuron I, which then inhibits neurons $Fast$ and $Slow$ using inhibitory transmission synapses (Eq. 5) with reversal potential E_{in} and a gain $K = -1$, to arrive at a maximum synaptic conductance of

$$g_{max,i,fast} = g_{max,i,slow} = -\frac{R}{E_{in}}. \tag{8}$$

Neurons I, $Slow$, and output neuron Out all have the same time constant, which approximately acts as the upper bound of the filter's passband. Neuron $Fast$ has a larger time constant and lower cutoff frequency than the other neurons, and the corresponding cutoff frequency results in setting the lower bound of the passband. Neuron $Fast$ inhibits neuron Out with a gain-controlled inhibitory synapse (Eq. 5), and neuron $Slow$ excites Out with a synapse designed to mirror $g_{max,fast,out}$, where

$$g_{max,slow,out} = \frac{g_{max,fast,out} \cdot (E_{in} - R)}{R - E_{ex}}. \tag{9}$$

This results in the state of neuron Out being the difference between the original signal in I being processed via two different low-pass filters, resulting in a band-pass effect. In practice, the value of the transmission gain K from $Fast$ to Out is found using the Brent method for scalar minimization [7] in SciPy [35] such that the change in magnitude during a step input is -1. All neurons in this subnetwork additionally have a constant bias input of R, since the bandpass filters in our network need to hyperpolarize during rising luminance levels, but omitting these bias terms and swapping the inhibitory and excitatory synapses would result in a more traditional band-pass filter [31].

3   Network Design

For a circuit diagram of the network described in this section, as well as the comparative structure present in the *Drosophila* optic lobe, please refer to Fig. 1. All synaptic parameter values can be found in Table 1, and all neural parameter values can be found in Table 2.

3.1   Input Processing

When presented with a visual stimulus, each input node (denoted In in Fig. 1B) acts as a temporal low-pass filter, performing an analogous operation to a *Drosophila* photoreceptor cell [8]. As this initial stage sets an upper bound on the frequency response for the rest of the circuit, we set the time constant for this filter τ_{fast} such that no frequencies in our desired input range are filtered out and our network dynamics remain stable. In this work, we set this as $\tau_{fast} = 10 \cdot \Delta t$ based on our simulation timestep Δt.

3.2   Initial Filter Stage

Similar to the cells present in the *Drosophila* lamina, we apply temporal filters to the output of the initial input filtering stage. While the primary lamina cells in the *Drosophila* motion pathway have slight differences in temporal behavior [11], for analytic simplicity both B_O and B_F have the same properties in this work. For reduced analytic complexity, all spatial receptive fields are condensed into single columns.

We apply a band-pass filter which hyperpolarizes to stimuli of increasing brightness within each pathway to the output of the input stage, analogous to the behavior of the L1 and L2 cells [6], and we refer to them as B_O and B_F. These are constructed in the manner described in Sect. 2.2, and the time constant of the fast side is set to τ_{fast}. For the slow side, we choose τ_{slow} so that for the fastest input stimulus, the response has time to settle to baseline over the course of a single input period. Approximating the settling period for a leaky integrator as 5τ, we write the time constraint as

$$5\tau_{slow} = \frac{\lambda}{2} \cdot \frac{1}{V_{fast}}, \tag{10}$$

where λ is the spatial wavelength and V_{fast} is the fastest spatial velocity of the input stimulus.

Similar to the L3 neuron in *Drosophila* [6], we include an additional low-pass filter (denoted as L in Fig. 1B) which is shared across both the On and Off pathways. In order to preserve the range of temporal information available for later processing, we set the time constant of L to τ_{fast}, causing this node to act as a delayed and inverted copy of the input stimulus.

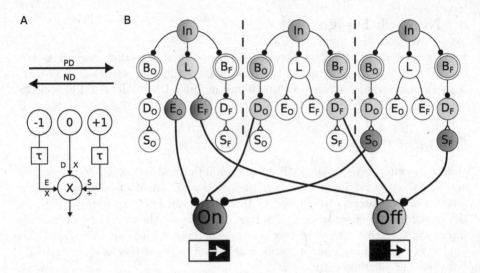

Fig. 3. A: Diagram of a three-arm Haag-Borst HR/BL EMD circuit [15]. **B:** Schematic of the three-arm motion detectors in this work, for both On and Off stimuli. PD denotes the preferred direction, ND denotes the not preferred (null) direction. Nodes without color do not contribute to behavior in this direction of motion.

3.3   Motion Detectors

For the design of the elementary motion detectors (EMD) in the On and Off pathways, we take inspiration from the Haag-Borst HR/BL three-arm EMD [15] (Fig. 3A). This structure has been shown to be capable of reproducing recordings from T4 [15] and T5 [16] cells, and connectomic analysis has found candidate cells for each input arm of the model [29]. In this model, the output neuron of each EMD (*On* for the On pathway, *Off* for the off pathway) receives input from three separate elements: a direct input from the cell in the same column, an enhancement input which enhances stimuli coming from the preferred direction, and a suppressor input which suppresses stimuli coming from the null direction. In this work we choose to model the EMD as a three-arm circuit instead of older models which used two arms to achieve either preferred-direction enhancement [17] or null-direction suppression [5], as the three-arm model generates finer directional selectivity and is less susceptible to noise [15].

In *Drosophila* the inputs in each arm can come from multiple neurons, which combine to create varied spatio-temporal properties [2,6,11]. For simplified analysis and reduced computational complexity, each arm is represented as a single neuron in this work. Additionally, while the cells in the medulla act as band-pass and low-pass filters with a variety of time constants, for simplicity we represent all of them as low-pass filters and reshape the activity from the higher-level filters (B_O, B_F, and L). In this work, neurons which perform enhancement are named E, direct stimulation D, and suppression S. Unless otherwise specified, all neurons can be assumed to have a time constant of τ_{fast}. This is only changed as needed for behavioral reasons, which will be explained below.

On Pathway. Recent studies have focused on the behavior of T4 cells and found potential mechanisms which generate motion-detection and direction selectivity using the cells which contribute to the On pathway [29], particularly in the work of Groschner et al. [14]. In their work, they modeled the T4 pathway and found that multiplicative behavior can occur during a period of low inhibition that creates a "window of opportunity" [10]. We adapt a similar mechanism here based on our previous work [31], with a circuit diagram in Fig. 3B and behavior shown in Fig. 4. Neuron D_O mimics the behavior of Mi1 and Tm3, S_O the response of CT1, and E_O is analogous to Mi9.

Direct: Neuron D_O receives input from B_O via an inhibitory transmission synapse (Eq. 5), and the gain is tuned via Brent's method [7] such that the peak during a step input is 1. It excites On with an excitatory transmission synapse, with the gain tuned again via Brent's method for an isolated peak response of 1.

Suppression: Unlike the other arms of the On EMD, S_O receives input from D_O instead of the filtering stage. This is similar to CT1 receiving indirect input from Mi1 [24,29]. This creates a slight delay in the response, which improves the ability of S_O to suppress stimuli in the null direction. The connection between S_O and On is tuned as an inhibitory target synapse (Eq. 6) which aims to bring the state of On to zero when D_O is signaling with peak strength.

Enhancement: In our model, E_O is responsible for the majority of the stimulus-dependent behavior of the On EMD. Starting with the temporal response, we set the neural time constant so that the state of E_O settles during the time it takes the signal to travel from one column to the next at the slowest desired velocity V_{slow}, assuming that the neuron settles after a time period of 5τ (Eq. 10). This is found with

$$\tau_E = \frac{\angle}{5 \cdot V_{slow}}, \tag{11}$$

where $\angle$ is the spatial resolution of the model (5° in this work). E_O stimulates On using a modulatory synapse with a division factor δ of 10 (Eq. 7), and is stimulated by L using an excitatory transmission synapse (Eq. 5) with unity gain.

Off Pathway. While studies have found the presynaptic neurons which generate direction selectivity within the Off motion detector circuit [24,29], current studies which model the Off pathway either omit the role of CT1 in suppression [20] or do not model chemical reversal potentials [21]. As such, we make some base assumptions based on the connectivity in order to produce direction selectivity. Neuron D_F implements the role of Tm1, Tm2, and Tm4, S_F is analogous to CT1, and E_F mimics Tm9.

Direct: D_F receives stimulation from B_F via an excitatory transmission synapse (Eq. 5) with a gain tuned such that the postsynaptic peak is 1 for a decreasing step response in brightness, and θ_{lo} and θ_{hi} of R and $2R$ respectively. It stimulates *Off* with an excitatory target synapse of target R (Eq. 6), with the conductance multiplied by ρ_D, where ρ_D is the percentage of direct stimulation. In this work, $\rho_D = 0.5$. We found that the peak of D_F is a primary factor in the magnitude of *Off*, so we select the time constant τ_{DF} so that the peak magnitude starts decreasing at our slowest input velocity V_{slow}. We first find the frequency of our slowest input as $f_{slow} = \frac{V_{slow}}{\lambda}$, and scale that to get $f_{DF} = 10f_{slow}$. A scaling factor of 10 is chosen because the gain of leaky integrators begins to decrease approximately 1 decade below the cutoff frequency on a logarithmic scale.

Suppression: S_F is tuned in a similar manner to S_O, receiving an excitatory transmission (Eq. 5) input from D_F that is optimized using Brent's method [7] for a peak magnitude of 1. S_F inhibits *Off* via an inhibitory target synapse with the same properties as the synapse between S_O and *On*.

Enhancement: E_F is tuned with the exact input and neural properties of E_O for simplicity. It stimulates *Off* with an excitatory target synapse (Eq. 6) with target R, and the conductance scaled by ρ_E where ρ_E is the percentage of enhancement stimulation and is constrained so $\rho_E + \rho_D = 1$.

4   Results

4.1   Simulation Setup

All simulations are done using SNS-Toolbox [25], a Python package for designing and simulating synthetic nervous systems (https://github.com/wnourse05/SNS-Toolbox). A Δt of 0.1 ms is used as the simulation step. In all simulations, the network was tuned for sensitivity to images with a spatial wavelength λ of 30° and a velocity between 10°/s and 180°/s across the visual field. Code to simulate the network and generate all of the figures presented here is available at https://github.com/wnourse05/Motion-Vision-SNS.

4.2   Individual EMD Stimulation

To verify the basic behavior of the EMD circuits, we applied square wave gratings with a spatial wavelength of 30° and a velocity of 30°/s to 3 adjacent columns. We focus on the behavior of the B channel neurons, which are tuned for sensitivity in motion traveling from left to right.

Shown in Fig. 4, we examine the behavior of the On pathway. When stimuli of increasing brightness move across in the preferred direction, E_O receives the stimulus change first and starts to hyperpolarize. In the time it takes for the stimulus to continue to the central column, E_O has decreased. This allows the

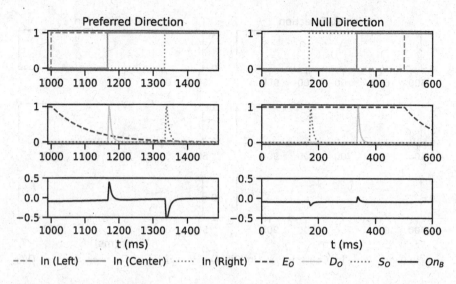

Fig. 4. Simulation of elements within the On pathway during a stimulus moving in the preferred (*Left*) or null (*Right*) directions. Dashed green traces correspond to Enhancement (E_O) signals, solid blue to Direct (D_O) signals, dotted pink to Suppression (S_O) signals, and solid indigo for the On EMD (On_B). *Top:* Traces of visual stimuli to the Enhancement, Direct, and Suppression columns of the motion detector; *Middle:* Traces of the Enhancement, Direct, and Suppression neurons which are presynaptic to the EMD neuron; *Bottom:* Trace of the final motion detector, which depolarizes for stimuli traveling from left to right (On_B).

direct stimulus from D_O to excite On with reduced inhibition. As the stimulus continues to the right column, S_O exhibits a bout of further inhibition. The timing relationship between E_O and S_O creates the speed-dependent behavior; as stimuli move more rapidly, the offset in time between these columns decreases and more inhibition is applied to On, causing a decrease in the activity caused by D_O. When stimuli move in the opposite direction, S_O and D_O are both activated while E_O is strongly depolarized, resulting in a significant reduction of peak magnitude in On.

Repeating the experiment for stimuli with decreasing brightness, as the off-edge stimulus moves in the preferred direction E_F in the Off pathway begins to depolarize. This is accentuated by a later pulse from D_F, followed by strong inhibition from S_F. As stimuli move in the opposite direction, E_F is either at rest or hyperpolarizing towards rest, depending on the timing of prior stimuli. The off-edge first arrives at S_F which strongly inhibits *Off*, followed by a pulse in excitation from D_F and then a separate increase in excitation from E_F. While the specifics of the mechanism are different between the On and Off pathways, the net behavioral result is the same: stimuli traveling in the preferred direction are enhanced to some degree, while stimuli in the opposite direction do not have as strong a response (Fig. 5).

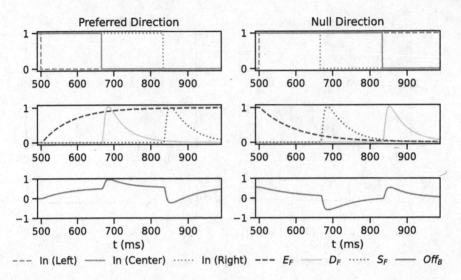

Fig. 5. Simulation of elements within the Off pathway during a stimulus moving in the preferred (*Left*) or null (*Right*) directions. Dashed green traces correspond to Enhancement. (E_F) signals, solid blue to Direct (D_F) signals, dotted pink to Suppression (S_F) signals, and solid olive for the Off EMD (*Off*$_B$). For further description refer to Fig. 4.

4.3 Velocity Response

Square-wave stimuli with $\lambda = 30°$ are applied to a network which consisted of 49 columns, arranged in a 7×7 grid. The velocity of stimuli is varied from $10°/s$ to $360°/s$, and data is recorded from the central EMD. As shown in Fig. 6, the peak magnitude of both the On and Off pathways decreases as the velocity approaches the maximum tuning range ($180°/s$). The On pathway has a high dynamic range, varying smoothly from 1 to near zero, and with peaks in the preferred direction always greater than the null direction. Changes in the magnitude of the Off pathway are more gradual as it approaches the desired maximum velocity, with a slow increase slightly before this point. The ratio between the preferred and null directions is always greater than 1, but to a lesser degree in the Off than the On pathway. Behavior in the *Drosophila* T4 and T5 cells are more similar to the On results shown in Fig. 6 than the Off results, with a peak response that decreases as the input velocity increases [23]. However, in *Drosophila* this decrease occurs as input velocity is both increased and decreased from a peak velocity.

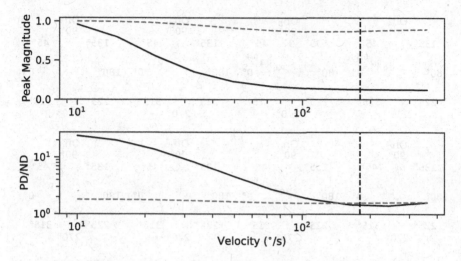

Fig. 6. Output behavior of the On (solid indigo) and Off (dashed olive) motion detectors when subjected to a square wave, translating from 10° to 360° per second. Target maximum velocity (180°/s) shown with a vertical dashed line. *Top:* Peak magnitude of the motion detector in the preferred direction; *Bottom:* Ratio between the motion detector in the preferred direction and the null direction.

4.4 Directional Selectivity

Stimuli of a consistent wavelength and velocity are applied to the same network described in Sect. 4.3 while the direction of travel is varied from 0° − 360° in 45° increments, with results shown in Fig. 7. The EMD for each cardinal direction exhibits enhanced sensitivity to stimuli in the preferred direction, and reduced sensitivity to the other directions. The On pathway is able to generate a finer level of directional sensitivity than the Off pathway, due to its multiplicative window of reduced inhibition. Further work is necessary to find a similar multiplication mechanism for the Off pathway.

As the networks for each cardinal direction are mirrored versions of each other, the resulting responses are identical except for their orientation. This is different than the tuning found in *Drosophila*, where the sensitivity of each cardinal direction is slightly different [23]. The general shape of our *On* and *Off* responses most closely matches the behavior of the T4b and T5b neurons in the animal, consisting of a sharp triangular point in the preferred direction and a slight bump in the null direction, however T5b is much more similar to T4b than our *Off* neurons are to the *On* neurons.

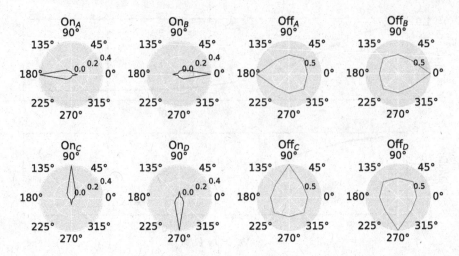

Fig. 7. Peak response of each motion detector in the On (*Left*) and Off (*Right*) pathways to a square wave grating with $\lambda = 30°$ and $V = 30°/s$. Preferred direction of each sub-type: *A*: right to left; *B*: left to right *C*: bottom to top; *D*: top to bottom.

5   Discussion and Future Work

In this work, we implement an SNS network which is a reduced model of the *Drosophila* motion vision system. The network performs optic flow measurement at each point in the visual field, and can be tuned for different ranges of input stimuli in a parametric manner. While some parameters are found via numerical optimization, most are chosen by hand via analytic rules. With further optimization, we expect that the performance of the network could be tuned to detect particular stimuli.

Compared to the circuit found in *Drosophila*, the model presented here is far reduced in complexity. In particular, the animal uses more neurons as inputs to the EMD cells, which allows for better temporal response and additional adaptation to factors such as changing input contrast [11]. Adding more neurons into the motion detection area in our network may be promising for future development. Another simplification in our model is that the initial filter stage only receives visual input within its own column. This is not the case for the lamina neurons in *Drosophila*, which perform spatial filtering over a $15° - 20°$ radius for each column [6]. Future work will extend our analysis to generate directional selectivity in the presence of wider spatial receptive fields.

While our implementation of the On pathway is derived from detailed biological models [14], less recordings and detail were available for the Off pathway. Our model attempts to model direction selectivity using current information about the structure of this system, but showcases some current gaps in understanding. In particular, the neuron in our model which is intended to act analogously to

Tm9 (E_F) does not provide a significant role in motion detection based on its connectivity. This differs strongly from biological experiments, where the effect of Tm9 in Off motion detection is greater than many of the other neurons combined [28]. As such Tm9 may have additional functionality and roles, as discussed in [29].

Much work has been done to study the effect of the visual system on walking control in *Drosophila* [9,12]. We aim to continue development of the network described in this work, so that it may be used to assist in the control of legged motion onboard our *Drosophila*-inspired robot, *Drosophibot* [13].

Table 1. Synapse Parameter Values.

Synapse	g_{max}	E_{syn}	θ_{lo}	θ_{hi}
$In \to B_{O,I}$	0.5	−2.0	0.0	1.0
$In \to B_{F,I}$	0.5	−2.0	0.0	1.0
$In \to L$	0.5	−2.0	0.0	1.0
$B_{O,I} \to B_{O,Fast}$	0.5	−2.0	0.0	1.0
$B_{O,I} \to B_{O,Slow}$	0.5	−2.0	0.0	1.0
$B_{O,Fast} \to B_{O,Out}$	1.329*	−2.0	0.0	1.0
$B_{O,Slow} \to B_{O,Out}$	0.997	5.0	0.0	1.0
$B_{F,I} \to B_{F,Fast}$	0.5	−2.0	0.0	1.0
$B_{F,I} \to B_{F,Slow}$	0.5	−2.0	0.0	1.0
$B_{F,Fast} \to B_{F,Out}$	1.329*	−2.0	0.0	1.0
$B_{F,Slow} \to B_{F,Out}$	0.997	5.0	0.0	1.0
$L \to E_O$	0.25	5.0	0.0	1.0
$L \to E_F$	0.25	5.0	0.0	1.0
$B_{O,Out} \to D_O$	0.546*	−2.0	0.0	1.0
$B_{F,Out} \to D_F$	1.173*	5.0	1.0	2.0
$D_O \to S_O$	0.262*	5.0	0.0	1.0
$D_F \to S_F$	0.250*	5.0	0.0	1.0
$E_O \to On$	9.0	−0.1	0,0	1.0
$D_O \to On$	0.262*	5.0	0.0	1.0
$S_O \to On$	0.5	−2.0	0.0	1.0
$E_F \to Off$	0.125	5.0	0.0	1.0
$D_F \to Off$	0.125	5.0	0.0	1.0
$S_F \to Off$	0.5	−2.0	0.0	1.0

*Found using optimization

Table 2. Neuron Parameter Values.

Name	τ (ms)	B	U_0
In	1.0	0.0	0.0
$B_{O,In}$	0.796	1.0	1.0
$B_{O,Fast}$	1.0	1.0	0.0
$B_{O,Slow}$	8.334	1.0	0.0
$B_{O,Out}$	0.796	1.0	1.0
$B_{F,In}$	0.796	1.0	1.0
$B_{F,Fast}$	1.0	1.0	0.0
$B_{F,Slow}$	8.334	1.0	0.0
$B_{F,Out}$	0.796	1.0	1.0
L	1.0	1.0	1.0
E_O	100.0	0.0	1.0
E_F	100.0	0.0	1.0
D_O	1.0	1.092*	0.0
D_F	47.746	0.0	0.0
S_O	1.0	0.0	0.0
S_F	1.0	0.0	0.0
On	1.0	0.0	0.0
L	1.0	0.0	0.0

*Found using optimization

References

1. Ache, J.M., et al.: Neural basis for looming size and velocity encoding in the Drosophila giant fiber escape pathway. Curr. Biol. **29**, 1073–1081.e4 (2019). https://doi.org/10.1016/j.cub.2019.01.079
2. Arenz, A., Drews, M.S., Richter, F.G., Ammer, G., Borst, A.: The temporal tuning of the Drosophila motion detectors is determined by the dynamics of their input elements. Curr. Biol. **27**, 929–944 (2017). https://doi.org/10.1016/j.cub.2017.01.051
3. Ayers, J., Witting, J.: Biomimetic approaches to the control of underwater walking machines. Philos. Trans. R. Soc. A: Math. Phys. Eng. Sci. **365**(1850), 273–295 (2007)
4. Bagheri, Z.M., Wiederman, S.D., Cazzolato, B.S., Grainger, S., O'Carroll, D.C.: Performance of an insect-inspired target tracker in natural conditions. Bioinspiration Biomimetics **12** (2017). https://doi.org/10.1088/1748-3190/aa5b48
5. Barlow, H., Levick, W.R.: The mechanism of directionally selective units in rabbit's retina. J. Physiol. **178**(3), 477 (1965)
6. Borst, A., Drews, M., Meier, M.: The neural network behind the eyes of a fly (2020). https://doi.org/10.1016/j.cophys.2020.05.004
7. Brent, R.P.: Algorithms for Minimization Without Derivatives. Courier Corporation (2013)

8. Clark, D.A., Demb, J.B.: Parallel computations in insect and mammalian visual motion processing (2016). https://doi.org/10.1016/j.cub.2016.08.003
9. Creamer, M.S., Mano, O., Clark, D.A.: Visual control of walking speed in Drosophila. Neuron **100**, 1460–1473.e6 (2018). https://doi.org/10.1016/j.neuron.2018.10.028
10. Denève, S., Machens, C.K.: Efficient codes and balanced networks (2016). https://doi.org/10.1038/nn.4243
11. Drews, M.S., et al.: Dynamic signal compression for robust motion vision in flies. Curr. Biol. **30**, 209–221.e8 (2020). https://doi.org/10.1016/j.cub.2019.10.035
12. Fujiwara, T., Brotas, M., Chiappe, M.E.: Walking strides direct rapid and flexible recruitment of visual circuits for course control in Drosophila. Neuron **110**, 2124–2138.e8 (2022). https://doi.org/10.1016/j.neuron.2022.04.008
13. Goldsmith, C.A., Szczecinski, N.S., Quinn, R.D.: Neurodynamic modeling of the fruit fly Drosophila melanogaster. Bioinspiration Biomimetics **15**, 065003 (2020)
14. Groschner, L.N., Malis, J.G., Zuidinga, B., Borst, A.: A biophysical account of multiplication by a single neuron. Nature **603**, 119–123 (2022). https://doi.org/10.1038/s41586-022-04428-3
15. Haag, J., Arenz, A., Serbe, E., Gabbiani, F., Borst, A.: Complementary mechanisms create direction selectivity in the fly. eLife **5** (2016). https://doi.org/10.7554/eLife.17421.001
16. Haag, J., Mishra, A., Borst, A.: A common directional tuning mechanism of *Drosophila* motion-sensing neurons in the on and in the off pathway (2017). https://doi.org/10.7554/eLife.29044.001
17. Hassenstein, B., Reichardt, W.: Systemtheoretische analyse der zeit-, reihenfolgen- und vorzeichenauswertung bei der bewegungsperzeption des rüsselkäfers chlorophanus. Zeitschrift für Naturforschung B **11**(9–10), 513–524 (1956)
18. Hunt, A., Szczecinski, N., Quinn, R.: Development and training of a neural controller for hind leg walking in a dog robot. Front. Neurorobot. **11** (2017)
19. Izhikevich, E.M.: Dynamical Systems in Neuroscience: The Geometry of Excitability and Burtsing (2007). https://doi.org/10.1017/S0143385704000173
20. Kohn, J.R., Portes, J.P., Christenson, M.P., Abbott, L., Behnia, R.: Flexible filtering by neural inputs supports motion computation across states and stimuli. Curr. Biol. **31**(23), 5249–5260 (2021)
21. Lappalainen, J.K., et al.: Connectome-constrained deep mechanistic networks predict neural responses across the fly visual system at single-neuron resolution. bioRxiv, pp. 2023–03 (2023)
22. Leuba, G., Kraftsik, R.: Changes in volume, surface estimate, three-dimensional shape and total number of neurons of the human primary visual cortex from midgestation until old age. Anat. Embryol. **190**, 351–366 (1994)
23. Maisak, M.S., et al.: A directional tuning map of drosophila elementary motion detectors. Nature **500**(7461), 212–216 (2013)
24. Meier, M., Borst, A.: Extreme compartmentalization in a Drosophila amacrine cell. Curr. Biol. **29**, 1545–1550.e2 (2019). https://doi.org/10.1016/j.cub.2019.03.070
25. Nourse, W.R., Szczecinski, N.S., Quinn, R.D.: SNS-toolbox: A tool for efficient simulation of synthetic nervous systems. In: Hunt, A., et al. (eds.) Biomimetic and Biohybrid Systems. Living Machines 2022. LNAI, vol. 13548, pp. 32–43. Springer, Cham (2022). https://doi.org/10.1007/978-3-031-20470-8_4
26. Scheffer, L.K., et al.: A connectome and analysis of the adult drosophila central brain. Elife **9**, e57443 (2020)

27. Sedlackova, A., Szczecinski, N.S., Quinn, R.D.: A synthetic nervous system model of the insect optomotor response. In: Vouloutsi, V., et al. (eds.) Living Machines 2020. LNCS (LNAI), vol. 12413, pp. 312–324. Springer, Cham (2020). https://doi.org/10.1007/978-3-030-64313-3_30

28. Serbe, E., Meier, M., Leonhardt, A., Borst, A.: Comprehensive characterization of the major presynaptic elements to the Drosophila off motion detector. Neuron **89**, 829–841 (2016). https://doi.org/10.1016/j.neuron.2016.01.006

29. Shinomiya, K., et al.: Comparisons between the on-and off-edge motion pathways in the *Drosophila* brain (2019). https://doi.org/10.7554/eLife.40025.001

30. Szczecinski, N.S., Hunt, A.J., Quinn, R.D.: Design process and tools for dynamic neuromechanical models and robot controllers. Biol. Cybern. **111**, 105–127 (2017). https://doi.org/10.1007/s00422-017-0711-4

31. Szczecinski, N.S., Hunt, A.J., Quinn, R.D.: A functional subnetwork approach to designing synthetic nervous systems that control legged robot locomotion. Front. Neurorobot. **11** (2017)

32. Szczecinski, N.S., Quinn, R.D., Hunt, A.J.: Extending the functional subnetwork approach to a generalized linear integrate-and-fire neuron model. Front. Neurorobot. **14** (2020). https://doi.org/10.3389/fnbot.2020.577804

33. Takemura, S.Y., Nern, A., Chklovskii, D.B., Scheffer, L.K., Rubin, G.M., Meinertzhagen, I.A.: The comprehensive connectome of a neural substrate for 'on' motion detection in Drosophila (2017). https://doi.org/10.7554/eLife.24394.001

34. Teeter, C., et al.: Generalized leaky integrate-and-fire models classify multiple neuron types. Nat. Commun. **9** (2018). https://doi.org/10.1038/s41467-017-02717-4

35. Virtanen, P., et al.: SciPy 1.0 contributors: SciPy 1.0: fundamental algorithms for scientific computing in Python. Nat. Methods **17**, 261–272 (2020). https://doi.org/10.1038/s41592-019-0686-2

36. Winding, M., et al.: The connectome of an insect brain. Science (New York, N.Y.) **379**, eadd9330 (2023). https://doi.org/10.1126/science.add9330

37. Yu, W., et al.: Visual-locomotion: learning to walk on complex terrains with vision

Driving Hexapods Through Insect Brain

Paolo Arena[1]($\boxtimes$), Emanuele Cannizzo[1], Alessia Li Noce[1], and Luca Patanè[2]

[1] University of Catania, Viale A. Doria 6, 95100 Catania, Italy
paolo.arena@unict.it
[2] University of Messina, Contrada di Dio, S. Agata, 98166 Messina, Italy
lpatane@unime.it

Abstract. Insects are really astonishing creatures if their learning and adaptation capabilities are considered. In this paper two specific characteristics of their tiny brain are taken into account: classification and sequence learning. A complex neural network architecture, refined in the last few years, is reviewed and applied to a neuro-inspired controller for a hexapodal robotic structure. Classification is performed using Morris Lecar neurons, that receive input stimuli from a lattice of spiking neurons, arranged similarly to the insect Mushroom Bodies neuropile. A specific network devoted to context formation is used to recall the learned sequences and to retain relevant subsequences. A typical example of a labyrinth solution through the capability of learning and recalling sequences of visual objects is dealt with. The computational model is reviewed, refined and experiments on a hexapodal structure are discussed.

Keywords: Insect mushroom bodies · bio-inspired control · spiking neurons · hexapod robot · sequence learning

1 Introduction

Nowadays Machine Learning algorithms are showing ever and ever impressing capabilities which are improving our quality of life. This comes at the expense of huge computational requirements and typically a constant web connection is necessary to provide real-time performance. Under this perspective, full autonomy would require all the needed computational resources on board. In all cases in which web availability is absent (like post-disaster conditions or deep space exploration), this quality is considered essential. Under this perspective, we can look at bio-inspired solutions: animals are fully autonomous since the brain possesses all the ingredients for solving the behavioral tasks needed by its ecological niche. In particular, to reproduce behaviours from the design of the underlying neural structures, investigation on fully evolved brains, like mammals, would be not rewarding. On the other side, there are animal realms whose brain structures are much simpler than mammals but are able to show impressive learning and adaptation capabilities. A typical example is related to arthropods (and in particular insects). These creatures possess a brain, many orders of magnitude smaller than their mammal counterparts. However, they are able to show such abilities as both temporal and spatial learning and memory, attention and expectation. They are able to

F. Meder et al. (Eds.): Living Machines 2023, LNAI 14157, pp. 381–397, 2023.
https://doi.org/10.1007/978-3-031-38857-6_28

count [18,46] and make decisions [50] even in front of contradictory cues. The most developed exemplars are able to form complex societies with member specialization [37], develop forms of language [25] and others [16].

The approach to distil an artificial nervous system for insectoids requires also a biomimetic counterpart aimed at producing suitable limb motions; under this perspective, several approaches are found in the literature [19,39]. Insect brain-inspired architectures using spiking and locally connected neural networks resembling a limited part of the insect brain (i.e., the Mushroom bodies) were designed to infer the sense of touch by estimating the ground reaction forces into a simulated quadruped robot [12]. In this paper two other functions of the insect brain, feature and sequences-of-features learning, are addressed to control navigation of a hexapod robot, allowing it to solve a simple labyrinth task resembling that one typically used in experiments with bees. The emerged functions in this work efficiently mimic their biological counterpart even with a significantly smaller network size. The insect brain, embedded into a hexapod robot while moving in an environment, will allow it to choose, among a number of concatenated choices to be potentially selected, that one maximizing a reward function. Since, as it is usually argued, one of the fundamental characteristics of a cognitive system is the capability of planning ahead [17], here a bio-inspired control system able to show cognitive capabilities is implemented and shown in action.

The research in this direction is twofold: from the one side there is a push in improving the dexterity of body-legs low-level architecture and control; from the other side, there is the need to build efficient high-level control routines [30]. Our approach to the latter need is to look at the biological counterpart and build algorithms for engineered brain structures at the software level, opening the way to neuromorphic implementations. We selected the fruit fly, *Drosophila melanogaster*, for our work, as it is often referred to as a model organism for neurobiological inspection. The benefits of using *Drosophila* include:

- a very short life cycle (10 days from fertilization to the adult stage);
- ease of raising, maintaining, and testing in a small laboratory;
- availability of genetic tools to create mutant flies offsprings in which specific classes of neurons can be silenced acting on specific control signals (light or temperature) [20]. This leads to the active control of mutation while the animal is behaving, verifying online the effect of gene mutations in the targeted neural centre under consideration on the behavioral responses [7,38,44].

The fly brain is one order of magnitude smaller than other insects such as bees. In the fly central brain, there are about 10^5 neurons organized in different neuropiles. These are involved in a multitude of interesting behaviors [16]. In recent years, research has been conducted by the authors on developing an insect brain computational model [3,5], mainly constituted by spiking neurons and bio-inspired synaptic connections [22], to mimic the architecture and function of two central brain neuropiles, Mushroom Bodies (MBs) and Central Complex (CX) [35]. The former is in charge of a multitude of behaviors, like olfactory learning [40], adaptive termination of behaviors [31], multimodal integration, decision making, and motor learning [24]. Moreover, upon implementing these basic functionalities of the MBs computational model, other emergent functions were addressed to be potentially hosted herewith, like attention, expectation, and delayed match-to-sample [6,8,9]. Neural processing in biology is also character-ized by the massive exploitation of time, which plays a primary role in sensory process-ing. For example, locusts encode olfactory stimuli into precise timings of neural activity [48]. The intrinsic recurrent nature of the biological neural network is reproduced as a primary feature in our model, able to elicit, in principle, a number of parallel behaviors, exploiting the rich dynamics generated by mutually interacting neurons in a space-distributed lattice. Our structure focuses on modeling the processes which manipulate highly pre-processed sensorial stimuli mimicking the MB structure. The MB processing is principally related to the olfactory sensory modality, although other sensory stimuli such as visual inputs are processed through indirect pathways. In the proposed work visual feature processing is adopted and applied for robotic experiments.

In *Drosophila melanogaster* (DM), the first neuropile encountered for the olfac-tory processing is the antennal lobe (AL). The AL is composed of olfactory sensory neurons which, together with the olfactory glomeruli, contribute to encoding the odour features [42]. The corresponding signals project through the projection neurons (PN), to the input stage of the MBs, namely the Kenyon cells (KC), concurrently innervating the Lateral Horn (LH). The reduced number of PN (about 150) and the much larger number of KCs (about 2500) implies a boost in dimensionality which is believed to be the basis for the representation space efficiency [14]. Studies in locusts verified that KCs spiking activity is regularly inhibited by LH [36]. The other key information for the development of our model comes from Cassenaer and Laurent (2007) [15], where KCs are cyclically activated by the AL and inhibited by the LH. In our model, this period was fixed at 96 ms. The developed architecture represents the KC layer as a complex spatial temporal pattern generator whose dynamics can be exploited to per-form multiple behavioral tasks like the biological counterpart [13,14]. After focusing on different spiking-based architectures [22], we modelled the KCs activity as a mainly locally connected Liquid State Network (LSN), a lattice very similar to a liquid state machine [28], that includes regular connectivity as in the Cellular Nonlinear Network structure, exploiting the axo-axonal connections among the KCs [15], explicitly found in the locust MBs.

Several models for the MBs have been previously created for classification using spiking neurons [34]. Our model adds another layer on top of the classification (i.e., the Context layer), to include sequence learning capabilities. Of course, we implemented a much down-scaled network with respect to the biological counterpart in order to have a feasible computational time in a robotic setup. Taking into account the spatial orga-nization of the MB lobe system into concentric rings [43], we modelled the context layer accordingly. Moreover, we assumed that the information flow within the con-centric rings of the context develops from the inner to the outer rings through time, implementing a form of a reaction-diffusion process. The context layer can build and recall, besides sequences of objects, also subsequences therein, which can be recalled in case of noisy sequences and can become relevant to solve uncertain situations. Even if actually *Drosophila* was found unable to show distinct sequence learning capabilities, but only to show persistence in repeating actions or action alternations [32], nevethe-less, adding the context layer to such a tiny brain, realises the capability of sequence learning. This would stimulate the design of ad-hoc experimental setups for further investigations.

The developed computational model was exploited to build a neural controller for visual navigation in a legged robot engaged in solving a labyrinth task inspired by experiments with bees [49]. They exploit the visual features of objects to take decisions while negotiating complex mazes after learning suitable rules. In our experiments, we also used visual cues, but in general, each input element could represent an odour, a visual pattern, or even an endogenously generated stimulus. After processing the input stimulus, the architecture imposes to the robot the associated motor action (e.g. left or right turn). During the testing phase, upon presentation of a given input, the possible sequences arising from such input are internally simulated and the most rewarding sequence of actions is selected and given to the robot. Another interesting feature of the architecture is the high capability of input noise filtering: if a presented object is noisy, thanks to the input layer learning skills, the network is able to reconstruct the missing feature, if the memorised patterns do not have a large number of features in common.

Among the similar approaches found in literature, the so-called Synthetic nervous system [39,45] aims at designing an artificial system starting from the basic functionalities known in living beings, implementing the corresponding functional rules and linking them together to reproduce the desired behavior. The strategy employed somewhat dissects a complex problem into sub-modules, each one devoted to solving a particular sub-function. This design method is really effective when modelling stereotyped low-level functions, such as locomotion. Our approach aims at moving one step up, trying to exploit the very complex nonlinear dynamics embedded into arrays of spiking neurons. Higher level "protocognitive" functions can so be considered as the result of an emerging property of huge dynamics attractors shaped by simple external readout maps. The results of this modelling phase lead to a structure that has similarities with the computational counterparts of liquid-state machines, with the addition of neurobiological details. On the other side, our approach suffers from the lack of interpretability, which is instead an added value for the Synthetic approach.

2   MB-Inspired Computational Model

The model consists of an input layer here organised in a 2×4 matrix of spiking neurons (mimicking the AL neurons, in a down-sized version) which record the features of the relevant objects acquired in the scene. These neurons are connected through synapses which create correlations among the different features (i.e. colour and shape) in case of noise or partially missing features [6]. AL layer is randomly connected (using a 25% probability) to the LSN layer. The input signal also stimulates the LH whose main modelled action is to apply an 96 ms delayed inhibition both to the ALs and the LSN. In this way, the input and KC layers are reset to host new input processing. Within this time window, there exists a dynamic spreading within the LSN: each LSN neuron dynamics is passed to the next layer via a weighted integration stage (within the so-called Sum Neurons) leading to the generation of a read-out map. Multiple read-out maps could be instantiated to provide different parallel responses from the same dynamics, according to different behavioral needs, following the Neural reuse paradigm [6,9]. Each class is here represented by a Morris-Lecar neuron, working as a resonator [33], trained with a supervised simple algorithm. In particular, the target is represented by a periodic wave

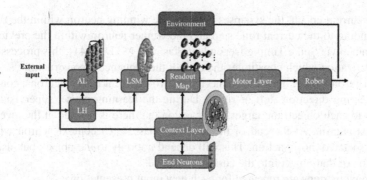

Fig. 1. Block scheme of the developed architecture: (see text for details) The relevant components are outlined: Antennal Lobes (AL), Lateral Horn (LH), Liquid State Network (LSN), Readout Map, containing the Sum neurons and the corresponding Morris-Lecar neurons.

which is supposed to be sent from a generic extrinsic neuron acting as the conditioner, with a frequency able to stimulate the corresponding resonant neuron. Multiple read-out maps can be created, according to the needs. The strategy adopted is a growing one, as explained below. Here the first read-out map is trained to generate a 62.5 Hz sine wave, upon presentation of the first input. If another input is provided, after the suitable noise removal or feature reconstruction at the input stage, if the already existing ML neurons do not fire, a new ML neuron is enrolled with a new frequency, and the corresponding read-out map is instantiated. Figure 1 schematically depicts the main components of the neural architecture. Further details can be found in the literature [10].

For the ML neurons, we selected a specific frequency range, from 60 Hz to 260 Hz. Here we used an integration step $dt = 0.08$ ms: this to host easily six different classes, through a reliable number of spikes for each ML neuron. LSN neural signals, after integration, are thresholded to filter out the noise and generate a robust impulse train of a specified frequency to properly stimulate the ML neurons. The context layer instead has concentric anatomy, resembling the MB organization of parallel fibers. If we call N_c the number of classes and with N_r the ring number (in or case 1, 2, 3 or 4) the number of neurons within each ring is $N_c^{N_r}$. The presence of a high neuron number in the context layer allows the reconstruction of both the complete sequences and the subsequences contained therein, much beyond the capabilities of reconstructing simple sequences. Also, neurons within the same ring mutually inhibit, generating a winner-takes-all dynamics. [23].

The stages of sequence learning are herewith described:

- An external input, or an internally generated stimulus, onsets a neural activity at the input layer and, through the LSN layer, stimulates a specific ML neuron. This neuron stimulates, in turn, the corresponding neuron for each ring of the context layer, starting from the inner one, representing the initial object within the sequence. A mutual inhibition among the neurons of the first ring improves noise robustness;
- during each time step, information propagates one ring ahead, from the inner to the outermost. So rings represent time steps characterising the sequence length;

- at the current epoch, the synapses between the winning neuron within the ring corresponding to the current time step and the winner neuron within the previous ring are trained via Spike Timing Dependent Plasticity (STDP) [41]; this process creates depolarization which constitutes the core of the sequence reconstruction;
- each neuron in the context is connected to two different motor neurons, controlling the steering direction (left or right). During the learning phase, supervision associates to each object, the target motor action that here is learned at the level of the context neuron. At the end of the learning phase, each context neuron will elicit the associated motor action. This will depend not only to the object, but also to the position of that object into the current sequence.
- the previous steps are repeated for each new input presentation;
- neurons belonging to the context layer are connected to the End Sequence neuron which belongs to a neuron array whose size is equal to the ring number;
- after completing a sequence, a rewarding signal activates the end sequence neuron, reinforcing the corresponding synapse; the amplitude of the reinforcing reward signal denotes the importance of the corresponding sequence;
- the activity in the Context layer is now reset and a new sequence can start to be processed.

The weights connecting the input layer to the LSN one are fixed to 1. The LSN lattice is represented as a regular grid. Here two generic LSN neurons i and j are characterised by a spatial distance $d_{i,j}$. Following the usual percentage between excitation and inhibition [29], they are connected to each other by 75% excitatory and 25% inhibitory connections, whose value is randomly distributed between -0.5 and 0.5. The connection probability depends on the presynaptic (i) to postsynaptic (j) neurons distance $d_{i,j}$:
$P_{ij} = k * C_{i,j}$, where $C_{inh,inh} = 0.2, C_{inh,exc} = 0.8, C_{exc,inh} = 0.4, C_{exc,exc} = 0.6$
[28] and $k = 1$ only for nearest neighboring neurons; $K = 0$ if $d_{i,j} > 2$, being $K = 0.5$
only if $1 < d_{i,j} \leq 2$.

In the LSN Toroidal boundary conditions were adopted. This implies that signals outgoing for example, from the last neuron of a given row, are received from the first neuron of the same row. Synapses within the LSN are characterised by a time constant randomly selected from the values $\tau = \{2.5, 5, 15, 25\}$ ms, to improve the richness of the dynamics. All the LSN neurons are connected to all the Sum neurons through the readout map weights, which are subject to learning. This is here realised through a simple Least Mean Square routine.

The whole network was built using different neuron models. In particular, we used:

- Izhikevich Tonic spiking model in the ALs, Context layer, and End Sequence neurons [26];
- Izhikevich Class I model in the LSN;
- the Morris-Lecar model (ML) in the classification layer [33].

2.1 Learning Details

Different learning strategies are used in the proposed MB architecture to generate the desired behavioral responses. In particular, three different learning strategies were used:

- STDP is employed to train the connections between the Context Layer and the End Sequence Neurons as well as within the context layer neurons. The reward is here an external input, provided to the End Sequence neuron when the robot accomplices the task assigned. The reward amplitude is proportional to the "value" given by the sequence that just ended. This is encoded as an input current, so the larger the reward level, the higher the spiking rate. During the testing phase, the various sequences can be simulated and the most rewarding one can be selected to be followed.
- The context neurons innervate both the ML and the AL neurons. For this, a simple Hebbian rule is used to update the corresponding weights. The role of these connections is manifold: from the one side that neuron in the context corresponding to the class actually elicited by the ML neuron is excited, whereas signals from the Context to the ML neurons inhibit all the ML neurons except that one representing the next expected class C_e whose synaptic weight is subject to learning during the sequence presentation. The learning process is used to update the synaptic weights when pre- and post-synaptic neurons are concurrently active. When such synapses, after learning, are sufficiently strengthened, the ML neuron corresponding to C_e will fire, stimulating C_e in the next ring of the Context. A similar process is duplicated, with synapses connecting the context layer to the AL neurons. In particular, the context neurons corresponding to the expected object stimulate the AL neurons representing the features of the expected object. This creates a bias in the following input presentation, which facilitates the next object to be better focalised in the AL against input noise. This concept plays an important role in object reconstruction, as detailed in the following.
- Spiking neurons in the KC lattice are fully connected to the Sum Neurons via plastic trainable synapses. A simple supervised learning method has been adopted based on the pseudo-inverse algorithm [27].

ML neurons spike only after a periodic input of a given frequency, whose specific value depends on the model parameters. A decay rate allows the system to work in dynamically changing environments: here the learned sequences could be forgotten if no longer rewarding. Interesting applications of this learning paradigm to biorobotics, together with details on the parameters, are reported in literature [4].

3   Simulation Results

The whole network was simulated taking into account some simple cases. In particular, objects with two different shapes (i.e., circle and rectangle) and with four colours (i.e., yellow, red, blue and green) compose the data set to build the different sequences. Taking into account Fig. 1, the input to the network (AL) is constituted by 8 Izhikevich neurons, whose spiking activity represents the presence of two distinct features constituting the object in the scene. These are arranged in a 2×4 matrix, depicted in Fig. 2. In particular, the first row of the sub-figures refers to the colour, whereas the second row represents the shape.

The input layer stimulates the LSN, which generates complex spatial dynamics during the 96 ms of temporal activity, corresponding to the first 1200 simulation steps (Fig. 3). In particular, the first 200 steps, i.e. 16 ms, are used to stabilize the input

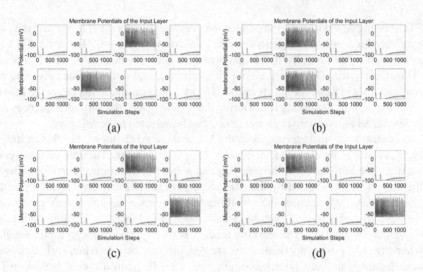

Fig. 2. Neural activity of the input layer, when a blue (a) and a red (b) rectangle, a blue (c) and a red (d) circle are presented to the network (Color figure online)

neuron spikes. The LSN spiking activity is integrated into the Sum Neurons, which are trained so as to generate sinusoidal signals useful for stimulating the ML neurons. Figure 4 depicts the trend of the signals for the four Sum neurons corresponding to the four images. These signals are rectified before stimulating the ML neurons, which, in this way, receive in input a square wave with a fixed frequency. Only the ML neuron resonating at that frequency will be active. This is depicted in Fig. 5. In parallel to the constitution of classes, at the level of the ML neurons, the context starts building sequences. The ML active neurons stimulate the corresponding neurons within the context. Figure 6 depicts the various phases of the sequence reproduction at the end of the learning phase. Here neuron activity is represented through the membrane potential averaged over the last 700 simulation steps. In detail, the ML neuron representing the class of the first presented object, say Rectangle-red R_r, stimulates the activity of the corresponding neuron in the first ring. This is clearly visible from the enhanced activity in one neuron (outlined in red). The second object presentation, say Rectangle-blue R_b causes the excitation of another ML neuron which stimulates all the corresponding neurons in all the rings of the context. The winning neuron in the second ring will be that one contemporary excited also from the winning neuron in the previous ring (one time step behind). The construction of subsequences requires that also another neuron, corresponding to R_b is activated in the first ring (see Fig. 6(b). The process continues until all the objects in the sequence are presented. The end sequence signal is triggered by the End Sequence neuron, whose intensity of activation is related to the Reward value.

3.1 Noise Robustness

In this example, we assessed the network's ability to reconstruct the distinctive features of a winning sequence under noisy conditions. By providing the network with the

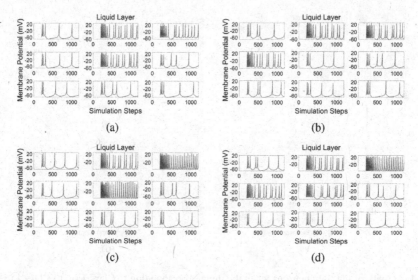

Fig. 3. Time evolution of the membrane potential for a subset of 3×3 neurons over the 8×8 neurons present in the liquid layer for the four inputs reported in Fig. 2.

starting point of the sequence (represented by the blue rectangle), (Fig. 7(a)) the context layer effectively predicted the subsequent input (represented by the red rectangle), creating a sense of expectation. Consequently, if the following element was corrupted by noise, the network demonstrated the capability to reconstruct it to some extent. To examine this phenomenon, we intentionally presented the network with an incomplete input (Fig. 7(b)), containing only the feature encoding the presence of a rectangle. Leveraging its memory of the context layer, which retained the information that a blue circle typically followed the red rectangle, the corresponding features were depolarized. In this specific configuration, we could also observe the impact of the input layer's ability to reconstruct the input using its internal plastic synapses, as well as the inhibitory interactions among neurons representing the same feature. The network associated the concept of a rectangle with both red and blue colours. Consequently, the presence of the sole shape feature depolarized both the red and blue colour features (Fig. 7(b)). Due to the inhibitory connections between these two neurons, we noticed that the winner neuron, excited by the context layer, was primarily the one corresponding to the red colour. This additional depolarization on the AL layer causes an increase in the spiking rate of the feature predicted by the context (i.e., red). Finally, in Fig. 7(c) and 7(d), we witnessed the network's spontaneous activity as it reconstructed the expected input without any external input stimulation, relying solely on feedback from the memory in the context layer.

It has to be noticed that these dynamics can be elicited also by noise present in the input layer. Even in the absence of any object, some noise intensity can lead to the emergence of one of the memorised objects which can autonomously onset the generation of a given sequence and the associated synaptic reinforcement, realising a kind of autonomous memory consolidation.

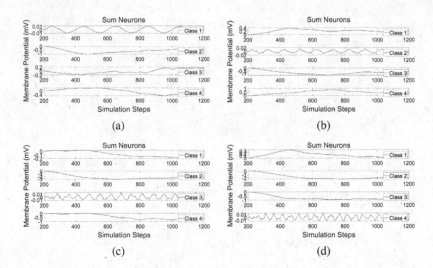

Fig. 4. Activity of the Sum neurons when the input corresponding to Class 1 (a) to Class 4 (d) is given to the network.

4   Experimental Results

The robot selected for the experiments is a modified version of a commercial hexapod, the PhantomX Hexapod Mark II of Interbotix Labs [47] (see Fig. 8). Indeed, the original structure was completely rearranged: in particular, the tibia links were specifically redesigned to host pressure sensors and conditioning electronics which were used for attitude control [11]. Each leg of the hexapod has three DoF with a total of 18 actuators. A mixing of Dynamixel AX-12A and AX-18A servomotors is used to actuate each DoF, reaching a good compromise between the torque required by each link to support the structure and the battery charge duration. The old onboard microcontroller was substituted by an Arduino Mega. This hosts the locomotion controller based on a Cellular Nonlinear Network Central Pattern Generator (CNN-CPGs), able to impose desired phase shift synchronization among the neural oscillators controlling the leg joints. The design leads to stable locomotion patterns exploiting results from the Partial Contraction Theory [1]. The high-level controller, implementing the proposed sequence learning architecture is currently implemented on an external PC connected to the robot via serial port. The visual information is acquired using a cellphone placed on the front part of the robot. The acquired images are transferred through a wireless channel to the PC where the landmarks present in the images are extracted and their features are used as inputs for the neural architecture.

The labyrinth realised for the experiment is shown in Fig. 9.

This is composed of an entrance followed by two T-mazes and only one final route to exit, outlined with the maximal reward value $R = 3$. In the labyrinth walls, a series of landmarks are fixed in specific positions (Fig. 9 - right-hand side). In this experiment, we trained the architecture using the following three different sequences:

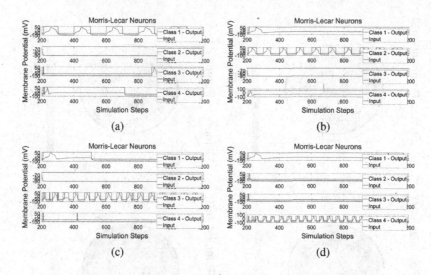

Fig. 5. Activity of the Morris-Lecar neurons for the four different classes.

- S1: {blue rectangle; red rectangle; red circle; blue circle}, with associated motor actions: {right; left; right; left} and Reward level R=3;
- S2: {yellow Circle; yellow rectangle}, with associated motor actions: {left; right} and Reward level R=1;
- S3: {blue rectangle; yellow rectangle; }, with associated motor actions: {left; left} and Reward level R=1.

In the simulations, as outlined before, coloured shapes were used as landmarks. During experiments, due to the poor light condition and the resolution of the images acquired by the camera endowed in the robot, the shape recognition was not very accurate, due to contour distortions; on the other side, colour identification was much more robust. To face this problem, the shape information was encoded inside an ArUco marker. This is also used to correct the robot trajectory while moving through the labyrinth. Simple and light routines exploit the ArUco markers for detecting the camera pose and correcting the robot heading when approaching an identified object, taking into account the estimated position of the marker center [21]. Moreover, the binary encoding makes them particularly robust, able to be detected even using low-resolution images. The robot is let to walk through the labyrinth, acquiring the landmarks. An image processing algorithm acquires the current frame and uses it in two distinct routines: one converts the frame in HSV format and then applies a mask for detecting a specific colour (for example, a red mask for detecting red-coloured elements) and the other detects the marker and returns the related id. These are passed to the input layer of the neural architecture which is run on the remote PC. The overall architecture simulated in the experiment has the following size:

- an input layer consisting of 8 Neurons arranged in a 2×4 matrix;
- an LSN consisting of an 8×8 locally connected spiking network;
- an output stage consisting of 8 Morris Lecar neurons;

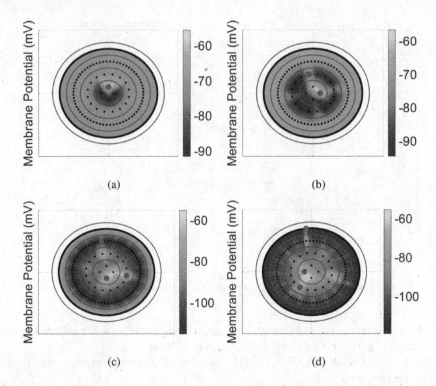

Fig. 6. Activity of the context layer when the sequence blue rectangle, red rectangle, blue circle and red circle is provided in the input. The mean of the membrane potential is reported for each neuron in the context (i.e. black circles). The winning neuron for each ring is also shown (i.e. red circle). (Color figure online)

- a context layer hosting 1554 neurons;
- 4 End Sequence neurons.

Whereas the learning phase is quite time-consuming (in our case of a PC Intel i5, 8GB RAM it takes about 2 min), a few seconds are needed to compute the winning sequence. During the testing phase the hexapod, starting from the entrance of the labyrinth, acquires the images of two landmarks (i.e. the yellow circle and the blue rectangle) representative of the first objects of two different sequences. As outlined above, each object is made up of two features: the colour is directly acquired from the onboard camera and detected through the HSV conversion, whereas the shape is extracted by processing the ArUco marker placed next to the landmark, using the OpenCV libraries. Each object is processed by the architecture: the two corresponding sequences, starting with each of the two landmarks, are internally simulated, and the most rewarding one is finally selected to give the robot the correct sequences of driving actions to follow that sequence. More in detail, the hexapod, once detected the object to be followed, tries to approach it until reaching a given distance from it. Due to the irregular walking of legged robots, heading control has to be assured: if the tracked object falls outside a fixed bounding box, a steering strategy is implemented. In particular, to implement

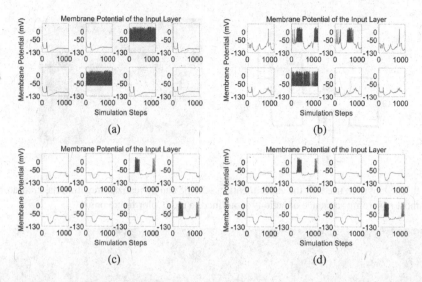

Fig. 7. Example of sequence reproduction in the presence of incomplete or absent external input: (a) first input presentation (blue rectangle); (b) external presentation of only the shape "rectangle" and reproduction of both possible colour (blu and red) features at the beginning of the simulation step. At the end only the red feature is retained due to the concurrent feedback from the context; (c): no external input is given to the network, and the AL is stimulated only by the context, eliciting the red circle and consequently the blue circle (d) (Color figure online)

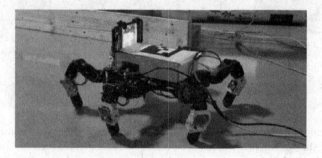

Fig. 8. The hexapod robot used in the experiments.

such steering, the robot stops its slow walking gait and performs a tripod gait enabling a turning on the spot [2]. Turning stops as soon as the following object belonging to the sequence is detected. Of course, it is possible that the robot, while turning, detects other objects in the visual scene. This issue is relieved by the information coming from the context layer increasing the robustness when following the selected sequence: expectation contributes to filtering out possible noise of lacking info in one of the object features. In Fig. 10, five trajectories, obtained using a tracking algorithm able to detect the robot while following the winning sequence, are depicted in coloured traces.

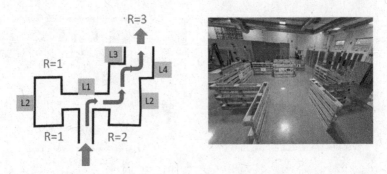

Fig. 9. The labyrinth used for the experiments: a scheme and its realization within the laboratory. The most rewarding sequence of actions is outlined in red (Color figure online)

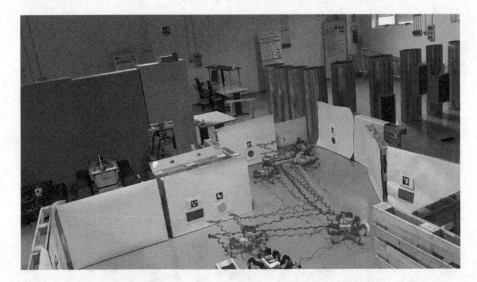

Fig. 10. Trajectories followed by the robot during the test phase. The most rewarding sequence learned during the training phase is followed (i.e., blue rectangle, red rectangle, red circle and blue circle. The robot's behavior over five trials of the test phase is reported. Besides the initial and final robot positions, intermediate configurations showing the robot soon after taking the action decision due to a landmark processing, are reported. (Color figure online)

5   Conclusions

In this paper, a complex spatial-temporal architecture, inspired by the main neural assemblies in charge of learning and memory in insects, namely the Mushroom Bodies, was reviewed and applied to drive a hexapod robot to solve a typical labyrinth task, as that one performed by bees. A neurocomputational model was reviewed, able to deal with classification, sequence and subsequence learning. The role of the Context layer is fundamental not only to build and retrieve sequences of objects but also to generate expectations about which object the robot will meet immediately after, allowing to resolve external images where part of the features is noise corrupted or even missing The model presented herewith can host also a number of different other behavior already presented in the literature, like persistence, and motor learning. Most of them are built upon the same LSN acting as a dynamic generator able to embed complex dynamics, to be exploited for eliciting different parallel behaviors, according to the Neural Reuse paradigm. A growing mechanism was adopted to create new classes according to the needs. Ongoing research is focused on an optimization of the structure, inspecting the possibility of a parallel hardware implementation to decrease the learning phase. The added value of such a bio-inspired architecture cannot be found looking for a simple comparison with the state-of-the-art artificial algorithms for solving the same tasks. Rather, the key specificity lies in having a unique architecture whose core is useful to solve a number of different behavioral needs, a possibility that classical architectures are not designed for. An example is represented by the use of the same LSN core to estimate the ground reaction force from a hexapod robot considering the motor torques. This is an important feature that would cope with the problem of expensive and prone to-fault sensors [12] Among the future refinements of the architecture, there is the selection of a different kind of neuron for implementing the classification stage, like an Izhikevick neuron in a specific configuration, which would decrease the computation time. The embodiment of such insect-inspired neural structures within the most performing robotic architectures would be an interesting step toward the next generation of insectoid robots, i,e, robots with the insect brain embodied into a performing biomimetic agent.

Acknowledgments. The work was supported PNRR MUR project PE0000013-FAIR.

The authors would like to thank the contribution of Eng. Marco Cali', from Amazon Web Services, UK, and former student from the University of Catania, for developing the initial version of the simulation code

References

1. Arena, E., Arena, P., Patanè, L.: Efficient hexapodal locomotion control based on flow-invariant subspaces. IFAC Proc. Volumes **44**(1), 13758–13763 (2011). https://doi.org/10.3182/20110828-6-IT-1002.02533. 18th IFAC World Congress
2. Arena, E., Arena, P., Patanè, L.: Modelling stepping strategies for steering in insects. In: Frontiers in Artificial Intelligence and Applications, vol. 8068, pp. 275–283 (2011). https://doi.org/10.3233/978-1-60750-972-1-275
3. Arena, P., Calí, M., Patané, L., Portera, A., Strauss, R.: A mushroom bodies inspired spiking network for classification and sequence learning. In: IJCNN, Ireland, pp. 1–8 (2015)
4. Arena, P., Fortuna, L., Frasca, M., Patané, L.: Learning anticipation via spiking networks: application to navigation control. IEEE Trans. Neural Netw. **20**(2), 202–216 (2009)
5. Arena, P., Patanè, L. (eds.): Spatial Temporal Patterns for Action-Oriented Perception in Roving Robots II. CSM, vol. 21. Springer, Cham (2014). https://doi.org/10.1007/978-3-319-02362-5
6. Arena, P., Patané, L., Stornanti, V., Termini, P., Zaepf, B., Strauss, R.: Modelling the insect mushroom bodies: application to a delayed match-to-sample task. Neural Netw. **41**, 202–211 (2013)

7. Arena, P., Patané, L., Strauss, R.: The Insect Mushroom Bodies: A Paradigm of Neural Reuse, pp. 765–772. MIT Press, Taormina (2013)

8. Arena, P., Patané, L., Termini, P.: Learning expectation in insects: a recurrent spiking neural model for spatio-temporal representation. Neural Netw. **32**, 35–45 (2012)

9. Arena, P., Patané, L., Termini, P.: Modeling attentional loop in the insect mushroom bodies. In: IJCNN, Brisbane, Australia, pp. 7–12 (2012)

10. Arena, P., Calí, M., Patané, L., Portera, A., Strauss, R.: A fly-inspired mushroom bodies model for sensory-motor control through sequence and subsequence learning. Int. J. Neural Syst. **26**(06), 1650035 (2016). https://doi.org/10.1142/S0129065716500350, pMID: 27354193

11. Arena, P., Furia, P., Patané, L., Pollino, M.: Fly-inspired sensory feedback in a reaction-diffusion neural system for locomotion control in a hexapod robot. In: 2015 International Joint Conference on Neural Networks (IJCNN), pp. 1–8 (2015). https://doi.org/10.1109/IJCNN.2015.7280544

12. Arena, P., Pia Cusimano, M.F., Meli, L.E., Taffara, S., Patanè, L., Poramate, M.: Ground reaction force estimation in a quadruped robot via liquid state networks. In: 2022 International Joint Conference on Neural Networks (IJCNN), pp. 01–08 (2022). https://doi.org/10.1109/IJCNN55064.2022.9892423

13. Aso, Y., et al.: Mushroom body output neurons encode valence and guide memory-based action selection in Drosophila. eLife **3** (2014). https://doi.org/10.7554/eLife.04580

14. Aso, Y., et al.: The neuronal architecture of the mushroom body provides a logic for associative learning. eLife **3** (2014). https://doi.org/10.7554/eLife.04577

15. Cassenaer, S., Laurent, G.: Hebbian STDP in mushroom bodies facilitates the synchronous flow of olfactory information in locusts. Nature **448**(7154), 709–713 (2007)

16. Chittka, L., Niven, J.: Are bigger brains better? Curr. Biol. **19**(21), R995–R1008 (2009). https://doi.org/10.1016/j.cub.2009.08.023

17. Cruse, H.: The evolution of cognition-a hypothesis. Cogn. Sci. **27**(1), 135–155 (2003). https://doi.org/10.1016/S0364-0213(02)00110-6

18. Dacke, M., Srinivasan, M.: Evidence for counting in insects. Anim. Cogn. **11**(4), 683–689 (2008). https://doi.org/10.1007/s10071-008-0159-y

19. Dürr, V., et al.: Integrative biomimetics of autonomous hexapedal locomotion. Front. Neurorobot. **13** (2019). https://doi.org/10.3389/fnbot.2019.00088

20. Duffy, J.B.: Gal4 system in *Drosophila*: a fly geneticist's swiss army knife. Genesis **34**(1–2), 1–15 (2002)

21. Garrido-Jurado, S., Muñoz-Salinas, R., Madrid-Cuevas, F., Marín-Jiménez, M.: Automatic generation and detection of highly reliable fiducial markers under occlusion. Pattern Recogn. **47**(6), 2280–2292 (2014). https://doi.org/10.1016/j.patcog.2014.01.005

22. Ghosh-Dastidar, S., Adeli, H.: Spiking neural networks. Int. J. Neural Syst. **19**(4), 295–308 (2009)

23. Giurfa, M.: Cognitive neuroethology: dissecting non-elemental learning in a honeybee brain. Curr. Opin. Neurobiol. **13**(6), 726–735 (2003)

24. Gronenberg, W., Lopez-Riquelme, G.: Multisensory convergence in the mushroom bodies of ants and bees. Acta Biol. Hung. **55**, 31–37 (2004)

25. I'Anson Price, R., Grüter, C.: Why, when and where did honey bee dance communication evolve? Front. Ecol. Evol. **3** (2015). https://doi.org/10.3389/fevo.2015.00125

26. Izhikevich, E.M.: Which model to use for cortical spiking neurons? IEEE Trans. Neural Netw. **15**(5), 1063–1070 (2004)

27. Jaeger, H.: Short term memory in echo state networks. GMD-Report German National Research Institute for Computer Science **152** (2002)

28. Maass, W., Natschlaeger, T., Markram, H.: Real-time computing without stable states: a new framework for neural computation based on perturbations. Neural Comput. **14**(11), 2531–2560 (2002)
29. Maass, W., et al.: A new approach towards vision suggested by biologically realistic neural microcircuit models, vol. 2525 (2002). https://doi.org/10.1007/3-540-36181-228
30. Manoonpong, P., et al.: Insect-inspired robots: bridging biological and artificial systems. Sensors **21**(22) (2021). https://doi.org/10.3390/s21227609
31. Martin, J., Ernst, R., Heisenberg, M.: Mushroom bodies suppress locomotor activity in Drosophila melanogaster. Learn. Mem. **5**(1–2), 179–191 (1998)
32. May, R., Wellman, A.: Alternation in the fruit fly *Drosophila melanogaster*. Neurosci. Biobehavioral Rev. **12**(Psychonomic science), 339–340 (1968)
33. Morris, C., Lecar, H.: Voltage oscillations in the barnacle giant muscle fiber. Biophys. J. **35**, 193–213 (1981)
34. Mosqueiro, T.S., Huerta, R.: Computational models to understand decision making and pattern recognition in the insect brain. Curr. Op. Insect Sci. **6**, 80–85 (2014)
35. Neuser, K., Triphan, T., Mronz, M., Poeck, B., Strauss, R.: Analysis of a spatial orientation memory in Drosophila. Nature **453**, 1244–1247 (2008)
36. Nowotny, T., Rabinovich, M., et al.: Decoding temporal information through slow lateral excitation in the olfactory system of insects. J. Comput. Neurosci. **15**, 271–281 (2003)
37. Patalano, S., et al.: Self-organization of plasticity and specialization in a primitively social insect. Cell Syst. **13** (2022). https://doi.org/10.1016/j.cels.2022.08.002
38. Pick, S., Strauss, R.: Goal-driven behavioral adaptations in gap-climbing *Drosophila*. Curr. Biol. **15**, 1473–8 (2005)
39. Rubeo, S., Szczecinski, N., Quinn, R.: A synthetic nervous system controls a simulated cockroach. Appl. Sci. **8** (2017). https://doi.org/10.3390/app8010006
40. Scherer, S., Stocker, R., Gerber, B.: Olfactory learning in individually assayed *Drosophila* larvae. Learn. Mem. **10**, 217–225 (2003)
41. Song, S., Miller, K.D., Abbott, L.F.: Competitive Hebbian learning through spike-timing-dependent plasticity. Nat. Neurosci. **3**, 919–926 (2000)
42. Stocker, R., Lienhard, C., Borst, A.: Neuronal architecture of the antennal lobe in *Drosophila melanogaster*. Cell Tissue Res. **262**, 9–34 (1990)
43. Strausfeld, N.J.: Organization of the honey bee mushroom body: representation of the calyx within the vertical and gamma lobes. J. Comp. Neurol. **450**(1), 4–33 (2002)
44. Strauss, R.: The central complex and the genetic dissection of locomotor behaviour. Curr. Opin. Neurobiol. **12**, 633–638 (2002)
45. Szczecinski, N., Hunt, A., Quinn, R.: A functional subnetwork approach to designing synthetic nervous systems that control legged robot locomotion. Front. Neurorobot. **11** (2017). https://doi.org/10.3389/fnbot.2017.00037
46. Triphan, T., Nern, A., Roberts, S., Korff, W., Naiman, D., Strauss, R.: A screen for constituents of motor control and decision making in Drosophila reveals visual distance-estimation neurons. Sci. Rep. **6** (2016). https://doi.org/10.1038/srep27000
47. TrossenRobotics: Trossenrobotics. https://www.trossenrobotics.com/phantomx-ax-hexapod.aspx
48. Wehr, M., Laurent, G.: Odor encoding by temporal sequences of firing in oscillating neural assemblies. Nature **384**, 162–166 (1996)
49. Zhang, S., Si, A., Pahl, M.: Visually guided decision making in foraging honeybees. Front. Neurosci. **6**(88), 1–17 (2012)
50. Zhao, F., Zeng, Y., Guo, A., Su, H., Xu, B.: A neural algorithm for Drosophila linear and nonlinear decision-making. Sci. Rep. **10**, 18660 (2020). https://doi.org/10.1038/s41598-020-75628-y

Weighting Elementary Movement Detectors Tuned to Different Temporal Frequencies to Estimate Image Velocity

Benjamin P. Campbell(✉) [iD], Huai-Ti Lin[iD], and Holger G. Krapp[iD]

Imperial College London, Exhibition Rd, South Kensington, London SW7 2BX, UK
b.campbell21@imperial.ac.uk

Abstract. Insects' ability to know the velocity they are flying is of interest to both biologists and roboticists. While the Reichardt detector is one of the most prominent models for insect motion vision, it has various limitations when extracting image velocity in a natural environment. Here we demonstrate a method for estimating image velocity by weighting the outputs of a population of Reichardt detectors where individual detectors are tuned to different temporal frequencies. By providing stimuli of different spatial frequencies and velocities, we then perform a convex optimisation on each average output to find weights. We show that when the weighted detector arrays are provided with different stimuli, the output reasonably approximates image velocity. Our results have implications for power-limited autonomous systems and suggest a potential mechanism for insect motion vision.

Keywords: Computer vision · Elementary movement detector · Image velocity · Bio-inspired

1 Introduction

Calculating the velocity of motion can be an important requirement for navigation in both, biological organisms, and mobile robots. Mobile robots frequently employ object tracking for simultaneous localisation and mapping (SLAM) [27], or gradient-based movement detectors with heavy filtering and windowing; such as the Lucas-Kanade algorithm [3]. Whereas, the Reichardt detector has been a popular model for explaining the analysis of directional visual motion in a wide range of insects [4]. It requires far less computational power than the computer vision classical methods in mobile robots [2] likely due to evolutionary pressures for energy efficiency [25]. Despite the low computational overheads, it is hardly ever implemented in robotic systems. This is presumably because the output of the Reichardt detector inherently depends on the spatial contrast distribution of the input pattern.

Supported by the Defence Science and Technology Laboratory (DSTLX1000161145).

There is some evidence for biology overcoming the challenges associated with the Reichardt detector. Ibbotson found cells in honeybees that are tuned to velocity [13], and it has even been shown that the optic flow-based path integration is communicated to other hive mates [10]. In addition, Shoemaker et al. found cells in the hoverfly *Eristalis tenax* that demonstrate what they call *velocity constancy*: cells whose output is invariant with spatial properties [33].

Here we propose a method to retrieve an output proportional to velocity and independent of spatial frequency, using an array of Reichardt detectors. Our work (i) demonstrates the feasibility of a method that biology could be using to extract velocity information, and (ii) makes the Reichardt detector a more competitive choice for the analysis of directional motion on low-power autonomous robots when computational power is at a prime.

The Reichardt detector, shown in Fig. 1, samples the light intensity at two points separated on the image plane. The delayed input at a_1 is multiplied by the current input at a_2. On average this leads to a higher output when there is a high correlation between what was at a_1 before the time delay, and what is currently at a_2. The opposite is then subtracted to mitigate the influence of changing lighting conditions. This leads to a direction-selective correlation-detector. By having arrays oriented at 90° direction-selective movement detectors can infer the 2D image velocity as shown in [28].

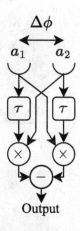

Fig. 1. Single Reichardt detector model parameterised by τ which is the time constant in a temporal low-pass filter; and $\Delta\phi$ which is the spatial sampling base. The × symbolises the multiplication of the two inputs.

For a single Reichardt detector, the dependence on spatial frequency of the input means that information on velocity is inaccessible: a slow-moving, high spatial frequency sinusoid induces the same response as a fast-moving, low spatial frequency sinusoid.

In the past, there have been three successful attempts at using a Reichardt detector to estimate the velocity of a simple sinusoidal stimulus. The first, presented by Zanker et al. uses an *imbalanced* Reichardt detector, where each side of the detector (half-detector) is unevenly weighted before subtraction. As a result, the detector's temporal frequency response is shifted, leaving an approximately linear response within a range of image velocities. However, uneven weighting is used at the expense of knowing the direction of motion, and at the expense of robustness to changes in light intensity. Also, the method Zanker et al. [37] provided only works for specific spatial frequencies. The second method, by Cope et al. uses ratios of *imbalanced* detectors with different parameters to estimate image velocity. This method was only demonstrated in the paper with sinusoidal and square wave stimuli [7]. Again, the use of *imbalanced* detectors comes at the expense of introducing a transient response when there is no motion but the light intensity changes. The third method by Riabinina and Philippides also uses a ratio of two channels. In their method, they attempt to suppress the temporal frequency tuning in one detector, by dividing the output by another detector with a clear temporal frequency dependence. Again, it is not demonstrated on naturalistic scenes [29].

A fourth method presented in this paper uses an array of *balanced* Reichardt detectors. The use of balanced detectors means that there is symmetric directional-selectivity, and there will be no transient output when there is changing light intensity but no motion. We were able to show that our approach also works for images that contain a composition of multiple spatial frequencies as found in natural scenes [26].

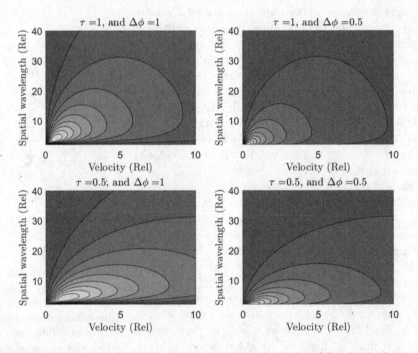

Fig. 2. Mean response of four differently parameterised simulated Reichardt detectors. The units have no absolute values; instead, the spatial wavelength is given relative to a single unit of sampling base, and velocity relative to a single unit of time constant. Hence, the values of the response have been omitted; yellow represents a large response, and dark green is a small response. By combining the two parameters there are two ways in which the mean response profile can be changed. Decreasing τ stretches the response in the velocity axis, and decreasing $\Delta\phi$ appears to compress the profile along both axes. (Color figure online)

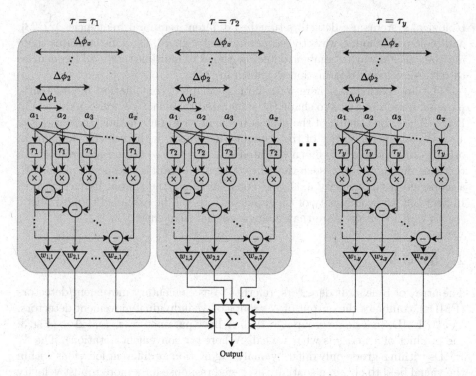

Fig. 3. Multiple weighted Reichardt detectors tuned to different temporal frequencies by varying the spatial sampling base $\Delta\phi$ and the time-constant τ. Within each box the spatial-sampling base is varied, and each box contains detectors with different time-constants. There are x different spatial sampling bases and y different temporal low-pass filters (parameterised by y values of τ)

Two parameters of the Reichardt detector, the time constant in the low-pass filter (τ) and the spatial sampling distance ($\Delta\phi$), shown in Fig. 1, control the optimal temporal frequency the detector is tuned to as shown in Fig. 2. The spatial sampling base in insects must be an integer number of interommatidial angles; where the ommatidia is an eye unit made up of a cluster of photoreceptors, and the interommatidial angle is the angle between two neighbouring ommatidium. Nalbach has suggested that crabs integrate the responses of detectors tuned to different temporal frequencies [23]. In addition, Maddess and Laughlin provided evidence of a variable low-pass filter time constant [21] in the motion vision system. There is also experimental evidence that the spatial sampling base of the inputs to the Reichardt detector may vary. Schuling et al. found that in the fly *Calliphora vicina* multiple spatial sampling bases, as opposed to the sole use of neighbouring ommatidia, are fed into the motion vision pathway [32]. The parameters change the response dynamics (Fig. 2), biological systems use detectors tuned to different temporal frequencies [21, 23], and biology has found ways to estimate velocity [10, 13, 33]. This indicates there may be a useful way to combine detectors tuned to multiple temporal frequencies to retrieve velocity information as shown in [34].

The approach taken here is to find a weighted combination of differently parameterised detectors to shape the integrated frequency response, as shown in Fig. 3. The target shape of the overall frequency response is independent of the spatial pattern properties of the stimulus and linear in the velocity domain. In other words, the aim is to find a weighted sum of response magnitude profiles, like the ones shown in Fig. 2, such that the result of the sum is a response plane with a slope along the velocity axis, and constant along the spatial frequency axis. In Sect. 3.2, the complexity of the input pattern will be extended to naturalistic scenes which contain more than a single spatial frequency.

2   Method

The array of Reichardt detectors, referred to as elementary movement detectors (EMDs), combines the output of N groups of M individual movement detectors. The M EMDs in a single group $n = 1, 2...N$ have parameters, τ_n and $\Delta\phi_n$ (Fig. 3; the product of x and y is what we call N here for convenient notation). The M EMDs within a group only differ by analysing motion at different locations within the visual field to obtain a spatially averaged response for a more robust velocity estimation.

Each group of EMDs is stimulated with an input video sequence of sinusoidal gratings moving with U combinations of spatial wavelength λ, and velocity v. The responses are averaged for each of the N groups of EMDs with given parameters τ and $\Delta\phi$, at each combination of spatial wavelength and velocity.

The results can be concatenated into a matrix A where, each row represents the average response of a single group of EMDs to U different combinations of velocity and spatial wavelength, and each column is the average response of each of the N groups of EMDs to a single combination of velocity and spatial wavelength. Therefore, $y_{u,n}$ where $u = 1, 2...U$, and, $n = 1, 2...N$, is the average output of an EMD with parameters τ_n and $\Delta\phi_n$, to an input sinusoid with parameters λ_u and v_u. By combining variables (variable n: the nth combination of τ and $\Delta\phi$, and variable u: the uth combination of λ and v) the results populate a two-dimensional matrix, a convenient format for optimisation. The vector $\vec{b}$ represents the ground truth velocities at each of the U combinations.

$$\underset{\vec{x}\in\mathbb{R}^N}{\text{minimise}} \qquad \|A\vec{x} - \vec{b}\|_2$$

where: •

$$A = \begin{bmatrix} y_{1,1} & y_{1,2} & \cdots & y_{1,N} \\ y_{2,1} & y_{2,2} & \cdots & y_{2,N} \\ \vdots & \vdots & \ddots & \vdots \\ y_{U-1,1} & y_{U-1,2} & \cdots & y_{U-1,N} \\ y_{U,1} & y_{U,2} & \cdots & y_{U,N} \end{bmatrix} \quad \vec{x} = \begin{bmatrix} w_1 \\ w_2 \\ \vdots \\ w_{n-1} \\ w_n \end{bmatrix} \quad \vec{b} = \begin{bmatrix} v_1 \\ v_2 \\ \vdots \\ v_{U-1} \\ v_U \end{bmatrix}$$

$$(1)$$

The result of the optimisation problem given in Eq. 1 is a vector of N weights that, when multiplied by the output of the N different groups of EMDs, produce a response that, on average, is proportional to velocity.

The array of EMDs for the sinusoidal stimulus was built so that each group includes $M = 200$ individual movement detectors, and there are $N = 25$ groups of EMDs with every combination of the parameters given in Table 1. For the naturalistic scenes stimuli the EMD array contained $M = 30 \times 570$ individual movement detectors, 30 vertically by 570 spread horizontally.

Table 1. Table of the parameters of each of the groups of EMDs that were chosen to optimally combine. The EMD parameters for the analysis using natural scene stimuli are also given, where the only difference was the sampling base variable ($\Delta\phi$) which was chosen to be smaller since the naturalistic scenes had higher spatial frequency content.

EMD parameter	Values for sinusoid/values for scenes	Units
Tau (τ)	2, 3, 4, 5, 6/2, 3, 4, 5, 6	frames (24 fps)
Separation ($\Delta\phi$)	1, 9, 17, 25, 33/1, 2, 3, 4, 5	pixels

For the sinusoidal test stimuli all 25 groups of EMD were subjected to input videos of sinusoidal gratings that were 256×256 pixels in size, 24 frames per second (fps), at every combination of the velocities and spatial wavelengths given in Table 2.

The video stimuli for the naturalistic scenes were created using one of three high-definition images (retrieved from Textures.com) wrapped around a cylinder in the software Blender. The "camera" was an equirectangular panoramic camera that was then rotated around the vertical axis inside the cylinder at different angular velocities, and simulated the capture of a 360° horizontal by 20° vertical field-of-view. The frames were rendered to 576×32 pixels meaning the horizontal angle between two neighbouring pixels (and therefore the smallest spatial sampling base $\Delta\phi$) is 0.625°. A single rendered frame of each of the three scenes is shown in Fig. 4.

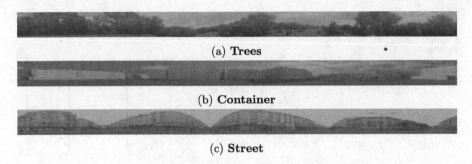

(a) **Trees**

(b) **Container**

(c) **Street**

Fig. 4. Shows the three naturalistic scenes to study the retrieval of velocity information using weighted groups of EMDs. The images' rectangular shapes are due to them being horizontally panoramic, 360° horizontal field-of-view, with 20° vertical field-of-view. (a) The first input pattern was a green natural scene with trees and some grass. It had a relatively high spatial frequency content. (b) The second scene was a panoramic view of a shipping container yard. This image contains many vertical lines where the phases of different frequencies align. (c) The third scene was a panoramic image at a junction in Paris. This had a high spatial frequency content. (Color figure online)

Table 2. Table of the sinusoidal stimuli parameters that were used in the optimisation.

Input variable	Values optimised at	Units
Spatial frequency	2, 3, 4, 5	256/wavelength in pixels
Velocity	2, 4, 6	pixels/frame (24 fps)

3   Results

3.1   Sinusoidal Stimulus

The weights to estimate image velocity were tested using videos with velocities and spatial frequencies that were not included in the weight optimisation. To show the advantage of using multiple temporal frequency channels the weighted response is compared with a single group of EMDs. The single EMD group was also subjected to the same stimuli that were used for weight optimisation. A single optimal weight (scaling factor) was calculated and applied to the single group of EMDs to allow for a fair comparison. Otherwise, the single group of EMDs (Fig. 1) would respond with a different order of magnitude when compared to the weighted responses of the 25 groups of EMDs (Fig. 3). The results shown in Fig. 5 give the output of both systems against the image velocity and spatial frequency, as well as the absolute error in velocity estimation. The output and absolute error of the single scaled-group of EMDs are given in Figs. 5a and 5b, respectively. The results from the weighted groups of EMDs tuned to different temporal frequencies are in Figs. 5c and 5d.

Figures 5c and 5d show the output and the error in velocity estimation for the system using weighted groups of EMDs, respectively. It is clear that within

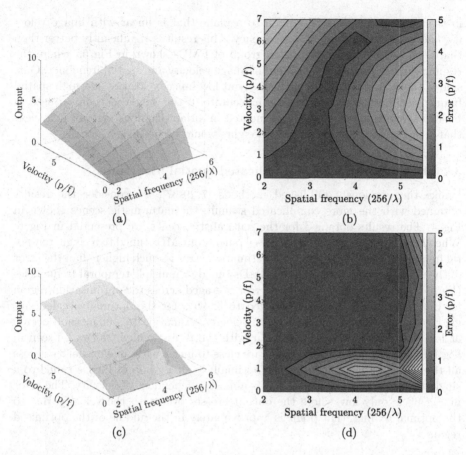

Fig. 5. Comparison between two methods to estimate image velocity from video sequences showing sinusoidal gratings of different spatial frequencies moving at different velocities. Velocity in the axes of the figures refers to image velocity and is in the units pixels per frame. The units of spatial frequency are the number of sine wave gratings, which is equivalent to $256/\lambda$ (where λ is the spatial wavelength). The two methods are optimally scaling a single group of EMDs, compared with an optimal weighting of 25 EMD groups tuned to different temporal frequencies. Figures 5a and 5b show the response and error in estimating velocity, respectively for the optimally scaled single group of EMDs as a benchmark. Figures 5c and 5d show the same for our approach of optimally weighting 25 EMD groups tuned to different temporal frequencies. The red crosses on the four plots show the stimulus parameters that were used in the weight optimisation. (Color figure online)

the region optimised (shown by the red crosses) that the error is low. The average absolute percentage error within the optimisation region for the multiple weighted groups' tuned to different temporal frequencies velocity estimate was 3.86%. This was significantly lower than the 42.57% for the single scaled-group in Fig. 5b. We also observe that the surface plot in Fig. 5c has the desired properties

in the optimised region: it is close to a plane that is linear with image velocity, and independent of spatial frequency. This result is significantly better than
that obtained by the single scaled-group of EMDs shown in Fig. 5a where the
response increases with the product of image velocity and spatial frequency. Outside of the optimised range, particularly at low image velocities and high spatial
frequencies, both methods become inaccurate. If this was a mechanism used in
biological systems, or it was implemented in an autonomous system, it is clear
that a method for re-adjusting the weights would be needed.

3.2   Extension to More Complicated Spatial Structures

Unlike the previously published methods [7, 29, 37], we consider the results
obtained with the more complicated stimuli, the naturalistic scenes shown in
Fig. 4. The results obtained for the naturalistic scenes are presented in Fig. 6.
When based on the optimally weighted output of EMDs tuned to a single temporal frequency (Fig. 6b) the velocity estimation error is much higher than the error
of the estimate from the weighted EMDs tuned to multiple temporal frequencies
(Fig. 6d). The absolute percentage error averaged across the optimisation region
for our method was 3.93% compared to 32.95% for the optimally scaled single group of EMDs. Some inaccurate velocity estimation by our method occurs
at low image velocities, in particular with the tree stimulus, as can be seen in
Fig. 6d. Other than that the results are close to linear with image velocity across
all three scenes. The output of the optimally scaled group of EMDs tuned to a
single temporal frequency (Fig. 6a) is almost independent of velocity. The error
in Fig. 6b is only low where the output crosses over with the velocity, due to
the optimal scaling, that point is approximately in the middle of the optimised
region.

4   Discussion

In summary, we have demonstrated that using EMDs tuned to multiple temporal
frequencies to estimate image velocity is more accurate and reliable than using
a group of EMDs tuned to a single temporal frequency. The behavioural work
on crabs by Nalbach appears to be the only study to suggest that biological
vision systems exploit this strategy [23]. Further support for the possibility of
using EMDs with different sampling bases, and thus temporal frequency tunings,
comes from studies of the blowfly motion vision pathway. Schuling et al. recorded
the activity of the directional selective H1-cell and found responses induced
by consecutive stimulation of ommatidia that were separated by much larger
distances than one interommatidial angle [32]. This could in principle be the
basis for establishing EMDs with different temporal frequency tunings. The other
parameter that can be altered to modify the temporal frequency tuning, the
time constant of the detector, has also been shown to be adaptable, either due
to motion adaptation [21] or changes in the animal's locomotor state [19].

   In previous attempts to estimate image velocity using elementary movement
detector models [7, 29, 37] naturalistic scenes as input patterns had not been

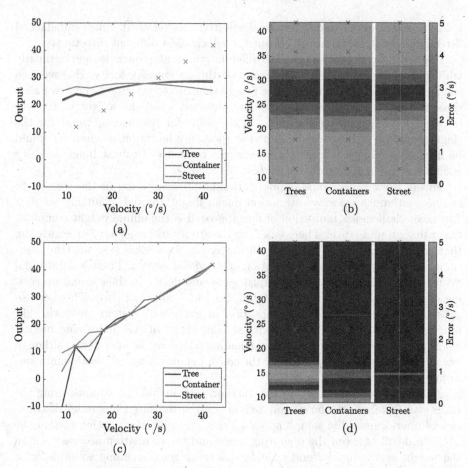

Fig. 6. Comparison between two methods to estimate image velocity from three video sequences of different scenes. The image velocity corresponds directly to an angular velocity since the video sequences are generated from rotational self-motion. The same comparison is made between a single optimally scaled detector array and 25 optimally weighted detector arrays. Figures 6a and 6b show the response and error in estimating image velocity respectively for the optimally scaled single group of EMDs as a benchmark. Figures 6c and 6d show the same for our method, optimally weighting 25 EMD groups tuned to different temporal frequencies. The red crosses mark values included in the weight optimisation for each scene. (Color figure online)

included. The successful testing of our approach when using moving naturalistic scenes suggests its suitability for implementation in autonomous robotic systems [22,31].

Additional advantages of this system result from using balanced Reichardt detectors, which previous studies did not exploit [7,29,37]. The first of these advantages is that there will not be a transient response when the light intensity changes. Imbalanced detectors produce a transient output when the light intensity changes, even without any directional motion. The second advantage of using balanced detectors is that directional selectivity is retained. Since imbalanced detectors have an asymmetric output for velocities in different directions.

Implementing detectors tuned to different temporal frequencies and optimally adding their outputs offers a method to estimate image velocity. However, no single weight vector was found that provided accurate velocity estimates for all three scenes. Accurate results were only obtained when the weight vector was re-calculated for each scene. This was the same for the scaling factor for the single group of EMDs - again implying that an adaptation mechanism would be needed in biological and robotic systems to enable a robust image velocity estimate across a wide range of scenes.

Future work will include online learning, and adaptation of the weights to enable continuous velocity estimation during flight through changing scenery. The most challenging limitation of our approach is the offline weight computation using ground truth. There is a high sensitivity to image statistics meaning that small changes can lead to significant errors. Biological systems may overcome this challenge through adaptation in the visual system. There is substantial evidence that biological systems adjust gains and delays in their visual processing depending on their locomotive state ([6,15,24,30], rev.: [20]). There is also substantial evidence for local adaptation in the visual system for both light intensity [18,35,36], and image contrast [12]. Many of the underlying mechanisms may provide guidance for implementing adaptive vision systems, although few of them have been exploited for the control of autonomous robotic platforms so far.

Additional improvements to this method may include (i) co-optimising the EMD parameters with the output weights, (ii) optimising the spatial distribution of inter-ommatidial sampling resolutions, and (iii) investigating further the likely trade-off between the operating range and the estimation accuracy. Often the weight vector had several weights that were zero, meaning some detector parameterisations were not integrated into the output. This reduces computational efficiency, as the visual input is still passed through these zero-weight parameterisations. Co-optimising both the output weights and EMD parameters could help reduce the number of different detectors needed. However, this co-optimisation would require a larger dataset of velocities and scenes. Furthermore, while we used a fixed resolution of 0.625°, compound eyes have different resolutions depending both on the species [16] and the location in the compound eye [17]. Spatially varying resolution across the visual plane has demonstrated advantages for robotic systems [8]. Therefore, systematic investigation into the performance using different resolution schemes could improve future performance.

The EMD, or Reichardt detector, is one amongst other detectors analysing directional motion [5] and its biological implementation is still ongoing. Specifically, in fruitflies, state-of-the-art experimental techniques including genetics tools have provided powerful methods to identify the neural elements corresponding to the EMD's functional components [9,11,14]. The results of those efforts have led to several amendments to the detector's original functional layout as shown in Fig. 1 that was based on a phenomenological model. This methodology is not limited to the Reichardt detector, and can, in theory, be applied to any model of EMD (some other models outlined in [1,5,9]).

In summary, combining known motor activity, local adaptation of visual processing, and weighted detectors tuned to different temporal frequencies could provide an energy-efficient method for online velocity calculation using simple elementary movement detectors. Our study provides a proof of concept that it is possible to estimate image velocity by summing the outputs of weighted Reichardt detector arrays tuned to different temporal frequencies.

References

1. Adelson, E.H.: The extraction of spatio-temporal energy in human and machine vision. In: IEEE Workshop on Motion: Representation and Analysis, pp. 151–155 (1986)
2. Aulinas, J., Petillot, Y., Salvi, J., Lladó, X.: The SLAM problem: a survey. In: Artificial Intelligence Research and Development, pp. 363–371 (2008)
3. Baker, S., Matthews, I.: Lucas-kanade 20 years on: a unifying framework. Int. J. Comput. Vis. **56**, 221–255 (2004). https://doi.org/10.1023/B:VISI.0000011205.11775.fd10.1023/B:VISI.0000011205.11775.fd
4. Borst, A., Egelhaaf, M.: Principles of visual motion detection. Trends Neurosci. **12**(8), 297–306 (1989)
5. Borst, A., Egelhaaf, M.: Detecting visual motion: theory and models. In: Visual Motion and Its Role in the Stabilization of Gaze, vol. 3, pp. 3–27 (1993)
6. Chiappe, M.E., Seelig, J.D., Reiser, M.B., Jayaraman, V.: Walking modulates speed sensitivity in drosophila motion vision. Curr. Biol. **20**(16), 1470–1475 (2010)
7. Cope, A.J., Sabo, C., Gurney, K., Vasilaki, E., Marshall, J.A.: A model for an angular velocity-tuned motion detector accounting for deviations in the corridor-centering response of the bee. PLoS Comput. Biol. **12**(5), e1004887 (2016)
8. D'Angelo, G., et al.: Event-based eccentric motion detection exploiting time difference encoding. Front. Neurosci. **14**, 451 (2020)
9. Eichner, H., Joesch, M., Schnell, B., Reiff, D.F., Borst, A.: Internal structure of the fly elementary motion detector. Neuron **70**(6), 1155–1164 (2011)
10. Esch, H.E., Zhang, S., Srinivasan, M.V., Tautz, J.: Honeybee dances communicate distances measured by optic flow. Nature **411**(6837), 581–583 (2001)
11. Groschner, L.N., Malis, J.G., Zuidinga, B., Borst, A.: A biophysical account of multiplication by a single neuron. Nature **603**(7899), 119–123 (2022)
12. Harris, R.A., O'Carroll, D.C., Laughlin, S.B.: Contrast gain reduction in fly motion adaptation. Neuron **28**(2), 595–606 (2000)
13. Ibbotson, M.: Evidence for velocity-tuned motion-sensitive descending neurons in the honeybee. Proc. Roy. Soc. Lond. Ser. B Biol. Sci. **268**(1482), 2195–2201 (2001)
14. Joesch, M., Weber, F., Eichner, H., Borst, A.: Functional specialization of parallel motion detection circuits in the fly. J. Neurosci. **33**(3), 902–905 (2013)
15. Jung, S.N., Borst, A., Haag, J.: Flight activity alters velocity tuning of fly motion-sensitive neurons. J. Neurosci. **31**(25), 9231–9237 (2011)
16. Kirschfeld, K.: The resolution of lens and compound eyes. In: Zettler, F., Weiler, R. (eds.) Neural Principles in Vision. LIFE SCIENCES, pp. 354–370. Springer, Heidelberg (1976). https://doi.org/10.1007/978-3-642-66432-8_19
17. Land, M.F.: Variations in the structure and design of compound eyes. In: Stavenga, D.G., Hardie, R.C. (eds.) Facets of Vision, pp. 90–111. Springer, Heidelberg (1989). https://doi.org/10.1007/978-3-642-74082-4_5

18. Laughlin, S.B., Hardie, R.C.: Common strategies for light adaptation in the peripheral visual systems of fly and dragonfly. J. Comp. Physiol. **128**, 319–340 (1978).
https://doi.org/10.1007/BF00657606

19. Longden, K.D., Krapp, H.G.: State-dependent performance of optic-flow processing
interneurons. J. Neurophysiol. **102**(6), 3606–3618 (2009)

20. Longden, K.D., Krapp, H.G.: Sensory neurophysiology: motion vision during motor
action. Curr. Biol. **21**(17), R650–R652 (2011)

21. Maddess, T., Laughlin, S.B.: Adaptation of the motion-sensitive neuron H1 is generated locally and governed by contrast frequency. Proc. Roy. Soc. Lond. Ser. B
Biol. Sci. **225**(1239), 251–275 (1985)

22. Milde, M.B., Bertrand, O.J., Ramachandran, H., Egelhaaf, M., Chicca, E.: Spiking elementary motion detector in neuromorphic systems. Neural Comput. **30**(9),
2384–2417 (2018)

23. Nalbach, H.O.: Three temporal frequency channels constitute the dynamics of the
optokinetic system of the crab, *Carcinus maenas* (L.). Biol. Cybern. **61**(1), 59–70
(1989)

24. Niell, C.M., Stryker, M.P.: Modulation of visual responses by behavioral state in
mouse visual cortex. Neuron **65**(4), 472–479 (2010)

25. Niven, J.E., Laughlin, S.B.: Energy limitation as a selective pressure on the evolution of sensory systems. J. Exp. Biol. **211**(11), 1792–1804 (2008)

26. Olshausen, B.A., Field, D.J.: Natural image statistics and efficient coding. Netw.
Comput. Neural Syst. **7**(2), 333–339 (1996)

27. Pritsker, A.A.B.: Introduction to Simulation and SLAM II. Halsted Press (1984)

28. Reichardt, W., Egelhaaf, M., Schlögel, R.: Movement detectors provide sufficient
information for local computation of 2-D velocity field. Naturwissenschaften **75**,
313–315 (1988)

29. Riabinina, O., Philippides, A.O.: A model of visual detection of angular speed for
bees. J. Theor. Biol. **257**(1), 61–72 (2009)

30. Rosner, R., Egelhaaf, M., Warzecha, A.K.: Behavioural state affects motion-
sensitive neurones in the fly visual system. J. Exp. Biol. **213**(2), 331–338 (2010)

31. Schoepe, T., Gutierrez-Galan, D., Dominguez-Morales, J.P., Jimenez-Fernandez,
A., Linares-Barranco, A., Chicca, E.: Neuromorphic sensory integration for com-
bining sound source localization and collision avoidance. In: 2019 IEEE Biomedical
Circuits and Systems Conference (BioCAS), pp. 1–4. IEEE (2019)

32. Schuling, F., Mastebroek, H., Bult, R., Lenting, B.: Properties of elementary movement detectors in the *fly Calliphora erythrocephala*. J. Comp. Physiol. A **165**(2),
179–192 (1989). https://doi.org/10.1007/BF00619192

33. Shoemaker, P.A., O'Carroll, D.C., Straw, A.D.: Velocity constancy and models for
wide-field visual motion detection in insects. Biol. Cybern. **93**(4), 275–287 (2005).
https://doi.org/10.1007/s00422-005-0007-y

34. Snippe, H.P., Koenderink, J.J.: Extraction of optical velocity by use of multi-input
Reichardt detectors. JOSA A **11**(4), 1222–1236 (1994)

35. Stöckl, A.L., O'Carroll, D.C., Warrant, E.J.: Neural summation in the hawkmoth
visual system extends the limits of vision in dim light. Curr. Biol. **26**(6), 821–826
(2016)

36. Van Hateren, J.: Processing of natural time series of intensities by the visual system
of the blowfly. Vis. Res. **37**(23), 3407–3416 (1997)

37. Zanker, J.M., Srinivasan, M.V., Egelhaaf, M.: Speed tuning in elementary motion
detectors of the correlation type. Biol. Cybern. **80**(2), 109–116 (1999). https://doi.
org/10.1007/s004220050509

Comparison of Proximal Leg Strain in Locomotor Model Organisms Using Robotic Legs

Gesa F. Dinges[ID], William P. Zyhowski[ID], C. A. Goldsmith[ID],
and Nicholas S. Szczecinski[✉][ID]

Neuro-Mechanical Intelligence Laboratory, CEMR Mechanical and Aerospace L4, West
Virginia University, Morgantown, WV, USA
nicholas.szczecinski@mail.wvu.edu

Abstract. Insects use various sensory organs to monitor proprioceptive and exteroceptive information during walking. The measurement of forces in the exoskeleton is facilitated by campaniform sensilla (CS), which monitor resisted muscle forces through the detection of exoskeletal strains. CS are commonly found in leg segments arranged in fields, groups, or as single units. Most insects have the highest density of sensor locations on the trochanter, a proximal leg segment. CS are arranged homologously across species, suggesting comparable functions despite noted morphological differences. Furthermore, the trochanter–femur joint is mobile in some species and fused in others. To investigate how different morphological arrangements influence strain sensing in different insect species, we utilized two robotic models of the legs of the fruit fly *Drosophila melanogaster* and the stick insect *Carausius morosus*. Both insect species are past and present model organisms for unraveling aspects of motor control, thus providing extensive information on sensor morphology and, in-part, function. The robotic models were dynamically scaled to the legs of the insects, with strain gauges placed with correct orientations according to published data. Strains were detected during stepping on a treadmill, and the sensor locations and leg morphology played noticeable roles in the strains that were measured. Moreover, the sensor locations that were absent in one species relative to the other measured strains that were also being measured by the existing sensors. These findings contributed to our understanding of load sensing in animal locomotion and the relevance of sensory organ morphology in motor control.

Keywords: Strain · Campaniform sensilla · Load · Walking · Insect

1 Introduction

The ability to monitor and respond to dynamic, mechanical stimuli is an important aspect of robust locomotion. Multiple sensory structures sensitive to proprioceptive stimuli can be found in insect legs (Fig. 1A). Their collective output can be integrated

---

G. F. Dinges and W. P. Zyhowski—These authors contributed equally to this work.

F. Meder et al. (Eds.): Living Machines 2023, LNAI 14157, pp. 411–427, 2023.
https://doi.org/10.1007/978-3-031-38857-6_30

in the nervous system to modify or reinforce motor output, contributing to adaptability. Sensing the magnitudes and dynamics of forces that arise during walking provides useful information to the locomotor system [1, 2]. Changes in force that each leg experiences are accompanied by changes in load. Because the gravitational load that the body exerts on the legs must be continuously supported [3], the measurement of forces in the legs can influence individual legs to transition between their stance and swing phases during walking [4], ultimately influencing interleg coordination [5, 6].

Campaniform sensilla (CS) are sensory organs that facilitate force measurements, monitoring resisted muscle forces through the detection of strains in the exoskeleton [7, 8] (Fig. 1A1). Resisted muscle forces arise as legs transition during stepping from the swing to the stance phase, during which body weight support is initialized. CS are embedded within the exoskeleton, with cap-like structures that deform when the surrounding cuticle is strained. Electrophysiological experiments have shown that CS fire during the onset of the anterior extreme position (anterior-most position at the onset of stance phase, AEP) [8, 9] (Fig. 1A2). This type of CS activity can enhance the magnitude of muscular contractions, increasing support for the added load [7, 10, 11]. CS also signal the termination of the stance phase at the posterior extreme position (posterior-most position at the termination of stance phase, PEP) [6, 12] (Fig. 1A2). Between the onset and termination of stance phase, the neuronal responses of CS adapt under exposure to force [2, 13].

Leg CS are generally located in the proximity of joints [14]. There, they can be found in fields, groups, or as single sensors [15–18]. In groups and fields, CS caps are commonly elliptical, with the orientation of their axes producing directional sensitivity [8, 13, 14, 19–21]. This is beneficial for two reasons, as multiple sensors with the same orientation allow for range fractionation in force encoding and redundant measurements reduce noise [1, 22]. Moreover, different components of forces can be measured depending on the orientation of a sensor relative to limb segments. For example, axial torques, as seen during supination and pronation movements, create helical forces that can be detected by sensors with a long-axis orientation of 45° relative to the limb's long axis [6, 13].

Groups and fields of CS are more commonly found in proximal leg segments [23]. The trochanter, a limb segment located between the coxa, the most proximal limb segment, and femur, the limb-segment between trochanter and tarsus, acts as a focal point for forces generated by multiple leg and body muscles [24, 25]. In the stick insect *Carausius morosus*, four fields of CS on the posterior, anterior, and dorsal faces encode external loads and strains [25, 26]. Within each field, the sensors' long-axis orientations are similar, creating functional subunits [26]. Extensive electrophysiological investigations in *C. morosus* have shown that groups G1 and G2 on the posterior and anterior trochanter monitor load in the posterior and anterior direction, respectively [19, 26, 27]. G3, on the dorsal trochanter, encodes increases in dorsal load and decreases in ventral load [25], while G4, also on the dorsal trochanter, shows mirrored directional sensitivities and directly responds to depressor muscle contractions [25]. Together, G3 and G4 encode the increases and decreases of load in the dorsal–ventral plane of the coxa–trochanter joint [25].

Other insects, even the significantly smaller and lighter fruit fly *Drosophila melanogaster*, have CS in some of the same leg locations, indicating potential functional homology; however, morphological differences have been noted [1, 17, 28]. The *D. melanogaster* trochanter contains the trochanter field (TrF), which is homologous to G3 + G4 and consists of two subunits [15, 17, 18]. Further, a group of three sensors can be found on the posterior trochanter, all with the same axis orientations. Unlike in *C. morosus* and the cockroach *Periplaneta americana*, *D. melanogaster* and the blow fly *Calliphora vomitoria* do not have anterior trochanteral CS [1].

Although both species have CS on their trochanter, the trochanter–femur joints' mobility may influence strain sensing in these locations. This joint in *C. morosus* is fused [29–31], while in *D. melanogaster* the joint's mobility has not been conclusively determined [32–35]. Changing the mobility of this joint may contribute to changes in the orientation of the leg, impacting force distributions across the various leg segments. In this manner, leg orientation has been found to directly affect CS discharge [25]. Although the principal aspects of locomotion are comparable between different insects, characteristics such as body weight, leg and sensor morphology, and average walking speed may influence the activity of leg CS. Body weight has been shown to be reflected in the range of cap sizes [1] as well as the number of CS. *C. morosus*, with an average mass of 800 mg, has more CS than the 1-mg *D. melanogaster*. However, the 30-mg juvenile cockroach contains a similar number of CS as *D. melanogaster*. This suggests that the fly's CS fields may monitor the same force despite the insect's size [1]. Nonetheless, flies are significantly smaller than the insects that have commonly been used to study leg CS function, which introduces methodological limitations.

A key element for investigating the function of load sensors within neuromuscular systems is understanding what strains arise in different limb segments during cyclic movements. While larger insects like cockroaches and stick insects allow for the direct measurement of strains [36] and neuronal activity [6, 13, 19, 23, 25, 26, 28, 37, 38], smaller insects like *D. melanogaster*, while advantageous because of its vast genetic toolbox, only produce minute forces that are difficult to monitor using modern tools. Thus, approaches like that of Zyhowski et al. (2023), which used a stick insect-inspired robotic leg to analyze strain patterns similarly to electrophysiological experiments in real animals, provide an opportunity to investigate strain in smaller insects.

In the present study, we utilized an updated robotic leg modeled from *D. melanogaster* [39] and a robotic leg modeled from *C. morosus* [40], with both legs dynamically scaled to each insect. These legs should experience inertial, viscous, elastic, and gravitational forces proportionally similar to the corresponding insect legs. We investigated what strains are detected by sensors with correct orientations and what is detected by the fields that are present in some species and absent in others. The results underlined that the sensor locations and leg morphology influenced the detected strains in the proximal leg segment, creating noticeable differences in which aspects of load changes throughout the stance phase were captured. Further, the "missing" sensor locations detected tensile strains similar to those detected by sensors in existing locations on the other animal. These findings aid our understanding of load sensing and the relevance of sensory organ morphology.

2 Materials and Methods

2.1 General Setup

Based on previous publications [39, 40], the legs consisted of three MX-28AT Dynamixel servomotors (Dynamixel, Seoul, Korea) connected in series via brackets and hollow 3D-printed limb segments manufactured with Onyx [41] using a Markforged Mark 2 (Markforged, Waltham, MA, USA). MATLAB (2021b; MathWorks, Natick, MA, USA) controlled the servomotor angles to execute footpaths based on the inverse kinematics published in Zyhowski et al. (2023; Fig. 1 B, C). For the *D. melanogaster* model, the inverse kinematics were calculated in the same manner; however, a shorter step trajectory was implemented based on published data [34]. Consequently, the legs stepped on a treadmill (as in Zyhowski et al., 2023), simulating an anteriorly directed body movement similar to those seen in walking animals. During the stance phase in each step, the leg supported the carriage's weight and simulated body weight using a linear guide (Fig. 1). To simulate different walking speeds, we altered the duration of the stance phase: (1) 2-s swing, 2-s stance; (2) 2-s swing, 4-s stance; and (3) 2-s swing, 6-s stance.

Strains were detected using strain gauge rosettes (C5K-06-S5198–350-33F; Micro-Measurements, Raleigh, NC, USA). Using operational amplifiers, their signals were amplified and converted to 12-bit digital signals using an OpenCM 9.04 microcontroller (Robotis Inc., Lake Forest, CA, USA). Strain gauges were placed onto the proximal-most end of the femur in each leg based on published scanning electron images of *C. morosus* [42] and *D. melanogaster* [15] (Fig. 1 Bi-B3, Ci-C3). Because CS are most sensitive to strains along their short axis, we oriented the strain gauges to match the short axis orientations of the majority of the CS within each location [8, 13, 14, 20, 21, 43] (Fig. 1A2). This also determined our labeling of each location, with *axial* describing the group with more short axes along the axial plane of the leg, and *transverse* the group with more short axes along the transverse axes of the leg. For locations with CS that have mirrored axes (G2, G3 + 4, TrF) we used two of the strain gauge axes, set perpendicular to each other by 90°, to capture the naturally occurring sensitivities of the CS fields. For the locations without a perpendicular subgroup (G1, TrG), we also recorded from two strain gauge axes to measure any strains that the animals do not capture (Fig. 1 B3, C3).

2.2 Legs

To compare how different leg morphologies may contribute to different proximal strains, we used two different robotic legs, one for each insect (Fig. 1 B1-B2, C1-C1). For the stick insect, we used a scale of 25:1, which is an upscaled version of the Zyhowski et al. (2023) leg. For the fly, we used an updated version of the Goldsmith et al. (2019) Drosophibot leg, scaled 400:1. By scaling the legs in this manner, both robotic legs had the same length dimensions.

In addition to scaling, the stick insect leg was further modified by adding a round, silicone foot. In preliminary experiments, this increased friction with the substrate, which prevented the leg from slipping on the treadmill. These types of friction-increasing components are common in insects such as the adhesive organs found on the *C. morosus* tarsus [44]. The same foot was also attached to the *Drosophila* leg (Fig. 1A1).

Figure 1B1 shows the robotic stick insect leg, which had 3 degrees of freedom and was modeled after the morphology detailed in Cruse et al. (1995). The leg consisted of the coxa, a fused trochanter–femur, and tibia (limb-segment between femur and tarsus) segments. The movement of the leg was generated by the thorax–coxa (ThC, θ_1), coxa–trochanter (CTr, θ_2), and femur–tibia (FTi, θ_3) joints. Figure 1C1 shows the robotic fly leg, which also had 3 degrees of freedom and was modeled in a similar fashion based on the design from Goldsmith et al. (2019, 2022). It is important to note that both legs had the same degrees of freedom but differed in their axes of rotation (how the movement is generated). Specifically, the ThC and CTr joints rotated the legs in different planes. The FTi joint had the same axis of rotation in both robotic legs.

2.3 Dynamic Scaling

Because the robot legs are much larger and more massive than insect legs, it is necessary to dynamically scale their motion relative to that of the insects. Elastic and viscous forces have been shown to dominate the dynamics of insect leg joints [45–47], with legs possessing gravity-independent posture that slowly returns to equilibrium when disturbed. In contrast, robot legs (in particular, servomotors) are massive, meaning that even moderate accelerations during motion may result in large inertial forces. Furthermore, when powered down, robot legs hang with gravity, in stark contrast to insect legs [46]. These differences in dynamics were accounted for here in two ways. First, when the robot leg was powered up, the servomotors at their joints had programmed equilibrium angles and produced torque proportional to the deviation from these equilibrium angles, functioning like springs and imbuing the leg with an "active" elasticity. Powered up legs no longer hanged with gravity. Second, increasing the stepping period of the robot reduced leg acceleration and, therefore, inertial forces. The resulting robot legs exhibited a balance of inertial, viscous, elastic, and gravitational forces comparable to an insect, despite the magnitude of these forces being much larger in the robot legs.

We scaled the stepping period of the robotic legs by maintaining the same ratio between the motion's frequency and the leg's natural frequency (which depends on the balance between it elastic and inertial forces) in the robot and the insect. For example, *C. morosus* has an approximate natural period of 0.132 s [40] and a step period of around 1 s [48]; a step is approximately six times longer than the natural period. The robotic *C. morosus* leg was similar in that its natural period was 0.63 s [40], with a step period of approximately 4 s. The robotic *D. melanogaster* step time was calculated with the same process, and its step period was also approximately 4 s [34, 39].

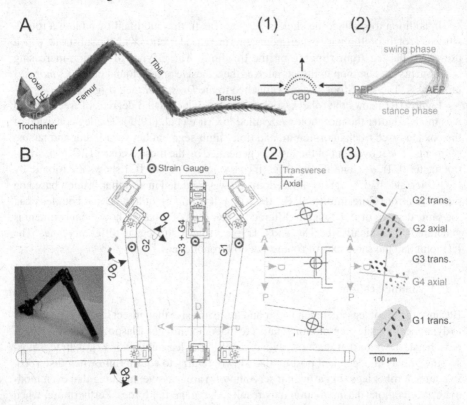

Fig. 1. Experimental Setup; (A) nano-CT rendered leg of *Drosophila melanogaster*. Image taken from Dinges et al., 2022, modified in color. Limb segment labels were added; TrF and TrG approximate locations were labeled; (A1) schematic drawing of a CS experiencing compressive strains, schematic cap undergoes lateral displacement; (A2) example trajectories of a *Drosophila* front leg step cycle. The trajectories were traced from tracked leg movements courtesy of the Büschges Lab (University of Cologne). PEP – posterior extreme position, AEP – anterior extreme position; **(B)** image of robotic stick insect leg; **(B1)** location of strain gauges on robotic stick insect leg; **(B2)** close up of **B1**, indicating axis orientations of strain gauges; joint angles are noted on the anterior face of the leg **(B3)** schematic drawing of CS morphology taken from published SEM images; gray circles indicate indentations in the cuticle; crosshairs display perpendicular compression axes at each location **(C)** image of robotic *Drosophila melanogaster* leg; **(C1)** location of strain gauges on robotic *D. melanogaster* leg; **(C2)** close up of **B1**, indicating axis orientations of strain gauges; joint angles are noted on the anterior and dorsal faces; **(C3)** schematic drawing of CS morphology taken from published SEM images; trans, transverse; both axial and transverse are relative descriptors. A, anterior face; D, dorsal face; P, posterior face.

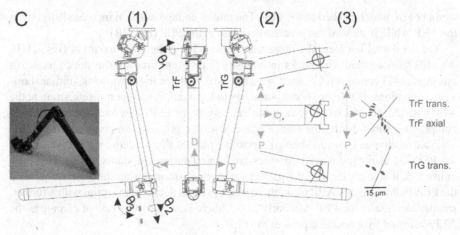

Fig. 1. (*continued*)

2.4 Data Analysis

Strain was detected over the course of 10 steps and averaged. The rate of change was calculated using averaged and smoothed strain data. All analyses were completed using MATLAB. Images were compiled using CorelDRAW (X8; Alludo, Ottawa, Canada).

3 Results

To investigate how insect leg morphology, stepping speed, and sensor presence and location affect strain monitoring during walking, we evaluated the strains that stick insect- and *Drosophila*-like robotic leg segments experience during treadmill stepping.

3.1 Strains Detected by CS-Like Sensors

To test how changes in stepping speed affect strain monitoring in the legs, we recorded strain during stepping on a treadmill at three different speeds. The speeds were modulated by altering the duration of the stance phase (2 s/4 s/6 s), ultimately prolonging the duration for which the leg was required to support the "body".

The two strain locations on the anterior face of the leg, G2 transverse and G2 axial, detected different strains during the stance period. G2 transverse contains 6 CS and G2 axial contains 12 CS in the stick insect, and the CS of each subfield share the same short-axis orientations, with the two groups perpendicular to each other (Fig. 1 B3). In the robotic leg, G2 transverse detected decreases in strain, peaking at the AEP of the stance phase, indicating tensile strain. The detected strains decreased gradually over time after the AEP, with a small peak at the PEP. The rate of change in strain reached its lowest value at the AEP and its highest at the PEP (Fig. 2B). The G2 axial group was exposed to the inverse during stepping (Fig. 2A). Unlike G2 transverse, this location was under compressive force during the stance phase. At the AEP, a gradual increase in detected strain began, which peaked at the PEP. The rate of change in strain increased slightly at the AEP, while it showed the greatest decrease at the PEP (Fig. 2B).

On the dorsal leg face, the more transverse G3 and the more axial G4 (Fig. 1B3), detected tensile strain with peaks in intensity at different times in the stance phase. In the animal, G3 contains 8 CS and G4 12 CS, with both locations showing similar short-axis orientations. G3 in the model, similarly to G2 axial, began monitoring strain at the AEP with the gradual increase in strain peaking at the PEP. This location experienced compressive force during the stance phase, with the greatest compression at the PEP. The rate of change in strain showed a positive peak at the AEP and a negative peak at the PEP. G4 also experienced compressive strains during the stance phase. However, unlike G3, it was exposed to the greatest amount of strain during the AEP rather than the PEP. Following this AEP peak, there was a gradual decrease in strain, with a further, smaller increase at the PEP. Similarly to G3, there was a positive rate of change at the AEP, followed by a negative peak at the PEP.

G1 is located on the posterior leg face in *C. morosus* and consists of 11 CS, which are largely oriented in the transverse direction (Fig. B3). Here, during stepping, G1 detected strain similarly to G4, with a primary peak at the AEP, followed by a gradual decline and a smaller peak at the PEP. It was also under compressive force during the stance phase. The rate of change in strain followed the same pattern as those of G2 axial, G3, and G4, with a positive peak at the AEP and negative peak at the PEP.

In the fly model, the anterior leg face contained no CS (Fig. 1C3); the CS closest to the anterior face (TrF transverse) detected tensile strain with a peak at the AEP. In the animal, this location contains five CS, all with the same short-axis orientation. This sensor location detected a rapid increase in strain with peak values at the AEP. The strain gradually decreased for the rest of the stance phase without a further increase at the PEP. The rate of change in strain only showed a positive peak at the AEP. This location was under compressive force during the stance phase. The more posterior subfield of the TrF, here referred to as TrF axial, contains 8 CS in the animal, all with the same short-axis orientation (Fig. 1C3). Similarly to TrF transverse, this location detected the greatest amount of strain at the AEP in our model; however, it detected tensile and not compressive forces. There was also a gradual decrease in strain through the rest of stance, with no further peaks. The rate of change in strain only showed a negative peak at the AEP.

The only remaining CS location of the fly, TrG, detected compressive strain. In the animal, it consists of three CS, all with the same short-axis orientation (Fig. 1C3). Similarly to TrF transverse, this location in our model experienced compressive forces and detected rapid increases in strain, peaking at the AEP. There was no further peak in strain measurement for the rest of the stance phase. Consequently, the rate of change in strain only increased at the AEP.

For all locations, independent of the modeled species, there were no apparent differences in the detected strains at different stepping speeds (Fig. 2A). This suggests that inertial forces do not dominate the dynamics and that the dynamic scaling of the leg was successful.

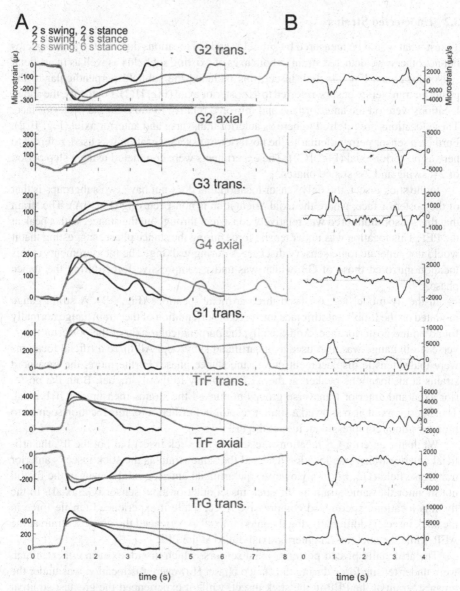

Fig. 2. Strain during stepping at different speeds; (A) strain recordings (microstrain) of the robotic stick insect (G2/G3/G4/G1) and *D. melanogaster* (TrF/TrG) at different stepping speeds; black line, 2 s swing, 2 s stance; grey, 2 s swing, 4 s stance; light grey, 2 s swing, 6 s stance; **(B)** rate of change (microstrain per s) curves for the 2-s swing/2-s stance strain recordings; trans, transverse; both axial and transverse are relative descriptors. Lines under plot G2 trans., schematize the swing phase using dotted lines, and stance phase using the solid line for each tested speed.

3.2 Undetected Strains

To test what would be measured by subfields and CS locations that exist in some species but not others, we detected strain in both axes of existing subfields as well as in artificial sensor locations. For the stick insect, this included the subfield perpendicular to the posterior transverse sensors, referred to as posterior axial (Fig. 1B2). For the fly, the added locations were on the anterior face and mirrored relative to those on the posterior face. These locations are referred to here as anterior transverse and anterior axial (Fig. 1C2). Further, a sensor perpendicular to the posterior transverse location was used, referred to here as posterior axial (Fig. 1C2). The experiments were completed using a step period of 2-s swing and 2-s stance phases.

In the stick insect, the only sensor location that does not have two subgroups is that of the posterior face, where the axial orientation is non-occurring (Fig. 3A). The strain that this sensor monitored was relatively consistent throughout the stance, with a peak at the PEP. This location was under tensile force during the stance phase, suggesting that it would not generate tonic sensory discharges during walking. The measurements at this location mirrored those of G3, which was under compressive force during the stance phase.

In the fly model leg, we used three artificial locations (Fig. 3B). A strain gauge mounted on the limb's anterior face mirrored the orientation of the strain gauge normally found on the posterior face. Additionally, the perpendicular axis of the posterior transverse strain gauge was also used as its artificial subgroup. All three artificial locations were under tensile displacement during the stance phase. Furthermore, the measured strains at all locations peaked at the AEP, similarly to the fly model. Both the posterior axial and anterior transverse groups mimicked the strains measured at TrF axial. The anterior axial also showed a similar response. Furthermore, this location seemed to monitor minor compressive forces at the PEP.

While the anterior CS locations are seen in the stick insect but not the fly, the artificial anterior transverse location detected the same strain as the stick insect's anterior transverse field (G2; Fig. 3). However, the artificial anterior axial sensor in the fly did not monitor the same strain as the stick insect anterior axial sensor (G2 axial). In the fly, this location experienced compressive force, while it experienced tensile force in the stick insect. Additionally, the fly anterior axial experienced the greatest strain at the AEP, while the stick insect anterior axial did so at the PEP.

The artificially placed posterior axial sensors, which do not exist in either animal, were under tensile force during the stance phase. However, this location was under the greatest strain at the PEP in the stick insect, while it experienced the greatest strain at the AEP in the fly.

4 Discussion

We compared changes in strain during stepping in two robotic legs, which were modeled after the morphology of two motor control model organism, *C. morosus* and *D. melanogaster*. We believe comparative studies not only benefit our understanding of proprioceptive function but also how species-specific morphology can affect homologous organs. The strains detected by the strain gauges reflected the onset of the AEP

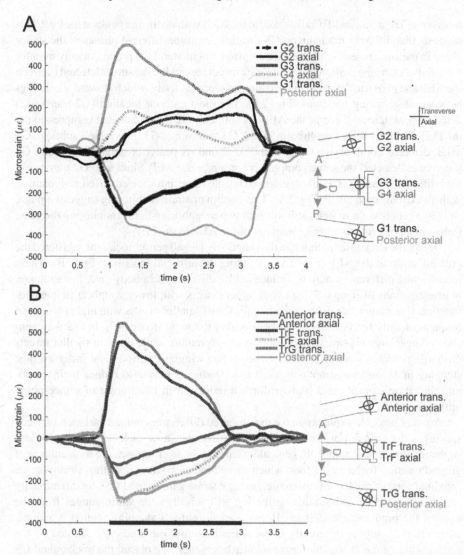

Fig. 3. All sensors on the robotic leg; (**A**) strain recordings of all strain gauges placed on the robotic stick insect leg; (**B**) strain recordings of all strain gauges placed on the robotic *D. melanogaster* leg; black lines mark proximal CS, colored lines mark artificially placed strain gauges; trans, transverse; both axial and transverse are relative descriptors. Bar along x-axes marks stance phase.

in both robotic legs. However, only the robotic leg model of *C. morosus* had sensors in locations predominantly sensitive to strains arising at the PEP, which is similar to results from electrophysiological recordings of all four stick insect trochanteral fields [25].

The stick insect G2 transverse, G4, and G1 transverse registered strain peaks at the AEP, while G2 axial and G3 peaked at the PEP. In the *D. melanogaster* model, TrF transverse, TrF axial, and TrG all peaked at the AEP, with no further peaks at the PEP. This suggests that different trochanteral CS locations monitor different phases of the stance phase in the stick insect, while *D. melanogaster* trochanteral CS predominantly monitor the onset of stance. Additionally, in the stick insect leg model, the strain detected between the AEP and PEP was reflected in the course of sensor activity, which showed similarities between neighboring locations (Fig. 2A). The most anterior location (G2 transverse) detected peak tensile force at the AEP. Its subfield, G2 axial, detected compression at the PEP, as did its dorsal neighboring field, G3 transverse. G3 transverse's subfield, G4 axial, detected compressive strain at the AEP, and its posterior neighboring field, G1 transverse, detected the same compressive strain at the AEP. Similar to G2 transverse, the artificially placed G1 axial experienced tensile force, but showed different dynamics, with an extreme at the PEP (Fig. 3A). This pattern of strain monitoring suggests a phase shift-like progression in field activity, with two neighboring fields monitoring the same strains in a posterior-to-anterior tracking of the AEP to the PEP.

Unlike the stick insect model, in the robotic fly leg, all sensor locations registered the greatest strain at the AEP (Fig. 2A), including the artificial locations (Fig. 3B). These fundamental differences may be influenced by differences in body size. For example, in investigations of wing CS, the CS of larger insects with lower wingbeat frequencies functioned as magnitude detectors, while the CS of smaller insects with higher wingbeat frequencies only fired at single instances within the wing stroke [49]. In this way, sensors in larger insects primarily detected force magnitude, while those in smaller insects primarily detected timing. Similar to the shorter wingbeat periods, the faster average stepping in *D. melanogaster* compared to *C. morosus* may also reduce their temporal integration capacity and, thus, enforce a reduction in monitoring of stance phase initiation [48–51].

Another possible explanation for the observed differences in load variation between species is the unique posture of the legs, in particular, how each leg is extended and supinated throughout stance. In general, extending the leg increases the moment arm of ground reaction forces at the foot, which should increase stress (and thus strain) on the proximal parts of the leg. Furthermore, because strain gauges (and CS) are directionally sensitive, pronating and supinating the leg will misalign the strain gauges from the axes of the predominant stresses. Because each animal's stepping motion is unique, these effects combine differently in each. Furthermore, our study was limited by the accessibility of the *D. melanogaster* robotic trochanter. We placed the trochanteral CS on the femur of both legs, which further changed their orientation throughout the step. In future investigations, we will extend the robotic *Drosophila* trochanter to fit the necessary CS and further explore the impact of the mobile trochanter–femur joint on load sensing.

For the stick insect, the leg extends to reach the AEP, flexes throughout the first half of stance, then extends throughout the second half of stance to reach the PEP [42]. As a result, the lever arm of the ground reaction force on the body starts large, then decreases, then increases. Simultaneously, the plane of the leg begins pronated and supinates throughout stance, meaning that stresses are initially not aligned with G4 axial, then align with G4 axial mid-stance, and finally misalign at the end of stance. These mechanisms appear to counterbalance one another, resulting in a relatively constant but ultimately "dual-peaked" profile in the stick insect G4 axial recording.

In contrast, the fruit fly leg remains quite flexed when reaching the AEP and then extends throughout stance to reach the PEP. Furthermore, the leg is neither pronated nor supinated at the AEP and is supinated at the PEP. These monotonic progressions from flexion to extension and from neutral to supination do not produce the same "dual-peaked" strain profiles seen in the stick insect. Instead, all the recordings from the fruit fly are "single-peaked". Although both species' legs perform the same roles of supporting and propelling the body, these differences in posture would certainly change the way that stress is applied to and resisted throughout the leg. Such postures may be the result of locomotion speed differences, as discussed above. An evolutionary and developmental survey of insect species, their locomotion speeds, their leg posture, and CS placement may reveal broader correlations between these behavioral and morphological properties.

The rate of change in strain at each sensor location may reflect neuronal activity during walking. CS discharges reflect both the amplitude and the rate of change of strain [2]. The aforementioned differences between the legs further suggest that the stick insect sensor locations monitor strain throughout the stance phase while those of *D. melanogaster* monitor strain solely at phase onset. Future investigations should model sensory discharges in response to the strain signals we recorded to gain insight into the features of loading that are emphasized within the nervous system. Potential experiments (i.e., using optogenetics) could illuminate if CS in *Drosophila* are active during the complete stance phase, during phases in which the rate of force changes, or solely at the onset of stance, as our experiments suggest.

The differences between the two legs in the functionality of the sensor locations legs, as discussed above, may also explain why *Drosophila* has fewer CS locations on its trochanter and the stick insect does not possess a G1 subfield. The *D. melanogaster* model's axial trochanter field detected tensile force at the AEP, which is what the missing locations would also monitor in this setup. The stick insect model's G3 transverse was under compression during the stance phase and detected similar strain developments as the missing posterior axial subfield. Additionally, all "missing" locations were exposed to tensile strain during stance phase, which may not lead to CS activity [43]. Notably, the present study was limited by the simplification of the sensor field by using strain gauges. The exact orientations of the caps within each field may vary, which could lead to sensory activation in individual sensors at different time points. Moreover, there may be differences in cellular properties between neurons associated with larger and smaller caps within one location.

In future studies, this experimental technique could be used to predict which CS fields and groups other insect species possess, based on the species' leg orientation and walking kinematics. Accurate predictions would support our main hypothesis that CS fields and groups that redundantly signal loads disappear over the course of evolution. Inaccurate predictions would suggest that this hypothesis is incomplete or incorrect. More closely examining the behavior of individual species may suggest other reasons for CS fields and groups changing over evolutionary time.

The present study investigated strains in a proximal limb segment in two morpho-logically different robotic legs. Generally, tension and compression were seen in the proximal limb segment of both robotic legs with amplitudes independent of the stepping speed. Furthermore, the waveform of the strain did not change with stepping speed, indicating that inertial forces were not dominating, and that the robotic models mimicked the dynamics of insect locomotion. In both legs, all but one of the morphologically correct locations were positioned in locations that are sensitive to compressive strains during the stance phase. There are, however, key differences, including the monitoring of both the AEP and PEP in the stick insect model and only the AEP in *D. melanogaster*. Further, there were clear differences between the models in the amplitudes of the rates of change of strain, with single peaks in the fly and dual peaks in the stick insect. These differences may be due to joint angles, loads, or CS morphology and orientation. To investigate this further, future experiments should analyze how joint movements may influence strain sensing and apply a dynamic discharge model to the recorded strain to understand how different sensors in different organisms may physiologically respond to load. These results can be taken into account in future animal experiments, as understanding how extremity morphology contributes to mechanosensory activity eases knowledge transfer between species. In conclusion, the current work contributes to the understanding of how differences in load sensors may influence neuromuscular systems and motor control.

Funding. G.F.D., W.P.Z., C.A.G., and N.S.S. were supported by NSF DBI 2015317 as part of the NSF/CIHR/DFG/FRQ/UKRI-MRC Next Generation Networks for Neuroscience Program. W.P.Z. and N.S.S. were supported by NSF IIS 2113028. G.F.D. was supported by DFG DI 2907/1-1 (Project number 500615768).

References

1. Harris, C.M., Dinges, G.F., Haberkorn, A., Gebehart, C., Büschges, A., Zill, S.N.: Gradients in mechanotransduction of force and body weight in insects. Arthropod Struct. Dev. **58**, 100970 (2020). https://doi.org/10.1016/j.asd.2020.100970
2. Zill, S.N., Dallmann, C.J., Büschges, A., Chaudhry, S., Schmitz, J.: Force dynamics and synergist muscle activation in stick insects: the effects of using joint torques as mechanical stimuli. J. Neurophysiol. **120**, 1807–1823 (2018). https://doi.org/10.1152/jn.00371.2018
3. Cruse, H.: Which parameters control the leg movement of a walking insect?: Ii. The start of the swing phase. J. Exp. Biol. **116**, 357–362 (1985). https://doi.org/10.1242/jeb.116.1.357
4. Cruse, H.: What mechanisms coordinate leg movement in walking arthropods? Trends Neurosci. **13**, 15–21 (1990). https://doi.org/10.1016/0166-2236(90)90057-H
5. Cruse, H.: The control of the anterior extreme position of the hindleg of a walking insect, Carausius morosus. Physiol. Entomol. **4**, 121–124 (1979). https://doi.org/10.1111/j.1365-3032.1979.tb00186.x
6. Dallmann, C.J., Hoinville, T., Dürr, V., Schmitz, J.: A load-based mechanism for inter-leg coordination in insects. Proc. R. Soc. B Biol. Sci. **284**, 20171755 (2017). https://doi.org/10.1098/rspb.2017.1755
7. Noah, J.A., Quimby, L., Frazier, S.F., Zill, S.N.: Sensing the effect of body load in legs: responses of tibial campaniform sensilla to forces applied to the thorax in freely standing cockroaches. J. Comp. Physiol. A **190**, 201–215 (2004). https://doi.org/10.1007/s00359-003-0487-y
8. Zill, S., Schmitz, J., Büschges, A.: Load sensing and control of posture and locomotion. Arthropod Struct. Dev. **33**, 273–286 (2004). https://doi.org/10.1016/j.asd.2004.05.005

9. Noah, A.J., Quimby, L., Frazier, F.S., Zill, S.N.: Force detection in cockroach walking reconsidered: discharges of proximal tibial campaniform sensilla when body load is altered. J. Comp. Physiol. A **187**, 769–784 (2001). https://doi.org/10.1007/s00359-001-0247-9
10. Kemmerling, S., Varju, D.: Regulation of the body-substrat-distance in the stick insect: responses to sinusoidal stimulation. Biol. Cybern. **39**, 129–137 (1981). https://doi.org/10.1007/BF00336739
11. Pearson, K.G.: Central programming and reflex control of walking in the cockroach. J. Exp. Biol. **56**, 173–193 (1972)
12. Zill, S.N., Keller, B.R., Duke, E.R.: Sensory signals of unloading in one leg follow stance onset in another leg: transfer of load and emergent coordination in cockroach walking. J. Neurophysiol. **101**, 2297–2304 (2009). https://doi.org/10.1152/jn.00056.2009
13. Zill, S., Moran, D.T.: The exoskeleton and insect proprioception. I. Responses of tibial campaniform sensilla to external and muscle-generated forces in the American cockroach, Periplaneta Americana. J. Exp. Biol. **91**(1), 1–24 (1981)
14. Pringle, J.W.S.: Proprioception in insects: I. A new type of mechanical receptor from the palps of the cockroach. J. Exp. Biol. **15**, 101–113 (1938)
15. Dinges, G.F., Chockley, A.S., Bockemühl, T., Ito, K., Blanke, A., Büschges, A.: Location and arrangement of campaniform sensilla in Drosophila melanogaster. J. Comp. Neurol. **529**, 905–925 (2021). https://doi.org/10.1002/cne.24987
16. Grünert, U., Gnatzy, W.: Campaniform sensilla of Calliphora vicina (Insecta, Diptera). Zoomorphology **106**, 320–328 (1987). https://doi.org/10.1007/BF00312006
17. Merritt, D.J., Murphey, R.K.: Projections of leg proprioceptors within the CNS of the fly Phormia in relation to the generalized insect ganglion. J. Comp. Neurol. **322**, 16–34 (1992). https://doi.org/10.1002/cne.903220103
18. Yasuyama, K., Salvaterra, P.M.: Localization of choline acetyltransferase-expressing neurons in Drosophila nervous system. Microsc. Res. Tech. **45**, 65–79 (1999). https://doi.org/10.1002/(sici)1097-0029(19990415)45:2%3C65::aid-jemt2%3E3.0.co;2-0
19. Delcomyn, F.: Activity and directional sensitivity of leg campaniform sensilla in a stick insect. J. Comp. Physiol. A **168**, 113–119 (1991). https://doi.org/10.1007/BF00217109
20. Hofmann, T., Bässler, U.: Response characteristics of single trochanteral campaniform sensilla in the stick insect, Cuniculina impigra. Physiol. Entomol. **11**, 17–21 (1986). https://doi.org/10.1111/j.1365-3032.1986.tb00386.x
21. Tuthill, J.C., Wilson, R.I.: Mechanosensation and adaptive motor control in insects. Curr. Biol. CB. **26**, R1022–R1038 (2016). https://doi.org/10.1016/j.cub.2016.06.070
22. Kaliyamoorthy, S., Zill, S.N., Quinn, R.D., Ritzmann, R.E., Choi, J.: finite element analysis of strains in a Blaberus cockroach leg during climbing. In: Proceedings 2001 IEEE/RSJ International Conference on Intelligent Robots and Systems. Expanding the Societal Role of Robotics in the Next Millennium (Cat. No.01CH37180), pp. 833–838. IEEE, Maui, HI, USA (2001). https://doi.org/10.1109/IROS.2001.976272
23. Akay, T., Haehn, S., Schmitz, J., Büschges, A.: Signals from load sensors underlie interjoint coordination during stepping movements of the stick insect leg. J. Neurophysiol. **92**, 42–51 (2004). https://doi.org/10.1152/jn.01271.2003
24. Marquardt, F.: Beiträge zur Anatomie der Muskulatur und der peripheren Nerven von Carausius Dixippus morosus Br.; Mit 5 Abb. im Text u. Taf (1939)
25. Zill, S.N., Schmitz, J., Chaudhry, S., Büschges, A.: Force encoding in stick insect legs delineates a reference frame for motor control. J. Neurophysiol. **108**, 1453–1472 (2012). https://doi.org/10.1152/jn.00274.2012
26. Hofmann, T., Bässler, U.: Anatomy and physiology of trochanteral campaniform sensilla in the stick insect, Cuniculina impigra. Physiol. Entomol. **7**, 413–426 (1982). https://doi.org/10.1111/j.1365-3032.1982.tb00317.x

27. Schmitz, J.: Load-compensating reactions in the proximal leg joints of stick insects during standing and walking. J. Exp. Biol. **183**(1), 15–33 (1993)
28. Zill, S.N., Neff, D., Chaudhry, S., Exter, A., Schmitz, J., Büschges, A.: Effects of force detecting sense organs on muscle synergies are correlated with their response properties. Arthropod Struct. Dev. **46**, 564–578 (2017). https://doi.org/10.1016/j.asd.2017.05.004
29. Bässler, U.: A movement generated in the peripheral nervous system: rhythmic flexion by autotomized legs of the stick insect Cuniculina impigra. J. Exp. Biol. **111**, 191–199 (1984)
30. Schindler: Funktionsmorphologische Untersuchungen zur Autotomie der Stabheuschrecke Carausius morosus Br. (Insecta: Phasmida). Zool. Anz., vol. 203, no. 316 (1979)
31. Bordage, E.: XXIII.—On the probable mode of formation of the fusion between the femur and trochanter in Arthropods. J. Nat. History (2009). https://doi.org/10.1080/002229399086 78095
32. Soler, C., Daczewska, M., Da Ponte, J.P., Dastugue, B., Jagla, K.: Coordinated development of muscles and tendons of the Drosophila leg. Development **131**, 6041 (2004). https://doi.org/10.1242/dev.01527
33. Lobato-Rios, V., Ramalingasetty, S.T., Özdil, P.G., Arreguit, J., Ijspeert, A.J., Ramdya, P.: NeuroMechFly, a neuromechanical model of adult Drosophila melanogaster. Nat. Methods. **19**, 620–627 (2022). https://doi.org/10.1038/s41592-022-01466-7
34. Goldsmith, C.A., Haustein, M., Bockemühl, T., Büschges, A., Szczecinski, N.S.: Analyzing 3D limb kinematics of drosophila melanogaster for robotic platform development. In: Hunt, A., et al. (eds.) Biomimetic and Biohybrid Systems, vol. 13548, pp. 111–122. Springer International Publishing, Cham (2022). https://doi.org/10.1007/978-3-031-20470-8_12
35. Sink, H.: Muscle Development in Drosophila. Springer, New York, NY (2006). https://doi.org/10.1007/0-387-32963-3
36. Dallmann, C.J., Dürr, V., Schmitz, J.: Motor control of an insect leg during level and incline walking. J. Exp. Biol. **222** (2019). https://doi.org/10.1242/jeb.188748
37. Akay, T., Ludwar, B.C., Göritz, M.L., Schmitz, J., Büschges, A.: Segment specificity of load signal processing depends on walking direction in the stick insect leg muscle control system. J. Neurosci. **27**, 3285–3294 (2007). https://doi.org/10.1523/JNEUROSCI.5202-06.2007
38. Zill, S.N., Moran, D.T.: The exoskeleton and insect proprioception: III. Activity of tibial campaniform sensilla during walking in the American cockroach, Periplaneta Americana. J. Exp. Biol. **94**, 57 (1981)
39. Goldsmith, C., Szczecinski, N., Quinn, R.: Drosophibot: a fruit fly inspired bio-robot. In: Biomimetic and Biohybrid Systems. Living Machines 2019. LNCS, vol. 11556, pp. 146–157. Springer, Cham (2019). https://doi.org/10.1007/978-3-030-24741-6_13
40. Zyhowski, W.P., Zill, S.N., Szczecinski, N.S.: Adaptive load feedback robustly signals force dynamics in robotic model of Carausius morosus stepping. Front. Neurorobot. **17**, 1125171 (2023). https://doi.org/10.3389/fnbot.2023.1125171
41. Onyx - Composite 3D Printing Material. https://markforged.com/materials/plastics/onyx. Accessed 22 Feb 2023
42. Haberkorn, A., Gruhn, M., Zill, S.N., Büschges, A.: Identification of the origin of force-feedback signals influencing motor neurons of the thoraco-coxal joint in an insect. J. Comp. Physiol. A **205**(2), 253–270 (2019). https://doi.org/10.1007/s00359-019-01334-4
43. Delcomyn, F., Nelson, M.E., Cocatre-Zilgien, J.H.: Sense organs of insect legs and the selection of sensors for agile walking robots. Int. J. Robot. Res. **15**, 113–127 (1996). https://doi.org/10.1177/027836499601500201
44. Bennemann, M., Baumgartner, W., Bräunig, P.-M.: Biomimicry of the adhesive organs of stick insects (Carausius morosus). Fachgruppe Biologie (2015)
45. Garcia, M., Kuo, A., Peattie, A., Wang, P., Full, R.J.: Damping and size: insights and biological inspiration. Presented at First International Symposium on Adaptive Motion of Animals and Machines (2000)

46. Hooper, S.L., et al.: Neural control of unloaded leg posture and of leg swing in stick insect, cockroach, and mouse differs from that in larger animals. J. Neurosci. **29**, 4109–4119 (2009). https://doi.org/10.1523/JNEUROSCI.5510-08.2009

47. Ache, J.M., Matheson, T.: Passive joint forces are tuned to limb use in insects and drive movements without motor activity. Curr. Biol. **23**, 1418–1426 (2013). https://doi.org/10.1016/j.cub.2013.06.024

48. Cruse, H., Bartling, C.: Movement of joint angles in the legs of a walking insect, Carausius morosus. J. Insect Physiol. **41**, 761–771 (1995). https://doi.org/10.1016/0022-1910(95)00032-p

49. Dickinson, M.H.: Comparison of encoding properties of campaniform sensilla on the fly wing. J. Exp. Biol. **151**, 245 (1990)

50. Berendes, V., Zill, S.N., Büschges, A., Bockemühl, T.: Speed-dependent interplay between local pattern-generating activity and sensory signals during walking in Drosophila. J. Exp. Biol. **219**, 3781 (2016). https://doi.org/10.1242/jeb.146720

51. Wosnitza, A., Bockemühl, T., Dübbert, M., Scholz, H., Büschges, A.: Inter-leg coordination in the control of walking speed in Drosophila. J. Exp. Biol. **216**, 480 (2013). https://doi.org/10.1242/jeb.078139

An Insect-Inspired Soft Robot Controlled by Soft Valves

Joscha Teichmann[1,2]([⊠]) [iD], Philipp Auth[1] [iD], Stefan Conrad[1,2] [iD], Thomas Speck[1,2] [iD], and Falk J. Tauber[1,2]([⊠]) [iD]

[1] Plant Biomechanics Group @ Botanical Garden, University of Freiburg, Freiburg, Germany
joscha.teichmann@livmats.uni-freiburg.de,
falk.tauber@biologie.uni-freiburg.de
[2] Cluster of Excellence livMatS @ FIT – Freiburg Center for Interactive Materials and Bioinspired Technologies, University of Freiburg, Freiburg, Germany

Abstract. Robots are becoming more and important and can support humans in all possible areas of life. Due to their inherent compliance, soft robots are ideal for human-machine interaction. In contrast to their material compliance, soft robots such as walkers are often still powered and controlled by rigid and bulky electronics. In this study, we show a walking compliant robot, which is 3D printed by FDM printers, controlled by soft, pneumatic logic gates, and powered only by a source of constant pressurized air. The robots form and gait are inspired by the stick insect (*Carausius morosus*). To mimic the walking gait in fast walking on horizontal planes and the interdependency of the legs, we developed bioinspired pneumatic actuators functioning as legs and implemented a novel pneumatic logic circuit. In this circuit, one pair of legs can only transition from stance to swing when the other pair of legs has touched the ground. Our results demonstrate how the field of soft robotics can advance with critical technology such as soft, pneumatic logic gates being printed on FDM printers. We envision that our system will continue to evolve with the incorporation of even more advanced control circuits, enabling the robot to operate at even higher speed. The lifting capacity has the potential to be further optimized and an on-board pressure supply system can be implemented, allowing for more efficient and effective performance. This will ultimately lead to a fully autonomous soft machine.

Keywords: soft valve · soft robot · insect locomotion · biomimetics

1 Introduction

1.1 Soft Robots

Robots are almost irreplaceable in modern industries and lift, manipulate, talk, roll and walk [1]. Millions of robots are already in use worldwide mainly in technical applications. Invented to help humans, they take on work that is dangerous, dirty, too heavy or too monotonous for example in the automotive industry [2]. Conventional robots are made of rigid materials and are driven by electrical actuators such as motors and solenoids or with pressurized fluids (hydraulically or pneumatically) [1].

© The Author(s), under exclusive license to Springer Nature Switzerland AG 2023
F. Meder et al. (Eds.): Living Machines 2023, LNAI 14157, pp. 428–441, 2023.
https://doi.org/10.1007/978-3-031-38857-6_31

The control of robotic drive systems such as motion control is a highly developed and challenging field [3]. Nevertheless, the control systems are often heavy and inefficient. While robots are capable of performing complex movements, the control required to do so is no less complex [4], and often shows drastic limitations. This is because they are essentially non-collaborative [5]. In industrial circumstances, it is often unsafe to allow robotic arms or welding robots to operate near humans or other fragile objects [6]. For this reason, a cage is often built around them, fencing off their complete workspace [7].

Unlike conventional "hard" robots, which are usually made of rigid elements connected by discrete joints, nature uses systems made of deformable bodies. With soft robots inspired by the bodies of cephalopods that are completely non-skeletal or by using stored elastic energy as in muscles, tendons or ligaments of vertebrates [8], it is possible not only to match but often even to exceed the performance of conventional robots in terms of complexity of motion compared with the required control [9]. Compliant robots based on this principle overcome many of the obstacles of their "hard" counterparts due to the intrinsic compliance of the materials systems used. They have continuously deformable structures [10] with actuators that resemble muscles. This allows them to adapt to confined environments and manipulate objects with unusual geometries due to their high adaptability [11]. To do so, they do not require complex control and complicated sensor monitoring as the material deforms until it matches the shape of the object [12]. Furthermore, they are usually much simpler in design than "hard" robots [13]. With this simplicity often comes simpler control, greater robustness, and lower cost [14] as the joints of compliant robots do not require motors, gears or roller bearings. The mobile platforms of these robots often utilize legs instead of wheels, eliminating the need for traditional propulsion [14].

Unfortunately, in most cases, hard valves and electronic components are still needed to control compliant robots. Typically, the control of the robot occurs externally, requiring the robot to remain tethered to the control unit in order to continue functioning [15, 16]. However, even on-board circuits have the problem that electromechanical components are not compliant, bulky, and unsafe to use in environments at risk of spark ignition.

1.2 Logic Modules

To solve the challenge of controlling compliant robots without the need for rigid electronics, we [17] and others [18–23] designed soft, pneumatic logic gates (Fig. 1 A). While the existing soft, pneumatic logic gates (PLG) are elegant in design, they do require manual casting of the parts and cumbersome assembly [18, 21]. There is a 3D printed PLG [23], but that version still requires manual removal of support material, the durability of the material is low and the polyjet 3D printing technology is not very accessible. At the same time the chosen materials can only handle low pressures [18, 21, 23].

The system presented in the following are easy and cheap to manufacture as they are 3D printable by common FDM printers in seven hours each, are ready to use after printing, can handle high pressures up to 400 kPa and are modular in design, making them very versatile. These logic modules consist of two sets of pneumatic chambers and tubes, forming two soft valves, and interacting analogously to electronic transistors (Fig. 1 A, B). Through the antagonistic combination of normally open and normally closed soft valves, the PLG functions like an electronic Schmitt trigger. Because of its hysteresis, the Schmitt trigger is the basis of oscillators and noise filters for digital signals [24]. In our pneumatic version, an overpressure signal at the shared socket S_T switches the output socket S_{Out} from being connected to input channel one, to being connected to input channel two (Fig. 1 C).

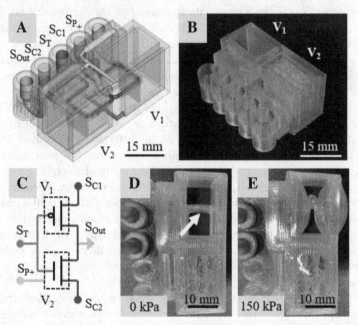

Fig. 1. Soft pneumatic logic gate. A: Model of the pneumatic logic gate (PLG) consisting of two soft valves V_1 and V_2. Two input channels S_{C1} and S_{C2} (green) lead through one valve each and merge in the output channel S_{Out} (pink). S_{P+} (orange) connects the lateral chambers of V_2 to a constant pressure supply, thereby kinking the tube of S_{C2} by default. A high signal at S_T (blue) switches the conductivity of the valves by closing V_1 and opening V_2. B: 3D printed PLG made of TPU A 70 using fused deposition modeling. C: Schematic CMOS diagram showing that S_T switches the conductivity of S_{Out}, connecting either S_{C1} or S_{C2} [17]. D: Atmospheric pressure at S_T creates a pneumatic equilibrium at the membranes, so that the tube (red arrow) is conductive. E: Overpressure of 150 kPa at S_T makes the membranes of the lateral chambers expand, thereby kinking the tube inside the central chamber.

In a pneumatic equilibrium the membranes between the chambers inside the valves are relaxed (Fig. 1 D), however when a HIGH signal in the form of overpressure is applied to the lateral chambers they expand, kink a tube inside the central chamber and inhibit the airflow (Fig. 1 E). When the lateral chambers are permanently pressurized and the signal is applied to the central chamber, the tube inside is unkinked, resuming the airflow [17].

The pneumatic logic gate (PLG) consisting of two valves can be configured to function like buffer, NOT, OR and AND digital logic gates. A buffer gate delays a signal by its response time and isolates two parts of a circuit from each other. It sets the output to HIGH, when its input gets a HIGH signal. A NOT gate inverts the input of S_T at the output S_{Out}, an OR gate sets the output to HIGH as soon as one of the inputs gets a HIGH signal, and an AND gate only sets the output to HIGH, when both inputs get a HIGH signal. The mode of operation only depends on the way the three input sockets S_{C1}, S_T and S_{C2} are connected.

The permissible range of operating pressure is 153 kPa to 400 kPa and the response time for a single PLG at 225 kPa operating pressure is around 100 ms. For further information including detailed configurations for the modes of operation and additional characterization please see [17].

1.3 Insect Leg Morphology and Walking Gaits

The legs of insects, specifically those of *Carausius morosus*, can be modelled as manipulators with three hinge joints, resulting in three degrees of freedom (Fig. 2) [25] from the proximal thorax-coxa joint (TC), over the coxa-trochanterofemur joint (CT) to the distal femur-fibia joint (FT). The TC joint is responsible for the protraction and retraction of the coxa, the CT joint enables the depression and elevation of the femur and the FT joint is responsible for the flexion and extension of the tibia [26]. While the TC joint is more complex than a hinge joint, most of its movement can be modelled by the rotation around a slanted axis [25] and the angles that define this axis vary only little during normal walking [27] (Fig. 2 A).

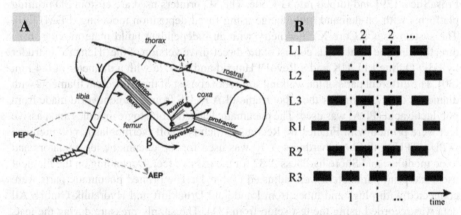

Fig. 2. Leg and fast walking gait of *Carausius morosus*. A: Sketch of a stick insect leg. The thorax-coxa joint (TC), coxa-trochanterofemur joint (CT) and femur-tibia joint (FT) can be modelled as hinge joints [25]. The interaction of these three joints results in a stance (or power stroke) beginning at the anterior extreme position (AEP) and transits into the swing (or return stroke) at the posterior extreme position (PEP). B: Schematic drawing of a typical fast tripod gait, marking the stance periods from AEP to PEP of each leg as a black bar. The left middle leg (L2), right front leg (R1) and right hind leg (R3) create one tripod (shown by dashed lines 1) and the left front leg (L1), left hind leg (L3) and the right middle leg (R2) create the other tripod (shown by dashed lines 2). A: Adapted with permission from [26] under Creative Commons CC BY license B: Adapted with permission by Royal Society publishing from [25].

To generate the walking gait of stick insects, a set of six coordination rules apply [28]. These rules - in a normal fast walking gait - make the left middle leg, right front leg and right hind leg move in synchronous swing and stance patterns (Fig. 2 B). Similarly, the left front leg, left hind leg and the right middle leg move in the same patterns, but phase shifted by one swing/stance. This ensures that there are always three legs touching the ground, forming a stable triangle with the center of gravity of the insect inside. Thereby always creating a statically defined stand. The resulting trajectory of the leg is that of a half-circle with its straight line from the anterior extreme position (AEP) to the posterior extreme position (PEP) touching the ground during stance.

1.4 Aim of the Study

In order to advance the research on compliant, efficient, autonomous robots, we employed our new soft logic gates [16] for developing a soft-legged walker. In this work, we lay the foundation for this by developing an FDM printed bio-inspired pneumatic actuator that functions like an insect leg and is controlled by a novel circuit of FDM printed pneumatic logic gates, implementing the walking gait of *Carausius morosus*.

2 Materials and Methods

All 3D printed objects were designed with a CAD-software. They were sliced with PrusaSlicer [29] and turned into G-Code. The 3D printers used are custom 3D printing platforms with on-demand tool-change using fused deposition modeling (FDM) [30]. The system uses a Core XY geometry with an independent build plate moving in Z-direction and the print heads consist of the direct-drive version of the "Hemera" extruder by E3D-Online Ltd. UK and a Revo™ Hotend and Nozzle with a diameter of 0.4 mm [30]. The different parts of the walking soft robot consist of three different filaments with diameters of 1.75 mm. For the robot frame PLA PLUS from Filamentworld made from polylactic acid (PLA) was used. The pneumatic leg actuators, logic modules and passive feet were printed with Filaflex by Recreus, which is a soft thermoplastic polyurethane (TPU). TPU with Shore hardness A 70 was used for the pneumatic leg actuators and logic modules, and Shore hardness A 82 for the passive feet. Depending on the filament used, the print parameters were adjusted (Table 1). The printed pneumatic parts were connected with plugs and tubes from Landefeld Druckluft und Hydraulik GmbH. All data was recorded using the test setup from [31]. The supply pressure during the tests was measured with a JUMO Midas Type 401001 pressure sensor by M.K. Juchheim GmbH & Co. connected to data acquisition devices (NI USB 6002 DAQ) by National Instruments controlled via LabView [32]. The airflow was measured with a red-y smart meter thermic flow sensor by Vögtlin Instruments GmbH and evaluated with get red-y [33]. The created motion trajectories of the legs were recorded with two Lumix cameras set to 100 fps and evaluated with Kinovea [34]. The times required to calculate the speed were measured with a stopwatch while the robot walked a defined distance of 1 m.

Table 1. Printing parameters used to create the soft robotic walker parts.

Parameter	PLA PLUS	TPU A 82 & A 70
Nozzle diameter [mm]	0.4	0.4
Print temperature [°C]	230	220
Bed temperature [°C]	60	60
Fan speed [%]	35 - 100	100
Bridges fan speed [%]	100	20
Layer height [mm]	0.2	0.1
Perimeters	3	5
Solid top and bottom layers	5	10
Infill density [%]	15	95
Print speed [mm/s]	Varied	10
Print speed bridges [mm/s]	45	20
Infill/perimeter overlap [%]	50	25
Extrusion multiplier perimeters [%]	100	125

3   Results

3.1   Insect Leg Actuator

Inspired by the legs of *Carausius morosus*, we designed pneumatic soft actuators that are able to act as hinge joints by bending, as is common practice in soft robotics [35]. As we wanted them to move forwards/backwards and upwards/downwards at the same time, we designed a four-chambered actuator (Fig. 3 A). Each of the chambers is responsible for bending the actuator in one of the four directions. By mirroring the chambers responsible for forwards/backwards movements (TC joint) vertically along the centerline, both are equally powerful and generate the same movement. They were placed closer to the suspension of the leg, thus profiting from the increased lever to the tip by increased movement (Fig. 3 A, B). The upwards/downwards chambers (CT joint) were horizontally mirrored along the centerline (Fig. 3 A) and are able to lift more weight because of the reduced lever to the tip. This mimics the placement of the TC and CT joints in the stick insect (Fig. 2). The upward chambers were tapered towards the end to allow the downward chambers to bend further during actuation. The leg actuators were printed lying on the untampered side of the downward chambers. The FT joint was not implemented in order to decrease complexity and increase printability.

The base of the insect leg actuator was designed in such a way that it can be attached to the frame of the robot via two vertical slots on each side, as well as pressurize the internal chambers by four air inlets. These inlets are connected to tubing by pneumatic connector plugs with a diameter of 4 mm. The ground contact is established by the tarsus inspired feet of the soft robot. Tarsi do not feature muscles, but instead conform passively to the surface structure. The robot feet are printed from slightly more rigid

TPU A 82 compared to the TPU A 70 of the rest of the leg. They are hollow inside, but not connected to the air inlets. Combining inwardly curved top and bottom surfaces with straight sides and a flat, elliptical tip (number 6 in Fig. 3 A), these feet yield in the vertical direction but remain stable in the horizontal. Similar to tarsi of stick insects, this allows them to conform and create a larger surface area. At the same time when fully engaged they offer a stable stand for the robot.

3.2   Control Circuit

The legs are controlled and supplied with pressurized air by four PLGs that form an oscillator, similar to Drotman et al. [36] (Fig. 3 C). The respective chambers of the right front and hind legs and the left middle leg are linked and form group one. The respective chambers of the three other legs are linked as well and form group two. The outputs of each logic gate of the oscillator are connected to one of the pneumatic chambers of the groups. However, unlike the circuit by Drotman et al. [36], the upwards and downwards bending chambers are not connected directly, but through preceding AND and OR gates. As such, the oscillator can only ever continue to oscillate once the downwards bending chamber of the group transitioning to stance is sufficiently pressurized.

3.3   Soft Robotic Walker

A lightweight frame was constructed, 3D printed and fitted with eight PLG and six insect leg actuators (Fig. 4 A). The PLG are spread across the entire frame to ensure an even weight distribution. They are fixed to the frame by printed brackets that hook into sockets in the frame. The six legs are fixed in connectors and have small protrusions to prevent them slipping out during movement. The connectors are screwed to the frame at a 30° downwards angle. This mimics the angle of the rotational axis of the TC joint during normal fast walking on a horizontal plane in stick insects [27]. Pneumatic connector plugs are pressed into the inlets of the insect leg actuators and the chambers of all legs of one group are connected respectively. This results in eight different tubes - one for each pneumatic chamber of each group of legs - connected to the different output sockets S_{Out} of the PLG. The PLG are connected to each other according to the diagram shown (Fig. 3 C). Additionally, all PLG require a constant pressure supply at one or two sockets, depending on the used gate type [17]. These sockets are also interconnected to a single tube, which can be connected to a compressed air pump. The total weight of the soft robotic walker including the frame, all tubing and screws is 433.9 g. The length of the robot is 383 mm, the width is 344 mm from the tip of the left middle leg to the right middle leg and the height is about 115 mm including the tubing. To equalize the load on the legs in each group, the frame was designed in such a way, that the distances from the center of gravity to the contact point with the ground are the same.

For characterization of the walking gait, the robot is connected to a compressed air pump with a constant supply of 225 kPa overpressure. The PLG begin transient oscillation for about 1.5 s, gradually building up to its full pressure amplitude and the soft robot starts walking (Fig. 4 B-E). The resulting gait consists of group one beginning its stance phase at their respective PEP with the downwards bending chambers becoming pressurized. The three legs lift the robot up into a statically defined stand and move

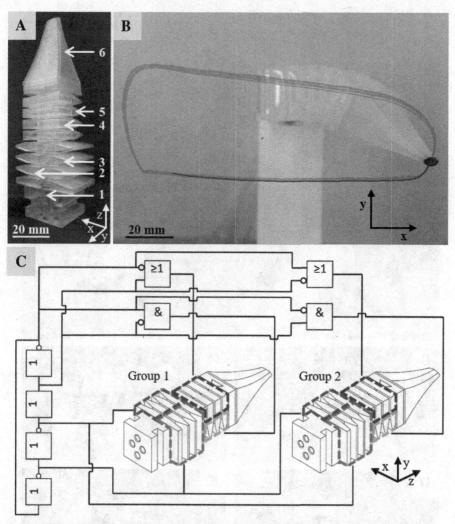

Fig. 3. Design and connection of the insect leg actuator. A: Soft, pneumatic insect leg actuator. The air inlets for the internal pneumatic chambers are located at the base of the actuator (1), with which the actuator is connected to the frame. The chambers for forward and backward bending (2) taper towards the sides, to allow the opposite side to bend further during actuation. The chamber for downward bending (4) – contrary to the chamber for upward bending (5) – is not tapered due to printing restrictions. A tapering is not needed, as the upwards bending is only needed for the foot (6) not to touch the ground during the swing phase. The foot is hollow and acts only as a passive element to conform to the ground. B: The achieved trajectory of the insect leg actuator in the plane. C: Schematic drawing of the control circuit. The general movement is controlled by a central oscillator of three NOT gates and a buffer (arranged in a column on the left). The forwards and backwards bending chambers (green and orange) are connected directly to the oscillator. Additional AND and OR gates with one input inverted ensure that the upwards bending chambers (pink) of one group of legs do not get pressurized, before the downwards bending chambers (blue) of the other group are pressurized.

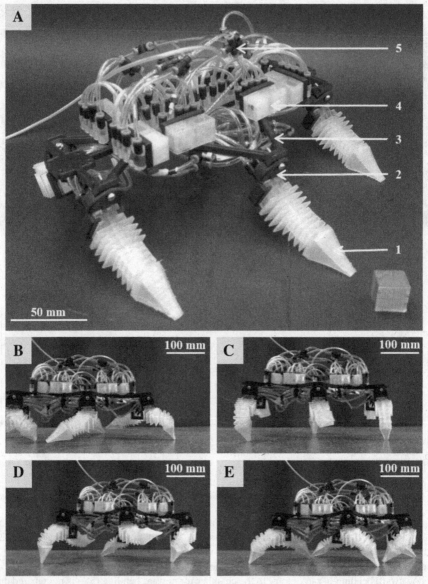

Fig. 4. Stick insect inspired compliant robot. A: The insect inspired leg actuators (1) are connected to the body of the robot via connectors that are tilted downwards at 30° (2). The PLA frame (3) serves as a platform for eight modular pneumatic logic gates (PLG), which control the walking pattern and distribute the pressurized air (4). The sockets of the pneumatic logic gates are connected via tubing and connectors (5) and lead to a single supply of constant pressurized air. B-E: Sequence of the soft robot walking from left to right. The right front and hind legs and the left middle leg form group one and move synchronously (here in stance phase). The other legs form group two (here in swing phase). Group one begins in their AEP (B), lifts the robot (C) and moves backwards (D), thereby generating forward thrust. As group one reaches their PEP, group two begins their stance phase (E).

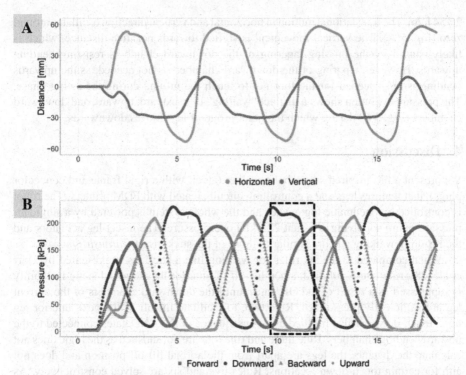

Fig. 5. Qualitative analysis of the actuation in a group of legs. A: Translational displacement of the tip of the pneumatic insect leg actuator. Positive horizontal distance indicates forward displacement and positive vertical distance indicates upward displacement. The origin for horizontal and vertical displacement is the resting position of the tip of the unactuated leg. B: Evolution of the pressure in the pneumatic chambers of one group of legs over time. The operating pressure for the entire pneumatic circuit is 225 kPa. The frequency of the oscillation is a result of friction in the tube acting as resistance, as well as the volumes in the robot acting as capacities. The downward chambers remain at overpressure longer than the other chambers, as they wait for the downward chambers of the group of legs to be pressurized (dashed black rectangle). Note: It has to be taken into account that the time scale of figure A is not directly related to the time scale of figure B and the two experiments were carried out independently from each other.

backwards, thereby pushing the robot forward. During this time, the other group of legs moves forwards while their upward bending chambers are pressurized. Once the AEP of the legs of group one is reached, they remain there, until the downward bending chambers of group two are pressurized at their PEP. The legs of group one depressurize and the weight of the robot is transferred to group two, ensuring that the robot body stays lifted from the ground. Now group two begins their stance phase with a power stroke backwards while group one begins the swing phase with a return stroke forwards.

At 225 kPa system pressure, the soft robotic walker moves at a speed of 0.061 m/s with a standard deviation of 0.003 m/s (N = 20). The required airflow during walking oscillates around 10.07 l_n/min (l_n: liter at 0 °C and 1013.25 mbar) due to pressurization and depressurization of the pneumatic chambers in the legs. This is the equivalent of

2.754 l_n/m. The translational motion in horizontal and vertical direction oscillates around zero (Fig. 5 A). The vertical movement is shifted towards negative distance, which is likely caused by the missing tapering of the downward chambers resisting bending upwards. However, tapering of the downward chambers is not needed, as the upwards bending is only needed for the foot not to touch the ground during the swing phase. The pressure evolution shows a distinct "waiting" of backward, upward, and downward chambers (Fig. 5 B) during which the other group of legs moves downwards.

4 Discussion

We present a bio-inspired soft robotic walker (albeit with a rigid frame and connector plugs), that features legs and a controlling circuit created with FDM printers. The robot is controlled by pneumatic logic gates and the whole system is powered by a single air pressure pump supplying constant 225 kPa overpressure. The insect leg actuators and the resulting walking gait are similar to those of the stick insect *Carausius morosus*.

When compared to the six rules for walking like a stick insect presented by Dürr et al. [28], rule one is fulfilled, since lift-off of anterior legs to avoid static instability is suppressed as a result of the OR gates, until the downward chambers of the current leg are sufficiently pressurized. Rule two, to facilitate lift-off of the next anterior leg upon touch-down, is also fulfilled as a consequence of the AND gates connected to the upward bending chambers. Rule three and rule four are not satisfied as the logic does not calculate the distance the legs are apart from the normal lift-off position and does not aim for certain touch-down locations. Rules five and six are solved constructively. As long as the robot walks on a horizontal plane, the propulsive force is distributed evenly across the legs, since all legs are equal distances apart from the center of gravity. There is also no need for a correction step to avoid stumbling, since the legs are short enough to never touch each other during walking.

When comparing the speed of our robot to similar soft robotic walkers, such as the one by Drotman et al. [36], our speed of 0.061 m·s^{-1}, which equals 0.16 body lengths per second, is higher than their speed of 0.090 body lengths per second. However, the 225 kPa system pressure we used is higher than the 150 kPa used by Drotman et al. [36] and no consideration was taken from our side to reduce the body length. Similarly, the straw-based robot with a PneuNet gripper by Decker et al. [37] is able to move 0.017 m·s^{-1} at 138 kPa (determined from their supplemented movie S4) and the Multigait soft robot by Shepherd et al. moves 0.005 m·s^{-1} in ambulating gait and 0.0006 m·s^{-1} in undulating gait at 48 kPa [15]. When comparing the various speeds achieved with the required pressure respectively, our robot is fastest at 0.271 m·s^{-1}·Pa^{-1} and can therefore be considered more efficient in terms of speed.

The speed can be increased by reducing leakage of flow in the various components of the robot. Due to the manufacturing technique and the hand-cut quality of the tubes installed, there is leakage within tolerable limits. Leakage can be thought of as a pneumatic resistance, increasing the response time of the PLGs. However, this does not impede the robot's gait, as long as the legs of each group still move synchronously. Since the legs in one group are interconnected and are essentially one volume, leakage affects them in the same way, keeping the synchronicity. Additionally, the speed of the robot might be increased at different frequencies of the oscillator.

We wish to add to the growing repertoire of knowledge for soft robots with this robot that has a statically defined stand at all times while walking. With our demonstration of a soft pneumatic circuit, we hope to advance the research on autonomy of soft robots. Additionally, similar pneumatic circuits could be used to increase the softness of other machines, for example by adding decentralized control structures for controlling single actuators.

In future work, we will continue to optimize the pneumatic circuits in order to translate even more complex biological walking gaits into soft robots. The FT joint was not implemented, as its interplay with the CT joint mainly serves the purpose of aiming for certain touch-down locations, to avoid stumbling or to correct leverage to better distribute propulsive forces [27]. In a controlled environment with horizontal, even ground this is not necessary, however, this is something to be investigated with additional experiments. In addition to comparing the speed with similar robots, comparing the required air flow will help to benchmark the efficiencies of these machines. As such it is planned to further characterize our robot, including the maximal lifting capacity, scaling of obstacles and coarse grounds, and walking on non-horizontal surfaces. Moreover, the overall softness could be increased by reducing the number of off-the-shelf components for example by gluing the tubing to the soft actuators similar to Yap et al. [38], this however increases the manual assembly required. Of exceptional interest are the possibilities of automation in terms of on-board pressure supply to enable untethered operation, as well as sensing of the environment and autonomous decision making, such as navigation.

References

1. Siciliano, B., Khatib, O. (eds.): Springer Handbook of Robotics. Springer, Cham (2016). https://doi.org/10.1007/978-3-319-32552-1
2. Graetz, G., Michaels, G.: Robots at work. Rev. Econ. Stat. **100**, 753–768 (2018). https://doi.org/10.1162/rest_a_00754
3. Hering, E., Martin, R., Gutekunst, J., Kempkes, J.: Antriebstechnik. In: Hering, E., Martin, R., Gutekunst, J., Kempkes, J. (eds.) Elektrotechnik und Elektronik für Maschinenbauer. V, pp. 379–417. Springer, Heidelberg (2018). https://doi.org/10.1007/978-3-662-54296-5_5
4. Cheah, C.C., Haghighi, R.: Motion control. In: Nee, A.Y.C. (ed.) Handbook of Manufacturing Engineering and Technology, pp. 1889–1932. Springer, London (2015). https://doi.org/10.1007/978-1-4471-4670-4_93
5. Bjoern, M., Susanne, O.-T., Harald, S., et al.: Injury risk quantification for industrial robots in collaborative operation with humans. In: ISR 2010 41st International Symposium on Robotics) and ROBOTIK 2010 (ed) ISR 2010 (41st International Symposium on Robotics) and ROBOTIK 2010 (6th German Conference on Robotics), pp. 1–6 (2010)
6. de Santis, A., Siciliano, B., de Luca, A., et al.: An atlas of physical human–robot interaction. Mech. Mach. Theory **43**, 253–270 (2008). https://doi.org/10.1016/j.mechmachtheory.2007.03.003
7. Krieger, R., Staab, H., Matthias, B., et al.: Industrieroboter als Produktionsassistenten für die Automobilmontage - Industrial Robots as Manufacturing Assistants for Automotive Assembly. VDI Berichte Band 2012, München (2008)
8. Dickinson, M.H., Farley, C.T., Full, R.J., et al.: How animals move: an integrative view. Science **288**, 100–106 (2000). https://doi.org/10.1126/science.288.5463.100

9. Wehner, M., Truby, R.L., Fitzgerald, D.J., et al.: An integrated design and fabrication strategy for entirely soft, autonomous robots. Nature **536**, 451–455 (2016). https://doi.org/10.1038/nature19100

10. Altenbach, H.: Kontinuumsmechanik: Einführung in die materialunabhängigen und materialabhängigen Gleichungen, 2nd edn. Springer, Heidelberg (2012)

11. Rus, D., Tolley, M.T.: Design, fabrication and control of soft robots. Nature **521**, 467–475 (2015). https://doi.org/10.1038/nature14543

12. Polygerinos, P., Wang, Z., Galloway, K.C., et al.: Soft robotic glove for combined assistance and at-home rehabilitation. Robot. Auton. Syst. **73**, 135–143 (2015). https://doi.org/10.1016/j.robot.2014.08.014

13. Polygerinos, P., Correll, N., Morin, S.A., et al.: Soft robotics: review of fluid-driven intrinsically soft devices; manufacturing, sensing, control, and applications in human-robot interaction. Adv. Eng. Mater. **19**, 1700016 (2017). https://doi.org/10.1002/adem.201700016

14. Whitesides, G.M.: Soft robotics. Angewandte Chemie (International ed. in English) **57**, 4258–4273 (2018). https://doi.org/10.1002/anie.201800907

15. Shepherd, R.F., Ilievski, F., Choi, W., et al.: Multigait soft robot. Proc. Natl. Acad. Sci. U.S.A. **108**, 20400–20403 (2011). https://doi.org/10.1073/pnas.1116564108

16. Martinez, R.V., Branch, J.L., Fish, C.R., et al.: Robotic tentacles with three-dimensional mobility based on flexible elastomers. Adv. Mater. (Deerfield Beach, Fla.) **25**, 205–212 (2013). https://doi.org/10.1002/adma.201203002

17. Conrad, S., Teichmann, J., Knorr, N., et al.: 3D printed digital pneumatic logic for the control of soft robotic actuators. Manuscript submitted for publication (2023)

18. Rothemund, P., Ainla, A., Belding, L., et al.: A soft, bistable valve for autonomous control of soft actuators. Sci. Robot. **3** (2018). https://doi.org/10.1126/scirobotics.aar7986

19. Preston, D.J., Rothemund, P., Jiang, H.J., et al.: Digital logic for soft devices. Proc. Natl. Acad. Sci. U.S.A. **116**, 7750–7759 (2019). https://doi.org/10.1073/pnas.1820672116

20. Preston, D.J., Jiang, H.J., Sanchez, V., et al.: A soft ring oscillator. Sci. Robot. **4** (2019). https://doi.org/10.1126/scirobotics.aaw5496

21. Xu, K., Perez-Arancibia, N.O.: Electronics-free logic circuits for localized feedback control of multi-actuator soft robots. IEEE Robot. Autom. Lett. **5**, 3990–3997 (2020). https://doi.org/10.1109/LRA.2020.2982866

22. van Laake, L.C., de Vries, J., Kani, S.M., et al.: A fluidic relaxation oscillator for reprogrammable sequential actuation in soft robots. Matter **5**, 2898–2917 (2022). https://doi.org/10.1016/j.matt.2022.06.002

23. Hubbard, J.D., Acevedo, R., Edwards, K.M., et al.: Fully 3D-printed soft robots with integrated fluidic circuitry. Sci. Adv. **7** (2021). https://doi.org/10.1126/sciadv.abe5257

24. Horowitz, P., Hill, W.: The Art of Electronics, 2 ed., 22. Printing. Cambridge Univ. Press, Cambridge (1989)

25. Cruse, H., Dürr, V., Schmitz, J.: Insect walking is based on a decentralized architecture revealing a simple and robust controller. Philos. Trans. A Math. Phys. Eng. Sci. **365**, 221–250 (2007). https://doi.org/10.1098/rsta.2006.1913

26. Schilling, M., Hoinville, T., Schmitz, J., et al.: WalkNet, a bio-inspired controller for hexapod walking. Biol. Cybern. **107**, 397–419 (2013). https://doi.org/10.1007/s00422-013-0563-5

27. Cruse, H., Bartling, C.: Movement of joint angles in the legs of a walking insect, Carausius morosus. J. Insect Physiol. **41**, 761–771 (1995). https://doi.org/10.1016/0022-1910(95)000 32-P

28. Dürr, V., Schmitz, J., Cruse, H.: Behaviour-based modelling of hexapod locomotion: linking biology and technical application. Arthropod. Struct. Dev. **33**, 237–250 (2004). https://doi.org/10.1016/j.asd.2004.05.004

29. Prusa Research PrusaSlicer 2.4, Prag (2022)

30. Conrad, S., Speck, T., Tauber, F.J.: Tool changing 3D printer for rapid prototyping of advanced soft robotic elements. Bioinspir. Biomim. **16** (2021). https://doi.org/10.1088/1748-3190/ac095a
31. Esser, F., Steger, T., Bach, D., Masselter, T., Speck, T.: Development of novel foam-based soft robotic ring actuators for a biomimetic peristaltic pumping system. In: Mangan, M., Cutkosky, M., Mura, A., Verschure, P.F.M.J., Prescott, T., Lepora, N. (eds.) Living Machines 2017. LNCS (LNAI), vol. 10384, pp. 138–147. Springer, Cham (2017). https://doi.org/10.1007/978-3-319-63537-8_12
32. Bitter, R., Mohiuddin, T., Nawrocki, M.: LabVIEW 2019 & 2020: Advanced Programming Techniques. CRC Press, Boco Raton (2006)
33. Vögtlin Instruments GmbH: get red-y 5.7.1.1, Muttenz (2022)
34. Joan Charmant and contributors: Kinovea (2019)
35. Mosadegh, B., Polygerinos, P., Keplinger, C., et al.: Pneumatic networks for soft robotics that actuate rapidly. Adv. Funct. Mater. **24**, 2163–2170 (2014). https://doi.org/10.1002/adfm.201303288
36. Drotman, D., Jadhav, S., Sharp, D., et al.: Electronics-free pneumatic circuits for controlling soft-legged robots. Sci. Robot. **6** (2021). https://doi.org/10.1126/scirobotics.aay2627
37. Decker, C.J., Jiang, H.J., Nemitz, M.P., et al.: Programmable soft valves for digital and analog control. Proc. Natl. Acad. Sci. U.S.A. **119** (2022). https://doi.org/10.1073/pnas.2205922119
38. Yap, H.K., Ng, H.Y., Yeow, C.-H.: High-force soft printable pneumatics for soft robotic applications. Soft Rob. **3**, 144–158 (2016). https://doi.org/10.1089/soro.2016.0030

Effects of Tarsal Morphology on Load Feedback During Stepping of a Robotic Stick Insect (*Carausius Morosus*) Limb

Clarus A. Goldsmith[1](✉) [iD], William P. Zyhowski[1] [iD], Ansgar Büschges[2] [iD], Sasha N. Zill[3] [iD], Gesa F. Dinges[1] [iD], and Nicholas S. Szczecinski[1] [iD]

[1] Department of Mechanical and Aerospace Engineering, West Virginia University, Morgantown, WV, USA
cg00022@mix.wvu.edu
[2] Institute of Zoology, University of Cologne, Köln, NRW, Germany
[3] Department of Biomedical Sciences, Marshall University, Huntington, WV, USA

Abstract. Sensory feedback from sense organs during animal locomotion can be heavily influenced by an organism's mechanical structure. In insects, the interplay between sensing and mechanics can be demonstrated in the campaniform sensilla (CS) strain sensors located across the exoskeleton. Leg CS are highly sensitive to the loading state of the limb. In walking, loading is primarily influenced by ground reaction forces (GRF) mediated by the foot, or tarsus. The complex morphology of the tarsus provides compliance, passive and active substrate grip, and an increased moment arm for the GRF, all of which impact leg loading and the resulting CS discharge. To increase the biomimicry of robots we use to study strain feedback during insect walking, we have developed a series of tarsi for our robotic model of a *Carausius morosus* middle leg. We seek the simplest design that mimics tarsus functionality. Tarsi were designed with varying degrees of compliance, passive grip, and biomimetic structure. We created elastic silicone tarsal joints for several of these models and found that they produced linear stiffness within joint limits across different joint morphologies. Strain gauges positioned in CS locations on the trochanterofemur and tibia recorded strain while the leg stepped on a treadmill. Most, but not all, designs increased axial strain magnitude compared to previous data with no tarsus. Every tarsus design produced positive transversal strain in the tibia, indicating axial torsion in addition to bending. Sudden increases in tibial strain reflected leg slipping during stance. This data show how different aspects of the tarsus may mediate leg loading, allowing us to improve the mechanical biomimicry of future robotic test platforms.

Keywords: tarsus · campaniform sensilla · robot · Carausius morosus · passive compliance

Supported by NSF/DBI NeuroNex 2015317 to NSS, DFG Bu857/125-1 to AB, NSF CRCNS 2113028 to NSS and SNZ, and DFG DI 2907/1-1 (Project number 500615768, grant no. 233886668/GRK1960) to GFD.

F. Meder et al. (Eds.): Living Machines 2023, LNAI 14157, pp. 442–457, 2023.
https://doi.org/10.1007/978-3-031-38857-6_32

1 Introduction

Sensory feedback is an important part of how the nervous system produces robust and agile walking. Dynamic feedback from sense organs throughout an animal's body helps continually influence activity in the low-level motor networks and high-level control centers, which in turn adjust limb movements [4,37]. Furthermore, the sensory feedback available to the nervous system is highly dependent on an animal's mechanical structure [9,28]. An example of the interplay between sensing and mechanics in insects is found in the campaniform sensilla (CS), mechanoreceptors in various locations across the insect exoskeleton that detect strains in the cuticle as a proxy for force [13,26]. Due to their sensitivity to strain, leg CS are highly impacted by the loading state of the limb, its geometry, and its material properties. The effect of loading state has been shown in recordings from CS groups found on the trochanter, femur, and tibia in a variety of insects [37]. In particular, these CS robustly capture the rapid force changes during lift off and touch down, as well as a measure of the tonic loading throughout stance [30,38,40,41].

Biomimetic robots have great potential to help scientists investigate how mechanics influence sensors like the CS by providing a simplified platform on which to conduct neurobiological experiments [5,31]. Several of the authors of this work have recently investigated CS discharge during locomotion by implementing biomimetic strain sensing on robotic insect limbs [17,18,42]. As part of these investigations, a robotic leg modeled after a stick insect, *Carausius morosus*, was developed with biomimetic strain sensing in reported CS locations on the leg segments [42]. The robotic model showed the effects of morphological and environmental factors such as increased body weight or end effector slippage on leg strain and phenomenologically-modeled CS discharge.

Although many insects have complex tarsal anatomy, the previously developed robotic leg modeled the tarsus as a single semi-spherical, rigid segment at the distal end of the tibia [42]. The insect tarsus is typically comprised of several nested segments connected via elastic membranes [1,2]. These tarsal segments are actuated by a singular tendon, the retractor unguis tendon, originating in the femur and tibia, running through the underside of the tarsus, and connecting to a plate in the final segment, the pretarsus [29]. The pretarsus contains the tarsal claws, and in many types of insects an adhesive pad called the arolium [2,16]. In insects such as stick insects, the other tarsal segments additionally include anisotropic frictional pads called pulvulli or euplantulae [7,11,39]. This complex morphology is difficult to recreate for a robot, meaning the tarsus is often excluded from biomimetic insect robots [24]. However, the tarsus has a strong capacity to influence CS firing by mediating ground-leg interactions and subsequently affecting how loads from the substrate distribute throughout the leg. A list of mechanisms in the tarsus that potentially affect loading and the morphological aspects that cause them include: (1) *Compliance* to the terrain due to elastic joint membranes (2) Increased *moment arm* between the most proximal point of ground contact and the long axis of the tibia due to angling of the tarsus; (3) *Passive grip* on ground surfaces from friction (euplantulae/pulvulli) and adhesive (arolium) pads; and (4) *active grip* with actuation of the claws.

To improve the biomimicry of our robotic animal models, and thus the accuracy of their predictions, it would be beneficial to understand the specific effects that these different tarsal mechanisms have on leg loading and the resulting CS firing. We could then design robotic tarsal segments that produce similar effects without the full biological complexity. However, it has not been investigated how individual aspects of tarsal morphology influence loading sensing in the leg during walking. Several biological experiments have investigated the influence of different tarsal mechanisms on overall walking capability, such as the material properties of the frictional and adhesive pads [3,7], how the adhesive pads and claws work together to grip a variety of substrates [6,8], how joint elasticity affects passive retraction of the claws [16], and how the unguitractor mechanism allows 'latching' of the claws to a certain position [19]. Biorobotic studies have also begun to move in this direction by developing insect-inspired tarsi with passive compliance [17] to decrease walking impacts or exploring how tarsi with variable rigidity enable walking on complex substrates such as mesh [35]. However, none of these studies have addressed the impact on load sensing in their investigations. Additionally, experimental studies of CS responses in the legs are rarely conducted in walking animals [25,27,36], and sometimes include ablation of all or a portion of the tarsus [38,40]. These methods make it difficult to determine experimentally the effect of tarsal function and morphology on leg strain during walking.

To quantify how different aspects of tarsal morphology affect leg strain during stepping in our robots, we have developed a series of tarsal segments for our robotic *C. morosus* leg with varying degrees of compliance, passive grip, and biomimetic structure. To mimic the elasticity of the joint membranes and cuticle, we designed compliant tarsal joints with a combination of 3D printed plastic and silicone. Although the relative sizes of the tarsus and tibia differ in flies and stick insects [25,40], we used nano-CT scans of the tarsal segments of adult *Drosophila melanogaster*, another model organism for studying walking, to inform the shape of the tarsomere segments. We characterized the linearity and magnitude of the stiffness in our tarsal joints across different deflection directions, batches of silicone, and tarsal segment morphologies, and found they were linear within joint limits. Readings of the femoral and tibial strain in the axial and transverse directions were recorded for an average step on a treadmill for each of the developed tarsi designs. We found that including a tarsus typically increased strain magnitude by increasing the moment arm between the point of ground contact and the CS. The moment arm also increased the sensitivity of the strain to joint and leg plane angles. Occasions when the tarsus slipped on the substrate became more apparent in the tibial transverse strain signal due to sudden increases. Increasing passive grip seemed to have minimal impact on strain magnitude, but did prevent slipping. This work demonstrates the importance of modeling the tarsus in biomimetic robots.

2   Materials and Methods

2.1   Tarsal Segment Scans

Nano-CT imaging was performed for tarsal segments in the metathoracic legs of female wild-type *D. melanogaster* (Berlin- K, RRID:BDSC_8522) as described in reference [15]. Images were captured at the tarsal segment joints between segments 1 and 2, 3 and 4, and 5 and the pretarsus. Segmentations were initially rendered in Blender (Blender Foundation, Amsterdam, Netherlands), then decimated using MeshLab [10] for importing into CAD software. Images of the renderings for segments 1 and 2 and 5 and the pretarsus are shown in Fig. 1A. *D. melanogaster* was selected for imaging instead of *C. morosus* due to recent advancements in neuromechanical data collection making *Drosophila* a more universally studied insect for nervous system research [21,23,32]. Given the homology of tarsal morphology across insect species [34], we do not expect that modeling tarsomere joints after *D. melanogaster* will greatly impact our model of *C. morosus* stepping. Further, presently obtaining images from *D. melanogaster* allows for greater specificity in future *Drosophila* neurorobotic investigations.

2.2   Robotic Tarsus Construction

Three distinct 'styles' of robotic tarsi were designed with different amounts of biological abstraction. Each tarsus was designed with an overall length scaled 15:1 to the insect tarsus. Two of the styles were manufactured with or without silicone grip at the contact surfaces, resulting in five total designs. As labeled in Fig. 1B, each tarsus is designated 1–3 based on its style, with a * to denote the inclusion of exterior silicone in the design to increase passive grip between the treadmill and the tarsus.

A summary of each design style is as follows: Style 1, referring to Designs 1 and 1*, is a rigid cylindrical segment positioned at a 45° angle from the long axis of the tibia. This style is meant to isolate the effect of the moment arm created by the tarsus. Style 2 (i.e Designs 2 and 2*) retains this cylindrical shape and 45° offset, but additionally includes a compliant tibia-tarsus (TiTar) joint. This compliance is created via a ball-and-socket joint filled with silicone rubber to replicate the elastic properties of the tarsal membranes and cuticle (Fig. 1C). Style 3 adds full compliance through a biomimetic recreation of the six tarsal segments in the stick insect connected with these compliant silicone joints. Table 1 summarizes the morphological aspects of each design.

In order to create a high degree of biomimicry in our Style 3 segments, we designed ball-and-socket joints similar to our collected nano-CT images. We also maintained a similar contouring of the tarsal segments while ensuring manufacturing feasibility. Figure 1A shows a comparison of the joints between segments 1 and 2 and 5 and the pretarsus in the *Drosophila* nano-CT scans and our corresponding Style 3 designs. Each segment length was scaled proportionally from scanning electron microscopy (SEM) images of the stick insect tarsus [3,40]. Figure 1D shows a detailed look at Design 3 with the corresponding biological

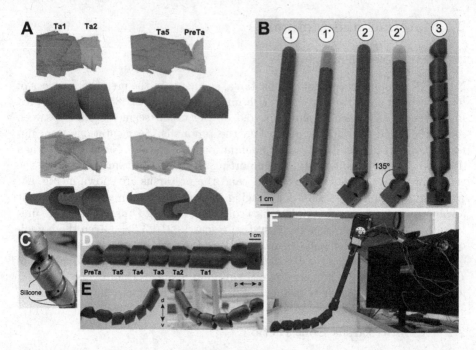

Fig. 1. Hardware designs for the robotic tarsal segments. (A) Comparisons of the nano-CT scans of *Drosophila* tarsal segments and the robotic segment designs for tarsal segments 1 and 2 (Ta1 and Ta2, respectively) and segment 5 (Ta5) and pretarsus. (B) The five tarsal morphologies labeled with their design designations. Three designs were tested with and without silicone grip components (silicone design denoted with a *). (C) Close-up view of the silicone interiors of the flexible segments, shown in Design 3. (D) Corresponding tarsal segments and notable biomimetic components labeled on Design 3. (E) Examples of the deflection capability of Design 3 in extension (left) and supination/pronation movements (right). (F) Leg setup with a Design 3 tarsus affixed.

Table 1. A summary of the morphological aspects of each tarsi design.

	Moment Arm	Compliance	Structure	Grip
Design 1	Yes	None	Simplified	No
Design 1*	Yes	None	Simplified	Yes
Design 2	Yes	TiTar	Simplified	No
Design 2*	Yes	TiTar	Simplified	Yes
Design 3	Yes	All Joints	Biomimetic	No

segments labeled. We omitted the claws and other aspects of active grip from our designs in this study due to the additional complexity of the tendon mechanism. Additionally, previous work in cockroaches suggests that removal of claws does not affect walking behavior on smooth surfaces where friction/adhesive pads would be dominant in maintaining grip [22].

Each tarsus design was manufactured from a combination of 3D printed Onyx composite nylon (Markforged, Watertown, MA) and Dragon Skin 10 silicone rubber (Smooth-On Inc., Macungie, PA). To create the silicone joints, rigid joint surfaces were first coated with DOWSIL 1200 OS Primer (Dow, Midland, MI) to increase silicone adhesion, then placed in external fixturing replicating the equilibrium position of the joint. Silicone was poured into the joint and left to cure for a minimum of five hours. Silicone pads were manufactured in a similar manner with molds creating the contours of the pads; external tarsus surfaces were coated with primer to aid silicone adhesion, and mold surfaces were coated with Mann Ease Release 200 (Mann Release Technologies, Macungie, PA) to ensure easy extraction from the mold.

2.3 Compliant Joint Characterization

The silicone joints between segments in Styles 2 and 3 permit a large degree of deformation in multiple directions (Fig. 1E for Style 3). Each tarsal joint is capable of deflecting 15° in its most flexible directions before the rigid plastic of the joints touch, which we defined as the typical joint limits. Within these limits, the joint is assumed to behave like a typical ball-and-socket joint. To relate the moment applied to the joint (τ) to its angular deflection ($\Delta\theta$) and evaluate the consistency of the manufacturing process, we collected force-deflection data with two different joint types: a tarsus-tarsus (TarTar) joint (i.e between two identical segments anywhere between segments 1 and 5 in Style 3; Fig. 2A) and a TiTar joint (found in Styles 2 and 3; Fig. 2B). For these tests, the proximal segment of each joint was affixed to the bottom plate of a Shimpo FGS-250W Manual Hand Wheel Operated Test Stand (Nidec-Shimpo America Corporation, Glendale Height, IL). A cable was routed through a hole in the distal segment and attached to the probe of a Shimpo FG-3008 Digital Force Gauge. The gauge was then vertically translated to apply force at intervals of 0.5 N. The angular deflection of the distal segment, $\Delta\theta$, and the angle of the cable from the vertical, θ_c, were both recorded through video capture. This process was repeated up to the limit of the joint. Figure 2C shows a picture of the test setup. Using these measurements along with the recorded force in the cable, T, the moment at each data point was calculated as $\tau = rT_{\parallel} = rT cos(\Delta\theta + \theta_c)$, where r is the moment arm length as shown in Fig. 2D. Each TarTar segment (n = 2) and TiTar segment (n = 1) was tested in dorsal and anterior-posterior deflection in at least two trials each. Ventral deflection was not tested due to the limited range of motion possible in the TarTar joint in this direction. The maximum force applied to the joint, and thus the number of data points per trial, varied depending on the deflection direction and joint morphology. For each trial, the stiffness coefficient k in Nm/rad was calculated as the slope of the curve fit to the τ vs. $\Delta\theta$ points with the y offset constrained to zero.

2.4   Stepping Experiments

Stepping experiments were conducted using a robotic leg modeled from the middle leg of a *C. morosus* stick insect walking on a treadmill (Fig. 1F). The leg setup is presented in full detail in ref. [42], but will be summarized briefly here. The leg is a 15:1 scale model of the insect's with the same segmental proportions. It includes actuated thorax-coxa (ThC), coxa-trochanter (CTr), and femur-tibia (FTi) joints. The ThC joint is mounted to a linear guide to allow free vertical movement, forcing the leg to support its weight as it steps. Two strain gauge rosettes are mounted on the leg to measure the transverse and axial strain data of each leg segment; one on the proximal dorsal face of the trochanterofemur (the trochanter and femur are fused in the stick insect), and one on the proximal dorsal face of the tibia. The locations and orientations of these rosettes are comparable to that of major CS groups 3 and 4, 6A and 6B, respectively [14,30]. To control the leg, a MATLAB (MathWorks, Natick, MA) script commands servomotor angles calculated from a desired footpath using inverse kinematics. The chosen footpath is modeled after that of *C. morosus* using a series of piecewise polynomials [12].

During a trial, a tarsal segment was affixed to the end of the tibia and the leg was commanded to step for six steps on the treadmill. Strain readings from each rosette were then recorded throughout stepping 60 Hz. The stride length of the footpath was adjusted to the scale of the robot leg, and the stepping period was set to 4 s to dynamically scale leg movements (i.e ensure a similar balance of inertial, viscous, elastic, and gravitational forces as in the insect; for more information, please see ref. [42]). The joint trajectories of the leg were not altered throughout these trials. No additional body weight was considered during these tests, meaning the leg was only lifting its own weight (similar to the "baseline" tests in ref. [42].

The strain data from the first step was discarded due to irregularities in the start position. The remaining five steps' data were filtered by a moving median filter with a window of 13 timesteps. This filter removed single-timestep fluctuations due to noise without affecting the strain profile over time. The filtered strain data for each step was then averaged to produce a typical stepping strain profile.

3   Results

3.1   Compliant Joint Stiffness

To characterize the stiffness of our compliant silicone joints, we measured the moment required for angular displacements of each joint on TarTar and TiTar joint types within joint limits. We were primarily interested in identifying the degree of directionality in the stiffness, as well as the degree of stiffness variation between silicone castings and joint morphologies. To quantify these differences, we calculated and compared the stiffness coefficient, k, for each trial and the

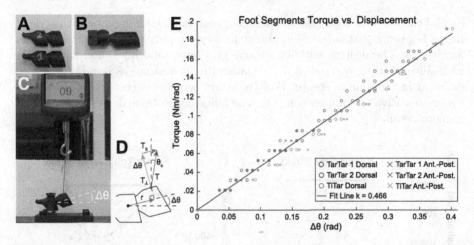

Fig. 2. Validation of the angular stiffness in our compliant silicone joints. (A) The two tarsus-tarsus (TarTar, i.e. between two identical segments anywhere between segments 1 and 5) joints tested. (B) The tibia-tarsus (TiTar) joint tested. (C) A frame from an extension trial with callouts showing the distal segment angular deflection, $\Delta\theta$ when force is applied. (D) A diagram of the force and angles present during deflection. (E) Torque vs. displacement graph for the TarTar (red for 1 and blue for 2) and TiTar (green) joints. Trials were conducted for extension (circle) and lateral movement (cross). The slope of the fit line (purple) to the entire dataset gives the stiffness coefficient of the joints. (Color figure online)

dataset as a whole. The results of all trials is presented as a torque vs. displacement graph in Fig. 2E. Each segment tested is represented by a different color; the first TarTar segment is blue, the second TarTar red, and the TiTar green. Dorsal deflection data points are represented by circles, and anterior-posterior deflection data points by crosses.

One immediately apparent feature of the data is the degree of linearity across trials. The average R-squared value of a line fit to a single trial's data was 0.994. Thus, the silicone-filled joints can be characterized as linearly elastic within typical joint limits. Furthermore, the segment stiffness does not appear to change drastically between different silicone pours, deflection directions, or joint morphologies. A line fit to the entirety of the dataset is shown in purple in Fig. 2E, with a slope of $k = 0.466$ Nm/rad. This line has an R-squared value of ≈ 0.98, indicating a highly linear fit to the data. As such, for future projects with similar tarsal segments we can assume a constant stiffness value of ≈ 0.46 Nm/rad across all segments for passive deflections within joint limits.

3.2 Strain Data

The primary purpose of this work is to explore how different aspects of tarsal morphology affect strain during walking. Thus, strain in the femur and tibia over an average step in the axial and transverse directions is presented in Fig. 3 for each of the five tarsus designs we manufactured. In the strain plots, each style of tarsus is given a particular color; orange for Style 1, purple for Style 2, and green for Style 3. The designs without silicone grip have solid lines, and the designs with silicone grip have dashed lines. Data without a tarsus as in ref. [42] is also included in blue for reference. Positive strain represents compression, because CS are sensitive to compression [14]. The following sections describe these plots in more detail.

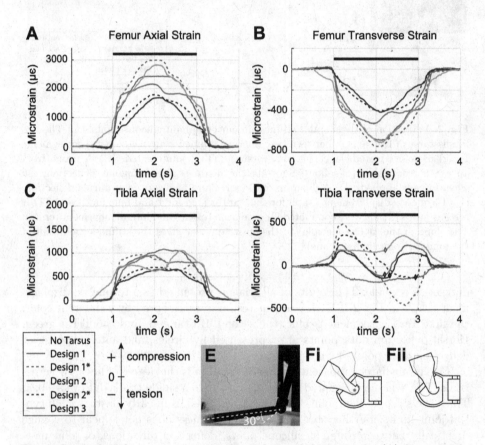

Fig. 3. Strain data for an average step for each tarsal design in the (A) femur axial, (B) femur transverse, (C) tibia axial, and (D) tibial transverse directions. Styles are given the same color, while the silicone grip designs are dashed and the non-silicone grip designs are solid. Data for no tarsus, as in ref [42], is included for reference (blue). The portion of the curve at which onsets of slip were observed are marked with diamonds in (D). (E) Position of the Design 2* leg during stance. (F) Diagrams of the movement of tarsal segment 1 within the compliant TiTar joint during deflection (i) within joint limits and (ii) outside of joint limits. The pivot point of the joint during these movements is marked as a red *. (Color figure online)

Trochanterofemur Strain. For Styles 1 and 3, the overall magnitude of the trochanterofemoral strains exceeded that recorded with no tarsus by 25–50% in both directions. Style 2's peak strain, however, was ≈20% less than that with no tarsus in both designs. The trochanterofemoral strains for different tarsus configurations also build and decay more gradually, resulting in a parabola-like curve typically peaking mid-stance.

Tibia Strain. Some effects from applying a tarsus occurred uniquely in the tibia strain data. Particularly in the transverse direction (Fig. 3D), strain readings became more sensitive to the pronation/supination of the leg. For Styles 1 and 2 this meant starting positive (compressive) in the first half of stance and becoming negative (tensile) as the tarsus became posterior to the FTi. This switch is most apparent in the Design 1* strain curve. Such strain propagation contrasts with the no-tarsus design, in which axial and transverse strains are scaled opposites, consistent with simple tension or compression of the leg surface (i.e. bending moments without axial torsion). However, every tarsus style broke this inverse-scale relationship, meaning that axial torsion was induced along the tibia. The Style 3 tarsus was the only design that created purely positive tibia transverse strain throughout the stepping cycle. Designs 1, 2, and 3 also exhibit a sudden increase in strain in the latter half of stance, approximately where they were observed to have slipped during testing (observed onsets of slip are marked with diamonds in Fig. 3D). Design 2* similarly produced a sharp increase in strain during the transition from stance to swing.

4   Discussion

In this study, we prototyped five tarsi for our robotic *C. morosus* leg to better understand which features of the tarsus, e.g., compliance, passive grip, and structure, most greatly impact the strain in the leg. As engineers, we seek the simplest design that will enable our robotic leg to accurately model the forces that the animal experiences during walking. To mimic the elasticity of insect joint membranes, we cast silicone hinges between tarsal segments. We characterized the stiffness and consistency of these joints. Finally, we recorded the strain experienced by the robotic leg as it stepped with each of the tarsi. The strain timecourses showed stark differences depending on the tarsus used. In subsequent sections, we propose explanations for the differences in leg strain among different Designs, comment on how the tarsus may aid in detecting leg slipping, and describe plans for future work.

4.1   Strain Magnitude

For Styles 1 and 3, the tarsus increased strain in the trochanterofemur and tibia segments relative to the no-tarsus baseline. This is likely because adding an angled segment increased the moment arm between the ground contact point and the FTi joint, increasing the strain of the tibia. However, Style 2's peak strain was less than the no-tarsus baseline. This difference is likely due to the high degree of deflection in the compliant TiTar joint. As shown in Fig. 3E, the TiTar joint is deformed ≈30 deg from equilibrium, 15 deg over what we define as the joint limit. When this limit is reached, the highly compliant interior of the joint allows the joint axis to change from the center of the 'ball' of the distal segment (Fig. 3Fi) to the contact point between the distal segment and the proximal segment's outer walls (Fig. 3Fii), creating further joint deflection. It is presently unclear the precise angular stiffness of this additional deflection, or if the stiffness is linear as within the joint limits. However, such deflection does lessen the impacts felt during touch down by increasing the time for deceleration of the foot. We believe that these lesser impacts were subsequently not enough to overcome the static friction present in our current linear guide. Thus, some of the body weight was supported in the guide, lessening the forces distributed throughout the leg. We plan to address this issue in future studies by redesigning our guide system, as well as investigating the precise stiffness characteristics of our elastic joints outside of their normal limits.

4.2   Strain Profile

The strain in both locations on our leg builds and decays more gradually for our different tarsi. In the trochanterofemur, these changes created a parabola-like curve typically peaking mid-stance. Such a strain progression is due to the tarsal moment arm increasing sensitivity to pronation/supination of the leg. Consider the axial strain in Fig. 3A. The leg angles during stance in our joint trajectories (as shown in Fig. 3A in ref. [42]) result in the leg plane being nearly vertical halfway through stance. This position minimizes the magnitude of ground reaction force (GRF) components passively resisted by the joint structure and maximizing resulting moments induced by the GRF on the femur. Further supinating the leg throughout stance angles the leg plane, decreasing the force components transferred to the femur and naturally producing a parabola-like curve similar to that of the joint angles.

In the tibia, the leg plane sensitivity produced a switch in strain polarity across stance in Styles 1 and 2. This sign change aligns with the tarsus tip traveling caudally along the body during stance. The tip begins anterior to the FTi joint in the first half of stance, producing moments that place the dorsal tibia surface in compression (Fig. 3D). As stance progresses, the tarsus travels posterior to the FTi, generating moments that place the dorsal surface in tension. For Style 3, the strain remained compressive across stance. The high degree of elasticity in the joints could account for this difference, as the tarsus was able to twist and bend to great degrees throughout stance to maintain its initial contact point with the treadmill. This deformation could potentially create unique moment arms. Regardless of their specific morphology, each tarsus produced axial torsion along the tibia instead of simple bending moments, highlighting how additional tarsal moment arms can alter the types of bending produced in the leg during stepping.

4.3 Slipping Detection

Four of the five tarsal designs exhibited a sudden increase in transverse tibial strain during the latter half of stance phase: Designs 1, 2, 2*, and 3 (Fig. 3D). In designs without grip components, this rapid increase corresponded to observations of slipping between the foot and the treadmill (marked with diamonds in Fig. 3D). For Design 2*, the increase occurred during lift off of the foot at the onset of swing. This change may be due to a 'snap back' effect in which stored elastic energy from tarsus deflection attempts to accelerate the tarsus back to equilibrium upon slip. This restoring movement reconnects the foot with the treadmill, creating a secondary impact that produces tensile limb strain. Design 2* did not slip, but the high elastic moments produced during stance phase (described in Sect. 4.2) could similarly accelerate the tarsus back into the treadmill surface as the leg begins to quickly lift off the ground.

The effects of slip during pronation/supination presented here combined with previous data collected for lateral slipping [42] demonstrate how CS may contribute to the detection of slipping. In pronation/supination, the tibia seems integral to detecting slip, as the femur recordings were largely unaffected in either direction. Including a tarsus then makes slip more prominent in the tibial data by increasing the strain magnitude, changing strain directions through axial torsion, and producing a 'snap-back' effect through joint compliance. Both of these datasets align with biological recordings from stick insects showing the encoding of slip by the tibial CS [20]. It remains unclear how information from different CS locations is used in the nervous system, but indications of slipping in the tibial strains is one possible reason for collecting sensory information from this location.

4.4 Compliant Joint Robustness

The silicone membranes between the joints in three of our five designs satisfactorily mimicked the elasticity of insect joint membranes in a consistent manner between castings and joint morphologies. The connections were also robust enough to complete our tests without any detachment or tearing. However, characteristics such as the useful life of these joints, the maximum weight the joints can support, and the maximum deflection the joints can undergo without damage, are presently untested. Anecdotally, previous iterations of Style 2 in which the TiTar equilibrium position had the tarsus parallel to the tibia (i.e. similar to Design 3) were found to fail within a handful of steps after repeatedly deforming ≈90°, giving a rough upper limit to joint deflection. Such failure was characterized by the "ball" of the distal joint un-adhering from the silicone. Thus, exploring methods to improve the bond between the plastic and the silicone could improve joint performance. Such methods will be explored in future work, alongside characterizing the precise mechanical robustness of the current joints.

4.5   Conclusions and Future Work

This study reveals several concrete effects that a tarsus has on the strain magnitude and profile in various leg locations during stepping. Such data shows the potential importance of including a tarsus in our future biomimetic robot designs when investigating leg CS. However, it is presently difficult to say how biomimetic the recorded strain are, as no explicit strain data has been recorded in insects. CS discharge has certainly been recorded, but it is presently difficult to say the precise conversion between mechanical strain and firing rate, for example. Several authors of this work have previously developed a phenomenological model of CS discharge in response to leg strain and used it to hypothesize firing during stepping [33]. In future work, we plan to run our data through this model and compare the resulting discharge to biological data. This process will allow us to determine which aspects of our current work most reflect animal mechanics.

We also plan to address necessary simplifications made during this work to contain our scope and lay groundwork for future investigations. One simplification was the use of the tarsal morphology of flies, in which the tarsal segments are proportionally much longer than in stick insects, that may have amplified the effects of tarsal compliance during walking. Another such simplification was the exclusion of active grip due to the additional complexity of the unguitractor mechanism attached to the claws. Previous biological data has highlighted the limited role of the claws on smooth surfaces [22]. However, claws improve the general robustness of ground contact by maintaining grip on rougher surfaces [8]. Additionally, the extra grip force produced by the unguitractor mechanism would further improve ground contact, possibly reducing slipping. As the additional moment produced in the tarsus by the unguitractor is in the same direction as the joint elastic restoring moments, active grip may increase the magnitude of the 'snap-back' effect on the strain we observed upon slip. We plan to investigate how to include active grip into our model in future work by replicating the unguitractor mechanism.

Another simplification we made was to use the same stepping kinematics in our leg for each tarsal design to make their strain data directly comparable. This is markedly different from the nervous system, which is able to modulate stepping kinematics to account for changes in leg structure (e.g., missing segments). Given the high dependence of the Style 3 tarsi ground contact to the initial touchdown location of the pretarsus, the biomimetic tarsi design would likely benefit from adapted joint trajectories that account for tarsus length.

References

1. Arnold, J.: Adaptive features on the tarsi of cockroaches (Insecta: Dictyoptera). Int. J. Insect. Morphol. **3**(3/4), 317–334 (1974). https://doi.org/10.1016/j.ymeth. 2019.07.013
2. Bässler, U.: Neural Basis of Elementary Behavior in Stick Insects. Springer, Berlin (1983). https://doi.org/10.1007/978-3-642-68813-3_6
3. Bennemann, M.: Biomimicry of the adhesive organs of stick insects (*Carausius morosus*). Ph.D. thesis, RWTH Aachen University (2015)

4. Bidaye, S.S., Bockemühl, T., Büschges, A.: Six-legged walking in insects: how CPGs, peripheral feedback, and descending signals generate coordinated and adaptive motor rhythms. J. Neurophysiol. **119**(2) (2018). https://doi.org/10.1152/jn. 00658.2017

5. Buschmann, T., Ewald, A., von Twickel, A., Büschges, A.: Controlling legs for locomotion-insights from robotics and neurobiology. Bioinspir. Biomim. **10**(4), 41001 (2015). https://doi.org/10.1088/1748-3190/10/4/041001

6. Bußhardt, P., Gorb, S.N., Wolf, H.: Activity of the claw retractor muscle in stick insects in wall and ceiling situations. J. Exp. Biol. **214**(10), 1676–1684 (2011). https://doi.org/10.1242/jeb.051953

7. Bußhardt, P., Wolf, H., Gorb, S.N.: Adhesive and frictional properties of tarsal attachment pads in two species of stick insects (Phasmatodea) with smooth and nubby euplantulae. Zoology **115**(3), 135–141 (2012). https://doi.org/10.1016/j. zool.2011.11.002, http://dx.doi.org/10.1016/j.zool.2011.11.002

8. van Casteren, A., Codd, J.R.: Foot morphology and substrate adhesion in the Madagascan hissing cockroach, *Gromphadorhina portentosa*. J. Insect. Sci. **10**(1), 1–12 (2010). https://doi.org/10.1673/031.010.4001

9. Chiel, H.J., Beer, R.D.: The brain has a body: adaptive behavior emerges from interactions of nervous system, body and environment. Trends Neurosci. **20**(12), 553–557 (1997). https://doi.org/10.1016/S0166-2236(97)01149-1

10. Cignoni, P., Callieri, M., Corsini, M., Dellepiane, M., Ganovelli, F., Ranzuglia, G.: MeshLab: an open-source mesh processing tool. In: Scarano, V., Chiara, R.D., Erra, U. (eds.) Eurographics Italian Chapter Conference. The Eurographics Association (2008). https://doi.org/10.2312/LocalChapterEvents/ItalChap/ItalianChapConf2008/129-136

11. Clemente, C.J., Dirks, J.H., Barbero, D.R., Steiner, U., Federle, W.: Friction ridges in cockroach climbing pads: Anisotropy of shear stress measured on transparent, microstructured substrates. J. Comp. Physiol. A **195**(9), 805–814 (2009). https://doi.org/10.1007/s00359-009-0457-0

12. Cruse, H., Bartling, C.: Movement of joint angles in the legs of a walking insect, *Carausius morosus*. J. Insect Physiol. **41**(9), 761–771 (1995). https://doi.org/10.1016/0022-1910(95)00032-P

13. Delcomyn, F.: Activity and directional sensitivity of leg campaniform sensilla in a stick insect. J. Comp. Physiol. A **168**(1), 113–119 (1991). https://doi.org/10.1007/BF00217109

14. Delcomyn, F., Nelson, M.E., Cocatre-Zilgien, J.H.: Sense organs of insect legs and the selection of sensors for agile walking robots. Int. J. Robot. Res. **15**(2), 113–127 (1996). https://doi.org/10.1177/027836499601500201

15. Dinges, G.F., Bockemühl, T., Iacoviello, F., Shearing, P.R., Büschges, A., Blanke, A.: Ultra high-resolution biomechanics suggest that substructures within insect mechanosensors decisively affect their sensitivity. J. Roy. Soc. Interface **19**(190), 20220102 (2022). https://doi.org/10.1098/rsif.2022.0102

16. Frazier, S.F., et al.: Elasticity and movements of the cockroach tarsus in walking. J. Comp. Physiol. A **185**(2), 157–172 (1999). https://doi.org/10.1007/s003590050374

17. Goldsmith, C.A., Szczecinski, N.S., Quinn, R.D.: Neurodynamic modeling of the fruit fly *Drosophila melanogaster*. Bioinspir. Biomim. **15**(6) (2020). https://doi.org/10.1088/1748-3190/ab9e52

18. Goldsmith, C., Quinn, R.D., Szczecinski, N.S.: Investigating the role of low level reinforcement reflex loops in insect locomotion. Bioinspir. Biomim. **16**, 065008 (2021). https://doi.org/10.1088/1748-3190/ac28ea

19. Gorb, S.N.: Design of insect unguitractor apparatus. J. Morphol. **230**(2), 219–230 (1996). https://doi.org/10.1002/(SICI)1097-4687(199611)230:2⟨219::AID-JMOR8⟩3.0.CO;2-B

20. Harris, C.M., Szczecinski, N.S., Büschges, A., Zill, S.N.: Sensory signals of unloading in insects are tuned to distinguish leg slipping from load variations in gait: experimental and modeling studies. J. Neurophysiol. **128**(5), 790–807 (2022). https://doi.org/10.1152/jn.00285.2022

21. Kohsaka, H., Nose, A.: Optogenetics in *Drosophila*. Adv. Exp. Med. Biol. **1293**, 309–320 (2021). https://doi.org/10.1016/j.ymeth.2019.07.013

22. Larsen, G.S., Frazier, S.F., Zill, S.N.: The tarso-pretarsal chordotonal organ as an element in cockroach walking. J. Comp. Physiol. A **180**(6), 683–700 (1997). https://doi.org/10.1007/s003590050083

23. Liessem, S., et al.: Behavioral state-dependent modulation of insulin-producing cells in *Drosophila*. Curr. Biol. **33**(3), 449-463.e5 (2023). https://doi.org/10.1016/j.cub.2022.12.005

24. Manoonpong, P., et al.: Insect-inspired robots: bridging biological and artificial systems. Sensors **21**(22), 1–44 (2021). https://doi.org/10.3390/s21227609

25. Merritt, D.J., Murphey, R.K.: Projections of leg proprioceptors within the CNS of the fly phormia in relation to the generalized insect ganglion. J. Comp. Neurol. **322**(1), 16–34 (1992). https://doi.org/10.1002/cne.903220103

26. Moran, D.T., Chapman, K.M., Ellis, R.A.: The fine structure of cockroach campaniform sensilla. J. Cell Biol. **48**(1), 155–173 (1971). https://doi.org/10.1083/jcb.48.1.155

27. Noah, A.J., Quimby, L., Frazier, F.S., Zill, S.N.: Force detection in cockroach walking reconsidered: discharges of proximal tibial campaniform sensilla when body load is altered. J. Comp. Physiol. - Sens. Neural Behav. Physiol. **187**(10), 769–784 (2001). https://doi.org/10.1007/s00359-001-0247-9

28. Pfeifer, R., Iida, F., Gómez, G.: Morphological computation for adaptive behavior and cognition. Int. Congr. Ser. **1291**, 22–29 (2006). https://doi.org/10.1016/j.ics.2005.12.080

29. Radnikow, G., Bässler, U.: Function of a muscle whose apodeme travels through a joint moved by other muscles: why the retractor unguis muscle in stick insects is tripartite and has no antagonist. J. Exp. Biol. **157**(1), 87–99 (1991). https://doi.org/10.1242/jeb.157.1.87

30. Ridgel, A.L., Frazier, S.F., Zill, S.N.: Dynamic responses of tibial campaniform sensilla studied by substrate displacement in freely moving cockroaches. J. Comp. Physiol. A **187**(5), 405–420 (2001). https://doi.org/10.1007/s003590100213

31. Ritzmann, R.E., Quinn, R.D., Watson, J.T., Zill, S.N.: Insect walking and biorobotics: a relationship with mutual benefits. Bioscience **50**(1), 23–33 (2000). https://doi.org/10.1641/0006-3568(2000)050[0023:IWABAR]2.3.CO;2

32. Scheffer, L.K., et al.: A connectome and analysis of the adult *Drosophila* central brain. eLife **9**, 1–74 (2020). https://doi.org/10.7554/ELIFE.57443

33. Szczecinski, N.S., Dallmann, C.J., Quinn, R.D., Zill, S.N.: A computational model of insect campaniform sensilla predicts encoding of forces during walking. Bioinspir. Biomim. **16**(6) (2021). https://doi.org/10.1088/1748-3190/ac1ced

34. Tajiri, R., Misaki, K., Yonemura, S., Hayashi, S.: Joint morphology in the insect leg: evolutionary history inferred from Notch loss-of-function phenotypes in *Drosophila*. Development **138**(21), 4621–4626 (2011). https://doi.org/10.1242/dev.067330

35. Tran-Ngoc, P.T., Lim, L.Z., Gan, J.H., Wang, H., Vo-Doan, T.T., Sato, H.: A robotic leg inspired from an insect leg. Bioinspir. Biomim. **17**(5) (2022). https://doi.org/10.1088/1748-3190/ac78b5

36. Zill, S.N., Moran, D.T.: The exoskeleton and insect proprioception III. Activity of tibial campaniform sensilla during walking in the American cockroach, Periplaneta americana. J. Exp. Biol. **94**, 57–75 (1981)

37. Zill, S., Schmitz, J., Büschges, A.: Load sensing and control of posture and locomotion. Arthropod. Struct. Dev. **33**(3), 273–286 (2004). https://doi.org/10.1016/j.asd.2004.05.005

38. Zill, S.N., Büschges, A., Schmitz, J.: Encoding of force increases and decreases by tibial campaniform sensilla in the stick insect, *Carausius morosus*. J. Comp. Physiol. A **197**(8), 851–867 (2011). https://doi.org/10.1007/s00359-011-0647-4

39. Zill, S.N., Chaudhry, S., Büschges, A., Schmitz, J.: Force feedback reinforces muscle synergies in insect legs. Arthropod. Struct. Dev. **44**(6), 541–553 (2015). https://doi.org/10.1016/j.asd.2015.07.001

40. Zill, S.N., Chaudhry, S., Exter, A., Büschges, A., Schmitz, J.: Positive force feedback in development of substrate grip in the stick insect tarsus. Arthropod. Struct. Dev. **43**(5), 441–455 (2014). https://doi.org/10.1016/j.asd.2014.06.002

41. Zill, S.N., Ridgel, A.L., DiCaprio, R.A., Frazier, S.: Load signalling by cockroach trochanteral campaniform sensilla. Brain Res. **822**(1), 271–275 (1999). https://doi.org/10.1016/S0006-8993(99)01156-7

42. Zyhowski, W.P., Zill, S.N., Szczecinski, N.S.: Adaptive load feedback robustly signals force dynamics in robotic model of *Carausius morosus* stepping. Front. Neurorobot. **17**(January) (2023). https://doi.org/10.3389/fnbot.2023.1125171

Correction to: Biomimetic and Biohybrid Systems

Fabian Meder⊙, Alexander Hunt⊙, Laura Margheri⊙,
Anna Mura⊙, and Barbara Mazzolai⊙

Correction to:
F. Meder et al. (Eds.): *Biomimetic and Biohybrid Systems*,
LNAI 14157, https://doi.org/10.1007/978-3-031-38857-6

The following chapters were originally published electronically on the publisher's internet portal without open access:

"A 3D-Printed Biomimetic Porous Cellulose-Based Artificial Seed with Photonic Cellulose Nanocrystals for Colorimetric Humidity Sensing", written by Kliton Cikalleshi, Stefano Mariani, Barbara Mazzolai;

"Bioinspired Soft Actuator Based on Photothermal Expansion of Biodegradable Polymers", written by Luca Cecchini, Stefano Mariani, Nicola M. Pugno, Barbara Mazzolai.

With the authors' decision to opt for Open Choice the copyright of the chapters changed on 13 September 2023 to © Authors, 2023 and the chapters are forthwith distributed under the Creative Commons Attribution 4.0 International License (http://creativecommons.org/licenses/by/4.0/deed.de), which permits use, copying, editing, distribution and reproduction in any medium and format , provided you give proper credit to the original author(s) and the source, include a link to the Creative Commons license, and indicate if changes were made.

The images and other third-party material contained in this chapter are also subject to the Creative Commons license mentioned, unless otherwise stated in the figure legend. If the material in question is not under the Creative Commons license mentioned and the action in question is not permitted by law, the consent of the respective rights holder must be obtained for the further use of the material listed above.

The updated versions of these chapters can be found at
https://doi.org/10.1007/978-3-031-38857-6_9
https://doi.org/10.1007/978-3-031-38857-6_12

© The Author(s) 2023
F. Meder et al. (Eds.): Living Machines 2023, LNAI 14157, pp. C1–C2, 2023.
https://doi.org/10.1007/978-3-031-38857-6_33

Funded by: the European Union Horizon 2020 research and innovation programme, Grant Number: 101017940.

Author Index

F. Meder et al. (Eds.): Living Machines 2023, LNAI 14157, pp. 459–461, 2023.
https://doi.org/10.1007/978-3-031-38857-6

Printed in the United States
by Baker & Taylor Publisher Services